The Cambridge History of
Literary Criticism

VOLUME 9
Twentieth-Century Historical, Philosophical and
Psychological Perspectives

The Cambridge History of
Literary Criticism

The Cambridge History of Literary Criticism will provide a comprehensive historical account of Western literary criticism from classical antiquity to the present day, dealing with both literary theory and critical practice. The History is intended as an authoritative work of reference and exposition, but more than a mere chronicle of facts. While remaining broadly non-partisan it will, where appropriate, address controversial issues of current critical debate without evasion or false pretences of neutrality. Each volume is a self-contained unit designed to be used independently as well as in conjunction with the others in the series. Substantial bibliographical material in each volume will provide a foundation for further study of the subjects in question.

VOLUMES PUBLISHED

Volume 1: *Classical Criticism*, edited by George A. Kennedy
Volume 3: *The Renaissance*, edited by Glyn P. Norton
Volume 4: *The Eighteenth Century*, edited by H. B. Nisbet
and Claude Rawson
Volume 5: *Romanticism*, edited by Marshall Brown
Volume 7: *Modernism and the New Criticism*,
edited by A. Walton Litz, Luke Menand and Lawrence Rainey
Volume 8: *From Formalism to Post-Structuralism*,
edited by Raman Selden
Volume 9: *Twentieth-Century Historical, Philosophical and Psychological Perspectives*, edited by Christa Knellwolf and Christopher Norris

VOLUMES IN PREPARATION

Volume 2: *The Middle Ages*, edited by Alastair Minnis
and I. R. Johnson
Volume 6: *The Nineteenth Century*

FOUNDING EDITORS

Professor H. B. Nisbet
University of Cambridge
Professor Claude Rawson
Yale University

The contribution of H. B. Nisbet and Claude Rawson in helping to specify and approve the shape of Volume 9, and in advising on preliminary synopses of the contributions, is gratefully acknowledged.

The Cambridge History of Literary Criticism

VOLUME 9

Twentieth-Century Historical, Philosophical and Psychological Perspectives

Edited by

CHRISTA KNELLWOLF AND
CHRISTOPHER NORRIS

Assistant Editor

JESSICA OSBORN

CAMBRIDGE
UNIVERSITY PRESS

PUBLISHED BY THE PRESS SYNDICATE OF THE UNIVERSITY OF CAMBRIDGE
The Pitt Building, Trumpington Street, Cambridge, United Kingdom

CAMBRIDGE UNIVERSITY PRESS
The Edinburgh Building, Cambridge CB2 2RU, UK
40 West 20th Street, New York NY 10011-4211, USA
10 Stamford Road, Oakleigh, VIC 3166, Australia
Ruiz de Alarcón 13, 28014 Madrid, Spain
Dock House, The Waterfront, Cape Town 8001, South Africa

http://www.cambridge.org

First published 2001

Printed in the United Kingdom at the University Press, Cambridge

Typeface Monotype Sabon 10/12 pt   *System* QuarkXPress™ [SE]

A catalogue record for this book is available from the British Library

ISBN 0 521 30014 2 hardback

Contents

Notes on contributors

Firdous Azim is a Professor in the Department of English, University of Dhaka, Bangladesh. Her areas of specialisation are feminism and post-colonialism. Her book, *The Colonial Rise of the Novel* (1993), traces the links between the colonial venture and the development of the novelistic form. Her current work is on English writing in nineteenth-century Bengal.

Timothy Bahti is Professor of Comparative Literature at the University of Michigan, Ann Arbor, and the author of *Allegories of History: Literary Historiography After Hegel* (1992) and *Ends of the Lyric: Direction and Consequence in Western Poetry* (1996). He is presently writing a monograph on styles of paradox in modern German-Jewish writing, and a theory of the lyric.

Manuel Barbeito is a Professor of Literary History at the University of Santiago, Spain. He has published a book on W. H. Auden (1988) and has edited *Paradise Lost: The Word, the World, the Words* (1991) and *Modernity, Modernism, Postmodernism* (2000). He is currently completing a work entitled *El drama de la identidad en siete obras de la tradición literaria inglesa*, and editing a book in honour of Terry Eagleton.

Andrew Bowie is Professor of German at Royal Holloway, University of London. He is the author of *Aesthetics and Subjectivity: From Kant to Nietzsche* (1990, new revised edition 2000), *Schelling and Modern European Philosophy* (1993), and *From Romanticism to Critical Theory: The Philosophy of German Literary Theory* (1997). He has also translated and edited F. W. J. von Schelling, *On the History of Modern Philosophy* (1994), F. D. E. Schleiermacher, *Hermeneutics and Criticism and Other Texts* (1998), and edited the book, *Manfred Frank: The Subject and the Text* (1997). He is at present writing books on music, meaning and modernity, on crossing the divide between European and analytical philosophy, and on German philosophy from Kant to Habermas.

Joseph Bristow is Professor of English at the University of California, Los Angeles. His books include *Effeminate England: Homoerotic Writing After*

viii

1885 (1995) and *Sexuality* (1997). He has edited several volumes, most recently *The Cambridge Companion to Victorian Poetry* (2000). He is currently at work on a full-length study of Victorian poetry, sex, and sexuality.

Alex Callinicos is Professor of Politics at the University of York. He has written extensively on Marxism and social theory. Among his many books are *Making History* (1987), *Against Postmodernism* (1989), *Theories and Narratives* (1995), and *Social Theory* (1999). He has recently completed a book on equality.

Clive Cazeaux is Senior Lecturer in Aesthetics at the University of Wales Institute, Cardiff. He is the editor of *The Continental Aesthetics Reader* (2000) and the author of articles on metaphor, synaesthesia, and the relationship between art and writing.

Brian Coates is a Lecturer in English and Cultural Studies at the University of Limerick. His most recent publications include two art catalogue essays, 'Deidre O'Mahony, Erratics' (1996) and 'Lingua occulorum' (1997). He is a joint editor (with Joachim Fischer and Patricia Lynch) of the IASIL Conference Proceedings 1998 on Irish writing 1798–1998 (forthcoming 2000).

Gary Day is a Principal Lecturer at De Montfort University. He is the editor of the three volume *Literature and Culture in Modern Britain* series (Longman). He is also the author of *Re-Reading Leavis: 'Culture' and Literary Criticism* (1996) and the forthcoming book *Class*.

John Drakakis is Professor of English Studies at the University of Stirling. He is the general editor of Routledge English Texts and the New Critical Idiom series. He is the editor of *Alternative Shakespeares* (1985), *Shakespearean Tragedy* (1992), and the New Casebook *Anthony and Cleopatra* (1984), and has contributed numerous articles, book chapters, and book reviews to volumes on Shakespeare and critical theory. He is currently editing *The Merchant of Venice* for the Arden 3 series, and is completing a monograph entitled *Shakespearean Discourses*.

Andrew Edgar is a Lecturer in Philosophy at Cardiff University in Wales. His research and teaching interests include twentieth-century German social and political philosophy, and the philosophy of art and music. He is the co-author of *The Ethical QALY* (1998) and of *Key Concepts in Cultural Theory* (1999).

Diane Elam is Professor of English Literature and Critical and Cultural Theory at Cardiff University in Wales. She is the author of *Romancing the Postmodern* (1992), *Feminism and Deconstruction: ms en abyme* (1994), and a forthcoming book, *The Injustice of Truth: Notes Toward a Feminist Politics*.

Rainer Emig is Professor of British Literature at Regensburg University in Germany. Previously he taught as a lecturer in English Litereature at Cardiff University in Wales, where he was also a member of staff in the Centre for Critical and Cultural Theory. Among his publications are *Modernism in Poetry* (1995), *W. H. Auden* (2000), and *Stereotypes in Contemporary Anglo-German Relations* (2000).

Dirk de Geest is a Professor in the Department of Literature of the Katholieke Universiteit Leuven, Belgium. He has published on systems theory, hermeneutics, and twentieth-century Dutch and Belgian literature. His books include *Literatuur als systeem, literatuur als vertoog* ('Literature as System, Literature as Discourse') (1996) and *Collaboratie of cultuur?* ('Collaboration or Culture?') (1997), a book on cultural collaboration in Belgium (1941–1944).

Ortwin de Graef is Senior Lecturer in the Department of Literature of the Katholieke Universiteit Leuven, Belgium. He has published *Serenity in Crisis: A Preface to Paul de Man, 1939–1960* (1993), *Titanic Light: Paul de Man's Post-Romanticism, 1960–1969* (1995), and on literary theory and nineteenth- and twentieth-century literature.

Paul Hamilton is Professor of English at Queen Mary and Westfield College, University of London, and was formerly a Fellow of Exeter College, Oxford. His works on Romanticism and historicism include *Coleridge's Poetics* (1983) and *Historicism* (1996), and his book on 'Metaromanticism' is currently in press.

Geoffrey Galt Harpham is Chair of the Department of English at Tulane University, where he has taught since 1986. His scholarly works include *The Ascetic Imperative in Culture and Criticism* (1987), *Shadows of Ethics: Criticism and the Just Society* (1999), and *One of Us: The Mastery of Joseph Conrad* (1996).

Ken Hirschkop is Senior Lecturer in English Literature at the University of Manchester. He is the editor of *Bakhtin and Cultural Theory* (1989) and the author of *Mikhail Bakhtin: An Aesthetic for Democracy* (1999). He is now working on the history of 'linguistic turns' in the humanities.

Renate Holub is Director of Interdisciplinary Studies at the University of California, Berkeley, where she teaches critical social theory and comparative European studies. She is currently the principal co-investigator (with Paul

Lubeck and Manuel Castells) of the International Collaborative Research Project on 'Multicultural Europe' at the Institute of European Studies, University of California, Berkeley. Among her publications is *Antonio Gramsci: Beyond Marxism and Postmodernism* (1992). Her current research focuses on 'Intellectuals and Islam in Europe'.

Robert C. Holub teaches German intellectual, cultural, and literary history in the German department at the University of California, Berkeley. Among his numerous publications on these topics are *Reflections of Realism* (1991), *Jürgen Habermas: Critic in the Public Sphere* (1991), and *Crossing Borders: Reception Theory, Poststructuralism, Deconstruction* (1992). He is currently working on an extended study of Friedrich Nietzsche.

Christa Knellwolf is a Fellow in the Humanities Research Centre at the Australian National University, Canberra. She has published a study of the gendered intellectual climate of eighteenth-century poetry, *A Contradiction Still: Representations of Women in the Poetry of Alexander Pope* (1998), and she is currently completing a cultural history of the scientific revolution, sponsored by the Swiss National Science Foundation. She has contributed articles to books and journals on the early modern period and on feminist literary history.

Peter Lamarque is Ferens Professor of Philosophy at the University of Hull. His books include *Truth, Fiction and Literature: A Philosophical Perspective*, co-authored with Stein Haugom Olsen (1994), *Fictional Points of View* (1996), and *Concise Encyclopedia of Philosophy of Language* (1997). He is the editor of *The British Journal of Aesthetics* and recently produced and contributed to a special issue entitled *Aesthetics in Britain* (2000).

Dan Latimer is Professor of English and Comparative Literature at Auburn University. His publications include *Contemporary Critical Theory* (1989) and essays in *Modern Language Notes, New Left Review, The Comparatist, Essays in Literature, New Orleans Review*, and other journals.

Simon Lee-Price has taught English at the University of Hawaii at Manoa and was an Associate Lecturer in cultural criticism at Cardiff University in Wales. He is currently editing an anthology on the subject of hybridity.

Kevin Mills is a Research Fellow in Literature and Theology at Westminster College, Oxford. His first book, *Justifying Language: Paul and Contemporary Literary Theory* appeared in 1995. Since then he has published widely, contributing to journals and collections of essays. He is a member of the European editorial board of the journal *Literature and Theology*.

Stephen Moller teaches Philosophy at Cardiff University in Wales and The Open University. His writings include articles on romantic theory, Italian humanism, Bosanquet, and the aesthetics of absolute idealism.

Christopher Norris is Distinguished Research Professor in Philosophy at Cardiff University in Wales, having previously (until 1991) taught in the Cardiff English Department. He has published more than twenty books to date on various aspects of philosophy and critical theory, including, most recently, *Against Relativism* (1997), *Quantum Theory and the Flight from Realism* (2000), and *Minding the Gap: Epistemology and Philosophy of Science in the Two Traditions* (2000).

Jessica Osborn is Research Assistant in Philosophy at Cardiff University in Wales. She is currently working on a dissertation on feminist approaches to rights, and is engaged in research for a project on 'Feminists and Wittgenstein'.

Michael Ryan teaches English at the Northeastern University. His books include *Marxism and Deconstruction* (1982), *Camera Politica: The Politics and Ideology of Contemporary American Film* (1988), *Politics and Culture: Working Hypotheses for a Post-Revolutionary Society* (1989), *Literary Theory: A Practical Introduction* (1999), *Literary Theory: An Anthology* (1998), *Film Interpretation: An Introduction* (forthcoming), and *Make Believe: Social Arguments in American Film* (forthcoming). His novels include *Gulliver* (1994) and *Over the Rainbow* (forthcoming). He has also translated works by Antonio Negri and Felix Guattari.

Duncan Salkeld is Senior Lecturer in the School of English at University College Chichester. He is author of *Madness and Drama in the Age of Shakespeare* (1993), and several articles on Renaissance drama, literary theory, and the history of sexuality.

Eveline Vanfraussen is Research Assistant in the Department of Literature at the Katholieke Universiteit Leuven, Belgium, where she is employed in a research project on 'Literature in Belgium (Flanders) during the period 1930–1945'. She is currently finishing a dissertation on the periodical of De Vlag (1937–1944), one of the main collaborating forces in Belgium.

Patricia Waugh is Professor of English at the University of Durham. Her books include *Metafiction: The Theory and Practice of Self-Conscious Fiction* (1984), *Feminine Fictions: Revisiting the Postmodern* (1989), *Practising Postmodernism/Reading Modernism* (1992), *Harvest of the Sixties* (1995), *Revolutions of the Word* (1997) and, with David Fuller (eds.), *The*

Arts and Sciences of Criticism (1999). She is currently completing a book entitled *Views From Nowhere: Literature, Science and the Good Society* on the two cultures debate, utopias and science, ethics and literature.

Chris Weedon is Reader in Critical and Cultural Theory at Cardiff University in Wales. Her publications include *Feminist Practice and Poststructuralist Theory* (second edition, 1996), *Cultural Politics: Class, Gender, Race and the Postmodern World* (co-authored with Glenn Jordan, 1995), *Postwar Women's Writing in German* (1997), and *Feminism, Theory and the Politics of Difference* (1999).

Introduction

CHRISTA KNELLWOLF AND CHRISTOPHER NORRIS

This volume of *The Cambridge History of Literary Criticism* is the last in a series of nine offering a scholarly survey of criticism and theory from classical antiquity to the present. Such a broad historical overview shows that the partiality of critical judgement has been recognised for almost as long as literature has existed; so much so, indeed, that the conscious attempt to make allowance for it marks the emergence of literary criticism as a discipline that seeks to achieve a certain judicious objectivity of viewpoint while perforce acknowledging its own dependence on rhetoric and strategies of persuasion. In the late twentieth century, moreover, critics have become so keenly aware of the cultural and ideological factors informing every act of interpretation that any claim to offer a fairly unbiased (let alone neutral or objective) survey of the field now seems more problematic than ever. Still it is essential to a project like this that such qualms should not be allowed to paralyse judgement or leave every sentence hedged around with qualifying doubts. As a matter of broad editorial policy, we have decided that the problem can best be confronted through a detailed discussion of historical context and emergent patterns of influence, along with a willingness to address such issues explicitly where need arises.

The guiding principle of Volume 9 is a sustained engagement with history, both in the sense that it raises issues of a markedly critical-historiographic import, and also in so far as it offers case studies of various historically situated movements and schools of thought. The last three volumes in the series are all concerned with twentieth-century developments, a weighting that might seem somewhat excessive, given the sheer chronological range of the series as a whole. However these volumes are strongly contrasted in terms of their distinctive emphases and governing interests. In particular the need has become clear for a survey of those various developments in the wake of French structuralism that are seen by many as posing a large – perhaps an insuperable – challenge to any project (such as ours) that entails the possibility of describing or narrating episodes of thought in some kind of historically intelligible sequence. This challenge has come from several quarters, among them poststructuralism, Foucauldian discourse-theory, deconstruction, postmodernism and new historicism. In each case, its most decisive effect has been to undercut the grounds for any confident appeal to matters of truth or historical fact. What these approaches chiefly share, despite differences of method and orientation, is their commitment to one or another form of the linguistic, discursive or textual 'turn' that has also been a prominent feature of other academic disciplines, not least philosophy and historiography. Where they chiefly differ is in the extent to which they still find room for some residual notion of historical truth behind the otherwise infinite play of textual significations, or how far they would endorse Fredric Jameson's claim that history is an 'untranscendable horizon' which will always in the end place limits on the scope for such forms of textualist licence.[1]

Roughly speaking, these tendencies can be ranged on a scale from full-fledged postmodernist scepticism, *via* the more sophisticated forms of 'left' poststructuralist theory, to the often strenuous attempts (by Jameson and others) to reconcile the claims of Marxist dialectical materialism with those of a moderate textualist approach that stresses the problems confronting any realist ontology or epistemology. Foucauldian approaches are distinguished in the main by their focus on the historically shifting forms of discursive representation and the way that these embody the covert operations of an ubiquitous Nietzschean will-to-truth whose driving force is the power vested in various disciplinary regimes.[2] Deconstruction is more difficult to place on this scale since – especially in the work of Jacques Derrida – it is concerned with a close philosophical analysis of the relationship between overt and covert *logics* at work in various kinds of text and not (or not primarily) with issues of literary representation.[3] Nevertheless deconstruction has often been seen, by proponents and detractors alike, as belonging very much to that wider postmodernist movement of thought which treats 'reality' as a purely textual or discursive construct. To this extent – as witness Richard Rorty's essay in the *Cambridge History*, volume eight – deconstruction can readily be enlisted on the side of a 'North Atlantic postmodern bourgeois liberal pragmatist' culture which would take literary criticism as its model for a new 'post-philosophical' style of thought. Such a culture would be one that placed high value on the writing of poets, novelists or strong revisionist interpreters and which had no time for the sorts of technical or specialised topic that have dominated philosophic discourse from Descartes and Kant to Frege, Russell and the modern analytic tradition.[4] Still the question remains – one taken up

[1] Fredric Jameson, *The Political Unconscious: Literature as a Socially Symbolic Act* (London: Methuen, 1981).
[2] See for instance Michel Foucault, *Language, Counter-Memory, Practice*, trans. and ed. D. F. Bouchard and S. Weber (Oxford: Blackwell, 1977).
[3] See especially Jacques Derrida, *'Speech and Phenomena' and Other Essays on Husserl's Theory of Signs*, trans. D. B. Allison (Evanston, Ill.: Northwestern University Press, 1973); *Of Grammatology*, trans. G. C. Spivak (Baltimore: Johns Hopkins University Press, 1976); *Margins of Philosophy*, trans. A. Bass (Chicago: University of Chicago Press, 1982).
[4] See also Richard Rorty, *Irony, Contingency, and Solidarity* (Cambridge: Cambridge University Press, 1989).

by various contributors – as to whether there might nonetheless be certain standards of truth or veridical warrant that would exercise a check on our freedom to extend such 'literary' modes of reading to the texts of philosophy, history, or the social and natural sciences.

Elsewhere (as for instance in the writing of postmodern historiographers like Hayden White) there is a strong claim for literary theory – in this case narrative poetics – as a means to revitalise the discourse of history and bring it up-to-date with the more advanced forms of present-day fictive representation.[5] What is so striking about these developments is the way that contemporary literary theory has moved from its erstwhile somewhat marginal position *vis-à-vis* those other disciplines to the status of a cutting-edge discipline perceived as having large implications for the conduct of enquiry in numerous other fields of thought. Thus, to take just a few salient examples from this volume, its effects have been felt – whether eagerly embraced or strenuously resisted – in such diverse fields as anthropology, ethnography, psychoanalysis, political theory, ethics, gender-studies, theology, postcolonial historiography, philosophy of science, modernisation-theory and the history of ideas. At one end of the spectrum, the claim very often is that literary theory now provides the best source of a radically transformative approach that would rescue those disciplines from their naive attachment to old-fashioned 'positivist' notions of truth and method. Or again, that literary theory is best equipped to take stock of that present-day cultural shift (the so-called 'postmodern condition') whose dominant sign is what Baudrillard calls the 'precession of the simulacrum', that is to say, the eclipse of reality and truth by various forms of hyperinduced media simulation.[6] This latter is just the most extreme sceptical variant of an outlook that permeates much present-day discussion and whose effects are a central topic of debate in this volume.

At the same time voices have been raised against the trend toward a wholesale textualisation of reality, a trend that is often viewed – not without justice – as cutting away the very grounds for any practice of historically informed, philosophically rigorous, ethically responsible or politically committed enquiry. Hence the urgent call for a 'new' historicism, an umbrella term that is often taken to embrace different localised variants, such as the (mainly) British movement that has come to be known as cultural materialism. Broadly speaking, this is a critical approach which leaves some room for judgements of historical truth while acknowledging the discursive and narrative dimension of its own interpretive strategies. However, new historicism has itself been much criticised – not least by cultural materialists – for leaning too far toward

---

[5] Hayden V. White, *Tropics of Discourse: Essays in Cultural Criticism* (Baltimore: Johns Hopkins University Press, 1978) and *The Content of the Form* (Baltimore: Johns Hopkins University Press, 1988).

[6] See for instance Jean Baudrillard, *Selected Writings*, ed. Mark Poster (Cambridge: Polity Press, 1989); also *The Revenge of the Crystal: A Baudrillard Reader* (London: Pluto Press, 1990).

a textualist position that would treat historical 'reality' as a purely discursive construct.[7] We have therefore made it a matter of editorial policy to recruit the widest possible range of viewpoints while asking our contributors to describe the field rather than adopt an overly partisan position. These differences of opinion will quickly strike any reader who follows the various threads of debate concerning (for instance) the issue between Marxism and poststructuralism, or that between the French and German traditions of critical theory, or the kindred yet (to some extent) rival methodologies of new historicism and cultural materialism, or again – most contentious of all – the quarrel over claims for a 'postmodern' science that would mark a decisive break with all the canons of hitherto accepted scientific method.[8] At any rate we have had the good fortune to assemble a team of exceptionally well-qualified writers who have managed to present a great diversity of views while maintaining an open and even-handed approach to their topics.

The present volume could well have been organised along somewhat different lines by picking out different patterns and affinities in the complex play of reciprocal influence between various schools of thought. In what follows we shall signpost the major topics and running themes of debate. The first section offers a range of views on the forms, genres and modalities of historical representation. A comparative treatment of historicisms past and present gives a strong sense of the way that historical approaches have lately been transformed through the advent of new theoretical resources and the questioning of older (though not for that reason presumptively discredited) modes of thought. The detailed discussion of the philosophical problems entailed by historical criticism is followed by a chapter which demonstrates their far-reaching implications for work in the history of ideas. Two chapters on cultural materialism and the new historicism draw out some salient points of contrast between these critical movements and seek to explain how the act of questioning conventional historiography produced new methods for studying the literature and culture of the past. An analysis of the complicity of literary criticism with fascist politics engages closely with the ideological premises of historical representation.

Marxism emerged as the earliest and most explicit critique of the politics of representation. Seeking to transform the conditions of social injustice which result from the exploitation of the working classes, Marxism produced a critical analysis of historical concepts and categories which was also – inseparably – an analysis of contemporary culture. The section on Marxism begins with a general survey of the history of Marxist critical practice. Marxist responses to deconstructionist criticism are discussed in a chapter on the

---

[7] See the various essays collected in Harold A. Veeser (ed.), *The New Historicism* (New York and London: Routledge, 1989).

[8] See especially Jean-François Lyotard, *The Postmodern Condition: A Report on Knowledge*, trans. G. Bennington and Brian Massumi (Manchester: Manchester University Press, 1984).

complex but productive alliance between Marxism and poststructuralism. The Frankfurt School, as a focal point of Marxist philosophy and social theory, is here subdivided chronologically into two phases: one chapter concentrates on the circle around Adorno and the second offers a contrastive survey of recent French and German developments.

Cultural studies shares with Marxism a commitment to analysing the relationship between culture, ideology and forms of political power. Its distinctive approach to literary criticism lies partly in its refusal to restrict itself to the choice of 'high' cultural artforms, instead aligning itself with popular culture, advertising and non-canonical literary texts. This section begins with a discussion of Mikhail Bakhtin, a Soviet critic and cultural theorist mainly active in the 1920s and 1930s whose work was rediscovered by western critics some four decades later and has since been subject to rival appropriations by Marxist, cultural-materialist and theologically inclined interpreters. A subsequent chapter examines the emergence of cultural studies as a thoroughgoing re-evaluation of the practice of literary criticism in the context of its deep affiliation with national culture. This treatment stresses the uneasy process of democratisation and its quest for some means of demystifying the authority attached to the written word. It also shows how dramatic changes in the institutional context over the past century have themselves affected the received self-image of 'English' as a field of study or an academic discipline in its own right.

The section on psychological and psychoanalytic approaches offers an overview from the first emergence of psychoanalysis in the early twentieth century to recent developments and applications. Concepts derived from psychoanalysis have informed a whole range of recent theories which seek to understand the premises of existing gender, race and class definitions, and which have thus become prominent in the study of ethnicity and gender. Gender studies and postcolonial criticism have each mounted a challenge to the discourse of traditional literary scholarship for its collusion with practices that act to marginalise or silence oppressed voices. The history of feminist criticism, like that of postcolonial and of gay or lesbian criticism, is a history of resistance in which direct action in support of equal rights and recognition of specific concerns is balanced against theoretically informed analysis of the complex workings of power. The first chapter here on twentieth-century feminist approaches examines the attempt to theorise representation and subjectivity through political readings and writings, alongside the feminist engagement with recent developments in the literary field. Drawing on deconstructionist methodology, the second interrogates the category of 'woman' and the idea of 'difference' in order to emphasise the grounds of solidarity among women. The third offers an overview of gay and lesbian criticism, indicating some of the problems encountered in maintaining gender definitions, and concluding with a survey of recent developments in queer and transgender theory.

It is impossible to overstate the role played by literature and representation in the construction of ethnocentric value systems and myths of western cultural superiority. African American literary history contests this deeply entrenched set of beliefs by describing how significant was the contribution by black people to North American culture and how their achievements were erased from the record by a white historiography. It offers a survey of black writers, both before and after emancipation, whose work has achieved belated acknowledgement through the process of challenging received canonical values. Along with this it provides an account of black struggles for recognition and a review of theoretical approaches to the construction of race as a concept which holds oppression in place. The chapter on postcolonial theory discusses the historical development of those countries which were formerly part of colonial empires, examining what new-found opportunities exist for oppressed people to find their own voices in a situation where the outlook of the colonial masters has been internalised through education, military service and a careers system imposed by the coloniser. A study of the methods and historical development of anthropology reveals the extent to which this discipline has often served to project the cultural norms of the observer onto the community or social system under observation. Such awareness has promoted a more self-critical mode of comparative analysis, introducing the concept of trans-national cultural studies in place of the old, supposedly neutral approach.

This leads on to a section concerned with the concept of periodicity as it has figured in various movements of thought during the twentieth century. Understanding how a particular orientation toward the future shapes the attitudes and choices of the present historical period requires a review of the various much-discussed modes of transition from modernism to postmodernism. But it also demands a theoretical engagement with concepts of modernisation and with notions of progress and historical development. Postmodernism is mostly thought to entail a sceptical questioning of Enlightenment values such as truth, knowledge and objectivity, along with a cultural-relativist stress on the sheer multiplicity of language-games (or 'first-order natural pragmatic narratives') by which different communities make sense of their lives. This chapter engages a wide range of views – explicit or implicit – with regard to some of the more sweeping claims put forward by exponents of the so-called 'postmodern condition'. More specifically, it assesses their implications for our thinking about literary theory, aesthetics and the ethics of criticism.

One feature that distinguishes this volume from other projects of a similar kind is its wide-ranging treatment of philosophical developments in relation to literary studies. Phenomenology and existentialism have often been noted as exerting a powerful influence on twentieth-century critical practice even though they currently enjoy nothing like the degree of interest or the fashion-

able following that has accrued to other movements of thought such as deconstruction or poststructuralism. Then there is the whole vexed issue of 'continental' *versus* 'analytic' philosophy, the latter referring – by academic
convention at least – to the kind of work carried on by mainly Anglo-
American philosophers in the wake of Frege's and Russell's revolution in the
fields of logic and philosophy of language. While a prominent approach in its
own right, analytic philosophy has held less attraction for literary theorists
than is manifest in the various successive 'turns' toward continental sources
and analogues. This situation has not been helped by the attitude of downright hostility evinced by many analytic philosophers, in particular as concerns deconstruction and what they take to be its outlook of breezy disregard
for elementary standards of rigour, consistency and truth. Most damaging
here was the notorious exchange between Derrida and John Searle on the
topic of Austinian speech-act philosophy, an exchange that did much to reinforce the old pattern of routine mistrust or contemptuous dismissal
bequeathed by the logical positivists.[9] Nevertheless, as the chapter on this
topic makes clear, the analytic tradition has produced some valuable work in
aesthetics and the philosophy of literary criticism which can be read with
profit by those who lean more towards recent continental thought.

The chapters on Italian idealism and on Spanish and Spanish-American aesthetics and criticism will probably cover some less familiar ground for many
readers of this volume. The first offers a case-study of the early twentieth-
century philosopher-critics Giovanni Gentile and Benedetto Croce, for whom
the possibility of an authentic literary criticism is grounded in a theory of
knowledge that seeks to maintain and preserve the universality of meaning. The
second examines the complex inter-relationship between theory, ideology and
artistic creation that marked the development of literary criticism in Spain and
Latin America throughout the twentieth century. They are followed by a chapter
on neo-pragmatism, a movement with various (mainly North American philosophical) sources, and one that has become closely identified with the curious
fashion of arguing 'against theory' in what remains all the same a highly theoretical mode of address. This section concludes with a comparative survey of
various approaches to the ethics of literary criticism, bringing out the centrality
of fictive or narrative examples in recent moral philosophy.

The final section deals with the powerful influence exerted by theories of
textuality on disciplines which have traditionally affirmed the existence of
objective truth-values and which have tended to shun the fictionality or the
kinds of 'poetic licence' associated with literature. Since it has nowadays
become increasingly difficult – so these theorists argue – to salvage objective
or straightforwardly veridical modes of description, the critique of language

---

[9] Jacques Derrida, *Limited Inc*, ed. Gerald Graff (Evanston, Ill.: Northwestern University Press,
1989); John R. Searle, 'Reiterating the differences', *Glyph*, vol. 1 (Baltimore: Johns Hopkins
University Press, 1977), pp. 198–208.

has extended its purview to every academic discipline, including history, sociology and even the natural sciences. With the presumed loss of a neutral mode of representation, boundaries between different disciplines have become increasingly fluid and subject to renegotiation. The demand for discipline-specific expertise has been counterbalanced by an urgent call for cross-disciplinary or interdisciplinary ventures. This has been motivated chiefly by the need to enable more productive communication between various specialised fields of knowledge. But there has also been a questioning of what is now seen as the 'constructed' or historically relative character of all such boundary-markers, whether between the various arts-and-humanities subjects or – in more adventurous claims of this sort – between the human and social sciences on the one hand and the natural sciences on the other. This development has no doubt received further impetus from the 'linguistic turn' across various disciplines, one effect of which – for better or worse – has been the widespread adoption of textualist or 'strong' hermeneutic approaches that count reality a world well lost for the sake of these new-found interpretative freedoms. Literary theory has thereby come to exert a powerful influence on thinkers in other disciplines, to the point where a comprehensive survey of the field would require treatment on a scale far beyond anything possible here. Two representative (though strongly contrasted) examples may be found in the chapters that discuss literary theory in relation to recent developments in theology and philosophy of science. On the other hand the point needs stressing that there is a great deal of work in other growth areas of interdisciplinary thought that the reader may wish to explore in keeping with his or her particular interests. At this point, therefore, we will pick out just a few such prominent lines of enquiry which, for reasons of space, could not be treated separately.

Thus, for instance, there is a whole flourishing movement of broadly deconstructionist legal theory which challenges the norms, procedures and values of traditional (mainstream-liberal) jurisprudence. This it does – in brief – by claiming to deconstruct the various cardinal distinctions which are taken to uphold that discourse, among them those between statute-law and case-law, or so-called 'easy' and 'hard' cases, or judgements arrived at by 'straightforward' application of a well-defined legal precedent and judgements arrived at through the exercise of interpretative tact, good sense or discretion. To mount such a challenge – so it is claimed – is to undermine the kinds of unquestioned authority or the 'commonsense' grounds of appeal that maintain an appearance of judicial neutrality while concealing the extent to which law operates as means of enforcing hegemonic values and sociopolitical interests.[10] Thus it is argued that contract law can be upheld – or rep-

---

[10] See for instance Matthew H. Kramer, *Legal Theory, Political Theory and Deconstruction: Against Rhadamanthus* (Bloomington: Indiana University Press, 1991); Peter Fitzpatrick and Alan Hunt (eds.), *Critical Legal Studies* (Oxford: Blackwell, 1987); Mark Kelman, *A Guide to Critical Legal Studies* (Cambridge, Mass.: Harvard University Press, 1987); Roberto M. Unger, *The Critical Legal Studies Movement* (Cambridge, Mass.: Harvard University Press, 1986).

resented as a matter of reciprocal trust between equal and fully consenting parties – only through the power of legal discourse to suppress or dissimulate the inequalities that always exist in any such situation. At this point Foucault is often invoked (along with poststructuralist theory) as a source for the idea of power/knowledge as the ubiquitous condition of all discourse, even (or especially) when masked behind a rhetoric of noble disinterest. Moreover, deconstruction is called upon as witness to the chronic instability of reference, or the fact that every term in legal discourse – from the most (apparently) concrete referring expression to the most (apparently) clear and unambiguous statute-law provision – can always be interpreted in various ways since its purport cannot be established beyond doubt by appealing either to framer's intention or to context as a regulative principle.[11] This shows, once again, how arguments that were first developed and applied in the field of literary theory have since taken hold – through a kind of colonising movement – in areas that might seem utterly remote from that original context. Thus it offers a singularly apt example of just the point that Derrida makes when he denies the possibility of defining 'context' in such a way as to fix or delimit in advance what shall count as a valid precedent or ground of appeal from one context to another.[12]

Hence, no doubt, the attractiveness of deconstruction to those in the Critical Legal Studies movement who cast themselves very much in an adversary role with regard to the normative values and assumptions of the dominant legal culture. Hence also its appeal to literary theorists with an interest in extending their own interpretative techniques to issues such as that of U.S. constitutional law where so much depends on the meaning assigned to certain (often highly abstract or vaguely formulated) principles. This goes some way toward explaining why deconstruction has provoked such controversy in the U.S. context, representing as it does the promise (or the threat) of a discourse that claims to breach disciplinary borders and which harbours ambitions far beyond the safe enclave of academic literary study. On the other hand there is room for doubt as to whether this kind of all-purpose radicalism really represents such a powerful challenge to the socio-juridical status quo. For it might just as well be argued that here, as in the case of postmodern historiography, there is little to be hoped or feared from a theory that seems to offer no purchase for counter-argument on reasoned or principled grounds. Certainly this is the point often made with considerable flair and relish by Stanley Fish, nimblest performer of the new-pragmatist or 'against theory' movement who delights in exposing such radical pretensions as so many sadly deluded examples of 'negative theory hope'.[13] At any rate it seemed to the editors that since we had to draw limits to the range of interdisciplinary approaches covered in

---

[11] Clare Dalton, 'An Essay in the Deconstruction of Contract Doctrine', *Yale Law Journal* 94 (1984), pp. 997–1114.　　[12] Derrida, *Limited Inc.*

[13] Stanley Fish, *Doing What Comes Naturally: Change, Rhetoric, and the Practice of Theory in Literary and Legal Studies* (Oxford: Clarendon Press, 1989).

this volume we should draw it at the point where literary theory becomes more a pretext than a source of inspiration for work in other fields. Besides, it would have given a skewed perspective to focus solely on these kinds of high-profile theoretical debate while ignoring the range of other developments under the 'law and literature' rubric, among them various thematic studies – treatments of law *in* literature – which may well prove to have a more enduring value.

A number of other recent growth-areas in the interdisciplinary zone deserve to be mentioned here. Many are located in the different branches of the visual and performing arts, suggesting that its received structure of generic and evaluative distinctions is currently subject to some far-reaching revisionist claims. In the visual-arts field, Svetlana Alpers was among the first to insist on the need to embed art-historical analysis in a broader conception of culture.[14] Her seminal work, *The Art of Describing*, argued that our visual responses to works of art cannot be divorced from the modes of seeing privileged by particular historical epochs or period-specific conventions. A comprehensive understanding of art requires that we seek out those contemporary modes of perception which produce the cultural specificity of genres and styles. Roland Barthes, among others, subjected the interpretation of images (and indeed all cultural phenomena) to a structural-semiotic analysis and claimed that its modes of signification could be treated as analogous with those of verbal art.[15] His pioneering essays can now be seen as having opened the way to an extensive re-thinking of the complex relationship between visual and textual or iconic and discursive modes of representation.

The new musicology is another discipline that has lately been making determined forays into various branches of literary theory, among them deconstruction and poststructuralism.[16] Of course there is nothing new about the general idea that music criticism might profit from contact with the more advanced forms of literary-speculative thought. This idea goes back to that early nineteenth-century period of intellectual ferment when post-Kantian idealists and Young Romantics such as Schlegel, Novalis and E. T. A. Hoffmann took music as a privileged topic for treatment in their hybrid style of philosophico-literary discourse and also as a challenge to its utmost powers of conceptual representation. More recently, there is the example of Charles Rosen's book *The Classical Style* (1971) which moves with impressive agility and grace between passages of close musical analysis and a mode of reflective commentary that draws on a wide range of extra-musical sources.[17] Thus Rosen discusses the music of Haydn, Mozart and Beethoven with

---

[14] Svetlana Alpers, *The Art of Describing: Dutch Art in the Seventeenth Century* (London: John Murray, 1983).

[15] Roland Barthes, *Image – Music – Text* (New York: Hill and Wang, 1977).

[16] Rose Rosengard Subotnik, *Developing Variations: Style and Ideology in Western Music* (Minneapolis: University of Minnesota Press, 1991).

[17] Charles Rosen, *The Classical Style* (London: Faber and Faber, 1971).

reference not only to cultural developments in their own time but also to various fruitful ideas from modern literary criticism, among them William Empson's quirkily brilliant treatments of ambiguity and pastoral. What is so distinctive about *The Classical Style* is Rosen's ability to integrate theoretical concerns – such as the hermeneutic issue concerning our access to earlier period conventions or expressive styles – with a marvellously quick and appreciative sense of how this music communicates subtleties of meaning despite and across such distances of cultural context. Thus he – like Empson – rejects the idea that analysis must somehow get in the way of a duly sensitive response, or that theoretical interests must prevent the interpreter from discovering what is actually there in the music or there to be discerned in the words on the page.

More recent approaches under the banner of the 'new musicology' have tended very often to make heavy weather of those same problems and thus to place a large obstacle between appreciative and other (analytic or theoretically oriented) modes of address. This has come about mainly through their keenness to adopt ideas from the more advanced branches of literary-cultural theory – deconstruction, poststructuralism, postmodernism – and then apply them to music (or to the discourse of mainstream musicology) in a somewhat over-generalised and procrustean fashion. Thus these writers take a lead from Paul de Man in denouncing the notion of organic form which they view as a species of 'aesthetic ideology', one that falls in with the conservative mystique of musical works as self-sufficient wholes transcending all mere contingencies of time and place.[18] Moreover, they argue, this conception carries across into the idea of musical history as a likewise 'organic' process of development wherein certain privileged *national* traditions – such as the hegemonic line of descent from Bach, *via* Haydn, Mozart, and Beethoven, to Schubert, Brahms and/or Wagner, Mahler and Schoenberg – are seen as evolving through a kind of predestined teleological necessity, itself duly mirrored in the works' internal ('naturally' evolving) structural form. For the new musicologists one main use of deconstructionist literary theory is to challenge this widespread aesthetic ideology and, along with it, the practice of musical analysis that takes for granted such sacrosanct values as organic unity, thematic integration or long-range tonal development. Sometimes this amounts to a full-scale attack on the very idea of 'structural listening', that is, the idea that *genuine* (as distinct from casual or inattentive) musical experience necessarily involves just the kind of sustained analytical activity on the listener's part that is made explicit in the writing of mainstream music theorists.[19] Elsewhere it takes the form of a selective emphasis on music that puts up maximum resistance to

[18] Alan Street, 'Superior Myths, Dogmatic Allegories: The Resistance to Musical Unity', *Musical Analysis* 8 (1989), pp. 77–123.

[19] Jonathan Dunsby, *Structural Ambiguity in Brahms: Analytical Approaches to Four Works* (Ann Arbor: UMI Press, 1981).

any such 'organicist' approach, especially mixed-genre pieces and sequences – like Brahms' late piano *Intermezzi* – which give an impression of somehow 'belonging together' while eluding any formal mode of analysis that would treat them as thematically related in the strong ('organicist') sense.[20]

For Adorno, conversely, 'structural listening' was a *sine qua non* of informed and cultivated musical response. Indeed it was Adorno's gloomy conviction – in his writings on the 'culture industry' – that such listening was everywhere relentlessly under attack, on the one hand from a mass-market drive to dictate and homogenise musical tastes, and on the other from those mass-induced habits of regressive or fetishised perception that fastened on favourite tunes, passages or fragments plucked out of context.[21] Thus the new musicologists' quarrel with Adorno tends to work out – and be repeated in other contexts – as a clash of views between, on the one hand, critics who uphold the 'modernist' values of formal complexity and art as a challenge to our routine, acculturated modes of response, and on the other hand critics of a broadly postmodernist persuasion who consider such views hopelessly out-dated as well as offensively elitist. These debates are taken up in various con-texts by several contributors to this volume so we shall not pursue them any further here.

Predictably, another main source of inspiration for the new musicologists is the literary new historicism, a movement which likewise maintains the inade-quacy of formal and structural modes of analysis, but which also rejects any old-style 'positivist' notion that we might gain access to historical truth through the methods and procedures of traditional scholarship. Rather, we should look at the sheer range of cultural contexts in which certain artefacts – whether literary or musical – have been written, composed, read, per-formed, produced, interpreted, revised, transformed, pressed into service and (in short) undergone all the shifting fortunes of their diverse reception-history. Again, this bespeaks a determined opposition to the idea of 'the work' as possessing some kind of organic unity or integral form, such as would protect it from the buffeting winds of cultural and socio-historical change. Also it marks a clear shift of emphasis from the more traditional Marxist (and indeeed cultural-materialist) stress on the original 'context of production' to a focus on the various contexts of reception that effectively debar any such appeal to some privileged point of origin. The new musicolo-gists have adopted this approach with considerable relish, deploying it both against scholarly arguments for the priority of 'authentic' (period-specific) instruments, orchestral forces, performing styles, etc., and also against the

---

[20] Ruth A. Solie, 'The Living Work: Organicism and Musical Analysis', *Nineteenth-Century Musicology* 4 (1980), pp. 147–156.

[21] Rose Rosengard Subotnik, 'Toward a Deconstruction of Structural Listening: A Critique of Schoenberg, Adorno and Stravinsky', in Eugene Narmour and Ruth Solie (eds.), *Explorations in Music, the Arts, and Ideas* (New York: Stuyvesant Pendragon Press, 1988), pp. 87–122.

fetishistic notion – in their view – of a work whose formal integrity assures the possibility of an 'authentic' (transhistorically valid) tradition of performance and interpretation.[22] In which case, clearly, there is no longer any place for those confident value-judgements that raised certain works to the status of accredited 'classics' and which did so, moreover, in the placid assurance that the criteria for greatness were (or should be) universally endorsed by those best qualified to judge. For it must now be apparent – so these theorists claim – that the musical canon (like the musical work) is a shifting and provisional construct which is always open to challenge on various theoretical, cultural or ideological grounds.[23] Thus new-musicological discussions of 'the canon' and its role in policing the boundaries of good (academically respectable) taste have mostly followed the agenda set by literary critics and theorists over the past decade and more.

Let us offer – in conclusion – a few brief remarks about coverage, sequence and editorial rationale. We have made every effort both to keep overlaps to a minimum and to ensure the greatest possible clarity of style and exposition. In some cases an apparent area of overlap in fact serves to highlight significant differences of emphasis or socio-cultural context. The sequence of sections and of chapters within each section has been chosen with a view to preserving some measure of thematic continuity while also pointing up relevant contrasts of method and approach. Some critics figure prominently in several chapters and are shown to have contributed in different ways to different (sometimes antagonistic) tendencies or schools of thought. This situation has often come about through the complex vicissitudes of reception-history within the field of literary studies and also – on occasion – through a detour *via* the social or natural sciences. Of course the most daunting expectation of the last volume in a series of nine is that it should somehow provide a comprehensive or at any rate truly representative coverage of the field. Unfortunately some important issues could be touched upon only in a cursory fashion or by way of cross-reference to other developments that have received more extensive treatment. However, we have made every effort to offer an internally balanced work of reference which picks up the dialogue at various points where previous volumes have left off. Finally, therefore, this returns us to the question of historiography and reminds us that a genuinely critical history must involve both reflection on its own theoretical premises and a constant awareness of the past as a challenge to present-day values and beliefs.

---

[22] Joseph Kerman, 'How We Got Into Analysis, and How to Get Out', *Critical Inquiry* 7 (1980), pp. 311–331.

[23] Marcia J. Citron, *Gender and the Musical Canon* (Cambridge: Cambridge University Press, 1992).

History

I

Historicism and historical criticism

Paul Hamilton

Old and new historicisms

Recent critiques of historical methodology have inaugurated a radically revised understanding of art, culture and society. Literary criticism has been at the forefront of these developments, an especially articulate advocate of their utility and their timeliness. The innovations of this new historicism, though, are bound to recapitulate old historicisms to some extent. In the heat of critical reaction to what went before, pioneers are inclined at first to neglect still earlier precursors of their own interpretative practice. Opponents of new historicism are, of course, quick to attack its claims to newness. In so doing, though, their criticism itself becomes historicist, one which historicises the historicisers. Historicism ought therefore to welcome their corrections. Indeed, the stage that historicist criticism has now reached is one which is keen to become more learned in past attempts to depart from a purely linear account of history, a chronology, in order to detect the art of historiography at work. An analysis of its rhetoric has thus become increasingly important. The tropes history uses, the choices it makes between the different kinds of available narrative, the realism which concerns of the present can bestow on supposedly correlative movements of the past are considered part of history's content. Critical fashion, in other words, may be historically informative, and the most critical aspect of historicism concerns the question of whether past and present concerns are so inextricable that they are in fact troping each other. Hayden White, in his immensely influential book *Metahistory*, found his major precedents for this historical self-consciousness in nineteenth-century German historical method.[1] The following chapter acknowledges earlier anticipations of current historicism while seeking to do justice to the idioms which it typically draws on now.

Historicism is a dialectical movement of thought. Its effort is threefold. First of all it encourages a properly historical understanding of the past: the past should be grasped on its own terms. Historical proprieties should be observed, anachronisms should be avoided. Secondly, though, it grasps the

---

[1] Hayden White, *Metahistory* (Baltimore: Johns Hopkins University Press, 1973); see also his *Tropics of Discourse: Essays in Cultural Criticism* (Baltimore: Johns Hopkins University Press, 1978).

nettle of hindsight. We cannot really pretend to understand the past on its own terms because we know so much more of what happened afterwards. Recovery of the exact boundaries of past knowledge would require an artificial forgetfulness of our difference from it. Historicism therefore next addresses the question of the degree to which hindsight should be allowed to revise our understanding of the past. The past, after all, must to some extent be characterised by how it sees its future, how it envisages the consequences of its actions. Our knowledge of what actually came to happen appears to give our assessments of the past an advantage over its own. But it would be a complacent, Whiggish form of historicism which assumes that hindsight is always superior and does not lay itself open to question for exactly the same reason that it presumes to correct an earlier period's judgement of its own significance.[2] By contrast, Collingwood's assertion that the past is nothing but 'the reconstruction of an ideal object in the interests of knowing the present' is double-edged.[3] Another, third act of qualification is set in motion, one which this time investigates the degree to which knowledge of the past should be allowed to reorientate or change present understanding rather than just confirm it. This third effort is necessarily open-ended, since it hypothesises the correction of present self-knowledge in a future still to come.

Some or all of these three moments of historicism have been central concerns of the western intellectual tradition. Their influence can be tracked from Plato's theory of knowledge as anamnesis or recollection to heroic and typically modern reversals of Plato such as Kierkegaard's idea of repetition, Nietzsche's doctrine of the eternal recurrence of the same and Walter Benjamin's attacks on the historical continuum cultural self-understanding takes for granted. Historicism has recently presented itself as an innovatory approach in Anglo-American criticism. Its plausibility in so doing has largely depended on its supposed contrast with an excessive formalism associated, rightly or wrongly, with the challenging poststructuralist techniques dominating current literary theory. But historicism's centrality to any western intellectual movement, poststructuralism included, should not be forgotten. And the new deconstructive techniques employed by poststructuralist criticism are the stock in trade of any new historicism worthy of the name. The following discussion will stress continuities and discontinuities between the explanations given by past and present critics and philosophers for the involvements of literature and history. Historicism ties criticism indissolubly to questions of philosophy and historiography. And historicist criticism is very partially understood when discussed in isolation from these problems which frame its interpretative decisions.

Historicism has become a very sophisticated business, and it is as well to

[2] For the 'Whig' view of history, see Herbert Butterfield, *The Whig Interpretation of History* (London: G. Bell & Sons, 1931).

[3] R. G. Collingwood, *The Idea of History*, rev. edn. with Lectures 1926–8, ed. Jan van der Dussen (Oxford: Oxford University Press, 1994).

begin with an honest statement of the complexities involved. Fredric Jameson, arguably, the most influential critical theorist writing in America today,[4] is a Marxist of sorts, and thus his criticism might be expected to assume an historicist monopoly. But the recent development of critical theory has found almost all critical methodologies, not just Marxist ones, proclaiming that their credentials are historicist. For however formalist other, competing choices of critical exposition may appear nowadays, however neglectful of local circumstantial detail, their practitioners are usually quick to advocate a comparable historicity for their procedures. In fact, the contemporary critical approaches most often accused of a transcendentalism neglectful of history – deconstruction and poststructuralism – frequently defend themselves by professing an historicism more fundamental and anterior to that understood by customary usage. By virtue of their location of historicism's workings in apparently ahistorical linguistic structures, these readings declare themselves to be wiser in and more knowing about the cunning of reason, as Hegel called it, than approaches which deal more ostensibly in the currency of historical context. History effaces itself with consummate, more self-defining artistry behind just those discursive mechanisms which appear to transcend it. For the deconstructive criticism of Paul de Man, say, questioning the means by which linguistic meaning is naturalised by historical reference is, paradoxically, historicism's proper task. The basis for a genuinely critical engagement with the subject is an awareness that the truly interested historical context of any utterance, the real McCoy, is actually lodged in those unreflective structures of presentation which apparently unsay or disavow historicism. De Man could have taken his cue from the start of Hegel's *Phenomenology of Spirit (Geist)*. There Hegel famously argues that the most apparently basic knowledge, the moment of apostrophe or demonstration when we point to a 'this', a 'here' or a 'now', is not the indisputable sense-certainty it seems to be. The immediacy of the gesture empties it of meaning: literally and unarguably *present* and nothing more, it cannot be conceptualised. Only the generalisation gained by locating it historically, differentiating the kind of thing it is from other historical events, can allow us to identify it and make it a subject of discourse, something we can talk and argue about. But then it is no longer a privileged, incorrigible presence, but one historical moment among others.[5]

So it is, perhaps, that deconstruction for Derrida engineers an ultimate convergence with Marx and other historicists whose spectres have in fact been haunting its intellectual trajectory all along. There is no immediacy with which we can seize on any moment, present or past. This logocentrism

[4] This 'slogan' is 'unsurprisingly . . . the moral of *The Political Unconscious*', Fredric Jameson, *The political Unconscious: Narrative as a Socially Symbolic Act* (London: Methuen, 1981), p. 9.

[5] The cunning of reason (*der List der Vernunft*) is demonstrated throughout Hegel's *Phenomenology of Spirit* (1807), trans. A. V. Miller (Oxford: Oxford University Press, 1977). For the discussion of 'sense-certainty' see pp. 149ff.

structuring our grasp of any event, however, is thought by anti-Hegelian post-structuralists to compromise understanding rather than innocently constitute it. They agree that we cannot think without concepts, certainly. To that extent Kant and Hegel are right. We should, though, acknowledge one of two things. Either we concede that differences between individuals may be elided when we conceptualise or subsume them under the same generalisation. The nominalist will then argue that such abstractions from individual diversity are merely verbal existences, the Platonist that they are essential because they name the thing itself freed of accidental circumstances. Or else, on another, more radical view, we should concede that it is our generalisations which alter with each historical application so as to fit different individuals.

Poststructuralists take the latter option. They argue that since we cannot shrug off concepts and apprehend immediately, we must show the distortion which, under the stress of the individual event, the supposedly immutable concept or universal necessary to ratiocination must suffer each time it is applied. They advocate what Theodor Adorno (taking Max Weber a stage further) called the 'disenchantment of the concept'.[6] This anti-generalising and polemically individualising philosophy now becomes clearly anti-Platonic as well as anti-Hegelian. But the motor driving its critique is always historicist. To acknowledge this is to grasp that we are always writing a Foucauldian history, a 'history of the present': a history, that is, of precisely these inventions of immediate access to reality by which we try to avoid the historical character into which we in fact perpetually translate reality. Our idea of what it is to be 'present' is peculiar to our own time. It differs, for example, from that of a sensibility belonging to an age prior to the age of anger and telegrams, never mind prior to that of television, e-mail and all the trappings of the communication revolution. Put philosophically, on this view Descartes' 'I am, I exist' may present him in the *Meditations* as listening only to himself, without any intermediary; but in fact his statement of self-coincidence is saturated with historical content, betrayed by the narrative strategies he uses to persuade us of his isolation.[7] Poststructuralists also argue against Heidegger, for instance, that even those pre-reflective experiences fundamental to human orientation in the world already inhabit a linguistic structure in which is inscribed our place in a specific historical epoch.[8] A criticism which historicises the present attacks with equal vigour both empiricism and ideal-

---

[6] Theodor W. Adorno, *Negative Dialectics*, trans. E. B. Ashton (London: Routledge and Kegan Paul, 1973), pp. 11–14. A helpful discussion of French attacks on what Adorno regarded as 'concept fetishism' can be found in Paul Patton, 'Strange Proximity: *Deleuze et Derrida dans les parages du concept*', in *Oxford Literary Review*, vol. 18.1–2 (1996), pp. 117–135.

[7] See Jonathan Reé's discussion of Cartesian narrative in *Philosophical Tales* (London: Methuen and Co., 1987).

[8] See Jacques Derrida, especially 'Différance' and '*Ousia* and *Grammé*: note on a Note From *Being and Time*', in *Margins of Philosophy*, trans. Alan Bass (Brighton: Harvester Press, 1982), pp. 1–69.

ism. Historicism opposes criticism which empirically identifies historical knowledge with history; but historicism is equally antagonistic towards a criticism which idealistically sees formalism as transcending historical consciousness rather than being a product of it.

Hermeneutical circles

What all this comes down to is that historicist criticism does not represent straightforwardly the literary expressions about which it wants to speak. Historicism does not offer unequivocal interpretations of the text in front of it in accordance with concepts of literary criticism, generalisations necessary to the coherence of its discursive practice. It is incorrigibly reflexive. For the historicist, criticism is to be understood by way of its consciousness of its own relativism in each and every judgement it makes. Unlike a full-blown historicist criticism, historical criticism achieves its ends by contextualising its interpretation of literary expression by reference to events or other discourses contemporary with that expression. Historicist criticism, though, interposes another plane of interpretation which takes as its subject those present prejudices or assumptions by which such historical critics decide that something is indeed historically relevant. To the sceptic, this sensitivity to the dangers of hindsight is problematic. Fastidiousness can disguise narcissism or else initiate an endless process of self-criticism. A hermeneutical circle is drawn from which the ostensible object of enquiry – a literary text other than the text discussing it – is forever excluded. But this dilemma is not peculiar to our own day. The Romantics were the masters of hermeneutics, although as a critical practice hermeneutics goes back to the Reformation idea that the interpretation of the scriptures is a source of revelation. Prior to that its etymology returns us to Hermes, most ambiguous of interpreters, who, incidentally, is also the messenger of the gods and the god of thieves; this explains why hermeneutical criticism can appear to steal its object's history for itself by claiming to offer a more sympathetic interpretation.

On the other hand, through this self-consciousness radical hermeneutics can seek historical correctives which help it to break out of the hermeneutical circle of self-regard in which it may appear to have imprisoned itself. For a post-Heideggerian philosopher such as Gadamer, historicist interpretation is a further disclosure of the existence of its object. To this way of thinking, hermeneutics does not necessarily obscure its object or traduce it but instead exhibits its historical effectiveness. Characteristic of any text, we might say, is its difference from what we want to make of it now. But this does not mean, as it did for the classical hermeneutics of Schleiermacher, that we understand the text better than its author or original readers. Our different, perhaps more 'enlightened' interpretations only go to show another aspect of a multifaceted common being shared by past and present, not a past mastered in present understanding. The modern critic establishes a critical tradition in which an earlier text can play along with contemporary critical protocols, simultaneously extending its and their existence. The 'fusion of horizons' effected by this tradition does not establish the superiority of one horizon over the other, but instead shows how contemporary criticism can endorse meanings outside its own protocols. Such a move allows for the possibility that these protocols are, in fact, open to development.

Understanding is what Gadamer calls a 'coming to understanding': a collaborative dialogue between past and present belonging exclusively to neither. Instead of seeing, for example, the revenge conventions of *Hamlet* as social norms that are now thankfully superseded, we might, looking backwards and shedding our progressive prejudices, feel chastened at the equally authentic form in which the same vengeful motivations are expressed in different circumstances by current notions of justice. For Michel Foucault also (to enlist an unlikely ally for Gadamer) literature of the past can allow the critic to detach power from the hegemonic forms in which the exercise of power is legitimate or acceptable in her own society, and learn to see power shockingly in the raw. This she does by becoming historically aware of the same energies and motivations at work under less congenial although equally valid descriptions.

In this scenario, we may still prefer our own morality; we may even still believe it more enlightened than the morality governing the tragedies of Shakespeare, Webster, Middleton and Tourneur. We are not, however, entitled to pretend that ours is anything other than a means of regulating power, a different way of doing the same thing. To some, though, the discontinuities by which this continuity between past and present interpretation is established smuggle in a disreputable metaphysics by the back door. Foucault, using Deleuze, warns explicitly against 'thinking that [this adaptation of Nietzsche's eternal] return is in the form of a content which is difference'.[9] Otherwise, postmodern hermeneutics relies on an unexamined concept of 'difference' which remains unexamined just because all historical and epistemological breaks between one era and another only serve to show difference in action. In this theory, they cannot fail to do so. What is the same is that the same is different each time. This is the metaphysical 'content' Foucault suspects. A higher order of connection is postulated each time a lower-order disconnection is overlooked. Edward Said's famous and supposedly Foucauldian reading of *Mansfield Park* shows, for example, that Jane Austen's inability to realise like us that her novel is about the slave-trade breaks through such criticism to speak loudly our different use of culture to euphemise all manner of

---

[9] Michel Foucault, *Language, Counter-Memory, Practice: Selected Essays and Interviews*, ed. and introd. by D. Bouchard (Oxford: Basil Blackwell, 1977), p. 196.

injustices now.[10] We identify a similarity of concern through our critical differences from it. But will this stand up to comparison with the logic of other discursive practices? We might, for instance, try to argue that just as in biology individual disagreements can be dissolved in a common genetic selfishness, so interpretative differences are over-ruled by a higher hermeneutical purpose.

But while it is *prima facie* plausible to assert, as Richard Dawkins has done, the existence of a macrocosmic genetic world measured through its transmission of genetic formations from one mortal species to another, the same is not obviously true of hermeneutics.[11] The individual, even the species, may be sacrificed to the furthered existence of genetic material. But what would be the higher principle to which specific critical interpretations would be sacrificed? Foucault calls it 'power', Deleuze and others call it 'difference'; but both of them are extremely wary of letting these categories reinstate a kind of negative metaphysics, a superior order of being or the substrate of individual differences. Were an *individual* to act like one of Dawkins' selfish genes, she would, with luck, be locked up quickly. We may be genetically programmed, but that would not stand up in court as an excuse for the abuse of others' rights. This shows the limitations of Dawkins' kind of explanation of human behaviour. But, unlike genetics, power and difference afford no access except from inside. We cannot have a perspective *on* them. They can never be ruled out of court; or, better, there is no further court of appeal in which they are not already sitting.[12] As a result, within poststructuralist hermeneutics contingency is repetition, failure becomes success, superiority to supposed primitivism or barbarism actually euphemises them. Yet, despite anti-metaphysical disclaimers, the faith required to believe in this can still sound theological. It echoes the conclusion of Bossuet's great *Discourse on Universal History*: 'that is why all rulers feel that they are subject to a higher power. They achieve either more or less than they plan, and their intentions have always led to unforeseen consequences . . . In a word, there is no human power which does not unintentionally serve other ends than its own.'[13] To describe in this way the common ground which makes historical interpretation of a text from radically different points of view possible is to hand over the responsibility for such unintended coherence to something like a providential agency, even if a Manichaean one. Full-blown historicism must steer a course between this Scylla and the Charybdis of total discontinuity.

---

[10] Edward Said, 'Jane Austen and Empire', in Terry Eagleton (ed.), *Raymond Williams: Critical Perspectives* (London: Polity Press, 1989).

[11] Richard Dawkins, *The Selfish Gene* (Oxford: Oxford University Press, 1976). See especially ch. 3, 'Immortal Coils'.

[12] For a magisterial discussion of what poststructuralism does to law, see Gillian Rose, *The Dialectic of Nihilism* (Oxford: Basil Blackwell, 1984).

[13] Jacques-Bénique Bossuet, *Discourse on Universal History* (1681), trans. E. Forster (Chicago and London: Chicago University Press, 1976), p. 375.

All-devouring Scyllas would include the Romantic 'Absolute', working its purpose out in nature and science, the 'life' of nineteenth-century *Lebensphilosophie* (a philosophy of life), Marx's dialectical materialism, Nietzsche's 'will to power', the Freudian 'unconscious'. These are all different devices with which critics have tried to ground the transhistorical understanding of different interpretations. They show the earlier one to be a disguised version of the later one, hiding its true content from an enlightened future understanding. The postmodern twist is to reverse the process, and escape Scylla by using historicism to argue in an anti-progressive direction. It employs the evidence of disguise or latent content to demystify or incriminate rather than vindicate the claim future understanding makes to enlightened hindsight. But the flexibility of this historicist criticism returns us to Charybdis, an old philosophical difficulty: the impossibility of formulating historical laws for a discourse, history, whose substance seems inescapably particular and exemplary, potentially unclassifiable. As Georg Simmel indicated, discontinuities in history are the least of the problems of historical interpretation; similarities between past and present can be equally unmanageable. In *The Problem of the Philosophy of History*, published in an expanded version in 1905, he points out that 'influences that do not have historical causes interrupt the immanent development of history. As a result, historical conditions which seem to be equivalent – and which seem to make knowledge of the future possible – produce unexpectedly different consequences.'[14] Simmel anticipates Popper's attack on an historicism which tries, in the manner of Condorcet and Marx, to predict the future from the past. In their different ways, both Simmel and Popper follow a tradition which goes back to Dionysius of Halicarnassus; they uncover a disciplinary division which regards history as philosophising by examples, not by scientific induction. Historical events, like art-works, while infinitely reproducible in different media are themselves irreducibly singular. In Popper's pithy summary, 'the most careful examination of one developing caterpillar will not help us to predict its transformation' into a butterfly'.[15] No more convincingly, as Hans Robert Jauss once showed, can a criticism with pretentions to being scientific, such as Russian formalism, predict the future reception or meaningful appropriations possible for works of art whose stage of development it otherwise appears to have pin-pointed in a progressively ironising process, a quantifiable unmasking by degrees or by successive generations of its own artistic devices. But is there a way of having historicism admit contingencies to its calculations without surrendering its explanations to arbitrariness? Can historicism retain a recognisable critical methodology which is neither narcissistic nor something which, because it must forego the ambition of reducing history to scientific law, lacks any unfolding, immanent logic at all?

[14] Georg Simmel, *The Problem of the Philosophy of History* (2nd edn., 1905), trans. and ed. Guy Oakes (London and New York: Macmillan, The Free Press, 1977), p. 125.
[15] Karl Popper, *The Poverty of Historicism* (London: Routledge & Kegan Paul, 1986), p. 109.

It is, therefore, in a sense different from that of the historicist predictions condemned by Simmel and Popper that a viable historicism must go back to the future, discovering in the past truths confirming or disturbing present assumptions about the past we were unaware of before. The future for the literary work created by reinterpretation is also the rejuvenation of the criticism extended by the same process. The Romantic critic Jerome McGann, for example, has moved on from the critical practice of simply demystifying Romantic ideology or any literature's self-conception to a less assured historicism in which 'the construction of what shall be possible' depends on the critic's failure to demystify completely. Texts as varied as the *Oresteia*, Blake's Prophetic Books and Pound's *Cantos* reflect back to the critics who have stirred them something other than the hegemonic ideas motivating both. In this heterology, the work departs from its original premises to satisfy a new interpretative function, but one it seems to have 'anticipated', even 'intended', one of which criticism may be the catalyst but is no longer the author.[16] The saving of hermeneutics from narcissistic self-analysis inevitably lets the genie of the future out of the bottle, justifying historicist criticism by making it a stage in something larger. This may sound Hegelian, as if all criticism were part of a larger system, but the unpredictable, expressionist aspect of the whole procedure frees it from Hegelian programming. Contingency is precisely what Hegel excludes and what historicism activates by not being able to describe.

Historicising historicism

Are some periods of criticism more historicist than others? My account so far appears only to permit the classification of different kinds of critical situatedness, equally true of all times. This indifference, though, might seem to fly in the face of a decidedly modern sensitivity to relativism and temporality characteristic of a break from previous sensibilities. Scientists such as James Clark Maxwell, Albert Einstein, Niels Bohr and Werner Heisenberg added another dimension to the popular sense of the extent to which our maps of reality might reflect our relative position or experimental methods instead of delivering some absolute truth. Their notions have had striking, if indirect, parallels. Sociologically, twentieth-century developments in communication can similarly be seen to have been valued as the cement of national cultures and as vehicles of communal consciousness rather than as instruments for revealing truth. We can deplore this triumph of culture over science, judging it, as did Theodor Adorno, to have set in motion a consumer industry so powerful that

---

[16] Jerome McGann, 'The Third World of Criticism', in Marjorie Levinson, Marilyn Butler, Jerome McGann, Paul Hamilton (eds.), *Rethinking Historicism: Critical Readings in Romantic History* (Oxford: Basil Blackwell, 1989), pp. 105–106.

it obscured any meaningful notion of truth altogether. Or we might extol its enfranchising potential, as does Walter Benjamin, seeing greater access to culture as a positive mobilisation of the masses against an elitist ideological apparatus, one which previously kept them in their place. Both views established definitive critical positions for the late twentieth century, and they did so by taking up different attitudes to an historicism typical of the modern era. Cultural studies, which has largely evolved out of English and sociology departments, typically focuses on the media by which experience is represented and often itself mutates into media studies. It discovers at all levels of cultural activity an appreciation of intertextuality no longer the preserve of specialists but characteristic of a popular hermeneutics which decodes the representations with which we are bombarded by media of all kinds. This relocation of the message in the medium is often believed to pinpoint postmodernity. At all events, it compensates for what Benjamin calls the devaluing of experience, and is the ebullient, knowing, upbeat Brechtian side to the Frankfurt School's otherwise pessimistic evaluation of historical changes to the idea of enlightenment.

Frankfurt, rather than Cambridge or Oxford, is a more likely source for the rationale of critical activities practised at the moment in Anglo-American academic departments of the humanities. Historicism is its basis, a historicism which argues the importance of relativising all interpretations in the light of modernist self-consciousness. The undermining of absolute values by the Holocaust has been influentially regarded by Adorno as a quintessentially modern phenomenon, impossible without the progress of technologies possessed of an apparently irresistible totalitarian momentum of their own. The difficulties in plotting the convergence of scientific knowledges have been compounded by changes in their paradigms. Polarised and rendered irremediably plural by those scientific revolutions recounted by Thomas Kuhn, such knowledges seem to escape inherited Whig notions of the progress of Science along a single continuum. Simultaneously the notion has emerged of an ecology which rationalises not our control over our natural environment, but its escape from that control, its reactive unpredictability. Typically, according to this ecology, unforeseen imbalances are precipitated by our so-called technological advances, not the unambiguously transparent benefits we intended and expected. Such generalisations, however bland, are necessary if we are to apprehend the sharpened sense of historicism reflected in the critical understanding of texts at the start of this century.

This impasse, though, has been arrived at by way of recurrent but different moments of historicist consciousness. Viewed through historicism, the usual periodisations of the recent history of ideas – early modern or renaissance, enlightenment, romanticism, modernist, postmodernist – look like repeated attempts to exhibit a different decisiveness in response to the vagaries of history. The renaissance has, more than other periods, looked as if it held a premium on the creative revival of the past as the texture of its own self-consciousness. But the strategic historicising typical of what the historian and political theorist J. G. E.Pocock has called 'The Machiavellian Moment' arguably released a characteristically modern secular consciousness of temporality. This allowed all subsequent ages to calculate their own decisiveness as a dialectic between virtue and fortune freed from divine eschatology. Each age generalised in its own way, claiming to provide a pattern for describing all the others. This was true for the universalising ambitions of the enlightenment, the individualistic nationalism of romanticism and the avant-gardism of modernism. It also holds good now for the scepticism of all stories the past has told about itself characteristic of the postmodern retrospective.[17]

To remember Machiavelli in this way is to interpret his political advice as signifying an epochal historicism. As a founder of modernity, Machiavelli adds to our understanding of the contingencies which historicism has to make room for in its own explanations. Neither the aleatoriness of postmodernism, nor the bookishness of the grand narratives whose explanations postmodernism attacks, appear to predominate here. Yet both are kept in play. Machiavelli's commendation of that *virtù* by which the great man copes with the unpredictabilities of fortune, and in fact is emboldened in *virtù* by just such challenges, now seems to rephrase what is required of current historicism.

Pocock's reading of Machiavelli has become influential on an English criticism traditionally wary of taking a theoretical turn. The fateful example of Coleridge, in particular his failure to produce a systematic critical theory, still looms large in the English critical imagination. Machiavellian historicism, though, is rooted in English literature, certainly since the Commonwealth period, and probably earlier. It pervades the length and breadth of Milton's *Paradise Lost*; in smaller focus, but with no less intensity, it drives Marvell's 'An Horatian Ode Upon Cromwell's Return from Ireland'. Its domestic sublime is revived in the Romantic period alongside the afflatus rationalised in Burke and German aesthetics.[18] Its emphasis on the power of example over prescription casts practical criticism from Arnold to Leavis in a new light. This is how new political agendas get generated: its quality of arguing by example does not necessarily shut poetry up in an isolated autotelic realm; it lets poetry set a pattern for what ought to happen outside. Why? Because the typically English preference for literary example over rules of criticism can suddenly be seen to model not the aesthetic transcendence of history but

---

[17] J. G. E. Pocock, *The Machiavellian Moment: Florentine Political Thought and the Atlantic Republican Tradition* (Princeton: Princeton University Press, 1975).

[18] For this 'domestic sublime' see David Norbrook, *Writing the English Republic: Poetry, Rhetoric, Politics* (Cambridge: Cambridge University Press, 1999), pp. 18ff; and Paul Hamilton, 'The Republican Prompt: Continuities in English Radical Culture', in T. Morton and N. Smith (eds.), *Radicalism in English Literary Culture* (Cambridge: Cambridge University Press, forthcoming).

rather the creative response to unforeseen historical circumstance. It pictures
the management of a dilemma without precedent. At this point, of course, it
can join forces with the continental emphasis on theorising which it appeared
to shun. The historical opportunism reflected in critical devotion to the
unparalleled literary example also instructs a postmodern attitude that rules
need to be adapted so as to suit the individual case.

Of course this is not the way the practical critic after the manner of Arnold
or Leavis would see it, and it is mischievous, but I hope productive, thus to
force the close reader and the theorist into society. The pervasiveness of historicism comes from the open-endedness I have been emphasising all along:
historicist criticism's facility, in response to a text, to table a new motion of
which it is no longer the author. In line with this thesis, historicism's reflexivity need not be narcissistic if it gestures towards a future understanding, one
set in motion by its dialogue with a text, but one as yet incomplete.
Historicism's most powerful expressions now are most probably to be found
in postcolonial and feminist criticism. Each of these enterprises negotiates an
enormous silence, a huge repression of the artificial and unjust social
mechanics which for ages enforced supposed normality. Since we cannot
imagine a larger unfairness at the root of an establishment, the criticism
attempting to redress such unparalleled inequity might reasonably be
expected to be systematically opposed to authoritarianism in the widest
sense.

Postcolonial criticism merges with the problem of providing a coherent
picture of multi-culturalism. New notions of integrity and selfhood need to
arise beyond the purview of a critique of colonial prejudice and a championing of opposition to it. Arguably that is why Franz Fanon's call at the end of
The Wretched of the Earth to 'work out new concepts, and set afoot a new
man' professes this aim.[19] When subalterns speak they are wise to 'the complicity between subject and object', perhaps too wise to think they can escape
complicity altogether, but definitely moving on, arriving somewhere else.[20]
But Gayatri Spivak's critical ambition here is the modest enough political
application of other, spectacular critical self-dissolutions of a subject always
in process. Deleuze's revival of the past as a difference whose content was
always still to be decided was portentously likened by Foucault to 'a lightning
storm'.[21] Deleuze returned the compliment after Foucault's death by reading
Foucault's own surpassing of Nietzsche – the account of the death of man by
which he trumped Nietzsche's account of the death of God – as the compar-
ably prophetic evocation of an elemental creature: one transgressing supposedly defining boundaries and exclusions, someone loaded with the animal,
the mineral, the organic. But, behind Foucault, Deleuze claimed to take his

[19] Franz Fanon, *The Wretched of the Earth*, preface, Jean-Paul Sartre, trans. Constance
Farrington (Harmondsworth: Penguin, 1967), p. 255.
[20] Gayatri Chakravorty Spivak, *In Other Worlds: Essays in Cultural Politics* (London: Methuen,
1987), p. 221.   [21] Foucault, *Language, Counter-memory, Practice*, p. 196.

inspiration from Rimbaud's project of the othering of the 'je'.[22] In each case, immediate apprehension of self-consciousness is shown up for the historical construction it really is, and the unprescribed future to be lived on such currently alienated terms is celebrated, celebrated as the call to a new kind of existence still to be appropriated as our own. In less individualistic terms, the same challenge is posed by multiculturalism. It belongs to this moment, it poses problems to ideas of unity and participation within a single politics as never before. But the new politics which must emerge if cultural difference is not to remain social contradiction reworks the model we have been examining: a historicist openness to self-redefinition engendered by or corresponding to a historicist generosity in judging the canons of past expression.

Feminism, especially from the 'new woman' debates of the late nineteenth century onwards, has always been interested in the conflicting drives of equality for woman as she is, and of the right for woman to escape any such imposed definition with its accompanying histories of distortion and containment. The debate continues in Germaine Greer's revival of a call for women's 'liberation' rather than mere equality of treatment. Post-feminism, she argues, has forgotten the true extent of re-creation open to a revolutionary movement freed of the determinants of class, culture, ethnicity and so on which have policed other revolutionary movements.[23] Such resistance to essentialism always takes further a resentment of the uniformity imposed by history. It contributes to that writing of a history of history typical of radical historicism. A critical theory which becomes implicated in historicism has therefore to choose between two possibilities. Both are ways of honouring Aristotle's dictum that the object of poetics is more philosophical than history.

The first possibility, roughly Hegelian, is to see the relativism of any period's self-understanding surpassed within a progressive narrative of ever-improving knowledge. The second, mutating from existentialism into postmodernism, is to see any relativising of the past as setting in motion a comparable potential for transformation in the historiciser, one which would immediately question, for example, any notion that hindsight was necessarily progressive, unquestionably an improvement on past knowledge. Most critical movements, such as new historicism, tend to dally between the two possibilities. And maybe this is right. Undoubtedly one wants to hang on to the belief in progress in some spheres of life, and condemn as reactionary those who do not agree. Equally, however, the arrogance of progress and its technological mystification can get in the way of any transfiguring notion of the good life. This apparently simple opposition, though, leads surely to the most complex of philsophical debates. Historicism is perhaps the most visible means by which critical theory is implicated in them at every turn.

---

[22] Gilles Deleuze, *Foucault* (Paris: Les Editions de minuit, 1986), pp. 140–141.
[23] Germaine Greer, *The Whole Woman* (London: Doubleday, 1999).

2

Literary criticism and the history of ideas

TIMOTHY BAHTI

The concept of the 'history of ideas' is associated with the work and legacy of a single person, the American philosopher Arthur O. Lovejoy (1873–1962). Literature, ideas and their possible *historical* interrelation are, however, problems of very wide interest and import for twentieth-century literary studies. Once the term 'criticism' covers all forms of literary study and once 'ideas' and their possible history are seen to overlap with – and to contest – other constructions that are available to make sense of literature, the topic of literary criticism and the history of ideas appears as but one version of the problematic relations between *literature* and *history* that dominate twentieth-century literary studies.

*

Lovejoy's masterwork, *The Great Chain of Being: A Study in the History of an Idea* was delivered in 1933 as the William James Lectures at Harvard and published in 1936;[1] it remains, together with some of his collected *Essays in the History of Ideas* (1948),[2] the signal contribution of the history of ideas to the concerns of literary criticism. Very briefly put, 'ideas' for Lovejoy are 'the persistent dynamic factors . . . that produce effects in the history of thought', 'the elements, the primary and persistent or recurrent dynamic units, of the history of thought' (pp. 5, 7). In an explicit analogy to chemistry, Lovejoy considers his objects of study to be 'component elements' of the larger compounds of thoughts, doctrines or systems in intellectual history, and he wishes to discriminate and trace the workings of such 'unit-ideas' (p. 3). In his magisterial history, 'the great chain of being' is studied not only as the more-or-less stable image and name for the universe across more than two millennia of western thought, but more importantly as a complex (or compound) of the related 'unit-ideas' of plenitude, sufficient reason, continuity, gradation and, ultimately, temporalisation. From Plato and neo-Platonism, across medieval scholasticism and early modern cosmology, to Spinoza and Leibniz and Enlightenment philosophers

---

[1] Arthur O. Lovejoy, *The Great Chain of Being: A Study of the History of an Idea* (Cambridge, Mass.: Harvard University Press, 1936). Subsequent references given by page number in the body of the text.

[2] Arthur O. Lovejoy, *Essays in the History of Ideas* (Baltimore: Johns Hopkins University Press, 1948).

and scientists, Lovejoy traces the endurance and flexibility of the 'unit-ideas' that constitute and maintain the great chain of being as a coherent assemblage of assumptions and understandings. But he is also everywhere attentive to the tensions and contradictions between component units therein, so that at the end of his history, with European Romanticism, the inherent strains give way under the pressure of the idea of temporalisation, and the great chain of being collapses as a comprehensive world-view capable of organising and guiding metaphysical and theological thought as well as scientific research.

The remarkable erudition and sustained analytic and narrative power of *The Great Chain of Being* make it one of the enduring works of twentieth-century intellectual history, but this extraordinary achievement does not exhaust its interest for literary criticism and literary history. For this, two further aspects of Lovejoy's work are salient. First, Lovejoy gives no distinctive status to literature: it is a mode of cultural expression – what we might today call a 'discursive field' – like many others, for the study of which one needs specialised disciplinary skills as well as broad linguistic experience and openness (Lovejoy was an early advocate of comparative literature), but which ultimately can be understood and evaluated in terms of the 'ideas' it contains and transmits. Dante and Milton, Pope and Young, Goethe and Hugo figure in his history for the versions of ultimately philosophical ideas they document. 'The interest of the history of literature', Lovejoy writes, 'is largely as a record of the movement of ideas . . . And the ideas in serious reflective literature are, of course, in great part philosophical ideas in dilution – to change the figure, growths from seed scattered by great philosophic systems' (pp. 16, 17).

Second, Lovejoy also gives no privileged status to the notion of a historical 'period'. While it has been much noted that Lovejoy attacked the term and concept of 'Romanticism' as a coherent movement or period in western literature, thought and culture[3] – it was too contradictory, with too many forms and tensions, to be known by one name – it has been less appreciated that the entire narrative of *The Great Chain of Being* finally works against the maintenance of the period terms it itself uses. Thus, while the history is still told in terms of familiar period categorisations such as 'medieval' and 'enlightenment' ('classical', 'Renaissance' and 'baroque' are less evident), the narrative argument is actually one that keeps thinkers and their basic thoughts, from Plato and the Schoolmen to Spinoza and Leibniz, vital and interacting beyond any historical delimitation by periodisation. Through its argument that a few 'unit-ideas' reappear in a restricted set of possible combinations in the primary and secondary thinkers of western culture, Lovejoy's history undermines one's ultimate confidence in the finer chronological discriminations of separable modes of philosophic and cultural expression. The tensions within the 'compound' idea, and between the 'unit-ideas', are permanent and there *ab ovo*, and think-

[3] Lovejoy, 'On the Discrimination of Romanticisms' (1924), *Essays in the History of Ideas*, pp. 228–252.

ers and scientists refer back and forth among these constitutive forces of contradiction. There is a single story *en bloc*, that of the chain and its tensile links. Indeed, the figure of a 'great chain of being' is the very master-figure of the continuity of western history as Lovejoy reconstructs it. If the period name of 'Romanticism' survives tenuously, it is as a name for the very *end* of the history that Lovejoy views and the narrative that he writes. Lovejoy's history is about arguments of seamless continuity – *natura non facit saltus*, in the formulation famous from the Scholastics through Leibniz – and his method and narrative similarly would deny the fundamental contingency and discontinuity that period concepts incipiently represent. 'Romanticism', in Lovejoy's history, finally does represent the unravelling of his argument and narrative.

The diminished status that literature and the period concept enjoy in his history leads to the fundamental interest that Lovejoy represents for literary criticism. For the question is whether literary criticism, literary history, and literary theory can do without both a privileging of literature *vis-à-vis* history and a privileging of historical periods within history. The answer to the question is, apodictically put, negative in its first part, affirmative in its second: serious literary study cannot do without a constitutive privileging of literature over its historical account, while it can do without period concepts.

In exploring this pair of answers to the problem that the history of ideas poses, we may observe that several of Lovejoy's distinguished colleagues in literature at the Johns Hopkins University were not unsympathetic to his doctrine. Charles Singleton, who was the premier Dantist of his time, Earl Wasserman, who was a leading intellectual-historical interpreter of English romantic poetry, and the great scholar of French literature and 'critic of consciousness' Georges Poulet were all entirely at home with Lovejoy's mixing of literature and philosophy and with his deployment of a master-figure such as the 'great chain of being', even if they did not each need to endorse or follow his historical argument in its sweep or in its details. But a fourth Hopkins colleague, Leo Spitzer, the preeminent practitioner of Romance stylistics in the twentieth century, poses a more significant difference respecting literature and its possible historical and period-specific forms. Like Lovejoy, Spitzer practises his mode of study across virtually all historical times and across many languages. And like Lovejoy, he is not shy about working across disciplines or discourses. So far, they are comrades-in-arms regarding transhistoric, comparative and cross-disciplinary studies. But their differences emerge at the two points we have thus far singled out: the privileged status of literature and the preeminent importance of the historical period. In his contribution to Lovejoy's *Journal of the History of Ideas*,[4]

---

[4] Leo Spitzer, '*Geistesgeschichte* vs. History of Ideas as Applied to Hitlerism', *Journal of the History of Ideas* 5 (1944), reprinted in Spitzer, *Representative Essays*, eds. Alban Forcione, Herbert Lindenberger and Madeleine Sutherland (Stanford: Stanford University Press, 1988), pp. 207–224.

Spitzer discusses Nazism and its alleged reappropriation of 'unit-ideas' from German romanticism in terms that precisely criticise Lovejoy's vaunted analytic method and chemical analogy. What counts for Spitzer are not contrived, abstract analytic 'ideas' that may be alleged to be continuous or recurrent across history, but the 'synthetic' and real bundles of cultural features that are specific and indeed unique to a historical place and time. Such a 'totality of features of a given period or movement', grasped 'as a unity',[5] is for Spitzer unabashedly the object and achievement of *Geistesgeschichte* and its key period-concept of a *Zeitgeist*, and this is hopelessly beyond the ken of the history of ideas.

The methodological specificity and preeminence of the period-concept are here apparent. It is also noteworthy that Spitzer's avowal of the historical period is of a piece with his privileging of literature and its distinctive features. While he studies discursive materials as diverse as political propaganda, commercial advertising and traditional philosophy, the overwhelming bulk of his massive bibliography is devoted to high literature. More importantly, his very notion and image of a 'totality of features' constitutive of a historical period is drawn from his practice and experience in literary stylistics. Most accessible in his programmatic essay, 'Linguistics and Literary History', but readily discernible in almost any of his voluminous stylistic studies, Spitzer's method confidently assumes and then confirms with great flair a continuity that moves from the smallest grammatical, syntactic and even morphological feature of style to the literary work as a whole and then on to the author's oeuvre and psyche as larger wholes, ultimately arriving at a characterisation of the period and the 'spirit of its time'.[6] This chain is not Lovejoy's narrative 'great chain of being', with its interlocking, tension-loaded but finally continuous links of recurring similarity; Spitzer's 'chain' is one of concentrically nesting synecdoches, each moving metonymically from part to adjacent whole in an expansion of literary signification and interpretive divination. The closest analogue to this, which also recalls their shared Leibnizian monadology, is Walter Benjamin's characterisation of 'historical materialism' – with the all-important difference that where Spitzer arrives at a stable endpoint, Benjamin arrives at an explosion. Benjamin writes in the seventeenth of his 'Theses on the philosophy of history': 'A historical materialist approaches a historical subject only where he encounters it as a monad . . . He takes cognizance of it in order to blast a specific era out of the homogeneous course of history – blasting a specific life out of the era or a specific work out of a lifework. As a result of this method the lifework is preserved in this work and at the same time cancelled; in the lifework, the era; and in the era, the entire

---

[5] *Ibid.*, p. 202.
[6] Leo Spitzer, *Linguistics and Literary History: Essays in Stylistics* (Princeton: Princeton University Press, 1948), pp. 10ff.

course of history.'[7] Spitzer's and Benjamin's equally synecdochal chains, while differing as nesting dolls do from a chain reaction, are likewise aimed at the 'homogeneous' chain-image of an analytically based narrative of history such as Lovejoy's history of 'unit-ideas'.

Spitzer, not unlike Benjamin, was temperamentally incapable of writing a literary history. But almost anywhere in his voluminous work – again, somewhat like Benjamin – one can find claims for historically specific knowledge that conforms to a period-concept (medieval, baroque, Romantic, etc.) and is formed of the specifically literary features (stylistic for Spitzer, allegorical for Benjamin) of the verbal work of art. As the last of the Hopkins literary colleagues' reactions to Lovejoy's history of ideas, Spitzer's position stands or falls on the import first of the historical period-concept (the *Zeitgeist*), then of the category of literature and its constitutive features (style). Moving now from this anecdotal-institutional juxtaposition of literary studies with Lovejoy to a more fundamental one, we confront the question whether there actually is in the historical record an alternative to the extreme polarity of Lovejoy's relatively seamless narrative absorption and even dissolution of literature within the history of ideas, and Spitzer's (or, *mutatis mutandis*, Benjamin's) episodic and fragmentary foregrounding of literature, which leaves it stranded like isolated islands amidst historical time.

A review of the record suggests that the answer is no. That is, one must admit how paltry and how poor have been the twentieth century's attempts at literary history and other forms of literary-historical study on anything resembling the scale of Lovejoy's *The Great Chain of Being*. René Wellek, simultaneously one of Lovejoy's most dogged critics and most fixated admirers, everywhere calls for literary history but nowhere either finds it to his satisfaction or writes it himself. With one exception we shall presently turn to, there are simply no distinguished, comprehensive, narrative histories of European literature after the century of Taine, Brunetière and De Sanctis. *Geistesgeschichte* lasted the longest in Germany, where it had its most solid foundation, and Georg Lukács' *Theory of the Novel* (1916) is prophetically one of the last breaths of comprehensive literary-historical aspiration in this atmosphere; it would have been more at home in the nineteenth century, but its famous thesis of the 'homesickness' of the novel reflects instead its own homelessness, loss of bearings and ultimate discontinuity in its native twentieth century.[8]

---

[7] Walter Benjamin, 'Thesen über den Begriff der Geschichte' (1940), English translation: 'Theses on the Philosophy of History', *Illuminations*, ed. Hannah Arendt, trans. Harry Zohn (New York: Harcourt, Brace and World, 1968), p. 263.

[8] Georg Lukács, *Die Theorie des Romans: Ein geschichtsphilosophischer Versuch über die Formen der grossen Epik* (1916); English translation: *The Theory of the Novel: A Historico-Philosophical Essay on the Forms of Great Epic Literature*, trans. Anna Bostock (Cambridge, Mass.: MIT Press, 1971).

In fact, apart from the occasional work that is typically restricted by national literature, by period, and by genre, the literary-historical achievements of twentieth-century literary studies are almost non-existent. After the striking but subterranean (indeed, geological) role that literature plays in his *Les mots et les choses* (1966)[9] – in the figures of Cervantes, Mallarmé, Artaud and Borges – there is neither literary history (or 'genealogy') by Foucault nor Foucauldian literary history. Ironically, the more one looks for literary history that would be at once transhistorical, comparative, multi-genred and successful, the less one finds any alternative to the Lovejovian model.

One famous example of a literary 'history' that productively bears comparison with Lovejoy's achievement is Ernst Robert Curtius' *European Literature and the Latin Middle Ages.*[10] Its title is slyly misleading: its coverage actually extends from Greek antiquity to the age of Goethe, and indeed into the twentieth century. Its linguistic and generic reach is virtually as comprehensive as its seemingly unending bibliography. And its conception of 'literature' – proceeding from rhetoric and its transmission through not only the literary genres but the entire educational practices of the west – is so broad as to absorb all kinds of cultural discourse. Precisely here is the first point where the comparison with Lovejoy becomes revealing.

Although, as far as I know, neither author made any recognition of his exact contemporary, Curtius' and Lovejoy's objects of study have considerable overlap. Lovejoy calls one aspect of his history of ideas 'an inquiry which may be called philosophical semantics – a study of the sacred words and phrases of a period or a movement', and he adds – against the very sense of containment that a period-concept would imply – 'it is largely because of their ambiguities that mere words are capable of this independent action ["the insensible transformation of one fashion of thought into another, perhaps its very opposite"] as forces of history' (p. 14). When the disciplinary propriety of the 'philosophical' is bracketed, these 'sacred formulas and catchwords'[11] of Lovejoy's that are 'forces of history' become indistinguishable from Curtius' objects of study, namely *topoi* or commonplaces, the dominant and recurrent tropes that every educated and not-so-educated person absorbs from the culture and without which thought and expression would be inconceivable. Lovejoy's 'ideas' are supposedly the stuff that appears in 'dilution' in literature, while Curtius' *topoi* are rather crystallised in the literary tradition and dissolved or permeating everywhere else. But when one looks at the materiality of the verbal record – the words themselves, and their forms – one has under whatever name the same tropological substratum. What Curtius the

---

[9] Michel Foucault, *Les mots et les choses: une archéologie des sciences humaines* (1966); English translation: *The Order of Things: An Archaeology of the Human Sciences* (New York: Pantheon, 1971).
[10] Ernst Robert Curtius, *Europäische Literatur und lateinisches Mittelalter* (1948); English translation: *European Literature and the Latin Middle Ages*, trans. Willard Trask (New York: Pantheon, 1953).   [11] Lovejoy, *Essays*, p. 9.

Romance philologist took as a 'literary' subject seeps, drifts and expands into a pancultural arena, while Lovejoy's 'philosophical' interest in the analysis of ideas works, at the end of the day, with the very same, that is, tropological material as literature.

If Curtius' privileging of literature – an understandable commitment, since he relies on the written record of ancient usages of the commonplaces – turns ironically into its dissolution, his sovereign *historical* reach also meets a paradoxical end, and in this, too, he bears comparison with Lovejoy. Beyond all distinctions by period, Curtius tells a story that has no end except that of fatigue and slow attrition without end: the 'end' of the western tradition's indebtedness to and embeddedness within its commonplaces is their *usure*, their wearing-down into our ignorance of our own tradition; it is their end in their very home, which is the commonplace of Tradition itself, without apocalyptic revelation, circular closure or violent rupture. Curtius has none of the narrative drive and skill of Lovejoy, but then again, he does not need them because he has no real *story* to tell. And yet, on the far side of his non-narrative history (or, more accurately, historical compendium), Curtius' account of his subject, like Lovejoy's, finds the means of his inquiry disappearing along its very course. Lovejoy's 'chain of being' survived as long as did the chain of his own narrative – with links always of the same 'units', and always in tension with one another – which is to say that the chain is the story of its own ending, its breaking apart and off. Curtius' *topoi* are the material of literary rhetoric and of its scholarly custody by philology and his melancholy study is one that knows everything up to the end-point of the means of its own knowledge.

Spitzer has the literary text's bundle of stylistic features, each time a synecdoche for the supposed essence of literature, representing 'synthetically' but no less synecdochally the 'totality of features of a given period or movement' – but he has no narrative literary history, no account of the succession of periods as the story of literature. Curtius has the constancy of literary *topoi* across the history of the west, but in the end he has neither literature in any restricted sense, nor, *a fortiori*, literary study, let alone a narrative literary history. Measured against the standard of Lovejoy's work, which is an historical narrative as well as *a history of* ideas, both preeminent philologists represent the failure of twentieth-century literary study to be at once literary *and* historical. In this, we arrive nowhere else but at René Wellek's and Austin Warren's doleful analysis of the fate of most histories of literature: 'One type is not a history of *art* [Curtius]; the other, not a *history* of art [Spitzer].'[12]

Wellek, unable himself to write a literary history but always able to fault others who failed, is nonetheless, despite his acerbic and often unpleasant manner, also very clear and tough-minded about what such a history should

---

[12] René Wellek and Austin Warren, *Theory of Literature*, 3rd edn. (New York: Harcourt, Brace and World, 1962), p. 253.

be. Following his Russian formalist beginnings, he maintains that literary-historical developments and periodisations must be 'established by purely literary criteria', by the study of 'system[s] of literary norms, standards, and conventions', and that literary history must be 'the tracing of the changing from one system of norms to another'. But Wellek cannot say why the development of literary periods 'has to move in the particular direction it has taken: mere see-saw schemes are obviously inadequate to describe the whole complexity of the process'. Baffled by 'a complex process varying from occasion to occasion . . . partly internal, caused by exhaustion and the desire for change, but also partly external, caused by social, intellectual, and all other cultural changes', Wellek's once-clear ambition is left trying to convert despair into a fuzzy idealism: 'The further and wider problem, a history of a national literature as a whole, is harder to envisage . . . histories of groups of literatures are even more distant ideals . . . Finally, a general history of the art of literature is still a far-distant ideal.'[13]

Always on the near side of these unreachable horizons, Wellek finds some solace – and here he refers explicitly to Lovejoy's critique of the period-concept of Romanticism – in the mental gymnastics of wrestling with the problem of literary history and its periodisation: 'the discussion of a period will at least raise all kinds of questions of literary history'.[14] Without narrative, we at least have ongoing discussion, the perennial raising of questions in which there is finally neither history as narrative nor criticism as satisfactory knowledge.

Throughout his work, Wellek pays almost as much attention – usually carping, sometimes begrudgingly admiring – to Lovejoy and his history of ideas as to any other modern practitioner of a history of discourse, literary or otherwise. The only other figure that repeatedly disappoints and yet re-attracts Wellek in like manner is Erich Auerbach and his literary history *Mimesis*.[15] Wellek's simplistic misunderstanding of Auerbach's masterwork need not concern us here. *Mimesis: The Representation of Reality in Western Literature* is, for our purposes, the only literary history in the twentieth century that measures up to, and finally yields an adequate measure of, *The Great Chain of Being* and its history of ideas.

It is superficial but instructive to recall how *Mimesis* meets the broadest criteria provided by Lovejoy's example: Auerbach's book is transhistorical, polyglot, comparative, and studies most genres (only lyric verse is neglected). If Lovejoy the analytic philosopher privileges philosophic 'unit-ideas', and includes literature only as their 'diluted' form, Auerbach the philologist privileges with symmetrical rigour literature's narrative and dramatic resources of

---

[13] Cf. *ibid.*, 264–268.   [14] *Ibid.*, p. 267.

[15] Erich Auerbach, *Mimesis: dargestellte Wirklichkeit in der abendländischen Literatur*; English translation: *Mimesis: The Representation of Reality in Western Literature*, trans. Willard Trask (Princeton: Princeton University Press, 1953).

representation and folds in religion, philosophy and social history only as their setting and stage. And most evidently, Auerbach's history has a bold and comprehensive thesis to match Lovejoy's. The 'great chain of being' is the compound of a handful of elemental ideas (plenitude, continuity, gradation, sufficient reason) that, despite but also because of their inherent tensions, constitute a coherent metaphysics, theology and scientific world-view – until, with the varieties of temporalisation that are coextensive with modernity, it no longer hangs together. Auerbach has an equivalently essential thesis regarding western literature – it is nothing less than the representation of reality – and he argues for its ever expansive achievements from antiquity to the fullest modern depictions of social reality (the French realists) and interior reality (Proust and Woolf).

Lovejoy's book is truly a history *of* ideas in that the ideas themselves – following the chemical analogy of elemental properties in their possible combinations and reactions – properly drive the history: '[t]his historic outcome of the long series of "footnotes to Plato" which we have been observing was also, so far as it went, the logically inevitable outcome' (p. 326). Thus, he needs neither familiar social accounts (the transition from feudal to bourgeois society) nor economic ones (mercantilism, industrialisation) nor political ones (the nation-state, colonialism) to assist his argument, and he even makes relatively little use of technology (although the telescope and microscope do figure importantly). It has been insufficiently noticed that Auerbach matches Lovejoy's purism, and in this, he alone meets Wellek's strictures that a true history of literature would be 'established by purely literary criteria'. There are, ultimately, only two such literary principles that are necessary and sufficient for Auerbach's history.[16] One is the doctrine concerning levels of style, where, in Auerbach's well-known argument, distinct generic and stylistic differences give way under the force of the Christian *sermo humilis* to yield the ever-more comprehensive representational power of western literature. The other principle is the figural representation of history, in which any two events in time (including a 'time' that would be, to use Lovejoy's term, 'otherworldly', time on the far side of human history, *sub specie aeternitatis*) can be coordinated as prefiguration and fulfillment, with the latter fulfillment being the 'real' or true representation of 'reality'.[17]

It is no secret that Auerbach's two principles draw upon the historico-theological discourses of the Judaeo-Christian tradition, just as his narrative also draws upon the inmixing of class distinctions across early-modern and modern western history as a parallel to his literary history of the leveling of

---

[16] The following interpretation is developed more fully in Timothy Bahti, *Allegories of History: Literary Historiography After Hegel* (Baltimore: Johns Hopkins University Press, 1992), pp. 137–155; see also Timothy Bahti, 'Vico, Auerbach and Literary History', *Philological Quarterly* 60 (1981), pp. 239–255.

[17] See Erich Auerbach, 'Figura' (1938), *Scenes From the Drama of European Literature*, trans. Ralph Mannheim (New York: Meridian, 1959), pp. 11–76.

stylistic differences. But it cannot be stated emphatically enough that the twin principles of stylistic and generic leveling and of figural representation of human time are nonetheless strictly literary. To overstate the matter only slightly, if the histories of the rise and spread of Christianity and of the modernisation of the social experience of classes in the west did not exist as backdrops for Auerbach's literary history, he would not even need to invent them. To put the same point more analytically, Auerbach's two principles are literary because they are the tropology of verbal art.

Both the relation of style to genre and the relation of one figure to another (prefiguration to its fulfillment) are tropological arrangements of *figurae verborum* and *figurae sententiae*, figures of speech and figures of thought. Together, they constitute the material and the method, the subject matter and the procedure, of *Mimesis*. The style of plain prose, which comes closest to what Hegel calls 'the prose of the world' and the genre of historical narrative which is Auerbach's historicism are combined in his literary history, in *Mimesis* itself, as the fulfillment and end of his history. And the structure of representation that aligned prefiguration and fulfillment first in their *décalage* in Homer and the Old Testament, then in their inversion of the otherworldly back into the this-worldly in Dante's *Inferno*, and then in their threateningly nihilistic realisation of experiential life in Flaubert's *Madame Bovary* – this structure is at once fulfilled and evacuated, left to collapse, at the end of *Mimesis*, when the achievement of the representation of interior reality as a stream of consciousness is left towering above a flattened, faceless and rubble-strewn reality that is the representation of the 'merely' historical west at the end of World War Two. Auerbach's one genre of historicist narrative yields as an afterimage – a *figura* beyond the fulfillment – the other genre of autobiography. Beyond Proust's and Woolf's fictional autobiographies, Auerbach's disguised autobiographical narrative – his book's interior 'representation of reality' – is and means (in figural language, it figures and fulfills) the afterlife of an almost nameless exile, survivor and victim of fatigue who is also, typologically, the post-war Everyman of 'real' historical reality.

From his material practices of philology and stylistics, Auerbach is uniquely able to fashion a history *of* literature. His literature remains literature, and his history remains and becomes literature – 'remains and becomes' because it becomes, in his hands, what it always already was, a genre of literary rhetoric developing from Homer's epics and the Old Testament narratives to modern historicism. Auerbach famously wrote that *Mimesis* could not have been written in any tradition other than that of Hegel and *Geistesgeschichte*,[18] and here we may recall as well that Hegel is conspicuously absent from Lovejoy's *The Great Chain of Being* – conspicuously so because Hegel is arguably the one western writer and philosopher who is able

---

[18] Erich Auerbach, 'Epilogomena zu *Mimesis*', *Romanische Forschungen* 65 (1953), p. 15.

to combine temporalisation with plenitude, continuity, gradation and sufficient reason to yield, in his late work, a chain of mental being (of *Geist*) that is sometimes narrative and historical, sometimes – in the *Logic* and the *Encyclopedia* – post-narrative. Lovejoy, in fact, appears from this perspective as Hegel *manqué* – as Hegel without the Hegelian post-narrative – and *The Great Chain of Being* as a narrative history that must tell its story of breakage and dissolution without an ultimate ending in Hegel's own fulfillment of history.

With Hegel situated alongside Auerbach and Lovejoy, we return again to our topic of literary study and the history of ideas. The topic is the *topos* or commonplace of the relation of an idea to a literary structure and – a subsidiary of this topic – of the relation of history to a literary structure. Hegel's *Aesthetics* is an argument, at once analytic and narrative, about how art, and preeminently the highest art that is literature, is its very development from sensuous and merely 'ideal' stages to the idea of itself. In becoming, via the stage of religion, the idea of itself, art becomes the philosophy that the *Aesthetics* itself, as narrative and discourse, is; thus, art confirms the *Aesthetics*, just as it fulfills art. The entire *Aesthetics*, as a historically informed and organised narrative (the symbolic, classical and Romantic 'stages' of art, the arrangement of the 'kinds' of art, etc.), is an attempt to work out – to think and write out, in the 'genre' of philosophy – the relations between the basic tropological structures that Hegel, like many before and since, calls 'symbol' and 'allegory', and their 'higher' comprehension as sheer linguistic materiality in the sign as 'mere sign' (*blosses Zeichen*): this, in summary, is the entire narrative and argumentative trajectory of the three volumes, from the symbolic in pre-classical architecture to the transition from music to poetry at the end of romantic art.[19] On the far side of Hegel, Lovejoy, and Auerbach, we here also approach the narrative and argumentative trajectory of Paul de Man's work. In 'The Rhetoric of Temporality', he postulates that the entirety of literary history could be understood as a 'dialectic' (albeit a negative one) between the rhetorical structures of allegory and irony.[20] In his last readings of Hegel, he argues that the philosophic idea is in truth – in the language of 'The Rhetoric of Temporality', it is the demystified allegory of – the sheer materiality of the letter, the linguistic signifier 'itself', if we could only know such a thing or condition.[21] Under this view, the 'great chain of being' is, in the end, language itself understood on de Man's radically materialist account.

The array of perspectives that we arrive at does not dissolve into perspectivism. Literature may be only 'dissolved' philosophy or ideas for Lovejoy, but

[19] This interpretation is presented more fully in Bahti, *Allegories*, pp. 95–133.
[20] Paul de Man, 'The Rhetoric of Temporality', in Charles Singleton (ed.), *Interpretation: Theory and Practice* (Baltimore: Johns Hopkins University Press, 1968), pp. 206–207.
[21] Paul de Man, 'Sign and Symbol in Hegel's *Aesthetics*', *Critical Inquiry* 8 (1982), pp. 761–775.

for literary studies in the twentieth century, Lovejoy remains exemplary 'literary' history in that he retells and re-presents the allegory of historical narratives of the west (its world-views, its literature, its culture) after and yet wishfully in the absence of Hegel: after but also without Hegel, philosophic history is sheer literary allegory, and its ideas are tropological structures (plenitude, continuity and gradation are forms of metonymy, sufficient reason is metalepsis, etc.). The singular example of Auerbach's *Mimesis* is that of the possibility of turning Hegel's basic assumption in the *Aesthetics* – the historical development of western art, via literature, to its truth – into an historical narrative that is very nearly purely literary, and that reveals its tropological (that is, figural) structure as both its vehicle and its truth – which is also, we must recall, the claimed truth of the west. But like Lovejoy's book, *Mimesis* also must end in the narrative of a collapse, and a collapse of its own narrative: the historical justification of the ways of ideas or literature to human understanding yields their unravelling into discontinuity, fraying, ruination. At the end of his work, de Man saw that his attempts at a comprehensive, comparative and historical understanding of European literary Romanticism had foundered not only on some proper names called 'Rousseau' and 'Hölderlin', but on the tropological structures of allegory, irony and parataxis, leaving only *fragments* of a possible, now impossible literary history.[22] Literary history cannot be solved by tropology, for tropology dissolves history. The idea of literary study after a history of exemplary philosophic, historical and literary achievements – after Hegel, after the history of ideas, after Spitzer, Curtius, Auerbach and de Man – is the non-historical, non-narrative, non-idealist, that is to say, properly tropological and material study of the exemplarity of language that we call literature.

[22] Paul de Man, *Allegories of Reading: Figural Language in Rousseau, Nietzsche, Rilke, and Proust* (New Haven: Yale University Press, 1979), p. xi; and Paul de Man, *The Rhetoric of Romanticism* (New York: Columbia University Press, 1984), pp. viii–ix.

3

Cultural materialism

John Drakakis

In the opening chapter of *The Long Revolution* (1961), Raymond Williams argues that '[e]verything we see and do, the whole structure of our relationships and institutions, depends, finally, on an effort of learning, description and communication'.[1] In what was to become a radical challenge to the dominant modes of literary and cultural study, Williams concluded that:

If all activity depends on responses learned by the sharing of descriptions, we cannot set 'art' on one side of a line and 'work' on the other; we cannot submit to be divided into 'Aesthetic Man' and 'Economic Man.'[2]

Williams goes on, in his chapter on 'The Analysis of Culture', to challenge an historical methodology based upon the assumption that 'the bases of society, its political, economic, and "social" arrangements, form the central core of facts, after which the art and theory can be adduced, for marginal illustration or "correlation"', and a literary methodology which privileged its own formal laws of composition while relegating this central core of facts to the status of 'background'. His call in 1961 was for a cultural history which had to be 'more than the sum of the particular histories, for it is with the relations between them, the particular forms of the whole organisation, that it is especially concerned'. Thus, Williams' 'theory of culture' could subsequently be defined as 'the study of the relationships between elements in a whole way of life'.[3]

Almost twenty years later, and some three years after he published *Marxism and Literature* (1977), Williams re-visited the theoretical foundations of his own thought in a collection of essays entitled *Problems in Materialism and Culture* (1980). Here he sought to align, more directly than hitherto, his own personal intellectual development with a much longer history of twentieth-century Marxist cultural theory. It had become clear after the momentous social and intellectual upheavals of the late 1960s that this tradition was in need of radical revision. In this later text Williams associated his own work with that general process of revision and at the same time gave a local habitation and a name to his own practice:

[1] Raymond Williams, *The Long Revolution* (London: Chatto & Windus, 1961), p. 54.
[2] *Ibid.*, p. 54.   [3] *Ibid.*, pp. 62–63.

It took me thirty years in a very complex process, to move from that received Marxist Theory [Engels, Plekhanov, Fox, Caudwell, West, Zdanov] (which in its general form I began by accepting) through various transitional forms of theory and enquiry, to the position I now hold, which I define as 'cultural materialism'.[4]

After naming the intellectual endeavour to which he was now committed, Williams then proceeded to describe his theory of culture as:

a (social and material) productive process and of specific practices, of 'arts', as social uses of material means of production (from language as material 'practical consciousness' to the specific technologies of writing and forms of writing, through to mechanical and electronic communications systems).[5]

Cultural materialism as an intellectual orientation had already been in existence long before Williams' explicit description of its practices and procedures in 1980. For example, within the English tradition, where the emphasis came to rest firmly on questions of social class, Richard Hoggart's *The Uses of Literacy* (1957) had sought to recover a demotic voice through analysing the cultural life and literary production of the British working classes, while in 1963 the socialist historian E. P. Thompson charted *The Making of the English Working Class* as part of a larger radical historical tradition whose roots may be traced back to the various dissenting movements in England during the mid-seventeenth century. Beyond Britain the investigation of 'culture' developed a distinct anthropological, sociological and ethnological focus, where the debate revolved, in part, around the conflict between empiricist concerns with 'patterns of behaviour' and idealist questions of 'ideas' and 'values'.[6] The shift away from 'patterns of behaviour' and towards 'other symbolic-meaningful systems as factors in the shaping of human behaviour'[7] opened the way for the study of culture as a 'semiotic field', and to the possibilities of reading culture as text.[8] Williams' own contribution to developments and refinements within a British context from the late 1950s onwards – and it is important to remember that Williams himself was Welsh, not English – extended a preoccupation with

[4] Raymond Williams, *Problems in Materialism and Culture: Selected Essays* (London: Verso, 1980), p. 243.   [5] *Ibid.*, p. 243.
[6] See Marvin Harris, *Cultural Materialism: The Struggle for a Science of Culture* (New York: Random House, 1979), pp. 279–280.
[7] Alfred Kroeber and Talcott Parsons, 'The Concept of Culture and of Social Systems', *American Sociological Review* 23 (1958), pp. 582–583; Harris, *Cultural Materialism*, p. 281. I am grateful to Terence Hawkes for having directed my attention to the work of Alfred Kroeber and Clyde Cluckholn.
[8] See Benjamin Lee Whorf, *Language, Thought and Reality* (Cambridge, Mass.: MIT Press, 1956); Edward Sapir, 'The Status of Linguistics as a Science', in David G. Mandelbaum (ed.), *Selected Writings of Edward Sapir in Language, Culture and Personality* (Berkeley and Los Angeles: California University Press, 1968); Claude Lévi-Straus, *Structural Anthropology* (New York and London: Basic Books, 1963), *The Savage Mind* (London: Weidenfeld & Nicolson, 1966); Clifford Geertz, 'Deep Play: Notes on the Balinese Cock-Fight', *Daedalus* 101.1 (1972), pp. 1–37. See also, Terence Hawkes, 'Language as Culture', *Shakespeare's Talking Animals: Language and Drama in Society* (London: Edward Arnold, 1975), pp. 9–23.

the relationship between 'literary' and non-literary textual production within the purview of a class politics that was latent in the work of the *Scrutiny* school, but remained undeveloped there. It was left to Richard Hoggart, Williams and, later, Terry Eagleton to extend this materialist concern with the manifest forms of cultural production. Also, within the British academy there was a more general acceleration of these interests in the wake of an explosion of continental 'theory'; this was very influential on the discipline of literary studies, which had itself gathered considerable momentum by the mid-1970s. Between 1968 and 1973 various works of Mikhail Bakhtin (also known as V. N. Volosinov) were translated, although their effects were not felt until over a decade later; Michel Foucault's *Madness and Civilization* was translated in 1967, Roland Barthes' *Mythologies* was translated in 1972, and throughout the 1970s the journal *Screen*, with its initially Althusserian trajectory, was the major forum for the discussion of the 'the relations between culture and signification';[9] in 1976 Jacques Derrida's *Of Grammatology* was translated, and two years later in 1978 his influential collection of essays, *Writing and Difference* was published in translation, the same year in which Pierre Macherey's *A Theory of Literary Production* appeared. In Britain there was a comparable acceleration of output. In 1976, under the auspices of the influential Centre for Contemporary Cultural Studies at Birmingham, Stuart Hall and Tony Jefferson edited a collection of essays entitled *Resistance Through Rituals*, in which the definition of culture as 'that level at which social groups develop distinct patterns of life, and give *expressive form* to their social and material life-experience' was later to be more fully developed in the work of Alan Sinfield.[10] A year before the publication of Williams' *Marxism and Literature* (1977), Terry Eagleton's influential *Criticism and Ideology* (1976) appeared, and also in that year the Essex Sociology of Literature Conferences began and continued annually at the University of Essex until 1984. In 1977 under the general editorship of Terence Hawkes, the first volumes in the New Accents series were published, which sought to make a range of theoretical concerns accessible to students. In addition to Hawkes' own *Structuralism and Semiotics* (1977), other influential early volumes in the series were Dick Hebdige's *Subculture: The Meaning of Style* (1979), Tony Bennett's *Formalism and Marxism* (1979), Catherine Belsey's *Critical Practice* (1980), Christopher Norris' *Deconstruction: Theory and Practice* (1982) and Peter Widdowson's edited collection, *Re-reading English* (1982). In 1977, Rosalind Coward and John Ellis' *Language and Materialism* was published, a dense and challenging overview of the intellectual revolution that followed in the wake of Saussurean structural-

---

[9] Antony Easthope, *British Post-Structuralism Since 1968* (London: Routledge, 1988), pp. 134–135.

[10] Stuart Hall and Tony Jefferson (eds.), *Resistance Through Rituals* (London: Hutchinson, 1976), p. 10. See also for an initial statement of this view of culture, Alan Sinfield, *Literature in Protestant England 1560–1660* (London: Croom Helm, 1983), p. 4.

ism. That year also, coincidentally, saw the publication of Jacques Lacan's *The Four Fundamental Concepts of Psychoanalysis* and a selection translated from *Écrits*, and in the wake of Lacan's revisions of Freud, Coward and Ellis insisted that it was no longer possible to see 'the concerns of psychoanalysis as pre-existing the social operations analysed by historical materialism'. Their positioning of the subject within discourse posed a challenge to traditional humanist definitions of identity, and this led them to a conclusion that was to have major consequences both for literary and cultural theory:

The sign and identity can no longer remain as homogeneous and non-contradictory, but are rather to be understood as produced in contradictory processes. Fixed, transgressed and renewed, there is only the discursive space of the subject in relation to a contradictory outside and ideological articulations. And this is always in process.[11]

Eagleton introduced the work of Pierre Macherey to British readers in 1976, and Coward and Ellis' challenge to classical Marxism made more accessible than hitherto the work of Roland Barthes, Julia Kristeva, Louis Althusser and Jacques Lacan. Later more extensive exposure to the work of Foucault, Bakhtin and Derrida was to complete a radical re-mapping of an entire intellectual terrain. In 1978 the first of a series of annual conferences entitled 'Literature/Teaching/Politics' was held at the Polytechnic of Wales and that series, accompanied by an annual journal, continued at different venues until 1984. By 1982 Peter Widdowson was able to write of 'the "crisis" in English' as an enquiry 'as to what English *is*, where it has got to, whether it has a future, whether it *should* be a discrete discipline, and if it does, in what ways it might be reconstituted'.[12]

Meanwhile, the migration of Theory from Europe to North America had already begun, and some of the translations, particularly those of Bakhtin and Derrida, emanated from the USA. Consequently, when Stephen Greenblatt's *Renaissance Self-Fashioning from More to Shakespeare* (1980) appeared, its engagement with questions of historicism harmonised in many ways with debates which were already well advanced within British Higher Education. The election of the right-wing Margaret Thatcher as Prime Minister of the United Kingdom in 1979, and that of the right-wing Ronald Reagan to the presidency of the United States, did much to sharpen the polemical tone and the political urgency of these debates. The forces of 'tradition' and reaction had begun to assert themselves in the political sphere. But they faced a radical assault in the 'cultural' sphere within English departments in British universities where the anti-theoretical formalism of Leavisite practical criticism, that had hitherto co-existed uneasily with traditional modes of literary-historical study, was challenged by new modes of thinking

[11] Rosalind Coward and John Ellis, *Language and Materialism: Developments in Semiology and the Theory of the Subject* (London: Routledge & Kegan Paul, 1977), p. 155.
[12] Peter Widdowson (ed.), *Re-reading English* (London: Methuen, 1982), p. 7.

emanating from influential journals such as *Tel quel, Screen* and *Representations*, and by an increase in the availability of translations of the work of European cultural theorists.

This, then, provides a very brief general context for the emergence of cultural materialism, one in which forms of revisionary Marxism, feminism, poststructuralism and psychoanalysis all came together in a series of productive tensions. In Britain the appeal of cultural materialism extended well beyond the academy, into the area of a more general cultural politics, in contrast to American new historicism which was far more rigidly confined to the academic circles which had called it into existence.

From Raymond Williams' initial delineation of the field of 'cultural materialism' in 1980, the name remained dormant for a brief period until it received a very specific focus in a collection of essays edited by Jonathan Dollimore and Alan Sinfield, *Political Shakespeare: New Essays in Cultural Materialism* (1985). Indeed, Williams himself contributed a magisterial afterword to this collection. In a brief foreword to the volume, Dollimore and Sinfield situated their approach in the aftermath of the disintegration of consensus 'in British political life during the 1970s' and the accompanying 'break-up of traditional assumptions about the values and goals of literary criticism'. They went on to point out that under the influence of various energetic strains of thought within Marxism, structuralism, feminism, psychoanalysis and poststructuralism, questions of a profound nature were now being raised 'about the status of literary texts, both as linguistic entities and as ideological forces in our society'.[13] They then offered their definition of cultural materialism:

Historical context undermines the transcendent significance traditionally accorded to the literary text and allows us to recover its histories; theoretical method detaches the text from immanent criticism which seeks only to reproduce it in its own terms; socialist and feminist commitment confronts the conservative categories in which much criticism has been hitherto conducted; textual analysis locates the critique of traditional approaches where it cannot be ignored. We call this 'cultural materialism'.[14]

Like Williams, Dollimore and Sinfield sought to emphasise the analytical rather than the evaluative sense of the term 'culture', and to include 'work on the cultures of subordinate and marginalised groups like schoolchildren and skinheads, and on forms like television and popular music and fiction'.[15] In focusing on 'Shakespeare' they also sought to extend their critique to 'artefacts and practices which have traditionally been prized within the evaluative idea of culture'.[16] In *Criticism and Ideology* (1976), Terry Eagleton had insisted that '[c]riticism is not an innocent discipline, and never has been',

---

[13] Jonathan Dollimore and Alan Sinfield (eds.), *Political Shakespeare: New Essays in Cultural Materialism* (Manchester: Manchester University Press, 1985), p. vii.   [14] *Ibid.*
[15] *Ibid.*, pp. vii-viii.   [16] *Ibid.*, p. viii.

that it has 'a history which is more than a random collocation of critical acts', and that it 'does not arise as a spontaneous riposte to the existential fact of the text, organically coupled with the object it illuminates'.[17] This had been, in part, the impetus behind a collection of essays edited by John Drakakis and also published in 1985, *Alternative Shakespeares*, where such propositions were expanded to provide a wide-ranging, radical, theoretically informed challenge to the ethos of traditional Shakespeare studies in a series of attempts to offer alternative methodologies. Dollimore and Sinfield, who also contributed an important essay to this collection, concurred with the general view that the discourse of 'high culture' was one of a range of signifying practices. But they also re-asserted the claim that culture is 'material' insofar as 'it does not (cannot) transcend the material forces and relations of production'. They eschewed the vulgar Marxist reading of culture as a reflection of 'the economic and political system', but they insisted that it could not be independent of its pressures either. For them, as for Williams, the focus was on the historically specific institutions through which culture is transmitted. They concluded that '[c]ultural materialism therefore studies the implications of literary texts in history'[18] where 'history' is defined as the dynamic movement of the forces and relations of production.

The focus on the English Renaissance, its material histories and the critical discourses that it has generated over some four centuries, was no accident. The English Renaissance offered a well-documented but very selectively narrativised account of the interaction of all of those social and cultural forces that led up to the English Revolution of 1642–60, and the subsequent birth of the 'modern' era. In Dollimore's introduction to the first edition of *Political Shakespeare* he acknowledged frankly some of the shared concerns of both cultural materialism and new historicism. Starting out from Marx's perception that 'men and women make their own history but not in conditions of their own choosing', he went on to observe the tension between the two parts of this statement: the one privileging human agency, and the other emphasising 'the formative power of social and ideological structures which are both prior to experience and in some sense determining of it'.[19]

To some extent *Political Shakespeare* might be read as a rapprochement between two allied but quite distinct methodolgies in that prominent new historicists such as Stephen Greenblatt and Leonard Tennenhouse contributed to the collection. But later in the introduction Dollimore went on to articulate a crucial difference between the two approaches. Whereas Greenblatt had come retrospectively to a realisation that his own perspective was implicated in the very process of historical enquiry, cultural materialism had insisted from the very outset that the interpretation of historical data and the perspective from which it is undertaken are inextricably intertwined:

---

[17] Terry Eagleton, *Criticism and Ideology* (London: NLB, 1976), p. 17.
[18] Dollimore and Sinfield (eds.), *Political Shakespeare*, p. vii.   [19] *Ibid.*, p. 3.

Explicitness about one's own perspective and methodology become unavoidable in materialist criticism and around this issue especially: as textual, historical, sociological and theoretical analysis are drawn together, the politics of the practice emerges.[20]

This entails a major shift from questions of received aesthetic value with their focus upon forms of consumption such as taste toward an emphasis on questions of *practice* and sites of *production*. In this, the specificity of Dollimore and Sinfield's project harmonises with Raymond Williams' exhortation 'to discover the nature of a practice and then its conditions'.[21] In the case of Shakespeare this means paying much more detailed attention to the theatre as an institution within which certain kinds of meanings circulated and to literature as a practice. But, as Sinfield argues in an essay added to the second edition of *Political Shakespeare* (1994), it also involves highlighting 'the modes of cultural construction that (re)produce the patterns of authority and deference in our societies (including the prestigious discourses of high culture)'.[22] Sinfield also identifies here a second project, very much present both in the first edition of *Political Shakespeare*, and in Dollimore's own path-breaking monograph of 1984, *Radical Tragedy: Religion, Ideology and Power in the Drama of Shakespeare and his Contemporaries*, but subjected to much wider subsequent scrutiny. This involves the theorisation of 'the scope for dissidence' as a response to those (re)produced patterns of authority and deference in our societies.[23] The question of dissidence, which distinguishes cultural materialism from new historicism, is one to which we shall return shortly, especially in connection with the practice of *reading*.

In his survey volume, *British Post-Structuralism Since 1968* (1988), Antony Easthope suggests that in the re-founding of literary studies it was not surprising that 'Shakespeare and Renaissance literature should become a main arena for contestation since it represents the hegemonic centre of conventional literary criticism'.[24] However, and more problematically, Easthope identifies a group consisting of Francis Barker (*The Tremulous Private Body: Essays on Subjection*, 1984), Jonathan Dollimore, John Drakakis, Alan Sinfield, Peter Stallybrass and Allon White (*The Politics and Poetics of Transgression,* 1986) as 'British Renaissance Foucauldians' strongly influenced by the work of Stephen Greenblatt, but both Marxist in its focus upon 'mode of production as real centre of the social and discursive formation', and also 'post-structuralist on the British model in its concern with the subject as a subject of discourse constituted in a subjectivity that is ineradicably historical'.[25] It is indeed the case that Barker's *The Tremulous Private Body: Essays on*

---

[20] *Ibid.*, p. 13.   [21] Williams, *Problems*, p. 47.
[22] Jonathan Dollimore and Alan Sinfield (eds.), *Political Shakespeare: Essays in Cultural Materialism*, 2nd edn. (Manchester: Manchester University Press, 1994), p. 260.   [23] *Ibid.*
[24] Antony Easthope, *British Post-Structuralism Since 1968* (London: Routledge, 1988), p. 179.
[25] *Ibid.*

Subjection was, in the main, Foucauldian in its concentration upon discontinuous subjectivity.[26] Moreover, Barker's concern with a revolutionary moment in English history which brought the bourgeois subject into existence does not depart significantly from a classic Marxist conception of periodisation. This is also the case with Dollimore's more wide-ranging treatment of the drama of Shakespeare and his contemporaries in *Radical Tragedy*. Dollimore's concern with subjectivity also draws, in part, on the work of Louis Althusser, but there is a strong Brechtian influence in the concern with contradiction and the way in which it informs both social process and identity.[27] In addition, Dollimore takes very much more seriously than most the view that the production of ideas themselves has material *effects*; consequently his emphasis on the *practice* of producing knowledge (philosophy), though occasionally misunderstood by his critics as a retreat into idealism, is, in fact, perfectly consistent with the legacy that cultural materialism inherited from Raymond Williams. In fact, the studied eclecticism of Dollimore's own complex position is mapped out in his introduction to the second edition of *Radical Tragedy* (1989). Here he re-affirms the tenets of a materialist criticism as one that 'attends to non-canonical texts and offers different conceptions of (for instance) human identity, cultural, social and historical process, as well as the activity of criticism itself'.[28] In a brief discussion of J. W. Lever's *The Tragedy of State* (1987), he distinguishes between an idealist commitment to the necessity of suffering and conflict in Tragedy (as exemplified in George Steiner's *The Death of Tragedy*, 1961), and Lever's own commitment to these categories as contingent, 'the effect of social and historical forces focused in state power'.[29] His re-statement of the 'subversion-containment' debate is an issue that will be dealt with in more detail shortly, but his emphasis on the significance of the concept of marginality extends the discussion that had earlier appeared in *Political Shakespeare* (1985). Dollimore remarks upon the emphasis that many contributors to that volume had given to marginality, to that which the dominant power occludes but upon which it depends for its own self-definition, and that points towards the symbolic centrality of all that is marginal.[30] But he goes on to insist that materialist theory 'rejects those ideologies which sustain the belief in an ultimate separation between the political, historical and social, on the one hand, and the subjective and spiritual on the other'.[31] He aligns himself with the projects of Francis Barker (*The Tremulous Private Body*) and Catherine Belsey (*The Subject of Tragedy*, 1985)

---

[26] Francis Barker, *The Tremulous Private Body: Essays on Subjection* (London: Methuen, 1984), p. 59.

[27] Jonathan Dollimore, *Radical Tragedy: Religion, Ideology and Power in the Drama of Shakespeare and his Contemporaries*, 2nd edn. (New York and London: Harvester Wheatsheaf, 1989), p. 246.   [28] *Ibid.*, p. xv.   [29] *Ibid.*, p. xviii.

[30] *Ibid.*, p. xxvi. See also Peter Stallybrass and Allon White, *The Politics and Poetics of Transgression* (London: Methuen, 1986), pp. 17–20.

[31] Dollimore, *Radical Tragedy*, p. xxvii.

in challenging 'the traditional reading of character, human nature and individual identity as they are found in studies of Shakespeare, of Renaissance literature and, more generally still, in the practice of English Studies'.[32] Dollimore's more audacious claim was that Renaissance drama itself had subjected the conception of 'God' to sceptical interrogation to the point that it '"deconstructed" providential legitimation' and, in the process, 'de-centred' man.[33] The resultant 'discoherences' were what traditional forms of criticism habitually filtered out of consideration. But up to a point, he argues, 'we can say that post-structuralism re-discovered what the Renaissance already knew: that identity is powerfully – one might say essentially – informed by what is not', and that this perception is a direct consequence of subsequent critiques of humanist conceptions of identity.[34] In this Dollimore appears to depart significantly from the residual humanism that prevailed in the work of Raymond Williams. But we shall see when we return to the question of agency, that cultural materialism redefines the contours of a radical humanism as a possible outcome rather than as an impulse to transformation, since it remains within the parameters of a broad critique of the factors that govern subjectivity. In response to the question of why *Radical Tragedy* draws so much attention to the de-centring of the subject, he argues:

if essentialist humanism involves a fundamental misrepresentation of literature and history, it does so in part with an ideology of a trans-historical human nature and an autonomous subjectivity, the second being an instantiation of the first; in short a metaphysics of identity occludes historical and social process. A critique of essentialism is about making history visible both within the subjectivity it informs, and beyond subjectivity, by, as it were, restoring individuals to history.[35]

It would be a mistake to read this as a reduction of the role of subjectivity (*pace* Althusser) to 'bearers' of history, *effects* of impersonal structures. Indeed, a little later in the argument he distinguishes between those such as Walter Cohen in *Drama of a Nation: Public Theatre in Renaissance England and Spain* (1985), who insist 'on the necessity of a totalising aspect, one which attends more to large historical changes than to issues of subjectivity, marginality and gender',[36] and those like himself who are concerned with the micro-political investigation of the over-determinations of subjective agency. To this extent Dollimore acknowledges the legacy of Foucault, but his contention is that the next level of theoretical enquiry involves the historical challenging of certain of its orthodoxies, through the deployment of history in the 'reading' of theory and vice versa.[37]

These two questions of agency and reading are of central importance to cultural materialism and, along with the concept of dissidence, establish points of contact with an extant, highly developed and complex British

---

[32] *Ibid.*, p. xxviii.   [33] *Ibid.*, p. xxix.   [34] *Ibid.*, p. xxxi.   [35] *Ibid.*, p. xxxii.
[36] *Ibid.*, p. xliii.   [37] *Ibid.*, p. xlvi.

Marxist tradition. Let us consider first the vexed question of agency. In his revisiting of the problem of 'base and superstructure' as it had been conceived
in classical Marxism, Raymond Williams arrived at the conclusion that too
literal and narrow a definition of 'economic base' resulted in the relegation to
the 'superstructure' of certain crucial productive and reproductive forces. He
argued that '[i]f we have the broad sense of productive forces, we look at the
whole question of the base differently, and we are then less tempted to dismiss
as super-structural, and in that sense merely secondary, certain vital productive social forces, which are in the broad sense, from the beginning, basic'.[38] In
a difficult attempt to square the circle Williams wants to hold on to the
concept of 'superstructure' in that it enables him to argue that 'laws, constitu-
tions, theories, ideologies, which are so often claimed as natural or as having
universal validity or significance, simply have to be seen as expressing and rat-
ifying the domination of a particular class'.[39] In a practical political sense,
Williams maintains that the class character of a society falls from view if these
claims of the dominant order 'to universal validity or legitimacy are not
denied and fought'.

As a way of resolving the problem Williams deploys the Gramscian concept
of 'hegemony' which he sees as a way of avoiding 'retreat to an indifferent
complexity'. He argues, 'In the practice of politics, for example, there are
certain truly incorporated modes of what are nevertheless, within those
terms, real oppositions that are felt and fought out', and he concludes:

The existence of the possibility of opposition and of its articulation, its degree of
openness, and so on, again depends on very precise social and political forces. The
facts of alternative and oppositional forms of social life and culture, in relation to
the effective and dominant culture, have then to be recognised as subject to historical
variation, and as having sources which are very significant as a fact about the
dominant culture itself.[40]

His formulation of the synchronic structure of culture involving a tripartite
tension between 'dominant', 'residual' and 'emergent' forces, where past
and new practices and meanings are incorporated into the dominant values
and practices of the present, reinforces a sense of the present as a site of
potential contest particularly at those junctures where the process of incorporation is incomplete or breaks down. These moments yield surpluses of
meaning, thereby offering the prospect of limited social transformation.
However, here the distinction between 'alternative' and 'oppositional'
becomes important. Williams defines the former as 'someone who simply
finds a different way to live and wishes to be left alone with it', and the latter
as 'someone who finds a different way to live and wants to change the society
in its light'.[41]

[38] Williams, *Problems*, p. 35.   [39] *Ibid.*, pp. 36–37.   [40] *Ibid.*, pp. 39–40.
[41] *Ibid.*, pp. 41–42.

It is this latter category that raises problems insofar as it lays claim to a morality that underpins practice. In a partly Lacanian critique of cultural materialism, Scott Wilson seeks to establish a connection between dissident challenge to the symbolic order and what he calls 'the imaginarily sustained subject', and an encounter with 'the real' where the imaginary and the symbolic are rejected *tout court* and which is the place, he argues, 'where subversion or dissidence, receives its dynamic energy'.[42] Wilson's claim (and it is as much a critique as a claim) is that cultural materialism does not encounter the Lacanian 'real' because it is 'first, an inherently moral, even theological, concept, and second, it delimits a restricted economy'. Wilson goes on:

The mutual reinforcement of the moral and the material is implied by the double meaning available to the term 'good'. For cultural materialism it is ultimately always a question of the good (or bad) production, distribution and consumption of good goods; good signs, good meanings, positive identities; or bad, ideological signs, cultural tokens, negative images, and so on. Yet dissidence has as much to do with the negativity activated by the traumatic encounter with the real, as with positive discursive struggle.[43]

Wilson seems here to be arguing that the commitment of cultural materialism to the theory of sign production is insufficiently constructivist, that its concerns are residually positivistic rather than enthusiastically poststructuralist. Moreover, in his wish to deploy George Bataille's radical emphasis upon theories of *consumption* as opposed to the Marxist theory of *production*, he neglects Raymond Williams' insistence upon 'class' as the primary dynamic force in society.

Cultural materialism, while focusing on the primary question of production, expands the analysis of dynamic force to include, more directly than Williams had done, questions of gender and race. It is here that the debt to Foucault is perhaps most clearly in evidence, and it is here that the dynamic operations of power in the strong Foucauldian sense of the term are explored. What Wilson brings into question is the 'material' base of materialism, that is, its preoccupation with the questions of production and reproduction of social relations. By contrast, cultural materialism would regard the essentially relational nature of the forces and relations of production as something that could not easily be collapsed in its entirety into discourse. Nor would it concede that the encounter with the Lacanian 'real', in the orthodox doctrinal sense that Wilson wishes to deploy, was anything more than a bourgeois existential luxury of limited explanatory force. Agency, therefore, in cultural materialism remains structural, and political intention remains collectivist, notwithstanding the contingent complexities of the social formation itself. What Wilson dismisses as the 'moral' element of cultural materialism is

---

[42] Scott Wilson, *Cultural Materialism: Theory and Practice* (Oxford: Blackwell, 1995), p. 37.
[43] *Ibid.*, pp. 37–38.

nothing other than the 'emergent', that which struggles to come into being despite the tendencies of the dominant order to incorporate it into existing structures. In the theoretical model proposed by Raymond Williams, political struggle was both an effect of structure *and* the consequence of actually lived social experience; and its objectives were to secure justice, equality and freedom. While the poststructuralist element in cultural materialism as it developed included a critique of essentialist humanism, and while it questioned the Enlightenment myth of progress, it did not relinquish a conviction that *desire* was generated by the processes of selectivity and occlusion, and that this provided a mechanism for the movements of history itself. The space where these conflicts are fought out is in the realm of representations, in 'culture' itself and its multiform manifestations, and, although the mechanisms are recognisably dialectical, there is never any guarantee of complete and total transformation. It is the anxieties of the present that serve to focus attention upon the past, not for the purpose of locating re-assuring certainties, but in order to establish *differences* within whose structures some form of provisional 'truth' may be located as a basis for future action.

These important qualifications notwithstanding, the emphasis upon contingency in cultural materialism demands to be seen within the context of Marxism, even if it is a Marxism that has been forced to address the consequences for its own practice of poststructuralist theories of signification and representation. Cultural materialism does not commit itself to any naive or uncritical understanding of the existence of an external physical world, but nor does it abandon entirely a 'realism' grounded in the conviction that at the root of all production, and the reproduction of the relations of production, is a series of complexly determined relations which it is the purpose of the dominant power to secure. Where it departs significantly from the 'base–superstructure' model is in the emphasis it places, *pace* Althusser, upon 'the point of view of reproduction'.[44] The production of meanings and values is invariably connected with the history of their reproduction. Consequently 'the real' is always perceived in terms of a series of relations, rather than in Lacanian terms as a point beyond symbolisation altogether. As Sinfield observes in the second edition of *Political Shakespeare* (1994), the objective was to 'construct a model of cultural production that did *not* fall into the determinism that had influenced earlier Marxist theories'.[45] Of course, as Raymond Williams had argued, there are two opposed meanings of 'determine', the one emanating from metaphysical accounts of the world, and the other emanating from a Marxist account that focuses on the material complexity of human activity. In resisting the language of external causation, Williams appeals to what he calls 'the experience of social practice' where determination involves 'setting

---

[44] Cf. Louis Althusser, *Lenin and Philosophy and Other Essays*, trans. Ben Brewster (New York and London: NLB, 1971), p. 136.

[45] Dollimore and Sinfield (eds.), *Political Shakespeare*, 2nd edn., p. 259.

limits, exerting pressures'.[46] This permits precisely the kind of flexibility towards which Sinfield's formulation works, and it involves a much more active engagement in the sphere of cultural activity than earlier, more mechanical notions of determinism might suggest.

Where new historicism is primarily *descriptive* in its procedures, even though it is self-consciously so, cultural materialism is *interventionist* as well as descriptive. Despite Isobel Armstrong's stringent critique of its early pessimism,[47] from the outset cultural materialism has always emphasised a practice of resistant reading, of reading literary and critical texts against the grain in order to disclose their contradictions or their occlusions, but it has also sought to emphasise the ways in which reactionary meanings and values have been proliferated and sustained. Two concepts that are crucial to its textual practice are 'dissidence' and 'resistant reading'.

In his book, *Faultlines: Cultural Materialism and the Politics of Dissident Reading* (1992), Alan Sinfield proposes to deploy the term 'dissidence' in preference to either 'transgression' or 'subversion'.[48] His reasons for doing so become clearer in a later chapter where he argues:

There can be no security in textuality: no scriptor can control the reading of his or her text. And when, in any instance, either incorporation or resistance turns out to be the more successful, that is not in the nature of things. It is because of *their relative strengths in that situation*.[49]

Sinfield derives dissidence from the system itself, and in this important respect he rejects both the new historicist concern with strategies of incorporation, or the possibility that dissident energy derives from some human impulse. Similarly, Jonathan Dollimore challenges the new historicist deployment of the subversion–containment model of the operations of power, even though, unlike Sinfield, he holds on to the terms 'transgression' and 'subversion'. In his *Sexual Dissidence: Augustine to Wilde, Freud to Foucault* (1991), he raises three objections: (i) that subversion and transgression 'necessarily *presuppose* the law, but they do not thereby necessarily *ratify* the law'; (ii) that the agency of change presupposed by the theory of containment is 'too subjective and a critierion of success too total', that is to say that agency in this model 'is usually assumed to be a local or a limited one, and often subjectivist or voluntarist'; (iii) that containment theory, like radical humanism, 'overlooks the part played by contradiction and dislocation in the mutually reactive process of transgression and its control'.[50] In his focus on the role of ideology in smoothing over contradiction, Dollimore seeks to uncover what he calls 'the

---

[46] Williams, *Problems*, p. 32.
[47] Isobel Armstrong, 'Thatcher's Shakespeare', *Textual Practice* 3.1 (Spring, 1989), pp. 1–14.
[48] Alan Sinfield, *Faultlines: Cultural Materialism and the Politics of Dissident Reading* (Oxford: Clarendon Press, 1992), p. x.   [49] *Ibid.*, p. 48.
[50] Jonathan Dollimore, *Sexual Dissidence: Augustine to Wilde, Freud to Foucault* (Oxford: Clarendon, 1991), pp. 85–86.

contingency of the social', and this can only be done in part 'by disarticulating or disaligning existing ideological configurations' in such a way that the process of making meanings cohere is reversed; his term for this reversal is 'discoherence', whereby 'meanings are returned to circulation, thereby becoming more vulnerable to appropriation, transformation, and re-incorporation in new configurations'.[51] Because subjectivity is rooted in the practice of ideology, the purpose of such a process of disarticulation, disalignment and subsequent re-making and re-articulation, is emphatically not to return subjectivity to an essential humanism whether that be radical or otherwise. It is for this reason that cultural materialism has interested itself in the contradictory process of the formation of the subject, and in this it proposes a very clear break with the radical humanism of Raymond Williams.

The focus on the textuality of cultural production, however, develops further Raymond Williams' project of disclosing 'the specific historical conditions in which institutions are organised by textualities', by insisting not only that these now be addressed in their historical specificity, but also, beginning from what Sinfield believes is a position that has scandalised literary criticism, 'that meaning is not adequately deducible from the text-on-the-page'. Louis Montrose has noted that a feature of the poststructuralist focus upon 'history' is what he calls a chiastic reciprocity: 'the historicity of texts and the textuality of history'.[52] As Sinfield makes very clear in a response to certain feminist anxieties about what he calls 'the derogation of the individual in cultural materialism', poststructuralism has done much to obscure what he calls 'the importance of collectivities and social location'.[53] What remains important is to resist the new historicist preoccupation with structural homology which, he argues, 'discovers synchronic structural connectedness without determination, sometimes without pressure or tension',[54] in favour of a dissident identity that arises from the individual's involvement 'in a *milieu*, a *subculture*'. It is through this Gramscian strategy that 'plausible oppositional preoccupations' might be generated,[55] and it allows Sinfield to hold on to the poststructuralist awareness of textuality while at the same time addressing the implausibility of its totalising claims. In this context 'fault-lines' are those discernible moments when the fissures in ideology become visible, necessitating *either* radical change, *or* the production of a new narrative designed to smooth over the disclosed contradiction.

We can now begin to see a little more clearly how 'dissidence' is connected to forms of 'reading'. The refusal of any aspect of the dominant in any aspect of the cultural formation is not something subjective or voluntarist in its being the product of individuals, but structural with the proviso that Sinfield

---

[51] *Ibid.*, p. 87.
[52] Louis Montrose, 'The Poetics and Politics of Culture', in H. Aram Veeser (ed.), *The New Historicism* (New York and London: Routledge, 1989), p. 20.
[53] Sinfield, *Faultlines*, pp. 37–38.   [54] *Ibid.*, p. 39.   [55] *Ibid.*, p. 37.

lays down. Moreover, unlike the historicist argument that underwrites an Enlightenment ethic of progress, neither dissidence nor its outcome can be pre-judged. In this the influence of Foucault's laws of the tactical polyvalence of discourse may be discerned, in which power *may* incorporate resistance into its structures, *or* that resistance may provide the basis for a departure from its structures.[56] As Terence Hawkes has observed, meanings are *made* through social interaction in determinate conditions, the corollary being that they can be unmade or re-made; the coherent narratives that our cultural institutions fabricate in order to sustain themselves are, by definition, selective. If meaning is irreducibly social then, as Hawkes concludes, there can be 'no final, essential or "real" meaning at the end of it. There is no end. There is only and always the business of "meaning by"'.[57] Sinfield adds to this the observation that cultural materialism undertakes to 'review those institutions that re-tell the Shakespeare stories, and will attempt also a self-consciousness about its own situation within those institutions'.[58] Beyond that, both Sinfield and Dollimore have extended this remit to cover a wide variety of cultural narratives, not simply in order to produce 'different readings', but as Sinfield himself puts it, 'to shift the criteria of plausibility'.[59]

More recently cultural materialist work has extended into the arena of gender politics and queer theory. Although *Political Shakespeare* addressed the issue of gender in some of the essays it contained, questions of sexual orientation did not figure in the editors' Foreword. However, in Dollimore's *Sexual Dissidence* (1991), and in Sinfield's *Cultural Politics – Queer Reading* (1994) and *The Wilde Century: Effeminacy, Oscar Wilde, and the Queer Moment* (1994), these issues are fully and explicitly addressed. Towards the end of *Sexual Dissidence*, Dollimore quotes Ania Loomba and counsels firmly against an ahistorical account of difference which in the field of post-colonial studies either devalues or romanticises 'native insubordination', or worse, 'tends to read colonised subjects through linguistic or psychoanalytical theories which, for some of us, remain suspiciously and problematically shot through with ethnocentric assumptions whose transfer to all subalterns is unacceptable'.[60] He extends this concern to consider the ways in which homosexual identity has been articulated historically, and how it may be more positively perceived as a '*creative* otherness' rather than as a negative 'other'.[61] In *Cultural Politics – Queer Reading* and *The Wilde Century*, Alan Sinfield

---

[56] Michel Foucault, *History of Sexuality, Vol. 1: An Introduction*, trans. Robert Hurley (New York: Viking Penguin, 1978), pp. 100–102.

[57] Terence Hawkes, *Meaning by Shakespeare* (London: Routledge, 1992), p. 8.

[58] Sinfield, *Faultlines*, p. 51.

[59] *Ibid.* See also Alan Sinfield, *Literature, Politics, and Culture in Postwar Britain* (Oxford: Blackwell, 1989); *Cultural Politics – Queer Reading* (London: Routledge, 1994); and *The Wilde Century: Effeminacy, Oscar Wilde and the Queer Moment* (London: Cassell, 1994); also Jonathan Dollimore, *Death, Desire and Loss in Western Culture* (London: Allen Lane The Penguin Press, 1998).   [60] *Ibid.*, p. 329.   [61] Dollimore, *Sexual Dissidence*, p. 332.

amplifies the history of this notion of negative otherness further through identifying the ways in which what he calls 'literary dissidence' is traditionally gendered:

Literary dissidence accepts – in the main very gingerly – a touch of the feminine. Its invocation of a 'human' protest depends on a strategic deployment of effeminacy: of culture against brutality, the spirit against the system, style against purpose, personal emotion against compulsion. Hence the commonplace that the great writer is androgynous. There mustn't be too much of the 'wrong' sex, though. The trick in artistic dissidence is to appropriate sufficient of the radical aura of androgyny, without more than is necessary of the disabling stigma. The great writer embraces something of the feminine, it is often said – but not too much.[62]

The matter of the historical articulations of sexual identity has always been a feature of cultural materialism whose abiding concern with the detailed study of cultural politics is both inclusive and challenging. In the concluding chapter of *The Wilde Century*, Sinfield states that '[t]he ultimate project of this book is to promote a questioning of the constructions through which we have been living'.[63] While the 'we' in this context refers to a specific social group, the methodologies deployed extend well beyond its stated parameters, and stand for a dynamic analytical repertoire of distinctive literary, cultural and political strategies.

[62] Cf. Sinfield, *Cultural Politics – Queer Reading*, p. 32.
[63] Sinfield, *The Wilde Century*, p. 177.

4

New historicism

DUNCAN SALKELD

New historicism emerged in the early 1980s as a turn to history in literary studies after the formalisms of New Criticism, structuralism and deconstruction. The label describes, as Stephen Greenblatt has observed in *Learning to Curse* (1990), 'less a set of beliefs than the trajectory' of related materialist, Marxist and feminist critical practices as they seek to interpret literary works amid the complexities of their own historical moment.[1] An American counterpart to British cultural materialism, its influence has been felt mainly in Renaissance studies, and, to a lesser extent, in eighteenth- and nineteenth-century studies of the novel and Romanticism.[2] Its Renaissance practitioners draw upon diverse strands in modern critical theory (especially Foucault and Althusser), upon the work of cultural historians (by Emmanuel Le Roy Ladurie, Carlo Ginzburg, Natalie Zemon Davis) and on social anthropology (especially Clifford Geertz), in order to read across the boundaries of literature and history. So far as it is possible to generalise about such a vast and varied field, new historicists seek to identify hitherto unacknowledged contexts of semiotic exchange between literary and cultural history.

Characteristically self-conscious in method, new historicist criticism frequently voices an acute awareness of its own procedural difficulties. A key problem, for example, has to do with what kind of sense may, indeed should, be made of the materials of literature and history. New historicism represents a sustained negotiation of those complex cultural, textual and political forces which intervene between past and present, then and now. Its central problem has thus to do with distanciation. On the one hand, the past must be minimally intelligible for history to bear any meaning at all; on the other hand, intelligibility always remains relative to the conditions in which interpretations are made. To give an example, early on in Plautus' *Bacchides*,

---

[1] Stephen Greenblatt, *Learning to Curse: Essays in Early Modern Culture* (New York and London: Routledge, 1990), p. 3.

[2] See, for example, Don E. Wayne, 'Power, Politics, and the Shakespearean Text', in Jean E. Howard and Marion F. O'Connor, *Shakespeare Reproduced: The Text in History and Ideology* (New York and London: Methuen, 1987); John Bender, 'Eighteenth-Century Studies', in Stephen Greenblatt and Giles Gunn (eds.), *Re-drawing the Boundaries: The Transformation of English and American Literary Studies* (New York: Modern Language Association, 1992); Stephen Copley and John Whale, *Beyond Romanticism: New Approaches and Contexts, 1780–1832* (New York and London: Routledge, 1992).

Pistoclerus shakes his fists at Parasite, who has pounded the door almost off its hinges:

PISTOCLERUS (*roaring*): By the Lord, that face of yours is precious close to a calamity, the way these toothcrackers here are itching![3]

The Plautine Latin for 'toothcrackers' in this line is 'dentifrangibula'. The joke translates across more than two thousand years of cultural and semantic change. Getting a joke means getting a culture's language games and here, in Plautus, connecting via language with the laughter of the past. Any such connection – indeed any reading of history – depends upon the translatability of the past into the present.[4] But translation is never a straightforward process. As Greenblatt, the most prominent of new historicist critics, points out in his essay 'Learning to Curse', when Caliban, in Shakespeare's *The Tempest*, promises to fetch Stefano and Trinculo 'scamels from the rock', no one yet knows what the word 'scamels' means.[5] Such 'opacity' he takes as resonant of the loss of an entire culture: if the cursing 'savage' Caliban is Shakespeare's type of New World Indian, he is also the dramatist's most eloquent sign of a sixteenth-century 'linguistic colonialism' of Western European over Indian speech: 'And so most of the people of the New World will never speak to us. That communication, with all that we might have learned, is lost to us forever.'[6] Language games may bear dark histories which reach beyond the aesthetic structure of the work of art. Greenblatt's is a new historicist reading insofar as it finds the play voicing certain powerful historical moves, audible only in the stumbling eloquence of the half-human monster Caliban. The question of how to construe the meanings of the past while respecting their difference leads therefore to more complex considerations of power as language, culture and ideology come into conflict with one another. New historicist use of example and anecdote to illustrate the repressive effects of discourse across a range of literary and non-literary genres reminds that no single answer to that question may pretend to finality.

Historicising Shakespeare and the Renaissance

Historical studies of literature are a comparatively recent development, having long been regarded as unnecessary. In the shadow of Coleridge and Romantic literary theory, early twentieth-century critics like H. H. Furness, E. E. Stoll and Mark Van Doren regarded Shakespeare's genius as transcending mere contingencies of early modern politics or history, a view F. R. Leavis

---

[3] Plautus, *Bacchides*, trans. Paul Nixon, Loeb Classical Library (Cambridge, Mass.: Harvard University Press, 1997), p. 387.

[4] Donald Davidson, *Inquiries Into Truth and Interpretation* (Oxford: Oxford University Press, 1984).   [5] Greenblatt, *Learning to Curse*, p. 31.   [6] *Ibid.*, p. 32.

applied to others he considered 'great writers'. A divergent group of critics, including H. B. Charlton, J. Dover Wilson, Alfred Hart, E. M. W. Tillyard and Lily B. Campbell maintained, however, that since Shakespeare was essentially a Renaissance Man, his works 'reflect' or 'picture' their 'historical background' – the beliefs, ideas and attitudes of his time.[7] Informative as these critics were, they tended to assume a clear distinction between fiction and reality, regarding history largely as a realm of objectively ascertained facts, truths and moral universals. Some, like Tillyard, ascribed Shakespeare's distinctiveness to his ability to grasp an entire conceptual scheme (an Elizabethan world picture). Others, like Campbell, stressed the Leavisite permanence of his moral vision. With the benefit of theoretical hindsight, however, recent historicists regard the idea that literature should mirror a historical background of objective facts or moral truths as ideologically positioned and seriously limiting. Instead, they treat literary works (including Shakespeare's) as plural, constructed by differing social discourses whose vocabularies intersect to constitute the text.[8] New historicism, at its most supple, seeks out different, occasionally surprising, conjunctures of historical and literary vocabulary as they render power visible and enable marginal or unheard voices to emerge. Although new historicists borrow quite freely from diverse works in cultural history, Marxism, psychoanalysis, theories of language and semiotics, the two key influences behind this approach to literature are the French historian of discourse Michel Foucault and the American social anthropologist Clifford Geertz.

The emergence of new historicism

Foucault argued, in studies of the histories of madness, medicine, representation, punishment and sexuality, that socially organising vocabularies ('discourses') voiced and guaranteed by powerful institutions, have constituted the body of knowledge which constitutes western subjectivity. Such analyses, each conducted from Foucault's Nietzschean perspective of knowledge as more or less identical with power, were absorbed by left-inclined literary critics in conjunction with other works of Marxist literary theory, including Mikhail Bakhtin's *Rabelais and his World* (English edn. 1968) and Pierre Macherey's *A Theory of Literary Production* (1966), to form a complex base for the literary theorisation of class, power, body and text.[9] Translated into

---

[7] Lily B. Campbell, *Shakespeare's Histories* (London: Methuen, 1947), pp. 3–7.

[8] See David Kastan and Peter Stallybrass (eds.), *Staging the Renaissance: Reinterpretations of Elizabethan and Jacobean Drama* (New York and London: Routledge, 1991), p. 2.

[9] See Alan Sheridan, *Michel Foucault: The Will to Truth* (London: Tavistock, 1980); M. Bakhtin, *Rabelais and his World*, trans. Helene Iswolsky (London and Cambridge, Mass.: MIT Press, 1968); P. Macherey, *A Theory of Literary Production*, trans. G. Wall (London: Routledge and Kegan Paul, 1978).

English throughout the sixties and seventies, Foucault's work thus not quite single-handedly set the agenda for subsequent studies of early modern literature. Foucault argued that those centralising, masterful discourses operative throughout history routinely denied a voice to the socially rejected – the mad or the criminal – in ways which the historian of discourse and, indeed, the literary critic might trace. To this extent, such historicising literary studies of early modern madness, violence and vagrancy as Carol Thomas Neely's 'Documents in Madness' (1996), Karin S. Coddon's 'Suche Strange Desygns' (1989), Francis Barker's *The Culture of Violence* (1993) and William C. Carroll's *Fat King, Lean Beggar* (1996) all trace established Foucauldian themes.[10]

The term 'new historicism' was coined in 1982 by Greenblatt to characterise a collection of Renaissance essays he had edited.[11] Two years earlier, he had published his landmark study, *Renaissance Self-Fashioning*, a scrupulously written book whose thesis, that subjectivities in the English Renaissance were complexly and publicly wrought only to be self-cancelled in murder or execution, bore subtle resonances with Foucault's work.[12] In the late seventies and early eighties, a number of studies including Stephen Orgel and Roy Strong's *Inigo Jones: The Theatre of the Stuart Court*, Orgel's *Illusion of Power*, Franco Moretti's '"A huge eclipse": Tragic Form and the Deconsecration of Authority' and Louis Montrose's 'The Purpose of Playing' focused upon the conditions, paradoxes and contradictions of power in Tudor and Stuart literature.[13] The British critic Derek Longhurst, in his 1982 article 'Not For All Time But of an Age', argued for an approach to Shakespeare which gave careful historical attention to 'contemporary concepts of order, authority, kingship, nature, women, marriage and the family, justice and law, usury, religious beliefs, reason etc'. In 1985 Greenblatt contributed to *Political Shakespeare*, a volume edited by Jonathan Dollimore and Alan Sinfield, in

---

[10] Carol Thomas Neely, 'Documents in Madness: Reading Madness and Gender in Shakespeare's Tragedies and Early Modern Culture', in Shirley Nelson Garner and Madelon Sprengnether (eds.), *Shakespearean Tragedy and Gender* (Bloomington: Indiana University Press, 1996); Karin S. Coddon, 'Suche Strange Desygns: Madness, Subjectivity and Treason in *Hamlet* and Elizabethan Culture', in *Renaissance Drama* 20 (1989), pp. 51–75; Francis Barker, *The Culture of Violence: Tragedy and History* (Manchester: Manchester University Press, 1993); William C. Carroll, *Fat King, Lean Beggar: Representations of Poverty in the Age of Shakespeare* (Ithaca and London: Cornell University Press, 1996).

[11] Stephen J. Greenblatt (ed.), *Allegory and Representation* (Baltimore and London: Johns Hopkins University Press, 1981).

[12] Greenblatt acknowledges the influence of Foucault's visits to the Berkeley campus between 1979 and 1984 in *Learning to Curse*, ch. 8, 'Towards a Poetics of Culture'.

[13] Stephen Orgel and Roy Strong, *Inigo Jones: The Theatre of the Stuart Court* (Berkeley: University of California Press, 1973); Stephen Orgel, *The Illusion of Power: Political Theatre in the English Renaissance* (Berkeley: University of California Press, 1975); Franco Moretti, '"A Huge Eclipse": Tragic Form and the Deconsecration of Authority', in Stephen Greenblatt (ed.), *The Forms of Power and the Power of Forms in the Renaissance* (Norman: University of Oklahoma Press, 1982), pp. 7–40; Louis Montrose, 'The Purpose of Playing: Reflections on a Shakespearean Anthropology', *Helios* 7 (1980), pp. 51–74.

which the editors outlined a now familiar three-stage process organising power relations across literary and non-literary Renaissance texts alike: consolidation, subversion and containment. Greenblatt's contribution, 'Invisible Bullets', illustrated this process by arguing that Prince Hal, in Henry IV, Part 1, actively creates a carnivalesque subversiveness only to contain it and so confirm the power of the monarchy, a process simultaneously identifiable in the colonialist narrative of Thomas Harriot written after his encounter with the natives of Virginia in the New World. Such a 'strong containment' thesis has been taken as distinguishing new historicism from the more liberatory left-wing political edge of British cultural materialism. However, in the 1994 second edition of Political Shakespeare, Dollimore states that Political Shakespeare was initially considered as 'an exploratory alliance' between the two critical perspectives, adding that it little matters how they coincide or diverge. After all, he avers, cultural materialism has always shared the new historicist concern to confront 'the forces which prevent change'.[14]

A poetics of culture

In 'Towards a Poetics of Culture' (Learning to Curse), Greenblatt professed that he had never intended to start a critical movement, indeed that he was 'giddy with amazement' at the way its (oxymoronic) name so rapidly caught on. Equally rapidly, he dropped it in favour of an earlier, more synchronic formulation of criticism as 'cultural poetics'. The phrase 'a poetics of culture' appears mid-way through the introduction to Renaissance Self-Fashioning, after Greenblatt has cited Geertz and others as major influences for this 'more cultural or anthropological criticism'. Geertz's notion of anthropology as 'thick description', the sustained reading of a culture's slightest signs, informs Greenblatt's close attention to semiotic and textual detail. Anthropology shares with historiography a similar (though not identical) problem of distanciation. The task of ethnography, Geertz stated in Works and Lives, is to 'enlarge the possibility of intelligible discourse between people quite different from one another in interest, outlook, wealth, and power, and yet contained in a world where tumbled as they are into endless connection, it is increasingly difficult to get out of each other's way'.[15] The same year, Greenblatt opened Shakespearean Negotiations with the statement: 'I began with the desire to speak with the dead . . . and if I knew that the dead could not speak, I was nonetheless certain that I could re-create a conversation with them . . . for the dead had contrived to leave textual traces of themselves, and those traces

---

[14] Jonathan Dollimore and Alan Sinfield (eds.), Political Shakespeare: New Essays in Cultural Materialism, 2nd edn. (Manchester: Manchester University Press, 1994), pp. 129–130.
[15] Clifford Geertz, Works and Lives: The Anthropologist as Author (Cambridge: Polity Press, 1988), p. 147.

make themselves heard in the voices of the living.'[16] Spectrality aside, Greenblatt's 'anthropological' historicism has continued to seek synchronic, spatial ways of theorising 'the poetics of culture'. *Shakespearean Negotiations* largely follows chronology in readings of the history plays via Thomas Harriot's colonialist *Brief and True Reporte*; *Twelfth Night* via Renaissance hermaphroditism; Harsnett's source for *King Lear* alongside the discourse of exorcism; and *Measure For Measure* and *The Tempest* through ecclesiatical manipulations of anxiety. It is structured, however, by the somewhat enigmatic concept of 'a circulation of social energy', Greenblatt's construal of the rhetorical force which sustains the manipulation, negotiation, transformation and exchange of cultural artefacts between discursive and aesthetic spheres.

This vocabulary of circulation and exchange, elaborated in 'Towards a Poetics of Culture', has invited criticism from the left that new historicism represents at best an acceptance of the fact of capitalism, and at worst a capitulation to 'money and prestige'. But if Greenblatt has resisted both Marxist (Jameson's) and postmodern (Lyotard's) conflations of the aesthetic and the social, a conflation literally embodied, he argues, by Ronald Reagan, B-movie actor and President of the United States ('Towards a Poetics of Culture'), this is ultimately to preserve a materialist perspective on the literary. His introduction to *Learning to Curse* squarely confronts that dichotomy by comparing Edmund Scott's sadistic account, in 1606, of the torture and murder of a Chinese 'spy' with the fictional torture of the unnamed Jew in Nashe's *The Unfortunate Traveller*, published in 1593. The fictionality or non-fictionality of these descriptions, Greenblatt points out, fundamentally alters our 'ethical relation to the text', and a rigorous criticism must be able to account for such imperatives. Hence, Greenblatt's critical practice has been to seek 'a new set of terms', able to capture effects of resonance, wonder and the marvellous, as they trace out the 'oscillation' of works of art between zones and demarcations of language. So it is, he writes with Giles Gunn, that 'in certain circumstances literature may pull quite sharply against interest and ideology, may even function precisely as their opposite'.[17] Such comment hardly amounts to what one critic has described as an end-of-history 'worship of the market', since it presents no more than a pragmatic refusal to have one's position contained in advance by ideological dogma. Charges of capitalist recidivism appear all the more ironic after the British Press heralded Greenblatt's general editorship of *The Norton Shakespeare* (based on the Oxford edition) as a full-scale unreconstructed Marxist *coup d'etat* over everything sacredly Shakespearean. Robert Smallwood and Rex Gibson

---

[16] Stephen Greenblatt, *Shakespearean Negotiations: The Circulation of Social Energy in Renaissance England* (Oxford: Clarendon, 1988), p. 1.
[17] Greenblatt and Gunn (eds.), *Redrawing the Boundaries*, p. 6.

sounded the alarm, warning that 'neo-Marxists' were now resurgent. An unnamed source was quoted as saying it was like 'ushering the wolf into the nursery'.[18]

Feminist responses and dissenting voices

Feminist approaches to early modern literature have maintained a cautious, somewhat sceptical dialogue with new historicism while sharing its concern to recover the marginal, excluded and the oppressed. The first ostensibly feminist collection of Shakespeare criticism, *The Woman's Part* (1980), engaged only tangentially with history. Juliet Dusinberre's *Shakespeare and the Nature of Women* (1975) maintained that Reformation Christianity broadly cultivated domestic equality between the sexes. In *Women and the English Renaissance: Literature and the Nature of Womankind, 1540–1620* (1984), however, Linda Woodbridge argued that Renaissance culture tended to accept and endorse 'male dominance'. Lisa Jardine's *Still Harping on Daughters: Women and Drama in the age of Shakespeare* (1983) took something of a 'via media' between these polarities, arguing that women experienced an increased domestic responsibility under Puritanism proportionate to their decline in power.[19] Such pioneering studies, however, underlined the need for close, nuanced investigations into the historical situations and experiences of women in Renaissance society and literature. In 'The Patriarchal Bard', Kathleen McLuskie argued, somewhat in line with Woodbridge, that the emotional organisation of *King Lear* is so structured against its women characters as virtually to preclude any feminist reading of the play at all. Whereas Dollimore in *Radical Tragedy* had pointed out that critical homiles on the play's evocations of pity mask the fact that Lear only pities other 'poor, bare, forked rascals' once he himself has experienced their destitution, McLuskie sees pity as violently exacted by the play's determinedly masculine structure.[20] Ann Thompson, in an essay under the title 'Are There Any Women in *King Lear*?', finds no easy answer to the question but exhorts feminist critics not to give up on the play altogether.[21]

A study that more than meets that challenge is Janet Adelman's richly

18 Richard Wilson, 'Historicising the New Historicism', in Richard Wilson and Richard Dutton (eds.), *New Historicism and Renaissance Drama* (London and New York: Longman, 1992), p. 9; *The Sunday Times*, 6 April 1997, p. 7.
19 Lisa Jardine, *Still Harping on Daughters: Women and Drama in the Age of Shakespeare* (New York and London: Harvester Wheatsheaf, 1983), p. 116.
20 Kathleen McLuskie, 'The Patriarchal Bard: Feminist Criticism and Shakespeare: *King Lear* and *Measure for Measure*', in Dollimore and Sinfield (eds.), *Political Shakespeare*.
21 Ann Thompson, 'Are There Any Women in *King Lear*?', in Valerie Wayne (ed.), *The Matter of Difference: Materialist Feminist Criticism of Shakespeare* (Ithaca: Cornell University Press, 1991), pp. 117–128 (p. 126).

rewarding *Suffocating Mothers* (1992) which carefully historicises its mainly psychoanalytic perspective on Shakespeare, and argues that Lear's identification of Goneril as 'a disease within my flesh', his exclamation 'hysterica passio' and his many allusions to women's bodies, all articulate dark, anxious fantasies of repressed maternal origins crucially felt within himself. The 'presence of the female' resides, Lear finds, within his own body.[22] Feminists have criticised new historicism for its reluctance to draw gender distinctions, and hence sought to widen the terms of debate. In 'Are We Being Historical Yet?' Carolyn Porter finds attention has been too narrowly paid to 'one set of discourses' which make up the 'dominant ideology' within literary texts, and in her follow-up article, 'History and Literature', she argues that resistant voices themselves should be read as 'multivoiced', neither wholly oppositional nor wholly contained. As if by way of answer to Porter's question, Lisa Jardine's *Reading Shakespeare Historically* presents just about as historical a study of literature as one could hope for. Her first chapter on *Othello*, 'Why Should He Call Her Whore?', focuses on the private situation in which Desdemona rejects Iago's imputations that she is a strumpet. As Jardine demonstrates from cases in the Durham Ecclesiastical Court archive, public defamation, or slander, could become 'an actuality' if not repudiated publicly. Words could easily grade into illocutionary 'events' if not openly denied since competing accounts of fault and blame required resolution within the community. Jardine's point is that this historical condition shapes words into events in *Othello*. Desdemona's protestations of innocence are made in private (unlike Bianca's) and once public doubt has hardened into certainty, she dies 'a whore's death for all her innocence'.[23] Traced across both historical and literary texts, Jardine argues, is a kind of ontological dynamic which governs historical agency, a dynamic made visible in the juridical status of defamatory speech in the Renaissance. The critic cannot restore agency to the female character, but may, she claims, 'retrieve' a recognition of the performative nature of slander against women, by locating the 'technical defamation' at stake in *Othello*. For Jardine, 'retrieval' describes the way in which the hermeneutic circle between past and present is closed. Her complaint against new historicists like Greenblatt is that when they undertake similar projects of retrieval, they tend to accept as given Renaissance codes of sexuality in which women are subjected. Criticism of *Hamlet*, Jardine argues, has unquestioningly accepted Hamlet's disgust at his mother: 'Gertrude's *sexuality* even convinces herself of her guilt.' Feminist historicism, then, must provide a sustained critique of the 'political tendency to deny responsibility for the oppressed . . . and to transfer to them culpability for their own predicament'.[24]

[22] Janet Adelman, *Suffocating Mothers: Fantasies of Maternal Origin in Shakespeare's Plays, Hamlet to The Tempest* (London: Routledge: 1992).
[23] Lisa Jardine, *Reading Shakespeare Historically* (New York and London: Routledge 1996), p. 31.   [24] *Ibid.*, pp. 38, 47, 157.

Similar ethical commitments sustain those seeking to lend a voice to gay and lesbian experience in the past. Jonathan Goldberg's *Sodometries* and Bruce R. Smith's *Homosexual Desire in Shakespeare's England* (1991) both offer powerfully argued, detailed readings of homoeroticism in works by Wyatt, Spenser, Marlowe, Shakespeare and others. Valerie Traub, following Alan Bray's claim that lesbianism is invisible in Renaissance history and literature, has argued persuasively that its effacement is registered in *A Midsummer Night's Dream*, as the intimate Hermia–Helena relationship becomes increasingly occluded by the Lysander–Demetrius plot, and eventually mourned once the play converts elegiacally to heterosexual order in marriage. More recently, Catherine Belsey has shown, in 'Cleopatra's Seduction', that the boys on Cleopatra's barge, like the *putti* in Renaissance paintings, participate subtly in the depiction of female seductiveness.

If feminist criticism has only partially assimilated new historicist paradigms, others have rejected them altogether. Broadly speaking, the principal antagonists have included William Kerrigan, Edward Pechter, Richard Levin, Brian Vickers and more recently Harold Bloom. Most, if not all, of these critics have condemned new historicism for its politicising left-wing commitment, its modish use of theory and its self-conscious, anecdotal style. But it is fair to say that none of these have substantially met the arguments of theoretical historicism with more convincing claims of their own. On the other hand, left-wing critics, such as Walter Cohen and Richard Wilson, have deemed new historicism insufficiently Marxist. Indeed, a commitment to marginality led Barker to conduct a full-scale critique of Greenblatt in the footnotes to his study of violence in early modern literature and culture.

Romanticism and the historical turn

Since the publication of Marilyn Butler's *Romantics, Rebels and Reactionaries* (1981), which broke decisively with New Critical, psychoanalytic, ironist and formalist approaches to Romantic literature, the number of historical studies of Romanticism has dramatically increased.[25] Jerome McGann's *The*

[25] David Aers, Jonathan Cook and David Punter, *Romanticism and Ideology: Studies in English Writing 1765–1830* (London: Routledge & Kegan Paul, 1981); Jerome McGann, *The Beauty of Inflections: Literary Investigations in Historical Method and Theory* (Oxford: Oxford University Press, 1985); Marjorie Levinson, *Wordsworth's Great Period Poems, Four Essays* (Cambridge: Cambridge University Press, 1986); Clifford Siskin, *The Historicity of Romantic Discourse* (New York and London: Oxford University Press, 1988); Vivien Jones, 'Women Writing Revolution: Narratives of History and Sexuality in Wollstonecraft and Williams', in Stephen Copley and John Whale (eds.), *Beyond Romanticism: New Approaches and Contexts, 1780–1832* (New York and London: Routledge, 1992), pp. 178–199; Robin Jarvis, 'Wordsworth and the Use of Charity', in Copley and Whale (eds.), *Beyond Romanticism*, pp. 200–236; Mary

Romantic Ideology (1983) sees the influence of Romantic concepts upon contemporary criticism as sustaining an opposition of poetry to 'the ruins of history'.[26] David Simpson's study, *Wordsworth's Historical Imagination* (1987), covers the major poems, drawing attention at every turn to their links with varieties of social discourse on labour and property, agrarianism and civic virtue, the French Revolution, vagrancy, education and religion. This book, and his article 'Literary Criticism and the Return to History', anticipated two major historicist engagements with Romanticism: the collaborative *Rethinking Historicism* (1989) and Alan Liu's magisterial *Wordsworth: The Sense of History* (1989). Marjorie Levinson's chapter 'The New Historicism: Back to the Future', in *Rethinking Historicism*, contextualises the shift in Romantic studies towards history and traces in Wordsworth's sonnet 'The world is too much with us' a series of historical disruptions to its calm aestheticism.[27] In the 1807 and 1815 editions, Wordsworth removed this poem from among the political sonnets and relocated it under 'Miscellaneous', a move which Levinson reads as an attempt to dispel its links with history and politics altogether. She notes that stanzas one to four of the 'Ode on intimations of mortality' were completed on the day the Peace of Amiens was signed, and finds in its wistful 'whither is fled the visionary gleam?' a faint nostalgia for evaporated revolutionary ardour.

Liu stages similar, if more detailed, versions of these arguments. He sees new historicism generally as a kind of pattern-making formalism, a criticism so devoted to creating its own 'picture-perfect' verbal structure that it lacks credibility as any reliable guide to the past.[28] Liu's Wordsworth hesitates repeatedly between the nationalisms of England and France, caught in 'a politics of the verge that was neither fully subversive nor contained'.[29] His own mode of historicising Wordsworth mingles formalism, biography and history with close readings of individual poems. He argues, for example, that 'Composed upon Westminster Bridge' records three processes: remembering, forgetting and recollection. What the poem remembers, he suggests, are those (for Liu, Anglo-French) 'troubles and disasters' mentioned in Dorothy Wordsworth's journal in 1802. The poem's subsequent 'forgetting' occurs in Wordsworth's later alteration (in the 1807 and 1815 editions) of its date from 1802 to 1803. This alteration removes it from the 1802 political 'Sonnets ded-

footnote 25 (*cont.*)

A. Favret and Nicola J. Watson (eds.), *At the Limits of Historicism: Essays in Cultural, Feminist and Materialist Criticism* (Bloomington: Indiana University Press, 1994).

[26] Jerome J. McGann, *The Romantic Ideology: A Critical Investigation* (Chicago and London: University of Chicago Press, 1983). p. 137.

[27] Marjorie Levinson, 'The New Historicism: Back to the Future', in Marjorie Levinson, Marilyn Butler, Jerome McGann and Paul Hamilton (eds.), *Rethinking Historicism: Critical Readings in Romantic History* (Oxford: Basil Blackwell, 1989).

[28] Alan Liu, *Wordsworth: The Sense of History* (Stanford: Stanford University Press, 1989), p. 466; see also his 'The Power of Formalism: The New Historicism', *English Literary History* 56.4 (1989), pp. 721–772.   [29] *Ibid.*, p. 428.

icated to liberty'. In what Liu describes as a 'recollection', visible in the editions after 1838, Wordsworth remembered and forgot history all over again, changing the date back to 1802 in the title, and linking his dream of a private utopia to an awareness of the 'vox populi'.[30] What Liu omits, however, is the most historically specific entry in Dorothy's recollections of 1802: 'It was a bad hop year. A woman on top of the coach said to me, "It is a sad thing for poor people, for hop-gathering is the women's harvest; there is employment about the hops both for women and children"'.[31] But not, the woman implies, this year. This question of women's labour, voiced by a woman to a woman, emerges neither in Wordsworth's poem nor in Liu's reading, even as the poem feminises and eroticises the sleeping metropolis: 'This city now doth, like a garment, wear/ The beauty of the morning; silent, bare . . . glittering'. Such echoes of Herrick contrast with the masculine sun and river and naturalise a female lack of work into tranquil slumber. Yet behind the poem's depiction of a womanly power in abeyance ('all that mighty heart is lying still') lie very specific historical material conditions of poverty and unemployment, disclosed not by the poet-critic (Wordsworth-Liu) but by the historicising journalist Dorothy, and her woman fellow-traveller.

Conclusion

Neither a school of critical thought nor a movement – nor indeed even a methodology – new historicism remains difficult, indeed unwilling, to be pinned down. Unease about its very name even among so-called practitioners warrants caution when summarising its concerns. If the subversion–containment debate is now regarded as sterile, it is yet unclear as to what a more sufficient and flexible vocabulary for literary-historical analysis would look like. The anti-humanist drift of much theory associated with Lacan, Althusser and Foucault – all to some extent precursors of new historicism – has tended to write off the possibility of human agency, or at least circumscribe it heavily amid wider structures of language, ideology and discourse. Lisa Jardine's work notwithstanding, agency remains a critical problem for those who read for signs of opposition or contestation. No consensus seems yet to have emerged as to the 'After' which new historicism awaits, though the ethical considerations it has raised may sustain the dialogue between Marxists, humanists and feminists in future critical debates.[32] But perhaps new

[30] *Ibid.*, p. 496.
[31] E. de Selincourt, *Journals of Dorothy Wordsworth*, vol. 1 (London: Macmillan, 1952), p. 173.
[32] See Greenblatt, *Learning to Curse*, introduction, pp. 1–15; Jonathan Dollimore, 'Shakespeare and Theory', in Ania Loomba and Martin Orkin (eds.), *Post-Colonial Shakespeares* (New York and London: Routledge, 1998), pp. 259–276; Lawrence Buell, 'Introduction: In Pursuit of Ethics', *PMLA*, Special Topic: Ethics and Literary Studies 114.1 (1999), pp. 7–19.

historicism's most enduring legacy will be its recognition that languages, discourses, vocabularies – call them what we will – work powerfully as effects and echoes in cultural history beyond the particular moment of their articulation. And that where those effects and echoes align in the very contingencies of language – in unexpected contexts, fragments and anecdotes – the inequities harboured in those discourses are most sharply disclosed.

5

Fascist politics and literary criticism

ORTWIN DE GRAEF, DIRK DE GEEST AND
EVELINE VANFRAUSSEN

Fascist aesthetics – more precisely, aesthetics informed by fascist conceptions of nation, society and human essence – is intricately and insidiously bound up with twentieth-century critical thought. This chapter discusses the origins and significance of fascist elements in twentieth-century criticism and aesthetics. It offers an analysis of theories of art expressive of, or simply receptive to, fascist ideology, taking the Belgian national context as a case study in the growth, diffusion and cultural resonance of fascist ideas.

The concept of fascism

The term 'fascism' derives its force from an incongruous yet potent mixture of novelty and imprecision. Arriving on the scene in 1919, Mussolini's *Fascismo* styled itself as a decisive tear in the mottled purple fabric with which liberal, conservative and socialist ideologies failed to cover the expanse of the political; it rapidly attained the status of a viable ideological alternative backed up by a distinct political force whose 'March on Rome' in October 1922 made it the first fascist movement 'autonomously to "seize" power'.[1] 'Fascism' has retained its significance as the name for a distinct, radically new political phenomenon, notwithstanding the semantic confusion wrought through its use as a generic term. Paradoxically, the generic term 'fascism' still has the performative power of a proper name, despite, on the one hand, its loose usage as a catch-all label for 'right-wing' or even just generally 'unpleasant' ideological beliefs, and, on the other hand, the numerous exercises in terminological hygiene seeking to distinguish between the dubious privilege of the proper name and the generic features constituting the 'fascist minimum'.[2]

The problematic status of the generic notion of fascism is typically thematised with reference to Germany and France. While it is commonly

[1] Roger Griffin, *The Nature of Fascism* (London: Pinter, 1991), p. 21.
[2] Zeev Sternhell, *Ni droite, ni gauche: l'idéologie fasciste en France*, rev. edn (Brussels: Complexe, 1987), p. 57. Unless otherwise indicated, all translations into English are ours.

assumed that the National-Socialist regime coming into power with Hitler's appointment as chancellor in 1933 is a prototypical example of fascism, a number of scholars have challenged this assumption, either by arguing for a distinction between movements approximating the Nazi model and movements closer to 'the Italian fascist pattern';[3] or by suggesting that this difference is so decisive as to become truly categorical.[4] Scholarly debate over fascism's historical origins prior to its emergence as a political regime remains no less unresolved. Here the most prominent bone of contention is arguably Zeev Sternhell's thesis that 'the true cradle of fascism' must be located in France.[5] 'The nature of a political ideology', Sternhell contends, 'is always clearer in its aspirations than in its application', and it is in France, in the 'great ideological laboratory of the Belle Epoque', that fascism's aspirations found their most sophisticated expression, which also helps to account for the remarkable proliferation of often highly articulate forms of fascism in France in the first half of the twentieth century.[6]

As it is not our intention here to flesh out these important questions of historical and conceptual clarification, we propose to take Roger Griffin's attempt to construct an 'ideal type' of fascism as our point of reference. Griffin's exercise in 'idealising abstraction', accompanied as it is by a lucid account of fascist scholarship, has the considerable advantage of being both flexible enough to accommodate most informal political uses of the term (including its application to National Socialism), and sufficiently sensitive to a broad cultural perspective to allow us to focus on the specific encounter between fascist politics and literary criticism.[7] The central point of Griffin's definition is the identification of fascism's 'mythic core' as 'a palingenetic form of populist ultra-nationalism'[8] (*palingenesis* meaning 'rebirth'). In fascism's 'mobilizing vision' the '(perceived) crisis of the nation' is read as 'betokening the birth-pangs of a new order' in which the 'national community' will rise 'phoenix-like from the ashes of a morally bankrupt state system and the decadent culture associated with it'.[9] The fascist myth is populist in

[3] Stanley Payne, 'Fascism in Western Europe', in Walter Lacqueur (ed.), *Fascism: A Reader's Guide* (London: Wildwood House, 1976), p. 301.

[4] See e.g. Zeev Sternhell, 'Fascist Ideology', in Lacqueur (ed.), *Fascism*, p. 317.

[5] Zeev Sternhell, Mario Sznajder and Maia Ashéri, *Naissance de l'idéologie fasciste* (Paris: Gallimard, 1989), p. 19.

[6] Sternhell, *Ni droite*, pp. 29, 59. For a survey of right-wing ideology in France, see Jean-François Sirinelli (gen. ed.), *Histoire des droites en France*, 3 vols. (Paris: Gallimard, 1992); Philippe Burrin's chapter 'Le fascisme' in vol. 1 of this study, pp. 610–617, contains a critical appraisal of Sternhell's analysis.

[7] See also Roger Griffin, 'Staging the Nation's Rebirth: The Politics and Aesthetics of Performance in the Context of Fascist Studies', in Günter Berghaus (ed.), *Fascism and Theatre: Comparative Studies on the Aesthetics and Politics of Performance in Europe, 1925–1945* (Providence: Berghahn, 1996).

[8] Griffin, *Nature of Fascism*, p. 26.

[9] Roger Griffin (ed.), *Fascism*, Oxford Readers Series (Oxford: Oxford University Press, 1995), p. 3.

that 'even if led by small elite cadres or self-appointed "vanguards" . . . [fascism] depend[s] on "people power" as the basis of [its] legitimacy'; it is ultra-nationalist in that it goes beyond, 'and hence reject[s], anything compatible with liberal institutions or with the tradition of Enlightenment humanism which underpins them'.[10]

In this 'matrix of fascist ideology', a number of further features receive varying degrees of emphasis in distinct instances of fascist politics: fascism is both anti-liberal and anti-conservative but does not essentially style itself as anti-socialist (rather, it claims to release 'true' socialism from its distortion in communism and recruits its supporters from all classes of society); it favours charismatic politics centred around the figure of the Leader; it is anti-rational; it is racist in its 'celebration of the alleged virtues and greatness of an organically conceived nation or culture' yet it does not preclude a form of internationalism conceived as a 'bond with fascists in other countries'; lacking a generally accepted canonical source comparable to the place Marx holds in socialism, fascism is extremely eclectic; and finally, but decisively, fascism is totalitarian.[11]

Indeed, as Sternhell has argued, fascism was 'the first political system to call itself totalitarian precisely because it encompassed the whole range of human activity', 'represented a way of life', and 'meant to create a new type of society and a new type of man'.[12] This involved, among other things, 'the creation of an elaborate machinery for manufacturing consensus through propaganda and indoctrination',[13] and it is in this respect that fascism's relation to art is of paramount importance. For if fascism styles itself as a total response to what it perceives as a historical crisis, it must also attempt to control the representations of that crisis and of the recovery it heralds: in order to achieve total hegemony in the representational field, it must engage with the actual representational mechanisms involved in the production and reproduction of, precisely, the 'aggressive' style which expresses its 'new ethical and aesthetic values'.[14] The fact that these values are often systematically incoherent lends a special urgency to this totalitarian representational programme and it has been suggested that 'fascism required an aesthetic *over-production* . . . to compensate for, fill in, and cover up its forever unstable ideological core'.[15] To the extent that the practice of representation particularly pertains to the province of art, then, fascism must also submit art to critical judgement, and the study of fascism must trace the criteria it employs in this judgement.

[10] Griffin, *Nature of Fascism*, pp. 36–37.   [11] See Griffin, *Fascism*, pp. 4–8.
[12] Sternhell, 'Fascist Ideology', p. 337.   [13] Griffin, *Fascism*, p. 6.
[14] Sternhell, Sznajder and Ashéri, *Naissance*, p. 27.
[15] Jeffrey T. Schnapp, 'Epic Demonstrations: Fascist Modernity and the 1932 Exhibition of the Fascist Revolution', in Richard J. Golsan (ed.), *Fascism, Aesthetics, and Culture* (Hanover, N.H.: University Press of New England, 1992), p. 3.

Aesthetics, literature, literary criticism

The reference to Walter Benjamin's 1936 characterisation of fascism as an 'aestheticization of politics'[16] has become an almost ritual obligation for enquiries into the relation between fascism and art. Two major strands may be discerned in the interpretation of Benjamin's dictum. The first starts out from the text Benjamin uses to illustrate his argument, viz. the Italian futurist Filippo Tommaso Marinetti's glorification of war as an experience of aesthetic excellence. Taking Marinetti's judgements in this tract at face value results in an understanding of fascist aesthetics as a wilfully extremist indulgence in violence as modernity's decisive modulation of Beauty itself. Although it is not difficult to find suitably shocking instances of fascist aesthetic doctrine to support this interpretation, it does tend to reduce the impact of fascist aesthetics by diagnosing it as an easily identifiable aberration comfortably alien to the development of true aesthetics. The second strand in the interpretation of Benjamin's analysis takes its cue from his insistence that fascist aesthetics should be read dialectically, that is, with specific attention to the political and socio-economic processes that determine it. For Benjamin this involves the recognition that the aesthetic glorification of war, far from being an idiosyncratic if influential deviation from the norm, is the logical culmination of the twin processes of massification and proletarisation revealing the discrepancy between capitalism's compulsive augmentation of the means of production and its refusal to radically reorganise the distribution of wealth: 'Only war makes it possible to mobilize the entirety of technical means of the present whilst preserving the property relations.'[17]

The strength of this diagnosis is that it can think together both the extremely destructive edge in fascist aesthetics and its manifold alternative strategies for representing the masses of modernity in accordance with the projection of a fascist utopia, including its predilection for the monumental, its obsession with mass rituals, pageants, festivals and exhibitions, its aggressive anti-individualism; in short, its cult of the People as the organic raw matter with which to refashion the Body Politic after the disillusionment created by the political crisis. 'The masses have a right to a change in the property relations; fascism seeks an *expression* of the masses whilst conserving these relations.'[18] Benjamin thus credits fascism with a full-blown aesthetic ideology (as opposed to a ragbag of halfbaked aesthetic mannerisms), thereby inviting us to take fascist aesthetics extremely seriously and to recognise its aggressive populist resurrection of the aura of authenticity and the authority of genius that, according to Benjamin's historical-materialist analysis, had been traditionally associated with art in the past. A similar appeal to take

---

[16] Walter Benjamin, 'Das Kunstwerk im Zeitalter seiner technischen Reproduzierbarkeit', *Illuminationen: ausgewählte Schriften* (Frankfurt a.M.: Suhrkamp, 1977), p. 169.
[17] *Ibid.*, p. 168.   [18] *Ibid.*, pp. 167–168.

fascist aesthetics seriously informs alternative inquiries that trace the fate of modern aesthetics itself from its critical articulation in the work of Immanuel Kant, through its reworking by Friedrich Schiller, to its systematic perversion in the work of Nazi ideologues such as Joseph Goebbels, who notoriously held that 'The statesman is an artist, too. The people are for him what stone is for the sculptor. . . Politics are the plastic arts of the state as painting is the plastic art of color. . . To transform a mass into a people and a people into a state – that has always been the deepest sense of a genuine political task.'[19]

The suggestion that fascism's investment in aesthetics is far from being a mere quirk in the course of (western) culture finds further support in the numerous studies of prominent authors (including Maurice Blanchot, Louis-Ferdinand Céline, T. S. Eliot, Ernst Jünger, Wyndham Lewis, Ezra Pound and W. B. Yeats)[20] whose work has been compromised in varying degrees by their embraces of, or brushes with, versions of fascism. While the existence (though not always the extent) of fascist connections in the work of most of these figures had been relatively well-documented for a number of decades, the 1987 revelation of the collaborationist cultural journalism published in the first years of the German occupation of Belgium by the distinguished deconstructive literary theorist Paul de Man (1919–83) came as a surprise that added fuel to the already acrimonious debate over the state of literary studies in the 1980s.[21] Earlier in the same year, Victor Farias' book on *Heidegger et le nazisme* had lent new intensity to the dispute over the German philosopher's involvement with National Socialism, and the fact that Heidegger is one of deconstruction's privileged points of reference raised the stakes in the controversy. Rather than pursue this particular controversy further, we propose to direct our attention to the specific genre to which de Man's wartime writings belong: the cultural and, especially, literary criticism published in channels supervised by the propaganda division of the particular brand of fascism that is National Socialism.

[19] Quoted in the editors' introduction to Friedrich W. Schiller, *On the Aesthetic Education of Mankind*, ed. and trans. Elizabeth M. Wilkinson and L. A. Willoughby (Oxford: Oxford University Press, 1967), p. cxlii.

[20] See Steven Ungar, *Scandal and Aftereffect: Blanchot and France Since 1930* (Minneapolis: University of Minnesota Press, 1995); Leslie Hill, *Maurice Blanchot: Extreme Contemporary* (London: Routledge, 1997); Philippe Alméras, *Les idées de Céline* (Paris: Berg International, 1992); Anthony Julius, *T. S. Eliot, Anti-Semitism, and Literary Form* (Cambridge: Cambridge University Press, 1995); Marcus Bullock, *Violent Eye: Ernst Jünger's Visions and Revisions of the European Right* (Detroit: Wayne State University Press, 1992); Thomas R. Nevin, *Ernst Jünger and Germany: Into the Abyss, 1914–1945* (Durham: Duke University Press, 1996); Fredric Jameson, *Fables of Aggression: Wyndham Lewis, the Modernist as Fascist* (Berkeley: University of California Press, 1979); Robert Casillo, *The Genealogy of Demons: Anti-Semitism, Fascism and the Myths of Ezra Pound* (Evanston: Northwestern University Press, 1988); Elizabeth Butler Cullingford, *Yeats, Ireland, and Fascism* (London: Macmillan, 1981).

[21] See Paul de Man, *Wartime Journalism, 1939–1943*, eds. Werner Hamacher, Neil Hertz and Thomas Keenan (Lincoln: University of Nebraska Press, 1996); also see Werner Hamacher, Neil Hertz and Thomas Keenan (eds.), *Responses: On Paul de Man's Wartime Journalism* (Lincoln: University of Nebraska Press, 1989) and the special issues of *Critical Inquiry* 15.1 (1989), *Diacritics* 20.3 (1990) and *South Central Review* 11.1 (1994).

The fact that this type of research is by no means the norm for investigations into fascist aesthetics is at once understandable and surprising. Understandable, because it involves the analysis of vast quantities of writings which, from the perspective of established aesthetics and literary scholarship, must appear utterly banal. Instead of the fascinating spectacle of highly articulate modulations of fascist aesthetics in the work of major figures, research into common or garden literary criticism pledging allegiance (often implicitly) to fascism seems to lead one into a dreary wasteland of trivial mediocrity. Yet it is precisely this apparently unsurprising textscape that the study of fascist aesthetics must also explore, for it is through the compulsive reproduction of the components of fascist belief *as* banalities that fascism summons the People whose palingenesis as a Nation it claims to represent – as is indeed implied in the historical meaning of the term 'banal', 'obligatory for all the tenants of a feudal jurisdiction'. The fact that the workings of this ideological reproductive apparatus are most prominent in 'minor' genres such as journalistic criticism does not of course prevent the emergence of fascist banalities in 'major' works: inasmuch as fascism is a totalitarian ideology intent on a homogeneous saturation of the representational field, the proper function of its ideological beliefs is banality, irrespective of the context in which they appear.[22]

It is nonetheless noteworthy in this respect that the 'major' authors now most frequently studied as representatives of fascist aesthetics often occupied less than prominent positions in the field of fascist culture at the height of fascism's political trajectory. The history of fascist politics shows a recurrent pattern in which fascism's rise to actual power, especially in nations where it is imposed by a foreign aggressor, is accompanied by a series of strategic political concessions intended to win over alternative important political factions. In its bid for cultural power fascism employed similar strategies of qualified compromise but it would appear that its mechanisms of representational control were relatively unsuccessful in fully accommodating potentially 'major' fellow travellers. This does not diminish the extent to which some of these 'major' figures were implicated in fascist ideology; rather, it may suggest a certain resistance to totalitarian homogenising strategies in practices characterised by a particularly acute fascination with the complexities of representation. The fact that this resistance is frequently also a matter of arrogant elitism on the part of self-appointed candidates for cultural canonisation should not be allowed to rule out the possibility that resistance to totalitarian banalisation is a critical, though by no means decisively democratic or enlightened, feature of representation itself. To the extent that this is indeed the case, even the discourse reproducing fascist aesthetics in its apparently

---

[22] On fascism and banality, see Alice Yaeger Kaplan, *Reproductions of Banality: Fascism, Literature, and French Intellectual Life*, foreword by Russel Berman (Minneapolis: University of Minnesota Press, 1986).

most coercively banal form is bound to show signs of representational strain. A brief sketch of Flemish 'fascist literary criticism' may serve to illustrate this hypothesis.

The discourse of fascist literary criticism

The pre-critical assumption that fascist literary criticism can be described in terms of a principled commitment to a stable corpus of texts and authors or to a fixed matrix of specific literary features does not survive a systematic encounter with instances of such criticism. In what follows we present some of the findings such a systematic encounter actually yields, basing ourselves on the extensive study of cultural discourse in occupied Belgium (specifically the Flemish part of the country) carried out by the Literature in the Second World War Research Centre at Leuven University.

This historical and geographical demarcation has at least three important implications. First, as is the case for fascisms everywhere, the 'fascism' represented in this discourse is shot through with features borrowed from the specific cultural tradition in which it takes shape. For Flanders this is predominantly the Catholic tradition, and it is often unclear whether recurrent features of fascist literary criticism are not just minimally transcoded elements of activist Catholicism.[23] Alongside this conservative Catholic-activist input, fascism in Belgium, as elsewhere, also incorporates 'left-wing' elements, the most prominent case in this respect being the influence of Hendrik de Man, 'theoretician of "left-wing fascism"'.[24]

Second, there is the specific location of Belgium on the border dividing Germanic culture and Latin culture, which makes it a particularly complicated example of the friction between the imperialist pan-Germanic strain in National Socialist fascism and the more neutralist or universalist tendencies of alternative fascisms.[25] Given the fact that Belgium consists of two linguistic communities of comparable size (the Flemish Dutch-speaking North and the Walloon francophone South), plus a small German-speaking community in the East, the politics of language play a decisive role in the formation of fascist tendencies in this country. Attempts to forge a Belgian People as an organic reality by fascist criteria never quite took hold, for fairly obvious cultural-historical reasons. Restricting ourselves to the Flemish situation, the most instructive conflict is arguably that between VNV (*Vlaams Nationaal Verbond*, Flemish National Union) and DeVlag (*Duits-Vlaamse Arbeidsgemeenschap/Deutsch-Vlämische Arbeitsgemeinschaft*, German-Flemish Labour Association). As its name suggests, the latter struggled for the Great-German ideal according to

---

[23] See Martin Conway, *Catholic Politics in Europe, 1918–1945* (London: Routledge, 1997), p. 53.
[24] Hendrik de Man, *Après coup (Mémoires)* (Bruxelles: Toison d'Or, 1941), p. 298.
[25] See Griffin, *Nature of Fascism*, pp. 48–49.

which Flanders is destined to figure as an integral part of the German Third Reich. The VNV, sharing the separatist agenda as far as the abolition of the Belgian nation was concerned (as witness their irritation with Hendrik de Man's 1940 'Manifesto to the Members of the Belgian Labour Party' which called for a 'national resurrection' of 'the Belgian people' in a politics of collaboration with the German occupant),[26] opposed DeVlag's Great-German aspirations and instead favoured a full integration with the Netherlands.

In a strict application of the working definition we have chosen, both these forms of Flemish secessionism fail to qualify as fascism – as Griffin indeed states, while admitting their kinship with fascism[27] – since they are not intent on the palingenesis of the nation 'properly speaking', i.e. as a territorially established political entity. This, however, would seem to underestimate the distinction between the nation as a historical political entity and the symbolic functioning of the nation as a culturally and linguistically homogeneous and ultimately 'natural' given coinciding with the People imagined by fascism itself. In fact, it can be argued that it is precisely in cases such as this, where convenient (albeit spurious) recourse to the existing nation as a ready-made mould for the People is impossible, that the formative resolve of fascism is tested to the full.

This confusing state of affairs is further compounded by a third aspect, involving the specific nature of National Socialist rule in occupied Belgium. Unlike the Netherlands, for instance, where a *Zivilverwaltung* of German civilian officials actively governed the country at all levels, Belgium was provisionally administered by a *Militärverwaltung*, consisting of a relatively small cadre of military executives who delegated the actual administration of the country, including its cultural life, to Belgian civilians, thus creating a wider margin for more or less significant deviations from Nazi orthodoxy.

Notwithstanding this heterogeneity and instability, it is possible to articulate dominant patterns in what we can still call (Flemish) 'fascist literary criticism' as a discourse of normative and institutionally determined statements assigning specific functions to literature and its reading in the service of the establishment and maintenance of the People as an organic reality. In what follows we propose a composite picture of a central strand of this discourse refracted through the prism of the body. The wide semantic spectrum generated by this notion (involving the body proper as well as the various figures of incorporation depending on it)[28] covers an important section of fascist representational practice and should allow us to assess the function of literature and criticism in mainstream Flemish fascist discourse.

[26] Peter Dodge (ed.), *A Documentary Study of Hendrik de Man, Socialist Critic of Marxism* (Princeton: Princeton University Press, 1979), p. 328.
[27] Griffin, *Nature of Fascism*, p. 169.
[28] See Jean-Luc Nancy, *Corpus* (Paris: Métailié, 1992); and Ortwin de Graef, 'Sweet Dreams, Monstered Nothings: Catachresis in Kant and *Coriolanus*', in Andrew Hadfield, Dominic Rainsford and Tim Woods (eds.), *The Ethics in Literature* (Houndmills: Macmillan, 1999).

The fascist body in criticism

The institutional determination of fascist literary critical discourse is perhaps its most readily visible feature, involving as it does the legitimation of this discourse through a complicated apparatus of cultural councils, party commissions and state organisations. The relations between these various organisations are often troubled even in a firmly established fascist regime such as Nazi Germany, so it is not surprising that cultural institutionalisation in countries occupied or controlled by Nazi Germany should be characterised by overt conflict, backstabbing and duplicity. Yet while the relation between the Councils for Culture founded on German directives in occupied Belgium and the many cultural organisations subordinated to them was indeed far from harmonious, it is the very fact of these institutionalising strategies that is important in that it reveals fascism's express intent to get a firm grip on the cultural system.

In the field of literary criticism, the effects of this intent become clear even at a cursory glance: the discourse on literature is compelled to style itself as an institutional performance. Literature is represented at official functions, in public speeches set up as photo opportunities for critics in uniform against a backdrop of banners and insignia, in publications in journals proudly sporting their official affiliations. This emphatic awareness of institutional space also informs the more strictly textual framing of this discourse: bylines often include references to the author's military rank or station and editorial comments rivet the text to the contemporary political situation. Even in its external trappings, then, the discourse of fascist literary criticism is obsessed with the sense of its own historical situation and compulsively confesses its participation in the People's struggle from crisis to rebirth.

This participation in the People's palingenesis takes on specifically activist overtones in the cultural elite's determined assumption of its salvific task. The notion of the 'People' in effect functions as a normative rather than a descriptive category. The People may figure in the essential core of fascist thought, but the people is in a state of crisis and will only become totally itself under the instruction of an elite that has fully recovered its essence and recognised its destiny. The implication of this normative transcription is that the sense of historical crisis and renewal powering fascist ideology is ultimately integrated in the transhistorical teleology of apocalyptic myth: the emphatic commitment to the present historical condition involves a reading of this condition as the last chance to end history properly in the final fulfilment of the People.

In order to accomplish its part of this mission, the discourse of fascist literary criticism needs norms with which to judge the works it must represent and perhaps its most typical routine in this respect is the projection of its own mission onto the author of the literary work. The fact that the biography of the author is a standard component of fascist literary criticism is hardly a distinctive characteristic in itself. What is striking is the sheer insistence with which these biographical data are hammered into exemplary shape. An appropriate model for this practice in English culture is the portrait of the Hero as Man of Letters in Thomas Carlyle's 1840 lectures *On Heroes, Hero-Worship and the Heroic in History*. For Carlyle, characterised by Harold Bloom as 'the true forerunner of twentieth-century Fascism',[29] the Hero as Man of Letters is 'the soul of all. What he teaches, the whole world will do and make. . . His life . . . is a piece of the everlasting heart of Nature herself: all men's life is, – but the weak many know not the fact, and are untrue to it, in most times; the strong few are strong, heroic, perennial, because it cannot be hidden from them.'[30]

If we change 'Nature' into 'People', Carlyle here captures the core of fascist literary criticism in its obsessive representation of the true Author as the exemplary incarnation of the People's purest essence. This representation typically follows the narrative patterns of epic and tragedy. Thanks to his extraordinary qualities, the Author is able to transcend all limitations, be they internal or external. He is man enough to recognise and redress errors in his personal past – the standard topos here being his conversion to literature of and for the People after a brief spell of unhealthy fascination with various vaguely-defined modernisms. He courageously deals with diverse instances of personal opposition which are readily identified as symptomatic of the decadence threatening the People in its time of crisis. The critical conditions diagnosed over and again in this connection are capitalist and individualist modernity; the ruins of parliamentary democracy and misguided technologisation; rampant urbanisation demonised in the vision of the city as a noxious melting pot of cultures whose effluvia threaten to asphyxiate the People; crass commercialisation and mercantilism typically portrayed in vicious vignettes of prostitutes and Jews; and in particular the internationalist literary movements whose villainous representatives flourish in this wasteland.

The argument undergirding this narrative dynamic is perfectly circular: the Author truly in touch with his People can only produce literature proper for the People; authors with foreign allegiances can never successfully represent the People they are strangers to or estranged from: at best they can strike an unconvincing pose, at worst they indulge in subtly perverse attempts to deceive that must be firmly condemned on grounds that are typically though not exclusively racist. This of course raises the question of the special status of foreign literature in a relatively small linguistic community: even assuming that this literature is a proper representation of and for the People to which its Author belongs, its function in the context of another culture remains problematic. A typical strategy in this respect is the reference to congenial literary-

[29] Harold Bloom (ed.), *Thomas Carlyle* (New Haven: Chelsea House, 1986), p. 14.
[30] Thomas Carlyle, *Sartor Resartus: On Heroes and Hero Worship* (London: Dent, 1908), p. 384.

critical representations of such Authors in their own culture; another subter-
fuge consists in exercises in special pleading intended to strike a balance
between the recognition of the merits of foreign literature and the programmatic preference for literature produced by representatives of the People at
home. The following 1942 statement by the Flemish critic Paul Hardy gives a
good impression of the unstable commixture of self-deprecation and self-
assertion this yields: 'Generally speaking our literature, the literature of a
small people, can evidently not be a match for that of the great European
countries; yet nobody would think of preferring the mother of his rich neighbour over his own just because his own happens to be less endowed with the
gifts of the spirit.'[31] The programmatic transformation of critical judgement
into filial commitment encapsulates the coercive dynamics of fascist literary
criticism in its structurally unstable intent to honour both the universal superiority of *genius* and the particular superiority of the *locus*.

A similar ideological-critical balancing act is required in the attendant
debate over the issue of popular editions. Here, the conflict is between commercial, ideological and aesthetic values: the People must be furnished with
their representation in the Body Popular, yet the popular market produces representations insufficiently infused with the representational project of fascism
or even wholly indifferent to it, while the writers among the people ready to
embrace this project are not always particularly 'endowed with the gifts of the
spirit' and consequently disseminate 'aesthetically inferior' and ideologically
unbalanced 'tendentious literature'. Faced with the popular appeal of this literature, fascist literary criticism takes it upon itself to adjudicate between the
people's mere need for representations, its 'hunger' for literature and its
genuine but fatefully obscured desire for the representation of its sacred
essence.

The amount of special pleading in articles concerning this problem indicates yet again the instability in the representational project of fascist discourse – an instability institutionally performed in the encounter between the
Flemish critic R. F. Lissens, writing in the francophone journal *Cassandre*
about Flemish literature, and Lothar von Balluseck, representative of the
'Reichsverband deutscher Zeitungsverleger' and director of the Belgian collaborating distribution house *Agence Dechenne*, represented here by Belgian
critic Paul de Man. Lissens had commented unfavourably on popular Flemish
editions distributed by *Dechenne*, and von Balluseck invited him, via his
editor Paul Colin, to an interview on this topic with his subordinate Paul de
Man.[32] The vertiginous perspectival shifts in this encounter are symptomatic
of the intractability of the literary field in the period: a dismissive 'French'

---

[31] Quoted in Dirk De Geest, Eveline Vanfraussen, Marnix Beyen and Ilse Mestdagh, *Collaboratie of cultuur?: een Vlaams tijdschrift in bezettingstijd (1941–1944)* (Antwerp/Amsterdam: Meulenhoff/Kritak/Soma, 1997), p. 248.
[32] Letter to Paul Colin, *Agence Dechenne*, 13 August 1942.

look at Flemish writing coming from a Flemish critic crosses a German glance
at the necessities of the representational programme, represented by a Belgian
critic-cum-secretary invariably championing 'properly aesthetic' and
'European' criteria. The interview never took place, but de Man did write an
article on the uses and abuses of popular editions in the collaborationist
newspaper *Het Vlaamsche Land* (20 October 1942), stating that 'The author
should not descend to the people but the people should rise to the level of the
artist'[33] – which may in itself be read as a classical 'properly aesthetic' statement all too ready for transcoding in the heroising discourse of fascist literary
criticism.

On the field of actual reading and writing, then, the Author as Hero is
crowded out by a plurality of alternative representations of the author as
entertainer: teller of tales, stories, anecdotes, which may or may not harbour
fascist aspirations of various hues. In the critical appreciation it must devote
to these insufficiently integrated, and hence potentially dissenting, yet
extremely familiar voices, fascist literary criticism is torn between its commitment to the integral representation of the People and its task of recognising
the people's representations in popular culture. On the field where it represents itself to itself, however, this discourse exorcises its internal scission by
repositing the Author as Hero in a monological incantation structured as
sheer repetition – spectacularly expert in figures of amplification, such as the
incremental repetition of synonyms and the successive development of
increasingly emphatic features, and in figures of pathos, such as hyperbole
and personification.[34] In its predilection for a performative stylistics, fascist
literary criticism turns its back on the requirements of rational articulation
and effectively imitates the prophetic and visionary mode it simultaneously
identifies as the proper voice of the genuine Author.

The drastic homogenisation of the literary-critical corpus resulting from
this representational strategy is entirely consistent with its express intent to
frame the Author's individual body in the Body Popular to which he is born.
This rhetorical conception of the People as a corporate organism finds its
concrete, but no less rhetorical, counterpart in the remarkable attention
devoted to the body of the Author, both in photographs and in prose impressions. The Author's body is typically staged in a vertical and monumental
position: he (and the ideal-typical author is invariably male) dominates his
surroundings and surveys them from above, his gaze qualified as steely, perceptive, penetrating. Whenever possible it is dressed up in military garb and,
even more importantly, over-coded as pre-eminently virile. The figure of the
self-enclosed virile body suggests a dynamic totality, self-sufficient in its difference from the symptoms of decadence and endowed with the capacity to

---

[33] De Man, *Wartime Journalism*, p. 333.
[34] See also Saul Friedländer, *Reflets du nazisme* (Paris: Seuil, 1982), pp. 49–51.

realise itself in the world of its People by reproducing its culture as in itself it really is: a 'living work of art'[35] which transforms the masses into the Body they have become alienated from.

The mythical frame of fascism

In its performance of this essentially racist 'national-aestheticist' phantasm,[36] fascist literary criticism must also engage with the fictional world created by the Author: it is the task of criticism to frame this fiction in the image of the People from which it derives its significance. To appreciate the nature of this enterprise, it is instructive to juxtapose the fascist framing of everyday life with the notion of *figura*, the key to 'the conception of reality in late antiquity and the Christian Middle Ages' in Erich Auerbach's 1946 classic *Mimesis*: 'In this conception, an occurrence on earth signifies not only itself but at the same time another, which it predicts or confirms . . . The connection between occurrences is not regarded as primarily a chronological or causal development but as a oneness within the divine plan.'[37] A simple translation exercise yields a helpful insight into fascism's framing of the quotidian: ordinary life receives its full significance in the context, not of a 'divine plan', but of the People's palingenesis. Ultimately, then, fascism's insistent awareness of the historical uniqueness of the contemporary condition of crisis is cancelled in its commitment to the transhistorical mythical reality of, to paraphrase Carlyle, 'the everlasting heart of the People itself'.

Fascist framing so conceived can be read as an alternative response to one of Auerbach's guiding questions, viz. the question as to the precise difference between medieval and modern realism. For Auerbach, modern realism is exemplified in the work of Woolf, Joyce and Proust, whose relative neglect for 'the great exterior turning points and blows of fate' and concomitant commitment to 'minor, unimpressive, random events' provides him with a tentative modern alternative for 'the divine plan' of medieval figural realism.[38] In its 'representation of the random moment in the lives of different people', a moment 'comparatively independent of the controversial and unstable orders over which men fight and despair', modern realism brings to light 'the elementary things which our lives have in common' and thereby bears witness to the fact that 'the differences between men's ways of life and forms of thought have already lessened' in 'an economic and cultural levelling process' which is taking place 'below', and 'through', the 'surface conflicts': 'It is still a long way to a common life of mankind on earth, but the goals begin to be visible'

---

[35] Philippe Lacoue-Labarthe, *La fiction du politique* (Paris: Bourgeois, 1987), p. 111.
[36] *Ibid.*, p. 112.
[37] Erich Auerbach, *Mimesis: The Representation of Reality in Western Literature*, trans. Willard Trask (Garden City: Doubleday Anchor Books, 1957), p. 490.   [38] *Ibid.*, pp. 484, 483.

and 'the complicated process of dissolution' initially mirrored in modern realism thus 'seems to be tending toward a very simple solution'.[39]

Considering the actual ramifications of what Auerbach refers to as 'the surface conflicts', including the fact of his writing *Mimesis* as a Jewish refugee in exile in Istanbul during the Second World War, this hopeful humanist projection of 'a common life of mankind on earth' as a resolutely secular alternative to the divine plan in pre-modern figural framing acquires a bitter taste. For the 'simple solution' advanced by fascist literary-critical discourse in the face of 'the complicated process of dissolution' is precisely intent on keeping the random at bay by representing it as ultimately incompatible with the homogeneous Body Popular whose constitutive components in the quotidian are radically dependent on the total struggle of the People to conclusively exorcise its others. Fascist literary criticism programmatically identifies the ordinary lives in the realism it favours as fascist *figurae* in a mimetico-mythical design whose commitment to simplicity and unity must appear irredeemably incommensurable with Auerbach's conception of a simple solution. As Auerbach indeed suggests: 'Perhaps [the very simple solution of a common life for mankind on earth] will be too simple to please those who, despite all its dangers and catastrophes, admire and love our epoch for the sake of its abundance of life and the incomparable historical vantage point which it affords. But they are few in number, and probably they will not live to see much more than the first forewarnings of the approaching unification and simplification.'[40] To the extent that they did see such forewarnings, the representatives of fascist literary criticism devoted themselves to combating this solution by way of a very different unification and simplification – it is that difference that must be addressed.

Solutions for a world in decline

In the pages immediately preceding the prospective framing of modern realism in 'the common life of mankind on earth', Auerbach clearly demonstrates that he is by no means blind to the dark side of the temptation of unity and simplicity that informs fascism. After a rapid rehearsal of the 'tremendous acceleration' in the 'widening of man's horizon', reflected in the fact that 'synthetic and objective attempts at interpretation are produced and demolished every instant', he specifically identifies fascism as a response to the 'violent clash of the most heterogeneous ways of life' attending this disintegration: 'The temptation to entrust oneself to a sect which solved all problems with a single formula, whose power of suggestion imposed solidarity, and which ostracized everything which would not fit in and submit – this tempta-

---

[39] *Ibid.*, p. 488.   [40] *Ibid.*

tion was so great that, with many people, fascism hardly had to employ force when the time came for it to spread through the countries of old European culture.'[41] In the literature of those countries, Auerbach continues, the 'increasing predilection for ruthlessly subjectivist perspectives is another symptom' of the 'confusion and helplessness' generated by 'the decline of our world': in much of modern realism, there is often 'something hostile to the reality which they represent', a 'hatred of culture and civilization, brought out by means of the subtlest stylistic devices which culture and civilization have developed, and often a radical and fanatical urge to destroy'.[42] Yet it is in this same modern realism that Auerbach notices 'something entirely different tak[ing] place too' – the prefiguration, through this literature's representation of the random, of, precisely, 'the common life of mankind on earth', the 'very simple solution' responding to 'the complicated process of dissolution' which also prepared the ground in which fascism struck its roots.

The lucidly implicit irony with which Auerbach thus establishes the connection between the 'sinister unification'[43] proposed in the 'single formula' of fascism and the 'approaching unification' of 'mankind on earth' he reads in modern realism's representations of the random, suggests that in order to oppose the forces of totalitarianism, the mere *positing* of the difference between the coercive frame of fascism and the frames fashioned to dissolve this coercion, may be too simple a solution. Rather, this difference has to be critically reconstituted, and for literary criticism this task can take shape as the careful insistence on the barely representable resistance to total incorporation which constitutes common life.

[41] Ibid., p. 485–486.   [42] Ibid., p. 487.
[43] Such was Kenneth Burke's diagnosis of *Mein Kampf*, quoted in Geoffrey H. Hartman, *The Fateful Question of Culture* (New York: Columbia University Press, 1997), p. 123.

Marxism and post-Marxism

6

Marxism and literary criticism

ALEX CALLINICOS

'Always historicise!' Fredric Jameson famously wrote, adding that this was 'the one absolute and we may even say "transhistorical" imperative of all dialectical thought'.[1] It is indeed a requirement one would expect anyone committed to Marx's theory of history to observe when studying cultural products. The most natural way of interpreting that theory implies that these products are, quite simply, unintelligible unless placed within the broader set of historically contingent social relationships from which they emerged. But how to historicise without causing the text to vanish into its historical context? This difficulty is especially acute when questions pertaining to the formal construction of the text are under consideration. Marx and Engels acquired from Hegel a hostility to divorcing form and content: 'the form is the indwelling process of the concrete content itself', as the latter put it.[2] But – once again – how to demonstrate that form is part of the process without subjecting it to the contingencies of historical specificity?

Literary theory did not, of course, figure high among the concerns of the founders of historical materialism. In his most celebrated statement of that theory, Marx contrasted the productive forces and the relations of production, which together formed the 'real foundation' of social life, with 'the legal and political superstructure' developing from that base: 'it is always necessary to distinguish between the material transformation of the economic conditions of production, which can be determined with the precision of natural science, and the legal, political, religious, artistic, or philosophic – in short, ideological forms in which men become conscious of this conflict and fight it out'.[3] Art is thereby firmly put in its place – included in the superstructure, and indeed subsumed under ideology; cultural production must be seen as subordinate to the rhythms of material production. At the same time, however, the idea that it is in these 'ideological forms' that human beings 'become conscious' of the contradiction within the economic base and 'fight it out' suggests that their role is more than passively to reflect the development of the productive forces.

---

[1] Fredric Jameson, *The Political Unconscious* (London: Methuen, 1981), p. 9.
[2] G. W. F. Hegel, *The Phenomenology of Spirit*, trans. A. V. Miller (Oxford: Clarendon, 1977), § 56, p. 35 (translation modified).
[3] Karl Marx, *A Contribution to the Critique of Political Economy*, trans. N. I. Stone (London: Lawrence & Wishart, 1971), pp. 20–21.

Engels, in his role as guardian of Marx's doctrine after the latter's death, indeed sought to underline this point: 'It is not that the economic situation is *cause, solely active*, while everything else is only passive effect. There is, rather, interaction on the basis of economic necessity, which *ultimately* always asserts itself.'[4] The imperative to historicise must thus be accomplished without reducing cultural products, along with the rest of the superstructure, to the economic base. The same flexibility is shown by Marx in his very extensive reading of classical and modern European literature. Great works of art (Marx is unabashed in his value-judgements) can provide profound insights into specific historical situations; they also, because of the relatively unalienated character of artistic labour, offer intimations of how work will become a means of self-fulfilment in a classless communist society. That such achievements are possible despite the overt intentions of the author is indicated by Marx's and Engels' immense admiration for Balzac, whom the latter called 'a far greater master of realism than all the Zolas *passés, présents et à venir*'. Balzac's greatness lies in how he 'was compelled to go against his own class sympathies and political prejudices' – his nostalgia for the *ancien régime* – and portray 'the progressive inroads of the rising bourgeoisie upon the society of nobles'.[5]

We see here emerging what Frank Kermode has called 'the discrepancy theory', according to which 'texts can under Marxist analysis reveal a meaning not intended by the author'.[6] Though, as we shall see below, greatly influential on Althusserian criticism, this idea remained in Marx's and Engels' writings merely an intriguing suggestion. One reason why it was not developed further is perhaps that an obvious strategy for eliciting the discrepancy between author-intention and meaning is to study the traces it might have left in the formal construction of the text. But, as S. S. Prawer observes, 'Marx does not often deal with questions of form.'[7]

This inattention to form became endemic in the Marxism of the first mass socialist movement in Europe, the Second International (1889–1914), which sought to codify a relatively reductionist and determinist version of historical materialism. Inasmuch as leading theoreticians such as Karl Kautsky and G. V. Plekhanov discussed literary texts it was to expose their dependence on material conditions. Of more potential value was Antonio Labriola's attempt in his *Essays on the Materialistic Conception of History* (1896) to distinguish historical materialism from a theory of distinct and interacting 'factors' – economic, political, cultural, etc. The Marxist theory of history rather conceived society as a *complexus* or integrated totality whose understanding

---

[4] Letter to H. Starkenburg, 25 January 1894, in Karl Marx and Friedrich Engels, *Selected Correspondence* (Moscow: Progress, 1965), p. 467.

[5] Letter to M. Harkness, April 1888, *ibid.*, pp. 402–403.

[6] Frank Kermode, *History and Value* (Oxford: Clarendon, 1988), p. 99.

[7] S. S. Prawer, *Karl Marx and World Literature* (Oxford: Oxford University Press, 1978), p. 413.

took priority over that of its component parts. This argument influenced Trotsky and anticipated Lukács' philosophical recasting of Marxism in *History and Class Consciousness* (1923).

It is indeed in Trotsky that we find the most sustained attempt to conceptualise the place of the literary within the social totality from the standpoint of classical Marxism. By far the most accomplished writer among the leading Marxists, he was therefore particularly well qualified to explore the relationship between form and historical context. His most important contribution, *Literature and Revolution* (1923), was an intervention in the intense aesthetic debates among Russian intellectuals which followed the revolution of October 1917. Trotsky is here fighting on two fronts. Thus he confronts the cultural movement known as *Proletkult* (glorification of the proletariat) which flourished in the first years of the new regime. *Proletkult*'s supporters argued that the workers' state should move rapidly to the creation of a 'proletarian culture' radically different from the artistic inheritance of bourgeois society. If this position represented a particularly crude form of economic reductionism, Trotsky also found himself at odds with the futurist avant-garde movement, which had emerged in Russia before the First World War. Many futurists rallied to the revolution but they were still influenced by the doctrine of autonomy of literary form most forcefully expressed by Shklovsky, Jakobson and other theorists of formalism.

In a brilliant polemic, Trotsky followed Marx and Engels in their insistence on starting from epochal socio-economic transformations but displayed a far greater sensitivity to the specificities of literary form. Thus he takes *Proletkult* to task for failing to recognise the material and cultural backwardness of the Russian working class. Making possible radically different forms of artistic creation from those of capitalist society will be part of a much broader process aimed at producing the economic and social conditions for a communist society in which all classes, including the proletariat, will vanish. From this perspective, the idea of 'proletarian culture' is a contradiction in terms, an attempt to absolutise the evanescent features of a transitional society. The bourgeois cultural heritage will provide valuable support in helping the working class to overcome its backwardness, as well as offering a source of insight into universal features of the human condition.

At the same time as Trotsky resists *Proletkult*'s nihilist attitude towards the art of the past, he denounces formalism as 'an abortive idealism when applied to the questions of art'. It breaks up the complex social whole into distinct factors, but fails to carry through this method to its conclusion: if 'the process of poetic creation' is merely 'a combination of sounds or words', why not use 'algebraic combinations and permutations of words' to generate all possible poems? (Trotsky here anticipates the future development of structuralism by Jakobson and Lévi-Strauss.) Formal analysis is indeed indispensable: 'the verbal form is not a passive reflection of a preconceived artistic idea, but an active element which influences the idea itself'. Yet the 'idea', the content, derives from the natural and social environment. 'Artistic creation' is 'a deflection, a changing and a transformation of reality, in accordance with the peculiar laws of art. However fantastic art may be, it cannot have at its disposal any other material except that which is given to it by the world of three dimensions and by the narrower world of class society.' And the forms themselves involve a dialogue between those inherited from the past and the historically shaped needs of a new generation of producers: 'Artistic creation is always a complicated turning inside out of old forms, under the influence of new stimuli which originate outside of art.' Thus: 'A work of art should, in the first place, be judged by its own law, that is, by the law of art. But Marxism alone can explain . . . who it was who made a demand for such an artistic form and not for another, and why.'[8]

Trotsky developed this conception of art most notably in a later essay on Céline's *Voyage au bout de la nuit*. Despite the author's morbid pessimism, his 'panorama of life's meaninglessness' is a work of both aesthetic and political subversion: 'To ease his conscience from terror in the face of life, this physician to the poor had to resort to new modes of imagery. He turned out to be the revolutionist of the novel. Generally speaking, that is the law governing the movement of art: it moves through the reciprocal repulsion of tendencies.' Writers seeking to forge a language appropriate to their circumstances are compelled, usually unconsciously, to rebel against the status quo:

Living creativeness cannot march ahead without repulsion away from official tradition, canonised ideas and feelings, images and expressions covered by the lacquer of use and wont. Each new tendency seeks for the most direct and honest contact between words and emotions. The struggle against pretence in art always grows to a lesser or greater extent into the struggle against the injustice of human relations. The connection is self-evident: art which loses the sense of the social lie inevitably defeats itself by affectation, turning into mannerism.[9]

Trotsky's writings on literature are a series of brilliant snapshots by an author mainly preoccupied with more immediate political questions, and increasingly reduced to the margins of the left by the triumph of Stalinism in the Soviet Union and in the Communist International (Comintern). Their most important influence was on a generation of young New York intellectuals who came to adulthood during the 1930s, many of whom were initially attracted towards Trotskyism. Trotsky's affirmation of 'the law of art' and his application of the discrepancy theory to authors such as Céline served to legitimise a positive reception of modernism, and, indeed (almost certainly

---

[8] Leon Trotsky, *Literature and Revolution* (Ann Arbor: University of Michigan Press, 1971), pp. 183, 172, 173, 175, 179, 178.
[9] Leon Trotsky, *On Literature and Art* (New York: Pathfinder, 1970), pp. 192, 201.

contrary to Trotsky's own views) to license Clement Greenberg's declaration of the autonomy of form in modern art.[10]

Modernism in any case represented a major test of the Marxist approach to art and literature. Here Lukács made a decisive, albeit contradictory contribution. In the first place, *History and Class Consciousness* (1923) offered a theoretical framework in which to address far more rigorously than before the relationship between literary form and social context. In effect Lukács displaced the base/superstructure model by affirming the methodological priority of the Marxist conception of social totality: *'The primacy of the category of totality is the bearer of the principle of revolution in science.'*[11] This move, which took its inspiration from Hegel, focused on the relationship between part and whole. To conceptualise this relationship Lukács invoked the theory of commodity fetishism which Marx had developed in *Capital*. Marx had argued that the fact that under capitalism the products of human labour were exchanged on the market led to the transformation of social relations into relations between things. What were in fact features of historically specific social arrangements appeared to be the consequences of universal natural laws operating outside human control.

Lukács now claimed that this process of reification, as he called it, permeated the entirety of social life. Drawing also on Max Weber's theory of rationalisation, he argued that capitalism was characterised by a systemic contradiction between partial rationality and global irrationality. Individual forms and institutions were progressively subject to rational organisation, yet the (social) totality remained unamenable to comprehension or control. Cultural products were as much as any other aspect of social life instances of this central contradiction. Lukács concentrated on illustrating this proposition through a virtuoso analysis of the development of modern philosophy, but there was no reason why the same should not be done with respect to other cultural forms.

The challenge for Marxist criticism was thus to trace the effects of commodity fetishism on literary form. Lukács himself did not take it up. Disappointment at the failure of the Russian Revolution to spread to Europe, alongside an intense campaign within the Comintern of vulgar denunciation of *History and Class Consciousness* led him in the late 1920s to repudiate his book for excessive idealism. He reformulated his Marxism under the right-Hegelian slogan of 'reconciliation with reality'. The revolutionary transformation of society would be a difficult long-term process involving many disappointments, detours and compromises. The task of the theorist was to detect the underlying historical tendencies and not to become enamoured of short-term trends. From this perspective, Lukács developed an aesthetic

[10] See Alan Wald, *The New York Intellectuals* (Chapel Hill: University of North Carolina Press, 1987).

[11] Gyorgy Lukács, *History and Class Consciousness*, trans. R. Livingstone (London: Merlin, 1971), p. 27.

theory systematically hostile to modernism. For him, the great nineteenth-century realist writers represented a period when the bourgeoisie had been a revolutionary class, striving to understand, within the limits allowed by its interest in entrenching a new form of exploitation, the nature of the social world. After 1848, however, the capitalist class is increasingly in the saddle. Objective insight is now a positive disadvantage to a class that needs to conceal, even from itself, its dependence on the extraction of surplus value. And so bourgeois literature becomes, even in its most skilled practitioners such as Flaubert, obsessed with surface sensation rather than underlying structures. Modernism is merely the transformation of this obsession into a self-conscious style. Writers such as Joyce are 'frozen in their own immediacy'. What for Trotsky was a strength in Céline is, according to Lukács, the modernists' chief weakness: 'they all develop their own artistic style . . . as a spontaneous expression of their immediate experience'.[12] Modernism is thus largely a symptom of bourgeois decline.

This critique of modernism depends on the perspective theory of ideology Lukács had developed in *History and Class Consciousness*, according to which it is a class's objective place within the relations of production, rather than any process of social manipulation or propaganda, which sets limits on its view of the world. Defended with great skill and not without insight, it met with a firm rebuttal by one of the leading Marxist practitioners of modernism, Bertolt Brecht. Brecht sought to turn the tables on Lukács, arguing that he, and not his modernist opponents, was guilty of formalism, by requiring contemporary writers to conform to an ideal type of literary style culled from classical realism. 'Realism is not a mere question of form.' It had to be understood broadly as 'discovering the causal complexes of society/ unmasking the prevailing view of things as the view of those who are in power/ writing from the standpoint of the class which offers the broadest solutions for the pressing difficulties in which human society is caught up/ emphasising the element of development/ making possible the concrete and making possible abstraction from it'. These objectives could be met through a variety of different forms: 'Methods become exhausted; stimuli no longer work. New problems appear and demand new methods. Reality changes; in order to represent it, modes of representation must change.'[13]

Brecht, like Trotsky, thus posited a dialectical relationship between literary forms and a changing social reality. Written in the late 1930s but only published posthumously, his critique of Lukács allowed Brecht to defend his epic theatre as a form of realism. It was left to two other German Marxists sympathetic to modernism, Walter Benjamin and Theodor Adorno, to explore more rigorously the relationship between form and reality. Both sought to turn

[12] Gyorgy Lukács, 'Realism in the Balance' (1938), in E. Bloch *et al.*, *Aesthetics and Politics* (London: NLB, 1977), pp. 36–37.   [13] Bertolt Brecht, 'Popularity and Realism', in *ibid.*, p. 82.

History and Class Consciousness against its author by using it to illuminate the formal development of Modern art. They did so, however, in distinctively different ways reflecting their contrasting aesthetic preferences. Benjamin championed those avant-garde artists such as Brecht and the surrealists who sought to connect formal innovation and political radicalism; Adorno, however, argued that the greatest critical charge was offered by those artists, such as Schoenberg and Beckett, who most rigorously prized abstraction.

Since Benjamin and Adorno are discussed extensively elsewhere in this volume, I consider their different methodologies only briefly here. Following Marx and Lukács, both saw capitalist society as permeated by commodity fetishism. For Benjamin, this structure consisted in the formal correspondences between material relations and cultural products. In his great unfinished *Passagen-Werk* he assembled a mass of evidence relating economic developments under the Second Empire to Baudelaire's poetry and the changing urban geography of Paris as it became a city governed by the rhythms of mass consumption. The juxtapositions of these fragments produced 'dialectical images' that simultaneously registered the commodification of social life and, by evoking memories of primitive communism, pointed towards a classless future. Adorno, though in many respects indebted to Benjamin, was highly critical of his method: merely juxtaposing disparate facts could easily collapse into the kind of economic reductionism both were trying to avoid; moreover, the theory of dialectical images seemed to require the suspect notion of a collective unconscious. The Lukácsian conception of the social totality remained indispensable as a means of demonstrating how commodity fetishism shaped the structure of works of art, as well as the particulars of everyday life – a claim most successfully made out by Adorno in *Minima Moralia* (1974). Yet the finest products of modernism in their dissonant forms both exemplified the suffering caused to humankind and to nature itself by social domination and implied the demand for an end to domination.

History and Class Consciousness thus remained a crucial reference point for Adorno, despite his suspicion of the totalising tendencies of the Hegelian dialectic. The other major Marxist school of critical theory to offer a positive appreciation of modernism was, by contrast, unambiguously hostile to the Hegelian influence on Marxism. For Louis Althusser and his followers, Lukács' conception of totality was an instance of what they called 'expressive totality'. Here all the different aspects of the social whole are conceived as expressions of a singular essence. Thus in Hegel himself, the whole movement of human history is the coming to self-consciousness of Absolute Spirit. In Lukács' apparently more materialist version, all the different phenomena of capitalist society replicate the basic structure of commodity fetishism. The result is an economic reductionism as complete as any to be found in Second International Marxism.

The authentic Marxist totality, Althusser argues, is a complex, structured whole, a plurality of different structures and practices. Within this whole, economic determination operates only 'in the last instance'. But while Althusser thus adopts Engels' formula, he gives it a different meaning. Every society has a 'structure in dominance', a set of hierarchical relationships in which one practice has primacy over the others. The economy plays its ultimately determining role by selecting whichever practice is dominant. Economic causality thus operates indirectly, through the structure in dominance, rather than as a direct influence on the superstructure. Individual practices develop according to their differential logic, within the limits laid down by the structure in dominance. The superstructure is thus 'relatively autonomous' of the economy.

Where do literature and art fit in? Althusser and his collaborator Pierre Macherey suggest that their relationship to the economy is even more oblique than that of other social practices. Indeed, it is unclear whether or not they belong to the superstructure at all. Their social anchorage is achieved via ideology, which Althusser conceives as the universal medium in which all human beings live their relationship to their material conditions of existence. The function of art is cognitive: 'The real difference between art and science lies in the *specific form* in which they give us the same object in quite different ways: art in the form of "seeing" and "perceiving" or "feeling", science in the form of *knowledge* (in the strict sense, by concepts).' Art's 'object' is ideology. Thus 'Balzac and Solzhenitsyn give us a "view" of the ideology to which their work alludes and with which it is constantly fed, a view which presupposes a *retreat*, an *internal distantiation* from the very ideology from which their novels emerged.'[14]

This version of the discrepancy theory asserts that writers are able to offer insights not despite, but in some sense because of their overt political beliefs: 'The fact that the content of the work of Balzac and Tolstoy is "detached" from their political ideology and in some way makes us see it from the *outside*, makes us "perceive" it by a distantiation inside that ideology, *presupposes that ideology itself*.'[15] This contradictory situation is revealed by the dissonant structure of the text itself:

The concealed order of the work is thus less significant than its real *determinate* disorder (its disarray). The order which it professes is merely an imagined order, projected onto disorder, the fictive resolution of ideological conflicts, a resolution so precarious that it is obvious in the very letter of the text where incoherence and incompleteness burst forth. It is no longer a question of defects but of indispensable informers. This distance which separates the work from the ideology which it transforms is rediscovered in the very letter of the work: it is fissured, unmade even in its making.[16]

---

[14] Louis Althusser, *Lenin and Philosophy and Other Essays*, trans. Ben Brewster (London: Verso, 1971), pp. 205, 204.   [15] *Ibid.*, p. 206.
[16] Pierre Macherey, *A Theory of Literary Production*, trans. G. Wall (London: Routledge and Kegan Paul, 1978), p. 155.

Here indeed we see the triumph of modernism over realism. All literary works, Macherey asserts, however finished their apparent form, however much they may ostensibly conform to the mimetic rules laid down by Lukács, conceal structures as misshapen and discordant as those of the most self-conscious products of modernism. Macherey stresses the inherent incompleteness of every text: 'the book is not self sufficient; it is necessarily accompanied by a *certain absence*, without which it would not exist'. But this absence does not simply refer us to other texts, in an endless play of signifiers. On the contrary, '[t]o know the work, we must move outside it'. Doing so 'reveals the work in so far as it entertains a specific but undisguised (which does not mean innocent) relation to history'. This process of recovering '*the unconscious of the work* (not of the author)' is not 'a question of introducing a historical explanation which is stuck on to the work from the outside. On the contrary, we must show a sort of splitting within the work: this division is *its* unconscious, in so far as it possesses one – the unconscious which is history, the play of history beyond its edges, encroaching on those edges.'[17]

Far, then, from there being a tension between literary form and historical context, the fractures in the text reveal its relationship to history. Macherey's conception of the task of Marxist criticism plainly had as its model psychoanalysis, though what is repressed here is not sexual desire but 'that intricate reality in which men – both writers and readers – live, that reality which is *their ideology*'.[18] *A Theory of Literary Production* remains one of the most important Marxist attempts to show how it is possible to historicise without effacing the text. It is, however, at least in part dependent upon the coherence and plausibility of Althusser's reconstruction of historical materialism. The most relevant difficulty lies in his distinctive conception of the totality: critics persistently argued that the idea of a plurality of relatively autonomous instances is indistinguishable from the kind of dissolution of the social whole into a mere aggregate of distinct factors against which Labriola and Trotsky had polemicised. Various 'post-Marxists' – for example Ernesto Laclau and Chantal Mouffe – have argued that this pluralism should not be shunned but rather embraced. From this perspective, the problem of relating text and context simply vanishes. Literary forms and social institutions are absorbed into the vast multiplicity of inherently contingent relationships that no form of thought can hope to master.

Nevertheless, the most intellectually distinguished response to postmodernism is a quite unabashedly Marxist experiment in totalisation. For Jameson postmodern art is best understood as representing the 'logic of cultural production' during a specific phase of capitalist development – what he calls 'late or multinational or consumer capitalism'.[19] This interpretation

---

[17] *Ibid.*, pp. 85, 90, 92, 94. [18] *Ibid.*, p. 155.
[19] Fredric Jameson, *Postmodernism, or the Cultural Logic of Late Capitalism* (London: Verso, 1991), ch. 1.

methodologically presupposes a remarkable reconciliation of Lukács and Althusser. Rejecting poststructuralist attempts to textualise history, Jameson glosses Althusser as arguing 'that history is *not* a text, not a narrative, master or otherwise, but that, as an absent cause, it is inaccessible to us except in textual form'. Similarly, 'the conception of totality in *History and class consciousness* must be read' as 'a methodological standard'. Ideology for Lukács consists in 'strategies of containment' which 'can be unmasked only by confrontation with the ideal of totality which they at once imply and repress'. Such exposures of the limits which ideologies impose on the texts which enact them presupposes Marxism 'as that thinking which knows no boundaries of this kind, and which is infinitely totalisable, but the ideological critique does not depend on some dogmatic or "positive" conception of Marxism as a system. Rather, it is simply the place of an imperative to totalise.'[20]

Thus, Jameson suggests, 'in some paradoxical or dialectical fashion, Lukács's conception may here be said to rejoin the Althusserian notion of History or the Real as an absent cause'. The rational kernel in Althusser's critique of Hegelian Marxism lay in its rejection of the homologies posited by Lukácsian critics such as Lucien Goldmann between literary texts and aspects of the social whole. Jameson argues that 'the interpretive mission of a properly structural causality will on the contrary find its privileged content in rifts and discontinuities within the work and ultimately in a conception of the former "work of art" as a heterogeneous and . . . a schizophrenic text'. This allows him not merely to endorse Althusser's and Macherey's version of Marxist criticism but even to take on board poststructuralism. Not simply do philosophies of difference, such as Deleuze's, presuppose some notion of totality in order to dismantle it, but '[t]he current poststructuralist celebration of discontinuity and heterogeneity is . . . only an initial moment in Althusserian exegesis, which then requires the fragments, the incommensurable levels, the heterogeneous impulses, of the text to be once again related, but in the mode of structural difference and determinate contradiction'.[21]

One may admire the dazzling virtuosity of this exercise while harbouring doubts both about the syncretist brio with which Jameson asserts that 'Marxism subsumes other interpretive modes or systems' and about the application of his methodology to postmodernism (an exercise which seems more reliant on the detection of homologies than, according to its own canons, it should be).[22] Nevertheless, his work bears witness to the vitality of a Marxist criticism which is not afraid either to historicise or to attend to formal subtleties. As I have shown, the most thoughtful Marxist writing on literature has struggled, in different ways, to relate form and context. At a time when much cultural theory has dissolved history into textuality, the strengths of this tradition provide a welcome contrast.

[20] Jameson, *Political Unconscious*, pp. 35, 52, 53.   [21] *Ibid.*, pp. 54–55, 56.
[22] *Ibid.*, p. 47. See Alex Callinicos, 'Drawing the Line', *International Socialism* 53 (1991), pp. 93–102.

7

Marxism and poststructuralism

MICHAEL RYAN

For Marxist critics, the way literature makes meaning out of the arrangement of words or the telling of life stories contributes to the way ruling groups maintain their power in society. In this light, a play like *King Lear* might be understood as not only telling a tragic tale of family betrayal but also promoting a vision of the world that would help assure the domination of the aristocracy in late Renaissance England. Marxist critics have also been interested in the way literature challenges unjust social arrangements and displays through its refractive mirror of history the weaknesses and fissures that make unjust social arrangements unstable and prone to radical transformation. For example, even as *King Lear* argues for aristocratic hegemony, the work demonstrates precisely those problems and social contradictions that would make inevitable the downfall of the aristocracy in the middle of the seventeenth century.

Marxism assumes that labour, broadly defined by Marx as human constructive activity on the world, is an essential and defining characteristic of human life. But, according to Marx, human labour is alienated under capitalism. The products of labour are taken from the producers and sold for a profit that benefits the capitalist class but not the workers. The intention of Marxism as a political project is to restore to workers control over what they produce so that the benefits accrue to them and not to a class of owners.

That step is impeded by force as well as by what Marx calls 'ideology'. All societies in which power and wealth are unequally divided and which depend on the subordination of one group to another require a set of ideas and cultural practices that license the existing inequalities by making them seem rational or natural or divinely sanctioned. Because for Marx consciousness is historical, practical and material, each new economic form makes possible a new way of thinking about and living in the world. Whereas social and economic interaction in the feudal world was shaped by ideas such as 'fealty' and 'duty', the emergent capitalist class required the shaping power of ideas such as 'liberty', 'individualism' and 'freedom'. Marx initially defined ideology as 'the ruling ideas of the ruling class'. The ideas that prevail in a culture tend by and large to be ones that certify as legitimate the shape of that society and to reinforce the hegemony of the ruling elite. For example, in the Middle Ages the highly unequal and hierarchical class structure of society was justified to its members (especially to the serfs out in the fields who had to do all the work) by the ideal of unconditional loyalty to one's master.

The term 'ideology' has become much more refined since Marx's day. It is now conceived as processes of cultural signification and personal formation that cannot be summed up merely as 'ruling ideas'. It also consists of training in certain practices of self-discipline or certain modes of self-identification. We all learn to think and act as if we were perfectly free, while simultaneously and unconsciously acceding to all sorts of regimens that betoken our obedience and submission. We learn to behave 'well', which is to say, in accordance with the dictates of the social system in which we live, but we do so voluntarily, as if they were not dictates at all. That is the magic of ideology: to make us do things that may be against our interests and to do them as if they were entirely self-willed.

Marxist literary criticism has traditionally been concerned with studying the embeddedness of a work within its historical, social and economic contexts. In order to make it on to the stage at all, Shakespeare's plays had somehow to address (which is to say, accept and further) the values and ideals of monarchical English culture. All literature is in this respect 'determined' by economics, by the translation into cultural limitations and imperatives of the sheer weight of how material life in a society is conducted. There are several strands of Marxist criticism, and I will review two of them. Reflection theory and cultural materialism (which is covered in another section of this volume) study the relations between literature and social history, while structuralist Marxist criticism is concerned with how texts put social contradictions on display.

Christopher Caudwell's work (*Studies in a Dying Culture*, 1938, to *Illusion and Reality*, 1937) is an example of reflectionist Marxist criticism. For Caudwell, literature embodies in images the dominant emotions of an epoch. For example, a new kind of self emerged in the Renaissance, the expressive, oftentimes violently wilful bourgeois individual, who sought wealth and power in the evolving world of early market capitalism. This self finds expression in Shakespeare's tragic characters, from Hamlet to Lear. Their self-expression or wilfulness is always depicted as tragic because Shakespeare himself, though a son of bourgeois parents, was a member of the court, a player for the king. His works thus cohere with the 'public world of emotion' of which he was a part. While expressing the 'bourgeois illusion' that the word is a field for the free play of self will, he also therefore argues, in *King Lear* especially, in favour of the court's 'coercive imposition of its will' on the emergent bourgeoisie. All of the wilful characters in his plays therefore must end tragically. Criticism of this kind is called 'reflectionist' because it claims that literature holds a mirror up to the historical world.

Structuralist Marxist critics are concerned with the placement of literature within social structures whose determining role cannot be effaced by literary ideology. The formal surface and thematic conclusions of a work, which for other schools of criticism might be the end-points of literary criticism, are just the starting point for structuralist analysis, which seeks to go beyond surface appearances and to grasp the underlying structural and structuring principle that gives rise to the work. Using Marx's model, they seek out the principle of literary production that lies below the text's surface and remains unsaid by the work. For example, Pierre Macherey (A Theory of Literary Production, 1966), argues that literature which promotes a certain ideology seeks to reconcile social contradictions (such as that between worker and capitalist or that between the ideology of individual freedom and the reality of material determination). Such a work of literature makes contradictions disappear by resolving them into such formal unities as a coherent narrative line or a seemingly originary heroic character, one who appears not to be limited or determined by material circumstances. But social contradictions and the realities of material determination are silently inscribed within the text, and the task of the critic is to expose the contradictions which the text seeks to reconcile and hold in formal equipoise. Even as they convert social contradictions into unified imaginative exercises, literary texts display symptoms of those contradictions in certain formal faults or breaks.

Macherey's Marxist literary criticism noticeably bears the imprint of another school of thought that came into being in France in the 1960s. Thinkers like Michel Foucault, Jacques Derrida, Julia Kristeva and Jean Baudrillard combined a structuralist interest in signs and language with a concern for rethinking critically some of the founding assumptions of rationalist philosophy and western civilisation. These poststructuralists share with Marxists a sense that capitalism is a form of domination, but they are more interested in analysing the forms of thought and cultural signification that maintain such domination. Moreover, influenced by the New Left of the 1960s, which distanced itself from traditional Marxist political forms such as the Leninist Communist Party, poststructuralists tend also to be post-Marxists.

Poststructuralists assume that culture constructs order out of the inchoate matter of the world and in so doing helps to maintain repressive social regimes. If structuralists found order in everything from kinship systems to fashion, poststructuralism argues that all such orders are founded on an essential endemic disorder in language and in the world that can never be mastered by any structure or semantic code that might assign it a meaning. It is less interested in knowing how systems work than in finding out how they might be undone, so that the energies and potentials that they hold in place might be liberated and used to construct an altogether different kind of society.

The first works of what would eventually be called poststructuralism began to appear in the early 1960s, and they reflected the growing influence on

French thought of Friedrich Nietzsche (whose works had been recently translated into French), a thinker whose value for younger French philosphers had to do with his rejection of both the rationalist tradition of objective description and the idealist tradition which dissolved empirical world events into non-empirical or hidden meanings or truths. Another major counter-structuralist influence was Martin Heidegger, a German thinker whose work had been highly influential in France since the 1940s (especially in the work of Jean-Paul Sartre, whose *Being and Nothingness* is in many ways a pre-text of poststructuralism in that it elaborates on themes – such as the foundationlessness of foundations – that would become major assumptions of such poststructuralist thinkers as Jacques Derrida). Michel Foucault's *Madness and Civilization* (1961) set the tone for the new tendency in French thought by noting how classical reason constructed itself by banishing alternative 'nonsensical' modes of thought and labelling them as 'madness'. People previously considered mystics were suddenly thought to be candidates for incarceration, and that switch was due to the invention of Reason as a guiding category for the Enlightenment. Reason assisted nascent capitalism by permitting utility or usefulness to be calculated and objects and people to be identified, assigned categories and controlled.

Another major early poststructuralist book, Gilles Deleuze's *Nietzsche and Philosophy* (1962) drew attention to Nietzsche's subversion of the rationalist ideal of knowledge and his caustic critique of the habit of Christian civilisation of locating spiritual meaning in everything. The material world is a play of forces in contention, not something that conceals spirit or meaning. It cannot be understood using rational categories like 'subject', or 'object', or 'will', or 'truth', because all categories necessarily 'lie'. By grasping the world of forces in differential flux, categories translate flux into stable identities, things that have nothing to do with the world. All our thinking is fiction making, forming a chain of metaphors that substitute stability for the inherent instability of existence and meaning for the eternally returning sameness of a material world; there remains no spiritual sense and the material world ultimately resists being translated into ideas or ideals like justice or truth or sin and redemption. Nietzsche's ideal philosopher-artist learns to accept this state of things, to refuse to assign meaning to things, to avoid categorisation, to accept the groundlessness of all our ways of thinking, to throw himself into the play of the world and dance with it.

In 1966 another book by Foucault – *Words and Things (Les Mots et les Choses*, translated as *The Order of Things*) – drew attention to the new way of thinking. Foucault examines rationalism historically and shows how it comes into being and changes over time. Reason is no longer to be understood as a light that was switched on at a point sometime during the seventeenth century and that continues to illuminate everything we do and think in the same consistent manner, locating an objective order in empirical events. The very notion of such an order, Foucault argues, was itself a historical invention, one that required the systematic displacement of earlier ways of knowing that did not make classificatory cuts in the world and that thought and spoke of the world as an order of resemblances and interconnected parts, one of which was language itself.

It was in the experimental literature of writers like Mallarmé, Lautréamont and Artaud especially, that the new French thinkers began to see an alternative current to the rationalism and repression that characterised modern capitalist culture. The new thinking sought to undo this repressive social order by harnessing the signifying potential of the signifier and with it all the heterogeneous elements that capitalist signification worked to restrain in the world signified. A new politics of the signifier began to emerge in the journal *Tel quel* (literally 'Just as it is') especially, which devoted much space to the new generation of poststructuralist thinkers like Julia Kristeva and Jacques Derrida.

The publication in 1967 of Derrida's three books *Of Grammatology, Writing and Difference*, and *Speech and Phenomena* marks a major turn in the evolution of poststructuralism. Derrida's critique of western rationalism includes Lévi-Strauss' structuralism, and Derrida finds an alternative to that tradition in the very artist-renegades, represented by Bataille and Artaud, who were being championed by the *telquellistes*. Western logocentric philosophy privileges reason and truth and banishes the artist-renegade. Reason demands that representation, signification and language be subordinated to its higher authority, but the renegades believe that signification itself begets truth and allows reason to operate. The order of priority is reversed, and the values and assumptions that order upheld – that reason precedes signs, that truth is outside and above representation, that authenticity and presence precede and determine the artificial play of signifiers – are set in play, become unsteady and enter negotiations they sought to avoid. Western philosophy has sought rational forms of authority that sustained social forms of authority, and the questioning of the first necessarily dovetailed with the radical critiques of social authority underway in the 1960s.

Kristeva is probably the thinker who most clearly embodies the radical spirit of *Tel quel*. In *Semeiotike: Towards a Semanalysis* (1969) and *Revolution in Poetic Language* (1974) she joins aesthetic to political radicalism. In the first, she links Marx's notion of production to semiotics and presents the work of Mikhail Bakhtin, especially his concept of dialogic ambivalence, to French readers for the first time. In *Poetic Language*, she argues that writers like Lautréamont, by undermining the orders of signification (which she associates with thetic statements that assume a separation of subject and predicate in a thesis statement such as 'I know x'), tap into a well of as yet unordered language processes and unarticulated sounds to generate new possibilities for thought and for society, greater freedom to signify and greater liberation from the capitalist regime of utility, functionality and work.

Deleuze, in *Difference and Repetition* (1968) and *The Logic of Meaning* (1969), had elaborated on his own earlier philosophic work on Nietzsche's concepts of play and the differences of force that constitute reality. With his collaborator of the 1970s, Felix Guattari, Deleuze becomes one of the most interesting and creative of the political poststructuralists. While the weld of Marx, Freud and poetic modernism in *Tel quel* in some respects inaugurates poststructuralism understood as a form of cultural politics, it remained for Deleuze and Guattari to take the additional step of going beyond Marx and Freud. Their *The Anti-Oedipus: Capitalism and Schizophrenia* (1972) and *A Thousand Plateaus: Capitalism and Schizophrenia* (1980) criticise Freudian oedipalism and elaborate a new post-Marxist political ontology. Against the then prevalent psychoanalytic myth of Oedipus, which describes desire as originating in absence or lack (of access to the forbidden mother), Deleuze and Guattari instead propose a positive concept of desire as a productive activity. They also announce a new set of concepts for understanding the world and our place within it. We are all machines, they argue, and the institutions we make for ourselves such as the family and the state are also machines that take the desiring-production of humanity and process it in useful ways for a particular social regime. The oedipal family is useful for capitalism because it represses desires that might be in excess of the limits the utilitarian capitalist system requires. In order to work functionally, we have to desire efficiently. But desire is innately reckless and inefficient, a flow of energy without bounds, and it should be understood as just one segment in larger flows of energy and matter that constitute the world as a mobile, varying, multiple flux with different strata that make up planes of consistency. We exist within such planes as lines of flight that can either escape or be captured and pinned down by signifying regimes, semantic orders that assign us meanings and identities as 'boy' or 'girl' or 'businessman' or 'wife'. All such stabilisations or codings constitute territorialisations in that they establish boundaries of identity that restrain temporarily the movement of the flows and the lines of flight. They hold them in place (demarcate a territory), but deterritorialisation is a more powerful force, and everything eventually breaks apart and flows anew, only once again to be recaptured and reterritorialised by another social regime of signification, made useful and meaningful at the same time.

Jean Baudrillard espouses an immediatist politics appropriate to the student movement of 1968, which demanded an immediate total revolution of society, in place of the deferred change or gradual amelioration sought by the unions and the left parties. Baudrillard's first book, *The System of Objects*, appeared, appropriately, in 1968. It lays out one of his central themes: modes of signification have taken the place of reality. About the shaping of desire and identity by advertising, *System* describes a world in which material needs have given way to codified equivalences between commodities and personal identity. Capitalist production has ceded primacy to the process of reproduction through the marketing of goods, and that marketing is entirely semiotic. The code dominates our lives and tells us who we are. There is no reality apart from it. Baudrillard would extend this argument in *Consumer Society* (1970) and *For a Critique of the Political Economy of the Sign* (1972), but his most scandalous book of this early period is *The Mirror of Production* (1973), an extended critique of Marx and of Marxism. Marx, he argues, merely holds up a mirror to capitalism by adopting its categories, such as 'production'. By doing so, Marx mortgages everyone's lives to the capitalist–rationalist ideals of deferred gratification and functional usefulness. Reform socialists (to this day) argue that the goal of social revolution is a shorter working day; Baudrillard argues that it should be the abolition of work as capitalism knows and imposes it – a system of equivalence that equates human lives with monetary signs and exchange values. No contradiction at the heart of production of the kind Marx adduced (between workers and owners, or between productive forces and productive relations) will end this system; change can only be brought about by dismantling the code of signification itself (which is what defines capitalist production itself as a set of equations between money, time and human life). Against the subsumption of all the radical energies opposed to this rationalist social system into parties or unions that as much control and restrain as direct them, Baudrillard proposes a negative strategy of disaffection, a withdrawal of support, a revolt against the code of valuation as such:

All the institutions of 'advanced democracy', all 'social achievements' in regard to personal growth, culture, individual and collective creativity, all of this is, as it has always been, simply the privilege of those with private property, the true right of the few. And for everyone else there are day-care centers and nurseries, institutions of social control in which productive forces are deliberately neutralized. For the system no longer needs universal productivity; it requires only that everyone play the game. This leads to the paradox of social groups who are compelled to fight for a place in the circuit of work and of productivity, the paradox of generations who are left out or placed off limits by the very development of the productive forces . . . Revolt emerged against the integration of labour power as a factor of production. The new social groups, de facto dropouts, on the contrary, proved the incapacity of the system to 'socialize the society' in its traditionally strategic level, to dynamically integrate them, even by violent contadiction at the level of production. And it is on the basis of their *total irresponsibility* that these marginal generations carry on the revolt.[1]

It is in this book as well that Baudrillard provides a capsule portrait of the artist radical:

[1] Jean Baudrillard, *The Mirror of Production*, trans. M. Poster (St. Louis: Telos, 1975), pp. 132–133.

The cursed poet, non-official art, and utopian writings in general, by giving a current and immediate content to man's liberation, should be the very speech of communism, its direct prophecy. They are only its bad conscience precisely because in them something of man is *immediately* realized, because they object without pity to the 'political' dimension of the revolution, which is merely the dimension of its final postponement. They are the equivalent, at the level of discourse, of the wild [*sauvage*, wild or uncontrolled] social movements [of May '68] that were born in a symbolic situation of rupture (symbolic – which means non-universalized, non-dialectical, non-rationalized in the mirror of an imaginary objective history).[2]

The Mirror of Production describes society in a manner that will influence Foucault's theory of the carceral or disciplinary society. For Baudrillard, society consists of very little else than institutions of social control and discipline. Like the Italian radical thinkers of his generation, especially Antonio Negri, he argues that the discipline of the factory floor has spread to all of society.

Baudrillard's work of the late 1970s and 1980s, especially *Symbolic Exchange and Death* (1976), portrays signification as having so replaced reality that now one can say that the world is altogether simulational, entirely generated by semiotic models that have no referent in a supposedly 'real world'. All of our desires are codified and manipulated as fashion; all of our thought is saturated with semiotic equations that make critique (the pose of standing outside the system and opposing it) futile; detached from any referent in the world, capitalist signs refer only to other signs within a closed system. Baudrillard's later work, especially *Seduction* (1979), *Simulacra and Simulations* (1981), *The Fatal Strategies* (1983) and *The Gulf War Did Not Happen* (1991), has attracted a great deal of attention amongst philosophers, cultural critics and artists (who perhaps have come to recognise in his deliberately provocative style a version of their own aesthetic radicalism). Baudrillard's work is the most resiliently leftist and political of his class of poststructuralists. Indeed, thirty years later, it is difficult to imagine that someone still manages to write so ably and accurately in the style of 1968.

Michel Foucault in the 1970s and 1980s broadened his historical critique of western regimes of knowledge and western social institutions such as the hospital to include what he called the general disciplinary power that saturates society as a whole and shapes our lives. Foucault's master work written in 1975, *Discipline and Punish: The Birth of the Prison*, is a history of the emergence in modern times of a 'carceral' or disciplinary society in which overt forms of public punishment of the kind that characterised the eighteenth century have given way to practices of self-discipline learned in institutions such as schools. Anxiety over behaving well has replaced fear of being publicly dismembered or burned. We have become our own prison guards, according to Foucault, and have learned to mould our behaviour in accordance with the

[2] *Ibid.*, p. 164.

needs of modern capitalism. The three volumes of Foucault's *History of Sexuality* (1976, 1984) dislocate gender traditionally conceived as a stable, ontologically grounded cluster of acceptable identities by arguing that sexuality and sexual practices have been the objects of disciplinary power/knowledge that have 'scientifically' constructed ideals of propriety by excising and rendering unwelcome sexual practices that earlier ages had no trouble in accommodating. Foucault's most provocative example is sexual love between men in ancient Greece, a practice celebrated by none other than Plato, the philosopher most fondly turned to by many contemporary social conservatives who oppose equal rights for gays and lesbians.

The work of Jean-François Lyotard quickly acquired the political tone that had been established in 1968 (what might be called 'revolutionary optimism'). In *Discours/Figure* (1971) he argues for a deconstructive understanding of figuration or rhetoricity as the spatial representation which makes the discursive ordering of objects possible while simultaneously undermining and eluding all rational intelligibility. His *Dérive à partir de Marx et Freud* ('Adrift after Marx and Freud') (1975) gives voice to the post-Marxism that would become a commonplace of French poststructuralist thought in the 1970s. Already in *Discours/Figure*, Lyotard had linked figuration to desire and to the operations of the unconscious, what he would in a later book call a 'libidinal economy'. In this book, social and political institutions like capitalism or the Party are described as mechanisms for restraining desires potentially in excess of socially acceptable limits. The task of radical politics is to liberate those desires. Lyotard accords priority to experimental art, which works radically with visual figuration itself rather than making it subordinate to meaning, over the traditional sloganising of the Left, which gives primacy to meaning over the artifice of figuration.

In *The Post-Modern Condition: A Report on Knowledge* (1979) Lyotard describes the contemporary historical situation in which the old western European master narratives of progressive subjective enlightenment and rational liberation (liberal humanism and Marxism especially) no longer apply to a world of micronarratives that cannot be dominated by any single legitimating metanarrative. Instead, a criterion of scientific and economic performativity or usefulness and technical/economic effectiveness has replaced the old rationalist ideal of a legitimating metalanguage, and it is linked to the growing power of corporations. By controlling scientific research, they are setting the terms of what can be construed as useful knowledge (and by implication, of what is construed as true). Truth is no longer the possession of a rational subject, nor is it a property of a reality that would be described objectively using objective scientific methods. Rather it is determined by the effectivity of knowledge within a particular economic situation dominated by corporations that have the power both to shape the world and to say what counts as scientific truth regarding that world. What will count as true is what is useful from their point of view. For example, tests on drugs that provide justification for marketability will be deemed true; tests that provided contrary results will be avoided.

Marxists have not always been comforable with the new ways of thinking about literature, culture and society offered by poststructuralism. Yet poststructuralism can be seen as a continuation of the project initiated by Marx and by other social and cultural critics interested in the building of a more just human community. As Derrida notes in *Specters of Marx* (1993), poststructuralist deconstruction is in some respects the next logical step in Marxism, but as such it is also necessarily a step away from Marxism towards what Derrida calls a 'New International', a programme for change that ranges from family dynamics to global institutional politics. It is indeed a 'general program', if a post-Marxist one.

8

Adorno and the early Frankfurt School

ANDREW EDGAR

Although the Frankfurt Institute for Social Research was founded in 1924, the work of the Institute took on its distinctive theoretical character only after 1930, when the philosopher Max Horkheimer (1895–1973) became its director. At the core of Horkheimer's programme for the Institute was a commitment to multi-disciplinary, empirical social science projects, articulated within a Marxist social philosophy.

The Institute's Marxism (initially developed by Horkheimer along with Herbert Marcuse, 1898–1979) was firmly within the scope of western Marxism opened up by Georg Lukács' *History and Class Consciousness* (1923). On the one hand, Marx was situated within the main tradition of German idealist philosophy, and thus as an inheritor of Kant and Hegel. On the other hand, Marx's own social and economic theories were developed in order to provide a more adequate account of twentieth-century capitalism than that provided by orthodox Marxism. The core concern of the Institute's research programme was the problem of the relationship between base and superstructure in late capitalism, articulated in terms of the connections between economic life, the psychological development of individuals, and changes within science, religion and art, law, custom, public opinion and popular culture. Psychological and cultural mechanisms were to be explicated in terms of their function in the continuing latency of objective class conflict. Thus, during the 1930s and 1940s, alongside the major Institute projects on anti-semitism, Nazism and authoritarianism, Institute members published on economic theory, class structure, trade unionism, law and the Asiatic mode of production, together with important theoretical and empirical work on mass and high culture. In addition, Herbert Marcuse and Erich Fromm, particularly, were responsible for exploring a fusion of Marxism with psychoanalysis, thereby providing not merely an account of socialisation appropriate to Marxist theory, but also a framework in which the fate of the individual in an increasingly authoritarian and bureaucratic post-liberal capitalist society could be explained.

In 1932, the Institute began publishing its own journal, *Zeitschrift für Sozialforschung*, where the Institute's first essays on literature appeared. Although not officially a member of the Institute until 1938, Theodor Wiesengrund Adorno (1903–1969) was teaching at the University of

Frankfurt and nevertheless published in the *Zeitschrift*. However, at this point, Adorno's major contribution to cultural theory was in the field of musicology and the sociology of music, not of literature. Adorno's contribution to literary theory would not come until the 1950s. This leaves Leo Lowenthal, who published *Zeitschrift* essays on Conrad Ferdinand Meyer, Dostoevsky, Ibsen and Knut Hamsun, and sketched an outline of a materialist literary theory, as the principal theorist and practitioner of a Frankfurt approach to literature.

Lowenthal published 'On Sociology of Literature' in the first volume of the *Zeitschrift*.[1] Here he responds to what he perceives as the atheoretical (and ahistorical) nature of contemporary literary criticism. By placing exclusive emphasis on those elements of artistic production which are not amenable to analysis or explanation, literary criticism does not merely cut itself off from any rational discourse about art, but also from any rational reflection upon its own methodology. The work of art is thereby credited with an ultimately mystical autonomy from social and historical forces. In contrast, Lowenthal suggests that both the form and content of a literary work can be understood, adequately if not exhaustively, through reference to the social and historical conditions within which the work is produced. The task of a materialist literary theory becomes that of accounting for 'the extent to which particular social structures find expression in individual literary works and what function these works perform in society'.[2] He illustrates this through a series of sketched analyses of German literature.

The social structures with which Lowenthal is most concerned are those of the economic base, and their manifestation in class conflict. In order to account for the link between social structures and art Lowenthal turns to psychoanalytic theory. Lowenthal's materialist theory of literature is concerned with 'mediation', by which he means the processes through which cultural (or superstructural) phenomena reproduce the base. The way in which an artist thinks will be expressed in his or her work. This manner of thinking will be influenced or determined by his or her position and development within a society characterised by class conflict. For example, Meyer represents an optimistic, feudally inclined upper class. This is manifest in the way in which his narratives frame the central events of the story, separating the glorious world of the upper classes from the diversity of mundane social reality. He denies historical progress, presenting mundane social life as nothing more than the backdrop to the achievements of great individuals. Lowenthal's suggestion is that 'literary studies are largely an investigation of ideologies', so that literature functions to form a false consciousness that conceals social contradictions behind illusions of social harmony.

---

[1] Leo Lowenthal, 'On Sociology of Literature', in S. E. Bronner and D. M. Kellner (eds.), *Critical Theory and Society: A Reader* (London: Routledge, 1989).   [2] *Ibid.*, p. 44.

Lowenthal's essay on the Norwegian novelist Knut Hamsun (1937) is, perhaps, his finest literary analysis.[3] The purpose of the essay is to reassess Hamsun's work as politically regressive, against the mainstream of critical interpretation. In later publications of the essay, Lowenthal congratulates himself on having identified Hamsun's authoritarianism, prior to his overt expression of sympathy for Hitler and Nazism. Lowenthal's analysis centres upon Hamsun's distinctive appeal to nature. Increasingly, in western culture, Lowenthal argues, the identification of the individual with nature represents the possibility of an escape from social pressures and conflicts. Hamsun takes this to an extreme, by celebrating the abandonment of the rational liberal individual to an irrational and unreflective collectivism in keeping with a supposedly natural order.

The thesis is explicated by drawing out a number of themes from Hamsun's novels, including an unreasoned opposition to urban life and capitalist manufacturing and finance, a celebration of the peasant, and a reduction of all human relations and practices to the dictates of supposedly natural rhythms and hierarchies. Hamsun thereby comes to illustrate a distinctive development in capitalist ideology. Whereas Meyer, for example, had sought to generate a coherent appearance that could conceal class conflict, and in the framework of Marcuse's more sophisticated account of 'affirmative culture' (published in the same year),[4] had promised a more authentic inner or private happiness in compensation for the struggles of the public world, Hamsun glorifies (rather than conceals) the hardship of economic struggle and political subordination, in what Marcuse calls 'heroic realism'. Hamsun thereby represents the psychology of the economically and politically insignificant classes. Unable to challenge or change their political impotence, they glorify it through a comparison to submission before the wasteful and destructive forces of nature. Hamsun's irrationalism is thus taken to be representative of an authoritarian personality, sacrificing the only intellectual means for resistance in its nihilistic surrender to domination and brutality.

While Lowenthal's work begins to outline the possibility of a materialist sociology, it falls short of the expectations that Adorno, and later Horkheimer, held for a materialist aesthetics. Crucially, for Adorno, it fails to give due, dialectical, credit to the autonomy of the art work. Lowenthal reduces works of art to the status of ideological counters in a class struggle. While his interpretations may situate those counters with a good deal of subtlety, they tend to suggest that the political interpretation of a work is exhausted once this class analysis is complete. In effect, the work of art is credited with no meaning or worth independent of its ideological position.

[3] Leo Lowenthal, 'Knut Hamson', in A. Arato and E. Gebhardt (eds.), *The Essential Frankfurt School Reader* (Oxford: Blackwell, 1978).
[4] Herbert Marcuse, 'The Affirmative Character of Culture', *Negations: Essays in Critical Theory* (Harmondsworth: Penguin, 1968).

A different view begins to emerge in Horkheimer's essay 'Art and Mass Culture.'[5] (This essay was first published in English in 1941, in the English language successor to the *Zeitschrift*, during the Institute's exile in the United States.) Horkheimer's approach shares much with Marcuse, not least by relating art to a private realm of personal imagination and, nostalgically, to the security of a middle-class childhood. This is explicated by recognising that an autonomous art is an historically recent phenomenon, marking the separation of aesthetic activity from social utility. As such, art is linked, not simply to a private realm of pleasure, but to a realm of freedom, and thus to human emancipation from economic need. For Horkheimer, unlike Marcuse, this freedom is realised not simply, or even primarily, through the consumption of art, but rather through its production. Artistic practice is inherently resistant to the demands of the economy.

Horkheimer continues by raising what may be seen to be the most fundamental challenge to Lowenthal's and Marcuse's approach, by throwing into question the communicative and emotive nature of contemporary art. Crucially, for Horkheimer and Marcuse alike, the difficulty of articulating a social theory that is adequate to twentieth-century capitalism becomes more acute during the 1930s. Relatively early in their theoretical development, they ceased to believe in the revolutionary potential of the proletariat. Late capitalism is rather to be understood in terms of the administrative integration of all classes into a single system. The contradictions of nineteenth-century high capitalism are seen to be increasingly managed by industrial and governmental bureaucracies. Administration extends into the private realm, be it that of 'well-to-do parents' adjusting their children to the demands of mass culture, or adult leisure time being subject to the routines of the ball park and the movie. At the extreme, the advance of administration is seen to undermine the possibility of imaginative fantasy, to erode even Marcuse's private aesthetic realm, and thus to question the very possibility of art as understood by Lowenthal and Marcuse.

Lowenthal presupposes that a work of art communicates with its audience. An appropriately sensitive reading of a literary work will therefore yield a coherent meaning, and a materialist social theory aids this reading process, not least in explicating the interpretative interests of the work's audiences. Similarly, Marcuse's analyses rest on the assumption that aesthetic pleasure is essential to the consumption of a work of art. Horkheimer, in contrast, points to the modernist avant-garde (figures such as Picasso and Joyce) which makes 'the masses draw back in horror'. Thus, while a Galsworthy novel may offer an illusion of harmony (much as Lowenthal suggests), to conceal the 'miserable, almost prehistorical existence' of contemporary humanity, Joyce and

---

[5] Max Horkheimer, 'Art and Mass Culture', *Critical Theory: Selected Essays* (New York: Continuum, 1982).

Picasso 'uncompromisingly express the gulf between the monadic individual and his barbarous surroundings'.[6] Paradoxically, precisely by communicating and giving pleasure, traditional art forms are seen today to deny the very realm of freedom to which they overtly appeal.

Horkheimer's assumption, therefore, is that if works of art were communicative, in the manner, say of a Disney cartoon, then they would be indistinguishable from any other cultural good. Experience of the mass media of communication, both in European fascist propaganda and the American entertainment industries, leads to an uncompromising questioning of the ideological nature of contemporary communication. In sum, the means of mass communication are seen as an integral part of the administrative forces of production of late capitalism. The very language that is used in mundane communication, and which is taken for granted as something natural, begins to be seen by Horkheimer as a material resource that works to inhibit critical reflection, insight and imagination. The last works of art, as Horkheimer calls them, survive and remain loyal to freedom, only insofar as they denounce these prevailing forms of communication, pursuing their own inherent logic, rather than the demands of economic existence, and thereby expose the natural as unnatural, disrupting the ideological illusion of social harmony. Horkheimer concludes by appealing to Dewey's comment that art can be indifferent to its immediate reception, if the artist has something new to say. While Dewey implies that a later generation will understand the work, Horkheimer is pessimistic about the possibility of such an audience (which is to say, a humanity that can, to some degree, again recognise a realm of freedom).

Paradoxically, Lowenthal's materialist approach to art is no more capable of acknowledging the aesthetic worth of these last works of arts, than would be an overtly conservative cultural criticism that equates worth with popularity (and thus puts Disney on a par with Shakespeare). It is thus incapable of recognising the realm of freedom within art. For Horkheimer, the despair of contemporary society can be inferred, using social theory, from any cultural good. In contrast, genuine works of art objectify this despair. This suggests that an adequate materialist aesthetics (as opposed to a sociology of art) will yield political insight by approaching the work in terms of its inherent artistic logic. For Adorno, expressing the same point, what Marcuse (and thus Lowenthal) overlook is the 'decisive' level of 'knowledge and discovery' embedded in art.[7]

During and after the war, the Frankfurt approach to literature and culture becomes ever more sophisticated, not least as Adorno developed Horkheimer's social philosophy in line with his own work in philosophy, cultural criticism

[6] *Ibid.*, p. 278.
[7] See Rolf Wiggerhaus, *The Frankfurt School: Its History, Theories and Political Significance* (Cambridge: Polity Press, 1994), p. 221.

and sociology. Prior to the war, Lowenthal's interpretation of Horkheimer's Frankfurt research programme presupposed a model of capitalist society as the independent variable in any interpretation of literature. This model is itself subject to revision and refinement in the light of scientific criticism, new empirical evidence and historical experience. Implicit in this approach is an orthodox model of class conflict, and thus the presupposition that the interests of the proletariat provide an Archimedian point of interpretation from which to judge the ideological implications of the work of art.

In the *Dialectic of Enlightenment* (1947), Horkheimer and Adorno throw into question the presupposition of any such fixed point of objectivity. The problem is not simply one internal to Marxism, grounded for example in the historical failure of the proletariat to mature as a revolutionary class. The problem lies more broadly in the nature of enlightened western scientific knowledge. Lowenthal had questioned the ahistorical and atheoretical nature of literary criticism, thereby accusing it of irrationalism. Horkheimer and Adorno turn this accusation (of being ahistorical and atheoretical) against rational inquiry. They argue that Enlightenment reason, originally motivated by the desire to dispel myth and superstition, has itself reverted to myth. This occurs insofar as a positivistic scientific methodology, grounded in the quantification and mathematical manipulation of data, supposes itself to be the only valid means of acquiring knowledge. By providing the most rigorous articulation of the concept of reification of all the Frankfurt authors, Adorno links this intellectual development to the economic base, arguing that Enlightenment thought manifests the same structure as capitalist commodity exchange. Commodity exchange presupposes the possibility of equating or identifying qualitatively distinct goods, insofar as the use-value (or the subjectively perceived utility) of the commodity is subordinated to its exchange-value (or price). In Marx's analysis of commodity fetishism, the exchange-value of the good, which is strictly a product of human culture, is mistaken for an objective property, just as the mythological properties of a religious fetish are assumed to be objectively present in it. Enlightenment thought reproduces this fetishistic structure, insofar as it presupposes that its analytical procedures immediately explicate structures inherent in objective reality. Science presupposes that the concept (not least where it can be reduced to a mathematical expression) exhaustively grasps its object. It may then proceed to manipulate the object, either through the rational development of industrial technology, or more ominously, through the application of the same instrumental reason to the administration of human beings and social life (in the bureaucratic administration of a company, or of a concentration camp).

From this, Horkheimer and Adorno draw two crucial implications. First, the entwining of enlightened scientific thought with industrial and administrative procedures suggests the impossibility of generating a viable critique of capitalism using current scientific methods. Second, the curtailment of critical self-reflection within Enlightenment reason suggests that authoritarian-ism, be it in the fascism of the capitalist west, or in Soviet Marxism, is a product of the Enlightenment. In summary, in its self-understanding, Enlightenment science and reason sunders itself from the historical, social and economic context of its own development, and by presenting itself as the culmination of universal reason, prematurely curtails its critical programme. Akin to a viable mythology, its existence as a product of a finite and histori-cally specific human imagination is concealed. Contemporary, post-Enlightenment society thereby becomes objectively incomprehensible by the criteria and methodology of its own science and reason.

This analysis can be reformulated by considering Horkheimer and Adorno's use of the concept of mediation (*Vermittlung*). Lowenthal argued that a literary work would manifest traces of its mediation by the economic and class structures of the society within which it was produced and con-sumed. Hence, he proposes little more than a social constructionist thesis, insofar as the literary work is understood as being constituted by its society. Horkheimer and Adorno go further, in order to argue that the very discipline used to understand and criticise such mediation in the object is also, itself, economically and culturally constituted. Mediation thus takes on an unfath-omable, and crucially dialectical, complexity. The relationship between the knowing subject and the known object can never be direct. The subject, understood both as that which perceives and understands the object and as that which acts upon the object, is not simply given, as something transcend-ing history. It is rather the unfolding product of an engagement with nature and the given cultural environment. Similarly, the object is constituted by the subject, in being a product of subjective perception, understanding and labour. The object, as encountered by the human subject, and which itself mediates the subject, is therefore a crystallisation of historically unfolding practice and thought. In this context, reification is the precise historical form in which the subjective moment in this dialectical relationship is concealed behind an appearance of immediacy.

The very possibility of articulating an objective model of society, and thus of establishing an Archimedian point from which to judge society, is thereby thrown radically into question. As an epistemological claim it presupposes the possibility of extricating the knowing subject from the historical coils of mediation. Politically, in curtailing critical reflection at an arbitrary point, it is revealed as a gesture of authoritarianism, implicitly siding with the dominant reified order by accepting that order as natural and given. The implications of this argument may be seen in Adorno's account of cultural criticism. The claim that the work of art has knowledge embedded within it will be expli-cated in terms of the possibility of the work of art articulating and revealing social mediation.

Adorno's essay on 'Cultural Criticism and Society' was written in 1949 while he was still resident in America.[8] What Adorno embraces under the term 'cultural criticism' takes the place of the orthodox approach to literature that was the subject of Lowenthal's attack. However, unlike Lowenthal, Adorno is not prepared merely to replace this approach with one grounded in a materialist sociology. Such 'transcendent critique', precisely in its presupposition of objective access to society, is as problematic as the 'immanent critique' characteristic of cultural criticism. Adorno's essay is therefore structured in terms of an exposition of the tensions found within each form of critique, and of the tensions between them.

While Adorno gives no specific examples of cultural critics, it may be suggested that, at least in the early part of the essay, 'cultural criticism' bears the associations of the scientific connoisseurship of, for example, Berenson. The critic combines a certain positivistic knowledge of art works with an ability to classify works within given evaluative categories. By concerning him or herself with matters that are immanent to the art work, the critic overtly seeks to separate culture from the material base. Cultural values are accorded an immediate validity. Yet, both autonomous art and criticism are linked, in their historical emergence, with the market. Just as the culture to which the critic responds is a product of the free capitalist market and the leisure of the bourgeoisie, so the original task of the critic was to orientate clientele within the market of intellectual goods. That is, in assigning value to art works, aesthetic evaluation is implicitly subordinated to economic value and the demands of the art market. Yet the tracing of this historical narrative is almost incidental to Adorno's argument. The fundamental relationship between the critic and the economic base lies not in the superficial service of class interests, but rather in the very structure of critical thought.

Adorno points to a contradiction within the concept of 'cultural critic'. The one who is overtly critical of culture, is also, as the historical narrative and concept of mediation reveals, a product of that culture. The contradiction may be understood as that between the particular work of art, which the critic evaluates, and the universal cultural sphere that provides the critic with values. Given the reification that characterises contemporary society (whereby all thought reproduces economic rationality), the critic, by presupposing an immediately valid objective order against which particular works can be judged, subordinates that work to the dominant economic and political order, in a model exercise of the curtailment of Enlightenment reason. By unwittingly subordinating particular art works to a naively presupposed universal standard, the cultural critic places them within the economic order as effectively as does the sociologist of culture (or indeed the apologist for Soviet realism). At best, the implications of critical thought can be differentiated from those of the sociologist only insofar as the former surrenders the art

---

[8] Theodor W. Adorno, 'Cultural Criticism and Society', *Prisms*, trans. Samuel and Shierry Weber (Cambridge, Mass.: MIT Press, 1981).

work to the remnants of the market, while the latter generates the data necessary for the administration of culture. Each denies the relevance of the contradiction between particular and universal (for the universal, be this an intellectual or a material order, is assumed to represent the objectivity of truth), and so nullifies what Horkheimer had identified as art's resistance to the economic order. Ironically, in the very attempt to raise culture above the economic order, and thus to acknowledge the intrinsic aesthetic purposes of the art work, the cultural critic abandons it to that economic order and the purposes of commodity exchange, precisely by failing to reflect upon the historical mediation of culture.

At this point Adorno's analysis appears to reach an impasse, and crucially one that mirrors the epistemological and political contradictions of Enlightenment reason. The contemporary economic order appears to allow for no resistance. The work of art is thereby understood to be serving economic interests whether it is treated as an autonomous, spiritual product, or as a mere social fact, determined by its place in the social structure. Adorno breaks this impasse, albeit tentatively and uncertainly, by shifting his focus from cultural criticism *per se*, in order to question its approach as immanent critique. The work is approached increasingly from the viewpoint of its production, not its consumption.

Immanent critique, properly understood in terms of its potential to acknowledge the cognitive element in art, shifts the site of contradiction into the work of art itself. The work is then not interpreted in terms of the positivistic documentation of its detail or what these details may represent. Rather, the genuine critic, in order to be critical of culture as a whole, turns to the form, material and technique of the work of art, and thus to purposes that are integral to the particular work. As Adorno notes elsewhere, the distinction between scientific knowledge and knowledge in art lies only in art's mode of presentation. The epistemic content of art works is thus taken to lie not in the messages that they may be able to communicate, but rather in the manner in which the articulation of inherently artistic material may encode something of society. Adorno notes of Kafka that he exposes the inhumanity of contemporary society without explicitly referring to monopoly capitalism. The spell of a repressive society is expressed, rather, in the tension between Kafka's matter-of-fact style of language and the extraordinary events recounted. The language reproduces contemporary social repression precisely in the mundane description of that which has to be 'thus-and-no-different'.[9]

In effect, while the connoisseur subordinates the goals of the particular work to those that are decreed by the dominant culture, Adorno treats art works as mutually antagonistic and inherently flawed particulars that are at odds with the universal. Only the sterile and lifeless works of the academy are constructed

---

[9] T. W. Adorno, *Aesthetic Theory*, trans. C. Lenhardt (London: Routledge, 1984), p. 327.

through conformity to a given set of aesthetic rules, values and purposes. The vital work takes as its starting point the inherent logic of the works that have gone before it, but not in order to confirm and reproduce that logic, but rather in order to take it to the point of contradiction. Crucially, while Adorno strives for an exhaustive, coherent interpretation of the art work (translating the aesthetic logic and development of the art work into the mundane language of criticism), and is thus motivated by the presence of inconsistency, this coherence is not achieved or expected. The profound work resists the attempt to classify and explain it. It remains contradictory, and as such undermines any security that the interpreter might have in their own standpoint.

Because the work is not understood in isolation from all other work, but rather as a response to the artistic tradition, the very task that defines the work is drawn from its engagement with the work that has gone before. Adorno compares art works to riddles.[10] Each work is an attempt to solve the riddles posed by its predecessors. It is interpreted as the exposition of the failure of the tradition, stripping away any illusion of consistency and success. Thus, for example, Adorno's interpretation of Beckett explicitly situates his work in relation to the tradition of European theatre since Shakespeare. Beckett's work is such that categories from traditional drama criticism are no longer applicable to it, thereby disrupting the critic's position. Yet the work must still be understood as a determinate response to the fate of categories, such as 'comedy' and 'tragedy', 'plot' and 'character', in contemporary society. Beckett is seen to expose the impossibility of writing drama today, and to respond, not by proposing a codifiable alternative such as 'the theatre of the absurd', but by tracing the historical collapse of the tradition. The taken-for-granted immediacy and coherence of traditional theatre is thereby irrevocably undermined.

Immanent critique can still lead to falsehood in both orthodox cultural criticism and artistic production. By focusing on that which is wholly inherent to the work of art, culture may again be falsely validated as an autonomous realm, and the art work reduced to mere ornament, not least by concealing the division between mental and manual labour upon which art is founded. Yet this division is at once the source of art's ideological falsehood and its utopian moment of truth. Adorno does not seek to overcome this contradiction, for art cannot avoid the falsehood of its privileged position within the division of labour. Rather, by forcing immanent critique to deal with the relationship between the aesthetic and material realms and thus to force artistic and critical practice to reflect upon the material conditions of their own possibility, immanent critique becomes what Adorno terms a social 'physiognomy'; through its very sensitivity to art, it transforms art into an image of the society in which it is produced and consumed.

[10] *Ibid.*, p. 186.

Immanent criticism celebrates what Horkheimer identified as the relationship between the art work and the realm of freedom (and thus truth). Considered as pure aesthetic activity, artistic production sunders itself from the economic realm of necessity. It is pursued for its own sake, independently of the dominant economic goal of profit maximisation and the extraction of surplus-value. Yet art, along with its materials and techniques, has a social origin. The technology that the artist uses (for example, painter's pigments or the instruments of a musician) are dependent upon contemporary forces of production; conceptual language is derived from everyday speech; and the very structures of artistic form manifest that mundane contemporary understanding (for example, in the grasp of space, time and narrative). The artist does not then create *ex nihilo*, but with materials and patterns of thought that have crystallised in human culture. The artist rehearses the logic of contemporary thought and practice, but in a sphere that is sundered from the presupposed ends of that practice. Material that would otherwise be subordinated to the ends of economic production (even if only through the demand to provide profitable entertainment) is set free. Adorno adopts and reinterprets Kant's formulation that art is 'purposiveness without a purpose'.[11] Art shares the disciplines of the rest of society, and is thus purposive, but exercises those disciplines free of the dominant economic purpose. Crucially, this entails that a successful work 'is not one which resolves objective contradictions in a spurious harmony, but one which expresses the idea of harmony negatively by embodying the contradictions, pure and uncompromised, in its innermost structure'.[12] The inconsistency of the art work is not then to be attributed to the failings of the individual artist, but rather to the impossibility of reconciling the diverse aspects of the (socially mediated) object.

In summary, the shock of modern art, from which, as Horkheimer noted, the audience recoils, marks art's negative knowledge of society. It marks the point at which the immediacy of that which is supposed to be natural is confronted by the unnatural. Art thereby avoids the reified language and thought of contemporary society, in that an expressive shock, having a negative and disruptive impact on the illusions of an harmonious cultural and social existence, replaces positive communication (which could only be of that which is known anyway). Immanent critique interprets this shock as the pursuit of an aesthetic logic to the point of inconsistency. It becomes social physiognomy at the moment at which it attempts to interpret aesthetic inconsistency as the mark of social contradiction. Only thus does it respect art's moment of resistance to economic reality.

In conclusion, Adorno may be understood, superficially, as an archetypal modernist. The dominant value of aesthetic autonomy is articulated through an understanding of works of art as monadic wholes, that strive for

---

[11] *Ibid.*, pp. 201ff.   [12] *Ibid.*, p. 32.

consistency and self-justification. (The young Adorno was once upbraided by his composition teacher, Alban Berg, when he expressed a naive enthusiasm for a new work by Richard Strauss. Berg took Adorno carefully through the score, pointing out the arbitrariness of so much of the musical argument.) Montage and aleatorical composition, as structural principles of art, are rejected, precisely because of the illogicality of the associations they establish between the parts of the art work. Adorno celebrates fantasy, but only as exact fantasy. This modernist approach leads Adorno to a conservative focus on the accepted canon of great literature and music. Yet Adorno's greatness as an interpreter lies in his simultaneous rejection of aesthetic autonomy, or more precisely, his recognition that aesthetic autonomy is as much the point at which art is to be condemned for collaborating with the evils of human history as the point at which it transcends those evils. The modernism to which he subscribes is thereby forced to become self-conscious regarding its failure and social responsibility. Crucially, the programme of the Frankfurt School, articulated by Horkheimer in the early 1930s, remained a modernist programme and thus one of Enlightenment. Adorno remains true to this programme by convicting all involved in it of their failure. Only thus is the self-critical reflection, that lies at the core of Adorno's thought, kept alive. The problem for Adorno is always one of too little Enlightenment (which is to say, too little or too superficial rational reflection), not too much.

9

The 'German–French' debate: critical theory, hermeneutics and deconstruction

ANDREW BOWIE

The development of literary theory in the Federal Republic of Germany was deeply affected by demands at the end of the 1960s for new critical analyses of the intellectual traditions which played a role in Germany's catastrophic past.[1] Despite the moves to 'de-Nazify' German society in the Federal Republic after the war, much of academic and other institutional life continued to be controlled by those who had at least been compromised during the Nazi period, if they had not been active Nazis. It was, above all, the Student Movement of the late 1960s and early 1970s which made an issue of the persisting role of such people, and of the affluence of a society that had so recently been morally, socially and economically bankrupt. The Student Movement concentrated on ideas in the Marxist tradition, including the Frankfurt School, which had been suppressed in the Nazi period and neglected in the immediate post-war years. These ideas were rather crudely deployed to question the legitimacy of capitalist economies in the west which were involved in supporting repressive regimes in the Third World. Such questioning was supposed to lead to revolutionary change, but it has since become clear that much of the energy invested in the idea of revolution in fact depended on feelings relating to the unresolved injustices of the Nazi period.[2] The effects of the Student Movement on the humanities were evident in a tendency to disregard aesthetic issues in favour of approaches which looked at literary texts in particular solely as the products of historical and ideological conflicts. Even though these approaches were reductive, they did draw attention to weaknesses in theories of the inherently humanising or revelatory effects of art, which were still widely held, despite the events of the Nazi period. At the height of the Student Movement the more differentiated critical resources available in the work of Adorno and other members of the Frankfurt School were largely neglected.

Attempts to introduce the ideas of Derrida and other poststructuralists into Germany had already been made, before his tragic early death in 1971, by the literary scholar Peter Szondi, but more widespread interest in these ideas took

---

[1] I shall not deal here with the question of the Marxist tradition in the GDR, or with the effects of German re-unification.
[2] This is effectively shown in the films and literary work of Alexander Kluge during the 1970s.

longer to develop.[3] Given poststructuralism's dependence on thinkers like Nietzsche and Heidegger, whose role both in Germany's past and in the orientation of the intellectual world of the FRG had come to be regarded with considerable suspicion, it was not surprising that many progressive German intellectuals, such as Jürgen Habermas, who was Adorno's assistant and became the main representative of the Second Generation of the Frankfurt School, were distrustful of it. However, one of the effects of the failure in both France and Germany of the more radical hopes of the Student Movement was to create space for the sceptical style of thought characteristic of poststructuralism, which continues to influence debates over literary theory, social theory and philosophy throughout the western (and now some of the eastern) world. In important respects the concomitant shift from hoped-for praxis to an intensification of theoretical reflection paralleled moves in Europe at the end of the eighteenth century. At that time the move from a utopian optimism inspired by the French Revolution to a more sober critical reflection upon post-feudal possibilities of understanding and transforming both society and the natural world was part of what occasioned, in Germany in particular, some of the most important philosophy of the modern period. Significantly, the main theoretical frameworks of the recent debates have relied upon a re-examination of ideas from the Kantian and post-Kantian period in Germany, which initiated what Habermas terms the 'philosophical discourse of modernity'.[4] Habermas' phrase indicates one of the major fault-lines in the German–French debate: his focus is modernity, not postmodernity, a term he rejects. The following outline of some widely held assumptions about modernity in Germany may suggest why German theorists have, despite sharing many of the same predecessors, often advanced very different views from their most prominent French counterparts.

The development of 'literature' as a culturally significant concept is itself part of the 'discourse of modernity'. Before the second half of the eighteenth century the primary function of language had been taken to be the representation of ideas or objects which already exist as such independently of language. The conceptions of language of J.-J. Rousseau, J. G. Herder, J. G. Hamann and others initiate a tradition concerned with the 'expressive' or 'constitutive' dimension of language, which makes possible the disclosure of aspects of the world and ourselves that would not become accessible without language. The justifiable point of the claim, on the part of these thinkers, that the first language was either poetry or music is therefore that language does not just re-present what is already there in the world. When these new

---

[3] See Robert Holub, *Crossing Borders: Reception Theory, Poststructuralism, Deconstruction* (Madison: University of Wisconsin Press, 1992), for the history of the German–French debates. Holub offers the important reminder that the most widely accepted form of literary theory by far in Germany in the late 1960s and the 1970s was the reception theory of Hans Robert Jauss and Wolfgang Iser.

[4] See Jürgen Habermas, *Der philosophische Diskurs der Moderne* (Frankfurt a. M.: Suhrkamp, 1985).

conceptions of language are linked to Kant's revolutionary insistence in the 1780s upon the active role of the mind in 'giving the law to nature' in the natural sciences and giving the law to ourselves in ethics, the Enlightenment idea that the truth about the world is 'ready-made' and can be represented in human thought is called into question. The idea that language does not just represent the world is also relevant to the new elevated status given at this time both to 'literature' and to music, which are seen as striving to articulate what other forms of language cannot, and to the emergence of a new concern with hermeneutics, the 'art of interpretation'. What are in question here are the foundations of humanity's new understanding of itself and the world, which can no longer be assumed to be already established by a divinity. This is the situation which Habermas considers to be definitive of modernity and which is the focus of the most significant theoretical work in Germany after the waning of the Marxism of the Student Movement.

The still unresolved disputes in modernity over the status of 'literature' are addressed in this observation by Habermas, which underlines how awareness of the Nazi period affects the German perception of these issues:

Contemporary debates show what insights we owe to the concentration on the world-constituting and eye-opening, and at the same time withholding (*vorenthaltende*) function of language and aesthetic experience. I see in this a specifically German contribution to the philosophy of the 20th century, which one can trace back via Nietzsche to Humboldt and Hamann. However much we stand in this tradition and feel ourselves indebted to it, for some of us equally specific experiences of this century have also left behind traces of scepticism. This scepticism is directed against an abdication of problem-solving philosophical thinking before the poetic power of language, literature and art.[5]

Elsewhere Habermas refers critically to Jacques Derrida's tendency to make the 'problem-solving capacity of language disappear behind its world-creating capacity'.[6] For Habermas, failure to acknowledge the civilising effects of the modern divisions between cognitive, ethical and aesthetic forms of 'communicative action' leads to a betrayal of rationality manifest both in the German experience of the twentieth century – Habermas' worry is suggested in Walter Benjamin's portrayal of fascism as the 'aestheticisation of politics' – and in the work of the most well-known French 'literary theorist'. The potential for controversy thus becomes very obvious.

Despite his misgivings about many of the ideas in poststructuralism, it was the Tübingen philosopher, Manfred Frank, who probably did most to get the ideas of Derrida, Foucault, Lyotard, Lacan and others taken seriously in Germany.[7] Building on the researches of the philosopher Dieter Henrich,

[5] Jürgen Habermas, *Texte und Kontexte* (Frankfurt a. M.: Suhrkamp, 1991), p. 90.
[6] Habermas, *Der philosophische Diskurs*, p. 241.
[7] See, in particular, Manfred Frank, *Was ist Neostrukturalismus?* (Frankfurt a. M.: Suhrkamp, 1984).

Frank established historical and conceptual links between poststructuralism, German idealism and early German Romanticism, which elucidate the tensions between the orientations represented by Habermas and Derrida. The story of modern philosophy which emerges from these researches is very different from the one presupposed in many accounts of literary theory.[8] A vital figure here is the philosopher and novelist F. H. Jacobi (1743–1819). Both Kant and Jacobi are concerned with the question of whether modern reason can establish foundations for itself without relying on theological support. Jacobi's essential contention is encapsulated in his assertion in 1799 to the philosopher J. G. Fichte that '[t]he root of reason (*Vernunft*) is listening (*Vernehmen*). – Pure reason is a listening which only listens to itself.'[9] Jacobi argued that the endeavours of Spinoza and Fichte to establish self-contained philosophical systems were necessarily narcissistic. Philosophy could construct a system only on the basis of what it had already presupposed: access to the real, on the other hand, depended upon a prior revelation which philosophy could not explain, because explanation itself relied upon that revelation. Jacobi therefore characterised his own work as 'unphilosophy' and saw the only answer to the dilemmas of modern philosophy in a return to theology. The German idealist philosophy of Fichte, Schelling and Hegel,[10] which develops in response to Jacobi and Kant and culminates in Hegel's system, was in part an attempt to refute Jacobi's objections to systematic philosophy by showing that reason could ground itself. The eventual importance for literary theory of Jacobi's remarkably influential claims about philosophy becomes apparent in Derrida's unconscious echo of Jacobi, when he claims that western metaphysics, from Kant and Hegel to Husserl, is based on the 'absolute desire to hear oneself speaking'.[11]

Jacobi had already mapped out another aspect of the structure essential to Derrida and other literary theorists in contributions to the controversy over Spinoza's atheism, which began in 1783.[12] Here Jacobi suggested that any relational system based on Spinoza's principle of 'all determination is negation' – the principle which structuralism would later employ when characterising language as a system of differences with no positive terms – led to the problem of how to ground the intelligibility of what was differentially constituted. Relational systems entail a regress, in which the intelligibility or

---

[8] See Andrew Bowie, *From Romanticism to Critical Theory: The Philosophy of German Literary Theory* (London: Routledge, 1997), for a detailed account of these issues.

[9] Friedrich Heinrich Jacobi, *Jacobi an Fichte* (Hamburg: Friedrich Perthes, 1799), p. 14.

[10] Schelling cannot always be regarded as a German idealist: see Andrew Bowie, *Schelling and Modern European Philosophy* (London: Routledge, 1993).

[11] Jacques Derrida, *La voix et le phénomène* (Paris: Presses Universitaires de France, 1967), p. 115. The pattern of influence which leads from Jacobi to Derrida is traced in Bowie, *From Romanticism to Critical Theory*.

[12] Above all in Friedrich Heinrich Jacobi, *Über die Lehre des Spinoza in Briefen an den Herrn Moses Mendelssohn von F.H. Jacobi* (Breslau: Löwe, 1789). For the details, see Bowie, *From Romanticism to Critical Theory*, chapter 1.

justification of one element is grounded in another element, and so on. What makes anything intelligible or justified at all in the first place is not explained by this and therefore requires something outside the system to ground its intelligibility, which consequently prevents the system being complete in itself.[13] Derrida presents a version of these ideas in his notion of '*différance*', the notion that no sign can ever definitively represent a meaning, because signs rely for their identity on a never-to-be-completed temporalised chain of other signs. The relationship of the question of grounding to 'literature' was already established by the early Romantic thinker Friedrich Schlegel, who was one of the first modern thinkers seriously to entertain the idea that the attempt to ground philosophy might be simply in vain, without making this an argument for a return to theology. In response to Jacobi, Schlegel maintains in 1800 that: 'Where philosophy ceases, literature (*Poesie*) must begin . . . One ought, for example, not just to oppose unphilosophy, but also literature, to philosophy.'[14] Philosophy 'ceases' when it cannot provide the final explanation of its own foundations: this can be seen either as leading to an existential abyss which could only be overcome by a theological leap of faith, or – as Schlegel sees it at this time, thereby prefiguring aspects of poststructuralism – as opening the way for endless new possibilities of interpreting and articulating the world in art.

Frank has shown that even though the German idealist and early Romantic conceptions of modern philosophy both originate in the attempt to overcome the problems Kant encountered in grounding knowledge in subjectivity, there is an essential difference between them, which has been ignored by Derrida and other poststructuralists. Idealism pursues the 'metaphysical' project of grounding in a systematic manner, whereas early Romanticism renounces this foundational project and seeks to come to terms with the finite nature of human reason.[15] Where Hegel talks of the 'end of art', because art's capacity for revealing truth is being superseded by the sciences, Romantic thinkers, like Friedrich Schlegel, Novalis, F. D. E. Schleiermacher, K. W. F. Solger and the early Schelling, whom Szondi, Frank and others make central to their own work on literary theory, see the inexhaustibility of meanings in art as revealing the essence of modernity.[16]

The debates in literary theory of recent years can be seen as continuing attempts to understand the relationships between 'problem-solving' (scientific) and 'world-disclosing' (literary) conceptions of language, of the kind

---

[13] This idea is later developed in detail by Schelling: see Bowie, *Schelling*.

[14] Friedrich Schlegel, *Kritische Schriften und Fragmente 1–6* (Paderborn: Ferdinand Schöningh, 1988), vol. 2, p. 226. *Poesie* has the Greek sense of *poiesis* and often refers to any creative art.

[15] See Manfred Frank, '*Unendliche Annäherung': die Anfänge der philosophischen Frühromantik* (Frankfurt a. M.: Suhrkamp, 1997). Frank talks of a 're-Kantianisation of philosophy' in Novalis and Schlegel.

[16] See Andrew Bowie (ed.), *Manfred Frank: 'The Subject and the Text: Essays in Literary Theory and Philosophy'* (Cambridge: Cambridge University Press, 1996).

that had already been made by Adorno, Benjamin, Heidegger and others. The competing positions echo the tension that first became manifest between idealist and Romantic conceptions of art's relationship to philosophy and natural science around the end of the eighteenth century, and the work of Frank, Karl Heinz Bohrer, Peter Bürger, Szondi, Albrecht Wellmer, Wolfgang Welsch and others, has often been concerned to elaborate stories of modern philosophy based on this tension. What makes the ensuing debates so controversial is epitomised by the differing conceptions of truth advanced by the participants. For example, instead of assuming, as do Nietzsche and many in France and elsewhere – like Jean-François Lyotard[17] – that the lack of definitive philosophical foundations leads to an arbitrary proliferation of incommensurable perspectives, Habermas maintains a conception of truth as a 'regulative idea', of the kind Frank has shown to have been central to early Romanticism. In this latter view the pursuit of truth is primarily ethical, entailing the acknowledgement to others that one's own beliefs have no claim to absolute validity: the vital question is how the ethical then relates to the cognitive and the aesthetic, which is where many disagreements are located.

Habermas' suspicion, despite his proximity to key Romantic ideas,[18] of the Romantic idea that *Poesie* is the privileged locus of the disclosure of truth derives both from his suspicion of forms of discourse which involve normative claims that are not susceptible to democratic consensus, and from two related aims of his theoretical project which also inform his criticisms of poststructuralism. The first aim is to invalidate the assessment of modernity proposed by Horkheimer and Adorno in the 1947 *Dialectic of Enlightenment*, for whom Enlightenment falls back into mythology, because of the 'subordination' of everything natural to the arrogant subject.[19] It appears to Habermas that Adorno is led by this assessment to a view of modern art as a kind of negative theology divorced from existing reality, because he regards other forms of human rationality as merely instrumental means of controlling nature. Habermas' second aim is a change of philosophical paradigm, away from the idea of grounding philosophy in subjectivity – which he sees as the source of Adorno's totalising critique of rationality – towards a conception in which 'language reveals itself to speaking subjects as something prior and objective, as the forming structure of conditions of possibility'.[20] Habermas thus seems to echo the priority expressed in the later Heidegger's famous claim that 'Language speaks. Man speaks to the extent to which he corresponds to

---

[17] See Jean-François Lyotard, *La condition postmoderne* (Paris: Minuit, 1979) and *Le différend* (Paris: Minuit, 1983).

[18] See Andrew Bowie, 'German Philosophy Today: Between Idealism, Romanticism and Pragmatism', in A. O'Hear (ed.), *German Philosophy Since Kant* (Cambridge: Cambridge University Press, 1999).

[19] Cf. Max Horkheimer and Theodor W. Adorno, *Dialektik der Aufklärung: Philosophische Fragmente* (Frankfurt a. M.: Fischer, 1971), pp. 3–5.

[20] Jürgen Habermas, *Nachmetaphysisches Denken* (Frankfurt a. M.: Suhrkamp, 1988), p. 51.

language':[21] in both cases language subverts any attempt by the subject to claim absolute authority.

Despite their common adherence to the idea of the subversion of the subject by language, there are obvious differences between Habermas, Heidegger and poststructuralism, which are reflected in approaches to literary theory. Habermas takes the crucial element in the shift of philosophical paradigm to be the differentiation of modern spheres of communication into the cognitive, the ethical and the aesthetic, each of which makes its own kind of intersubjectively binding demands. Heidegger's move against the perceived dominance of subjectivity in the modern world involves a kind of truth he thinks is to be heard only in the 'essential' modern poets like Hölderlin and Rilke (which brings him closer to certain aspects of Adorno's position).[22] Poststructuralism, while to some extent adopting Heidegger's conception of the relationship of language to the subject, highlights the subversive 'aesthetic' moment in claims to rationality by arguing that the very notion of communicative consensus disguises a repression of differences between incommensurable language games, of the kind supposedly characteristic of subject-centred 'Western metaphysics'.

The main German participants in the debate of the last thirty years over the ramifications of Critical Theory for literary theory adopt positions either closer to Heidegger or closer to Habermas. The divergences between the positions of Bürger and Bohrer exemplify this, with Bohrer representing the 'French' side of the debate, though the debate is, of course, not defined by geography or national identity. Bürger's *Theory of the Avantgarde* (1974) was written partly as a response to discussions in the Student Movement. It seeks to do justice to Marxist insights into the social function of art, while at the same time coming to terms with the attacks directed by the avantgarde movements of this century against the very idea of art. Bürger's key notion is the 'institution of art', which is 'both the apparatus which produces and distributes art, and the dominant ideas about art at a particular period that essentially determine the reception of works'.[23] He maintains that the development of the idea of the autonomy of art from society in the aestheticism of the second half of the nineteenth century enables the avant-garde to criticise art for its lack of social consequences. The avantgarde attack on autonomy makes visible the institution of art in bourgeois society, most vividly in Marcel Duchamp's making of a urinal into a work of art for the art-market.

---

[21] Martin Heidegger, *Unterwegs zur Sprache* (Pfullingen: Neske, 1959), pp. 32–33. Heidegger's move towards this conception of language begins in the 1930s, but it becomes predominant after the end of the war.

[22] Adorno is often closer to Habermas than Habermas allows: see Bowie, *From Romanticism to Critical Theory*, chapter 9. Adorno makes his differences from Heidegger very clear in his essay on Heidegger's interpretations of Hölderlin: see *Noten zur Literatur III* (Frankfurt a. M.: Suhrkamp, 1965).

[23] Peter Bürger, *Theorie der Avantgarde* (Frankfurt a. M.: Suhrkamp 1982), p. 29.

Academic study of works of art – Bürger is referring to all the arts, including literature – should therefore now be concerned with the 'analysis of the function' of the work within the specific contemporary forms of the institution of art, not with norms that are supposed to transcend that institution. Bürger's account of the emergence of aesthetic autonomy accords with Habermas' account of the separation of the modern spheres of communicative action. However, he does not worry, as Habermas does in the wake of his mentor Adorno, that bringing art back into everyday life might lead to a regressive erosion of its ability to sustain a domain of specific meaning not articulated in the other spheres of modern life.

Bürger's concentration upon the ways in which art can be integrated into other forms of understanding is one of the targets of Bohrer's attempt to show, in the light of the early Romantics and Nietzsche, and against Hegel and his contemporary heirs, that the significance of art in modernity, far from being diminished by the massive new growth of warrantable knowledge, gains a radical new dimension. Whereas Bürger is concerned with the 'mediation' of art as something to be comprehended in terms of its relations to society, Bohrer thinks this approach ignores the 'immediacy' vital to modern art, particularly since Baudelaire, which he terms 'suddenness'.[24] He therefore defines 'aesthetic appearance' as 'the particularity of the aesthetic artefact which is not legitimated by any logos or any reference to society'.[25] Like Lyotard in his work on the sublime, Bohrer concentrates on the moment of terror associated with the sublime, which he deems to be the central moment in modernist art, linking it to Nietzsche's idea of beauty as the temporalised counter to the 'Dionysian' horror of being, and to Adorno's notion of the 'non-identity' evident in modern art's resistance to being made discursively accessible.

Bürger's and Bohrer's conceptions raise paradigmatic questions. Bürger can be seen as occluding the enduring potential for semantic novelty of works from the past by simply classifying them in accordance with already existing criteria. Bohrer's insistence on showing that art is resistant to being converted into conceptuality – hence his reliance on music-oriented thinkers like Nietzsche and Adorno – renders the status of his own general theoretical claims about modern art problematic. Given the discussion of modernity above, it is significant that the opposition between Bürger's 'mediation', and Bohrer's 'immediacy' echoes the opposition between Hegel and Romanticism. Hegel was concerned to show that nothing is ultimately immediate, because immediacy itself is only intelligible via its opposite, which means that it is really still an aspect of 'mediating' thought. The Romantic claim, deriving from Jacobi, was that mediation leads to a regress of mediations, which require an immediate, conceptually inarticulable ground in order for the

---

[24] Karl-Heinz Bohrer, *Plötzlichkeit: zum Augenblick des ästhetischen Scheins* (Frankfurt a. M.: Suhrkamp, 1981).   [25] *Ibid.*, p. 90.

world to be intelligible in the first place. The recent German–French debates can, therefore, be understood as a series of disagreements between theories of texts and other artefacts which rely, like much of the work of the Frankfurt School, on their relationships to what is already known about language and society, and theories which think such approaches fail to do justice to the irreducibly particular aesthetic moment. The strength of the best work of Adorno, which has again become a focus of recent discussion,[26] lies in its attempt to combine these two conflicting approaches, thus pointing to a possible reconciliation of some of the following oppositions, which have set the terms of this German–French debate.

In the view associated with Lyotard and others, in which the influence of Nietzsche and the later Heidegger is apparent, the particularity essential to the aesthetic is employed as the basis of a more universal characterisation of modern thought, in which rationality is regarded as inherently involving a repressive imposition of identity on difference by the modern subject. The perceived exclusions generated by modern rationality are then opposed in the name of a new 'postmodern' openness to irreducible 'alterity', of the kind also suggested by Bohrer's 'suddenness'. The legacy of Nietzsche and Heidegger is, though, itself deeply ambiguous. Derrida, for instance, while relying on the later Heidegger's problematic notion of a language of metaphysics, pursues an incessant Nietzschean undermining of interpretative claims, on the grounds that any such claim pretends to an impossible 'metaphysical' correspondence of signifier and signified. Heidegger's pupil Hans-Georg Gadamer asserts on the other hand – thereby coming closer to Hegel – that 'understanding is never a subjective relationship towards a given "object", but belongs rather to the effective history, and that means: to the being of that which is understood'.[27] Understanding for Gadamer is, therefore, not thought of as entailing the problematic sceptical consequences implied by Derrida, even though neither Gadamer nor Derrida thinks that interpretation can be metaphysically foreclosed.[28]

Habermas' Gadamer-influenced revisions of critical theory, in contrast, aim to show that the intersubjective nature of communicative action invalidates descriptions of modernity couched solely in terms of the dominance of subjectivity, and so obviates the need for a radical critique of rationality. Frank has, however, questioned both German and French versions of the role of the subject in modernity. He contends that the Jacobi-influenced arguments of

---

[26] See, e.g., Christoph Menke, *Die Souveränität der Kunst: ästhetische Erfahrung nach Adorno und Derrida* (Frankfurt: Suhrkamp, 1991).

[27] Hans-Georg Gadamer, *Wahrheit und Methode* (Tübingen: J.C.B. Mohr, 1975), p. xix.

[28] Gadamer's attempt in the 1980s at a public dialogue with Derrida about hermeneutics was a complete failure, which was compounded by Derrida's showing no evidence of having read any more of Gadamer's work than the paper presented at their meeting: see Diane P. Michelfelder and Richard E. Palmer (eds.), *Dialogue and Deconstruction: The Gadamer-Derrida Encounter* (Albany: SUNY Press, 1989).

the Romantics show that modern philosophical thinking about subjectivity has anyway not been exclusively based on Cartesian self-presence and the subject's resultant dominance of its other, which means that much of the philosophical story of modernity told by Heidegger, Derrida and Lyotard is untenable. He and Henrich argue that any wholesale move to the linguistic paradigm, whether in Derrida's or Habermas' version, fails to account for the non-propositional individual awareness of myself that is essential to the very possibility of my understanding language, and thus to any account of rationality, let alone to accounts of the production and understanding of innovative forms of language or music. This leads Frank to the claim, derived from Schleiermacher, that the effect of attention to literature in modernity lies not least in the emergence of awareness of literary 'style', as a manifestation of the individuality of the subject which cannot be reduced to general terms. He contrasts this view with Habermas', Gadamer's and Derrida's view of the subjection to language inevitably incurred by those who speak it.[29]

The main disagreements in literary theory have, then, increasingly revealed themselves to be part of the continuing debate about the status of modern rationality in the face of the loss of belief in transcendent authority. In a notable polemic which epitomised one of these divisions,[30] Frank concurs with Habermas' argument that the search for non-coercive democratic consensus is the only possible basis of 'post-metaphysical' rationality against Lyotard's insistence on the *différend*, the discursive conflict which is totally undecidable because a 'universal rule of judgement between heterogeneous types of discourse is lacking'.[31] Awareness of the undecidability of a discursive conflict, Frank argues, already excludes the possibility of wholly 'heterogeneous types of discourse': without some residual agreement by both partners on what is at issue in a dispute (including the fact that they are in dispute) neither can claim to be involved in a dispute at all, irresolvable or not.[32] The essential question here is the extent to which insights based on the particularity of the aesthetic, of the kind Lyotard relies on for his notion of the *différend*, are to inform thinking about truth and meaning. Here the issues are anything but straightforward: Frank, for example, rejects strict divisions between the cognitive, the ethical and the aesthetic, and thus gives a more significant role to the 'literary' than Habermas. The locus of these debates has, though, begun to shift. Given the continuing lack of constructive engagement by Derrida and most other poststructuralists with the criticisms of Habermas, Frank and others, there has been a widespread move in Germany

---

[29] See Manfred Frank, *Stil in der Philosophie* (Stuttgart: Reclam, 1992).

[30] Manfred Frank, *Grenzen der Verständigung: ein Geistergespräch zwischen Lyotard und Habermas* (Frankfurt a. M.: Suhrkamp, 1988).

[31] Lyotard, *Le différend*, p. 9.

[32] For a similar argument, see also Donald Davidson, 'The Very Idea of a Conceptual Scheme', *Inquiries Into Truth and Interpretation* (Oxford: Oxford University Press, 1984).

away from concern with poststructuralism, towards development of the dialogue, already established in the 1970s by Karl-Otto Apel and Habermas, with pragmatic and other traditions of American analytical philosophy. Whether this dialogue with traditions that are more oriented towards the natural sciences will lead to a neglect of the inheritance of Romanticism and German critical theory remains to be seen.

10

Post-war Italian intellectual culture: from Marxism to cultural studies

RENATE HOLUB

Post-war Italian intellectual culture can be analysed by way of three distinct yet overlapping phases. The first period – 1944 to 1968 – is characterised mainly by a drive by intellectuals to establish Marxism as the dominant critical theory. During this period, against opposing ideas from the centre (Crocean liberal secularism and catholic modernity) and the right of centre (conservative Catholicism), Marxism increasingly came to dominate the public sphere; so much so indeed that influential intellectual currents – phenomenology, hermeneutics, semiotics, positivism, existentialism, textual criticism, Neo-Hegelianism, structural linguistics – looked to Marxist ideas as points of reference against which to set themselves off. 1968 was the year which signalled the triumph of Marxism in Italy; a second period, lasting from 1968 to 1986, was marked by a massive production of cultural knowledge from within the Marxist paradigm. However, it was also characterised by an increasing fragmentation of the left. As a result, it was during this period that turbulent struggles arose between various Marxist forces.

This fragmentation also created a space for the re-emergence of philosophical theories inspired by Husserl, Heidegger, Levinas and others that opposed Marxist interpretations of history, the subject and agency. Thus, the third period, from 1986 to 1999, witnessed a dismantling of the Marxist project to the extent that positions derived from French postmodernism gradually displaced Marxism altogether. It was also during this last phase that Italy's cultural politics – which had previously been organised in relation to modernist notions, such as the territorial state, high cultures and national identities – were gradually opened up to new conceptions of culture, reflecting an increasing awareness of global issues.

The triumph of Marxism

In the period leading up to 1968, the success of Marxist cultural politics cannot be viewed in isolation from the political power of the communist party and the symbolic capital it commanded in western socialism at large. Due to its leadership role in the resistance against fascism, the communist party had considerable success in its promotion of socialist ideas in general and classical

Marxism in particular; such was at least the case during the immediate post war era.[1] Italian Marxists – Mario Alicata, Giorgio Amendola, Delio Cantimori, Lucio Colletti, Renzo De Felice, Galvano della Volpe, Palmiro Togliatti and others – continued to refine and disseminate their cultural politics through the fifties and sixties. They did so in spite of considerable international pressure to promote liberal, rather than Marxist, political cultures. They also had to overcome domestic obstacles, such as the influence of the catholic church in educational and cultural institutions. It was in this intellectual climate that the *Prison Notebooks* of Antonio Gramsci were published,[2] although, since Gramsci represented for the communist party primarily a political leader rather than a theorist, the originality of Gramsci's cultural analysis remained largely unexplored at this time. Classical Marxist aesthetics, as promoted by Zhdanov in the Soviet Union or by Georg Lukács' aesthetic theory, remained extremely influential until 1956. Yet it should also be pointed out that leading Marxist intellectuals such as the political scientist Norberto Bobbio, the philosopher Galvano della Volpe, linguists and semioticians such as Ferrucci Rossi-Landi and Umberto Eco and writers such as Elio Vittorini and Pier Paolo Pasolini, among many others, persistently argued for open dialogue with new forms of knowledge developed outside the Marxist paradigm. In this sense, even during periods of heightened Marxist orthodoxy, there always existed strong alternative or dissident versions of Marxism.

Until 1956, what Marxist intellectuals shared above all with non-Marxist thinkers was a desire to internationalise Italian culture. This was clearly a response not only to the provincialism imposed by fascism but also to Italy's relative inexperience in dealing with the institutional opportunities modern liberalism had to offer. Hence *Rinascità* and *Società*, major communist journals, promoted North American writers and philosophers by way of familiarising their audience with institutional practices from other western cultures. These journals fostered broad discussion of issues drawn from pragmatism, positivism and scientific methodology, and helped to disseminate the works of writers such as Faulkner, Steinbeck, Whitman and Hemingway. This strategy was not dissimilar from that of liberal journals, such as *Il mulino* (*rivista mensile di cultura politica*) and *Belfagor* (*Rassegna di varia umanità*), which also regularly featured the writing of Anglo-American, French and German authors. There was also, during this period, a significant interest in geopolitical topics on the one hand, and in the idea of a unified Europe on the other.

[1] See Renate Holub, 'The Cultural Politics of the CPI 1944–1956', *Yale Italian Studies* 2 (1978), pp. 261–283.

[2] These first major editions of Gramsci's writings in prison divided the material so that it reflected the cultural politics of the CPI during the post war years, rather than Gramsci's own organisation of his materials. Valentino Gerratana's edition of Gramsci's works respected his original order and it became the standard edition: for the Italian original, see Antonio Gramsci, *Quaderni del carcere*, ed. Valentino Gerratana (Turin: Einaudi, 1977).

Again, Italian Marxists shared these interests with liberal and catholic intellectuals alike, and their debates focused on anti-colonialist struggles, developing nations, the influence of Islam and related concerns. However, in the
aftermath of 1956, marked by the Soviet invasion of Hungary and, above all,
by the increasing flow of information about the human costs of Stalin's
authoritarian regime, the Italian communist party distanced itself from the
Communist International in Moscow, and embarked on its own distinctinve
road towards socialism, eventually called the 'via italiana al socialismo'.
Marxist cultural politics were deeply affected by this shift. Until the late
fifties, Italian Marxists had vigorously participated in the project to internationalise Italian culture through activities which related Italy to wider global
concerns. However, they now vigorously launched upon what we may call a
re-nationalising of their Marxist project. While this move is not unique to
Italy – in France and Germany nascent discourses on globality were likewise
briefly influential – its effects in the Italian context were especially marked. To
the extent that Marxism evolved into a powerful political force, calling forth
activities of the unions, student and women's movements, it also turned into
an intellectual force that reflected not so much on the application of Marxist
ideas in the global realm, but on their applications in a distinctive local
context.

By the late sixties, as Italian Marxists came to the fore, they quickly set up
positions of power in many institutions involved with the dissemination of
knowledge. Publishing houses, journals, university departments, cultural
centres and local governments all contributed to the production of a Marxist
public sphere.[3] A Marxist framework, committed to a belief in the collective
subject's ability to forge its own history, had virtually come to colonise Italy's
cultural unconscious. Major categories from within classical Marxism, such
as that of the base/superstructure distinction, or the dialectical relation of
politics, society and culture to the economic sphere, greatly influenced
the organisation of multi-volume encyclopaedias and historical studies in the
area of philosophy, literature, art and culture. Thus, for instance, one of the
most important research tools in Italian historical studies, the *Storia d'Italia*,
is clearly marked by distinctions derived from classical Marxism.[4] In addition,
the managers and editors of such projects set up formidable interdisciplinary
research collectives which included economic historians, political philosophers and social historians. Since these scholars shared a Marxist understanding of history and culture, many of these multi-volume projects are superb
examples of theoretical coherence, first rate scholarship and remarkable
breadth. Moreover, the disciplines rating a high status in Italy's for the most

---

[3] While local governments organised free cultural events, the communist party staged a yearly
'festa dell'unità', where the public could enjoy music, inexpensive food and book exhibits.
[4] See, for example, Carlo Salinari, *Storia d'Italia: dall'unità a oggi* (Turin: Einaudi, 1975), one
volume of a large project dealing with recent Italian history.

part humanistically oriented educational system – philosophy, literature and history – soon showed signs of a turn towards Marxism. All the studies written during this period are organised along Marxist analytical lines. Examples are Carlo Salinari's *Profilo storico della letteratura italiana* (1972) or Giuseppe Petronio's *Letteratura e società: storia e antologia della letteratura italiana* (1972) and Alberto Asor Rosa's *Sintesia di storia della letteratura italiana* (1975).[5]

From economic analysis to cultural critique

While 1968 marks the triumph of Marxism in Italy, it should also be noted that the kind of Marxism that emerged at this time was by no means homogeneous, but rather encompassed many different theoretical positions. In this sense it is more accurate to speak of the triumph of heterogeneous Marxisms. The diversity of Marxist theories is tied to Italy's geography and to various disciplinary peculiarities. While the intellectual centres of the North tend to measure themselves against secularising French and German streams of thought, centres of the South display greater independence and flexibility. It is in southern centres, for example, that subjects like liberation theology, which combine Marxist principles with religious debate, find their most congenial base. On the other hand, disciplines such as philosophy define themselves mainly in relation to German philosophy. Accordingly, the critics Salinari, Petronio and Asor Rosa promoted a Marxist aesthetics in the tradition of dialectical materialism. Their aesthetics is founded on the premise that literature and art reveal the elements of class struggle and ultimately reflect, irrespective of the artist's intention, a search for freedom throughout a linear (western) history. Hence it is the critic's function to locate the history of class struggle in cultural texts. This position was called into question by a second major Marxist trend, namely the structural Marxism of Galvano della Volpe.[6] Here Marxism is postulated not as an ideology or a cultural instrument of transformation, but as a scientific method. As such, it is an explanation of the world and not (or not primarily) a tool for change. Della Volpe rejects the idea of a dialectical relation between base and sociocultural super-

---

[5] Carlo Salinari, *Profilo storico della letteratura italiana* (Rome: Editori Riuniti, 1972); Giuseppe Petronio, *Letteratura e società: storia e antologia della letteratura italiana* (Palermo: Palumba, 1972); Alberto Asor Rosa, *Sintesia di storia della letteratura italiana* (Rome: Editori Riuniti, 1974; 1st edn. 1967). See also Giuliano Manacorda, *Storia della letteratura italiana contemporanea (1940–1965)* (Rome: Editori Riuniti, 1974; 1st edn. 1967).

[6] Galvano della Volpe, *Logica come scienza storica* (Rome: Riuniti, 1969); see also his *Rousseau e Marx* (Rome: Riuniti, 1974; 1st edn. 1956) and his *Storia del gusto* (Rome: Riuniti, 1971), which has been translated as *Critique of Taste*, trans. Michael Casar (London: MLB, 1978). See also John Fraser, *An Introduction to the Thought of Galvano della Volpe* (London: Lawrence and Wishart, 1977).

structure, and, above all, the power of the dialectic to effect social change, as propounded by Hegelian Marxism. Here, as in the structuralist model of Louis Althusser, cultural transformation is not tied to the logic of changes dictated by the modes of economic production, but can develop a logic, and a power, of its own. As a result, della Volpe can decouple culture and art from the rationale of capitalist modes of production while simultaneously summoning art to revolutionary ends. Hence also he can appreciate those aesthetic assumptions which inform the art not so much of realists but of expressionists, surrealists and other avantgardes. He approves writers such as Bertolt Brecht, whose epic theatre promotes the production of critical yet open-ended interaction between audience, actors, playwrights and stage directors. This theoretical development from within Italian Marxism, although anti-Hegelian, has ideological affinities with the cultural theory of the Frankfurt School. It also facilitated a critical elaboration of French structuralism. All the same, it was not able to pose an ideological challenge to developments in the fields of semiotics, semiology and linguistics, where intellectuals in Italy, more than in other western regions, have produced pioneering work. Paradoxically, although Gramsci's theoretical framework might well have facilitated productive encounters between his analytical concepts and those of the Frankfurt School, structuralism and linguistics, in Italy such encounters have remained marginal to this day.[7]

While classical Marxism provided Italy's radical movements of the late sixties with analytical tools with which to study the rise of capitalism in the west, it also insisted on the primacy of economic factors in historical change. In addition, Leninist versions of Marxism had insisted on the leadership of the working class, in the form of a vanguard party, as an essential prerequisite to the success of any revolution. Yet attentive readings of Lukács, Korsch, Luxemburg and Gramsci had suggested that the structure of capitalism, as described by the later Marx, no longer corresponded to those structures of capitalism which had evolved throughout the twentieth century. Moreover, analyses of post-World War Two societies suggested that a new service economy, buttressed by technologies of information, had increasingly displaced a narrowly industrial capitalism. Thus strategies for change would have to be anchored in theories which reflected the changing nature of the economy and society. The critical theory of the Frankfurt School, structuralism and critical semiotics all offered a basis for developing such theories. What they chiefly had in common was an analysis of the symbolic reproduction of power and domination, whereby a critique of social and cultural practices, of the media and the structures of everyday life displaced the analysis of

---

[7] See Renate Holub, *Antonio Gramsci: Beyond Marxism and Postmodernism* (London: Routledge, 1992). This volume examines Gramsci's relation to the Frankfurt School, to Marxist linguistics and to phenomenology.

politics and economics. Through recourse to concepts developed by the
Frankfurt School, such as the authoritarian family structure (Horkheimer),
the one-dimensionality of existence (Marcuse) and high art as resistance to
mass culture (Adorno), major Marxist journals and publications explored the
validity of cultural critiques as instruments for social change.[8] These explorations evolved against the background of polemics for and against the cultural
programme of the communist party. Crucial in these debates were thinkers
like Lucio Colletti, along with Massimo Cacciari and Gianni Vattimo.[9] By the
same token, intellectuals such as Maria Antonietta Macciocchi and, somewhat later, Antonio Negri maintained strong theoretical relations with
Althusserian structuralism.[10] Finally, theorists inspired by the work of
Ferrucci Rossi-Landi and Umberto Eco pursued systematic research in the
area of semiotics.[11] Indeed, if traditional Marxists and neo-Marxists inspired
by the Frankfurt School adhered to a concept of culture which privileged high
culture over mass culture, it was in research devoted to semiotics, and not in
the context of philosophy and history, that Marxist intellectuals discovered
the structures they took to govern the practices of everyday life.[12]

With the advent of neo-Marxism, structuralism and semiotics, Italian
Marxism shifted its priorities from economic production to the cultural
spheres. Critiques of culture were now credited with the power to effect substantive political and social change. Yet there was another important shift that
accompanied these debates. With the advent of neo-Marxism, structuralism
and semiotics, Italian Marxists abandoned their penchant for historicism,
history and historiography. This shift of focus towards the present, rather
than the past, also re-validated the social sciences, which in Italy had been

[8] Gian Enrico Rusconi, *La teoria critica della società* (Bologna: Il Mulino, 1968).
[9] See Lucio Colletti, *Marxism and Hegel*, trans. Lawrence Garner (London: Verso, 1973);
Massimo Cacciari, *Krisis: saggio sulla crisi del pensiero negativo da Nietzsche a Wittgenstein*
(Milan: Feltrinelli, 1976); Gianni Vattimo, *Il soggetto e la maschere: Nietzsche e il problema
della liberazione* (Milan: Bompiani, 1974).
[10] Cf. Maria Antonietta Macciocchi, *Letters From Inside the Italian Communist Party to Louis
Althusser*, trans. Stephen M. Hellman (London: MLB, 1975). For a discussion of Antonio
Negri, see his *Marx Beyond Marx*, ed. Jim Fleming, trans. Harry Cleaver, Michael Ryan and
Maurizio Viano (South Hadley, Mass.: Bergin and Garvey, 1984; Italian original 1979).
[11] See for example, Ferruccio Rossi-Landi, *Linguistics and Economics* (The Hague: Mouton,
1977); or *Language as Word and Trade: A Semiotic Homology for Linguistics and Economics*
(South Hadley, Mass.: Bergin and Garvey, 1983). For Umberto Eco, see his *A Theory of
Semiotics* (Bloomington: Indiana University Press, 1976); *Semiotics and the Philosophy of
Language* (Bloomington: Indiana University Press, 1984).
[12] The most important research in the area of language and society has been produced by the
institute of philosophy and language sciences at the University of Bari in Southern Italy under
the direction of Augusto Ponzio. Among his publications are *Produzione linguistica e ideolo-
gia sociale* (Bari: Di Donato, 1973); see also his *Signs, Dialogue and Ideology* (Amsterdam:
Benjamins, 1992). See also more recent work from within this circle by Patrizia Calefato,
Europa fenicia, identità linguistica, comunità, linguaggio come pratica sociale (Milan: Franco
Angeli, 1994).

under fierce assault from Croce's anti-positivism, Mussolini's anti-scientism and the prestige of the historically oriented humanities in the educational system.

Where traditional Marxists and neo-Marxists would therefore agree, in spite of all their differences, is in their belief that society could and should be rebuilt along egalitarian lines. With the accent on the potential of culture to effect social change, it should come as no surprise that all major Marxist traditions in Italy debated the leadership roles of the intellectuals. This is so not only because questions pertaining to the 'intellectual' are central preoccupations in Gramsci's political programme. The question of the moral leadership of intellectuals is indeed one of the most persistent themes that emerges from many centuries of Italian culture. Mainstream liberals and catholics renewed their interest in this issue under the impact of the dynamic sixties, and the more they reflected on it, the further they moved to the left. Every major intellectual journal that had sytematically questioned the foundations of Marxism in the fifties had itself become Marxist by the early seventies. Representative examples are two journals from Northern Italy, namely *Aut Aut* from Milan, and *Il mulino* from Bologna.

From cultural critique to cultural studies

There is no doubt that Marxism in Italy was more widespread than anywhere else in the west. Up until 1976, over half of the Italian population voted for left-wing parties. Since historically there had been no significant political tradition at the centre, the other half of the population voted for the conservatives or the right. While this polarisation of the electorate empowered the left to an unprecedented degree in the early seventies, it endangered the left in equal measure by the early nineties, when new right-wing movements tipped the political balance in the opposite direction. This emphatic move from left to right is well documented, as it was preceded by powerful challenges to the belief in the possibility of social transformation: in the late sixties intellectuals still believed in the capacity of reason and the public sphere to effect social change, yet ten years later, by the late seventies, left-wing intellectuals had retreated into the private sphere. A crisis of reason was declared.[13] Prestigious journals exchanged optimism for pessimism and chose Nietzsche over Marx. Under the impact of French poststructuralism, Hegelian history was to make room either for Foucauldian histories without subjects, or for Heideggerian

---

[13] See Renate Holub, 'Towards a New Rationality? Notes on Feminism and Current Discursive Practices in Italy', *Discourse: Berkeley Journal for Theoretical Studies in Media and Culture* 4 (1981–82), pp. 89–108. See also Aldo Gargani (ed.), *Crisi della ragione: nuovi modelli nel rapporto tra sapere e attività umane* (Turin: Einaudi, 1979).

subjects without histories. Phenomenology and hermeneutics were called upon to authenticate a minimum of meaning in a postmodern age condemned to witness its own epochal decline. Central to debates about the crisis of reason were intellectuals such as Aldo Gargano, Remo Bodei, Carlo Ginzburg and Gianni Vattimo. The latter formulated his theory around concepts such as the 'weak subject', a 'new rationality' and 'weak thought'.[14] To this day, many intellectuals who identify with the discipline of philosophy have continued to pursue a critique of reason, a critique premised on the unknowability of global processes and the impossibility of substantive social change. The work of Franco Rella, Giorgio Agamben and Maurizio Ferraris are typical of this trend.[15]

As in other western nations, feminism in Italy evolved very much in tandem with the student movement in the late sixties.[16] Given the hegemony of the Marxist paradigm, Italian feminisms are marked by major divisions within the left, and by the left's penchant for focusing on national and western rather than global issues, although Rossana Rossanda and Mariarosa Dalla Costa developed global agendas.[17] By the middle of the seventies, a solid and widespread feminist culture, established on the basis of centres and collectives that sprang up in many cities, enabled the dissemination of feminist ideas.[18] Among the leading feminist intellectuals were Lidia Campagnano, Carla Lonzi, Dacia Maraini, Lea Melandri and Lidia Menapace. As the male philosophical intelligentsia retreated in the late seventies, these feminist intellectuals took the opportunity to seize the public sphere with some highly original work. The Woman's Bookstore of Milan, along with the Diotima group of Verona, headed by Adriana Cavarero and Luisa Muraro, developed the theoretical model of a social-symbolic practice between women. Discussions of this model dominated the public sphere until the early nineties.[19] Influenced by the philosophical writings of Luce

---

[14] See Gianni Vattimo and Pier Aldo Rovatti (eds.), *Il pensiero debole* (Milan: Feltrinelli, 1983).

[15] See also Gianni Vattimo, *La società trasparente* (Milan: Garzanti, 1989); and Peter Carravetta, 'Repositioning Interpretive Discourse: From "Crisis of Reason" to "Weak Thought"', *Differentia: Review of Italian Thought* 2 (1988), pp. 83–126.

[16] Lucia Chiavola Birnbaum, *Liberazione della donna: Feminism in Italy* (Middletown, Conn.: Wesleyan University Press, 1986).

[17] See Rossana Rossanda, *Anche per me: donna, persona, memoria dal 1973–1986* (Milan: Feltrinelli, 1986); and Mariarosa Dalla Costa, *Paying the Price: Women and the Politics of International Economic Strategy* (London: Zed Books, 1995; Italian original 1993); see also her *Donne, sviluppo e lavoro di riproduzione: questioni delle lotte e dei movimenti* (Milan: Franco Angeli, 1996).

[18] Paola Bono and Sandra Kemp, *Italian Feminist Thought: A Reader* (Oxford: Basil Blackwell, 1991).

[19] Diotima (group), *Mettere al mondo il mondo: oggetto e oggettività alla luce della differenza sessuale* (Milan: Tartaruga, 1990); and *Il cielo stellato dentro di noi: l'ordine simbolico della madre* (Milan: Tartaruga, 1992); see also Renate Holub, 'Strong Ethics and Weak Thought: Feminism and Postmodernism in Italy', *Annali d'Italianistica* 9 (1991), pp. 124–143.

Irigaray, Diotima intellectuals built a model which focuses on a symbolic restructuration – linguistic and conceptual – of both consciousness and the unconscious. Their project of liberation was based on the idea that conceptual and symbolic processes are not separable from the male and female bodies that produce them, and that social and political equalities are attainable only by addressing the cultural conditions of symbolic and conceptual production. The theoretical model devoloped by the Diotima group remains the most original contribution to western second wave feminism by Italian feminists.

Feminists maintained a commitment to Marxist thinking until the early nineties. Under their influence, Italy's leading intellectuals mounted a last-minute campaign to prevent the demise of Marxism. With their journal *Micromega*, subtitled 'reasons of the left', Norberto Bobbio, Franco Crespi, Gianni Vattimo, Danilo Zolo and others engaged in a battle for the left as late as 1986. What is significant here is that humanists finally joined hands with social scientists. The Italian public sphere was soon to be haunted by scandals involving the corruption of political leaders, left and right alike. It would also be haunted by the widespread corruption of its magistrates and its juridical system. But more importantly, Italy was about to participate in the radical transformations taking place through the process known as European Unification. In terms both of its content and its contributors, *Micromega* registers these transformations. On its pages, work by pragmatic social scientists replaces that of utopian humanists. Massimo D'Alema and Walter Veltroni, who write for this and other journals, are public intellectuals, economists and political scientists, with occasional ministerial posts in the left of centre coalition known as Ulivo.[20] Under their influence, *Micromega* had abandoned its allegiance with the left by 1994. Like many other Italian publications, it renewed its interest in the study of regional and local cultures, in the structure of cities and the nature of dialects. Thus it shifted from a position of cultural critique to an approach more closely aligned with cultural studies, thereby, however, losing a good deal of its critical edge. Yet this shift also signals an acknowledgment of the formidable challenges to received categories of analysis and critique. With the decline of the modern state, cities and regions will play an increasingly important role. They will be called upon to mediate conflicts which Italy, as part of the European Union, will henceforth need to confront. Today, these conflicts result very largely from the flow of immigrants and refugees from many parts of the world who enter Italy. Under the impact of migration, particularly from Muslim majority countries, cultural theorists need to rethink issues that go beyond Italy. And, however belatedly, a search

[20] Massimo D'Alema, Claudio Verlardi and Gianni Cuperlo, *Un paese normale* (Milan: Mondadori, 1995); Walter Veltroni, *La bella politica* (Milan: Rizzoli, 1995).

has begun for new political and cultural models that can accommodate diversity. Debates on the future of Islam in Europe have intensified, and new disciplines, such as Mediterranean Studies, have lately gained prominence. The newly established University of the Mediterranean in Rome exemplifies the trend away from national towards regional studies. And interests in global and European issues, already apparent in the fifties, are now being pursued again with renewed vigour.[21] Such attention to global and local issues reflects the emergence of a form of society which bears witness to the ever more complex interrelation between the local and the global.[22]

[21] Gian Enrico Rusconi, *Nazione, etnia, cittadinanza in Italia e in Europa* (Brescia: La Scuola, 1993); Massimo Cacciari, *Geo-filosofia dell'Europa.*(Milan: Adelphi, 1994); Remo Bodei, *Repenser l'Europe* (Bruxelles: Editions de l'Université de Bruxelles, 1996); Luisa Passerini, *Identità culturale europea* (Florence: Nuova Italia, 1999).

[22] For a recent volume on cultural studies in Italy, see David Forgacs and Robert Lumley (eds.), *Italian Cultural Studies: An Introduction* (Oxford: Oxford University Press, 1996).

From cultural poetics to
cultural studies

11

Mikhail Bakhtin: historical becoming in language, literature and culture

KEN HIRSCHKOP

Mikhail Bakhtin wrote at length about the history of the novel and its roots in popular-festive culture, and his historical writing is often celebrated for its extraordinary erudition and breadth of reference. Nevertheless it often conveys the impression that history is simply a canvas on which Bakhtin is painting philosophical, political and maybe even religious pictures. This is partly due to the wild historical generalisations one finds throughout Bakhtin's works, generalisations for which Bakhtin scholars have always had to invent unconvincing excuses, but is more a matter of the aggressive, partisan, almost celebratory tone of Bakhtin's literary-historical writing. For Bakhtin did not see literary history as a succession of events. He saw the passage of time as a mountainside down which flowed, with an initially erratic and faltering momentum, an ever deepening, ever more forceful current of historical 'becoming', which, by the time it struck bottom, had become a torrent sweeping all before it. History was the focus of his writing not in the sense of a discipline or a field of problems and concerns, but as the great achievement of modern European culture, to be protected and cherished by critical and philosophical thought.

From roughly the middle of the 1930s until his death in 1975, Bakhtin argued that the European novel was the purest cultural embodiment of this historical becoming, and that, consequently, the theory of the novel was an act of supreme historical self-consciousness. In the many essays and notes he dedicated to the history and theory of this genre, he insisted on both its uniqueness and its centrality to the modern age. The novel was not just 'another' genre. It was

the only genre which is in a state of becoming, therefore it more profoundly, essentially, sensitively and rapidly reflects the becoming of actuality itself . . . The novel became the leading hero of the drama of the literary development of modernity precisely because it best of all reflects the tendency of the modern world to become; it is, after all, the only genre born of this modern world and in every respect of a piece with it.[1]

---

[1] M. M. Bakhtin, 'Epic and Novel: Toward a Methodology for the Study of the Novel', *The Dialogic Imagination: Four Essays by M.M. Bakhtin*, ed. Michael Holquist, trans. Caryl Emerson and Michael Holquist (Austin, Tex.: University of Texas Press, 1981), p. 7. Here and throughout I have amended all translations from Bakhtin's work.

The novel embodies this historical 'becoming' not only in the sense that it is a genre which is infinitely plastic and adaptable (almost an anti-genre, as some have claimed), but in the sense that it presents time and the world as 'historical: they unfold, albeit at first unclearly and confusedly, as becoming, as uninterrupted movement into a real future'.[2] The novel therefore not only has a history but is itself the means by which history moves forward: the story of its development is the story of how history itself, through centuries of experiment and experience, discovers its proper shape and true vocation. To understand the novel is therefore to understand modernity, or, to put the matter more forcefully, to become fully modern oneself. Through its new 'dialogical' style and its new ideal of narrative *Bildung* (formation), the novel had changed the very function of literary writing, and only the most adventurous kind of literary study would allow us to catch up with its achievement.

What added daring to literary studies was philosophy. Only an 'authentic philosophical and sociological approach', Bakhtin claimed in his first great essay on the genre, 'Discourse in the Novel' (1934–35), would allow one to 'sense behind individual and period-bound shifts the great and anonymous destinies of artistic discourse'.[3] Only philosophy would continually ask what literature was for, and would therefore be alert to the moment when literature as a whole might change direction. By all accounts, Bakhtin would have been dismayed to find himself embedded in the 'history of literary criticism', for he insisted until the very end of his life that he was really a 'philosopher' who had been forced into the narrower confines of literary criticism by historical circumstances.[4] And indeed, at the beginning of his working life, Bakhtin seemed set on an interesting philosophical career.

As a young intellectual in the 1920s Bakhtin had enormous ambitions. The circle of intellectuals with whom he met in this period (they moved around more or less as a group, and are known today as the 'Bakhtin circle') embarked on what Bakhtin would later describe – under interrogation – as 'the difficult and laborious work of the revaluation and testing of all our previous knowledge and convictions', a revaluation which, however, took its bearings from the European and Russian philosophical traditions.[5] For Bakhtin this revaluation assumed the form of a book on Dostoevsky, only completed in late 1928, and a systematic work of 'ethical philosophy', which addressed the crisis of Europe in grand philosophical style. Neither completed at the time nor picked up later, all that remains of this ambitious work are a fragment of an introduction, now known as 'Towards a Philosophy of the Act', a good part of a chapter devoted to aesthetics, now called 'Author and Hero in Aesthetic

[2] *Ibid.*, p. 30.
[3] M. M. Bakhtin, 'Discourse in the Novel', *The Dialogic Imagination*, p. 259.
[4] See S. G. Bocharov for Bakhtin's confession to him on this matter, 'Conversations with Bakhtin', trans. Vadim Liapunov and Stephen Blackwell, *PMLA* 109.5 (1994), pp. 1012–1013.
[5] KGB Archive, Leningrad region, d. 14284, t. 3, l. 7; cited in Iu. P. Medvedev, 'Na puti k sozdaniiu sotsiologicheskoi poetiki', *Dialog Karnaval Khronotop* 2 (1998), p. 47 n85.

Activity', and notes taken by a listener to a lecture which may have summed up the contents of a planned chapter on religion.

The crux of its argument would have been familiar to a European intellectual of the time: as a consequence of science and individualism, European culture had lost its legitimacy, its ability to motivate people's acts, and 'as a result, the performed act sinks to the level of elementary biological and economic motivation, that is, it loses all its ideal moments'.[6] When scientific reasoning, embodied in the 'universally valid judgement', became the norm for cultural creation, the result was 'a fundamental split between the content or sense of an act/activity and the historical actuality of its being'.[7] Values which were supported by objective statements and arguments, modelled on the scientific judgement, had no need of individuals, but by the same token had no call on them either. Lacking what Bakhtin called the quality of 'oughtness', this 'theoreticised' culture could no longer serve as the means by which individuals could embed themselves in a world whose values transcended their immediate impulses and needs. 'The world of culture' had become fundamentally separated from the 'world of life', to the detriment of both.[8] If history was to be more than either a random succession of acts or the inexorable yet meaningless 'progress' of culture, the two spheres would have to be reintegrated. In the 1920s Bakhtin seemed to think that what was needed was not a new culture or a new set of values, but a new kind of individuality, able to appreciate and feel bound by the values already on offer.

No abstract demonstration of moral principles, no matter how compelling or ingenious, would make the individual consciousness more 'responsible' or 'responsive' to the values around it. The moral attitude or orientation which modernity demanded had to be 'phenomenologically disclosed', that is, described for – and then hopefully acknowledged by – readers, the acknowledgement itself being something which 'cannot be adequately expressed in theoretical terms, but can only be described and participatively experienced'.[9] And the reason for this was fairly straightforward, if somewhat paradoxical: what made the individual responsible was precisely the recognition that there were no 'individuals' as such. 'Man-in-general', Bakhtin announced, 'does not exist: *I* exist and a particular concrete *other* exists.'[10]

According to Bakhtin, there was an ineluctable split in our experience of culture: 'an inner experience and mental whole can be concretely experienced – can be inwardly perceived – either in the category of *I-for-myself* or in the category of the *other-for-me*, that is, either as my experience or as the experience of this definite singular other person'.[11] Our own thoughts, feelings and

[6] M. M. Bakhtin, *Towards a Philosophy of the Act*, trans. Vadim Liapunov, eds. Vadim Liapunov and Michael Holquist (Austin, Tex.: University of Texas Press, 1993), p. 55.

[7] *Ibid.*, p. 2.   [8] *Ibid.*   [9] *Ibid.*, p. 40.   [10] *Ibid.*, p. 47.

[11] M. M. Bakhtin, 'Author and Hero in Aesthetic Activity', in *Art and Answerability: Early Philosophical Essays by M. M. Bakhtin*, eds. Michael Holquist and Vadim Liapunov, trans. Vadim Liapunov and Kenneth Brostrom (Austin, Tex.: University of Texas Press, 1990), p. 24.

sensations are experienced as part of a consciousness which is intent and always pressing forward; they and the world around us sound in the key of 'forward-directed life'. But the thoughts, feelings and experience of *others* are accessible to us only as language, gesture and expression, that is, in a distant and indirect form which renders them worldly and almost physical. The modern category of the all-purpose 'individual' hides this split from view, by creating the illusion of a third-person perspective from which all individuals, including our own *Is*, looked the same.

Once acknowledged, the split not only made responsible life possible – it made such a life unavoidable. The *I-for-myself* which sensed its distinctiveness would no longer be able to look at the problems it faced as somehow of a piece with those faced by others: their imbrication in *its* life gave them a uniquely compelling character and left the subject with, as Bakhtin put it, 'no alibi in Being'. At the same time, the difference between the *I-for-myself* and *others-for-me* was what made possible the ethical act par excellence: the act of empathy, which Bakhtin, following Max Scheler, saw as wholly dependent on the ineradicable distance between *I* and *other*.[12] 'When I empathize with the suffering of another,' Bakhtin observed, 'I experience it precisely as *his* suffering, in the category of the *other*, and my reaction to it is not a cry of pain, but a comforting word and an act of help.'[13] Subjects which recognised the *I/other* split would, by this act alone, transcend their isolation, for they would then feel compelled to embed themselves in a network of empathetic relations which would sew together their lives and their culture. Or put more brutally, they would exchange their liberal individualism for the life of a merciful Christian.

The uncertainty of modern historical experience was to be replaced by the security offered by faith. And there matters might have remained, but for an ambiguity which plagued Bakhtin's philosophy from the outset. For although Bakhtin called his philosophy 'ethical', he reserved a privileged place within it for art, on the basis that in art we came closer to the knowledge of the great split than in any other sphere. 'It is about the other', he claimed, 'that all plots are composed, that all works are written, that all tears are shed, for the other that all monuments are erected.'[14] Art was not the expression of one consciousness, but the framing and valuing of a second, different consciousness through the 'othering' eyes of a first. Its distinctiveness lay in its ability to render the ordinary contents of life on a different, distanced plane, empathising with them while not being caught up in the pressing urgency of their

---

[12] On this topic see Brian Poole's groundbreaking article, 'From Phenomenology to Dialogue: Max Scheler's Phenomenological Tradition and Mikhail Bakhtin's Development from *Towards a Philosophy of the Act* to his Study of Dostoevsky', in Ken Hirschkop and David Shepherd (eds.), *Bakhtin and Cultural Theory*, 2nd rev. edn. (Manchester: Manchester University Press, forthcoming).   [13] Bakhtin, 'Author and Hero', p. 26.

[14] *Ibid.*, pp. 111–112.

demands. As a consequence, art could chart the historical progress of a life or lives in a manner impossible from the inside: it endowed with form and wholeness a narrative which the *I-for-myself* could never draw together.

All those critics who argued with literary characters, thinking it was the latters' opinions that made them compelling, had therefore missed the point entirely. While the aesthetic work 'does not erase the boundary between good and evil, beauty and ugliness, truth and falsehood', it nevertheless subsumes them under an 'all-accepting loving affirmation of the human being', that is to say, it makes them moments of a life-story deemed valuable in itself.[15] No one's characters, of course, elicited more argument than those of Dostoevsky, who was thus a natural subject for Bakhtin's first book in 1929. There Bakhtin showed that arguing with the characters made the ideas themselves, rather than the lives of the heroes – the substance of the confession, rather than the act of confession – the important thing. Dostoevsky had evoked the all-important distinction of *I* and *other* not by argument, however, but by finding the means to endow the developing, 'becoming' human spirit of his characters with artistic form. And this was a secular artistic achievement, different in principle from both Dostoevsky's own spiritual torments and those of his characters.

Furthermore, it turned out to be a distinctively linguistic achievement. Having established that Dostoevsky's triumph had been to remain outside his characters, Bakhtin, suddenly shifting argumentative gear in the second half of the book, went on to show that establishing and maintaining this distance was a matter not of plot or characterisation, but of language and style. *Problems of Dostoevsky's Art* was a strange, bifurcated book, split between philosophy and stylistics, which read as if halfway through some external force had knocked it sideways onto a linguistic path lying parallel to the one it had been travelling along.

There was indeed an external force: Bakhtin's friend Voloshinov, who had been studying and working at the Institute for the Comparative History of Eastern and Western Languages and Literatures since 1924, ostensibly as a student of literature but also as a student of some of the most important linguists of the time. At about the time Bakhtin was finishing his work on Dostoevsky, Voloshinov was coming to the conclusion that language, which was at once the medium of individual commitment and cultural achievement, was what permitted the individual to transcend itself in culture without losing itself in abstraction. And to the extent that this transcendence depended on the empathetic framing of an individual's speech by an author, it was identical to the problem of reported speech in literature – the stylistic business of direct quotation, indirect style and the like had, so to speak, a philosophical core. For the minute stylistic choices which made reported speech at once the

---

[15] Bakhtin, *Towards a Philosophy of the Act*, pp. 63–64.

utterance of an author and that of a hero perfectly enacted the need to empathise and objectify at the same time.

Voloshinov had a name for this linguistic empathy, which Bakhtin adopted and expanded in his Dostoevsky book – 'dialogism'. To draw the hero out of isolation, Dostoevsky had to engage in dialogue with him: not by literally posing questions to him, but by writing a 'double-voiced discourse' which simultaneously embodied the intentions of the character and the distancing, shaping intentions of the artistic whole. To catch human beings in the process of real development one could neither address them directly nor let them speak directly: one had to address them through the novel, so that even the motion of plot seemed a permanent provocation to their deepest anxieties and concerns.

Dostoevsky ensured that the key turning points, the historical 'moments of truth', were the focus of this double-voicing by placing the action on the terrain of 'ultimate questions', the resolution of which he assumed would dictate the characters' life-course in all its essential moments. When Bakhtin decided that dialogism was not just Dostoevsky's achievement but the defining feature of all novelistic writing, history itself became the frame which drew characters out of their isolation. In a series of essays on the novel stretching from 1934 to 1946, Bakhtin claimed that in dialogical writing the double-voiced quality is 'fertilized by a profound connection with the language-stratifying forces of historical becoming'.[16] The relation of author to character which had interested Bakhtin earlier was recast as the relation of the novelist to language, the latter now being the object which had to be empathised with, entered into, yet also distanced and given objective form.

Language was given form in the sense that it became something which 'not only represents, but is itself represented',[17] and it was represented in the form of what Bakhtin called 'socio-ideological languages'. 'In the novel formal markers of languages, manners and styles are symbols for social points of view': the smooth and even surface of the novel's discourse was broken up, so that rather than being composed of language, it seemed to be composed of competing languages or, as Bakhtin called them, 'images of a language', each of which embodied a worldview, a speaker and a context.[18] 'Double-voiced' writing in the novel therefore presumed a 'deliberate sense of the historical and social concreteness and relativity of living discourse, a sense of its participation in historical becoming and social struggle'.[19]

It is commonly assumed that by 'dialogism' Bakhtin meant a confrontation within the work between several readily identifiable social languages. But this confrontation could take place only on the basis of a more basic dialogical encounter, in which the materials of everyday speech had been reframed by the novelist and made properly historical. For the antithesis of novelistic

16 Bakhtin, 'Discourse in the Novel', p. 325.   17 *Ibid.*, p. 336.   18 *Ibid.*, p. 357.
19 *Ibid.*, p. 331.

writing was not writing in which all speech sounded the same or where there were no arguments: it was writing in which speech differences remained private, at the level of 'individual dissonances, misunderstandings or contradictions', which 'however tragic, however firmly grounded in individual destinies', could never evoke a fundamental difference between worldviews or social contexts.[20]

The point was not, however, to 'place' the individual in a discrete context, but to integrate him or her into a world shaped by historical 'becoming'. Mere social realism would therefore not do the trick, and Bakhtin was permanently suspicious of novel-writing in which 'the representation of the real is knit together with the representation of something average and small (normal)', the realism of the small group in an 'indoor little world'.[21] When 'the event of life is played out on the most pacified inner territory, at a maximum distance from its borders, from beginnings and ends, both real and semantic', the individual loses touch with the fact that culture is historical in its essence, and that the justification of all values depends on a constant orientation to the future.[22] To be realistic meant not merely empirical social observation, but empirical observation informed by the belief that every existing value and way of life was straining towards its own future transformation and possible redemption. 'An acute sense (and a distinct and sharp awareness) of the possibility of a completely different life and a completely different worldview than the life and worldview of the present is a presupposition of the novelistic image of present life.'[23] But this acute sense could not itself be an ideology or worldview; it was embodied in a distinctive kind of language.

Bakhtin therefore effectively reinterpreted a whole series of stylistic effects: irony, parody, the stylisation of languages, the use of inserted genres and unreliable narrators, the Russian tradition of oral narration known as *skaz*. The point of all this was not only to evoke the 'heteroglot', stratified nature of language, its worldliness and context-dependence, but to make possible 'a new mode in the life of language'.[24] It was in language, understood as the medium of cultural creation, that the individual would be able to transcend the limitations of life and death and place, that he or she would participate in a continuously 'becoming' culture. But this could be achieved only if their own language was set in a context which emphasised their participation in the social shifting and striving which literally makes history.

[20] *Ibid.*, p. 325.
[21] M. M. Bakhtin, 'O Maiakovskom' ('On Mayakovsky'), *Sobranie sochinenii v semi tomakh, tom 5, Raboty 1940-kh – nachala 1960-kh godov* ('Collected works in seven volumes, vol. 5: Works from the 1940s to the beginning of the 1960s'), eds. S. G. Bocharov and L. A. Gogotishvili (Moscow: Russkie slovari, 1996), pp. 57, 55.
[22] Bakhtin, 'O Flobere' ('On Flaubert'), *Sobranie sochinenii*, vol. 5, p. 131.   [23] *Ibid.*, p. 132.
[24] M. M. Bakhtin, 'Iazyk v khudozhestvennoi literature' ('Language in artistic literature'), *Sobranie sochinenii*, vol. 5, p. 287.

Overcoming the isolation of the individual life was not only a matter of style, however. In the mid-1930s Bakhtin embarked on a study of the European *Bildungsroman* which would demonstrate how historical 'becoming' could be embodied in a distinctive kind of narrative. In this never completed study, the artistic paradigm was to be Goethe, whom Bakhtin believed to have perfected the 'novel of becoming', in which the striving of the hero was united with the movement of the plot. While earlier novels had either fixed the hero while varying the scene (as in, for instance, the Greek romance and the picaresque novel) or defined the environment as a fixed place ready to teach a malleable hero 'the way of the world' (as in many nineteenth-century examples of *Bildungsroman*), in the novel of becoming the hero

becomes *together with the world*, he reflects within himself the historical becoming of the world itself. He is no longer within an epoch, but on the border of two epochs, at the point of transition from one to the other. This transition is achieved in him and through him. He is forced to become a new, unprecedented type of human being. The issue here is precisely the becoming of a new person; the organizing force of the future is therefore extraordinarily great and it is, of course, not a private-biographical future, but an historical future. It is the *foundations* of the world that change, and the person must change with them.[25]

An historical, rather than a private-biographical future: this starkly defines what Bakhtin thought were the two available options. The latter meant a life lived by apparently solid values and conventions, which nevertheless might be swept away by the tide of history (a circumstance of which Bakhtin had direct experience, of course). The former meant recognising that only through others – in particular the many others who would remember your life, interpret its meaning, and give it a wholeness and context after it has ended – could your life be rendered permanently meaningful. It was the task of the novel to make such an historical existence imaginable.

Did anything stand in its way? In the essays on 'dialogism' Bakhtin claimed that a popular sense of historical 'becoming', embodied in the low genres of popular-festive culture, had always run beneath the surface of European culture, only occasionally bursting into the open. When he came to write his book on Rabelais (1940; published 1965), Bakhtin argued that the historical force of the latter's work was drawn directly from these popular sources, which gave it not just techniques, but a philosophy of culture. In this text and in notes composed for its revision, Bakhtin hypothesised that this popular historical consciousness had always been kept in check by the exercise of centralising political power.[26] The rulers, it seems, had their own designs for

[25] M. M. Bakhtin, 'The *Bildungsroman* and its Significance in the History of Realism', *Speech Genres and Other Late Essays*, eds. Caryl Emerson and Michael Holquist, trans. Vern W. McGee (Austin, Tex.: University of Texas Press, 1986), pp. 23–24.

[26] See M. M. Bakhtin, *Tvorchestvo Fransua Rable i narodnaia kul'tura srednevekov'ia i renes-sansa* ('The art of François Rabelais and the popular culture of the Middle Ages and

transcending the limitations of the here-and-now, but these depended not on historical consciousness, but on the prolongation of what already existed. Rather than write novels, the rulers would build monuments. Animated by 'the thirst for glory and immortality in the memory of one's descendants, for one's *proper name* (and not nickname) in people's mouths', the rulers sought to ensure the continuity of the name above all.[27] 'To name is to establish for centuries beyond, to secure something in being forever, inherent in it is a tendency to ineradicability, for it cannot be washed away, it wants to be cut as deeply as possible in the hardest and most solid possible material, and so on.'[28]

The implication was, of course, that all such attempts to secure the individual against the tide of change were doomed: the monuments of the ancient rulers fell into ruin, while the popular culture of their subjects remained a living force. This touching, but perhaps naive, comment on the limitations of power reminds us that Bakhtin's vision of historical becoming may not have been as self-reflective as it should have been. For Bakhtin did not acknowledge the possibility that the idea of history as a constant orientation to the future may itself have been the product of historical development. He preferred to think of it as a constant, always alive in the recesses of language, more evident in the practice of popular culture. To this extent, however much he praised the achievements of secular modernity, he remained indebted to ideals of faith and redemption which he inherited from the ancients.

Renaissance'), (Moscow: Khudozhestvennaia literatura, 1965; reprinted with new pagination in 1990); and Bakhtin's 'Dopolneniia i izmeneniia k "Rable"' ('Additions and amendments to "Rabelais"'), *Sobranie sochinenii*, vol. 5, pp. 80–129.

[27] Bakhtin, 'Dopolneniia i izmeneniia k "Rable"', p. 84.   [28] *Ibid.*, p. 100.

12

Cultural studies

CHRIS WEEDON

Since the 1960s the discipline of cultural studies has taken root throughout the English-speaking world and beyond. It has developed a wide range of approaches to the study of culture which are usually characterised by attention to political, ideological, social and historical factors, in particular the relationship between culture and power.[1] In the course of its development cultural studies has challenged established cultural canons and disciplinary boundaries and has focused attention on those aspects of culture which have been excluded by longer established humanities disciplines. Thus, for example, cultural studies has looked extensively at cultural theory, popular culture and the media. The development of cultural studies, in its turn, has influenced other disciplines, for example, literary studies, encouraging a more inclusive approach to the range of texts studied and greater attention to theory, context and the institutions that constitute the literary discursive field.[2]

Since the late 1960s cultural studies has become an established international discipline, yet its early roots are to be found in Britain, where they are closely intertwined with the development of literary studies. In its formative years cultural studies defined itself both *in relation to* and *against* what is known in Britain as the 'culture and civilisation' tradition, i.e. that tradition of English literary and cultural criticism that begins with Matthew Arnold in the 1860s.

For Arnold, culture was an explicitly political question, directly linked to class relations in nineteenth-century Britain. With the expansion of literacy among the working classes, the implementation of compulsory elementary education and the rise of trade unionism, social unrest and even social revolution increasingly came to be seen as real threats to existing social relations. As the title of his seminal work, *Culture and Anarchy* (1869) suggests, for Arnold, culture – that is high culture – played a crucial role in the construction of those shared meanings and values which were necessary for social

---

[1] For British cultural studies, see Graeme Turner, *British Cultural Studies: An Introduction*, 2nd edn. (London: Routledge, 1996) and Antony Easthope, *Literary Into Cultural Studies* (London: Routledge, 1991).

[2] For a more detailed discussion of the relationship between cultural and literary studies, see Andrew Milner, *Literature, Culture and Society* (London: UCL Press, 1996).

cohesion.[3] Arnold argued for the centrality of a canon of national literature in education, suggesting that, since it was more widely accessible than the classical languages and literature taught in the public schools and old universities, it could better promote shared national values, irrespective of class or other social differences. For Arnold and his followers, literature's new ethical and moral project was akin to that of religion and, without its civilising role, anarchy might well break loose. It was, indeed, more a question of culture *or* anarchy.

The culture and civilisation tradition of literary history and criticism which developed in the wake of Matthew Arnold's writing was liberal-humanist in character. It both assumed the inevitability of progress in western societies towards a higher state of civilisation and stressed the inalienable right of the individual to realise him/herself to the full. It privileged the role of culture, and literature in particular, in this process of self-development. Liberal humanism in its cultural form gradually penetrated thinking in education and by the 1920s had become the shaping discourse behind the influential Newbolt Report 'On the Teaching of English in England' of 1921. This report argued that what was needed was

not merely a means of education, one chamber in the structure which we are hoping to rebuild, but the true starting point and foundation from which all the rest must spring. For this special purpose, there is but one material. We make no comparison, we state what appears to us to be an incontrovertible primary fact, that for English children no form of knowledge can take precedence of a knowledge of English literature and that the two are so inextricably connected as to form the only basis possible for a national education.[4]

Here the national literature was envisaged as a privileged site for the articulation of universally true meanings and values which should ground a common culture, values and identity. The privileging of the national literature assumed a canon of exceptional texts which, if read properly, would shape the subjectivity, identity and values of the reader. The construction of this national canon was an ongoing process shaped by the educational, cultural and publishing institutions governing literary history and criticism.

The privileging of literature as the source of shared meanings and values reached a high point in the work of F. R. Leavis in Cambridge from the 1930s to the 1950s. Leavis, like Arnold before him, was interested in the links between culture and society, a theme which would become perhaps the key focus in the later development of cultural studies. Leavis stressed, in particular, what he saw as the negative effects of industrialisation – both in the

---

[3] Matthew Arnold, *Culture and Anarchy* (London: Smith Elder, 1869).
[4] Newbolt Report, *The Teaching of English in England* (London: Board of Education, HMSO, 1921), p. 14. See also George Sampson, *English for the English* (Cambridge: Cambridge University Press, 1921). For more on the ideological role of literature see Margaret Mathieson (ed.), *The Preachers of Culture* (London: Allen & Unwin, 1975).

workplace and in cultural production – on the development of civilisation. Indeed 'the movement of civilisation' and the links between culture and society were among the main issues raised in *Scrutiny*.[5] In 1933, Leavis, together with Denys Thompson, published *Culture and Environment* which looked at the links between industrial mass production and contemporary culture. For Leavis, high culture was set against what he saw as a stultifying, mass, popular culture, typified by Hollywood cinema. Unlike pre-industrial, organic, 'folk' culture, mass culture, Leavis suggested, bore no relation to the lives of ordinary people. In his view a healthy, national culture required an 'organic unity' between high and popular culture. In the absense of an organic popular culture, rooted in the lives of ordinary people, the educational task of great literature was all the more pressing.

In the face of the 'dumbing down' effects of mass culture, Leavis argued for the study of canonical English literature as the source of knowledge about life and a repository of the true values of the national culture. This approach to literature and the canon was publicised in his writings, in particular, *Mass Civilisation and Minority Culture* (1930), *Fiction and the Reading Public* (1932, written with Q. D. Leavis) and in the journal *Scrutiny* (1932–1953). His influence over generations of Cambridge students, many of whom themselves became teachers, was also a significant factor in popularising Leavisite criticism and it became the canonical approach to literature in secondary and higher education in the postwar period.[6]

Leavisite criticism relied on a process of canon formation in which certain texts came to be defined as 'great' and others as inferior and, therefore, less worthy of serious study. The criteria involved in selecting the canon were ostensibly those of universally recognisable aesthetic values which would be apparent to the perceptive reader. The ability to recognise great literature was acquired through the reader's encounter with great texts.[7] Simultaneously the reader would acquire moral sensibility – a sense of what was true and good – which transcended social differences. Both the ideological assumptions of this approach and its elitism would become focuses of critique as cultural studies, in its early years, sought to develop new conceptions of both culture and criticism. Cultural studies would insist that not only apparently 'universal' aesthetic criteria, but also the establishment of a body of canonical texts, were the effects of particular social and political processes embedded in the practices of a range of institutions such as education, publishing and literary criticism. Indeed the formation of the canon of English literature was an effect of

---

[5] Cf. the first issue of *Scrutiny* 1.1 (1932), p. 3.

[6] F. R. Leavis, *Mass Civilization and Minority Culture* (Cambridge: Gordon Fraser, 1930); Q. D. Leavis and F. R. Leavis, *Fiction and the Reading Public* (London: Chatto and Windus, 1932); *Scrutiny: A Quarterly Review*, eds. L. C. Knight and Donald Culver (Cambridge, 1932–53). For a history of *Scrutiny* and the Leavisite project, see Francis Mulhern, *The Moment of 'Scrutiny'* (London: New Left Books, 1979).

[7] See F. R. Leavis, *The Common Pursuit* (Harmondsworth: Penguin, 1962).

power that involved the exclusion of particular groups of writers, for example, working-class writing, most women's writing, writing by authors of colour and popular fiction. These excluded areas of literary culture would become important in early cultural studies in Britain.

A second significant influence on the development of cultural studies and its relation to canonical literature was a concern with class. Whereas the culture and civilisation tradition saw literature's role as transcending and even resolving class conflict, other approaches, in particular Marxism, privileged the study of the relationship between culture and the reproduction of class relations in capitalist societies. Marxist critiques reached a high point in the 1930s in a range of left-wing journals and cultural organisations. Particularly important in Britain were the Writers' International journal *Left Review* and the work of Christopher Caudwell.[8] Like liberal humanist critics, Marxists, too, worked with a canon of great literature which was often remarkably similar to the Leavisite canon. Indeed some of the contributors to *Scrutiny* also contributed to *Left Review*. However their ways of reading the canon were different from those of Leavis and his followers, even when the texts selected for study were the same.

Interwar Marxists also shared the Leavisite abhorrence of what was termed 'mass culture', in particular cinema and popular fiction. Neither tradition valued working-class culture or popular culture, both of which tended to be seen as aesthetically inferior and morally and ideologically corrupting. (There were, however, intermittent attempts on the left to encourage a class conscious working-class writing.)[9] Marxist approaches to literature and culture more broadly were developed in the Plebs League, in the educational work of the Communist Party and in various journals, particularly *Plebs*, *The Highway* and *Left Review*.[10] In both liberal humanist and Marxist approaches to literature in adult education up to 1945, moves were made to extend the canon of works studied to include texts of particular interest to working-class readers – for example the work of Charles Dickens and Jack London. Yet these texts were more often seen as a bait for working-class readers which would lead them on to 'higher' things.

The immediate post-war decades, marked as they were by revelations about the Stalinist Soviet Union and by events such as the Soviet invasions of Hungary (1956) and Czechoslovakia (1968), were not productive years for

---

[8] See *Left Review* (The Writers' International, British Section, London, 1934–38) and Christopher Caudwell, *Illusion and Reality* (1937) (London: Lawrence and Wishart, 1973) and *Studies and Further Studies in a Dying Culture* (1938) (New York and London: M.R., 1971).

[9] See Chris Weedon, *Aspects of the Politics of Literature and Working-Class Writing in Interwar Britain*, unpublished Ph.D. thesis, University of Birmingham, Centre for Contemporary Cultural Studies, 1984. See also Glenn Jordan and Chris Weedon, *Cultural Politics: Class, Gender, Race and the Postmodern World* (Oxford: Blackwell, 1995), pp 67–90.

[10] *The Plebs* (1919–) (previously published as *The Plebs' Magazine*, 1909–1919, London: Plebs' League; from 1928 onwards, London: National Council of Labour Colleges). *The Highway* (1908–) (London: Workers Educational Association).

Marxism. The main exception was the Frankfurt School which, however, perpetuated the hostility to popular culture found in interwar Marxism.[11] From its earliest years, cultural studies would take Marxism very seriously, but would distance itself from any easy dismissal of popular culture. Indeed, Marxist cultural criticism saw a revival in the 1970s, in tandem with the development of cultural studies, when, drawing on Althusser and Gramsci, it developed new and more sophisticated theories and approaches to culture and ideology.[12]

Adult education played an important role in the development of cultural studies and was the arena in which first attempts were made to extend the canon. From the turn of the nineteenth century onwards, both the culture and civilisation and Marxist traditions of literary and cultural criticism had been realised to varying degrees in the practice of adult education in Britain. For example, the Workers' Educational Association and university extension classes took up the Arnoldian project of extending high culture to the 'masses'. Whereas Arnold had called for working-class access to literature as a political necessity which would promote shared national values and counteract the forces of social revolution, exponents of liberal humanist adult education in the twentieth century saw access to literary culture as a question of rights. Here culture represented the highest achievements of humanity and should be accessible to all. This emphasis developed in the context of a utilitarian bias in elementary schooling which stressed the acquisition of basic skills and a suitably deferential attitude and reserved the study of literature for the grammar schools to which most people had no access prior to the education reforms of 1944.

In the post-war period adult education became the seedbed for the development of cultural studies.[13] The key protagonists in the development of British cultural studies – Richard Hoggart, Raymond Williams and Stuart Hall – all studied English literature and spent time working in adult education, an arena in which it was possible to transcend the constraints of canonical literature. Each of them worked to extend the range of texts studied to include, for example, working-class culture, popular culture and the media.[14]

[11] See, for example, Theodor Adorno, *Negative Dialectics*, trans. E. B. Ashton (New York: Saebury, 1973) and *Aesthetic Theory*, trans. C. Lenhardt (London: Routledge and Kegan Paul, 1984).

[12] See, for example, the Communist Party literary journal, *Red Letters* (London: Communist Party of Great Britain); or one issue of the journal published by the Centre for Contemporary Cultural Studies, *On Ideology: Working Papers in Cultural Studies 10* (1977; also published separately: London: Hutchinson, 1978). See also Raymond Williams, *Marxism and Literature* (Oxford: Oxford University Press, 1977).

[13] For more on the roots of cultural studies in adult education see Tom Steele, *The Emergence of Cultural Studies 1945–65: Cultural Politics, Adult Education and the English Question* (London: Lawrence & Wishart, 1997).

[14] For work on residual forms of working-class culture, see Richard Hoggart, *The Uses of Literacy* (London: Chatto and Windus, 1957) and *Speaking to Each Other*, vol. 1: *About*

The 1950s and 1960s saw a marked development of interest in working-class culture – evident both in the development of labour history (for example the development of 'history from below' and oral history), and in the kinds of cultural analysis developed by Hoggart and Williams. In the field of history, the main proponent of the new culturalist approach was E. P. Thompson. His pathbreaking study, *The Making of the English Working Class* (1963), argued for the importance of 'lived culture' and agency in working-class history, whilst insisting that culture itself is a site of struggle, shaped by competing class interests.

In the nascent area of cultural studies, Hoggart's and Williams' work from the 1950s and 1960s was concerned, in part, with the recovery and interpretation of older forms of working-class culture, which they saw as under threat from the development of the mass media, in particular cinema and television. Hoggart, for example, published his influential text *The Uses of Literacy* in 1957. Here he applied the techniques of close reading, familiar from literary analysis, to a wide range of popular cultural texts such as newspapers, magazines, music and popular fiction. The book depicts a rich and complex working-class life and culture in the north of England before the Second World War. Echoing themes which, in Leavis, are restricted to pre-industrial culture, Hoggart's account of interwar working-class life stresses its organic quality. As he moves on to the post-war period, Hoggart argues that organic working-class culture has been lost as a result of the postwar expansion of mass popular cultural forms which are not rooted in the life and experience of working-class communities. *The Uses of Literacy* is marked by a radical shift from high culture to the culture of working-class communities, yet its rejection of so-called 'inorganic' mass culture arguably limits its ability to do justice to post-war popular culture. Raymond Williams' work on class and culture would transcend these limitations and begin the cultural studies project of taking popular culture seriously. An important move in this direction was *Communications* (1962) in which Williams placed the development of modern media within the narrative of human liberation through democratic struggle that he had outlined in *The Long Revolution* (1961).[15]

One early event which marked the shift of emphasis away from canonical literature toward popular culture – a move fundamental to early cultural studies – was the conference on popular culture and the media organised by the National Union of Teachers in 1960. This event gave rise to Hall and

footnote 14 (*cont.*)
    Society (London: Chatto and Windus, 1970). For early analyses of the media and other forms of popular culture, see Raymond Williams, *Communications* (Harmondsworth: Penguin, 1962); Raymond Williams, *Television, Technology and Cultural Form* (London: Fontana, 1974); and Stuart Hall and Paddy Whannel, *The Popular Arts* (London: Hutchinson Educational, 1964).
15 Raymond Williams, *The Long Revolution* (Harmondsworth: Pelican, 1965).

Whannel's book *The Popular Arts* (1964) which applied strategies of close reading to television and other forms of popular culture, suggesting that it was possible to distinguish good from bad popular culture by looking closely at form. Research on the media and popular culture subsequently became central focuses of early work at the Centre for Contemporary Cultural Studies at the University of Birmingham which rapidly introduced semiology into the study of the media and popular culture.

Cultural studies, in its early years, was not only discursively related to literary studies, it was also institutionally an offshoot from the discipline of English literature. Thematically it drew on many of the concerns of the culture and civilisation tradition and applied literary modes of close reading to a much extended range of texts. Whilst early work in cultural studies in adult education developed in the context of English studies, cultural studies first became institutionalised as a discipline within British higher education with the founding of the Centre for Contemporary Cultural Studies at the University of Birmingham. Initially cultural studies had been part of the English department, but gained independent status in 1964 when Richard Hoggart, then a professor of English at Birmingham, became its first director. Hoggart was succeeded in 1968 by Stuart Hall.

Among other things work in cultural studies at Birmingham in the late 1960s and early 1970s was profoundly influenced by Raymond Williams' important texts *Culture and Society* (1958) and *The Long Revolution* (1961).[16] These texts rearticulated Arnold and Leavis' concerns with culture and society and marked the beginnings of new ways of studying culture in a broader social and ideological context. *Culture and Society* explored the development of the idea of culture from 1780 to 1950. In *The Long Revolution* Williams mapped the emergence of modernity via the democratic revolution, the industrial revolution and the revolution in communications. In the conclusion to *Culture and Society* and in *The Long Revolution*, Williams articulated his influential approach to culture in which it is defined not just as a body of intellectual and imaginative work but as a whole way of life. Throughout his work Williams suggested that culture is a very complex word with several distinct meanings. These are succinctly defined in *Keywords* (1976) as ranging from 'a general process of intellectual, spiritual and aesthetic development', through the 'works and practices of intellectual and especially artistic activity', to culture as a way of life.[17] Williams initiated a far reaching critique of canonical culture with his suggestion that the Arnoldian and Leavisite equation of culture with canonical 'high' culture is but one possible meaning which has elitist social implications since it legitimates the non-valuing of everything that it excludes.

---

[16] Raymond Williams, *Culture and Society* (London: Chatto and Windus, 1958).

[17] Raymond Williams, *Keywords: A Vocabulary of Culture and Society* (London: Fontana, 1976), p. 80.

While English literature focused on a specific tradition of 'great literature', cultural studies took as its object all types of culture. In its early years this was principally working-class and popular culture. Whereas F. R. and Q. D. Leavis and Marxist critics in the 1930s, and the Frankfurt School in the post-war period, were worried about what they saw as the detrimental effects of 'mass culture', in particular cinema and popular fiction, cultural studies did not assume in advance that popular culture was bad. It was interested in the social and ideological role of the popular in shaping meanings, values, subjectivities and identities and in offering spaces for the articulation of resistance to dominant cultural and social relations. One of the most important implications of cultural studies' challenge to exclusive literary and artistic cultural canons was the move from a unified idea of culture to a plural idea of *cultures* which are governed by social determinants such as class, gender, race and ethnicity. This shift of focus has involved the deconstruction of the high/low cultural divide, a process which reveals how such classifications are made. It has further involved a move to the popular which recognised that popular culture is more complex than many Marxist models have suggested.

In the field of literature, cultural studies initiated moves to include within the curriculum excluded forms of writing and writing by marginalised groups: working-class writers, women writers and writers of colour. Thus, for example, the exclusive literary canon was subject in the 1960s and 1970s to critiques for its failure to include working-class writing and working-class culture more generally and work began within cultural studies on the recovery of lost working-class writers. From the mid-1970s onwards, as feminism and issues of race made crucial impacts on cultural studies, this critique was expanded to include the absence of women's writing and writing by people of colour.[18] Gradually this development was taken up within more traditional literary studies where syllabuses were extended to include women's writing, forms of popular fiction and new literatures in English.

A further important aspect of the influence of cultural studies on the study of literature was its deconstruction of disciplinary boundaries and its stress on interdisciplinarity. Challenging existing disciplinary boundaries, cultural studies drew on questions, theories and methods taken from literary studies, history, sociology, film and media studies. In the process literature was no longer privileged as the bearer of universal values. Literary texts were read alongside other modes of writing as one cultural process among others. Moreover attention was focused not only on texts but on the process of writing, publishing, distribution and readership. This marked a shift from theories of 'literariness' as a fixed, recognisable aesthetic quality to 'literariness' as a social category produced via the institutional practices of publish-

---

[18] See for example, Janet Batsleer, Tony Davies, Rebecca O'Rourke and Chris Weedon, *Rewriting English: Cultural Politics of Gender and Class* (London: Methuen, 1985).

ing, education and literary criticism. As Milner argues in his book *Literature, Culture and Society* (1996), in cultural studies, '[t]he "literariness" of literature is not a property of a certain type of writing but rather a function of the ways in which different kinds of writing are socially processed, both by writers themselves and by readers, publishers, booksellers, literary critics and so on' (p. 22). Work on readership drew on reception theory and was extended to popular fiction and to specific audiences, such as women.[19] Thus, the 1970s saw the beginnings of research into particular genres of popular fiction with their specific, often gendered readerships. For example, cultural studies has produced a range of analyses of the role of romance fiction in the perpetuation of patriarchal social relations and of the role of reading romance in women's lives.

Cultural studies in Birmingham in the 1970s, under the directorship of Stuart Hall, was marked by a turn not only to social context but to cultural theory. Work in cultural studies engaged with a wide range of theorists and theories, drawing on semiology, Marxism, feminism, psychoanalysis, post-structuralism and theories of race and colonialism. (This new interest in theory was also shared by film and media studies elsewhere in Britain: see for example the journal *Screen*.)[20] The turn to theory was motivated by the critical ideological project of cultural studies which focused on understanding the role of culture in the reproduction of social power relations, above all exploitative relations of class, gender and race.

Among the most important influences on cultural studies in the 1970s were the French structuralist Marxism of Louis Althusser and the Italian Marxist Antonio Gramsci's theory of hegemony. Published work from the Centre for Contemporary Cultural Studies, for example *On Ideology* (1978) and *Culture, Media, Language* (1980), played an important role in making this theory known to a wider readership.[21] Both Althusser and Gramsci ascribed an important role to culture in the reproduction of social relations. Althusser's theory of ideological state apparatuses and of the interpellation of the individual as the subject of ideology were taken up in literary studies by Pierre Macherey whose influential work *A Theory of Literary Production* (1966) was published in English in 1978.[22] Althusser and Macherey became

---

[19] For reception theory, see Hans Robert Jauss, *Towards an Aesthetic of Reception*, trans. Timothy Bahti (Minneapolis: University of Minneapolis Press, 1982) and Wolfgang Iser, *The Act of Reading: A Theory of Aesthetic Response* (Baltimore: Johns Hopkins University Press, 1978).

[20] *Screen* (1969–), published by the Society for Film and Television, London; from 1990 onwards, by the Logie Baird Centre.

[21] Centre for Contemporary Cultural Studies, *On Ideology* (London: Hutchinson, 1978); and *Culture, Media, Language* (London: Hutchinson,1980).

[22] See Louis Althusser, 'Ideology and Ideological State Apparatuses: Notes Towards an Investigation', *Lenin and Philosophy and Other Essays* (London: New Left Books, 1971); and Pierre Macherey, *A Theory of Literary Production* (1966), trans. G. Wall (London: Routledge and Kegan Paul, 1978).

widely known in English departments through Terry Eagleton's *Criticism and Ideology* (1976) and Catherine Belsey's *Critical Practice* (1980).[23]

The study of literature as an institution within cultural studies gained momentum from its engagement with Pierre Bourdieu's theory of cultural capital, developed in his study of the French educational system. Bourdieu argues that education is as much about the acquisition of class specific cultural capital as knowledge. Thus the children of the middle classes are provided with the necessary skills for accessing an elite or 'high' culture which marks them off as different from the lower classes.[24] This perspective fed into critiques of cultural and literary canons. The project of understanding culture in social terms thus led to a focus not just on reading texts differently but on the circuit of cultural production and consumption.[25]

The work produced in the 1970s from within cultural studies, in particular on theories of ideology, reading and interpretation, was eventually taken up. Theory courses were introduced which promoted new ways of reading the canon and encouraged both its expansion and deconstruction. Cultural studies fed back to literary studies a concern with the importance of the process of literary production, the role of literary institutions and readership. Shifts in the discipline of English have thus led to a convergence with aspects of cultural studies. As Milner argues:

Leavisite literary criticism has thus been progressively superseded by much less prescriptive versions of literary studies, which have sought to analyze and explain how writing is written, read, distributed and exchanged. Thus reformulated, literary studies threatens to become part of that much wider intellectual enterprise which has increasingly come to be known as 'cultural studies'. For if literature is no longer the 'canonical' other of non-literature, as in the old antitheses between literature and fiction, minority culture and mass civilisation, then it becomes merely some texts amongst many, each in principle analysable according to analogous intellectual procedures and operations.[26]

When approached from a cultural studies perspective, literature becomes one element in the study of broader questions of culture, ideology and cultural history. Questions of aesthetic value are no longer free floating and apparently universal. Cultural studies also insists on a wider set of questions than those found in traditional text-based literary studies such as the study of the social and ideological role of popular literary forms and the raising of questions of readership. Cultural studies has relocated canonical literature in the context of the broader field of texts and forms of writing which it excludes. In the process, the canon itself has been extended and transformed.

[23] Terry Eagleton, *Criticism and Ideology* (London: New Left Books, 1976); Catherine Belsey, *Critical Practice* (London: Methuen, 1980).

[24] See Pierre Bourdieu and Jean-Claude Passeron, *Reproduction in Education, Society, and Culture*, trans. R. Nice (London: Sage, 1990).

[25] See Stuart Hall (ed.), *Representation: Cultural Representations and Signifying Practices* (London: Sage, 1997).

[26] Milner, *Literature, Culture and Society*, pp. 10–11.

13

Literature and the institutional context in Britain

GARY DAY

Exploring the relationship between literary criticism – English as an academic discipline – and the university during the course of the twentieth century, this essay argues that demands made on the university by the state have had a formative influence on the conception of literary criticism. At the beginning of the century the study of literature in Britain was seen both as a means of promoting pride in national identity and as a corrective to the materialist tendencies of the age.[1] As the millennium approaches, there is widespread scepticism about whether 'literature' can maintain its status as a superior form of writing, which has resulted in a shift of focus from privileged works – the canon – to a study of the diversity of cultural forms and the relations between them. Such changes take place in the context of a move from the university as the provider of a liberal education, concerned with the development of the individual, to a more vocational one, concerned with the needs of the economy.

From the 1870s there was increasing pressure on the universities to forge closer links with industry. This was due to fears of slow growth and the increasing intensity of foreign competition, particularly from Germany. To meet this need, civic colleges were created in industrial cities such as Manchester, Birmingham and Liverpool. The attitude of the two ancient universities to this development is summed up in J. S. Mill's remark that '[u]niversities are not intended to teach the knowledge required to fit men for some special mode of gaining a livelihood. Their object is not to make skilful lawyers and physicians or engineers, but capable and cultivated human beings.'[2] This was to be achieved through the teaching of traditional subjects such as classics, pure mathematics and philosophy. However, the view expressed by Mill, widely shared in the mid century, became more difficult to sustain by its end when pressure was brought to bear on the universities to help Britain become more competitive. Herbert Spencer, for example,

---

[1] An excellent overview of these developments can be found in Brian Doyle, *English and Englishness* (London: Methuen, 1988). A similar case is made for English studies in America in a work which makes a number of references to parallel arguments that were going on in England; see Gerald Graff, *Professing Literature: An Institutional History* (Chicago: Chicago University Press, 1987).

[2] J. S. Mill, 'Inaugural Address Delivered to the University of St. Andrews, 1 February 1867', in John M. Robson (ed.), *J. S. Mill: Collected Works*, vol. XVIII (Toronto: University of Toronto Press, 1977), pp. 139–186 (p. 147).

challenged the idea that the study of the classics was the mark of a civilised person since, in his view, it was science which made civilisation possible.

At the same time as the universities were being urged to develop closer ties with industry, moves were afoot to establish English as an academic discipline. During the nineteenth century the rhetorical tradition of teaching English – studying generally acclaimed writers as models of style – gave way to the teaching of English as cultural history while the *belles lettres* tradition now emphasised 'the moral power of great literature', demonstrating 'a belief in its humanising influence' which was supposed to be capable of counteracting malignant forces in a rapidly changing society.[3] These two views of English reflect its contradictory relationship with modern society. On the one hand, English serves as a means to unite the nation and to enhance productivity while on the other it is the discourse which deplores the depredations of industrialism. The establishment of English in the form of cultural history as a university subject, and also as the basis of the school curriculum, was part of a much wider process designed to promote pride in the nation's heritage. English literature, like the National Portrait Gallery (1896) and the Dictionary of National Biography (1885–1900), figured as a symbolically central concept expressive of a common culture that was also intended to be a spur to improved economic performance.[4] This view of English, whose most eloquent expression is found in the Newbolt Report (1921), complements one of the claims made to justify the inclusion of economics on university syllabi, namely that it would help to heal those social divisions which were painfully apparent in the late nineteenth and early twentieth century. The Cambridge economist Alfred Marshall argued in this vein that the study of economics enabled students to see a problem from the perspective of both workers and management, thus making them better placed, if they entered industry, to deal successfully with potential conflicts.

The endeavour to establish economics as university discipline occurs at the same time as that to establish English.[5] Despite the obvious differences between the two subjects, they each figured as a means of achieving social unity and, in that respect, they can both be understood as strategies designed to counter the revival of socialist politics at the turn of the century. Created as an alternative to the divisive politics of socialism, English appeared as the non-political expression of a unified culture. As a result, its ability to

---

[3] D. J. Palmer, *The Rise of English Studies: An Account of the Study of English Language and Literature From its Origins to the Making of the Oxford English School* (London: University of Hull and Oxford University Press, 1965), p. 15; cf. also Stanley Leathes, 'The Teaching of English at the Universities', *English Association Pamphlet* 24 (1913), p. 6.

[4] Doyle, *English and Englishness*, p. 18.

[5] A work which examines in detail the historical relations between literature and economics is John Guillory, *Cultural Capital: The Problem of Literary Canon and Formation* (Chicago: University of Chicago Press, 1993). See also Marc Shell, *Money Language and Thought: Literary and Philosophic Economies from the Medieval to the Modern Era* (Baltimore: Johns Hopkins University Press, 1982).

condemn sucessfully the reductive effects of industrialism was considerably weakened: the 'humanising powers' of the new academic discipline were enfeebled by not being related to a wider conception of the social order.

The justification for the academic study of English was conducted in terms which evoked the principles of liberal education, which meant that it was certainly not established with the intention of offering a critique of capitalism. Moreover, at the beginning of the twentieth century, English was still being defended in nineteenth-century terms, caught up as it was in the tradition of *belles lettres*. This explains why, as E. M. W. Tillyard complained, 'the dominant trend' of criticism at Cambridge before the foundation of the English Tripos (1917) 'was towards gossipy, and often highly metaphorical, description and unspecific praise'.[6] This was also true of Oxford where Walter Raleigh, who helped found the English School there (1908), was seen by some as more of an aesthete than an academic because of his distrust of examinations and his apparent neglect of scholarship. In both these universities, English later came to be defined, in part, against a studied dilettantism or excessive emotionalism.

The work of I. A. Richards, who was largely responsible for the introduction of the Practical Criticism paper in the Cambridge Tripos (1926), represents a more objective approach to the study of literature. This new orientation is partly the result of an increased awareness of the contributions made to England's victory in the first world war by science and technology. Ezra Pound's advice to poets to 'consider the ways of the scientist' was offered in a Britain dominated by 'the cult of technology'.[7] Richards' work shows how scientific and bureaucratic values were beginning to enter the study of English. In the first place, there was an empirical emphasis on the work itself rather than on the reader's perception of it. In the second place, Richards' claim that there was an objective response to the work which could be distinguished from a subjective one downplayed the importance of what that work could mean to any given individual. This can be seen as an extension of T. S. Eliot's famous doctrine of impersonality, most famously captured in his remark that 'poetry is not an expression of personality, but an escape from personality'.[8] Such assertions fitted well with the Fordist methods of production and large-scale bureaucratic organisations characteristic of modernity.

The inter war years saw a further consolidation of the relationship between the universities and industry as well as a rise in the university population from around 40,000 in the mid 1920s to around 50,000 in the 1930s. The effect of

---

[6] E. M. W. Tillyard, *The Muse Unchained* (London: Bowes and Bowes), p. 84.
[7] Ezra Pound, 'Rhythm and Rhyme', in Peter Jones (ed.), *Imagist Poetry* (Harmondsworth: Penguin, 1976), pp. 132–134 (p. 132); and Michael Sanderson, *The Universities and British Industry: 1850–1970* (London: Routledge, 1972), p. 235.
[8] T. S. Eliot, 'Tradition and the Individual Talent', *Selected Essays* (London: Faber and Faber, 1932 and 1951), p. 21.

these changes on English was to intensify existing tensions in the subject rather than to develop it in new directions. The most important figure of this period was F. R. Leavis who seemed to be exactly the kind of lecturer envisaged by the Newbolt report; a missionary who would 'wean' people away from 'sensational periodicals' by introducing them to the beauties of English literature.[9] Leavis believed that the university was a symbol of cultural tradition 'that should check and control the blind drive onward of material and mechanical development with its human consequences'.[10] English literature embodied this tradition and imparted a sense of significance to life which was otherwise missing from modern existence. For Leavis, English was a vehicle of protest against the spiritual and cultural impoverishment of the nation, brought on by the industrial revolution.

Leavis' conception of English, however, embodied the values of an increasingly technocratic yet socially conservative order. His claim, made in the context of the continued rise in the number of university students, that only a minority were capable of a just appreciation of literature, seemed like a justification for social hierarchies. The contradictory relationship to the social order in Leavis' work stems from the clash in his criticism between humane and professional values; between literature as a moral and cultural force in the life of society and literature as the object of specialised study by experts in universities. The origin of this clash goes back to the debate at the turn of the century over whether English was a proper academic subject or whether, in E. A. Freeman's famous phrase, it was 'mere chatter about Shelley'. The argument for the existence of English as a discipline as good as that of classics or philology was made on the grounds of its links with history and its being 'a systematic training of the imagination and sympathies, and of a genial and moral sensibility'.[11] It was precisely this sort of thinking which justified the view of English as having a major role to play in the cultural life of the nation.

Leavis shared this idea but certain aspects of his language suggest how deeply the study of English can become entangled with other discourses whose values it opposes. Specifically, his vocabulary evokes that of scientific management whose influence in Britain in the 1930s and 1940s was immense, when Leavis was writing about the critical discipline. Devised by Frederick Winslow Taylor, the object of scientific management was to increase productivity. Taylor placed great emphasis on the training and supervision of workers who were viewed as units of production rather than rounded human beings. The impact of scientific management on Leavis is evident in his view

---

[9] Cf. the arguments put forward in the report, *The Teaching of English in England: Being the Report of the Departmental Committee Appointed by the President of the Board of Education to Inquire into the Position of English in the Education System* (London: HMSO, 1921), p. 148, pp. 149–150.

[10] F. R. Leavis, *Education and the University* (London: Chatto and Windus, 1943), p. 16.

[11] John Morley, 'The Study of Literature', *Aspects of Modern Study, Being University Extension Addresses* (Oxford: Clarendon, 1889), p. 63.

of criticism as a form of production and in the value that he gives to training.[12] For him criticism is 'producing a poem from the black marks on the page' and the aim of training is 'to improve one's apparatus, one's equipment, one's efficiency as a reader'.[13] Such terminology is at odds with Leavis' conception of human creativity, placing it in the service of mechanistic production rather than cultural renewal.

The various connections between Leavis' criticism and scientific management mean that the values of English cannot simply be opposed to those of economics.[14] Furthermore, Leavis' elaboration of a professional vocabulary for English distances it from engaging with wider social concerns. Instead of authorising a cultural mission, the idea of English literature as an expression of national identity now validated the field of professional study. This reflects a new relationship between the university and society. Previously the traditional universities offered a liberal education which fitted their privileged students for high-ranking positions in government, the church and the civil service. By the 1930s, the increasingly techno-scientific character of industry demanded graduates who had studied business, statistics and industrial administration. The university was no longer required to civilise society but to improve its economic performance. It would be wrong, however, to believe that English was completely divorced from this development even in practical terms. Many firms employed English graduates as managers because they believed their lack of specific training would enable them to cope better with the demands of the modern organisation than graduates who had specialised in commerce. English as a valuation of human experience was being replaced by English as a career qualification.

The extension of higher education was part of the post-war settlement built around the welfare state with its promise to open up British society. In terms of English, this meant there was more of an attempt to understand popular culture than to dismiss it for its alleged inferiority to 'high' culture. Leavis' influence began to diminish while the work of Raymond Williams and Richard Hoggart became increasingly important. These were critics who broadened the meaning of the term 'culture' to include descriptions of a particular way of life and who severely attacked the elitist conception of 'high' art.[15]

Corresponding to these developments was the determination by the new universities (founded in the 1960s) to break away from the tight departmental structures of the old ones. In contrast to the traditional single honours degree, universities such as Essex and Sussex offered broader subject groupings to

---

[12] I discuss this question in my book *Re-reading Leavis: 'Culture' and Literary Criticism* (Basingstoke: Macmillan, 1996). See also Guillory, *Cultural Capital*, pp. 134–175.

[13] F. R. Leavis, *The Living Principle: 'English' as a Discipline of Thought* (London: Chatto and Windus, 1975), p. 36; and *How to Teach Reading: A Primer for Ezra Pound* (Cambridge: Minority Press, 1932), p. 73.   [14] See Guillory, *Cultural Capital*, pp. 269–339.

[15] For a discussion of the redefinition of the meaning of 'culture', see the chapter on cultural studies in this volume.

promote interdisciplinary studies. The emphasis in English now was less on whether works qualified for inclusion in the canon and more on seeing them in their social and historical context. The new universities were playing their part in the wider process of social emancipation.

Peter Scott, however, has argued that the new universities in their own ways reproduced the traditions of the old. The new universities were criticised because their undergraduate courses did not lead sufficiently or directly into industrial production while their graduate courses were condemned as 'at best irrelevant to industry and, at worst, a deterrent from entering it'.[16] It was left to the polytechnics to supply the skilled labour that had been one of the main reasons for the expansion of higher education in the 1960s. The democratic impulse to widen opportunity was not accompanied by a change in the approach to education which was still divided between academic and vocational study. Although the new universities were critical of 'high' culture in the courses they offered, as institutions they nevertheless perpetuated the social divisions of which 'high' culture was an expression. For most new universities aimed to affirm the connection between higher education and elite occupations[17] and no other British university went as far as Warwick in its 'determination to have a close relationship with industry and commerce' and to regard 'research collaboration with industry as an essential part of [its] programme'.[18]

Scott has pointed out that 'the university, for all its assumed antiquity, is a thoroughly modern institution'.[19] Only eighteen were established before the death of Queen Victoria while sixty-one were created during 1960s. The correlation between the nature of the economy and university expansion has an effect on the idea of what a university should be and the kinds of course it should offer. Already in the late sixties there were concerns that the number of students studying for humanities degrees 'posed a serious risk for the future of industry'.[20] Moreover, student militancy in the late sixties and early seventies seemed attributable, at least in part, to subjects like sociology. Thus not only were the universities failing to provide industry with the calibre of graduates they needed, they were also producing students who were critical of the values of capitalism. These two factors have led, in the past two decades, to reform of the universities, beginning with the severe cutbacks in university funding in 1981 made by the Conservative Prime Minister Margaret Thatcher.

[16] *The Flow into Employment of Scientists, Engineers and Technologists* (London: Committee for Monitoring of National Development 3760, 1968), p. 35.
[17] Peter Scott, *The Meanings of Mass Higher Education* (Buckingham: Open University Press, 1995), p. 118.
[18] *Reports of the Vice Chancellor, University of Warwick 1965–8* (Warwick: University of Warwick Publications, 1969), p. 12.
[19] Scott, *The Meanings of Mass Higher Education*, p. 118.
[20] *The Bosworth Report: Graduate Training in Manufacturing Technology* (London: HMSO, 1970), p. 9.

On a methodological level, the dissemination of the ideas contained in the work of Terence Hawkes and Catherine Belsey, among others, meant that conventional practical criticism was coming to be replaced by a new critical practice.[21] The critic no longer contemplated the work but produced it; no longer placed it in a tradition but opened it up to history; no longer evaluated it but utilised it as part of a politics of resistance. At the same time as the adherents of theory proclaimed that they were breaking with the past, Mrs Thatcher was declaring an end to the post-war consensus. The rise of theory, here, cannot be divorced from the growth of the free market or seen in isolation from the longstanding relationship between English and economics. The language of economics pervades the discourse of theory. This is true in a very general way, for example in Derrida's remark that language is always a 'problem of economy and strategy' but also in much more specific ways that can only be hinted at here. These include the connection between theory's attack on the unity of the text and the deregulation of the economy; also the idea of the free play of meaning mirrored in that of the free play of market forces.[22]

The rationale behind academic funding, moreover, dictates that institutions have to compete with one another for research money. Over the last twenty years, the universities have been increasingly subject to tighter political controls and the establishment of formal audit and assessment systems. In 1992, these developments culminated in the creation of a unified system of higher education in place of the former binary division between universities and polytechnics. This inaugurated the era of mass access, transforming university education into an investment good. The modular degree, a new development which demonstrates commitment to student choice, differs from the traditional honours course in that the student is free to devise his or her own particular framework of expertise, even though it may be difficult to reconcile it with the principle that all English graduates should have a common body of knowledge.

To the extent that a greater variety of writing is now available for study, it can be argued that English has been democratised. The influence of mainly French critical theory has led to a politicising of the study of English, where texts are interpreted in terms of their subversion of the established order. The difference between the traditional and theoretical approaches is, however, perhaps one of emphasis rather than substance since both fashion themselves in opposition to the prevailing ethos of society. Its assault on tradition similarly underwrites the new experience of time in a post-industrial society

---

[21] Terence Hawkes was the general editor of the New Accents series which was chiefly responsible for publicising the new methodology; see for instance his own *Structuralism and Semiotics* (London: Methuen, 1977) or Catherine Belsey's *Critical Practice* (London: Methuen, 1980).

[22] Jacques Derrida, *Writing and Difference*, trans. Alan Bass (London: Routledge, 1990), p. 282.

which Scott characterises as an 'extended present'.[23] The conventional sequences of past, present and future are transcended by the increasing presence of technological aids in teaching and learning, such as the video recorder and the internet.

As universities have grown in size and complexity so an academic culture has given place to a managerial one. This has resulted in commercial practices being imported into the universities. Appraisal systems such as the British RAE (Research Assessment Exercise) are designed to make academics more productive while temporary contracts and part time staff save on salaries. Management culture has also had an impact on teaching and assessment methods such as the introduction of distance learning and credit accumulation, both of which weaken the student's relationship to an institution. The tutorial system of Leavis' Cambridge, which made it possible for him to practise criticism as a form of 'creative collaboration', has been supplanted by a whole apparatus which encourages the student to develop skills conforming to what Scott calls the need to demonstrate 'individual enterprise and social application'.[24] Not surprisingly, some writers on management have lately started to appropriate the ideas and terminology of theorists. This illustrates the extent to which criticism endorses the values of commerce as they are brought to bear on the university even as it seeks to oppose them.[25]

[23] Scott, *The Meanings of Mass Higher Education*, p. 157.   [24] *Ibid.*, p. 186.
[25] See e.g. Paul Bate, *Strategies for Cultural Change* (Oxford: Butterworth-Heinemann, 1995).

Psychoanalytic approaches

14
Literary criticism and psychoanalytic positions

RAINER EMIG

Storytelling is the obvious link between psychoanalysis and literature. Sixty years before Jacques Lacan described the unconscious as structured like a language, its method was labelled the 'talking cure' by an early patient.[1] Most psychoanalytic methods produce texts, and most use texts such as dreams, narratives, slips of the tongue, jokes, but also bodily symptoms for their investigations. Freud employs Greek myths (most prominently Oedipus and Narcissus) for his crucial concepts. Jung scrutinises fairy tales and folklore, eastern and western religion, even alchemy. Neither differentiates between stories by actual patients and those inherited by literature and culture. This trend continues into the late twentieth century, as is evident in Lacan's analysis of Edgar Allan Poe's story 'The Purloined Letter'. Eventually, psychoanalytic texts themselves have become objects of analysis, as in the writings of Abraham and Torok, who analyse Freud's analysis of the pathological case study the 'Wolf-Man'.[2]

Text-based in its methods, psychoanalysis shares with literature the poiesis of images and expressions, the poetics of their arrangement, the grammar of narratives, but also a theory of interpretation. The latter frequently abandons the idea of an origin of symptoms (in empirical fact or transcendent metaphysics) and instead refers to other texts, previous traumas or archetypal images and stories that are closely related to myths. Modern literary theory calls this 'intertextuality'. Psychoanalytic theories also refer to their material in literary terms: the poetry of dreams, the drama of ur-scenes, and the narratives that emerge from them. Moreover they have inspired texts in all these genres: from the poetry of Sylvia Plath via Hitchcock's psycho-drama to fiction such as D. M. Thomas' *The White Hotel* and the works of Angela Carter.

---

[1] Sigmund Freud and Joseph Breuer, 'Fräulein Anna O.' (1895), in *Studies on Hysteria*, trans. James Strachey, ed. Angela Richards, *Pelican Freud Library*, 15 vols. (London: Penguin, 1973–85), vol. III, pp. 73–102 (p. 83). All subsequent citations of Freud's works refer to the *Pelican Freud Library* unless otherwise stated. See also Jeffrey Berman, *The Talking Cure: Literary Representations of Psychoanalysis* (New York: New York University Press, 1985).

[2] Nicolas Abraham and Maria Torok, *The Wolf Man's Magic Word: A Cryptonymy*, trans. Nicholas Rand, Theory and History of Literature Series (Minneapolis: University of Minnesota Press, 1986).

The following is an overview of psychoanalytic positions that have influenced literary theories. It will present the seminal texts these positions have produced, but also their own strategies of text production – and ultimately the relation of psychoanalytic positions to textuality itself.

Sigmund Freud (1856–1939) and Freudian positions

Today it is hard to imagine how much Freud's *The Interpretation of Dreams* (1900) must have offended the empiricist and positivist sciences of its time. Although in part based on physiological models of streams and blockages (images that later find a literary equivalent in the modernist 'stream-of-consciousness' technique), it also aligned the emerging discipline with contemporaneous fads, such as spiritualism and mysticism, and openly declared its debt to storytelling and literary analysis. For reasons that have no obvious therapeutic purpose, Freud describes the temporality of dreams and the origins of their 'timeless' quality as *condensation* and *displacement*. The linguist Roman Jakobson picks up on these terms in his essay 'Two Aspects of Language and Two Types of Aphasic Disturbances' (1956) and equates them with metaphor and metonymy.[3] The equation has since become canonical in structural literary analysis. Lionel Trilling pinpointed this intersection as early as 1947, when he claimed that '[t]he Freudian psychology makes poetry indigenous to the very constitution of the mind' and called psychoanalysis 'a science of tropes, of metaphor and its variants, synecdoche and metonymy'.[4] The aesthetic effect of 'timelessness' in turn became another literary ideal and shaped the modernism of W. B. Yeats, Virginia Woolf and James Joyce.

Apart from providing a structural link between the psyche and poetics, Freud's study also outlined a complex model of interpretation. On the one hand, dream interpretation as well as case studies followed the traditional hermeneutic surface–depth model. It assumes that underneath the layer of images or narrative a 'true meaning' can be deciphered. More problematically, reductive readings of Freud introduced, via the soon popularised 'Freudian symbols', an almost exclusive concentration of interpretation on the personal conflicts of the author and a set pattern of libidinal frustrations. Its general shape is outlined in Freud's essay 'Repression' (1915). While the number of Freudian-inspired analyses of literature is now impossible to assess, some texts have become particularly prominent objects, and some readings especially influential. Joseph Conrad's *Heart of Darkness* can accordingly be read as an incestuous Oedipal return to the mother. Poe has already been men-

---

[3] Roman Jakobson, 'Two Aspects of Language and Two Types of Aphasic Disturbance', *Studies on Child Language and Aphasia* (The Hague: Mouton, 1971), pp. 49–73.

[4] Lionel Trilling, 'Freud and Literature', *The Liberal Imagination* (London: Heinemann, 1964), pp. 34–57 (pp. 52–53).

tioned. Henry James, and in particular his short story 'The Turn of the Screw', has attracted many psychoanalytic critics.[5] The most fertile material for a Freudian reading, however, has undoubtedly been Shakespeare's *Hamlet*. A famous early example is Ernest Jones' study *Hamlet and Oedipus* (1949).[6]

In their extreme forms, simplistic applications of Freudian concepts have led to approaches that regard all creative activity as the result of psychological disturbance, a compensation for insufficient or aberrant fulfilment of libidinal urges. Freud's libidinal ideal is genital heterosexual sexuality, while deviations lead to narcicissm, fetishism, homosexuality, etc. He pursues this argument in some of his essays on art and literature, for example his studies of Leonardo da Vinci and Dostoevsky. While Freud is careful not to make pronouncements about an 'essence' of art, he describes the artist as someone who has perfected what is daydreaming for ordinary people. This productive employment of repression is called *sublimation*. It is regarded as the origin of most cultural production.[7]

Yet Freud himself ultimately proved dissatisfied with a simple opposition of 'false' symptoms, images, and stories and their 'true' significance, in which the Oedipal model of the child's anxiety concerning its position towards the parents is dominant. Although the internalised castration complex forms the basis of his early division of the psyche into *unconscious* and *conscious*,[8] already in *The Interpretation of Dreams* the suspicion is voiced that, ultimately, dream content might represent anything. This free flotation of significance is later taken up by poststructuralism. With *transference*, a concept which describes the projection of libidinal impulses from the analysand onto the analyst, Freud introduced a further problem into his project of interpretation.[9] These impulses structure and distort the messages that are produced during the analysis and thus ultimately become analogous to fictional strategies. At the same time, a related distortion occurs on the side of the analyst.

[5] See for example Frederick Crews, *Out of My System: Psychoanalysis, Ideology, and Critical Method* (New York: Oxford University Press, 1975); Marie Bonaparte, *The Life and Works of Edgar Allan Poe: A Psycho-Analytic Interpretation* (1933), trans. John Rodker (London: Imago, 1949); Shoshana Felman, 'Turning the Screw of Interpretation', in Felman (ed.), *Literature and Psychoanalysis: The Question of Reading: Otherwise* (Baltimore: Johns Hopkins University Press, 1982), pp. 94–207.

[6] Ernest Jones, *Hamlet and Oedipus* (New York: Norton, 1976). See also Jacques Lacan, 'Desire and the Interpretation of Desire in *Hamlet*', in Felman (ed.), *Literature and Psychoanalysis*, pp. 11–52.

[7] Sigmund Freud, 'Leonardo da Vinci and a Memory of his Childhood' (1910), and 'Dostoevsky and Parricide' (1927), in *Art and Literature*, trans. James Strachey, ed. Albert Dickson, *Pelican Freud Library*, vol XIV, pp. 143–231, esp. p. 167 and pp. 435–460. See also Sigmund Freud, 'Creative Writers and Day-Dreaming' (1907), in *Art and Literature*, pp. 129–141.

[8] Sigmund Freud, 'The Unconscious' (1915), in *On Metapsychology*, trans. James Strachey, ed. Angela Richards, *Pelican Freud Library*, vol XI, pp. 159–222.

[9] Sigmund Freud, 'Fragment of an Analysis of a Case of Hysteria ("Dora")' (1901), in *Case Histories I: 'Dora' and 'Little Hans'*, trans. James Strachey, ed. Angela Richards, *Pelican Freud Library*, vol. VIII, pp. 29–164 (pp. 157–161).

He or she also has a libidinal investment in the patient and the analytic process, desires that create what Freud calls *counter-transference*. The patient in turn feeds, frustrates and plays with the analyst's desire. Michel Foucault's theories of knowledge and power derive their basic model of the confession partly from Freudian transference.[10] Freud's concept also shares some of its aspects with philosophical hermeneutics, where the desire to uncover a supposed hidden meaning often meets the resistance of texts.[11] Reader-response theory, with its central idea that so-called 'gaps of meaning' provoke analysis in the first place and then continue to structure it, but also the debates concerning the 'death of the author' as a guarantor of meaning and the alternative idea of the involvement of the reader in literary analysis owe crucial impulses to the Freudian model.[12]

Freud abandons the binary model of unconscious and conscious in favour of a tripartite one in 'The Ego and the Id' (1923). In the new model the *id* generates libidinal urges which the *ego* needs to master in order to make the self a stable and social one. Yet all the time, the ego is itself controlled by the *super-ego* or *censor* that represents internalised personal, but also cultural, inhibitions. Freud paves the way for theories that acknowledge individual motivations while placing them within cultural formations and regimes for which the term *discourses* has become common (again mainly through the works of Foucault). Feminist theories, those of gender and sexuality, and, more recently, postcolonial criticism have taken up this model.

What has proved inspirational in the complex tripartite model of super-ego, ego and id is that it acknowledges an ultimate lack of control. It replaces it with a concept of tension and struggle and adds an equally strong element of repetition: while the uncontrollable id remains predictable in its urges, the equally uncontrolled super-ego in fact repeats many familiar personal as well as cultural injunctions. The fact that what appears threatening is at the same time familiar is allegorised in Freud's analysis of the *uncanny* in E. T. A. Hoffmann's tale of 'The Sand-Man', who is an evil figure that haunts the child protagonists, but who also bears a striking resemblance to the ultimate linchpin of familiarity and authority: the father.[13] Later theorists of literature and culture have taken the uncanny to represent more general concepts, such as the inextricable entanglement of the alien with the known, and the

---

[10] See, in particular, Michel Foucault, *The History of Sexuality*, vol. 1: *An Introduction*, trans. Robert Hurley (Harmondsworth: Penguin, 1981).

[11] Hans-Georg Gadamer, *Truth and Method*, 2nd edn., trans. William Glen-Doepel, eds. John Cumming and Garrett Barden (London: Sheed and Ward, 1979).

[12] Wolfgang Iser, *The Act of Reading: A Theory of Aesthetic Response* (London: Routledge and Kegan Paul, 1978); Roland Barthes, 'The Death of the Author', *Image – Music – Text*, trans. and ed. Stephen Heath (London: Fontana/Collins, 1977), pp. 142–148; Michel Foucault, 'What is an Author?', in David Lodge (ed.), *Modern Criticism and Theory: A Reader* (London and New York: Longman, 1988), pp. 196–210.

[13] Sigmund Freud, 'The "Uncanny"' (1919), in *Art and Literature*, pp. 335–376.

related idea that models of normality require an identification of its opposite, not outside it, but as part of its constitution. Sander L. Gilman and Slavoj Žižek are exponents of this critical trend, while, on an abstract philosophical plane, Gilles Deleuze has investigated *Difference and Repetition* (1969).[14]

Freud had in fact already questioned the binary model of the psyche in his essay 'Beyond the Pleasure Principle' (1919–20). In it he posits a radical model of the psyche that no longer rests on stable planes, but involves two mutually exclusive and destructive forces, the *pleasure principle* and the *reality principle* or *death drive*. Deconstruction later employs this conflictual and ultimately self-destructive model to support its own activity of 'reading against the grain' that ultimately rejects the idea of unified meaning altogether. Radical redeployments of the death drive focus on psychoanalytic models themselves in their critique of culture and politics. The most prominent example is Gilles Deleuze and Félix Guattari's *Anti-Oedipus* (1972),[15] a study that attacks the reliance of Freudian psychoanalysis on the capitalist model of the nuclear family. Its radical counter-concept employs the schizophrenic body that imagines itself as transient and self-destructive. Yet even this schizophrenic 'desiring machine' shares with the Freudian subject the feature that is of interest here: in its continual rejection and ejection of itself in terms of symbolic signification, it continually produces text.

Even more recently, theoretical engagements with death as a constitutive element in culture have taken the debate into the sphere of philosophy. Jacques Derrida is the French exponent of this trend in writings such as *The Gift of Death* (1992), while Simon Critchley provides a British counterpart in *Very Little . . . Almost Nothing* (1997).[16] The antagonistic and violent elements in Freud's theories have been reassessed by Leo Bersani, above all in his studies *A Future for Astyanax* (1976) and *The Freudian Body* (1986), where he rereads the Oedipal triangle in relation to art and literature.[17] A similar approach is employed in René Girard's works *Deceit, Desire and the Novel* (1965) and *Violence and the Sacred* (1979).[18]

[14] Sander Gilman, *Difference and Pathology: Stereotypes of Sexuality, Race and Madness* (Ithaca: Cornell University Press, 1985); Slavoj Žižek, *The Sublime Object of Ideology* (London: Verso, 1989); Gilles Deleuze, *Difference and Repetition*, trans. Paul Patton (London: Athlone, 1994).

[15] Gilles Deleuze and Félix Guattari, *Anti-Oedipus: Capitalism and Schizophrenia*, trans. Robert Hurley, Mark Seem and Helen R. Lane (London: Athlone, 1984).

[16] Jacques Derrida, *The Gift of Death*, trans. David Wills (Chicago: Chicago University Press, 1995); Simon Critchley, *Very Little . . . Almost Nothing: Death, Philosophy, Literature*, Warwick Studies in European Philosophy Series (London: Routledge, 1997).

[17] Leo Bersani, *A Future for Astyanax: Character and Desire in Literature* (Boston: Little, Brown & Co., 1976); and *The Freudian Body: Psychoanalysis and Art* (New York: Columbia University Press, 1986).

[18] René Girard, *Deceit, Desire and the Novel: Self and Other in Literary Structure*, trans. Yvonne Freccero (Baltimore: Johns Hopkins University Press, 1965); and *Violence and the Sacred*, trans. Patrick Gregory (Baltimore: Johns Hopkins University Press, 1979).

Carl Gustav Jung (1875–1961) and archetypal criticism

The controversy between Freud and Jung introduced the first major schism in the newly established discipline. While Freud assessed the evolution of the individual in a particular cultural setting, Jung extended his theories to the history of humanity. Both aspire towards universal validity. While Freud's scenarios are consequently based on the family (itself, in its nuclear variety, the product of the nineteenth century), Jung employs anthropological models that seemingly encompass all cultures. Ultimately, both remain troubled by the challenge of historicity. Freud requires a starting point for his libidinal impasses in the conflicts of an imaginary ur-tribe, a scenario that he outlines in *Totem and Taboo*.[19] Jung posits an 'always already' in the shape of an inherited collective set of images, values and meanings that he calls *archetypes*.[20] His pseudo-genetic model of a *collective unconscious* is thus indebted to Darwin's theory of evolution. Neither Freud nor Jung can ultimately answer the question concerning the origin of ur-scenes and archetypes. In order for decisive ur-traumas or the creation of archetypes to occur, a situation is required in which that which is to come about must already exist (in the shape of the dominant father in Freud or an already existing arrangement of archetypes in Jung). Jung's most prominent archetypes are those of *anima* and *animus*, representing feminine and masculine qualities respectively.[21] Archetypes have fascinated many scholars, mainly because (like Freudian symbols) they exist in abundance in cultural and literary artefacts.

While Freud's model is ultimately based on conflict, Jung's upholds harmony as its starting point and ultimate goal. In order to posit an originally harmonious self, Jung separates this self from culture and society. These pollute the pure self through their interference, as do the contradictory impulses of libidinal urges. What helps it find an alternative path that leads neither through social conformity nor rampant egocentrism are the inherited traces of harmony with a universal nature that resurface in archetypal images. Jung calls this struggle 'individuation'.[22] The force that enables the individual to harness these messages is creativity. Like Freud, Jung refuses to define an essence of art, although he also regards artistic creativity as crucial for his ideas. Unlike Freud, however, he refrains from analysing the artist in terms of neuroses, or the work in terms

---

[19] The problematic intersection of Freudian theory and history is discussed in Peter Gay, *Freud for Historians* (New York and Oxford: Oxford University Press, 1985). A recent investigation of the paradoxical basis of Freudian theory is Gerald Siegmund, 'Freud's Myths: Memory, Culture and the Subject', in Michael Bell and Peter Poellner (eds.), *Myth and the Making of Modernity: The Problem of Grounding in Early Twentieth-Century Literature*, Studies in Comparative Literature Series, 16 (Amsterdam and Atlanta: Rodopi, 1998), pp. 197–211.

[20] Carl Gustav Jung, *The Archetypes and the Collective Unconscious* (1934/1954), trans. R. F. C. Hull, ed. Herbert Read, Michael Fordham and Gerhard Adler, *Collected Works*, 20 vols (+ 4 unnumbered vols) (London: Routledge and Kegan Paul, 1959), vol. IX, part 1, p. 6.

[21] Carl Gustav Jung, 'Anima and Animus' (1928), *Two Essays on Analytical Psychology*, *Collected Works*, vol. VII, pp. 186–209.

[22] Jung, 'A Study in the Process of Individuation' (1950), *Archetypes*, pp. 290–354.

of symptoms. Instead, he insists that it be approached as a process from the perspective of aesthetics.[23] Again this means a comparison to a map of archetypal patterns. He insists on their status as symbols and accuses Freud of calling symbols what are mere signs or symptoms – of 'morbid psychic phenomena' rather than higher truths.[24] The tautological character of Jung's procedure becomes evident in claims such as: 're-immersion in the state of *participation mystique* is the secret of artistic creation'.[25]

Jungian concepts resemble the purification rituals of primitive cultures and many religions. They are clearly anti-rational, and indeed often vilify consciousness, contrary to at least early Freudian theories that see it as the safe haven into which libidinal chaos has to be translated. Like Freud, Jung splits human experience into planes, the rational one where archetypes must be recognised in their significance, and the underlying dream-like world in which archetypes are formed. He often describes the latter in terms of formlessness and water.[26] In its 'back to nature' mysticism, Jungian theories have informed important cultural trends of the twentieth century, such as Rudolph Steiner's Anthroposophical movement. They also fascinated writers intent on using primitivism as a critique of modern civilisation, such as D. H. Lawrence (who produced some attempts at a revisionist psychoanalytic theory himself). The seemingly higher spirituality that resulted from the disregard of society and the simultaneous chastising of the libidinous self also appealed to authors such as W. B. Yeats.[27] In the post-war period, many cultural and literary trends associated, for example, with ecological and New Age movements can be shown to have roots in Jungian thought. Most critiques of myth in literature and culture are either indebted to his ideas or, like Barthes' *Mythologies* (1957),[28] disavow an essence of mythologies and their supposedly universal significance in clear opposition to Jung.

The essentialism of Jungian archetypes also resurfaces in some poststructuralist feminist theories. While Camille Paglia rather unsubtly reasserts the anti-cultural force of sexuality (in terms that have long been employed by misogynist positions), even a more complex theorist such as Hélène Cixous with her concepts of 'writing in mother's milk' and fluid femininity harks back to archetypal models.[29]

---

[23] Carl Gustav Jung, 'Psychology and Literature' (1930), *The Spirit in Man, Art, and Literature, Collected Works*, vol. XV, pp. 84–105.

[24] Carl Gustav Jung, 'On the Relation of Analytical Philosophy to Poetry' (1922), *The Spirit in Man*, pp. 63–83 (p. 70).

[25] Jung, 'Psychology and Literature', p. 105.

[26] Jung, *Archetypes*, pp. 21–22.

[27] Compare James Olney, *The Rhizome and the Flower: The Perennial Philosophy – Yeats and Jung* (Berkeley: University of California Press, 1980).

[28] Roland Barthes, *Mythologies*, trans. A. Lavers (London: Paladin, 1973).

[29] Camille Paglia, *Sexual Personae: Art and Decadence from Nefertiti to Emily Dickinson* (New Haven: Yale University Press, 1990); Hélène Cixous, 'Sorties', trans. Ann Liddle, and 'The Laugh of the Medusa', trans. Keith Cohen and Paula Cohen, in Elaine Marks and Isabelle de Courtivron (eds.), *New French Feminisms* (Brighton: Harvester, 1981), pp. 90–98 and 245–264.

Apart from the many vulgar Jungian literary critics that function on a
similar level as the Freudian ones, Northrop Frye provides a more interesting
position with his use of archetypes as part of a structural model of literature.[30] His endeavour to outline ever-recurring patterns in literature, although
motivated by his Catholicism, shares common ground with structural critics
of myth such as Claude Lévi-Strauss. The assumption behind Frye's model,
that there exists a universal experience of nature, is debatable – as is the
implicit assumption that archetypal characters, such as the epic hero or the
quester for meaning and salvation, can be viewed independently, or indeed *a
priori*, of cultural and ideological formations.[31]

Maud Bodkin offers an alternative, but equally problematic use of Jungian
concepts in literary studies. Her *Archetypal Patterns in Poetry* (1934) returns
Jungian models to the individual, in particular the artistic individual, who
finds self-realisation in art with the help of archetypal symbolism. Great art
in turn enables its audience to achieve similar fulfilment through empathic
interpretation.[32] Apart from the obvious intentional fallacy of such a reading,
the conceptual problem is again that recurring cultural images are taken to
represent pre-cultural truths. Yet these 'truths' are only ever realised inside
culture and inform and often strengthen the ideological status quo (especially
in terms of gender and power), even when they are supposed to interrogate it.

Melanie Klein (1882–1960): reassessing the other

Klein's theories have their starting point in the maternal body. Rather than
regarding the mother as the embodiment of castration and, therefore, as a
mere reminder of the father's phallic power, as in Freud, or as the symbol of
archetypal femininity, as in Jung, Klein reassesses the relation of mother and
child from an empirical perspective: the fact that the mother provides protection and emotional stimulus as well as nourishment for the infant.[33] Klein's
move can be seen as a rejection of both masculine views of infantile psychological development and the restricted role allocated to women in the male-
oriented theories of Freud and Jung. Yet Klein refuses to create an idealised
alternative model. The relationship between infant and mother is troubled.
The maternal body is simultaneously the provider and guarantee of all things

---

[30] Northrop Frye, *Anatomy of Criticism: Four Essays* (Princeton: Princeton University Press,
1957).

[31] See Carl Gustav Jung, 'The Origin of the Hero' (1911), in *Symbols of Transformation*,
Collected Works, vol. V, pp. 171–205.

[32] Maud Bodkin, *Archetypal Patterns in Poetry: Psychological Studies of the Imagination*
(London: Oxford University Press, 1934).

[33] Melanie Klein, 'Some Theoretical Conclusions Regarding the Emotional Life of the Infant'
and 'On Observing the Behaviour of Young Infants', in Joan Rivière (ed.), *Developments in
Psycho-Analysis*, International Psycho-Analytical Library, 43 (London: Hogarth Press, 1970),
pp. 198–236 and 237–270.

positive for the infant (a function summed up in the concept of the 'good breast') and the potential source of all frustration (the 'bad breast').[34] The split into ideal and its opposite is not the effect of the law of the father (as in Freud), or of the alienation from a mystical nature (as in Jung), but the result of the actual presence of the mother.

The effect of this ambivalence towards the original source of fulfilment is a first awareness of separateness that becomes the prerequisite of individuation. It confronts the emerging self with a crucial libidinal ambivalence: the combined love and hate for the maternal body. This body is the goal of the infant's first attempts at exerting power, but also the stumbling block that makes the child realise that it is far from omnipotent. But more than merely providing yet another model of the self in competition with those of Freud and Jung, Klein's thinking also encompasses the 'Other', the 'object' in Freud's object cathexes or the obstacle in Jung's quest for harmony. Object-relations remain forever tainted by the ambivalence first experienced with and through the mother: the self remembers its union with her and wishes alternately to be part of her and to make her part of itself. Klein calls the effects of these desires *projection* and *introjection*. Their consequence is the placing of the problematic aspects of the self (its frustrated desires as well as its idolised body) and the desired objects (the mother and those objects that eventually replace her) in an intermediate realm where they are neither subject nor object. Klein calls their status that of 'part-objects'.[35] The self eventually learns to reject and even hate the frustrating Other in what has become known as *abjection*. Abjection links the suppression of desire not with neuroses, as does Freud, but with aggression, an aggression that is always partly directed against the subject itself. This abjection of the same as the alien and the desired as the detested has become an influential model for rethinking binary opposites in literary and cultural criticism.

By identifying the scenes of individuation as pre-linguistic, Kleinian thought has helped to establish what is now known as the distinction between the *semiotic* (the sphere of the unformed unity with the maternal Other) and the *symbolic* (the realm of individuated, if ultimately ungrounded, signification with the self as its central concept). Kleinian psychoanalysis also shares features with the 'transitional objects' that are crucial to the play theory of D. W. Winnicott. There, both role play and the changing investment of self and objects are regarded as central to the development of the self and its relation to its environment.[36] Although play theory had its heyday in the 1970s, its

---

[34] Melanie Klein, 'Notes on Some Schizoid Mechanisms' (1946), in Rivière (ed.), *Developments in Psycho-Analysis*, pp. 292–320 (pp. 297–300).

[35] Klein, 'Notes on Some Schizoid Mechanisms', pp. 298–305. The link between 'part-objects', melancholia and depression is discussed in 'A Contribution to the Psychogenesis of Manic-Depressive States' (1934), in Melanie Klein, *Contributions to Psycho-Analysis 1921–1945*, International Psycho-Analytical Library, 34 (London: Hogarth Press, 1968), pp. 282–310.

[36] D. W. Winnicott, *Playing and Reality* (Harmondsworth: Penguin, 1974).

theoretical legacy can be felt in the continuing vogue for the much earlier writings of Mikhail Bakhtin (whose concepts of the carnivalesque and dialogism
have similarities with Winnicott) and terminologically in the poststructuralist
formula of the play of signification.

Julia Kristeva has based many of her writings, in particular her seminal
Revolution in Poetic Language (1974), on the role of the *abject* in signification. Rather than relating abjection primarily to the body, she traces it as a
constitutive principle in western thought. She demonstrates how Hegelian
dialectic materialism and that of his followers Husserl and Frege, when read
through a Freudian lens, only ever manages to establish a position of being
(and thus a critical vantage point) through negativity. By splitting and rejecting heterogeneous matter from the self, by creating oppositions that is, these
theories achieve positions that Kristeva calls thetic. Yet Kristeva also outlines
that the thetic and its constitutive difference between the symbolic and the
semiotic remains troubled when the *chora*, the undiffentiated babble of language that is an echo of what she calls the maternal semiotic sphere, continues to rupture the symbolic. This is where Kristeva's earlier interest in the
works of Bakhtin and his ideas of dialogism and the carnivalesque come to
the fore and enter a productive allegiance with her linguistic interest in the
materiality of language, its sounds, rhythms and graphic representations, in
what she calls 'semanalysis'.[37] *Desire in Language* (1977) and *Powers of
Horror* (1980) extend the inquiry in a critical reassessment of the Freudian
uncanny (and also, perhaps less obviously, Jung's tales of individuation) in
their literary and cultural manifestations. In turn, Kristeva has been criticised
by feminists for privileging the maternal body as an area that precedes the discursive formations of culture.[38]

Cixous has already been mentioned as another exponent of Jungian
thought. She participates in the rethinking of binaries and even posits a form
of writing that unhinges the semiotic/symbolic distinction in favour of a disrupted style that she identifies as *écriture feminine*. Yet labelling a style essentially feminine and linking it biologistically with the female body are
problematic moves inside a model that wishes to overcome binary opposites.
While attempting to challenge the dominance of the alienated symbolic, *écriture feminine* might ultimately, despite itself, subscribe to a symbolic and
patriarchal concept, even though it has stimulated a number of interesting
feminist readings, especially of modernist literature.

An even more radical revision of Kleinian ideas takes place in the writings
of Luce Irigaray. Trained both as a linguist and a Lacanian psychoanalyst,
Irigaray attempts to liberate the feminine from traditional patriarchal concep-
tualisations which only ever grant women the right to express themselves in

---

[37] Julia Kristeva, *Séméiotiké: recherches pour une sémanalyse* (Paris: Éditions du Seuil, 1969).
[38] See Judith Butler, *Gender Trouble: Feminism and the Subversion of Identity* (London:
Routledge, 1990), pp. 80–81.

masculine terms. In order to develop an alternative to this model, she uses the Kleinian object-relation in a radical way. Rather than subscribing to male-oriented definitions of women and their sexuality in relation to phallic significance and power, she reads women's lack of the phallus as positive rather than as a symbol of deficiency or loss. The female body is, according to Irigaray, characterised by an essential doubling with its evidence in the female genitals. This undoes a unified gender definition: women are therefore, in the terms of the title of one of her books, a 'sex that is not one'.[39] It also enables women to be in constant dialogue with themselves. Like Cixous, Irigaray has been a stimulating force behind re-evaluations of women's writing and radical styles. At the same time, her recourse to biology has provoked accusations of essentialism. Another problem implicit in her theories is that they can be seen to envisage communication between the sexes as mere appropriation, amounting to a rejection of productive dialogue.[40]

Jacques Lacan (1901–81): psyche as text – text as psyche

Lacan's notoriously complex thinking is best approached by its obvious link with literary analysis: his re-readings of Freud through the linguistic theories of Ferdinand de Saussure. For Saussure language is a system of differences without positive terms. The significance of elements is only determined by their relation to other elements.[41] In terms of the psyche, this means a radical farewell to clear positionings of unconscious and conscious, id, ego and superego, but also individual, lifeworld and the sphere of archetypes. It produces a theory of the psyche based on the related processes of identification as misrecognition and desire and its frustration.

Lacan locates the origin of the frustrated desire for identification in the so-called 'Mirror Stage', Lacan's story of the infant's enthusiastic response to its mirror image.[42] According to Lacan, the child observes its detachment (again from the maternal body), the restricted control over its own body, and most crucially its misrepresentation even in the act of recognition (since the mirror

[39] Luce Irigaray, *This Sex Which is Not One*, trans. Catherine Porter with Carolyn Burke (Ithaca: Cornell University Press, 1985); and *Speculum of the Other Woman*, trans. Gillian C. Gill (Ithaca: Cornell University Press, 1985).

[40] Luce Irigaray, *Marine Lover of Friedrich Nietzsche*, trans. Gillian C. Gill (New York: Columbia University Press, 1991), *L'oubli de l'air chez Martin Heidegger* (Paris: Éditions de Minuit, 1983), *Divine Women*, trans. Stephen Muecke (Sidney: Local Consumption, 1986), and *Je, tu, nous: Towards a Culture of Difference*, trans. Alison Martin (New York and London: Routledge, 1993).

[41] Ferdinand de Saussure, *Course in General Linguistics*, eds. Charles Bally and Albert Sechehaye with Albert Riedlinger, trans. Roy Harris (London: Duckworth, 1983).

[42] Jacques Lacan, 'The Mirror Stage as Formative of the Function of the I as Revealed in Psychoanalytic Experience' (1949), *Écrits: A Selection*, trans. Alan Sheridan (London: Tavistock, 1977), pp. 1–7.

reverses and flattens the body). The allegorical scene shows that the incomplete self is forever driven to identify an 'Ideal-I' and forever suffers a distortion of what it aims to define. Yet rather than producing mere frustration, this generates desire as a productive force that in turn continually creates a chain of signification. The product of this lack is text. This Lacanian model bears an affinity to poststructuralist theories of continually ungrounded textuality, a link which has frequently been exploited. Simultaneously, Lacan's insistence on the visual, on the gaze as the constitutive factor in processes of (mis-) recognition has stimulated theories of the visual arts and film.[43]

The reason why signification must forever remain ungrounded and unfinished is expressed by Lacan in a symbolic term that proves his debt to Freud. The 'name of/"no" of the father' (Lacan puns on the French homonyms *nom du père/non du père*) ultimately refers to the 'law' created by the productive withholding of the phallus and its power.[44] In Freud's oedipal theories of castration anxiety and penis envy, the phallus is a real bodily feature: it is the penis that the boy experiences as part of himself, as an emblem of the father's power and as traumatically absent in his mother and sisters. In Lacan the phallus, or *objet grand a*, is a symbolic concept that does not represent a physical organ, but instead acts as the paradoxical foundation of signification: 'it is the signifier intended to designate as a whole the effects of the signified, in that the signifier conditions them by its presence as a signifier'.[45]

The ego, the central concept in Freud's theories of tension and the ideal in Jung's concept of individuation, is consequently a painful delusion for Lacan. His radical attack on Freud's formula 'Where the id was there ego shall be' is its reformulation as a cultural (rather than an individual) imperative in the paradoxical phrase 'it is my duty that I should come into being'.[46] Maud Ellmann reads this rejection of the ideal ego (which is also a rejection of popular 'ego-psychology') as an attack on 'the fiasco of the humanist tradition based on the Socratic dictum – *know thyself*'.[47]

If Lacan's concepts of misrecognition and the absence of unified selves as well as stable meanings are indebted to Freud and blend with poststructural-

---

[43] See Ernst Gombrich, *Art and Illusion: A Study in the Psychology of Pictorial Representation* (London: Phaidon, 1977), trans.; Christian Metz, *Psychoanalysis and Cinema: The Imaginary Signifier* (1977), trans. Celia Britton, Annwyl Williams, Ben Brewster and Alfred Guzetti (London and Basingstoke: Macmillan, 1990); Peter Fuller, *Art and Psychoanalysis* (London: Writers and Readers, 1980); Jacqueline Rose, *Sexuality in the Field of Vision* (London: Verso, 1986); and Laura Mulvey, *Visual and Other Pleasures* (Bloomington: Indiana University Press, 1989).

[44] Jacques Lacan, 'The Function and Field of Speech and Language in Psychoanalysis', *Écrits*, pp. 30–113 (p. 67).

[45] Jacques Lacan, 'The Signification of the Phallus', *Écrits*, pp. 281–291 (p. 285).

[46] Jacques Lacan, 'The Freudian Thing, or the Meaning of the Return to Freud in Psychoanalysis', *Écrits*, pp. 114–145 (pp. 128–129).

[47] 'Introduction', in Maud Ellmann (ed.), *Psychoanalytic Literary Criticism*, Longman Critical Readers Series (London and New York: Longman, 1994), pp. 1–35 (p. 2).

ism in their acceptance of the endless chain of signification, they also contain a problematic near-transcendental concept at their core. Feminists have rightly attacked Lacan's privileging of the phallus.[48] The metaphysical dimensions of Lacan's *objet grand a* and the problematic ontology it posits have also been criticised by Derrida.[49] In Lacan the insight into the continual absence of the phallus produces desire and ultimately text. Yet if this is a liberation of linguistics in Freudian thinking, as Fredric Jameson argues,[50] then it ultimately leads to a further impasse, this time a textual one. It translates lack and desire into a monolithic textuality in which that which is undermined by the absence of *objet grand a* becomes projected onto the many *objects petit a*, the signifers that are the doomed attemps at sense-making. They ultimately derive from the desiring and frustrated gaze of the incomplete subject on to that whose returned gaze it desires.[51] This interpellative concept of subjectivity in turn links Lacan with the ideological theories of the Marxist Louis Althusser who claims that the subject is called into being by the appeal of ideology and its apparatuses.[52]

On an obvious level, Lacan tries to reject both the imaginary and the symbolic order by setting them against what he calls the *Real*. This Real is neither a truth nor an objective empirical reality. Rather it is the ruptures in representation caused by that which remains unrepresentable. Here is a clear link of Lacanian theory with disputes concerning mimesis and realism in literature, all of which are strategies of mastering a reality outside textuality and evidence of ultimate failure. Lacan calls this failed encounter with the real the source of traumas,[53] which quality, however, also predisposes it to be understood as the creative principle in literary theory.

Yet rather than truly identifying the symbolic with failure, Lacan's disavowal (in the absence of the phallus, the negativity of the 'no', the theological uncertainty or taboo of the name of the father) ultimately turns the symbolic into the only significant sphere. This can be detected in Lacan's ingenious use of terms and concepts as place-holders of the lack and also by his

---

[48] See Elizabeth Grosz, *Jacques Lacan: A Feminist Introduction* (London: Routledge, 1990), pp. 50–51; Juliet Mitchell and Jacqueline Rose (eds.), *Feminine Sexuality: Jacques Lacan and the École Freudienne* (London: Macmillan, 1982), pp. 1–57.

[49] Jacques Derrida, *Positions*, trans. Alan Bass (London: Athlone, 1981), pp. 108–109. Lacan's, Derrida's and Barbara Johnson's positions concerning Lacan's seminar on Poe's 'Purloined Letter' are published as *The Purloined Poe: Lacan, Derrida, and Psychoanalytic Reading*, eds. John P. Muller and William J. Richardson (Baltimore: Johns Hopkins University Press, 1988).

[50] Fredric Jameson, 'Imaginary and Symbolic in Lacan: Marxism, Psychoanalytic Criticism, and the Problem of the Subject', in Felman (ed.), *Literature and Psychoanalysis*, pp. 338–395 (pp. 386–387).

[51] Jacques Lacan, 'Of the Gaze as *objet petit a*', in *The Four Fundamental Concepts of Psycho-Analysis*, trans. Alan Sheridan, ed. Jacques-Alain Miller (New York and London: Norton, 1978), pp. 65–119.

[52] Louis Althusser, 'Freud and Lacan', in *Lenin and Philosophy and Other Essays*, trans. Ben Brewster (London: New Left Books, 1971), pp. 88–108.

[53] Lacan, 'Of the Gaze', pp. 69–70.

recourse to the most abstract symbolic notation: algebra.[54] In terms of literature and its relation to psychoanalysis, it divorces the two again and ultimately opts out of an engagement with the psyche altogether and instead focuses entirely on textuality and signification.

While this is not particularly troublesome for poststructuralist literary critics who feel uneasy about the mere notion of referentiality (in the shape of a psyche, for example), it undercuts the implications of the Lacanian project. It takes psychoanalysis out of the dialogue of disciplines and threatens to turn some forms of Lacanian literary criticism into the structuralist maze of texts communicating their mere textuality, or reiterates a related phenomenon, New Criticism's insistence on the text as an ultimately self-sufficient artefact – despite Lacan's insistence on process and open-endedness.[55] Consequently, some followers of Lacan have disentangled their analyses from questions of the self altogether. Catherine Belsey's *Desire: Love Stories in Western Culture* (1994) uses Lacanian terminology less to examine subjectivities, and more to analyse the cultural status of relationships and their failure in 'western culture' (by which she means British and French traditions).[56]

Disremembering psychoanalysis: deconstructive outlooks

While all the above approaches use psychoanalytic concepts to investigate the psyche and its supposed manifestations, equivalences, or distortions in texts, assessments of psychoanalytic writings in terms of their textuality are a relatively recent phenomenon. Shoshana Felman and Geoffrey Hartman have edited collections that paved the way for an emphasis on what had been implicit in psychoanalytic theory and practice all along: their status as textual artefacts. The *Yale French Studies* issues dedicated to *Literature and Psychoanalysis* of 1970 and *Psychoanalysis and the Question of the Text* of 1978 continue to be very influential for the way in which they used styles of writing as an analytic tool with which to address psychoanalysis – and thus partly redressed what was perceived as a weakness of psychoanalytic inquiry concerning literature: its problematic imposition of a split between form and content and its often one-sided attention to the latter.[57] Barbara Johnson's

[54] Jacques Alain-Miller, 'Action de la structure', in *Cahiers pour l'analyse* 9 (Paris: Graphe, 1968), pp. 96–97; quoted in Slavoj Žižek, 'Two Ways to Avoid the Real of Desire', in Ellmann (ed.), *Psychoanalytic Literary Criticism*, pp. 105–127 (p. 111).

[55] For a subtler approach, see James M. Mellard, *Using Lacan, Reading Fiction* (Urbana and Chicago: University of Illinois Press, 1992). An overview of Lacanian positions is Robert Con Davis (ed.), *The Fictional Father: Lacanian Readings of the Text* (Amherst: University of Massachusetts Press, 1981).

[56] Catherine Belsey, *Desire: Love Stories in Western Culture* (Oxford: Blackwell, 1994).

[57] Felman (ed.), *Literature and Psychoanalyis*; Geoffrey Hartman (ed.), *Psychoanalysis and the Question of the Text: Selected Papers from the English Institute, 1976–77* (Baltimore and London: Johns Hopkins University Press, 1978).

The Critical Difference (1980) was a crucial step towards a merger of decon-struction and psychoanalysis via textuality.[58] The most extreme facet of this trend can be examined in Nicolas Abraham and Maria Torok's already men-tioned rereading of Freud's analysis of the 'Wolf-Man' and their concern for his 'magic word'. Their 'cryptonymic' approach is indebted to Derrida's anal-yses of Freudian theory as simultaneous event and problematic truth. In essays such as 'Freud and the Scene of Writing' (1967), 'The Purveyor of Truth' (1975) and 'Psyche: Inventions of the Other'(1987), Derrida has both demonstrated the indebtedness of deconstruction to the psychoanalytic enter-prise and criticised what he perceives as the latter's entanglement in sub-merged ontologies.[59] That he himself has not forgotten Freud can be seen in the slyly entitled essay 'Let Us Not Forget – Psychoanalysis' and, more spec-tacularly, in the resurrection of the uncanny in relation to the apparent failure of socialism in *Specters of Marx*.[60]

As regards the engagement of literary scholarship with psychoanalytic the-ories, the debate was reopened, after what appears in retrospect as a retreat into either structuralist or biographical positions, by the *Psychology and Literature* issue of *New Literary History* in 1980 and eventually the special 1990 edition of *The Oxford Literary Review*.[61] Several collections that appeared during this period and since are listed in the bibliography below. These continuing critical reassessments demonstrate that psychoanalysis has remained a stumbling block and point of contention for literary and cultural theory in the late twentieth century. Yet they also hint at the potential of psychoanalysis to offer a crucial and necessary link between disparate post-structuralist theories. It could act as a reminder of the continual translations and transformations that happen in literary and cultural theories, their implicit and explicit desires, tensions and frustrations. At the same time, by partly forming the object of critical investigation itself, psychoanalysis has avoided an undue harmonisation and homogenisation that might have turned it into the super-theory that it never set out to be.

[58] Barbara Johnson, *The Critical Difference: Essays in the Contemporary Rhetoric of Reading* (Baltimore: Johns Hopkins University Press, 1980).

[59] Jacques Derrida, 'Freud and the Scene of Writing', *Writing and Difference*, trans. Alan Bass (Chicago: University of Chicago Press, 1978); 'The Purveyor of Truth', *Yale French Studies* 52 (1975), pp. 31–113: 'Psyche: Inventions of the Other', trans. Catherine Porter, in *Reading Paul de Man Reading*, eds. Wlad Godzich and Lindsay Waters (Minneapolis: University of Minnesota Press, 1989), pp. 25–65.

[60] Jacques Derrida, 'Let Us Not Forget – Psychoanalysis', *Oxford Literary Review* 12.1–2 (1990), pp. 3–7; and *Specters of Marx: The State of the Debt, The Work of Mourning and the New International*, trans. Peggy Kamuf (New York: Routledge, 1994). See also Peter Buse and Andrew Stott (eds.), *Ghosts: Deconstruction, Psychoanalysis, History* (Basingstoke: Macmillan, 1999).

[61] See the special edition of *New Literary History* 12.1 (1980), *Psychology and Literature: Some Contemporary Directions*; and Nicholas Royle and Ann Wordsworth (eds.), *Psychoanalysis and Literature: New Work*, special edition of *The Oxford Literary Review* 12.1–2 (1990).

Gender and sexuality

15

The history of feminist criticism

CHRISTA KNELLWOLF

The term 'feminism' first emerged in the English language in the 1890s, a significant historical moment when there was an urgent need to name the activities of the women's movement, which was vibrant and popular as never before. Late nineteenth-century feminism joined together women from different classes and social backgrounds. Although the initial enthusiasm was to be dampened and many found their interests ignored by the politics adopted by the leading figures, it achieved the status of a social movement. While more recent feminist criticism warns against understanding 'women' as a homogenous category and emphasises the mistake of eradicating the unique characteristics of different groupings, in the late nineteenth century the emergence of a solidarity across national and class barriers was perceived as so novel that the common factor of being a woman was perceived as outweighing the differences. Among other things, the working conditions of female labourers were so appalling that the primary objective was to strive for some improvement: for instance pregnant women were not infrequently forced to work right up to the delivery of the baby and indeed sometimes gave birth in the factory itself. Like any politically oriented movement, the women's movements which formed in different national settings had to deal with the grossest social injustices of their daily experience; only then could it begin to think about equal rights among its members.[1]

A theoretical engagement with the claims and rights of women concentrated on representation, both in the sense of protesting against political disenfranchisement and challenging the insidious power of literature to propagate views about women's inferiority. This chapter examines the development of feminist criticism in the twentieth century. It begins with a review of early twentieth-century feminism (first-wave feminism) and then provides a detailed account of second-wave feminism, illustrating different critiques of observed instances of women's oppression.

---

[1] For a discussion of socialist indictments of the exploitation particularly of female labourers in the nineteenth century, see Lise Vogel, *Marxism and the Oppression of Women: Toward a Unitary Theory* (New Brunswick, N.J.: Rutgers University Press, 1983), pp. 41–92; see also Sheila Rowbotham, *Hidden From History: 300 Years of Women's Oppression and the Fight Against It* (London: Pluto Press, 1977).

First-wave feminism

The struggle for women's rights was no new phenomenon in the late nineteenth century: countless female writers who have recently been retrieved from a silence imposed by a patriarchally biased historiography testify to a longstanding tradition of protest against women's supposed physical, moral and intellectual inferiority. Women have always protested about the injustice of gender discrimination. In the British context, Mary Astell and Mary Wollstonecraft, eminent voices of the late seventeenth and late eighteenth centuries respectively, produced thorough critiques of the double standards of conventional morality.[2] They are among the most famous, but by no means the first thinkers, to argue that the normative definition of femininity reflects the wish to perpetuate women's dependent position and that the education of girls is abused as a means of teaching them to internalise a sense of their intrinsic inferiority.

While it could draw on previous work by both thinkers and activists, early twentieth-century feminism also contained a new component: it produced theoretical analyses of women's position within society, such as Charlotte Perkins Gilman's *Women and Economics* (1898) or Olive Schreiner's *Woman and Labour* (1911), which were embedded in broad political campaigns for the vote, for the right to own property, for fairer legislation concerning divorce, for equal access to education, culture, the arts, the sciences and the professions.[3] More than just exposing the injustice of women's economic dependence, Olive Schreiner explains the links between gender discrimination and economic oppression, which leads her to demand that women be recognised as equally important producers of social and economic value. Schreiner demonstrates that women possess the skills of writing sociological studies even without formal training in the discipline, thus doubly justifying her claim that women's critique of society and ideology is a valid and necessary innovation. The campaigns of the nineteenth-century women's movements provoked a wide public resonance of feminist ideas in most western countries.[4] The awareness that they could show some significant progress in changing legislation when women finally gained the right to hold property after 1880, encouraged further steps towards the ideal of gender equality. For the activists of this period, equality was the goal. While second-wave feminism after the Second World War appealed to difference as a basis for the formulation of political claims, early twentieth-century activists emphasised same-

---

[2] See Mary Astell, *Political Writings*, ed. Patricia Springborg (Cambridge: Cambridge University Press, 1996) and Mary Wollstonecraft, *A Vindication of the Rights of Woman* (Harmondsworth: Penguin, 1975).

[3] For a collection of women's claims to have their rights recognised, see Miriam Schneir (ed.), *The Vintage Book of Historical Feminism* (London: Vintage, 1996).

[4] See Sheila Rowbotham, *Women in Movement: Feminism and Social Action* (London: Routledge, 1992).

ness: they pursued egalitarian politics so as to ensure the success of their claims for equal legal and political status.

When it adopted the campaign for access to the culturally prestigious professions as one of its most important issues, early twentieth-century feminism had a decisively middle-class and white bent. The argument over women's rights to embark on a professional career reflects the struggle of middle-class women to enter the world of their male social equals and prioritises the political forum as the place to promote their interests. Working women as such were no new phenomenon. Working-class women and women of colour had long been going out of their homes to work as domestic servants. Women had worked on the fields, and ever since factories were built in the early nineteenth century, women formed a significant percentage of the labour force. Towards the end of the nineteenth century, the number of mostly unmarried working-class women who worked outside their homes was rising dramatically. The fact that women significantly outnumbered men in many western countries in the nineteenth century, moreover, heightened indignation that more than half of the population had no civil rights except in so far as they were derived from the rights of male relations. In Britain, certain women (those over thirty who held a certain economic status) were given the vote in 1918 as a reward for women's services during the war; the restricting qualifications were dropped ten years later.[5]

In view of the longstanding attack on the dramatic inequality between the education of boys and girls, it comes as no surprise that Virginia Woolf's classic *A Room of One's Own* (1928) should begin with the famous description of how women are prevented from entering into libraries and universities. She insists that the experience of being excluded from academies and educational institutions, on the one hand, and economic dependence, on the other hand, are instances of how women are systematically demoralised. Woolf relentlessly attacks the poverty of women, showing that even at the moment when women were allowed to hold property, they still had only a small share in the wealth of their respective social class. In spite of her class-based approach to women's economic condition, she shows that it is largely due to economic factors that old stereotypes about women's inferiority are held in place. Woolf made practical proposals concerning the foundation of women's colleges, a women's newspaper and a women's party, she formulated concrete claims about minimum wages and pensions for women, and, as is illustrated in *Three Guineas* (1938), was a committed pacifist who did not care for national honours. Woolf maintains that the female gender is defined as the opposite of what counts as the chief object of interest: masculinity. Her argument that women function as looking glasses which aggrandise male preoccupations with war and the heroic ethos of conventional historiography exposes

[5] Diane Atkinson, *The Suffragettes in Pictures* (Stroud: Sutton Publishing, 1996).

the prevalent devaluation of the experience and preoccupations of female writers. Finally, she posits the existence of a 'woman's sentence' arguing that women register and express experience differently, which thus calls for a revision of the standards used to evaluate women's artistic productions.

Woolf pursued a practical approach to the evaluation of gender roles and expressed herself in a style which subverts the possibility of maintaining firmly defined views – what Toril Moi calls her 'deconstructive form of writing'.[6] By contrast, the second eminently influential thinker for later twentieth-century feminism, Simone de Beauvoir, embarks on a theoretical discussion of the meaning of gender. In her work, _The Second Sex_ (1949), she makes the following famous claim: 'One is not born, but rather becomes, a woman',[7] and draws a careful distinction between sex and gender. Her philosophical enquiry into the premises of definitions of difference explains that the man is taken as the positive norm and woman as the negative, second (in the sense of less important) or deviant which figures as the 'Other'. She points out that the reasons behind the oppression of women are a particular interpretation of reproduction and the wish to control women's fertility, and by no means the biological facts as such. By showing that the factors responsible for gender difference are part of the ideological repertoire of culture and only indirectly evolve from biological factors, she criticises western thought for its biological determinism.

Second-wave feminism

The most important objective of second-wave feminism was a detailed analysis of 'difference' in its daily guise in the public and private spheres. Evocative slogans like 'the personal is political' or 'sisterhood is powerful' served as means to emphasise the gendered rationale underpinning the distinction between supposedly all-important public issues and unimportant domestic matters. When feminists tore down the barrier between private and public, issues such as domestic violence and the sexual abuse of children were brought to light. Rape crisis centres and women's refuges were established. Pornography came under attack for propagating misogynist images and for claiming that women enjoyed the role of the passive victim of male sexual aggression. The fight against violence towards women and struggles for childcare facilities, abortion on demand, protection against sexual harassment and discrimination on the grounds of gender and sexual orientation were prominent on the feminist agenda. Women's liberation tackled the sensitive issue of marital rape and protested against a culture which gives men unimpeded

---

[6] Toril Moi, _Sexual/Textual Politics: Feminist Literary Theory_ (London: Methuen, 1985), p. 9.
[7] Simone de Beauvoir, _The Second Sex_, trans. H. M. Parshley (Harmondsworth: Penguin, 1953), p. 295; the French original version, _Le deuxième sexe_, was published in 1949.

access to women's bodies. The culturally central concept of the 'family' (particularly in the guise of the western nuclear family) came under attack as a barrier to new attempts to conceptualise gender identity. Since these issues were all in some ways dependent on physical difference or rather on how culture used arguments of physical difference to defend its gendered division of labour, it was necessary to show in what ways such supposedly objective criteria of difference were discursively constructed; in what ways biological facts were emphasised by fashion and literary representations and how the disproportionately high value placed on the 'facts' was due to their symbolically central position and not to any biological necessity.

Feminist writers in the sixties and seventies came from various backgrounds: from journalism, the social sciences, linguistics, the media and the arts. Many worked at the margins of the conventionally defined disciplines and through their shared political interest created the sense of interdisciplinarity which still characterises women's studies. The feminist approach to the study of literature pursued several goals: a revisionist engagement with history and literary history, a revision of aesthetic standards and a radical critique of the representation of gender and gender roles as part of a larger critique of cultural self-definition.

On the political front, the sixties were a radical period. Many women were active in socialist movements but found that their claims were openly disregarded and that they were washing the dishes while their male colleagues were discussing radical politics. Being pressurised to return to a type of femininity, which serviced male interests, after they had held responsible positions during the war and feeling disappointed by leftist politics, women felt that they had to join forces. As an attempt to counteract age-old strategies of silencing female interests, women's groups began to spring up in the sixties and seventies. The focus on consciousness raising, one of the chief goals of the time, was a means of gaining distance from externally imposed definitions so that it might be possible to discover an authentic understanding of female experience. Another aim of workshops was to fend off the judgement of women's intrinsic lack of skill at creative and intellectual tasks which was felt to be all the more important because much of the imaginative wealth of women's artistic self-expression remained excluded from main-stream art centres and theatres, and the well established universities were hostile to the politics implicit in such experiments. However, the broad interest in feminist issues created the space for courses specifically designed for women's needs, mostly established in unprestigious institutions like city colleges and some unorthodox new universities.

The question of how culture produces and propagates gender stereotypes was one vital issue on the feminist agenda. Betty Friedan's *The Feminine Mystique* (1963), a work which exposes the socially enforced dependence of women, set the scene for American feminism, while Germaine Greer's *The*

Female Eunuch (1971) was a pioneering work that came out of British feminism. Greer analysed the ways by which cultural conventions and stereotypical modes of thought deprived women of the means of developing their own potentials. Conventional views about women's passive bodies and minds, as her title implies, reduces them to the position of disempowerment. The fact that these works by Friedan and Greer were understandable to a readership without previous knowledge ensured that they almost immediately turned into feminist classics.

Kate Millett's book *Sexual Politics* (1971) takes issue with ways in which representations of gender and sexuality reflect contemporary stereotypes of women's inferiority. When dealing with some of the chief figures of twentieth-century literature, such as Henry Miller, D. H. Lawrence and Norman Mailer, she takes them to task for their celebration of an aggressive type of male sexuality which reduces women to objects for the gratification of brutal instincts. Millett not only reveals the misogyny of culturally privileged literary works but also shows that the reasons for this bias reside in current definitions of literary value.

In their immensely influential book, *The Madwoman in the Attic* (1979), Sandra Gilbert and Susan Gubar explore the difficulties facing women writers of the nineteenth century. More than just struggling against what Harold Bloom calls the 'anxiety of influence',[8] they had to deal with the overt hostilities of their male contemporaries, and even more importantly they had to come to terms with their internalised sense of guilt about breaking the sacred definitions of gender when asserting themselves as independent and mature intellects with a claim to genius. Discussing the characteristics of the female protagonists described in Victorian novels and poetry, they conclude that it is by no means accidental that the writing by women circles around closeted heroines who are either mad or on the brink of madness. The nineteenth century established madness as an inevitable result if women invaded the masculine privilege of writing, and hence it figured as sanction for the intellectually active woman. It comes as no surprise, therefore, that their imaginative work keeps returning to the figure of madness in a self-conscious attempt of the artist to understand and justify her position within culture.

Initially hesitant quests for female writers, painters, artists and informed audiences almost immediately brought to light an unexpectedly large number of names. Books like Dale Spender's *Mothers of the Novel: 100 Good Women Writers Before Jane Austen* (1986) emphatically overturned the previously held assumption that women had never participated in the literary market.[9] The discovery of these many forgotten works required new ways of reading.

[8] Harold Bloom, *The Anxiety of Influence: A Theory of Poetry* (Oxford: Oxford University Press, 1975).
[9] Dale Spender, *Mothers of the Novel: 100 Good Women Writers Before Jane Austen* (London: Pandora, 1986).

Since women had always been the object of a mode of representation that was aimed at a male readership, a feminist reader-response theory, therefore, had to ask how women can deal with a body of literature that is firmly defined by male interests.[10]

Studies such as Patricia Spacks' *The Female Imagination* (1975), Ellen Moers' *Literary Women* (1976), Elaine Showalter's *A Literature of Their Own* (1977) and Mary Ellmann's *Thinking about Women* (1979) are amongst the first of hundreds of critical projects which investigate women's position within literary history. The attempt to understand why all of the female novelists before Jane Austen were erased from cultural memory revealed that the definition of literary value privileged male writers' engagement with warfare or politics over the more domestically centred literary works by female authors. Moreover, as Christine Battersby's incisive study of the cultural meaning of genius demonstrates, the masculine perspective and the gendered view of aesthetic appreciation belonging to it are deeply ingrained in standards of artistic merit.[11] Not only did the search for forgotten female writers turn out to be a study of silences but as the title of Tillie Olsen's autobiographically inspired study of female writers, *Silences*, eloquently expresses it, an engagement with silence, or rather with the systematic suppression of female voices, is a precondition of the career of a writer.

The influence of French feminism

American feminists vigorously denounced Freud, believing in the political power of the women's movement. By contrast, French feminists were strongly involved in the heady political – chiefly Maoist – climate which in 1968 led the intellectuals to proclaim a revolution without sufficient followers. Their inevitable disillusionment, as Toril Moi puts it, made them turn to psychoanalysis as 'an emancipatory theory of the personal and a path to the exploration of the unconscious, both of vital importance to the analysis of the oppression of women in patriarchal society'.[12] The work of the French feminists is characterised by a thorough, intensely sceptical engagement with the theories of Jacques Lacan. Hélène Cixous, Luce Irigaray and Julia Kristeva, to mention the most prominent figures, studied the psychic development of the child, concentrating on the moment when it leaves behind its imaginary unity with the mother and enters into the symbolic order. They were aware that one motive behind Freud's analysis of gender was that of holding back those who

---

[10] Cf. Patrocinio Schweickart, 'Reading Ourselves: Toward a Feminist Theory of Reading', in Robert Con Davis and Ronald Schleifer (eds.), *Contemporary Literary Criticism: Literary and Cultural Studies* (New York: Longman, 1989), pp. 118–141.

[11] Christine Battersby, *Gender and Genius: Towards a Feminist Aesthetics* (London: The Women's Press, 1989).   [12] Moi, *Sexual/Textual Politics*, p. 96.

attempted to break away from conventional definitions of gender roles. Realising that psychoanalysis had figured as a powerful tool to enforce the dictates of patriarchy, they still decided to use it for their purposes. So they consciously took one of the master discourses of patriarchy to study patriarchy and to seek for means to escape from the binary gender division informing its system of reasoning.

Embedding their interventionist projects in a complex discussion of the western philosophical tradition, French feminists sought to find a language and a means of representation suited to women's needs and psychic potentials. They came up with the concept of *écriture féminine*, a peculiarly female mode of expression which is supposed to reflect the physical closeness between infant and mother. Wishing to break away from patriarchal representations and their normative function in the socialisation of boys and girls, they proposed the language of irrationality as a possible subversion of the rigours of logic. Hysteria was hailed as a specifically female transgressive language (most eloquently put forward in Kristeva's thesis, *Revolution in Poetic Language*, 1974). Its chaotic language and pattern of associations became the antidote to literary styles and modes of philosophical reasoning which defined women as inferior to men. When they posited such a female/feminine form of writing (note that the French language does not distinguish between these two adjectives and *féminine* covers the meaning of both), they pointed to the irrationality contained in the discourse of male philosophy. However, by celebrating the opposite of patriarchal rationality as woman's imaginative and intellectual sphere, they alienated many women who felt that this position was a stab in the back to the longstanding struggle to have women's rationality recognised.

Juliet Mitchell was one of the first English-speaking feminists to take on board the liberating potential of French feminism, and Elaine Showalter was one of the prominent figures in American academia to be inspired by the concept of *écriture féminine*. Pursuing the project of revising the literary canon taught at the universities she coined the term 'gynocriticism' which she defines as 'the study of women *as writers*, and its subjects are the history, styles, themes, genres, and structures of writing by women; the psychodynamics of female creativity; the trajectory of the individual or collective female career; and the evolution and laws of a female literary tradition'.[13] Showalter uses the concept of *écriture féminine* as a biologically grounded category, which explains why women conceptualise the experience of their bodies and reproductive functions differently. Building on such an embodied understanding of difference, she posits a gendered literary experience and argues for the necessity of setting up courses designed to study the literary tradition of women writers.

---

[13] Elaine Showalter, 'Feminist Criticism in the Wilderness', in Elaine Showalter (ed.), *The New Feminist Criticism: Essays on Women, Literature and Theory*, (London: Virago, 1985), p. 248.

Countless feminist works showed that the view of women's inferiority is ingrained at the very structural levels of syntax and semantics; in other words, it is expressed both as a part of *what* is said and of *how* it is said. Language enforces gender difference by, for instance, projecting men into the position of linguistic agency and authority and women into the position of objects who cannot go beyond expressing their failure to gain autonomous subjectivity. As Dale Spender points out in her book *Man Made Language* (1980), language is no neutral medium of representation but is systematically shaped to serve male interests. In response to studies of language, numerous projects emerged which sought to change linguistic practices and to remove the sexism in language. Attempts to acknowledge women's contribution to literary and social meaning consequently required that the 'writer' and the 'reader' should no longer be exclusively referred to by the masculine pronoun 'he'.

Critiques and interventions

Misogyny was seen to reside at every level of language: the supposedly unmarked generic term 'man' was indicative of a systematic wish to exclude women and went hand in hand with the argumentative gender bias which Gayle Rubin ('The Traffic in Women', 1975), for instance, discovers in Lévi-Strauss's work on kinship which laid the foundation for the academic discipline of anthropology. Lévi-Strauss concludes that gender roles are rooted in social practices without objecting to the fact that women are reduced to objects in the social relations which come about over and above the exchange of women.

Women's groups, feminist newsletters and journals contributed to the redefinition of some previously derogatory terms for women, such as 'witches', 'crones', 'hags' and 'spinsters'. The positive revaluation of abusive stereotypes went hand in hand with the project of rewriting patriarchy's myths: fairy tales were recognised as insidious instruments through which children were socialised so as to identify with their respective gender roles. In an attempt to intervene in the construction of culturally central stereotypes, writers produced completely rewritten versions of these archetypal narratives. Provocative attempts to reject patriarchal standards and to valorise female power were a creative counterpart to the theoretical analysis of cultural myths. Mary Daly's call for radical separatism (her most widely read book being *Gyn/ecology*, 1978) emphasises women's erotic potential and calls for women to discover their own powers and to celebrate behaviour which had hitherto been classified as transgressive.

Theoretical rejections of hostile views were one side of the story; the other involved concrete attempts to change legislation. Catharine Mackinnon is one of the most prominent American figures who worked on having women's rights statutorily recognised. Together with Andrea Dworkin, she also became famous for daring to take the pornographic industry to court for its dehumanised representation of women.

In order to draw attention to the fact that much feminist work pursued the interests of white women, Audre Lorde wrote an open letter to Mary Daly, criticising her for patronising black women and reducing them to the role of powerless victims in her radical attack on the myths of western culture.[14] Quests for a positive idea of community led Alice Walker, among others, to posit a black aesthetics in which the black woman writer would emerge from the dual silencing due to race and gender.[15] Women of colour and ethnic backgrounds argued that they were subject to renewed oppression because of their inferior position within the women's movement. When Patricia Spacks, Elaine Showalter and others sought to reveal a female tradition, they were nevertheless complicit with the silencing of black women in conventional historiography. As Hazel V. Carby points out, black women's studies, as a movement which challenged the homogenous character of the supposedly disinterested discipline of women's studies, was established to make available a literary tradition which engages with the experience of women from non-western backgrounds, and discusses the fact that their sense of alienation and their fear of urban culture is linked to the much higher statistical likelihood of being raped or subjected to inappropriate medical treatment (such as unnecessary hysterectomies).[16] The collection of essays entitled *This Bridge Called my Back: Writings by Radical Women of Color* (1983) was an outcry against discrimination which also lay the foundation for a vibrant new field of studies.[17]

Sexuality and representation

Studies which built upon Simone de Beauvoir's pioneering claim that sexuality and reproduction were the reasons for women's oppression treated women's fertility both as a symbolic and a material corner stone in a male-dominated society. Feminist critiques, therefore, concentrated on analysing in detail the means used to control it. While some critics like Shulamith Firestone hoped that technological solutions to reproduction would do away with biologically grounded reasons for keeping women in the home, work on health and the medicalisation of the female body (particularly gynecology) recognised that technology subjected women's bodies to more stringent

[14] Audre Lorde, 'An Open Letter to Mary Daly', *Sister Outsider* (Trumansburg, N.Y.: The Crossing Press, 1984), pp. 25–34.
[15] Cf. Alice Walker, *In Search of Our Mothers' Gardens* (London: The Women's Press, 1984).
[16] Hazel Carby, *Reconstructing Womanhood: The Emergence of the Afro-American Woman Novelist* (Oxford: Oxford University Press, 1987), p. 18.
[17] Cherríe Moraga and Gloria Anzaldúa, *This Bridge Called my Back: Writings by Radical Women of Color* (New York: Kitchen Table Press, 1983).

control and was at odds with the ideal of a non-violent, non-intrusive approach to health and sexuality which gave responsibility to women for their physical and mental well-being.[18]

The seventies was an idealistic period, radical and imaginative in its manner of proposing social experiments. In response to the attempt by mainstream feminism to ignore lesbian issues, lesbians became active on the political front. Separatism, however, was not only a lesbian solution but it was also proposed as a practical experience of female bonding and a woman-identified culture; hence as the fastest route towards gender equality. The struggle for gay rights became a prominent issue on the feminist agenda and lesbian criticism spearheaded the women's liberation campaigns in many ways.[19] The critics Charlotte Bunch and Adrienne Rich produced detailed analyses of the educational strategies used to force children to identify with their respective gender roles and to curb any forms of deviance. In her article 'Compulsory Heterosexuality and Lesbian Existence' (1980), Adrienne Rich examines the pressures at work in romance and other forms of cultural propaganda to inscribe the heterosexual norms on the adolescent mind and to obliterate all non-heterosexual desire. What she calls the 'lesbian continuum' offers a revised understanding of female sexuality. She takes as her point of departure the psychoanalytic claim of the infant's original bisexuality. By showing that psychoanalysis erases the initial closeness between mother and child while it overemphasises the significance of a later emotional attachment to the father, she demands that the early experience of the baby's physical and emotional dependence on the mother be recognised as a formative element of adult sexuality. The concept of a 'lesbian continuum' points toward potentially indeterminate sexual preference as a means of emphasising that sexual orientation is culturally constructed. Emphasising that homosexuality is not a deviation from a supposedly natural heterosexual matrix, she calls for a theory of gender which moves away from the binary opposition between man and woman. She demands that it should be possible to conduct an open-minded quest for one's sexual inclination. The search for suppressed historical evidence leads Bonnie Zimmerman to entitle her overview of lesbian criticism: 'What Has Never Been' (1985).

Adrienne Rich's other influential book *Of Woman Born* (1976) studies the relationship between mothers and children to show how women are used to propagate the ideology of their own inferiority in a world of men. When she discusses motherhood as an institution which applies massive sanctions to failures to comply with its norms, she produces an apt analysis of the gender

[18] Donna J. Haraway, *Simians, Cyborgs and Women: The Reinvention of Nature* (London: Free Association Books, 1991), produces a complex critique of technology as a potentially liberatory innovation which is, however, used as a means to exert unlimited control over nature.

[19] Cf. Chris Weedon, *Feminism, Theory and the Politics of Difference* (Oxford: Blackwell, 1999), pp. 51–76.

politics involved in parenting. Many socialist studies of the oppression of women likewise arrived at the conclusion that the function of the family was that of reproducing the gendered ideology of capitalism.[20]

As Olive Schreiner had argued at the beginning of the century, gender and class, or patriarchy and capitalism, were two oppressive systems which were interlocked but which were by no means coextensive. Therefore, attempts were made to emphasise women's role in the capitalist system that suppressed their contribution to the national economy by refusing to assign value to their labour. A feminist revision of the Marxist theory hence argued that women's role in reproducing the labour force be recognised (by means of child-birth and passing on the capitalist values to their offspring). This argument was supported by demonstrations which demanded that housework and child-rearing should receive financial reward. Juliet Mitchell, Sheila Rowbotham, Nancy Hartsock, Heidi Hartmann, Michèle Barrett, Catharine Mackinnon and others, examined the economic subordination of women. They pointed out that women had almost exclusively low-paid part-time jobs in addition to their work inside the home. Within the field of literary criticism, such studies stimulated countless political readings of, above all, the novel.

Perspectives

Towards the late 1970s, consciousness raising proved to be no longer enough, and the witty and provocative but populist and simplifying writings of the pioneers gave way to more complex discussions of gender. So as to justify their struggle to break away from the biologically grounded stereotypes of femininity, most feminists welcomed the idea that gender was socially con-structed. Binary conceptions of gender were deconstructed in a radical cri-tique and replaced by an understanding of gender difference which expressed itself in different subject positions (which were emphatically separated from biological criteria).[21] A consequence of this was that a debate evolved as to whether men could write as feminists, that is to say speak from the feminist position. While a lot of men were very sympathetic to the feminist issues or indeed recognised that the study of gender concerned them as well, the female subject position, of course, cannot be adopted by choice but is the product of the life-long experience of being positioned in the female role. Recognising that gender is constructed as an effect of certain practices, therefore, led critics like Teresa de Lauretis to formulate a theory which centres on the

---

[20] See, for example, Juliet Mitchell, 'Women: The Longest Revolution', *New Left Review* 40 (1966), pp. 1–39.

[21] Works like Judith Butler's *Gender Trouble: Feminism and the Subversion of Identity: Essays on Theory, Film, and Fiction* (New York: Routledge, 1990), which concentrate on these issues, are discussed at length in Diane Elam's chapter in this volume: 'Feminism and Deconstruction'.

necessity of changing the habits and customary practices which reduce women to an inferior position.[22]

When poststructuralism denounced the idea of a metadiscourse, it brought politically inspired critiques of culture and society to a point of crisis. The study of how perceived categories of difference affect women's lives remained the core issue; only the theoretical terminology changed which demanded that the premises be expressed in historically specific and non-essentialist terms. While it was sometimes felt to be hostile to feminist politics, poststructuralism at its best, as Chris Weedon argues, can create a space in which to respond to criticisms concerning class, race and the heterosexual bias of feminism.[23]

My study began with first-wave feminism and ends with the remark that the contemporary situation is characterised by the telling term 'feminisation of the labour market'. Far from referring to a success of lengthy campaigns for genuinely equal opportunities on the basis of sufficient child-care facilities and maternity leave without imminent job loss or a victory over sexual harassment, the term stands for a devaluation of paid work (by men and women) in a situation of dramatically high unemployment in which women hold up to 55 per cent of the jobs. Now that we are facing an increasing powerlessness of the individual *vis-à-vis* large international corporations, it is more than ever important to be aware of the significance of economic factors for views about gender; changes in the economic structure have a dramatic impact on the understanding of gender roles, after all. Workers' rights are being eroded to a point where the working class is itself 'feminised'. While feminism needs to pay attention to the diversity between women world-wide, it also needs to respond to a situation in which fundamentalist governments, for instance, seek to remove women from education or to restrict them to jobs of low esteem. An immediate engagement with such issues may create a new solidarity which enables women to speak out against oppression.

---

[22] See Teresa de Lauretis, *Alice Doesn't: Feminism, Semiotics, Cinema* (Bloomington: Indiana University Press, 1984).

[23] Chris Weedon, *Feminist Practice and Poststructuralist Theory* (Oxford: Blackwell, 1987).

16

Feminism and deconstruction

DIANE ELAM

Feminism and deconstruction have influenced literary criticism by rethinking the terms of sexual difference, politics and ethics. Emphasising indeterminacy, the openness of interpretation and the importance of difference, their alliance has given rise to powerful interrogations of representations of women across a range of literary fields.[1]

While the alliance between feminism and deconstruction is acknowledged by literary criticism, there is not a simple formula for how they work together. Their relationship takes a variety of shapes, partially because feminism and deconstruction continuously redefine one another. The resulting instability produces a fluid relationship, in which neither term is subordinated.

It is important to note, though, that however many shapes it has the potential to take, the alliance between feminism and deconstruction was initially met with scepticism. In what is probably one of the clearest statements he has ever made, Jacques Derrida claimed that 'deconstruction is *certainly* not feminist . . . if there is one thing that it must not come to, it's feminism'.[2] For Derrida, feminism 'is the operation through which a woman desires to be like a man, like a dogmatic philosopher, demanding truth, science, objectivity'.[3] Feminism is therefore accused of eliding difference and judged to be just another form of western metaphysics, pinning its hopes on truth and objectivity.

---

[1] For a more detailed account of the arguments about the relationship between feminism and deconstruction, which are presented in this chapter, see Diane Elam, *Feminism and Deconstruction: ms. en abyme* (London: Routledge, 1994).

[2] Jacques Derrida, 'Deconstruction in America', *Critical Exchange* 17 (Winter 1985), p. 30.

[3] Jacques Derrida, *Spurs: Nietzsche's Styles*, trans. Barbara Harlow (Chicago: University of Chicago Press, 1978), pp. 62–65. Translation modified. While trying to maintain deconstruction's distance from a certain form of feminism, Derrida has, however, also come out in support of women's studies in 'Women in the Beehive: A Seminar with Jacques Derrida', in Alice Jardine and Paul Smith (eds.), *Men in Feminism* (New York: Methuen, 1987), p. 196. For essay collections that reflect specifically on the intersections between Derrida's work and feminism, see Ellen K. Feder and Mary C. Rawlinson (eds.), *Derrida and Feminism: Recasting the Question of Woman* (New York: Routledge, 1997); Nancy Holland (ed.), *Feminist Interpretations of Jacques Derrida* (University Park: Penn State University Press, 1997). For an especially astute deconstruction of Derrida's deconstruction of the figure of woman, see Gayatri Chakravorty Spivak, 'Displacement and the Discourse of Woman', in Mark Krupnick (ed.), *Displacement: Derrida and After* (Bloomington: Indiana University Press, 1987), pp. 169–195.

If Derrida has tried to push feminism away from deconstruction, a number of feminists have also attempted to push deconstruction away from feminism, although for a different set of reasons. Deconstruction is against feminism, according to Denise Riley, because it has 'no political allegiances'.[4] Jane Tompkins worries that deconstruction simply 'subsumes everything in language'; while Margaret Whitford puts it even more strongly when she argues that deconstruction 'attempt[s] to neutralize feminists' because 'the possibility of women's difference has not entered the deconstructive imagination'.[5] In short, the charge levelled on behalf of feminism is that deconstruction does not take sexual difference seriously, reduces the world to language and fails to provide a proper ground for political action.

However, Derrida's portrayal of feminism is now more of a caricature than a fair characterisation; other feminisms are not so easily dismissed in deconstructive terms. And while feminist reservations about deconstruction should be taken seriously, feminism and deconstruction are still able to forge an alliance that confronts questions of sexual difference, examines the relation of language to materiality and gives rise to political action.

The category of women

To begin with, feminism and deconstruction stress that there is no thematic identity to the category 'women'. While there are established notions about what women are and what women can do, the possibility remains that women are an indeterminate category. The question of indeterminacy arises in two ways: first of all, is the definition of the category of women a question of ontology or a question of meaning? If it is a question of ontology, then feminism and deconstruction promise neither to restore nor create the original woman, the natural woman, the whole woman. Appeals to individual experience, rational analysis or transcendental *a priori* knowledge will never be able to describe an essence. The alliance of feminism and deconstruction, therefore, makes us more aware of the infinite possibilities of women: women will never be exhaustively represented, never be brought together under one, undivided concept of 'woman'. Accumulations of representations seem to narrow the options and leave less room for uncertainty only if we forget that there are an infinite number of images of women.

Representation here works in a double register: women will never be defi-

---

[4] Denise Riley, *'Am I that Name?': Feminism and the Category of 'Women' in History* (Minnesota: University of Minnesota Press, 1988).
[5] Jane Tomkins, 'Me and My Shadow', in Linda Kauffman (ed.), *Gender and Theory: Dialogues on Feminist Criticism* (Oxford: Blackwell, 1989), p. 135; Margaret Whitford, *Luce Irigaray: Philosophy in the Feminine* (London: Routledge, 1991), p. 137.

nitely calculable either as object or as subject. This can be a problem for feminism, insofar as feminism has often set as one of its goals women's attainment of the position of the subject. Yet, as Derrida points out, the arrival at such a goal does not guarantee freedom.[6] Subjectivity may seem to offer agency, but women become subjects only when they conform to specified and calculable representations of themselves as subjects.

If the category of women is a question of meaning, however, feminism and deconstruction pose still another challenge. They argue that descriptivist accounts are normative and inadequate; it is not possible to describe the true identity of women, provide a definitive description articulating all possible differences. Attempts to conflate ontology with meaning, to take meaning to be an ontological issue, will not solve this problem either: the category of 'women' would then be useless because there is no corresponding essence.

What deconstruction can do here is provide feminism with more than a simple anti-essentialism. By offering a radical account of meaning as *deferral*, deconstruction suggests that 'women' as a category would be indeterminate in a second way. While 'women' would not be determinable as purely a question of either ontology or meaning, neither would they be determinable *within* the category of meaning because meaning itself is ultimately indeterminate, always subject to deferral.

Sex and gender

Deconstruction's terms of deferral and indeterminacy thus help to articulate the claim that feminism's struggle can perhaps best be understood not simply as a struggle to assert identity but as a struggle to assert difference. And feminism cannot get to the end of that struggle by just being more careful about listing a number of qualifiers every time it mentions women. Women may exist in relation to a complex matrix of differences, but as Judith Butler points out, 'it would be wrong to assume in advance that there is a category of "women" that simply needs to be filled in with various components of race, class, age, ethnicity, and sexuality in order to become complete'.[7] More differences, more meanings, will always remain to be articulated and contested. 'Women' is a permanently contested site of meaning, where meaning is always deferred, ultimately indeterminate.

It could be said, then, that women pose questions *for* feminism as much as they provide the basis *of* feminism. And one such crucial question involves the

[6] Jacques Derrida, 'Sending: On Representation', *Social Research* 49.2 (Summer 1982), p. 317.
[7] Judith Butler, *Gender Trouble: Feminism and the Subversion of Identity* (New York: Routledge, 1990), p. 15.

framework of gender and sex: how do 'women' stand in relation to gender
and sex? A deconstructionist feminist analysis responds by interrogating the
very distinction between sex and gender, suggesting that it is time to rethink
the position that sex is a biological, natural attribute onto which cultural
notions of gender are grafted. Making a crucial move, Joan Scott calls for 'a
genuine historicization and deconstruction of the terms of sexual difference',
shifting the emphasis away from sex so that gender could be 'redefined and
restructured in conjunction with a vision of political and social equality that
includes not only sex but class and race'.[8]

Teresa de Lauretis is even less satisfied with the distinction between sex and
gender. De Lauretis promotes a deconstruction of the sex/gender relationship
so that gender is no longer seen as either an imaginary construct or as unproblematically proceeding from biologically determined sex. She contends that
'gender is not a property of bodies or something originally existent in human
beings'; rather it is a 'product and process of a number of social technologies'
that create a matrix of differences that cross any number of languages as well
as cultures.[9] Significantly, de Lauretis draws the feminist line at this point,
arguing that 'gender marks the limit of deconstruction'.[10] She finds Derrida
guilty of 'displacing the question of gender onto an ahistorical, purely textual
figure of femininity'.[11]

However, feminism's alliance with deconstruction need not be abandoned
here. Butler sees no reason why sex, as natural fact, must precede cultural
inscriptions of gender. It would be more precise to say that sex is the product
of gender, that cultural notions of gender create the very notion that there is
an originary biological sex. As Butler puts it:

It's not that there is some kind of *sex* that exists in hazy biological form that is
somehow *expressed* in the gait, the posture, the gesture; and that some sexuality then
expresses both that apparent gender or that more or less magical sex. If gender is
drag, and if it is an imitation that regularly produces the ideal it attempts to
approximate, then gender is a performance that *produces* the illusion of an inner sex
or essence or psychic gender core . . . In effect, one way that genders get naturalized is
through being constructed as an inner psychic or physical *necessity*.[12]

The relationship between sex and gender is a continuously self-deconstruct-
ing one: it produces structures that are called natural only because we have
forgotten they are structures.

The problem that remains, however, is how it is possible to acknowledge the

---

[8] Joan Wallach Scott, *Gender and the Politics of History* (New York: Columbia University Press, 1988), p. 50.
[9] Teresa de Lauretis, *Technologies of Gender* (Bloomington: Indiana University Press, 1987), p. 3.   [10] *Ibid.*, p. 48.   [11] *Ibid.*, p. 24.
[12] Judith Butler, 'Imitation and Gender Insubordination', in Diana Fuss (ed.), *Inside/Out: Lesbian Theories, Gay Theories* (New York: Routledge, 1991), p. 28.

self-deconstructive nature of the sex/gender relation, while at the same time functioning within the established terms of sexual difference. As Drucilla Cornell reminds us, 'we can't just drop out of gender or sex-roles and pick them up again when we feel like it'.[13] Cornell's solution is that 'we must take off from within sexual difference and not simply pretend to be beyond it'.[14] She contends that one of the important aspects of deconstruction is the move it makes beyond binary or oppositional definitions of sexual differences. This would consist, in Derrida's terms, of recognising 'the multiplicity of sexually marked voices', 'of non-identified sexual marks whose choreography can carry, divide, multiply the body of each "individual"'.[15]

Critics have argued that such a position is hopelessly utopian, but for Cornell it is precisely the utopian quality that is of value for feminism. This is not a utopianism of ideal models (model women, model feminism or model deconstruction), but rather a 'literal' utopianism, a 'no [non-existent] place' (ou topos), that questions existing models of thought. Cornell describes Derrida's writing as 'explicitly utopian in that it evokes an elsewhere to our current system, in which sex is lived within the established "heterosexual" matrix as a rigid gender identity'.[16] This kind of utopian impulse, which is characteristic of the work of deconstructionist feminism, is of such value, according to Cornell, because it 'demands the continual exploration and re-exploration of the possible and yet also the unrepresentable'.[17]

Language, materiality and the body

The radicality of questioning the sex/gender divide leads on to a rethinking of the opposition between language and materiality. Derrida begins this work by attempting to denaturalise the rhetoric of the female body.[18] Concentrating on the hymen and the process of invagination as graphic entities, he argues against assigning any natural or essential femininity to them. The hymen has no proper meaning, belongs to no woman in particular; invagination and the hymen exist outside the discourse of biology. As such, they may mark a space of material difference, but there is no real space of difference to mark. For Derrida, bodies are always discursive, always both inscribed and inscribing.

Luce Irigaray, while not always strictly a deconstructionist thinker, also makes use of morphological language in her search for new linguistic avenues

---

[13] Drucilla Cornell, Beyond Accommodation: Ethical Feminism, Deconstruction, and the Law (New York: Routledge, 1991), p. 182.   [14] Ibid., p. 110.

[15] Jacques Derrida and Christie McDonald, 'Choreographies', Diacritics 12.2 (Summer 1982), p. 76.   [16] Cornell, Beyond Accommodation, p. 19.   [17] Ibid., p. 169.

[18] See Jacques Derrida, 'The Double Session', Dissemination, trans. Barbara Johnson (Chicago: The University of Chicago Press, 1981), pp. 173–286.

that can begin to speak about women's unspeakable pleasure, pleasure that
exists but is not able to be articulated within the terms of patriarchal discourse. For Irigaray, woman is never a sex that is one – singular or divisible
into one. Her pleasures are always multiple, occurring in multiple places on
the body. She is not limited to a single pleasure in a single place on her body;
her pleasures are not even limited to individual bodies with clearly drawn divisions: 'the passage from the inside out, from the outside in, the passage
between us, is limitless. Without end. No knot or loop, no mouth ever stops
our exchanges.'[19] Moving away from hypostatisations of the female body,
Irigaray's use of the rhetoric of biological discourse reconfigures anatomy in
terms which refuse to situate the body as a substance or essence. Irigaray is
effectively 'writing the body', to use Hélène Cixous's phrase, by writing
through and *with* the body rather than simply writing *about* the body.[20]

What becomes evident in both Derrida's and Irigaray's work is that language and materiality always entail one another. Or as Butler puts it, 'language and materiality are never fully identical nor fully different'.[21] Butler
takes the position that 'every effort to refer to materiality takes place through
a signifying process which, in its phenomenality, is always already material . . . Language both is and refers to that which is material, and what is
material never fully escapes from the process by which it is signified.'[22] What
women are, therefore, is not simply a question of language (an abstraction) *or*
a question of matter (raw bodies); they are both at the same time. As a way of
addressing this condition, Butler believes that feminism should turn its attention to the sexual hierarchy implicit in theories of materiality – where traditionally women have been seen to be on the (inferior) side of matter, men on
the (superior) side of form and abstraction – and deconstruct the lan-
guage/materiality binary altogether.[23]

Negotiating the limits of identity politics

By undermining ontological readings of the category of women and providing serious challenges to descriptivist accounts of women's identity, deconstructionist feminism argues that women are a political not a metaphysical
category. In making this move, though, it also questions the terms through
which we understand the political. Since deconstruction has persistently
refused to accept the category of the subject as coherent, self-evident or
natural, a deconstructive account of politics does not ground itself in a

[19] Luce Irigaray, *This Sex Which is Not One*, trans. Catherine Porter (Ithaca: Cornell University
Press, 1985), p. 210.
[20] Hélène Cixous and Catherine Clement, *The Newly Born Woman*, trans. Betsy Wing
(Minneapolis: University of Minnesota Press, 1986).
[21] Judith Butler, *Bodies That Matter: On the Discursive Limits of 'Sex'* (New York: Routledge,
1993), p. 69.   [22] *Ibid.*, p. 68.   [23] *Ibid.*, p. 91.

subject free to make its own decisions. It moves instead to consider what it would mean to do politics without a subject as such.[24]

However, it is this same deconstruction of the subject that has so often incited 'palpable feminist panic', as Wendy Brown puts it.[25] By challenging the sovereignty of the subject, deconstruction also hits at the heart of much feminist activism, with its recourse to identity politics. In its various forms, identity politics has, in the past, had as one of its primary goals that of obtaining an equally valorised definition of subjectivity for women, and to promote this end it has demanded that women join together politically on the basis of what they have in common.

Deconstruction calls attention to the problem that identity conventionally functions as a normative ideal, and when politics takes identity as its foundation it often not only ignores but also tries to erase differences among women. Identity politics tends to fall apart when it tries to account for the fact that not all women are facing the same set of political problems and that difference is more than a series of identity categories: women of colour, lesbians, working-class women and so on.

The alliance of feminism and deconstruction can negotiate the limitations of identity politics and offer possibilities for doing politics differently. Which is not to say that the political will simply be reformulated around difference instead of identity. As Trinh Minh-ha explains, 'difference does not annul identity. It is beyond and alongside identity.'[26] The infinite possibilities of the category of 'women', in Trinh's terms, emerge not only as a differences between women but as differences within women, where difference itself cannot be reduced to the same difference. As Trinh points out, 'Difference not as an irreducible quality but as a drifting apart within "woman" articulates upon the infinity of "woman" as entities of inseparable "I's" and "Not-I's."'[27] The hope, then, would be to affirm political solidarity without losing sight of the difference within and alongside it. As a way to accomplish this, feminism and deconstruction together position the political as the realm of continual negotiation, of ongoing judgement, of indeterminacy.

---

[24] This especially concerns politics based on securing certain fundamental rights for women subjects. Deconstruction reminds rights politics that subjects do not define rights; rights produce subjects who can hold them. Political subjects are thus always provisional. Cornell tries to escape this bind with her proposal for 'equivalent' rather than 'equal' rights for women. See Drucilla Cornell, 'Gender, Sex, and Equivalent Rights', in Judith Butler and Joan W. Scott (eds.), Feminists Theorize the Political (New York: Routledge, 1992), pp. 280–296.

[25] Wendy Brown, States of Injury: Power and Freedom in Late Modernity (Princeton: Princeton University Press, 1995), p. 39.

[26] Trinh Minh-ha, Woman, Native, Other: Writing Postcoloniality and Feminism (Bloomington: Indiana University Press, 1989), p. 104.

[27] Ibid., p. 104. Trinh importantly goes on to point out that 'the idea of two or more illusory separated identities, one ethnic, the other woman (or more precisely female), again partakes in the Euro-American system of dualistic reasoning and its age-old divide and conquer tactics', p. 104.

Groundless solidarity and the search for justice

This understanding of the political as the indeterminate is not about refusing to make decisions: it is about making judgements and taking actions without the assurance of a self-present subject. So when, for instance, Barbara Johnson argues that 'there is politics precisely because there is undecidability', she is not trying to escape action or avoid making judgements. Johnson instead uses this point to explain why, for instance, political action on the abortion question is possible precisely because of the recognition of the place of the undecidable. Her literary readings reveal that 'the question of "when life begins" is complicated partly because of the way in which language blurs the boundary between life and death'.[28] The instability of the legal definition of 'a person' that partially proceeds from this blurring creates a further ontological indeterminacy that drives abortion debates.

Deconstruction would not suggest that a feminist politics could or should pronounce on these matters once and for all, thus removing any question of undecidability from abortion politics. Rather, the political alliance between feminism and deconstruction would be more on the side of the pro-choice movement that relies on a solidarity based on difference, on the possibility of a respect for differences when it comes to a woman's right to choose whether or not she wants an abortion. The pro-choice movement works because of the recognition of difference within the movement itself; it acknowledges that universal laws are not needed to decide whether or not a woman should have an abortion. No two women are in the same position, and their differences make an ethical difference.

To speak in these terms is to define the political not as a discourse of social truth (a practice that aims to establish the truth about society in society) but as a discourse of social justice (a realm of opinion and judgement). The introduction of the ethical here is a way of problematising social responsibility and thinking the question of community without appeal to the truth of identity. For feminism and deconstruction, the ethical marks a necessary margin of undecidability in the question of political organisation. No social form will put an end to the problem of justice. So while deconstructionist feminism may articulate a politics that seeks social justice, it will neither be able nor want to define what counts as a just society, once and for all.

While this may sound to some like a pessimistic proposal on behalf of feminism and deconstruction, it is instead a hopeful acknowledgment that the search for the rule that may do justice to the case – justice to the case of women – is necessarily endless. The politics of deconstructionist feminism does not give rise to consensus, does not seek a political common ground.

---

[28] Cf. Barbara Johnson, 'Apostrophe, Animation, and Abortion', *A World of Difference* (Baltimore and London: The Johns Hopkins University Press, 1987), p. 194.

Rather, there is an endless deferral of consensus, a proliferation of differences, a lack of grounds.

This possibility of a community which is not grounded in the truth of a pre-social identity could be called 'groundless solidarity': solidarity forms the basis, although not the foundation, for political action and ethical responsibility. More precisely, groundless solidarity is a stability but not an absolute one. As Derrida explains, 'to account for a certain stability (by essence always provisional and finite) is precisely not to speak of eternity or of absolute solidity; it is to take into account a historicity, a nonnaturalness, of ethics, of politics, of institutionality, etc. . . . A stability is not an immutability; it is by definition always destabilizable'.[29] Groundless solidarity could thus be understood as a political coalition brought together on the basis of shared ethical commitments at a certain time. It would make no claim to inclusiveness or immutability; it would not suggest that it was in any way natural, arising out of any sense of the true nature of women. Instead, the community of groundless solidarity is open to being destabilised by the difference both within and outside the community, a difference that works even to destabilise any clear separation between individual and community, between self and other. Individuals are not autonomous and only responsible for their own actions; they are caught up in a network of obligations to others, to otherness, that cannot be calculated.

The ethics that results from the groundless solidarity suggested by the alliance between feminism and deconstruction is not derived from first principles, nor does it seek justice as a matter of calculation. There is no meta-language that can negotiate difference. Instead, deconstructionist feminism proposes that ethical judgements are themselves open to judgement: we can never be certain that we have judged justly or committed the right political act – done justice to women or done justice on women's behalf. As Cornell points out, 'we cannot be excused from our role in history because we could not know so as to be reassured that we were "right" in advance'.[30] Faced with uncertainty and contingency, yet required to act politically and pass ethical judgements, feminism and deconstruction form a groundless solidarity in their endless search for justice.

[29] Jacques Derrida, 'Afterword: Toward an Ethic of Discussion', *Limited Inc* (Evanston, Ill.: Northwestern University Press, 1988), p. 151.
[30] Drucilla Cornell, *The Philosophy of the Limit* (New York: Routledge, 1992), p. 169.

17

Gay, lesbian, bisexual, queer and transgender criticism

JOSEPH BRISTOW

The title of this chapter puts in roughly historical order related types of criticism that concentrate on varieties of what might be loosely termed sexual dissidence.[1] All of these labels emerge from dynamic mid- and late twentieth-century struggles to emancipate anti-normative sexual desires and gender identities from legal, medical and moral oppression. The word gay, for example – if traceable to male homosexual parlance of the Victorian era – became a politically charged term around which the short-lived Gay Liberation Front (GLF) of the late 1960s and early 1970s could mobilise demonstrations, festivals and marches that celebrated same-sex desires. Repudiating the clinical and pathological connotations often attached to the category homosexual (in use from at least the 1890s onwards),[2] the GLF upheld gay as an expression of pride in those desires between persons of the same sex that western cultures had for centuries outlawed and punished. In the annals of sexual history, GLF came into its own after the police attempted to raid the Stonewall Inn, a gay bar located in Greenwich Village at New York City, on 27 June 1969. Rather than succumb to police harassment, the Stonewall's customers fought back at the authorities for two nights. Soon referred to simply as Stonewall, this upsurge of militancy immediately provoked – in John D'Emilio's words – 'intense discussion of what many had begun to memorialise as the first gay riot in history'.[3]

Spreading rapidly across the United States, the GLF soon established itself in other western nations such as Australia, Canada and the United Kingdom. This movement derived its political energy from a broad repertoire of socialist

---

[1] The influential term 'sexual dissidence' is usually attributed to Jonathan Dollimore; see his theoretical study of (largely male) homosexual desire and sexual transgression, *Sexual Dissidence: Augustine to Wilde, Freud to Foucault* (Oxford: Clarendon Press, 1991).

[2] Chris White observes that among the various late-nineteenth century terms for same-sex desire – including ones 'derived from classical mythology, or from a carefully "scientific" differentiation of normal and abnormal instincts' – the one to persist 'into modern language' is 'homosexuality'; the word (with its Greek prefix and Latin noun) 'was coined in 1869 by a man named Benkert, who has gone down in history as a Hungarian doctor' but was in fact 'a Swedish campaigner for the rights of those he called "homosexuals"': 'General Introduction', in Chris White (ed.), *Nineteenth-Century Writings on Homosexuality: A Sourcebook* (London: Routledge, 1999), p. 4.

[3] John D'Emilio, *Sexual Politics, Sexual Communities: The Making of a Homosexual Minority in the United States, 1940–1970* (Chicago: University of Chicago Press, 1983), p. 233.

and leftist thought that energised Civil Rights groups, such as the Black Panthers and the Women's Liberation Movement (WLM), in North America. Black politics, with its emphasis on Black pride, helped to shape the GLF's promulgation of gay pride. At this time, many activists involved in the GLF and the WLM were inspired by the writings of the Freudian theorist Herbert Marcuse, who in books such as *Eros and Civilisation* (1956) contested what he saw as the repressive attitudes towards eroticism afflicting modern culture.[4] But as with many radical movements, internal divisions – as well as lack of central organisation – quickly dissipated the GLF's revolutionary fervour. Some critics such as Simon Watney argue that the movement lost direction when its members failed to agree on whether or not sexual emancipation remained subordinate to class struggle.[5] Further tensions resulted from the ways in which lesbians often felt marginalised within what had turned into a male-dominated political alliance. As a result, some women activists found the WLM a more suitable environment in which to pursue a revolutionary politics that championed lesbian desire. Even though the term lesbian had been used from at least the early 1900s (the period when lesbian subcultures began to thrive in cities such as Berlin, London, New York and Paris), the word became deeply politicised in the WLM during the early 1970s: the decade when the celebration of lesbian identity sought to make female homosexuality socially visible. Towards the end of that decade, when the concept of sexual politics influenced social thought, it became increasingly common practice to acknowledge the gender differences within campaigns for homosexual emancipation by referring to lesbian *and* gay liberation, pride and rights.

The political ferment of the GLF and the WLM encouraged lesbian and gay intellectuals to devise critiques of how and why western cultures often violently proscribed same-sex desires. To be sure, much sexological research – originating in innumerable case studies compiled from the mid- to late nineteenth century onwards and taking their statistically most elaborate form in the two Kinsey Reports of 1948 and 1953[6] – threw extensive light on homosexual activities, behaviours and identities. Indeed, some of these investigations by writers such as the German sex radical Magnus Hirschfeld emerged from scientific inquiries whose goal was homophile reform.[7] But the influential

[4] Herbert Marcuse, *Eros and Civilisation: A Philosophical Inquiry into Freud* (London: Routledge and Kegan Paul, 1956).

[5] Simon Watney, 'The Ideology of GLF', in Gay Left Collective (eds.), *Homosexuality* (London: Allison and Busby, 1980).

[6] Alfred C. Kinsey, Wardell B. Pomeroy and Clyde E. Martin, *Sexual Behavior in the Human Male* (Philadelphia: W. B. Saunders, 1948); and Alfred C. Kinsey, Wardell B. Pomeroy, Clyde E. Martin, Paul H. Gebhard, *et al.* (eds.), *Sexual Behavior in the Human Female* (Philadelphia: W. B. Saunders, 1953).

[7] Hirschfeld's position in the German homophile movements has been traced in James D. Steakley, *The Homosexual Emancipation Movement in Germany* (New York: Arno Press, 1975).

classificatory models first devised by theorists like the Austrian sexologist Richard von Krafft-Ebing (who, it should be noted, eventually supported the repeal of Paragraph 175 of the German Penal Code that condemned homosexual acts) set an influential trend that led a large proportion of scientists, medical practitioners and lawyers to treat same-sex desire as an intolerable deviation that threatened the moral fabric of society. GLF-inspired research took a defiant stance against those medical frameworks that categorised homosexuality as a perversion. Although GLF-orientated studies not uncommonly met with hostility in universities and colleges (preventing certain noted scholars from advancing their careers), the 1970s and 1980s nevertheless witnessed an immense number of distinguished essays and monographs that analysed such topics as the history of homophile movements in the west, the existence of homosexual subcultures in earlier periods like the Renaissance, and indeed the medical profession's enduring interest in those individuals classified as sexual perverts. By 1993 this body of material had established itself so firmly in disciplines across the humanities and social sciences that a major publisher issued an imposing volume, titled *The Lesbian and Gay Studies Reader*, featuring some forty-two essays of considerable critical complexity.[8]

But just at the moment when it appeared that lesbian and gay studies had emerged as an academic field in its own right, a younger generation of activists and thinkers contested what they saw as the complacent and exclusionary politics of this newly legitimated area of inquiry. In 1990 Queer Nation arose from the pro-active campaigning of the AIDS Coalition to Unleash Power (ACT UP). In an act of deliberate provocation, this movement reclaimed the word queer – a term that had frequently been used in the past to shame homosexual men and women. They eagerly resignified the meaning of queerness in the face of what they saw as an inert lesbian and gay politics that commonly refused to admit anyone into its ranks who did not subscribe to an inflexible homosexual politics of identity. In its comparatively brief life span, Queer Nation staged imaginative and confrontational political actions to unite all individuals (not just homosexuals) whose stigmatised desires refused to comply with the normative ideals of heterosexuality. Queer, according to Michael Warner in 1993, posed a challenge to all 'regimes of the normal'[9] – a normality defined by the very idea that heterosexuality could and should exist as the only form of erotic intimacy.

In the polemical context of queer thought, two sexual constituencies grew increasingly vocal in their criticism of the ways in which many lesbians and gay men had for at least two decades insisted that homosexual political identities

---

[8] Henry Abelove, Michèle Aina Barale and David M. Halperin (eds.), *The Lesbian and Gay Studies Reader* (New York: Routledge, 1993).
[9] Michael Warner, 'Introduction', in Warner (ed.), *Fear of a Queer Planet: Queer Politics and Social Theory* (Minneapolis: University of Minnesota Press, 1993), p. xxxvi.

provided a privileged site of resistance to an oppressive heterosexual and patri-archal society. Bisexual people articulated serious dissatisfaction with those les-bians and gay men who believed that anyone who professed to experience both same- and other-sex desires remained complicit with heterosexual oppression. By the late 1980s, bisexual thinkers proposed that lesbian and gay politics remained hamstrung by a limited monosexual approach to human intimacy. From this perspective, bisexual thinkers challenged the presiding belief that human sexuality could be understood in stark binary terms (*either* heterosex-ual *or* homosexual). Bisexuality, they claimed, confounded any hard-and-fast opposition between same- and other-sex desire. Concurrently, the expansive term transgender began to circulate widely to define individuals who expressed their desires through a broad – though not interchangeable – ensemble of gender-crossing and gender-effacing practices, including such different phe-nomena as androgyny, transsexuality and transvestism. As the 1990s drew to a close, bisexual theorists and transgender intellectuals had created impressive bodies of research that scrutinised how strict adherence to the paired categories of masculinity and femininity and heterosexuality and homosexuality limited much lesbian and gay thinking when analysing the complex manner in which human beings experienced both gender and eroticism.

Given that critiques of sexuality have diversified so much since Stonewall, it now seems likely that each of the labels listed in the title to this chapter will undergo further transformation – to the point that in the early twenty-first century innovative models for understanding ideas of gender, sex and sexual-ity may radically modify, if not altogether dispense with, them. In the remain-der of this discussion, I explore some of the landmark works of cultural, literary and political criticism that emerged as the terms gay, lesbian, bisex-ual, queer and transgender in turn came to represent significant moments in struggles to liberate dissident sexual communities.

Gay criticism

Dennis Altman's groundbreaking *Homosexual: Liberation and Oppression* (1971) counts among the most zealous critical interventions emerging from the GLF. 'Until very recently', Altman observes, 'homosexuals wrote about themselves in only very personal terms, usually in heavy tones of guilt and self-hatred.'[10] By contrast, he contends that 'human liberation rests on our ability to liberate that part of ourselves, homosexual or heterosexual, that we have repressed. We all need to come out of our particular closets.'[11] Altman accordingly devotes his opening chapter to the political urgency of 'coming

---

[10] Dennis Altman, *Homosexual: Oppression and Liberation*, rev. edn. (London: Allen Lane, 1974), p. 9.   [11] *Ibid.*, p. 13.

out' in public from the private 'closet' where lesbians and gay men have too often hidden their sexual preference from an antagonistic society. Much of his analysis concentrates on a partly autobiographical account of how 'coming out' involves a psychological and social process from 'the discovery that one is predominantly attracted to others of the same sex' to 'the development of a way of dealing with this'.[12] He maintains, however, that 'coming out' proves immensely difficult when, as he describes it, the limited 'gayworld' available to most male homosexuals comprises a somewhat repressive environment of bars and clubs 'providing a pseudo-community, held together largely by sexual barter'.[13] To transcend this dispiriting subculture, Altman advocates gay men's participation in a revolutionary movement committed to raising consciousness about the dignity, pride and self-esteem of homosexuals. A major barrier, however, is oppression – especially internalised self-loathing – that prevents male homosexuals from achieving a fulfilling sexual selfhood. Echoing Marcuse, Altman summarises his viewpoint as follows: 'The oppression of homosexuals is part of the general repression of sexuality, and our liberation can only come about as part of a total revolution in social attitudes.'[14] In conclusion, he speculates on how the GLF will bring about the 'end of the homosexual' – in the sense that a politicised gay identity could ensure that 'the homosexual as we know him or her may indeed disappear'.[15] Though written principally from the perspective of a political theorist, *Homosexual* noticeably develops an interdisciplinary analysis – one that would become familiar in subsequent gay criticism – that draws much of its understanding of the pressures exerted on men who desire intimacy with their own sex from a large number of literary sources. (Altman takes the works of writers such as James Baldwin, Jean Genet, Allen Ginsberg, Christopher Isherwood and John Rechy as key points of reference.)

Where the GLF motivated Altman to envision a future of homosexual emancipation, the movement encouraged Jeffrey Weeks to take research on gay liberation in an opposite historical direction. His ambitious project sought to situate the GLF in relation to the various homophile movements that developed in Britain between the 1870s and the 1970s. The resulting study, *Coming Out* (1977), remains a standard work of reference in the history of sexuality. Weeks frames his account of lesbian and gay attempts to secure legal reform by quoting Altman's influential remark that 'to be a homosexual in our society is to be constantly aware that one bears a stigma'.[16] But even if Altman's significant work shows that 'homosexuality is now a subject that is much discussed', Weeks argues that same-sex desire 'is still apparently little understood'. Indeed, he suggests that 'little effort has been made to understand the homosexual consciousness'. *Coming Out* looks mainly at the various small-scale sexual reform movements to establish 'some more general

---

[12] *Ibid.*, p. 20.   [13] *Ibid.*, p. 42.   [14] *Ibid.*, p. 71.   [15] *Ibid.*, p. 239.   [16] *Ibid.*, p. 14.

comments about the nature of the changing homosexual situation in Britain over the past hundred years'.[17] He prefaces his discussion, however, with concise accounts of how powerful institutions sought to define, regulate and punish same-sex desire. Like practically every part of his book, Weeks' opening chapters provided a platform upon which other scholars could build more specialised investigations into the proscription of male homosexuality in Britain during the nineteenth and twentieth centuries.

Coming Out begins with a survey of the changing legal prohibitions on male same-sex desire, pointing out that although '[l]aw does not create public opinion' it can indeed 'shape and reinforce it'.[18] Weeks carefully traces how the law formally removed the death penalty for buggery in 1861 (though executions for this offence terminated in 1836). Thereafter, his attention turns to the passing of the Labouchere Amendment to the Criminal Law Amendment Act (1885). This amendment – which remained on the statute book until the partial decriminalisation of male homosexuality in 1967 – outlawed acts of 'gross indecency' between males even in private. At the end of three humiliating trials in the spring of 1895, the noted Irish writer Oscar Wilde received the maximum sentence for committing this offence: two years in solitary confinement with hard labour. Weeks discusses how the much-publicised controversy surrounding Wilde's imprisonment formed part of the growing awareness of male homosexuality among influential members of society, notably through the Dublin Castle scandal of 1884 and the Cleveland Street affair of 1889–90. He indicates how and why sexual relations between men drove at the heart of cultural anxieties that arose from a wide range of late-Victorian ideologies, including the social purity crusades, eugenics-orientated debates about 'national efficiency' and the stranglehold that lower middle-class codes of respectability had on attitudes to morality.

Although Weeks' breadth of vision often means that he covers much complex material briefly, *Coming Out* sketches an illuminating picture of how the medical profession often sought to classify and pathologise homosexuality as a form of degenerate perversion. Thereafter, he considers how homosexual subcultures dating from the seventeenth century onward produced definitions of men-loving men. He observes, for example, that Edward Ward's *The Secret History of London Clubs* (1709) 'records the existence of "The Mollies" Club', where a 'curious band of fellows' met in a tavern in the City and held parties and regular gatherings.[19] He notes, too, the development of a subcultural homosexual slang called 'parlare': 'a language for evaluating appearances and mannerisms'.[20] Weeks makes it clear, then, that in the face of fierce hostility male homosexuals none the less devised means of communicating socially and sexually with one another, if mainly in urban settings like

[17] Jeffrey Weeks, *Coming Out: Homosexual Politics in Britain from the Nineteenth Century to the Present*, rev. edn. (London: Quartet, 1990), p. 1.   [18] *Ibid.*, p. 11.
[19] *Ibid.*, p. 36.   [20] *Ibid.*, p. 42.

London. All of this information elucidates the cultural context in which the earliest generation of homophile reformers embarked on the journey whose 'ultimate step' was 'the acceptance of homosexuality as a "way of life"'.[21]

Weeks' exploration of the reform movements in Britain then looks in turn at three pioneering figures – John Addington Symonds, Havelock Ellis and Edward Carpenter – who were among the first to speak out against the British legal ban on male homosexuality. *Coming Out* reveals that the two essays on desire between men written by the critic and poet Symonds for strictly private circulation drew on a variety of discourses to show that male-male eroticism not only had a long and distinguished history but also took a variety of congenital and acquired forms. His comments on Symonds' *A Problem in Greek Ethics* (1883) discloses how this respected Victorian man of letters devised a deeply scholarly analysis of how and why a particular ethics and moral discipline informed intimacy between men in ancient Greek culture. Likewise, Weeks' attention to Symonds' second pamphlet – *A Problem in Modern Ethics* (1894) – explains how the author put emergent sexological ideas about homosexual desire under scrutiny. By taking to task a range of influential criminological, medical and psychological researchers (including Cesare Lombroso and Paul Moreau), Symonds supported – though not without criticism – the views that the German homophile campaigner Karl Heinrich Ulrichs put forward on the various kinds of 'sexual invert' (whose fundamental type could be characterised as *anima muliebris virile corpore inclusa*: a female soul enclosed in a male body). Further, Weeks reveals how the controversial 'Calamus' poems of Walt Whitman inspired a generation of homophile thinkers like Symonds to imagine a modern society in which the American poet's enthusiasm for 'comradeship' took a central role. Carpenter, one of Whitman's greatest English enthusiasts, combined the Whitmanian model of 'comrade love' with his firm belief that homosexual – or, as he preferred to call it, homogenic – attachment formed part of a new evolutionary type that blended masculinity and femininity in new and better ways. In *The Intermediate Sex* (1908), which adapted Ulrichs' models of 'inversion', Carpenter declared: 'I believe it is true that Uranian [i.e. homogenic or homosexual] men are superior to the normal men . . . in respect of their love-feeling.'[22] In the same period as Carpenter theorised the 'intermediate sex', Ellis devised his liberal-minded study – one that drew selectively on Symonds' research – titled *Sexual Inversion* (1897): a sexological work that repudiated the idea that unconventional gender and sexual identities were inferior. Ellis made *Sexual Inversion* the first of seven volumes brought together under the general title *Studies in the Psychology of Sex* (1897–1928) that became some of the most authoritative works of their time.

[21] *Ibid.*, p. 44.
[22] Edward Carpenter, *The Intermediate Sex: A Study of Some Transitional Types of Men and Women*, 4th edn. (London: George Allen and Unwin, 1916), p. 128.

These studies of Symonds, Carpenter and Ellis provide the basis on which Weeks structures his compendious account of the uneven struggles for sexual reform organised by groups such as the British Society for Sex Psychology, whose pamphlets published from 1914 through the 1920s marked important advances in liberal opinion on same-sex eroticism. He shows how Australian sex educator Norman Haire furthered the aims of these early groups in the late 1940s. Weeks' study concludes with three chapters that investigate the cultural and political circumstances that led to the publication of the Wolfenden Report (1957) whose recommendations for removing the 1885 ban on 'gross indecency' would take another decade to pass into law. This extremely well-documented history culminates in an analysis of the GLF during its heady days of activism during 1970–72. Even though Weeks claimed with some disappointment in 1977 that '[t]he historic wave that GLF seemed to promise has not yet surged forward',[23] he could see from the vantage-point of 1990 – when the second edition of *Coming Out* appeared – 'that the real achievement of the gay liberation movement was to stimulate the growth of the lesbian and gay community'.[24] In 1990 he also noted some of the shortcomings of his 1977 study, in particular the small space devoted to lesbian struggles for liberation and his neglect of 'the complex interrelationship between race and sex'.[25]

Eight years after *Coming Out* attracted wide public attention, Eve Kosofsky Sedgwick published *Between Men: English Literature and Male Homosocial Desire* (1985) – an impressive study, based mainly on close readings of nineteenth-century writings, that employed an entirely fresh vocabulary for comprehending the complexities of male-male desire within an apparently heterosexual culture. In the middle of her eloquent book, Sedgwick reveals that her theoretical model owes much to Weeks' formulation that the 'homosexual role' – a term adopted from an innovative 1968 essay by Mary McIntosh[26] – 'has two effects: it first helps to provide a clear-cut threshold between permissible and impermissible behaviour; and secondly, it helps to segregate those labelled as "deviants" from others, and thus contains and limits their behaviour pattern'.[27] Pursuing this line of inquiry, Sedgwick suggests that the 'homosexual role' belongs to 'the larger category of male homosocial desire' that, in intricate ways, consolidates certain social bonds between men while repudiating sexual contact between them. Describing

[23] Weeks, *Coming Out*, p. 206.   [24] *Ibid.*, p. xiii.

[25] *Ibid.*, p. xiv. Emily Hamer's research helps to clarify developments in both lesbian consciousness and critical debates about female homosexuality in modern Britain that Weeks omits from his study; see *Britannia's Glory: A History of Twentieth-Century Lesbians* (London: Cassell, 1996). For a selection of documents that reveal the embedded nature of racial thought in sexological debate, see Lucy Bland and Laura Doan (eds.), *Sexology Uncensored: The Documents of Sexual Science* (Cambridge: Polity Press, 1998), pp. 201–230.

[26] Mary McIntosh, 'The Homosexual Role', *Social Problems* 16 (1968), pp. 182–192.

[27] Weeks, *Coming Out*, pp. 3–4.

'homosocial desire' as 'a kind of oxymoron', she says that this – her own distinctive invention – indicates 'the potential unbrokenness of a continuum between homosocial and homosexual – a continuum whose visibility, for men, in our society, is radically disrupted'.[28] Sedgwick emphasises that her model of a 'continuum' rebuts the idea that homoeroticism lies '"at the root of" other forms of male homosociality'.[29] Instead, her analysis focuses on how western cultures endorse a patriarchal imperative that often encourages men to work in the social interests of other men by subordinating women.

In Sedgwick's view, such homosocial bonding occurs most recognisably in the research of structural anthropologists such as Claude Lévi-Strauss who in the mid-twentieth century investigated the exchange of women through marriage. Drawing on René Girard's famous exploration of 'erotic triangles' in 'the male-centered novelistic tradition of European high culture', Sedgwick suggests that his inquiries show that, even when 'two males are rivals for a female', it is 'the bond between males that he assiduously uncovers'.[30] In her view, such analyses reveal that the ensuing rivalry creates tense forms of 'emulation and identification' between the male suitors – in a variety of sexual and non-sexual manifestations. The upshot of this analysis is to expose how and why male homosocial bonding remains inextricable from types of eroticism that western societies seek to banish through homophobia. In sum, Sedgwick's resourceful theoretical model indicates that the phobic, sexual and social elements structuring relations between men bear a precarious relation to one another.

Lesbian criticism

Lesbian-affirmative critical enquiries into female homosexuality pre-date GLF by more than a decade. In 1956 Jeannette H. Foster – who worked as librarian of the Kinsey Institute from 1948 to 1952 – published *Sex-Variant Women in Literature*, the result of twenty-one years of research whose remarkable bibliographical scope has ensured that the study remains an indispensable resource. Even though the pre-GLF era witnessed important advances in understandings of lesbianism, through community journals such as *The Ladder* (in the United States) and *Sappho* (in the United Kingdom), Foster's immensely scholarly book was the first to show that women classified as 'sex-variant' – a term 'not as yet rigidly defined nor charged with controversial overtones'[31] – maintained an enduring presence in countless literary

---

[28] Eve Kosofsky Sedgwick, *Between Men: English Literature and Male Homosocial Desire* (New York: Columbia University Press, 1985), pp. 1–2.   [29] *Ibid.*, p. 2.

[30] *Ibid.*, p. 21. Sedgwick's analysis refers to René Girard's chapter, 'Triangular Desire', in *Deceit, Desire, and the Novel: Self and Other in Literary Structure*, trans. Yvonne Freccero (Baltimore: The Johns Hopkins University Press, 1966), pp. 1–52.

[31] Jeannette H. Foster, *Sex-Variant Women in Literature*, 3rd edn. (Tallahassee: Naiad Press 1985), p. 11.

writings, all the way from Sappho to Jean-Paul Sartre. Owing to her exceptionally wide reading, Foster's discussion enables readers to see developments
in understandings of lesbianism across a number of European and American
literary traditions, often advancing views either ignored or dismissed in the
literary criticism of her contemporaries. In her detailed chapter titled 'From
the Romantics to the Moderns', for example, Foster traces a pattern of female
homeroticism linking Samuel Taylor Coleridge's 'Christabel' (1816) with
Christina Rossetti's 'Goblin Market' (1862); she boldly claims that the latter
'is generally regarded as variant or even lesbian',[32] a point anticipating feminist analyses of the 1970s. Although Foster often remains cautious in categor-
ising any woman writer as definitively lesbian, midway through her book she
offers a thoughtful 'Conjectural Retrospect' on authors whose lives 'most
readily yield suggestive hints' and whose works 'correlate such hints with corresponding traces' that may further our knowledge of their same-sex
desires.[33] Included in this section are Charlotte Charke, Eleanor Butler and
Sarah Ponsonby ('The Ladies of Llangollen'), George Sand, Michael Field
(Katherine Bradley and Edith Cooper) and Emily Dickinson, all of whom
have been the focus of detailed lesbian criticism produced since the time of the
GLF and the WLM.

The increasingly liberated climate of the 1960s certainly saw the publication of sympathetic accounts of lesbian desire, such as Vera Brittain's important study of the trial of Radclyffe Hall's novel, *The Well of Loneliness*, for
obscene libel in 1928.[34] But it was not until the advent of the GLF and the
WLM before critics devised positive celebrations of lesbian identity, community and creativity. Among the books that presented an unapologetic viewpoint on the need for lesbian liberation is Sidney Abbott and Barbara Love's
Sappho was a Right-On Woman (1972). Opening with a survey of widespread
social hostility to female homosexuality and the resulting feelings of guilt and
shame among many lesbians, they maintain that '[l]ike the schizophrenic, the
Lesbian creates a false self . . . which she interposes between herself and the
world'.[35] They contend that lesbians produce a 'false self' not only because of
the daily need to keep their desires in the closet but also because of what they
see as the distinct limitations to the lesbian subculture that has developed in
many western cities. In particular, they express discontent with the types of
butch and femme sexual identities that lesbians adopt in the bar scene. Such
role-playing, according to Abbott and Love, means that 'the Lesbian will find
it hard to be herself, to know who she is'.[36]

In the following year, Jill Johnston's energetic *Lesbian Nation: The
Feminist Solution* (1973) made equally forthright claims about the gendered

[32] *Ibid.*, p. 75.   [33] *Ibid.*, p. 117.
[34] Vera Brittain, *Radclyffe Hall: A Case of Obscenity?* (London: Femina, 1968).
[35] Sidney Abbott and Barbara Love, *Sappho Was a Right-On Woman: A Liberated View of
Lesbianism* (New York: Stein and Day, 1972), p. 65.   [36] *Ibid.*, p. 40.

styles developed in lesbian subcultures: 'The butch or diesel dyke is a stylistic imitation of the male whose structures she thought she had to transpose in relation to herself to obtain gratification. Likewise the femme.'[37] But in stressing impatience with what she witnessed as a depressing lesbian mimicry of heterosexual norms, she took her analysis a step further to declare that other-sex desires underwrote the oppression of all women:

The man retains the prime organ of invasion. Sexual congress between man and woman is an invasion of the woman, the woman doesn't get anything up to participate in this congress, and although a woman may be conditioned to believe that she enjoys this invasion and may in fact grow to like it if her male partner makes rare sacrifices of consideration in technical know-how, she remains the passive receptive hopeful half of a situation that is unequal from the start.[38]

Johnston's belief that heterosexual intercourse violated women's bodies because it represented the structural inequality between the sexes would be developed in many areas of radical feminist debate, particularly the critiques of rape and pornography produced in the late 1970s and early 1980s by such writers as Susan Brownmiller, Andrea Dworkin and Robin Morgan.[39] Further, Johnston's firm belief that love between women remained the only form of resistance to oppressive heterosexuality led to the formation of political lesbianism: a type of sexual separatism that by the mid-1970s often claimed to stand at the vanguard of feminism. In her memorable study, Johnston asks her readers to entertain a number of possible alternatives to heterosexuality for women. Does the answer, she asks rhetorically, lie in the test-tube baby that would release women from the reproductive function? From her perspective, the answer is no because women must look to other women – not the male medical profession – to achieve autonomy from patriarchy. 'Lesbianism', she contends, 'is the solution'; this is, she adds, 'another way of putting what Ti-Grace Atkinson once described as Feminism being a theory and Lesbianism the practice. When theory and practice come together we'll have a revolution. Until all women are lesbians there will be no political revolution.'[40]

The rise of lesbian-feminism during the 1970s provided a hospitable context in which Lillian Faderman could research her historically wide-ranging volume, *Surpassing the Love of Men* (1981). Covering some of the same ground as Foster's book, Faderman's highly regarded work adopted the

[37] Jill Johnston, *Lesbian Nation: The Feminist Solution* (New York: Simon and Schuster, 1973), p. 176.   [38] *Ibid.*, pp. 165–166.

[39] Susan Brownmiller, *Against Our Will: Men, Women, and Rape* (London: Secker and Warburg, 1975); Andrea Dworkin, *Pornography: Men Possessing Women* (London: Women's Press, 1981); and Robin Morgan, 'Theory and Practice: Pornography and Rape' (1974), *Words of a Woman: Feminist Dispatches, 1968–1992* (New York: W. W. Norton, 1992), pp. 78–89.

[40] Johnston, *Lesbian Nation*, p. 166. For a detailed account of the rise of political lesbianism within the WLM in the United States, see Alice Echols, *Daring to be Bad: Radical Feminism in America, 1967–1975* (Minneapolis: University of Minnesota Press, 1989), pp. 210–241.

concept of 'romantic friendship' – originally an eighteenth-century term that 'signified a relationship that was noble and virtuous in every way'[41] – from an earlier study by Elizabeth Mavor that explored the lives of Butler and Ponsonby, who in 1780 eloped from their wealthy Irish families and settled at Llangollen in north Wales.[42] In Faderman's view, 'romantic friendship' characterised close bonds of attachment that were not always – indeed rarely – eroticised through genital contact. Noting 'the lack of overt sexual expression' in the voluminous writings that she explores, Faderman concludes that 'it is likely that most love relationships between women during previous eras, when females were encouraged to force any sexual drive they might have to remain latent, were less physical than they are in our times'.[43] In the case of Butler and Ponsonby, for example, Faderman observes that 'even had there been a sexual relationship between them, it is doubtful they would have committed a discussion of it to paper'.[44]

Later critics would certainly call into question Faderman's hypothesis about the largely non-erotic but intensely romantic character of love between women who lived before the nineteenth century. In one of the most informed studies of lesbianism in the period from which the term 'romantic friendship' derives, Emma Donoghue remarks that this concept – if historically grounded – has fairly limited uses. Writing in 1993, Donoghue admits that 'Faderman's theory is a useful rebuttal of the mid-twentieth-century assumption that passion between women has always been a matter of a small, sick or sinful minority.'[45] Likewise, she believes that 'Faderman's thesis still helps us to make sense of the many early texts which present female friendship, even its jealousies and embraces, as sexless and innocent.' But from Donoghue's perspective, 'romantic friendship' – with its tendency to desexualise passionate attachments – 'fails to address' such phenomena as 'texts about "tribades" and "Sapphists" masquerading as romantic friends, or texts in which sex between women takes place in a context of female social friendship'. Moreover, 'Faderman's argument that women were only suspected of sexual deviance if, as transvestites, for instance, they were seen to be usurping a male prerogative, does not explain why some women who passed as men were given royal pensions, while some romantic friends were attacked in print.'[46] Instead of making any overarching claim about the diverse materials that she covers in her own book, Donoghue openly declares: 'I have found no simple answer to the question of whether women who loved women were socially acceptable.'[47] In many ways, where Faderman sought to contain passion

---

[41] Lillian Faderman, *Surpassing the Love of Men: Romantic Friendship and Love Between Women from the Renaissance to the Present Day* (New York: William Morrow, 1981), p. 16.

[42] Elizabeth Mavor, *The Ladies of Llangollen: A Study of Romantic Friendship* (London: Michael Joseph, 1971).   [43] Faderman, *Surpassing the Love of Men*, p. 19.

[44] *Ibid.*, p. 123.

[45] Emma Donoghue, *Passions Between Women: British Lesbian Culture, 1668–1801* (London: Scarlet Press, 1993), p. 19.   [46] *Ibid.*, p. 19.   [47] *Ibid.*

between women within a non-erotic identity, Donoghue focuses on how female homosexuality took many different – indeed, uneven and contradictory – forms.

The increasing attention to differences among lesbians became visible in a range of radical writings of the 1980s. Joan Nestle, for example, articulated strong criticisms of lesbian feminists who condemned butch-femme relationships. Looking back on her participation in the lesbian bar culture of the 1950s, Nestle offers this viewpoint: 'butch-femme relationships, as I experienced them, were complex erotic statements, not phony heterosexual replicas. They were filled with a deeply Lesbian language of stance, dress, gesture, loving, courage and autonomy.'[48] In the same decade as Nestle rethought the 'sexual courage' among women-loving women before the advent of the WLM, the voices of sadomasochist (SM) activists posed a challenge to lesbian-feminist disdain for any forms of eroticism involved with seemingly unequal power roles. In 1981, Gayle Rubin asserted that, '[g]iven prevailing ideas of appropriate feminist behavior, S/M appears to be the mirror opposite. It is dark and polarized, extreme and ritualized, and above all, it celebrates difference and power.'[49] In Rubin's opinion, the emergence of a visible lesbian SM subculture meant that 'sex – not just gender, not just homosexuality – has finally been posed as a political question'.[50] Anticipating by almost a decade issues that would become central to queer theory, Rubin declares that '[t]he sexual outlaws – boy-lovers, sadomasochists, prostitutes, trans-people – have an acute perception of the sexual hierarchies in society and how they work'.[51]

During this era, lesbian theorists of colour concentrated on questions of ethnic and racial difference to refocus how intellectuals considered sexual hierarchies. The African-American poet Audre Lorde emerged as one of the most articulate voices addressing what she witnessed as the biases of class, race and sexuality embedded in academic feminism. In her well-known speech titled 'The Master's Tools Will Never Dismantle the Master's House', delivered at the 'Second Sex Conference' at New York City in 1979, Lorde put the spotlight on 'the academic arrogance' that could 'assume any discussion of feminist theory without examining our many differences, and without a significant input from poor women, Black and Third World women, and Lesbians'.[52] Acutely aware of her marginal status at this event, Lorde remarked: 'I stand here as a Black Lesbian feminist, having been invited to comment within the only panel at this conference where the input of Black feminists and lesbians is represented.'

[48] Joan Nestle, 'Butch-Femme Relationships: Sexual Courage in the 1950s', *A Restricted Country: Essays and Short Stories* (London: Sheba, 1988), p. 100.
[49] Gayle Rubin, 'The Leather Menace: Comments on Politics and S/M', in SAMOIS (ed.), *Coming to Power: Writings and Graphics in Lesbian S/M* (Berkeley: SAMOIS, 1981), p. 213.
[50] *Ibid.*, p. 224.   [51] *Ibid.*
[52] Audre Lorde, 'The Master's Tools Will Never Dismantle the Master's House', *Sister Outsider: Essays and Speeches* (Freedom, Calif.: The Crossing Press, 1984), p. 110.

Ten years after Lorde contended that feminists should respect difference by taking a more inclusive approach to the diverse economic, ethnic and geopolitical identities of women, the Chicana lesbian writer Gloria Anzaldúa discussed the work of Mexican philosopher José Vasconcelos to propose a way of thinking about the differences that exist within what she calls '*mestiza*' subjectivity. Inhabiting a linguistic, social and political border zone between Mexico and the United States, the idea of *la mestiza* advances a theory of inclusiveness that results from 'the transfer of the cultural and spiritual values of one group to another'. In other words, *la mestiza* emerges from the interweaving of different cultures, languages and political environments, a process that necessarily involves certain contradictions, tensions and paradoxes. This is how Anzaldúa presents her *mestiza* predicament:

As a *mestiza* I have no country, my homeland cast me out; yet all countries are mine because I am every woman. (As a lesbian I have no race, my own people disclaim me; but I am all races because there is the queer of me in all races.) I am cultureless because, as a feminist, I challenge the collective cultural/religious male derived beliefs of Indo-Hispanics and Anglos; yet I am cultured because I am participating in the creation of yet another culture, a new story to explain the world and our participation in it, a new value system with images and symbols that connect us to each other and the planet.[53]

Excluded in some contexts yet integrated in others, Anzaldúa's *mestiza* consciousness offered a powerful model for thinking about the internal instabilities – as well as the transformational potential – of human subjectivity. Her style of thinking would at points coincide with theoretical debates within bisexual, queer and transgender criticism that began to proliferate in the 1990s.

Bisexual, queer and transgender criticism

Attending to questions of difference within and between sexual identity-formations, the divergent fields of bisexual, queer and transgender criticism in many respects extended and refined the points raised by such thinkers as Nestle, Rubin and Anzaldúa. In a roundtable discussion on bisexuality held in the mid-1990s, Ann Kaloski remarked: 'Like many of us, when I first started to theorize bisexuality there was very little around that related to how I experienced or thought about my sexuality.'[54] But readings in areas of French fem-

---

[53] Gloria Anzaldúa, 'La consciencia de la mestiza: Towards a New Consciousness', in Alma M. García (ed.), *Chicana Feminist Thought: The Basic Historical Writings* (New York: Routledge, 1997). Anzaldúa develops her model *mestiza* consciousness from José Vasconcelos, *La raza cósmica: missión de la raza Ibero-Americana* (Mexico: Aguilar S.A. de Ediciones, 1961).

[54] Ann Kaloski, 'Editors' Roundtable Discussion: The Bisexual Imaginary', in BI ACADEMIC INTERVENTION (ed.), *The Bisexual Imaginary: Representation, Identity and Desire* (London: Cassell, 1997), p. 204.

inist and postmodern feminism, if not directly addressed to bisexuality, enabled Kaloski to imagine 'ways of thinking about the self as a hotch-potch of processes and understandings'. 'I found', she added, 'Anzaldúa's work particularly useful as her thinking is focused around a hybridity which has "real" material consequences.' Kaloski's explorations of female bisexuality certainly stand at considerable distance from Johnston's contention made in 1972: 'Bisexuality for women in the revolution in any case is collaboration with the enemy.'[55] While Kaloski began to seek out theoretical models to conceptualise bisexual desire, experience and identity, Merl Storr contested one of the precepts informing lesbian and gay histories of sexuality – namely, the view 'that sexuality is regulated by a binary opposition between heterosexuality and homosexuality which was either inaugurated or consolidated by . . . sexologists' such as Krafft-Ebing and Ellis in relation to such concepts as inversion.[56] Storr maintained that homosexual critical frameworks mistakenly occlude 'bisexuality both as a historical – indeed, historiographical – concern and as a contemporary issue'.

Like much bisexual thought, queer theory emerged from a sense of considerable unease with the ways in which the GLF and the WLM often claimed that the only alternative to heterosexuality was its polar opposite: homosexuality. Much queer research absorbed the cardinal points made in the introductory volume of French thinker Michel Foucault's *History of Sexuality* (1976) – translated into English in 1978 – that theorised the complex relays of power emerging at the moment when the sexual category *homosexual* produced the idea of 'a personage, a past, a case history, and a childhood, in addition to being a type of life, a life form, and a morphology, with an indiscreet anatomy and possibly a mysterious physiology'.[57] In a study contemporaneous with the rise of queer thought, Sedgwick remarks that she takes as 'axiomatic' Foucault's view of how 'modern Western culture has what it calls sexuality in a more and more distinctively privileged relation to our most prized constructs of individual identity, truth, and knowledge'.[58] Foucault suggested that, prior to the time that sexology classified persons according to object-choice, societies generally understood same-sex intimacy in relation to acts and behaviours. Such a being was defined 'less by a type of sexual relations than by a certain quality of sexuality or sensibility', thus making the 'homosexual' an identifiable 'species'.[59] His introductory essay on the history of sexuality proposes a theory of how discursive regimes have consolidated what his followers would later call identitarian understandings of sexuality. Focusing on the

[55] Johnston, *Lesbian Nation*, pp. 179–180.
[56] Merl Storr, 'The Sexual Reproduction of "Race": Bisexuality, History and Racialization', in BI ACADEMIC INTERVENTION, *The Bisexual Imaginary*, p. 74.
[57] Michel Foucault, *The History of Sexuality*, vol. 1: *An Introduction*, trans. Robert Hurley (London: Allen Lane, 1979), p. 43.
[58] Eve Kosofsky Sedgwick, *Epistemology of the Closet* (Hemel Hempstead: Harvester Wheatsheaf, 1991), p. 5.   [59] Foucault, *The History of Sexuality*, vol. 1, p. 43.

social power exerted by the ways in which institutions created sexual identities through particular taxonomies, Foucault's singular critical approach had a strong impact on the work of several thinkers who became associated with the reconceptualisation of the term queer and its anti-essentialist mode of inquiry.

Drawing on different strands of poststructuralist thinking (including Derridean grammatology and Lacanian psychoanalysis), Judith Butler advanced an ambitious view of how western societies produced and perpetuated ideas of gender, sex and sexuality. Her mainly philosophical exploration frequently integrated Foucauldian insights into her analysis of the ways in which modern culture tended to use sexual categories as if they were natural, rather than socially constructed. She pointed out, for example, that an 'identity-sign' such as lesbian possessed no essential content but remained instead a signifier that operated within a field of contestatory representation. In an essay dating from 1991, Butler explained how the idea that she might go to a conference to 'be a lesbian' may at first sound frivolous but in fact involved forms of significatory play that, in complex ways, constituted what 'being lesbian' might mean:

To say that I 'play' at being one [a lesbian] is not to say that I am not one 'really'; rather, how and where I play at being one is the way in which that 'being' gets established, instituted, circulated, and confirmed. This is not a performance from which I can take radical distance, for this is deep-seated play, psychically entrenched play, *and this 'I' does not play its lesbianism as a role*. Rather, it is through the repeated play of this sexuality that the 'I' is insistently reconstituted as a lesbian 'I'; paradoxically, it is precisely the *repetition* of that play that establishes the *instability* of the very category that it constitutes.[60]

Instead of assuming that a lesbian essence must strive to come out publicly intact, Butler argued that the *performance* of that sexual identity must, through contextually variable structures of repetition, seek to constitute what it means to be lesbian. Like poststructuralist thinkers following the work of Ferdinand de Saussure, Butler stated that there is no *a priori* bond between a word and its meaning. For this reason, she proved highly responsive to French writer Monique Wittig's attention to the ways in which key components of discourse produced the ideological belief that other-sex desire remains utterly natural. In one of her brief but incisive essays from the 1980s, Wittig stated: 'The category of sex is the political category that founds society as heterosexual . . . The category of sex is the one that rules as "natural" the relation that is at the base of (heterosexual) society and through which half of the population, women, are "heterosexualized" . . . and submitted to a heterosexual economy.'[61] Concurring with Simone de Beauvoir's famous remark – 'One is

---

[60] Judith Butler, 'Imitation and Gender Insubordination', in Diana Fuss (ed.), *Inside/Out: Lesbian Theories, Gay Theories* (New York: Routledge, 1991), p. 18.
[61] Monique Wittig, 'The Category of Sex', *The Straight Mind and Other Essays* (Hemel Hempstead: Harvester Wheatsheaf, 1992), p. 5.

not born but becomes a woman' – Wittig proclaimed that 'Lesbian is the only concept I know which is beyond the categories of sex (woman and man), because the designated subject (lesbian) is *not* a woman, either economically, or politically, or ideologically.'[62] In many ways, Wittig put greater pressure than any other theorist on the idea that discourse creates 'sex'. Her viewpoint certainly coincided with the tenor of Butler's contention that 'compulsory heterosexual identities, those ontologically consolidated phantasms of "man" and "woman", are theatrically produced effects that posture as grounds, origins, the normative measure of the real'.[63] Together, Butler's and Wittig's lines of thinking prompted intellectuals to consider in greater depth how sexual identities emerged from sometimes unpredictable processes involving many different types of representation – linguistic, somatic, visual.

The queer emphasis on representational play, discursive construction, and differential instability contributed to debates about postmodernism: a large field of inquiry that preoccupied theorists during the 1980s. More than a decade later, an incipient transgender studies interrogated some of the commonplace postmodern axioms of queer thought abstracted from writings such as Butler's that advanced the view that the body existed as a somatic surface upon which meanings of gender remained in a state of significatory ambivalence. In 1998 Jay Prosser's sustained and thought-provoking transgender analysis of queer-orientated research opened by questioning the terms on which Butler derived influential ideas such as 'gender performance': the concept most commonly associated with Butler's acclaimed study, *Gender Trouble* (1990). According to Butler, 'gender performance' involved the representational production of gender upon a bodily surface. In other words, this structure of gendered representation could be seen as a metaphorical type of theatrical performance. To clarify the performative structure of gender, Butler concluded her 1990 study by drawing on the example of gay male drag; she declared: '*[i]n imitating gender, drag implicitly reveals the imitative structure of gender itself – as well as its contingency*'.[64] Her memorable formulation, which noticeably featured a cross-gendered practice, suggested that gender always remained within a domain of performative irresolution that defied any notion of authenticity. Prosser's valuable critique of Butler's work argued that various forms of transsexual experience present 'the limit case for queer studies', since transsexuality demands attention, not to performative play, but to precisely those kinds of bodily 'literality and referentiality' that queer thinking has sought to expose as essentialist and thus conceptually naive.[65]

[62] Wittig, 'One Is Not Born a Woman', *The Straight Mind*, p. 20; Wittig is quoting Simone de Beauvoir, *The Second Sex*, trans. H. M. Parshley (Harmondsworth: Penguin, 1953), p. 295.
[63] Butler, 'Imitation and Gender Insubordination', p. 21.
[64] Judith Butler, *Gender Trouble: Feminism and the Subversion of Identity* (New York: Routledge, 1990), p. 137.
[65] Jay Prosser, *Second Skins: The Body Narratives of Transsexuality* (New York: Columbia University Press, 1998), p. 58.

Prosser's research encouraged critics to respect that living in the 'wrong body' – an experience that can motivate transgender people to progress first to hormone therapy and then to surgical reassignment to the other sex – required a revised understanding of how Freud developed his theory of 'bodily ego' in 'The Ego and the Id' (1923). Taking his cue from psychoanalytic theorists such as Didier Anzieu, Prosser insisted that the skin remains 'a psychic/somatic interface': 'a locale for the physical experience of body image and surface upon which is projected the psychic representation of the body'.[66] Such reasoning contrasted sharply with the kind of gender 'literality' that lesbian-feminist critic Janice G. Raymond advanced in *The Transsexual Empire* (1979), where she stated that 'a society that produces sex-role stereotyping functions as a primary cause of transsexualism'. From Raymond's perspective, transsexuality resulted from a limited understanding of the supposed sexual antithesis of masculinity and femininity. As a consequence, she asserted that the desire to transition from one sex to another can only reinforce 'the fabric by which a sexist society is held together'.[67] Raymond thus concluded that in no respect could transsexuality be understood as a subversion of gender categories. Prosser's supple argumentation indicated that sexual identity was neither a form of natal embodiment central to much lesbian-feminist thought of the 1970s nor a type of significatory imitation celebrated by queer theory of the early 1990s. Further, he pointed out that historians of sexuality have often been misguided in assuming that sexological concepts such as inversion were largely or exclusively connected with homosexuality when in fact they may be more accurately understood within a transgender framework. Building on Prosser's valuable historical and theoretical intervention, transgender studies will doubtless continue to further our reassessment of the insights that have advanced the critical vision of each phase of gay, lesbian and queer criticism that I have outlined here.

[66] *Ibid.*, p. 72. Prosser's inquiries into the Freudian 'bodily ego' are informed by Didier Anzieu, *The Skin Ego: A Psychoanalytic Approach to Self*, trans. Chris Turner (New Haven: Yale University Press, 1989).

[67] Janice G. Raymond, *The Transsexual Empire* (London: Women's Press, 1980), pp. xviii–xix.

Colonialism, post-coloniality, nation and race

18

Post-colonial theory

FIRDOUS AZIM

Post-colonial theory or post-colonialism can be said to have been inaugurated with the publication of Edward Said's *Orientalism* in 1978. This seminal work heralded a revolution in the field of literary studies. It shows how no form of intellectual or cultural activity is innocent of power hierarchies, highlighting the collusion between literary representation and colonial power. *Orientalism* demonstrates how every branch of knowledge, scientific as well as that broadly denoted 'the humanities', is not merely tinged with, but part and parcel of, the establishment of European political hegemony through the process of colonial conquest and domination. However, it is the stress on the literary text that has marked out and at the same time circumscribed, the field of post-colonial studies.

In the two decades since the publication of *Orientalism*, post-colonialism has developed into a sprawling academic discipline. Its purview has expanded and in its examination of the power/knowledge nexus, post-colonialism has ranged over a wide variety of subjects, including the history of colonial conquests, of anti-colonial struggles, the exigencies of post-colonial nation formations and the politics of cultural domination. In geographical terms, it covers the whole world, examining the cultural ramifications of political and economic domination. Historically, it had begun by looking at post-colonial periods, *after* the process of colonisation had started, that is from the eighteenth and nineteenth centuries, and thus was part of the deconstructive questioning of the European Enlightenment. More recently, post-colonial scholars have begun to delve further back in time and, in a healthy partnership with new historicism, are now examining the process of Renaissance self-fashioning, as it pertains to travel and the 'discovery' of 'new lands'.

A theory or a field of study that encompasses the broad range that has been outlined above naturally runs into problems, and post-colonialism itself is a deeply contested discipline. Both within academia and certainly outside it, there is profound doubt and distrust about post-colonial theory, so that, twenty years on, scholars in the field are frequently faced with the problems of how to define post-colonialism; of understanding how it can be seen as different from the fields that it separates itself from, and in once-colonised countries, of assessing its usefulness in understanding social formations and struggles. There is a real obligation on the post-colonial scholar, whether within or outside academia, to answer these questions. As a theory that sets out to examine the power/knowledge nexus, and the processes of intellectual and cultural domination, it must address itself to the issues as they arise in the 'real' world and work towards eradicating some of these inequalities. In this way, it is akin to feminism, where a constant effort has been made to link feminist literary academic theory with feminist activism, to engage in a form of intellectual activity where the two feed into each other.

Post-colonial subjects

Orientalism had concentrated on literary representations and on the ways that the exigencies of colonial rule had led to an exoticised representation of other cultures (of the Middle East, in Said's example). A limitation of that work is that it pictures the colonised as mute and passive, and the coloniser as victorious and ubiquitous. Later post-colonial theorists sought to redress this balance. The theoretical interventions of Homi Bhabha, for example, look at colonisation as a process of subject formation. Bhabha examines various aspects of this process, using Lacan's concept of the mirror image where coloniser and colonised are seen to be locked in a dialectical relationship. In Bhabha's formulation the old binaries – master/slave, coloniser/colonised or European/other – are broken down and a new 'hybrid' identity is seen to emerge. Thus:

the image of the post-Enlightenment man is tethered to, not confronted by, his dark reflection, the shadow of colonised man, that splits his presence, distorts his outline, breaches his boundaries, repeats his action at a distance, disturbs and divides the very time of his being.[1]

A straightforward supremacist position is belied, as the dark reflection does not only position Black (other) races in a condition of Otherness, but also draws both subjects together into the ambivalence and the fear/desire oscillation of the Lacanian mirror-image.

Bhabha's description of post-colonial subject formation thus draws both coloniser and colonised into a close relationship, and deconstructs the binaries that Said's earlier study had exemplified. The subjects of colonial domination – the colonised – are now allowed chinks in the colonial armour through which they can speak or be seen. The new colonial subjectivity that emerges then becomes a strange amalgam – a hybrid, born out of mimicry of colonial forms. The effect of this is that power positions do not remain well-defined any longer, but are rendered ambivalent within the colonial encounter.

It is this notion of ambivalence, and specially the ambivalence of power, that is perhaps the most striking aspect of Bhabha's contribution to the field

[1] Homi Bhabha, *The Location of Culture* (London: Routledge, 1994), p. 44.

of post-colonial theory. In another essay, 'Signs Taken for Wonders', Bhabha emblematises the moment of the reception of the western book as the trope for western cultural domination. This essay examines in detail the notion of the hybrid subject and the subversive nature of colonial mimicry. The western book, in the new colonial sphere, undergoes variant readings, and in the very moment of its reception or acceptance is transformed into new, even unrecognisable forms, which in turn change and render ambivalent the subject-positions of both coloniser and colonised. In Bhabha's words, 'the colonial presence is always ambivalent, split between its appearance as original and authoritative and its articulation as repetition and difference . . . Such a display of difference produces a mode of authority that is *agonistic* (rather than antagonistic).'[2] It is within this ambivalence – these interstices (to use Bhabha's term) – that the potential for change and transformation lies.

Bhaba sees these interstitial spaces, where interaction between the various subject-positions occurs, as sites of negotiation. Liberated from the constraints of a binary chimera, the post-colonial subject is now seen to occupy a space which is *'neither the one nor the other'*, but a new space of translation which results in the heterogeneous hybrid subject.[3] This notion of hybridity, and the diffusion of power, while moving away from the stereotype of passive colonial subjectivity in *Orientalism*, does not satisfactorily account for the rise of colonial resistance. Moreover, it occludes what many have seen as the violence and brutality that marked the colonial enterprise, processes that have necessarily played a crucial role in the formation of colonial subjectivities.

Another very influential way of looking at postcolonial subject formations is that adopted by Subaltern Studies, a school of thought represented by Indian historians. In *Writings in South Asian History and Society*, Ranajit Guha institutes a break with the elite focus of Indian historiography in order to examine the history of Indian nation-formation through the eyes of subaltern groups. The new historical method being proposed here brings in the category of 'the people' and shows that conventional historical writing 'fails to acknowledge, far less interpret, the contributions made by the people *on their own*, that is, *independently of the elite*, to the making and development of this [i.e. Indian] nationalism'.[4]

This focus changes the binary structure of the coloniser/colonised into a situation in which diverse subject positions constitute once-colonised societies. Guha's introduction to the project states that subaltern studies will examine post-colonial nations and societies for the ruptures and fissures *within* them. Notions of ambivalence are not altogether eschewed, insofar as the elite and the subaltern are seen to be locked in a binary relationship, where

[2] *Ibid.*, pp. 107, 108; emphasis added.   [3] *Ibid.*, p. 25; emphasis in the original.
[4] Ranajit Guha, 'On Some Aspects of the Historiography of Colonial India', in Ranajit Guha (ed.), *Subaltern Studies*, Vol.1: *Writings in South Asian History and Society* (New Delhi: Oxford University Press, 1982), p. 3; emphases in the original.

accounts of the one cannot ignore the role of the other. So even while insisting on the 'autonomous domain' occupied by the subaltern, Guha's introduction goes on to state that there were inevitable points of contact between them.[5] 'Contact', 'overlap' and a 'braiding together' of elite and subaltern politics are mentioned, but the main aim is the study of hitherto uninterpreted and unresearched areas of national history. The elite and the subaltern are defined in terms of each other, as well as in their relation to the colonial power. Even in framing this dichotomy, Guha divides the elite into the 'national' and the 'local' elite, and comments on the shifting nature of this division, such that local elites may well be subaltern in a wider or a different context. The ambivalence and ambiguity involved in such subject positioning cannot be overlooked even in this account.

Though the subaltern studies project had not originally emerged as an intervention in the field of post-colonial theory, it is important to examine the notions of colonial subject-positioning that it draws out. Its rereading and rewriting of the history of the Indian nation-state brings into view the idea of a heterogeneous, or at least a bifurcated, colonial terrain, and focuses on the hierarchies of power among colonised peoples.

Gayatri Spivak, reading the subaltern studies project 'from within but against the grain', asks the crucial question 'Can the Subaltern Speak?' in her essay of that title, first published in 1988. Spivak's engagement with and reading of the subaltern project also finds expression in the essay 'Subaltern Studies: Deconstructing Historiography'.[6] The kind of subjectivity that the subaltern school describes shows that 'subaltern consciousness is subject to the cathexis of the elite, that it is never fully recoverable, that it is always askew from its received signifiers, indeed that it is effaced even as it is disclosed, that it is irreducibly discursive'.[7] Spivak's translations and readings of two of Mahasweta Devi's short stories, contained in the same volume, may be seen as her way of dealing with the subaltern consciousness through fictional representation. Many of these stories deal with tribal insurgencies in Bengal and Bihar, and the utter failure of mainstream Indian administration to deal with them. Spivak's translations are indeed beautifully rendered, drawing out the nuances of language use that mark the heterogeneity of linguistic cultures in once-colonised societies.

Spivak's essay on the possibility of deciphering the voice of the subaltern takes us back to the question of representation, and to the nature of the voices that can be heard from under the weight of cultural and political domination. This essay also adds to the rich on-going discussion on sati.[8] Examining the

---

[5] *Ibid.*, p. 6.
[6] Gayatri Spivak, *In Other Worlds: Essays in Culture and Politics* (London: Methuen, 1987), pp. 197–221.   [7] *Ibid.*, p. 203.
[8] Sati, or the custom of widow-immolation, has been a much-debated topic. See Lata Mani, 'Contentious Traditions: The Debate on Sati in Colonial India', in K. Sangari and S. Vaid (eds.), *Recasting Women: Essays in Colonial History* (New Delhi: Kali for Women, 1989); also Gayatri Spivak 'Can the Subaltern Speak?', in L. Chrisman and P. Williams (eds.), *Colonial*

various discussions of the scriptures and Hindu law that were circulated between Brahmin pundits and the British administration, Spivak is unable to decipher the voice of the sati or the woman burning on her husband's funeral pyre. It is as though 'Between patriarchy and imperialism, subject-constitution and object-formation, the figure of the woman disappears, not into a pristine nothingness, but into a violent shuttling which is the displaced figuration of the "third-world woman" caught between tradition and modernization.'[9] Spivak considers the project of 'recovering' the voice of the subaltern as one that is doomed to failure. However, she does not dismiss the project altogether but posits a new strategy – what she terms the 'strategic use of a positive essentialism' – as regards the recovery of the subaltern consciousness.[10] The project of looking at subaltern actions and histories needs to go on, but it is now the task of the intellectual to stand in and speak on behalf of this irrecoverable voice of the subaltern. Thus: 'The subaltern cannot speak. There is no virtue in global laundry lists with "woman" as a pious item. Representation has not withered away. The female intellectual as intellectual has a circumscribed task which she must not disown with a flourish.'[11]

Spivak's engagement with the post-colonial project is also important for the ways that it draws in the figure of the woman as the silenced other of colonialism. In an essay written in 1985, 'Three Women's Texts and a Critique of Imperialism', Spivak reads three novels by women, Mary Shelley's *Frankenstein*, Charlotte Brontë's *Jane Eyre* and Jean Rhys' *Wide Sargasso Sea*.[12] She refuses to read the last novel, as has usually been done, as a recounting of *Jane Eyre* from the standpoint of the other or colonised woman. Antoinette/Bertha Mason, a white creole, cannot be seen as a representative of the colonised races. The other woman of the colonised races is figured as the black servant, Christophine, who is shown to be 'tangential to the narrative' and completely effaced under the processes of colonialism and patriarchy. Benita Parry engages with Spivak in a lively debate regarding the figure of the other woman and its status within narrative discourse.[13] This debate emblematises many of the differences within post-colonial theory about the formation of colonial subjectivity and the practice of bringing to light the discourse of the colonised subject. *Orientalism* had highlighted the erotic dimensions of colonial conquest, where conquered lands were depicted as passive women waiting to be ravished. Spivak takes the analysis further to

---

Discourse and Post-Colonial Theory: A Reader (London: Harvester Wheatsheaf, 1993); and Rajeswari Rajan, *Real and Imagined Women* (London: Routledge, 1993).
[9] Spivak, 'Can the Subaltern Speak?', p. 102.
[10] For a detailed discussion of this term, see Gayatri Spivak, *Outside in the Teaching Machine* (London: Routledge, 1993), pp. 1–24. [11] Spivak, 'Can the Subaltern Speak?', p. 104.
[12] Gayatri Spivak, 'Three Women's Texts and a Critique of Imperialism', *Critical Inquiry* 12.1 (1985), pp. 243–261.
[13] Benita Parry, 'Problems in Current Theories of Colonial Discourse', *Oxford Literary Review* 9 (1987), pp. 27–58.

show that colonial domination renders the woman/subaltern mute, making it impossible to decipher her voice except in a tangential and masked manner.

Bhabha and Spivak, from their very different theoretical positions, have been most influential in shaping theories of post-colonial subject formation and, together with Said, have drawn out the main contours of this very eclectic field of study, amalgamating as it does discourse analysis, deconstruction and psychoanalysis. Its very broad range has been a source of strength, but has also made post-colonialism a highly uneven terrain, and the post-colonial critic is always placed in a position where his/her theoretical and political moorings are in question.

Bhabha's theories of post-colonial subject formation are themselves indebted to the work of Frantz Fanon. In fact, Bhabha first spelt out his theory of a hybrid colonial subjectivity in a preface to Fanon's *Black Skin, White Masks* in 1986. In the above text, as well as in other books such as *The Wretched of the Earth* (first published in 1961), Fanon had looked at concepts of national culture, trying to refocus attention from a wide pan-Africanist view of negritude to the particularities of the nation and the history of its anti-colonial struggles.

The concept of negritude gained currency as part of an intellectual artistic movement and provided impetus to anti-colonial movements in West Africa in the 1950s. It found its most famous delineation in the works of Leopold Senghor who called it the 'sum of the cultural values of the black world'.[14] Conceptually it can perhaps be said to occupy a position opposite to that of the subaltern studies group. Against the subaltern idea of the fragmented indigenous or colonised field, the concept of negritude signifies a pan-African spirit, where all black peoples are seen as culturally unified. It is a powerful expression of cultural pride, where all things African are seen in opposition to the European, and which celebrates the African way 'of speaking, singing and dancing, of painting and sculpturing, and even of laughing and crying'.[15] The concept of negritude has also influenced African Americans and Afro-Caribbeans in their search for a cultural identity.

However, not all African thinkers found themselves in agreement with this view. Opposed to the notion of pan-Africanism, Fanon concentrates on the growth and development of a national culture which grows out of an engagement with the colonial presence. This engagement is at times oppositional, and at others collusive. In the three-part division that Fanon ascribes to the growth of national culture in *The Wretched of the Earth*, the concept of negritude can be seen to apply to the second, where the colonised subjects place themselves in polar and deliberate opposition to the colonial culture. 'National' culture, however, would differ in different parts of the African world itself, and definitely in different 'Negro' worlds, and would emerge out of the processes of national struggle against the forces of colonisation.

[14] Leopold Senghor, 'Negritude: A Humanism of the Twentieth Century', in Chrisman and Williams (eds.), *Colonial Discourse and Post-Colonial Theory*, p. 28.   [15] *Ibid.*, pp. 27–28.

Post-colonial theories can thus be seen to occupy a vast and fraught arena, using many tools and occupying very different positions in their delineation of colonised cultures, and in their examination of the relationship between coloniser and colonised.

Post-colonial theory and post-colonial studies

If post-colonial theory is too wide-ranging and amorphous, it is even more difficult to define and fix the object or the scope of post-colonial studies. As an academic discipline, what does post-colonialism study? Given its origins in literary studies, post-colonialism has remained largely a literary endeavour, engaging in and contributing to the widening and contesting of the boundaries of literature. Said's *Orientalism* had begun by reading the texts of European colonialism as represented in the works of Renan and Flaubert. This literary project is carried forward in his later *Culture and Imperialism* (1993). This book contains a rereading of canonical European texts like *Mansfield Park* or *The Outsider*, in conjunction with other texts by the Indian historian Ranajit Guha or the Caribbean theorist C. L. R. James. Here the colonialist texts are read together with texts representing responses articulated by diverse subjects of the colonial venture. *Culture and Imperialism* also helps to direct the focus of post-colonial concerns away from a strict concentration on literary writing.

Post-colonial studies are, in most cases, institutionally housed in departments of literature, especially English literature. In fact their association has added a fresh dimension to the deconstruction and widening of the scope of English literature. Although a neat chronological charting of the influence of post-colonial theory on literary studies would be misplaced, a schematic division is nevertheless able to pinpoint a primary effect in the reinterpretation of the established literary canon where certain texts such as Shakespeare's *The Tempest* or Defoe's *Robinson Crusoe* are read to bring out the thematic and formal links with colonising processes.[16] This stage can be characterised as an examination of canonical English literary texts, ranging from rereadings of texts like the above to studies of the specifically colonial writings of writers like Rudyard Kipling, Joseph Conrad or E. M. Forster. An important, though often overlooked, feature of this kind of post-colonial criticism was the establishment of links between colonialism and literary forms. Thus studies of the novel focus on the development of the narrative voice through theories of colonial subjectivity.[17] When post-colonial literary criticism reads texts not only for their themes but for the formal devices and

[16] See David Dabydeen, *The Black Presence in English Literature* (Manchester: Manchester University Press, 1985) for an example of this kind of reading.
[17] Cf. Firdous Azim, *The Colonial Rise of the Novel* (London: Routledge, 1993).

structures of literary representation, colonial culture is exposed as all-pervasive, and not limited to texts that deal directly with colonial themes. Gayatri Spivak's statement that nineteenth-century British literature cannot be read 'without remembering that imperialism, understood as England's social mission, was a crucial part of the cultural representation of England to the English' is worth remembering in the context of this rereading of the English canon.[18]

A secondary, although perhaps simultaneous, addition to this project has been the recognition of writing in English from once-colonised countries or other anglophone cultures. The concept of 'other' Englishes has effectively challenged conventional English syllabi, and has added to the number and widened the range of texts that have habitually been the concern of English departments. It is now difficult to come across an English department that does not have the writings of V. S. Naipaul, Salman Rushdie or Chinua Achebe on their reading lists. This widening of the literature syllabus, however, has been the contribution not just of post-colonial theory, but also of movements such as feminism, cultural studies or new historicism. Post-colonial studies are part of these processes, so that history and literature, other forms of culture and literature, and studies of power hierarchy and literary/cultural production ideally merge together in this project. However, the task of adding more and other texts to the literature syllabus, though dynamic in itself, is not a sufficient challenge to conventional English studies. To be true to its own theoretical and critical spirit, post-colonial literary practice would insist on a constant examination of the power hierarchies involved in cultural production and dissemination. The discovery and recognition of newer material and different forms of writing tend to create a premature euphoria, distracting from the more difficult and challenging task of theorising and problematising the position of these texts, even as they are given canonical status.

Theories of post-colonial literature have concerned themselves with issues ranging from the problem of nomenclature and definitions, to questioning the concept as a whole. While the links between English or European literature and colonialism have been established to a certain extent, theorising about 'other' Englishes has proved to be difficult. The scholar-critic in this instance seems to be stuck in a double bind, and veers between theorising about the general principles that govern what can be called 'post-colonial' literature, and looking at the more specific instances of such literary production. The publication of anthologies – of Indian, Pakistani, African, Caribbean and Pacific writings – goes on apace. Again the richness and diversity of the field – geographically, thematically and stylistically – give enough reason for the post-colonial critic to feel that a vast and hitherto untapped

---

[18] Spivak, 'Three Women's Texts', p. 243.

mine has been brought to light. Certain works have tried to foreground the relationship of this body of writing to the colonising project. For example, in *The Empire Writes Back* (1989), English writing from places other than England is seen as a triumphant and assertive resistance to cultural domination.[19] This book is perhaps the most prominent effort to generalise the common tenets of this literature, trying to tease out, from the diverse terrains spanning the whole globe from which post-colonial writing in English emerges, common factors that can then be used to characterise this literary output as post-colonial.

The Empire Writes Back also engages with the vexed question of nomenclature. Terms used to describe other literatures in English had included 'commonwealth literature', 'third world literature' and most recently 'post-colonial literature'. The authors of this book opt for the term 'post-colonial' literature as it conveys the notions of political domination and resistance. It also highlights the importance of location, as writers have different points of entry into the world of English writing and have different ways of engaging with the language and literature.

Aijaz Ahmad, through his book *In Theory: Classes, Nation, Literatures* (1992), examines this vexed issue of nomenclature.[20] He asserts that it is the term 'third world literature' that is most applicable, because the new post-colonial literary canon adheres to the political power divisions envisaged by the three worlds theory. In the most scathing criticism of the post-colonial project, Aijaz Ahmad says that this task of bringing into canonicity writings in English from other parts of the world is effected by publishing and academic media which are fully complicit with the cultural dominance of the western world. Hence any form of writing or critique that emerges as a result of collusion with these institutions should be examined carefully. In fact he questions the transformative potential of the project as a whole.

Post-colonialism, concentrating as it does on cultural domination, cannot limit itself to the literary text. The concept of negritude used the term 'culture' to mean every aspect of being African, taking as its object of study the rhythms of African life. Today, even within the precincts of the departments of English in which post-colonial studies are housed, literary studies are opening up to include studies of popular culture. The revolution in the audio-visual industry calls for a thoroughgoing critical and theoretical examination of literary methods. However, cultural studies, even more than literary studies, has a tendency to uncritically celebrate the plethora of images and productions. Cultural studies, linked to multicultural movements in the west, seems to overlook the need for examination of the processes by which these images – and voices – are brought into play and view.

[19] B. Ashcroft, G. Griffiths and H. Tiffin, *The Empire Writes Back*, (London: Routledge, 1989).
[20] Aijaz Ahmad, *In Theory: Classes, Nations, Literatures* (London: Verso, 1992).

A question of language

Post-colonial studies are engaged in examining the history of cultural domination. The most potent tool for the establishment of colonial cultural domination has been the insertion of English literary studies into the educational
curriculum of colonised regions, a process which first occurred in nineteenth-
century Bengal. The reasons behind the Anglicist policy and the introduction
of English literature have been widely researched by Gauri Viswanathan in
Masks of Empire: Literary Study and British Rule in India.[21] The introduction of English into the colonial educational curriculum and its status as the
focal point of that curriculum has been seen as an alienating factor for the
young colonial child, separating it from its own culture. Ngugi Wa Thiongo in
Decolonising the Mind: The Politics of Language in African Literature examines the status of English in the educational establishment and the entrenching of colonial political domination.[22] In his own life, he sees his gesture of
giving up writing in English for writing in his native Gikuyu as part of an anti-
colonial movement. There has always been in post-colonial societies a debate
about the merits of using indigenous tongues or using the colonial language
for literary expression. Post-colonial studies, housed as they are within
English studies, seem to collaborate with the coloniser, and do not seem to be
able to question effectively the supremacy of that position. However, it is
post-colonial theory that can be an expedient means of studying the relationship between the colonial venture and writings in 'native' languages such as
Bengali, Swahili or Urdu. Examples of studies of the development of the novel
form and its relationship to colonialism do exist (for instance, in Bengali), but
these works need to be included within the reading lists of what counts as
'post-colonial'.[23] Other branches of cultural studies, such as anthropology or
history, have also become subject to the post-colonial examination of cultural
forms.

Post-colonial studies has indeed made it possible to examine the links
between cultural practice and political domination, and to establish the historical basis of these processes. The introduction of the European literary text
into the colonial domain and the bifurcated use of language in colonised societies, switching as it does between colonial official tongue and native mother
tongue, makes the status of language very interesting for the post-colonial
scholar. For the choice of English (or any other European language) as a
medium of expression for the writer from once-colonised societies is loaded

---

[21] Gauri Viswanathan, *Masks of Empire: Literary Study and British Rule in India* (London:
Faber and Faber, 1990).

[22] Ngugi Wa Thiongo, *Decolonising the Mind: The Politics of Language in African Literature*
(Nairobi: Heinemann, 1988).

[23] A good example of such a reading is Nirad Chaudhuri's *Bangali jibane ramani* (Calcutta:
Mitra and Ghose Publishers Ltd., 1968), which examines the changes in domestic and affective
life under colonialism and their literary expression in the novel.

with that history of domination and resistance. Thus the present tendency to celebrate the new literatures in English needs to be put through a post-colonial scrutiny for a more nuanced appreciation of the ways in which contemporary cultural production is tied in with the new world order. The metropolis and its cultural forms – language, the new technologies – govern cultural production, and the post-colonial writer/practitioner has to learn how to plug into these processes even while asserting independence and difference.

In recent times, post-colonial theoretical readings are indeed coming out of the literary enclave to look at more wide-ranging issues. An important intervention in this area is Gayatri Spivak's *A Critique of Postcolonial Reason: Towards a History of the Vanishing Present* (1999), a work which combines literary and philosophical readings with analysis of the new manufacturing processes of the global economic order. Specific studies such as Akhil Gupta's *Postcolonial Developments: Agriculture in the Making of Modern India* (1998) also help to widen the scope of post-colonial analysis to include politics and economics, as a way of studying the lives and nations formed in the contemporary world. Post-colonial theory had first appeared on the academic agenda with a political and interventionist promise. The inclusion of political and economic issues, therefore, should be understood as a development through which post-colonial theory can live up to this initial promise. The strength of post-colonial theory, after all, lies in the links that it makes between literary and cultural production, and economic and political processes.

19

African American literary history and criticism

SIMON LEE-PRICE

I do not care a damn for any art that is not used for propaganda.

W. E. B. Du Bois[1]

I have wanted always to develop a way of writing that was irrevocably black.

Toni Morrison[2]

A history of African American literature has to include some discussion of those deceptively transparent terms 'literature' and 'African American' and the issues raised by their juxtaposition. In recent years poststructuralist and postmodern critical practices have dismantled literary canons and called into question the very notion of literature, yet few literary anthologies are as daring in their selection of texts as *The Norton Anthology of African American Literature*, published in 1997. The inclusion of folk tales, work songs, spirituals and sermons, as well as a speech and prison letter by Martin Luther King, Jr., an extract from *The Autobiography of Malcolm X* and lyrics by the rap band Public Enemy, suggests something of the challenge that African American cultural production presents to a conventional understanding of literature. The anthology, which comes complete with CD, dissolves the distinction between 'high' and 'low' culture and demands a theory of literature which can take account of oral traditions, musical forms and the spoken voice, as well as the often explicitly political content and context of black cultural production. Such a theory of literature, which reconsiders the primacy of the written text and the relation of art to politics and propaganda, would also need to include a recognition of the enforced illiteracy of African Americans during slavery and the role that the concept of writing and literature played in ideologies of white supremacy.

[1] W. E. B. Du Bois, 'Criteria of Negro Art' (1926), *The Norton Anthology of African American Literature*, eds. Henry Louis Gates, Jr. and Nellie Y. McKay (New York: W. W. Norton, 1997), p. 757.
[2] Toni Morrison, cited in Paul Gilroy, *The Black Atlantic: Modernity and Double Consciousness* (London: Verso, 1993), p. 78.

The hybrid term 'African American', which is used, paradoxically, to figure the identity of a body of writing, raises a number of complex issues that will also be addressed in this chapter. What, for instance, does it imply about the relationship of black writing in America to the cultural texts, practices and traditions of African and other black diaspora populations? Just as importantly, what is the place of African American writing in 'mainstream' American literature? Should the African American literary tradition be viewed as supplementary to the national canon of mostly white authors, or can it be read as challenging the whole *rationale* behind the selection of the literary works which help define American identity?

In order to explore these questions it is useful to conceptualise the African American literary tradition as an implicit criticism of existing literary practices: as talking *back* and talking *black*, that is, conducting an ongoing struggle for liberation and self-definition in racist America. However, recognising that African American literature is at some level always a response to racism and that the experience of racism is arguably its dominant theme is not to reduce this diverse body of writing to the status of 'social science fiction', as one critic has described it.[3] To view African American writing in 'extraliterary terms' is, as Robert Stepto shows, a manifestation of racism within literary criticism itself.[4]

A literary history inevitably reveals the agenda of the critic in its structuring metaphors and the authors and texts it chooses to consider. For African American literature, the issues of critical perspective and selection of texts are especially sensitive as works by black authors have often been inadequately treated by dominant interpretative paradigms or excluded from literary history altogether. This chapter is presented as a critical reflection on the process of writing an African American literary history and thus seeks to demonstrate the self-conscious engagement of this literature with dominant interpretative values, conventions and paradigms. It introduces a number of key literary and critical texts, against the changing background of racism in America, and highlights issues and themes that have preoccupied authors and critics in their attempts to create and define the nature of a writing that talks back and talks black.

Slave narratives

In 1773 Phillis Wheatley, an eighteen-year-old slave living in Boston, became the first African (and second woman) to publish a book in English in America. So astonishing was the debut of the black voice in literature that Wheatley's

---

[3] Albert Murray, cited in Robert Stepto, 'Afro-American Literature', in Emory Elliot (ed.), *Columbia Literary History of the United States* (New York: Columbia University Press, 1988), p. 787.   [4] *Ibid.*

Poems on Various Subjects, Religious and Moral was prefaced by a two-para-graph 'Attestation' signed by a committee of Boston's most prominent citizens, 'assur[ing] the World, that the POEMS specified in the following Page' were indeed the original work of 'a young Negro Girl'.[5] The world certainly needed assurance on this matter, since the mastery of the formal written language that Wheatley demonstrated contradicted received wisdom which held blacks to be incapable of intellectual accomplishment. Some of the most influential Enlightenment philosophers including David Hume, Immanuel Kant and G. W. F. Hegel represented Africans as a race incapable of developing a culture or contributing to civilisation and made disparaging remarks about the capacity of Africans for intellectual development. Echoing these views in the New World, Thomas Jefferson argued, on the basis of his observation of slaves, that 'in memory they [blacks] are equal to the whites; in reason much inferior . . . never yet could I find that a black had uttered a thought above the level of plain narration'.[6]

The act of writing demonstrated the existence of reason, a quality unique to 'man', the autonomous subject of progress. Africans, held to have little or no capacity for rational thought, were regarded as scarcely human at all and their status as slaves explained as the natural and inevitable result of this failing. Wheatley's literary debut mounted a serious challenge to the ideology of essential racial types which legitimised slavery. To write as a 'Negro' in the slave society of colonial America was a profoundly subversive and political act, and *Poems* is a founding text in a literary tradition which originated with the unique task of proving the humanity of an entire race. Shortly after the publication of *Poems*, Wheatley achieved her manumission and has the distinction of being, perhaps, the first African to write herself into the 'human' community. In the course of the next century the relationship between literacy and liberty would emerge as a dominant theme in writing by African Americans.

From the late colonial period until the outbreak of civil war in 1861, published writing by African Americans generally took the form of autobiographical narratives and frequently contributed to the propaganda of the abolitionist movement. These slave narratives, as they came to be called, ranged in length from brief statements in newspapers and political tracts, to full-length books which were often serialised in periodicals. Although not the first to be published, Olaudah Equiano's *Interesting Narrative of the Life of Olaudah Equiano, or Gustavus Vassa, the African* (1789) is considered to be the precedent-setting slave narrative and exhibits the key features of the genre which are developed by later writers such as Frederick Douglass and Harriet A. Jacobs. Equiano's narrative offers an eye-witness account of the sufferings

---

[5] Cited in the 'Preface', in Gates and McKay (eds.), *The Norton Anthology*, p. xxxii.
[6] Emmanuel Chukwudi Eze (ed.), *Race and the Enlightenment: A Reader* (Cambridge, Mass.: Blackwell Publishers, 1997), pp. 98–99.

endured by slaves on plantations, condemns America's 'peculiar institution' in moral and religious terms, and recounts the narrator's road to literacy and freedom. According to Henry Louis Gates, Jr. and Charles T. Davis the 'slave narrative arose as a response to and refutation of claims that blacks *could* not write',[7] and by relating his own struggle for both liberty and literacy, Equiano makes explicit the politics inherent in the very act of writing as a person of African descent. The concern with literacy is even more apparent in the genre's most famous text, *Narrative of the Life of Frederick Douglass, an American Slave, Written by Himself* (1845). As with other slave narratives, the bold declaration of authorship 'written by himself' (or less often 'herself') testifies to the performativity of the text, for in addition to charting Douglass' journey from bondage to freedom, from slave to human being, the linguistic mastery which the published text demonstrates contributes itself to that transformation of status. In proclaiming their mastery of the written language, black authors were also registering their defiance of laws which, notwithstanding the 'natural inferiority' of Africans, were deemed necessary to keep slaves in a state of illiteracy. Following slave uprisings in South Carolina in 1739, for instance, legislation was introduced to prevent slaves from reading and writing or serving in any capacity which utilised these skills.[8]

Slave narratives were hugely popular both in America and Europe and Douglass' *Narrative* sold in excess of thirty thousand copies within the first five years of publication. However, although slave narratives are considered the basis of the African American literary tradition, the genre's own status as literature was and remains disputed. Traditional definitions of literature and even autobiography which emphasise the autonomy of the artist and the originality of the creative work have difficulty embracing a body of writing which evolved as abolitionist propaganda and adheres to rigid conventions. Indeed, since the primary purpose of the slave narrative was to offer a 'true testimony' to the horrors of slavery and win converts to the abolitionist movement, any significant deviation from the established codes of representation would tend to be counterproductive as it would raise doubts about the narrative's authenticity. On this basis James Olney suggests that slave narratives bear 'much the same relationship to autobiography in a full sense as painting by numbers bears to painting as a creative act'.[9] In contrast, however, a contemporary reviewer of Douglass' *Narrative* believed that slavery had 'become the prolific theme of much that is profound in argument, sublime in poetry, and thrilling in narrative'.[10] Recent scholarship on slave narratives seldom makes such aesthetic judgements but it is committed to demonstrating the often subtle and

---

[7] Charles T. Davis and Henry Louis Gates, Jr. (eds.), *The Slave's Narrative* (New York: Oxford University Press, 1985), p. xv.   [8] Gates and McKay (eds.), *The Norton Anthology*, p. xxix.

[9] James Olney, 'I Was Born: Slave Narratives, Their Status as Autobiography and as Literature', in Davis and Gates (eds.), *The Slave's Narrative*, p. 150.

[10] Cited in the 'Preface', in *The Norton Anthology*, p. xxvii.

sophisticated formal relationships between these texts and also explores their strategic deployment of the conventions of other literary genres, such as the picaresque and the Gothic. Of particular interest to critics is Jacobs' *Incidents in the Life of a Slave Girl* (1861) which, in its revision of a tradition dominated by male writers, addresses the neglected issue of the sexual exploitation of female slaves and draws on the conventions of sentimental fiction and the domestic novel. Furthermore, slave narratives are considered to have had an immeasurable influence on two of the most widely read novels of the nineteenth century, *Uncle Tom's Cabin* (1853) and *Huckleberry Finn* (1883).

Slave narratives continued to be produced after the formal abolition of slavery. During the 1920s and 30s the Federal Writers' Project collected the testimonies of 2,500 former slaves and it is estimated that in total 6,000 slave narratives have been published. More significantly, perhaps, slave narratives established a tradition of black autobiography which is developed in works like Richard Wright's *Black Boy* (1945), *The Autobiography of Malcolm X* (1965) and Toni Morrison's *Beloved* (1987).

While slavery remained the dominant theme of African American writing until the Civil War, authors did not restrict themselves to the form of the autobiography in their attacks on America's 'peculiar institution'. In 1853 Douglass published 'The Heroic Slave', which is generally regarded as the first work of long fiction in African American literature. And two years later William Wells Brown, already the author of a best-selling slave narrative, published the first full-length African American novel, *Clotel, or the President's Daughter: A Narrative of Slave Life in the United States*. Brown was a prolific writer and turned his hand to drama, poetry, essays and travel writing in the course of his long career.

Double consciousness

The Civil War led to the abolition of slavery but despite the initial promise of Reconstruction failed to achieve equality for African Americans and did little to change their image in the public mind. The decades around the turn of the century, which have been termed 'the Nadir', saw an increase in racial violence and the notorious Supreme Court ruling in *Plessy v. Ferguson* (1896) that relegated African Americans to the status of second-class citizens. In line with almost every other American business and institution, publishers discriminated on the basis of race and, when accepted, African American authors were severely restricted in the subjects and themes they were expected to treat. Nevertheless, by the end of the nineteenth century a young black poet, Paul Laurence Dunbar, had emerged as one of America's most popular literary figures. Dunbar wrote essays, fiction, 'standard' English verse and experimented with a range of regional dialects but won recognition largely for his

'Negro' dialect poetry. These dialect poems mark an important stage in the development of a black literary aesthetic; however, Dunbar's representation of African American vernacular expression is deeply problematic. Some critics argue that his dialect poetry catered to the demands of the publishing industry and readers for stereotypical representations of the 'darky' and utilised the conventions and language of the plantation tradition associated with white writers like Joel Chandler Harris (author of the popular Uncle Remus stories) and Thomas Nelson Page. Yet whatever position they take on the 'authenticity' of his black voice, almost all critics agree on Dunbar's important place in an evolving African American literary practice and consider his most famous poem 'Why We Wear the Mask' (1895) as deeply expressive of the black experience.

Charles Waddell Chesnutt also used the African American vernacular in his collection of short stories, *The Conjure Woman* (1899). These tales, narrated in dialect by an ex-slave Uncle Julius McAdoo, plunge the reader into the supernatural world of hoodoo (the African American equivalent of voodoo) and challenge the sentimental view of slavery promoted by the novels of the plantation tradition. At the risk of alienating publishers and readers, Chesnutt tackled the racial problems of the era more directly in *The Wife of his Youth and Other Stories of the Color Line* (1899) and his novel *The House Behind the Cedars* (1900), works which speak out against the 'color line' that excluded blacks from American social, cultural and economic life.

The richness of African American culture and the problem of the 'color line' are the twin themes of W. E. B. Du Bois' multigeneric work, *The Souls of Black Folk: Essays and Sketches* (1903). In this work, Du Bois introduces the seminal concept of 'double-consciousness' to define African American being-in-the-world. Double consciousness, he explains, 'is a peculiar sensation . . . of always looking at one's self through the eyes of others, of measuring one's soul by the tape of a world that looks on in amused contempt and pity'. As a result, '[o]ne ever feels his two-ness, – an American, a Negro; two souls, two thoughts, two unreconciled strivings; two warring ideals in one dark body, whose dogged strength alone keeps it from being torn asunder'. Importantly, Du Bois maintains that despite the contempt in which the 'Negro' is held by the nation, '[h]e would not bleach his Negro soul in a flood of white Americanism, for he knows that Negro blood has a message for the world. He simply wishes to make it possible for a man to be both a Negro and an American, without being cursed and spit upon by his fellows, without having the doors of Opportunity closed roughly in his face.'[11]

The Autobiography of an Ex-Colored Man (1912) by James Weldon Johnson explores in fictional form the ambivalence which Du Bois suggests structures the African American sense of self. In this novel, Johnson strategi-

---

[11] W. E. B. Du Bois, *The Souls of Black Folk: Essays and Sketches*, eds. and introd. David W. Blight and Robert Gooding-Williams (Boston: Bedford Books, 1997), pp. 38–39.

cally deploys a light-skinned African American as narrator (a talented ragtime musician who dreams of becoming a composer of Negro folk music in classical form) in order to emphasise the arbitrariness of the 'color line' and the narrative charts his attempts to 'identif[y] with a people that could with impunity be treated worse than animals'. Electing finally to pass as white after witnessing an horrific lynching, the narrator's sense of inner division or duality remains and is expressed in his guilt-ridden conviction that he has 'sold [his] birthright for a mess of pottage'.[12]

In its exploration of racial identity and cultural heritage, and celebration of African American cultural and expressive practices such as the 'cakewalk', ragtime and spirituals, Johnson's novel anticipates many of the concerns of the 'Negro' or Harlem Renaissance which would bring African American literature to national prominence during the 1920s and early 30s. Indeed, as editor and critic, Johnson played a leading role in preparing the way for this literary flowering, and in the Preface to the Book of American Negro Poetry (1922), the first collection of its type to be published in America, he stressed the importance of literature in the struggle for racial equality. 'No people that has produced great literature and art', he argued, 'has ever been looked upon by the world as distinctly inferior', and he insisted that 'a demonstration of intellectual parity by the Negro through the production of literature and art' would change social conditions in America. Demonstrating literary excellence rather than proving a capacity for literacy was now the task, and Johnson proposed that 'Negro' literature needed 'to find a form that will express the racial spirit by symbols from within rather than by symbols from without . . . a form expressing the imagery, the idioms, the peculiar turns of thought, and the distinctive humour and pathos, too, of the Negro'.[13]

Johnson's conviction that African American literary excellence could, in time, transform racial attitudes was shared by other black intellectuals and political leaders, including Du Bois and Alain Locke, who edited The New Negro (1925), the signal text of the Harlem Renaissance, which featured art, poetry, fiction and essays, and celebrated black assertiveness and cultural achievement. Locke encouraged African American writers to explore all subjects and championed poets as different in their formal expression as the orthodox Countee Cullen and the experimental Langston Hughes, and novelists as contrasting in their representations of black life as Nella Larsen and Claude McKay. Du Bois, on the other hand, outlined a more conservative position in his 'Criteria of Negro Art' (1926). He argued that to fulfil its role as 'propaganda' for the race African American writing was duty bound to strive for 'the creation of Beauty . . . the preservation of Beauty . . . the

---

[12] James Weldon Johnson, The Autobiography of an Ex-Colored Man, ed. and introd. William L. Andrews (New York: Penguin, 1990), pp. 139, 154.
[13] James Weldon Johnson, 'Preface', in The Book of American Negro Poetry (1922), in Gates and McKay (eds.), The Norton Anthology, pp. 861, 881.

realization of Beauty'.[14] Thus Du Bois objected strongly to Claude McKay's *Home to Harlem* (1928) on the grounds that it 'set out to cater for that prurient demand on the part of white folk for a portrayal in Negroes of that utter licentiousness which conventional civilization holds white folk back from enjoying'.[15]

Du Bois, Johnson and Locke have been taken to task for overestimating the role that the creation of high art and literature could play in winning equality for the African American masses.[16] Yet in developing an understanding of African American literary practice as derived from black verbal culture, expressive practices and folk traditions, their work pointed the way forward for black literary criticism.

Perhaps no other text of the Harlem Renaissance had such an influence on the development of a black literary aesthetic as *Cane* (1923), and its author, Jean Toomer, was hailed as 'a bright morning star of a new day of the race in literature' by the prominent black critic William Stanley Braithwaite.[17] *Cane* is a mixture of poetry, lyrical sketches and drama, and aims to represent the folk culture and distinctive voice of the black south which Toomer felt were doomed to extinction in modern America. The issue of formal experimentalism is often raised in critical discussions of *Cane*, and Toomer's association with American modernists like Waldo Frank and Sherwood Anderson, and the influence of Ezra Pound and the imagists on his writing point to the need to consider African American writing in relation to developments in American and European literature. It is important however, as Stepto warns, not simply to fit African American writers into existing critical paradigms like modernism but to challenge their universalist assumptions through close analysis of black texts.[18]

The poetry of Langston Hughes is central to any discussion of a black modernist aesthetic. In breaking with traditional poetic forms, Hughes tried to imitate the rhythms and sounds of jazz and the Blues. For Hughes jazz represented an expressive practice which defined the black experience in America, combining musical traditions of Africa and innovations in the New World and also linking the folk culture of the rural south to black experience in the city. In an essay 'The Negro Artist and the Racial Mountain' (1926), Hughes described jazz as 'one of the inherent expressions of Negro life in America; the eternal tom-tom beating in the Negro soul', and urged African

14 Du Bois, 'Criteria of Negro Art', p. 757.
15 W. E. B. Du Bois, 'Two Novels' (1928), in Gates and McKay (eds.), *The Norton Anthology*, p. 759.
16 See Nathan Irvin Huggins, *The Harlem Renaissance* (New York: Oxford University Press, 1971) and David Levering Lewis, *When Harlem was in Vogue* (New York: Oxford University Press, 1989).
17 William Stanley Braithwaite, 'The Negro in American Literature', in Alain Locke (ed.), *The New Negro*, ed. and introd. Arnold Rampersad (New York: Atheneum, 1992), p. 44.
18 Stepto, 'Afro-American Literature', p. 786.

American artists to follow the examples of the Blues singer Bessy Smith and the sculptor Aaron Douglass and 'express [their] dark-skinned selves without fear or shame'.[19] At the same time Hughes himself and other writers associated with the Renaissance were keenly aware of the deep ambivalence towards cultural heritage and black identity which results from 'double consciousness'. Countee Cullen's poem 'Heritage' (1925) asks in its first line 'What is Africa to me'; and Nella Larsen's two short novels, *Quicksand* (1928) and *Passing* (1929), tackle the vexed issues of 'miscegenation', 'passing for white' and divided racial heritage.

Larsen's novels are also of interest to critics because they focus on African American women and offer a sophisticated treatment of black female sexuality. They are often read as presenting a powerful critique of the patriarchal bias of the Renaissance. Published too late to be included in many discussions of the Harlem Renaissance, Zora Neale Hurston's *Their Eyes Were Watching God* (1937) also makes gender politics central to the representation of black experience in America as it charts the coming to voice of its female protagonist. In this 'speakerly' text which asserts the creative potential of oral traditions, Hurston, a trained anthropologist and folklorist, uses her familiarity with a range of black vernacular expressive forms such as sermons, spirituals and folk tales to develop a style of writing to which Alice Walker and Toni Morrison, amongst others, acknowledge a debt.

Social protest and the Black Aesthetic

The author and political commentator, Richard Wright, who emerged in the aftermath of the Great Depression and against a background of increasing class conflict in America and Europe, is often taken to be a transitional figure in histories of African American literature. According to one critic, his work lays the foundations of a new 'school' of black writing which registers a powerful 'protest' against racism through a portrayal of 'tough urban scenarios, the dehumanizing cycle of oppression, entrapment, and a view of individual fate as determined overwhelmingly by skin color and poverty'.[20] As early as 1937, in an essay 'Blueprint for Negro Writing', Wright signalled his rejection of 'the so-called Harlem school of expression' by asking a critical question about the role of black literature: 'Shall Negro writing be for the Negro masses, molding the lives and consciousness of those masses toward new goals, or shall it continue begging the question of the Negroes' humanity?' Wright's answer is a literary aesthetic which is informed by a Marxist analysis

---

[19] Langston Hughes, 'The Negro Artist and the Racial Mountain', in Gates and McKay (eds.), *The Norton Anthology*, pp. 1270–1271.

[20] Robert A. Lee, *Black American Fiction Since Richard Wright* (Durham: British Association for American Studies, 1983), p.16.

of society and committed to radical social change. He urges black writers to transcend sectional interests and adopt a perspective in their writing which connects the experiences of African Americans with the international proletariat and the 'hopes and struggles of minority peoples everywhere'.[21] His most famous work, *Native Son* (1940), is, consequently, uncompromising in its portrayal of the devastating psychological and social consequences of poverty and racism and designed to rouse the reader to the necessity for radical social change in America.

Just as Wright defined himself in opposition to an earlier generation of writers associated with the Harlem Renaissance, a number of authors, initially close to Wright, began to challenge the black literary realism or naturalism he came to represent. Ralph Ellison, who, like Wright, had been associated with the communist party, initially praised *Native Son*, but departed radically from his former mentor's literary aesthetics in *Invisible Man* (1952), a self-consciously modernist novel which flaunts its textuality, its status as written artefact and defamiliarises the black literary subject. James Baldwin, too, rejected the aesthetics of protest developed by Wright and pointed to an uncanny resemblance between *Native Son* and *Uncle Tom's Cabin* in their portrayal of their central black protagonist. Protest fiction, Baldwin argued in a characteristically passionate and rhetorical essay, mistook sociology for literature and indulged a 'passion for categorization' which denied the humanity of African Americans.[22]

Although he published several novels, Baldwin is most widely known for his collections of essays, in particular *Notes of a Native Son* (1955) and *The Fire Next Time* (1963), carefully crafted works which demonstrate his deep commitment to the struggle for civil rights. By the 1960s, however, the integrationist philosophy underlying the Civil Rights movement and Wright's literary aesthetic was facing mounting criticism. Out of anger at the failure of Federal legislation to improve the conditions of African Americans and in response to uprisings in many of America's major cities, the separatist Black Power movement emerged. The militant political activism associated with this broad-based movement provides an important context for understanding developments in African American writing and the challenges it presents to conventional definitions of literature. During the 1960s first-person representations by African American activists and political leaders, published in the form of diaries, letters, prison writings and autobiographies, such as *The Autobiography of Malcolm X* and Eldridge Cleaver's *Soul On Ice* (1968), were among the most widely read and influential black-authored texts. At no

---

[21] Richard Wright, 'Blueprint for Negro Writing' (1937), in Angelyn Mitchell (ed.), *Within the Circle: An Anthology of African American Literary Criticism from the Harlem Renaissance to the Present* (Durham: Duke University Press, 1994), pp. 105, 99, 104.

[22] James Baldwin, 'Everybody's Protest Novel' (1949), in Gates and McKay (eds.), *The Norton Anthology*, p. 1657.

time since the Abolition era did so many African Americans turn to autobiographical writing as a means of self-definition and political intervention, and this writing was defiant, shocking and explicitly propagandist. However, unlike slave narratives, black self-representation in the 1960s did not strive to appeal to whites or simply demand social equality for blacks; rather it was addressed primarily to other blacks and emphasised black pride and distinctiveness – objectives facilitated by the growing number of black-owned presses and black-owned or edited journals.

Another major influence on African American writing was the Black Arts movement which began in the mid-sixties and was closely allied to Black Power. The writer/activists associated with the movement such as LeRoi Jones (Amiri Baraka) and Larry Neal tended to employ and develop the literary forms of performance poetry and drama, which could convey the distinctive character of the black vernacular and allowed for a dynamic interaction between artist and audience. The Black Arts movement also included spoken-word artists and musicians like Gil Scott Heron whose influence is apparent in the work of rap artists today.

Those associated with the Black Arts movement also reflected upon the role and unique characteristics of black writing. While agreeing with Wright that black literature had an essentially political function in fighting racist oppression, they objected to protest fiction, claiming, as Wright had once claimed about the work of earlier black writers, that it relied on an appeal to the good conscience of whites and, therefore, was not empowering. Black Arts critics demanded a literature that spoke directly to African Americans in their own language. A black literature worthy of the name, then, would have its own distinctive forms, conventions and linguistic usage drawn from the black vernacular and would not be amenable to interpretations by the white critical establishment. Critics argued that a separate 'Black Aesthetic' was necessary for comprehending or appreciating black literature. Linking the practice of black writing to political struggle, Neal proposed:

Black Art is the aesthetic and spiritual sister of the Black Power concept. As such, it envisions an art that speaks directly to the needs and aspirations of Black America. In order to perform this task, the Black Arts Movement proposes a radical reordering of the western cultural aesthetic. It proposes a separate symbolism, mythology, critique, and iconology.[23]

The Black Arts movement has been criticised for essentialising blackness and presenting a masculinist view of black America. Nevertheless it is acknowledged for drawing attention to the unspoken 'white aesthetic' of mainstream critical practice which marginalised black writing and excluded all but a few black authors from literary anthologies or serious critical treatment. Its innovative creative work, as well as its defiant stance towards the literary and

[23] Larry Neal, 'The Black Arts Movement' (1968), in Mitchell (ed.), *Within the Circle*, p. 184.

critical establishment and commitment to demonstrating the richness and complexity of black writing, helped to win for African American authors the national and international reputations they have today.

Gender and theory

Arguably the most radical revision of the African American literary tradition was started by black feminists in the early 1970s and is still being carried on today. Responding initially to Anglo-American feminists, whose work generally ignored black women, and also to the masculinism of the Black Arts movement, black feminists sought to articulate the relationship between gendered and racial oppression and assert a positive and empowering identity for black women. At its simplest level black literary feminism is interested in the history and experiences of African American women and examines their representations in literary and critical texts. Consequently much valuable scholarship has gone and continues to go into recovering the neglected or marginalised works of black women writers and developing reading strategies for 'women-centred' narratives which the male-dominated black critical establishment has traditionally disregarded, trivialised and even condemned. The work of black feminist bibliographers, for instance, has drawn attention to forgotten narratives by female slaves and nineteenth-century women poets; and Alice Walker, though better known as a novelist, played a leading role in recovering Hurston, who was (in)famously dismissed by Wright and largely ignored for over thirty years. Along with Walker, the author Toni Morrison is closely associated with this project of recovering black women's history and experience. With a few exceptions the works of these two pre-eminent authors focus on female characters and place a female consciousness at the centre of the narrative. Walker's introduction of a female perspective on black history and experience has proved the more controversial, and *The Color Purple* (1982), which portrays sexual exploitation and domestic violence in the black family, has been the subject of heated exchanges between black critics.

Black literary feminism is far from monolithic. Critics like Hortense Spillers utilise interpretative techniques from deconstruction, psychoanalysis and other theoretical discourses in their work while others place considerable emphasis on personal experience and testimony. Black feminists are tireless in their criticism of masculinist assumptions embedded in the black literary tradition and dedicated to establishing a connection with black women writers of the past; however, their ultimate objective is not to construct a separate black female literary tradition but to outline a more representative African American literary history. As Mary Helen Washington points out: '[t]he making of a literary history in which black women are fully represented is a search for a full vision, to create a circle where now we have but a segment'.[24]

During the 1970s those working in African American literary studies made increasing use of formalist and structuralist methods of reading with the twin objectives of critiquing the essentialism of the Black Arts movement and 'yielding a "literary" understanding' of black literature.[25] For Gates, the black critic can gain by drawing on theories of interpretation that 'defamiliarize the black text', and he suggests his own turn to theory was motivated by a desire to 'see the text as a structure of literature and not as a one-to-one reflection of (my) life'.[26] The assertion by critics of the 'literariness' of African American writing should also be seen as a strategic response to a long tradition of reading black texts reductively as sociological, biographical or historical documents. While embracing theory, however, black critics are careful in their readings not to disregard the social text of race. The work of pioneering black theorist Houston A. Baker, Jr. is exemplary in this respect. Baker has advanced a number of compelling theories of African American literary production which consider the formal properties of texts (both 'literary' and 'non-literary') as well as black history and experience in America. Baker's work is clearly influenced by the insights and demands of Black Aesthetic criticism, and his attentive readings of novels, poems, autobiographies and essays are guided by tropes which derive from the black vernacular and black expressive practices such as the Blues.[27]

In their re-interpretations of the black literary tradition, Baker, Gates and other critics show the influence of poststructuralism on their thinking and privilege the formal relationships between texts (intertextuality) over any external social, historical or biographical referent. Pointing out that 'black writers read and critique other black texts as an act of rhetorical self-definition', Gates goes on to insist that '[o]ur literary tradition exists because of these precisely chartable formal literary relationships'. This observation is central to Gates' influential critical concept, 'signifyin(g)', a term drawn from the black vernacular which he uses to denote the formal repetitions and revisions that are apparent in the works of succeeding generations of black writers. Thus for Gates, Ellison's self-reflexive modernist novel 'signifies' on the naturalism of Wright:

The play of language, the signifying, starts with the titles. *Native Son* and *Black Boy* – both titles connoting race, self, and presence – Ellison tropes with *Invisible Man*,

---

[24] Mary Helen Washington, '"The Darkened Eye Restored": Notes Toward a Literary History of Black Women', in *Within the Circle*, p. 451.

[25] Henry Louis Gates, Jr., 'Introduction: "Tell me, sir, ... what *is* 'black' literature?"' *PMLA* 105 (1990), p. 17.

[26] Henry Louis Gates, Jr., *Figures in Black: Words, Signs, and the 'Racial' Self* (New York: Oxford University Press, 1989), p. xxiv.

[27] Houston A. Baker, Jr., *Blues, Ideology, and Afro-American Literature: A Vernacular Theory* (Chicago: University of Chicago Press, 1984).

invisibility an ironic response of absence to the would-be presence of 'blacks' and 'natives', while 'man' suggests a more mature, stronger status than either 'sons' [sic] or 'boy.'[28]

Baker's commitment to a formal as opposed to a historical or sociological understanding of black literary production is demonstrated in his important revaluation of the Harlem Renaissance. Breaking with a negative critical trend which judged the Renaissance's literary output to be 'a single, exotic set of "failed" high jinks confined to less than a decade', Baker locates the movement's cultural production within a broader black discourse of 'renaissancism', a 'resonantly and continuously productive set of tactics, strategies, and syllables that takes form at the turn of the century and extends to our own day'.[29]

However, the turn to theory by black literary scholars has not been without its critics, and Gates himself warns against 'the mistake of confusing the enabling mask of theory with our own black faces'.[30] Barbara Christian recognises other dangers and has spoken out against 'the race for theory', arguing that it is a worrying symptom of the professionalisation of black literary studies, continues western cultural hegemony by other means, and diverts critics from reading and engaging with new literary works by black and third-world writers.[31]

Crossing the 'color line' and the black Atlantic

The task of demonstrating that African Americans have produced a rich and complex literature that is rooted in their own specific cultural and expressive traditions has been complemented in recent years by a critical project which interrogates the self-identity of black and mainstream (white) literary traditions in America. Arguing against the prevailing ideology of cultural pluralism which places African American literature (along with other ethnic literatures) in a supplementary relationship to mainstream literature, Morrison calls instead for a radical 're-interpretation of the American canon'. Her challenge to critics is to examine canonical works for the '"unspeakable things unspoken"; for the ways in which the presence of African Americans has shaped the choices, the language, the structure – the meaning of so much American literature'.[32] Many critics who have taken up

---

[28] Gates, *Figures in Black*, p. 242, pp. 245–246.
[29] Houston A. Baker, Jr., *Modernism and the Harlem Renaissance* (Chicago: University of Chicago Press, 1987), pp. 91–92.
[30] Henry Louis Gates, Jr., 'Canon-Formation, Literary History, and the Afro-American Tradition: From the Seen to the Told', in Houston A. Baker, Jr. and Patricia Redmond (eds.), *Afro-American Literary Study in the 1990s* (Chicago: University of Chicago Press, 1989), p. 29.
[31] Barbara Christian, 'The Race for Theory', in Mitchell (ed.), *Within the Circle*, pp. 348–359.
[32] Morrison, 'Unspeakable Things Unspoken: The Afro-American Presence in American Literature' (1988), in Henry B. Wonham (ed.), *Criticism and the Color Line: Desegregating American Literary Studies* (New Brunswick: Rutgers University Press, 1996), p 23.

Morrison's challenge also point out that, since African American writers from Wheatley onwards have read, critiqued and been formally influenced by white authors, it is wrong to suggest or imply that intertextuality adheres to the binary configuration of the 'color line'.[33] Informed by these observations, an often controversial body of scholarship has emerged in which the works of black and white authors are taken to constitute a hybrid national literature that is the product of a 'complex dialectic between "white" and "black" cultures'. The work of critics adopting this approach frequently explores such narrative themes as 'passing', minstrelsy and doubling (as in Eric J. Sundquist's comparative reassessment of Mark Twain and Chesnutt), examines the interplay of racial voices in the text and problematises the relationship between author and cultural tradition. Sundquist suggests, for instance, that '[Herman] Melville is a writer whose contribution to African American culture is worth careful attention.' He argues that '[t]his point is worth making because it defines my sense that as readers, teachers, or critics, we make a serious error if we imagine that race alone determines an author's capacity to cross cultural boundaries with something approaching understanding of the other race's imaginative matrix or its necessarily different legacy and perspective'.[34] The 'color line' which divides the social body of America is figured, in paradoxical fashion, as the productive basis of its national literature. According to Henry B. Wonham:

Significant expression occurs along the color line because it is there that American identity is most at issue, there that the racial 'Other', whether black or white, is most insistent and hardest to conceal. The task of criticism . . . is to document the 'embarrassing' presence of this 'Other' in cultural places where one least expects to find it, to historicize, rather than to deny the cultural exchanges that *produce* American identity.

Wonham himself recognises the potential dangers of this critical project which 'celebrate[s] transgressions of the color line' and might work to 'cancel or neutralize black difference, thereby confirming the dominant culture's right to define black identity according to its own ideological purposes'. However, he is firm in his insistence that it is not the objective of the project to 'erase the color line but historicise a mutually constitutive relationship between African and European cultures in America'.[35]

Whether critics emphasise the ethnic distinctiveness of the African American literary tradition or expose within it the black/white dialectic which produces American identity, there tends to be a common underlying assumption that black literature can be interpreted within the confining national

---

[33] Shelley Fisher Fishkin, 'Interrogating "Whiteness", Complicating, "Blackness"', in Wonham (ed.), *Criticism and the Color Line*, pp. 272–273.

[34] Eric J. Sundquist, *To Wake the Nations: Race in the Making of American Literature* (Cambridge, Mass.: The Belknap Press of Harvard University, 1993), pp. 2, 22–23.

[35] Wonham, 'Introduction', *Criticism and the Color Line*, pp. 6, 14.

borders of America. In *The Black Atlantic* Paul Gilroy takes issue with this approach and the 'volkish popular cultural nationalism' apparent in the work of a number of African American scholars.[36] Examining slave narratives and the writings of Du Bois, Wright and Morrison alongside black musical forms, Gilroy charts instead a network of diasporic affiliations and exchanges which traverse the Atlantic between Africa, the Caribbean, America and Europe. Black cultural production, he argues, is essentially transnational, and he opposes the subversive image of the moving ship to the static modern nation state with its fixed boundaries. His readings draw attention to the themes of travel, exile, displacement and migration in the life and works of African American writers and political leaders. The contours of Gilroy's black Atlantic are discernible in a number of African American literary texts such as the novels *Banjo* (1929) and *Banana Bottom* (1933) by McKay, who was Jamaican by birth. More recently the Antiguan-born novelist and short story writer, Jamaica Kincaid, has made migration, the complex histories and cultures of the Caribbean and the experiences of Afro-Caribbeans in America the subject of her work.

In view of the ongoing dialogue amongst black scholars on issues of gender, textuality and the relation of black writing in American to the national canon and the black diaspora, any African American literary history is necessarily provisional. However, a tentative conclusion can be offered. While the notion of propaganda is limiting, it does begin to suggest the distinctiveness of a literary tradition which arose in response to slavery and racist stereotyping and has consistently spoken out against the many forms of racist oppression in America and elsewhere. It is not just the content of black writing which is political however; in order to talk back, black authors have deployed a variety of 'literary' forms and turned to oral and musical traditions. The dynamic interplay of political engagement and aesthetic experimentation – Du Bois' commitment to art as propaganda and Morrison's attempt to develop 'a way of writing that [is] irrevocably black' – is a constitutive feature of the African-American literary tradition.

[36] Gilroy, *The Black Atlantic*, p. 15.

20

Anthropological criticism

BRIAN COATES

Anthropological criticism refers, broadly speaking, to a form of criticism that situates the making, dissemination and reception of literature within the conventions and cultural practices of human societies. Such an undertaking has become increasingly suspect in the twentieth century as critiques of the idea of the centred subject and of a stable field of knowledge have been voiced. One critic has referred to its 'history of complicity variously with racism and slavery . . . its readiness to facilitate colonial governance'.[1] Another has asserted: 'Every focus excludes: there is no politically innocent methodology for inter-cultural interpretation.'[2] These questions have occupied prominent thinkers such as Jean-Paul Sartre, Claude Lévi-Strauss, Edward Said and Jacques Derrida. Anthropology is seen as upholding a privileged position whereby the dominant codes of western culture, including patriarchy and imperialism, survey, classify and govern the cultures of the east, the third world, of people of colour, women and those of different sexual preferences. As such, the discipline appears to perpetuate the same/other binary that is a part of the logocentric tradition of western culture. These matters will be discussed in the course of this essay. To begin with, I will present a brief summary of the relation of anthropology to literary criticism during this century.

Anthropological criticism came into sharp prominence during the early years of the twentieth century. The Cambridge school of classical anthropology took up the work of Sir James Frazer and applied the methods of his *magnum opus*, *The Golden Bough*, to the study of Greek drama. The conclusions of this loosely knit group of scholars and writers, sometimes known as the 'ritualists' (Jane Harrison, F. M. Cornford, A. B. Cook and Gilbert Murray), were that a pre-history of myth and ritual is present in Greek drama. Classical drama was thus read as a displaced narrative of much older, pagan ceremonial forms.

The influence of this school was reinforced by the modernist interest in mythic structures. Both James Joyce and T. S. Eliot incorporate mythic material into their work to show how, as Eliot wrote in his review of *Ulysses*,

---

[1] Robert Young, *Torn Halves: Political Conflict in Literary and Cultural Theory* (Manchester: Manchester University Press, 1996), p. 107.
[2] James Clifford, 'Travelling Cultures', in L. Grossberg, C. Nelson and P. Treichler (eds.), *Cultural Studies* (London: Routledge, 1992), p. 97.

modern literature 'manipulat[es] a continuous parallel between contemporaneity and antiquity'.[3] Other routes led through tribal and exotic cultural forms: Picasso's appropriation of African masks and Pound's attempt to reinvigorate the European poetic tradition through the use of Chinese hieroglyphics are examples of this search for 'authenticity' in the modernist aesthetic. Eliot explicitly acknowledges *The Golden Bough* and Jessie Weston's *From Ritual to Romance* as sources for *The Waste Land*; and his use of *The Tempest* as a ritual of rebirth strongly echoes Colin Still's *The Timeless Theme*, a Frazer-inspired study of the play. W. B. Yeats and D. H. Lawrence similarly rely upon a variety of western and eastern mythic narratives which they use as scaffolding for their historical and psychological interpretations of multiple consciousness and complexity in relationships, as well as to provide a good deal of incidental symbolism. Such issues took on a particular intensity in the conflict-ridden years of the first world war, the Russian Revolution and the Easter Rising in Ireland. Peter Nicholls, discussing Eliot's essay on Joyce, advances a series of reasons for the modernist preoccupation with myth: 'First, modernity is anarchic and lacking in any sense of direction; secondly, something which is not "history" and which is alien to modernity may be invoked as an *external* principle of order; and thirdly, in his discovery of this "mythical method", Joyce has killed off the novel once and for all.'[4] The stark formulae of myth offered a short-cut to that classical heritage that, for many modernist artists, represented a golden age of organic artistic practice.

A point of interest in this return to primitive source material lies in the apparent contradiction between its anthropological stance and 'practical criticism', the critical orthodoxy of the day, which stressed the need to attend to 'the words on the page'. Historical analysis and the study of questions which might seem to lie at the margins of the text were, however, more frequently practised in the close reading techniques developed at Cambridge than is often recognised. Even though *Scrutiny*, the house journal of 'Cambridge English', had a generally conservative agenda, the moral seriousness of F. R. Leavis, I. A. Richards and William Empson introduced challenging discussions on the social framework of the arts. Study of developmental psychology was also a prominent feature of Richards' scholarship. The quasi-scientific dictates of the Cambridge ritualists gave their work an appealing appearance of system, then badly needed by the new English Tripos; this is how 'myth' became an accepted element in the new literary schematic.

Though modernism is generally presented as a new departure, a response to the changing social, political and economic conditions of the nineteenth and early twentieth century, the anthropological motif links it to much earlier

[3] T. S. Eliot, '*Ulysses*, Order and Myth', *The Dial* 75 (1923), p. 483.
[4] Peter Nicholls, *Modernisms: A Literary Guide* (Basingstoke: Macmillan, 1995), p. 255.

articulations of the creative and critical mind. The modernist tenet that literary criticism is a specialised, professional activity was more often preached than practised.

In the early eighteenth century, the discipline of 'criticism', then an academic newcomer, was formed from eclectic sources. Alexander Pope's injunction that one should know a writer's

> . . . Fable, Subject, scope in ev'ry page;
> Religion, Country, genius of his Age . . .[5]

was a commonplace of literary criticism at the time. As René Wellek, in his pioneering work on this subject, points out: 'Nothing is more frequent in the eighteenth century than insistence on studying the environment of the poet, on entering sympathetically into his mind and conditions.'[6]

Wellek quotes Johnson, Lowth, Warton, Gibbon and Temple on this theme and notes that Robert Wood 'actually travelled in the land of Homer . . . and studied it with great care, in order to verify the correctness of every detail'.[7] Whilst this search for an empirical basis for literary representation based on such qualities as climate, landscape and culture may appear oddly misdirected to the mainstream twentieth-century critic, there are several points of principle located within this approach that are once again being put to service in modern philosophically based studies of literature. In Terry Eagleton's treatment of eighteenth-century critical thought, the 'ethical humanism' of early critical studies is stressed as well as the breadth of the critical discourse of the day. As he puts it: 'the examination of literary texts is one relatively marginal moment of a broader enterprise which explores attitudes to servants and the rules of gallantry, the status of women and familial affections, the purity of the English language, the character of conjugal love, the psychology of the sentiments and the laws of the toilet.'[8]

The myth of progress that motivated these Enlightenment attitudes inform such compilations as Percy's *Reliques of Ancient English Poetry* (1765) which aimed to 'show the gradations of our language, exhibit the progress of popular opinions, display the peculiar manners and customs of former ages, or throw light on our earlier classical poets'.[9] By ordering the volume chronologically, Percy seeks to produce a division between the authentic folk ballad and the modern imitation. It is ironic, in retrospect, to note that two of the most popular 'authentic' volumes of 'ancient' poetry at this time were those of Thomas Chatterton and James MacPherson, famous modern frauds of their day. Of particular relevance here is Jacques Derrida's essay 'Structure,

---

[5] Alexander Pope, *Essay on Criticism*, in William K. Wimsatt (ed.), *Alexander Pope: Selected Poetry and Prose* (New York: Rinehart, 1955), I. 120–121, p. 66.
[6] René Wellek, *The Rise of English Literary History* (New York: McGraw-Hill, 1966), p. 52.
[7] *Ibid.*, p. 57.
[8] Terry Eagleton, *The Function of Criticism: From 'The Spectator' to Poststructuralism* (London: Verso, 1985), p.18.   [9] Wellek, *Rise of English Literary History*, pp. 143–144.

Sign and Play in the Discourse of the Human Sciences' critiquing Lévi-Strauss' effort to privilege nature over culture. What Lévi-Strauss adjudges to be a *scandal* (incest is the subject of cultural prohibition yet it has a 'universal character') is read by Derrida as a necessary consequence of the establishment of a binary system. For Derrida, the scandal exists only 'within a system of concepts which accredits the difference between nature and culture'.[10]

In the nineteenth century, several attempts were made to put literary criticism on a firmer footing. One particular model of literary criticism which takes the context of human cultural endeavour into account is that of Hippolyte Taine (1828–93), whose taxonomy of literary production combined 'forces arising from racial inheritance . . . physical, social and political environment . . . and the moment of time in which the literature or the historical figure emerged'.[11]

This formula appears to blend universal and specific conceptions of the literary work but in fact operates as a meta-discourse which assumes that contextual classification will translate and tame the work in terms of a generalised set of human norms and cultural conventions. The suppressed agenda here is that of a master narrative able to produce an understanding of cultural practice yet standing outside cultural production itself. This assumption has haunted literary criticism up to the present day. 'Il n'y a pas de hors-texte', a much-misunderstood coinage of Jacques Derrida in a commentary on Rousseau, is an attempt to redress this assumption by pointing up the continuous entanglement of concepts which seek to universalise human attributes, capabilities and forms of expression with orders of discourse stemming from a particular (privileged) world-view.[12] Derrida notes the special roles which Rousseau gives to speech, lyric, melody and design as expressive of the spontaneous human being. Yet as Rousseau pursues the discussion, he comes up against the problematic insight that 'melody has its principle in harmony',[13] that colour is essential to design, that writing informs the codes of speech.

In Britain, Matthew Arnold (1822–88) argued that culture is, at root, an educational and moral force (1869):

There is a view in which all the love of our neighbour, the impulses towards action, help, and beneficence, the desire for removing human error, clearing human confusion, and diminishing human misery, the noble aspiration to leave the world better and happier than when we found it, – motives eminently such as are called social, come in as part of the grounds of culture, and the main and pre-eminent part.[14]

---

[10] Jacques Derrida, *Writing and Difference*, trans. Alan Bass (London: Routledge and Kegan Paul, 1981), p. 283.

[11] Paul Harvey and J. E. Heseltine, *The Oxford Companion to French Literature* (Oxford: Oxford University Press, 1969), p. 694.

[12] Jacques Derrida, *Of Grammatology*, trans. Gayatri Chakravorty Spivak (Baltimore: Johns Hopkins University Press, 1982), p. 158.   [13] *Ibid.*, p. 104.

[14] Matthew Arnold, *Culture and Anarchy* (1869), ed. J. Dover Wilson (Cambridge: Cambridge University Press, 1960), p. 44.

Arnold's emphasis here is on the incorporation of culture into the social nexus through its effects on an audience. Culture testifies to the power of a society to remake itself. The imaginative power of the literate classes projects (and renders possible) a morally improved social world; it is the task of artists and teachers (this distinction is blurred in Arnold) to initiate the public into a utopian vision whereby 'the moral, social and beneficent character of culture become manifest'.[15] Taine's consideration of the 'forces' impelling literary production can usefully be considered alongside Arnold's interest in cultural reception. Both writers seek to present a coherent, totalised meaning that is valid for all cultural production. This production is, in turn, defined by a set of values that include tradition, educative power and moral force.

In 1957, the Canadian critic Northrop Frye published *Anatomy of Criticism*, a text that blends the moralism of Arnold with the speculative insights of the Cambridge ritualists. The sheer inclusiveness of Frye's work, together with the close and rigorous readings which he presents, have given this work the status of a twentieth-century classic, a 'masterwork of modern critical theory'.[16] Frye's system projects the seasonal cycle on to the four narrative categories of comedy, romance, tragedy and irony. These generic markers are crossed with patterns of isolation (the tragic) and integration (the comic). In western literature, these narrative and thematic elements are the territory of a hero who is, respectively, mythic, romantic, tragic, comic and ironic; this 'ironic' hero (as created by Joyce and Kafka for instance) is seen as a renewer of the cycle: 'Irony . . . begins in realism and dispassionate observation. But as it does so, it moves steadily towards myth and dim outlines of sacrificial ritual and dying gods begin to reappear in it.'[17]

As this brief account indicates, Frye's scheme theorises the literary imagination in terms of mythic archetypes, a communal consciousness that shuttles between the poles of utopian longing and dystopian fear. The slippage between literature and myth appears to disconnect Frye's theory from the social issues which are frequently raised in his writings. Consciousness of this disconnection is reflected in Mary Douglas' attacks on the ritual and social myths centred around purity and pollution. As she puts it, 'myth sits above and athwart the exigencies of social life. It is capable of presenting one picture and then its opposite.'[18] Frye, for his part, stresses the 'sequence of contexts and relationships in which the whole work of literary art can be placed'.[19]

[15] *Ibid.*, p. 46.

[16] Vincent Leitch, *American Literary Criticism From the Thirties to the Eighties* (New York: Columbia University Press, 1988), p. 136.

[17] Northrop Frye, *Anatomy of Criticism: Four Essays* (New York: Atheneum/Princeton University Press, 1957), p. 42.

[18] Mary Douglas, *Implicit Meanings: Essays in Anthropology* (London: Routledge and Kegan Paul, 1975), p. 289.   [19] Frye, *Anatomy*, p. 73.

This organised vision of human society set out in the *Anatomy* has attracted much comment. Eagleton summarises Frye's position thus: 'Frye stands in the liberal humanist tradition of Arnold, desiring, as he says, "society as free, classless and urbane." What he means by "classless", like Arnold before him, is in effect a society which universally subscribes to his own middle-class liberal values.'[20] This criticism offers a useful way into the complexities of Frye's view of the function of criticism. However, while the encyclopaedic, universalising character of the enterprise does suggest a systematic meta-narrative of control, there is also a strong affiliation between Frye's 'system' and the line of emancipatory narratives inspired by contemporary experience of social dislocation and changes to the structures of work and education in the twentieth century. Marx and Freud, central figures in this area, are co-opted by Frye for their offering of 'mythological expressions of concern in which man expresses his own attitude to the culture he has built'.[21]

In terms of twentieth-century critical methodologies, one of Frye's greatest achievements lies in his steady resistance to the insidious lure of New Criticism with its promise of a safe, technically proficient literary method. His object has been to maintain and elaborate the links between social structure and literary artefact: 'criticism will always have two aspects, one turned toward the structure of literature and one turned toward the other cultural phenomena that form the social environment of literature'.[22]

Frye's method was quickly overtaken in European literary theory by the rise of a structuralist literary criticism. This model of analysis, stemming from Russian formalism and the structural linguistics of Ferdinand de Saussure, received a new lease of life through the post-war anthropological texts of Claude Lévi-Strauss. Lévi-Strauss seeks to demonstrate that the language system, like other sign systems, reveals the structure of culture, that the linguistic model can be applied in a wide variety of contexts including those of food and clothing. This structure is regulated, as is language, by rules and usages which seek to enculturate the natural, to produce 'human' meanings. Language 'constitutes "at once the prototype of the cultural phenomenon (distinguishing men from the animals) and the phenomenon whereby all the forms of social life are established and perpetuated"'.[23] The structuralist movement sought to identify the 'codes' of literature; instead of close reading, the task of criticism was to note the 'mythologies' (Barthes) and patterns (Greimas) inscribed in the processes of reading and writing. The value-laden term 'literature' is replaced by the objective term 'écriture' in the cultural poetics of this group of (mainly) French thinkers.

The last forty years of anthropologically based criticism owes much to the

[20] Terry Eagleton, *Literary Theory*, 2nd edn. (Oxford: Blackwell, 1996), pp. 81–82.
[21] Northrop Frye, *The Stubborn Structure* (Ithaca: Cornell University Press, 1970), p. 54.
[22] Northrop Frye, *The Critical Path* (Bloomington: Indiana University Press, 1971), p. 25.
[23] Quoted in Terence Hawkes, *Structuralism and Semiotics* (London: Routledge, 1992), p. 33.

seismic shift in literary theory that the rise of poststructuralism and, in particular, postcolonialism has brought about. In his 1973 collection, *The Interpretation of Cultures*, Clifford Geertz suggested that the term 'thick description' (a coinage of Gilbert Ryle) offered a powerful means of articulating a new model of anthropology.[24] 'Thick description' seeks to outline 'the multiplicity of complex conceptual structures, many of them superimposed upon or knotted into one another, which are at once strange, irregular, and inexplicit'.[25] For Geertz, human behaviour represents a dense signalling system which can only be comprehended through an imaginative engagement with the cultural contexts of its occurrence. The toolkit of the observing anthropologist includes the kinds of linguistic and visual sensitivity that belong to artistic practice: '. . . the line between mode of representation and substantive content is as undrawable in cultural analysis as it is in painting'.[26]

Geertz's position, rooted in the semiotics of the 1960s, unsettles the subject/object relationship that was a founding doctrine of the anthropological discipline, and initiates that shift toward the discourse theory of the social sciences that is current today. The literary critic Edward Said, in a series of illuminating texts, also interrogates the foundations of anthropology and has suggested that the examination of cultural practices is inevitably tainted with the 'sameness/difference' binary that produces a cultural value for self/other, man/woman, west/east, and civilised/primitive.

In a feminist contribution to this topic, Sherry B. Ortner maps domestic/public skills and concrete/abstract thought on to the nature/culture division. Woman's oppression is located in a biologically grounded understanding of difference. It is owing to this that she is reduced to a 'structurally subordinate domestic context', and systematically socialised so as to identify with the maternal role, that she appears to be 'rooted more directly and deeply in nature'.[27] *The Elementary Structures of Kinship* by Claude Lévi-Strauss, which contains the discussion of the incest taboo, has also been viewed as a text which seeks to naturalise a dominance/submission pattern in male/female gender roles in that its theory of a primeval 'exchange of women' associates these roles with the origin of culture. Gayle Rubin exposes the sexism inherent in cultural practices when she argues that the expression 'exchange of women' 'is a shorthand for expressing that social relations of a kinship system specify that men have certain rights in their female kin, and that women do not have the same rights either in themselves or in their male kin'.[28]

[24] Clifford Geertz, *The Interpretation of Cultures* (New York: Harpercollins, 1973).
[25] *Ibid.*, p. 10.   [26] *Ibid.*, p. 16.
[27] Sherry B. Ortner, 'Is Female to Male as Nature is to Culture?', in M. Z. Rosaldo and L. Lamphere (eds.), *Woman, Culture and Society* (Stanford: Stanford University Press, 1974), p. 184.
[28] Gayle Rubin, 'The Traffic in Women: Notes on the "Political Economy" of Sex', in R. N. Reiter (ed.), *Toward an Anthropology of Women* (New York and London: Monthly Review Press, 1975), p. 177.

Such race and gender issues have intensified concerns about the legitimacy of anthropology as a discipline. The 'theory wars' in English studies have deepened this discussion as a result of the poststructuralist turn in literary criticism. The Enlightenment had posited a claim for a centred, stable subject, purposive, rational and expressive relationships between people and a stable epistemological framework. The poststructuralist critique of these claims reduces cultural binary distinctions to issues of signification, the interpretive needs of particular communities, and so on. Postcolonialism has, on the whole, taken a more robust view of the issues of representation and language, seeking to implement a radical politics of difference as a strategy in the critical analysis of western intellectual narratives.

One of the earliest models of interventionist criticism that reads 'anthropologically' in order to point up the ideological determinants of textual meaning is an essay on Conrad's *Heart of Darkness* by Chinua Achebe (1977). Achebe sees the novel as saturated in racism; he reads its misrepresentations of Africa as typical of the prejudices of the European observer. The canonical authority of Conrad's text makes this critique all the more telling:

Africa as setting and backdrop which eliminates the African as human factor. Africa as a metaphysical battlefield devoid of all recognizable humanity into which the wandering European enters at his peril. Can nobody see the preposterous and perverse arrogance in thus reducing Africa to the role of props for the break-up of one petty European mind?[29]

What is notable (or notorious) about this critical act is Achebe's unfashionable assumption that literary texts are political documents; the aesthetic is not a bar but a bridge to the ethical implications of the politics of the text. His reading notes the metaphoric structure, the layering of narrative voices, the modernist economy of means, yet refuses to ignore pressing human issues. In this, his essay acts as augury of a philosophic position that is of key importance in recent critical debates. Christopher Norris, in a discussion of J. Hillis Miller's *The Ethics of Reading,* cogently summarises the view that literature has a meaning relevant to the aims, interests and purposes of human beings: 'it is wrong to think of literature as a realm apart, as enjoying an exemption from the normal modes of truth-telling discourse or speech-act entailment . . . Such notions . . . create what amounts to a false sense of ontological security by thus fencing literature off within a separate aesthetic domain.'[30]

The links between this broader view of literary meaning and the eighteenth-century conception of literature as an artefact constructed from a nexus of elements drawn from social life can readily be seen. The further point can be made that at a certain stage in this conceptual enlargement, the term 'literature' becomes absorbed into the more general category of culture.

[29] Chinua Achebe, *Hopes and Impediments* (Oxford: Heinemann International, 1988), p. 8.
[30] Christopher Norris, *The Truth About Postmodernism* (Oxford: Blackwell, 1993), p. 185.

This is the process that has resulted in literary studies becoming pressed into the service of cultural studies in many academic institutions.

Cultural studies thus opens up the anthropological aspects of literary study from two directions. The first is represented by a group of scholars whose expertise was formed in a literary studies context but who now use literary theory as a provider of tools for many different kinds of analysis. Homi K. Bhabha, Robert Young, Gayatri Chakravorty Spivak and Frederic Jameson would be among this group of scholars. The second direction is taken by anthropologists seeking to foreground the issues of textuality and often using similar source material to that developed by the new literary theory for their projects. James Clifford and Clifford Geertz have applied discourse studies to the conceptual field of their discipline and have produced, from this practice, a striking renewal of a discipline that has worked for some time to marginalise the empirical (and value-laden) context of its origin. An anthology entitled *Writing Culture* provides a useful introduction to the hybrid discipline that has resulted from this convergence. James Clifford argues in his introductory essay that 'writing has emerged as central to what anthropologists do',[31] and that, '[m]ost of the essays, while focusing on textual practices, reach beyond texts to contexts of power, resistance, institutional constraint, and innovation'.[32] Much of the material gathered in this text deals with the underlying assumptions, power systems and mechanisms of production that enable texts to be articulated and circulated. Race, gender, class, religious affiliation, sexuality and mental, social or physical disadvantage would be among the factors that lead to gain or loss in this respect. As Paul Rabinow suggests, 'we need to anthropologize the West: show how exotic its constitution of reality has been'.[33]

This aim bears a striking resemblance to the literary based work of Frederic Jameson and Homi K. Bhabha. For instance, Jameson's attempt to shift the critique of narrative into the political arena considers the 'textual revolution' as that which 'drives the wedge of the concept of a "text" into the traditional disciplines by extrapolating the notion of "discourse" or "writing" onto objects previously thought to be "realities" or objects in the real world, such as the various levels or instances of a social formation; political power, social class, institutions and events themselves'.[34]

Anthropological criticism appears, in these recent formulations, to be returning to the motives that first propelled it into existence. The preoccupation with language, discourse and textuality that inspired the 'new science' of

---

[31] James Clifford and G. E. Marcus (eds.), *Writing Culture: The Poetics and Politics of Ethnography* (Berkeley and London: University of California Press, 1986), p. 2.   [32] *Ibid.*
[33] Paul Rabinow, 'Representations are Social Facts: Modernity and Post-Modernity in Anthropology', in *ibid.*, p. 241.
[34] Fredric Jameson, *The Political Unconscious: Narrative as a Socially Symbolic Act* (Ithaca: Cornell University Press, 1981), pp. 296–297.

the Enlightenment in the late seventeenth and eighteenth centuries prompted the attempt at an objective account of the phenomenal world. The new fields of law, medicine, education, art and science were driven by this revolution. Yet this great leap forward has been haunted by a history that was once forgotten and is only now being repeated. A subsidiary definition of anthropology in the *Oxford English Dictionary* refers to it as '[a] speaking in the manner of men'. This curious phrase takes on a topical resonance when read with an awareness of the self-reflexive critique that many anthropologists now bring to the originating ideology and linguistic structure of their discipline. For it suggests that anthropology is not a master-narrative (despite the term 'men') but a narrative that is always under construction, a staging of presence, a framing of subjectivity inside the linguistic field. Such notions lie close to the line of modern philosophy that links Adorno and Benjamin to Foucault and Derrida. Memory, mark, inscription and trace are key terms in this work as it preserves, celebrates and mourns the privileged and marginal moments of the happening of a 'rational' civilization. An eloquent account of this position is given in an essay by Gayatri Chakravorty Spivak as she writes of

the recognition, within deconstructive practice, of provisional and intractable starting points in any investigative effort; its disclosure of complicities where a will to knowledge would create oppositions; its insistence that in disclosing complicities the critic-as-subject is herself complicit with the object of her critique; its emphasis upon 'history' and upon the ethico-political as the 'trace' of that complicity – the proof that we do not inhabit a clearly defined critical space free of such traces; and, finally, the acknowledgment that its own discourse can never be adequate to its example.[35]

In this quotation, an agenda for an ethical deconstruction of the sameness/otherness binary is put forward. The critic, while aware of the way in which language, race, gender and class affect her ability to speak 'in the manner of' others, still seeks a speaking position that intervenes in the political world and that values the subject, however dubious the springs of its being.

[35] Gayatri Chakravorty Spivak, *In Other Worlds* (London: Methuen, 1987), p. 180.

Modernity and postmodernism

21

Modernism, modernity, modernisation

ROBERT HOLUB

Modernism has always been a confusing and disputed term. In architecture it has been used to describe a design strategy based on rationality and functional analysis, such as those found in industrial architecture in the United States or in the Bauhaus projects of Germany, and it is most often distinguished from a vague 'traditionalism' that was its predecessor, and an equally ill-defined postmodernism that succeeded it. In music modernism refers most often to those composers who broke with the conventions of tonality and recognisable rhythmic patterns and structures, introducing instead musical style marked by dissonance, discontinuity, fragmentation and experimentation in sound and form. In dance the notion of modernism has been employed in connection with twentieth-century practitioners whose work reflected themes of contemporary life, but also with dance that focused on movement and form inherent in the human body. In pictorial art we find modernism emerging as a break with traditional and academic styles; in its incipient years it often served as commentary on social life, but as it developed, it came to explore visual representation as such, rather than any specific subject or topic. Literary scholars have most often viewed modernism as part of a reaction to both historical changes in the social order and aesthetic imperatives inherited from the nineteenth century, in particular those adopted by classicists and realists. Literary modernism eventually seems to reject representation as an artistic exigency, resorting instead to experimentation in forms and with words, although it often does not wish to relinquish an impact on readers. It is difficult to determine precisely what unites these various forms of modernism, but one suspects that if a unifying principle does exist, it is to be located in a specifically European consciousness that emerged in the late nineteenth century and continued into the decades of the next century.

Although we may situate modernism as a movement historically in the late nineteenth and early twentieth century, we can readily see that the consciousness of being modern was anything but original at that time and cannot be used to distinguish modernism from earlier ventures. It appears that the notion of being modern is itself very old and dates at least from the fifth century in Rome, where Christians employed it to distinguish the new Christian age from the epoch of paganism. At times, of course, there have been different valuations placed on the notion of modernity, and some of the most celebrated debates have resulted from taking sides for or against tradition. For the history of literature and aesthetics the most important marker is the celebrated *Querelle des anciens et des modernes*, which took place in two important stages: in France in the late seventeenth century, and in Germany approximately one hundred years later. At issue in these controversies was how to resolve a paradoxical situation. On the one hand it seemed evident that modern societies evidenced advances in certain areas of knowledge. The science and technology of the moderns were surely better than the science and technology of ancient societies (Greece and Rome). On the other it appeared that in the aesthetic arena – in architecture, sculpture, literature and art – the works of the ancients were at least equal to, if not better than, anything the moderns could produce. A careful analysis of the various stages of this debate would demonstrate the gradual emancipation of art from the hegemony of classical norms.[1] But it would also show an evolution in concepts and in consciousness. By the time we reach the early nineteenth century and the stage of the conflict has shifted to Germany, the operative terms in the aesthetic realm are less often 'modern' and 'ancient' than 'romantic' and 'classic', and the resolution lies less in taking one side or the other than in viewing the demise of classical art and the rise of romantic art as part of a larger historical process. In essence the transformation is from a recognition of difference to one of evolution and process, from a universe that is governed by eternal laws and rules to one that admits modification over time, from an appeal to perfection in ahistorical accomplishment to a call for originality and creativity. The prerequisite for the consciousness of nineteenth- and twentieth-century modernism, understood as a break with tradition, has its intellectual roots in the romantic endeavour to distinguish itself historically from classicism.

The aesthetic sphere and the dangers of the avant-garde

There are two additional aspects of modernity originating in the philosophical atmosphere of German idealism that are essential for our understanding of the consciousness that underlies modernism. These aspects are described best in the writings of Jürgen Habermas, a philosopher and social theorist who, in contrast to most theorists of the 1980s and 1990s, advocates a completion of the modernist project, rather than a turn to various forms of postmodernity. In his works Habermas has developed two historico-philosophical narratives to describe the modernist situation, one that is ultimately Kantian, which deals with the real tendencies of modernity, and one Hegelian, which captures the way in which the problems of modernity are reflected and solved in thought. According to the first, modernity is characterised by the separa-

---

[1] See Hans Robert Jauss, 'Literarische Tradition und gegenwärtiges Bewußtsein der Modernität', *Literaturgeschichte als Provokation* (Frankfurt: Suhrkamp, 1970), pp. 11–66.

tion of three types of activity – science, morality and art – into individual spheres. This scheme, drawn from Max Weber, is ultimately related to Kant's three critiques, which circumscribe the same general topics from the perspective of human subjectivity. With the disintegration of a unified religious or metaphysical world-view, each sphere achieves an autonomy and is assigned a particular question and domain: truth, conceived as an epistemological matter, is ascribed to natural science; normative rightness, formulated in terms of justice, is assigned to morality; and the determination of authenticity or beauty is ascertained through judgements of taste in the realm of art. Habermas continues these tripartite divisions by identifying a specific rationality with each sphere: cognitive-instrumental for science, moral-practical for ethics and aesthetic-expressive for art. Only with the advent of modernity do we witness an immanent history for each of these three realms; only in the modern era do these spheres begin to operate under internally developed laws and imperatives.

There exist, however, inherent dangers in this process: with the development of modern societies we encounter an increasing specialisation within each sphere, which Habermas, following Weber, calls rationalisation. For Habermas, rationalisation is a descriptive term that encompasses both positive and negative valences. Since the differentiation of activity removes it from dogmatic exigencies that had formerly defined it in traditional societies, subjecting it instead to reflection and justification based on evidence and argument, rationalisation is a necessary and welcome process in the progress of humankind. But some of its by-products are pernicious and appear to counteract the democratic and participatory tendencies of modern societies. Habermas notes that the instantiation of separate spheres for science, morality and art fosters a culture of experts that excludes collective decision-making. What Niklas Luhmann, the German sociologist of systems theory, greets as increased functional differentiation, Habermas bemoans as an impoverished lifeworld, since individuals are excluded from spheres that have a direct bearing on their lives and happiness. The project of modernity, which in Habermas' view is a continuation of the Enlightenment, is to promote the increased rationalisation of each sphere, while simultaneously releasing 'the cognitive potentials of each of these domains to set them free from their esoteric forms' (p. 9).[2] As formulated in the eighteenth century the goals of the three spheres are objective science, universal morality and autonomous art. The Enlightenment held the hope of employing the accumulated knowledge in each sphere for a more satisfying, enriching and rational organisation of everyday life, and Habermas believes that this hope can still be realised in our own times.

---

[2] Parenthetical citations in this section are taken from Jürgen Habermas, 'Modernity versus Postmodernity', *New German Critique* 22 (1981), pp. 3–14.

Modernism, for Habermas, is aesthetic modernity. It is the result of the differentiation of a sphere of art from a formerly unified and encompassing world-view. The tendency of art since the middle of the eighteenth century has been toward increased autonomy, toward a separation of aesthetic products of culture from a connection with truth (as conceived by science) or goodness (as a moral postulate). Kant's *Critique of Judgement* (1790) may not have been the inaugural document in this process, but it was certainly one of the most important. With Kant the trajectory for modern art was firmly established. An aesthetic realm, based on a universal notion of taste, separates itself out from the cognitive and ethical sphere. Although in the enlightenment philosophy of Kant a *sensus communis* still underlies our faculty of judgement, making beauty a matter of intersubjectively valid judgements of taste, the process of specialisation soon takes hold. Art as an end in itself leads ineluctably to a severing of the connections between art and the more general public. Eventually the type of formal experimentation and elitism we associate with twentieth-century art becomes the norm, as the various branches of art purify themselves, focusing on their constitutive elements: as we have seen above, in dance modernism is concerned with the inherent movements of the body; in music tone and rhythm are foregrounded; in literature and the pictorial arts representation gradually relinquishes its sway and is replaced by a foregrounding of the media themselves. Lines, color, shapes, sounds, words or even letters become themselves aesthetic objects. Gradually art relinquishes its appeal to the larger community and begins to aim at experts and connoisseurs.

One branch of modernism, usually called the 'avant-garde', challenges this inherent tendency in art by calling into question the separation of the aesthetic sphere from other human activities. Peter Bürger has best analysed this rebellious side of modernism, which criticised autonomous art by pointing to its own historicity as an institution. Duchamp's urinal or the collages of the surrealists are meant to radicalise the content of art and to reconcile the aesthetic with the everyday. Art as a smug and safe refuge for bourgeois appreciation and fine taste is the ultimate target of the avant-garde's assault; the destruction of the boundaries between art and life is the ultimate goal.[3] Behind this challenge Habermas detects an endeavour to recuperate the 'promise of happiness' that emanates from the original modernist project. But the surrealist 'warfare' against autonomous art fails in two regards. First, removing the aura from art, declaring everyone to be an artist, destroying the legitimacy of aesthetic forms, as the avant-garde had done, does not necessarily lead to the desired liberation: '[w]hen the containers of an autonomously developed cultural sphere are shattered, the contents get dispersed. Nothing remains from a desublimated meaning or a destructured form; an emancipatory effect does not follow' (p. 10). More importantly, the surrealist challenge

[3] Peter Bürger, *Theory of the Avant-Garde* (Minnesota: University of Minnesota Press, 1984).

ignored the need for communicative practices that cross all domains: cognitive, moral-practical and expressive. The rationalisation of the lifeworld cannot be countered by actions against a single sphere. 'A reified everyday praxis can be cured only by creating unconstrained interaction of the cognitive with the moral-practical and the aesthetic-expressive elements. Reification cannot be overcome by forcing just one of those highly stylised cultural spheres to open up and become more accessible' (p. 11). In short, the avant-garde represents a false path of aesthetic modernity: in contrast to traditional modernism, it initiated a false or one-sided negation of art that did not lead to an all-encompassing emancipation, but rather to a reaffirmation of the very aesthetic categories it sought to efface.

The Hegelian narrative and aesthetic irrationalism

The second narrative, which Habermas develops at length in the *Philosophical Discourse of Modernity* (1987), has slightly different implications for modernism. Although Kant and Fichte established subjectivity as the constitutive concept for modernity, Habermas claims that Hegel was 'the first philosopher for whom modernity became a problem' (p. 43).[4] Emancipating itself from the dogmas of religion and the past, modernity sets itself the task of creating its normativity out of itself. Hegel assumes this to be the central problem for his philosophical system and it leads him to the view that the modern age is 'marked universally by a structure of self-relation that he calls subjectivity' (p. 16). Subjectivity, as conceived by Hegel, has connotations and implications that reach into all areas of life and thought. Perhaps most important for Habermas, it establishes the essential forms in which modern culture will develop: along the lines suggested by Kant in his three critiques. With the subject no longer externally restrained the natural sciences are now free to confront a disenchanted nature unconstrained by the fetters placed on inquiry by extra-scientific dogma. Morality develops according to the notion of free subjects exercising free will, resulting in individual freedom and universal rights. And modern art, labelled romantic in Hegel's aesthetic theory, becomes characterised by its absolute inwardness. The spheres of science, morality and art, based on principles of truth, justice and taste were not only separated from belief, but also encompassed under the principle of subjectivity. The philosophical narrative developed from Hegel's philosophy thus includes as an important by-product the differentiated spheres of science, morality and art, but its goal is ultimately the grounding of modernity in self-contained subjectivity.

---

[4] Parenthetical citations in this section are taken from Jürgen Habermas, *The Philosophical Discourse of Modernity*, trans. Frederick Lawrence (Cambridge: MIT Press, 1987).

According to Habermas' reading, Hegel was unable to accomplish his goal satisfactorily, because he solved the problem of modernity 'too well' (p. 42). We can understand the difficulty as a victory of reason over the individual subject. By taking subjectivity and a philosophy of reflective self-consciousness as a starting point, Hegel propounds not only the freedom and unity of the subject, but also its objectification and alienation as object of its own subjectivity. The pernicious consequences of Hegel's solution become even more evident in his writings about the state. Habermas notes that the subject encounters itself both as universal subject embodied in the state and as individual subject or citizen of the state. In a potential conflict between the two, the concrete absolute of the state takes precedence. 'For the sphere of the ethical, the outcome of this logic is the primacy of the higher-level subjectivity of the state over the subjective freedom of the individual' (p. 40). The consequences of investing reason or self-conscious subjectivity with absolute authority is a deprecation of individual experience and criticism. 'Hegel's philosophy satisfies the need of modernity for self-grounding only at the cost of devaluing present-day reality and blunting critique. In the end, philosophy removes all importance from its own present age, destroys interest in it, and deprives it of the calling to self-critical renewal' (p. 42). Hegel's awareness of the necessity for the modern age to ground itself in self-conscious subjectivity paradoxically leads him to depreciate the exigencies of his own era.

Habermas detects an alternative to the philosophy of consciousness or subjectivity in Hegel's early works in which he wrote of the Christian community. The road Hegel does not choose, that of intersubjectivity, becomes foundational for Habermas's thought, and the writings that culminate in his *Theory of Communicative Action* (1984, 1987) are an endeavour to complete this discarded Hegelian approach and thus to solve the dilemmas of modernity in something other than a 'philosophy of consciousness'. Mainstream philosophy, however, continues to try to reconcile the demands of modernity with what Hegel had established as the philosophy of modernity. In the aftermath of the Hegelian solution Habermas outlines three directions that emerge, all of which criticise a notion of reason grounded in self-conscious subjectivity. The first, associated with the Young Hegelians, turns to a philosophy of practice that seeks to liberate a rationality pent up in its bourgeois forms. This group, whose most celebrated figure was Karl Marx, remains true to the spirit of the Enlightenment, but feels that its goals can only be accomplished by turning to the material world. For Marx the concept of labour replaces subjectivity as the key to modernity, and the solution to modernity's problems is envisioned in a proletarian revolution. The second group affirms Hegel's notion of the state and religion as compensation for the disruptions and alienation of modern society. Originally identified with right Hegelians, this group is the progenitor of the neoconservatives in contemporary times. Defending institutions and traditional values against radical critique, neoconservatives

such as Daniel Bell or Arnold Gehlen want nothing more than to allow bourgeois society to unfold according to its own dynamic.

The perils of this narrative in the aesthetic sphere do not lie with an artistic
avant-garde that extends endeavours to explode the aesthetic sphere and
produce a one-sided revolution, but in the aestheticisation of reflection itself.
For a third direction opts against extending reason, as the left and the right
Hegelians did, and instead, recognising the impasse of a philosophy of consciousness, turns against the Enlightenment and embraces art. Starting with
Nietzsche, whose reliance on the Dionysian is a transposition of aesthetic
experience into the archaic realm, the philosophers associated with postmodernity form an alliance with aesthetic modernity in their rejection of reason as
a vehicle for progress. Nietzsche's significance lies in his conception of a critique of modernity without any emancipatory content. Although his
anti-enlightenment philosophy, including its Dionysian dimension, has its
roots in the romantic tradition, his was the most congenial and influential
starting point for subsequent thinkers. Habermas notes two strands of his
thought that had the most impact for the twentieth-century theory. The first
conceives of an aesthetically based critique of western philosophy that would
oppose all claims to truth by valorising the will to power. The anthropological, psychological and historical aspects of such a subversion of reason have
been examined in recent times by Bataille, Lacan and Foucault respectively.
The second avenue that Nietzsche opens up attempts to uncover the metaphysical roots of the philosophical tradition without relinquishing its own
claims to philosophical rigor. This internal critique of metaphysics is associated with the works of Heidegger and his French disciple Derrida. Neither
of these alternatives escapes the problematic of modernity, however, since
according to Habermas they both accept the terms of the Hegelian tradition
and argue from within the conceptual framework of a philosophy of consciousness. The outside, or other, or 'post' that is envisioned as an alternative
is thus always just the irrational mirror image of reason conceived as self-contained subjectivity.

Modernisation and the challenge of the market

There is yet another way to understand the advent of modernity. The separation of spheres of human activity or the realisation of self-contained subjectivity are ultimately part of processes associated with the development of
modern societies. Often these processes are referred to in a short-hand form
as modernisation. Contemporary social scientists dealing with modernisation are careful to point out the foibles of their predecessors. Both Marxists
and modernisation theorists of the post-war era regarded economic factors as
the sole driving force in the rise of modern societies, but today commentators

consider the economy to be only one of the contributing factors. We have also come to recognise that modernisation is not an even process: it occurs in different regions of Europe at different times, and it proceeds at an uneven pace. The political dimension of modern societies is likewise not uniform, and throughout Europe different sorts of governmental structures, from dictatorial regimes to liberal democracies, were consonant with modernisation processes. The same can be said of societal aspects, which exhibit vast differences in hierarchical structures and social differentiation. Despite these caveats, a unified notion of modernisation can still be a useful term for describing the process whereby traditional societies became modern industrial societies, and although there is no ideal type or normal development, the results have been fairly uniform. Max Weber's description of modern European civilisation, as articulated in the introduction to *The Protestant Ethic and the Spirit of Capitalism* (1958), continues to be a compelling account of the consequences of modernisation, while the body of *The Protestant Ethic* (1978) and the unfinished *Economy and Society* provide a persuasive commentary on the modernisation process.

Weber's various analyses present no single defining characteristic for modernisation. He points out that there are a number of features that distinguish western civilisation from the rest of the world. Only in the west has science, defined in terms of empirical knowledge about the world and experimentation, achieved such a preeminent status. The west also evidences differences in its organisation of historical scholarship, in its music and in architecture. Certain political formations also are peculiar to occidental cultures, and Weber points in particular to parliamentary government with its rule by law according to a written constitution and its extensive administrative apparatus. In his earlier work Weber argues that capitalism, although it has existed worldwide, has developed in the west in qualitative and quantitative ways that have not been duplicated elsewhere. The key difference, he claims, is to be found in the organisation of formally free labour, although he also mentions the importance of the separation of business from the household, and of the introduction of rational bookkeeping, of applied science or technological innovation, and of legal and administrative structures for western developments. But even in his early thought, where economics appears to be the centrepiece, Weber places equal or greater emphasis on consciousness. Economic rationalism, the ethos of western capitalist development is intimately related to ascetic Protestantism, and at points Weber appears to be offering what amounts to an idealist explanation for modernisation. In later works, other topics come to the fore. Political organisation and its legitimacy, and the increasingly complex bureaucratic structures of industrial societies, are focal points for understanding how modern Europe has defined the modern age.

The exact process of modernisation might be complex, and each society may have travelled along different paths, but it is possible to distinguish modern societies from their traditional counterparts, as Stuart Hall does, on the basis of four encompassing features. (1) Power is secular, rather than religious, and it is defined in terms of a nation-state operating within geographically secure borders and based on conceptions of sovereignty and legitimacy. (2) Economies are based on money; there is large-scale commodity production and consumption regulated by free markets. Private property is enshrined in law. Long-term capital accumulation is established as a goal and rationale. (3) Fixed social hierarchies, such as existed in traditional societies, are replaced by more dynamic social stratification. Industrial societies produced new classes and a different relationship between the sexes. (4) We encounter the demise of religious world views and the concomitant ascent of secular and rationalist ways of interpreting the world and our actions in the world. Gradually individualist and instrumental forms of thinking prevail.[5] These four features overlap significantly with the views of Weber in his mature writings, and they reflect a world order in which change is enshrined as a central characteristic. Representative governments, capitalist economies, fluid social hierarchies and individualist worldviews suggest a world in flux, and it is not coincidental that a chief motif of modernist literature and commentary has been the transient, the fleeting, the contingent and the ephemeral. In contrast to traditional societies, the modern social order thrives on change, which can translate into apprehension and angst, as reflected in some of the seminal works of aesthetic modernity, or into the excitement and exhilaration that accompanies revolution and novelty in other writings.

But another aspect of modernist consciousness is related to art's status as one commodity among other commodities. With the withdrawal of governing bodies into largely administrative and bureaucratic apparatuses, the demise of the church as a patron, and the disappearance of aristocratic largesse, the artist, like the worker, was set free in the world of production and compelled to sell his or her wares on the market. The commodification of art is a process that started long before the advent of aesthetic modernity; its roots lie in the Renaissance; the eighteenth and early nineteenth century advanced its cause by destroying structures that had promoted commissioned artistic production. But by the time we reach the end of the nineteenth century, the notion of art as a commodity is no longer questioned, and the place of the artist as the producer for anonymous others is the accepted norm. The autonomy of art in the aesthetic sphere is in some sense an idealistic reflection of art's commodification, and the exalted creativity and originality of the artist are symptoms of market realities, as well as representing an individual aspiration for accomplishment. Modernisation presents new challenges for writers and artists producing commodities. Some choose to foreground the fetishised nature of art,

[5] Stuart Hall, 'Introduction', *Modernity: An Introduction to Modern Societies* (Cambridge: Polity Press, 1995), p. 8.

as we see in the dadaist and surrealist enterprises. Others, such as Rilke, Pound or Eliot, withdraw from conscious production for the market, remaining aloof and elitist, and focusing on formal perfections and innovations. Still others turn to the audience, whether out of political aims, such as Brecht, or even mercantile motives.

Alternative modernist revolutions

The modernisation process has also led theorists of modernism to reflect on the relationship of art to its material conditions of production. Two opposing views, represented by Walter Benjamin and Theodor Adorno, emerge as alternative ways to rupture the constraints of a capitalist social order. For Benjamin the modern situation is characterised by the technical possibilities for reproduction. Formerly works of art exuded an authenticity and uniqueness, which Benjamin captures in the notion of 'aura'. It is not coincidental that Benjamin selects a term that emphasises the religious and cultic nature of art; for his point is that the modernisation process, far from distorting some essence of art, presents an opportunity for art to emancipate itself from its earlier limitations. Benjamin is concerned with defining another praxis for art in the modern age, one that will allow it to contribute to a progressive politics. A main interest for him, therefore, is the conflict between painting and photography around the turn of the century. This debate, which revolved around the advent of a technology of reproduction, signals the conscious demise of the autonomy of art, since autonomous art, from the perspective of the social embeddedness of all products of human culture, was merely an illusion of bourgeois ideology. Benjamin's central example of a 'technically reproducible art form' is film. In this medium for the first time we witness an elimination of aura. Because the public is replaced by the camera, the mechanical spectator, so to speak, the aura associated with representation is destroyed. Regardless of how we evaluate particular aspects of Benjamin's arguments, his overall view is clear: the material conditions for modern art have changed, and art must become conscious of these changes if it is going to promote social revolution.

Adorno's view presents an alternative. He too recognises that the conditions under which art is being produced have changed, and that the autonomy of art is no longer predominant in the cultural sphere. But for Adorno, the separation of art into high and low forms has cheapened artistic value and threatens to marginalise authentic aesthetic accomplishment. Indeed, the 'culture industry' in the United States, like fascism and communism in Europe, has eliminated the individuality associated with art and contributed to the damaged subjectivity of the modern age. Adorno bemoans the commodification of art, and he recognises that art has become infused with technology; what is problematic for him is that the technology preferred in capitalist societies has led us away from individual control and creativity and toward the mass production of a degraded art. The seductiveness of the culture industry leads the audience to identify with it, completing the insidious circle of production and consumption. Art in advanced capitalist societies is thus no longer the site of authenticity, but of pseudoindividuality. Adorno's alternative, focused on the materiality of art as form and content, as well as art's immanent social quality, is associated with what we might call 'high modernism'. Despite the lack of overt political commitment in their works, modernist writers such as Marcel Proust, Samuel Beckett or Paul Celan, offer us a glimpse of domination-free intersubjectivity by remaining outside of conventions. Modernist art, like Adorno's philosophy itself, is valued as a means to explode from the inside the normalcy of a social order characterised by fettered subjectivity.

The contrasting views of Benjamin and Adorno on art and their emphasis on different art forms and artists in the twentieth century can easily seduce us into affirming the increasingly popular proposition that there is not one modernism, but several modernisms. It has become comfortable in an age we dub 'postmodern' to avoid a conceptual mode that would unify historical moments or artistic tendencies. Modernism assists us in this intellectual fragmentation because the writers and artists associated with it advocated a variety of different political, social and historical views; indeed, it would be difficult to make a comprehensive list of modernists, or of characteristics in modernist works. Pound and Brecht certainly cannot be politically reconciled; Eliot and Dos Passos did not share the same cultural outlook or aspirations. The usefulness of modernism as a unified concept, however, is that it tells us something essential about how artists and writers responded to a set of circumstances, not that they responded in a similar fashion. Modernisation in European societies and in the United States during the late nineteenth and early twentieth century confronted artists and writers with cultural phenomena they had not yet encountered, or at least not in this form or to this extent. The circumstances were accompanied by certain philosophical and historical developments in the realm of ideas and aesthetics, themselves influenced by modernisation. Within the particularities of modernisation and modernity, modernism emerged, and what we mean when we speak of modernism is not a single, unified, aesthetic movement, but rather the range of responses by artists and writers to an identical historical, philosophical and aesthetic predicament.

22

Postmodernism

PATRICIA WAUGH

> Where are the primary causes on which I can take my stand,
> where are my foundations? Where am I to take them from?
> I practise thinking, and consequently each of my primary
> causes pulls along another, even more primary, in its wake,
> and so on *ad infinitum*.
>
> Fyodor Dostoevsky, *Notes From Underground* (1864)

Naming the unnamable: what is postmodernism?

In 1979, Jean-François Lyotard proclaimed that Enlightened modernity was now caught in a 'legitimation crisis' from which it could not recover. By the mid-eighties, *La condition postmoderne* enjoyed hierophantic status as the book which had completed the Nietzschean project of persuading us of the death of the 'grand narratives' of God, metaphysics and science. Twenty years on, the discourse which named that crisis seems to have developed its own terminal symptoms. In a rather Beckettian image, Lyotard has recently declared that postmodernism is now an 'old man's occupation, rummaging in the dustbin of finality to find remains'.[1] Richard Rorty (defender of consensus but hardly secret sharer of Lyotard's postmodern anti-foundationalism) has also come to see the term as so elastic as to be useless even for his own neo-pragmatic purposes. He has, he now tells us, 'given up on the attempt to find something common to Michael Graves' buildings, Pynchon's and Rushdie's novels, Ashberry's poems, various sorts of popular music, and the writings of Heidegger and Derrida'.[2] So, has postmodernism become a victim of that very built-in obsolescence which was central to its diagnosis of all intellectual or artistic culture within late capitalism? Is it possible any longer to define postmodernism? Perhaps the task is comparable to an attempt to force a rainbow back through the geometrical contours of Newton's prism.

---

[1] Jean-François Lyotard, *The Postmodern Condition: A Report on Knowledge*, trans. Geoffrey Bennington and Brian Massumi (Manchester: Manchester University Press, 1984); Lyotard, quoted in Geoffrey Bennington, *Lyotard: Writing the Event* (Manchester: Manchester University Press, 1988).

[2] Richard Rorty, *Philosophical Papers 2: Essays on Heidegger and Others* (Cambridge: Cambridge University Press, 1991), p. 1.

Still, if we accept Fredric Jameson's belief that the value of postmodern expression lies precisely in its attempt to name the unnameable, to find a form in which to represent the seemingly unrepresentable global networks of technologised late capitalist culture, then there is some historical justification in attempting, yet again, to name the unnameable which is postmodernism. Because postmodernism has always been a constitutive as much as a descriptive term, definitions were bound to be value-laden. Even in its earliest literary phase, the same work of art might be dismissed as a perversion of the genuinely radical energies of an earlier avant-garde, a mere reflection of the depthless surfaces of consumer culture, or it might be celebrated (as in the early writing of Ihab Hassan) as auguring a radically new and global post-Cartesian 'gnostic' consciousness. More moderately, it might simply be seen as making the best of what is available, providing, for example, through its parodic form of repetition with distance, the only form of critique remaining in a world in which there can only be a perspectival seeing.[3]

What is the relationship between postmodernism considered, negatively or positively, as the dominant 'mood' of western late capitalism; as a legitimation crisis in western epistemologies and political structures; as a variety of aesthetic or cultural practices; or postmodernism as all those discourses which attempt to theorise late or post-modernity? If postmodernism has taught us that we cannot separate the object of knowledge from the various language games through which it is constructed, then why should we accept any historical 'grand narrative' of postmodernism itself? The term has come to designate a bewilderingly diverse array of 'little narratives' as well as a more broadly epistemic sense of crisis in the foundational philosophical and political discourses of the European Enlightenment. From its very inception, and more so than cultural modernism, postmodernism was created as much by academic categorisation and intellectual reformulation as by aesthetic manifestos and the development of identifiable literary or cultural movements. Theorists of postmodernism are endlessly caught in the performative contradictions of obsessively naming the unnameable even as they decry the activity of naming as incipiently totalitarian. It is no accident that one of the key reference points for postmodernists has always been that oft-quoted sentence from Nietzsche, warning us that: 'We obtain the concept, as we do the form, by overlooking what is individual and actual: whereas nature is acquainted with forms and no concepts. . . but only with an X which remains inaccessible and undefinable for us.'[4] One

---

[3] See Fredric Jameson, 'Postmodernism or the Cultural Logic of Late Capitalism', *New Left Review* 146 (1984), pp. 53–92; Terry Eagleton, *Against the Grain* (London: Verso, 1986); Linda Hutcheon, *A Poetics of Postmodernism: History, Theory, Fiction* (New York and London: Routledge, 1990).

[4] Friedrich Nietzsche, 'On Truth and Lies in a Non-Moral Sense', in *Philosophy and Truth: Selections From Nietzsche's Notebooks of the Early 1870s*, trans. D. Breazeale (New Jersey: Humanities Press, 1979), p. 83.

can accept Nietzsche's warning against intellectual arrogance, however, whilst resisting a full-blown postmodern nominalism. Accordingly, I will argue that postmodernism can be understood as a gradual dissolution of the modern idea of the separate autonomies of the spheres of art, science and morality or politics, and can be viewed as an increasingly pervasive aestheticisation of all spheres of knowledge and experience, from philosophy to politics and finally to science. Furthermore, I shall argue that postmodernism exists in a 'strong' and in a 'weak' form and that each of these may take on either a deconstructive (epistemological) or a reconstructive (ethical) orientation.

The postmodern 'mood' began to gather in the 1960s when changes in western societies (the emergence of post-industrialisation; increased technologisation; expanding consumerism and 'lifestyle niche' advertising; widening democracy and access to secondary and higher education; the growth of youth and sub-cultures; the global spread of information technology, mass media and the 'knowledge' industries; the retreat from both colonialism and utopianism in politics and the rise of new identity politics around race, gender and sexuality) coincided with changes in literary and artistic expression (pop art, anti-modernism in architecture, self-reflexivity in literature) and with a new scepticism towards science and positivism in thought. The changes gradually seemed to add up to both a rejection of modernism and a disillusionment with, and hence repudiation of, Enlightenment and post-Enlightenment rationalist ideas about the unity of the self, the concept of universal justice in politics, the role of the state, the idea of underlying laws of history, the possibility of certainty in thought and science. Since the Enlightenment itself, there had, of course, always been an anti-Enlightenment current in philosophy and art (Dostoevsky's aforementioned novel *Notes From Underground*, for example, challenges everything from Kantian and utilitarian ethics to scientific socialism and gender-blind universalism, in terms remarkably prescient of much postmodern thought), but never before had it seemed to chime so convincingly with the changes taking place in western societies. The retreat from utopianism had already been foreshadowed in the forties and fifties, in the responses of philosophers such as Karl Popper, Hannah Arendt, Michael Oakeshott and Isaiah Berlin, for example, to the horrors of the Holocaust and the rise of totalitarianism. Whilst western governments were busy trying to rebuild the post-war state within the framework of compromise now referred to as 'welfare capitalism', analytic philosophy increasingly turned introspective, political philosophy toward concepts of piecemeal reform or Berlin's 'agonistic liberalism' (a repudiation of all rationalist attempts to derive a collective social Good from the scientific laws of history).

Bertrand Russell had earlier defended Enlightenment rational scepticism as a criticism of knowledge which, though unable to 'tell us with any certainty what is the true answer to the doubts which it raises, is able to suggest many possibilities which enlarge our thoughts and free them from the tyranny of custom'.[5] By the 1970s, those doubts had increasingly turned back on the instruments of their own articulation and analysis, so that objects of knowledge become not so much entities on which language reflects as artefacts actually constructed through and within language. By 1979, when Lyotard published his influential book, new and burgeoning forms of epistemological and cultural relativism were already well out of their infancies. Truth, Knowledge, Self and Value were no longer to be regarded as foundational categories, but as rhetorical constructions masking relations of power and strategies of oppression and marginalisation. In the modern condition, philosophy had claimed the position of privileged metanarrative, claimed to be the discourse which might discover that final vocabulary which would ground the very conditions of knowledge. Postmodernists now claimed to have cut away this final ground in recognising there were only ever vocabularies to invent.

Broadly, postmodernism can be understood as a gradual encroachment of the aesthetic into the spheres of philosophy, ethics and, most recently, science; a gradual displacement of discovery, depth, truth, correspondence and coherence with construction, surface, fictionality, self-reflexive narrative and ironic fragmentation: realism giving way to idealism and then to an all-pervasive textualism. Jameson has described this as a pathology of auto-referentiality; Jean Baudrillard, as a condition of hyperreality where aestheticisation has turned on itself, where even art 'is dead, not only because its critical transcendence is gone, but because reality itself, entirely impregnated by an aesthetic which is inseparable from its own structure, has been confused with its own image'.[6] More specifically though: how did postmodernism gradually seep out of its earliest containment within debates about the value of literary, artistic and architectural modernism and into the fields of philosophy, social and political theory, and finally science studies? What are the value claims made for and against it? What are its political ramifications? What has been its effect on literary criticism? Where is the debate at the end of the century? Can we encompass the entire field of different postmodernisms with a broad map of types and tendencies? How may we trace its intellectual precursors? The rest of this essay will attempt to offer brief answers to some of these questions by considering the emergence of postmodernism: as a formal aesthetic; as a model for political engagement; and as a philosophical critique.

---

[5] Bertrand Russell, *The Problems of Philosophy* (1912) (Oxford: Oxford University Press, 1967), p. 91.
[6] Fredric Jameson, *Postmodernism or the Cultural Logic of Late Capitalism* (London and New York: Verso, 1991) p. ix.; Jean Baudrillard, *Simulations* (New York: Semiotext(e), 1983), pp. 151–152.

The irresistible rise of postmodernism: from art to science

The term 'postmodernism' was first used in the 1950s by literary critics to describe new kinds of literary experiment arising out of, but moving beyond, the terms of aesthetic modernism. It was associated with an emphasis on immanence or situatedness, on contingent experience and cultural complicity, and set in opposition to a modernism confirmed in New Critical theorising and in abstract expressionist aesthetics as conceived in terms of objectivity, transcendence and impersonality. Poets such as Charles Olsen and critics such as William Spanos (editor of the important journal *Boundary 2*) named the existence of a new non-anthropocentric literature whose Heideggerian anti-humanism was directed at seeing 'man' as a being in the world, as radically sit-uated as any other object. A similar tendency appeared at the same time in the *chosisme* of the French new novel and in Susan Sontag's rejection of an intel-lectualised depth/surface model of interpretation in favour of an acceptance of the experience of art as sensuous surface, an 'erotics' of the text. John Barth talked of abandoning the literature of exhaustion for an essentially parodic mode of replenishment. Leslie Fiedler spoke of a new and radically democratic art which would spurn the elitism of high modernism, bridge the gap between mass and high culture, and undo the much vaunted and loftily proclaimed 'autonomy' of modernist aesthetics.[7] For such critics, postmod-ernist 'surface' was the contemporary period's more democratic equivalent of Adorno's negative aesthetics of modernism. By the early eighties, however, the term had shifted from the description of a range of aesthetic practices involving 'double-coding', playful irony, parody, parataxis, self-conscious-ness, fragmentation and the mixing and meshing of high and popular culture, to a use which encompassed a more general shift in thought and which seemed to register a pervasive cynicism towards the progressivist ideals of modernity.

Postmodernism, at this point, began to take on the familiar cultural iden-tity discussed earlier; it was now used in Jameson's sense to designate a new cultural epoch in which distinctions between critical and functional knowl-edge break down as capitalism, in its latest consumerist phase, invades even the unconscious and the Third World, leaving no remaining space and no Archimedean point (philosophical or aesthetic) outside of culture. By 1984, postmodernism was firmly established as a constellation of discourses and preoccupations involving various repudiations of foundationalist thinking, a range of aesthetic practices which similarly disrupt the modernist concept of formal aesthetic autonomy and a variety of analyses of the present cultural

---

[7] These essays are collected in Patricia Waugh, *Postmodernism: A Reader* (London and New York: Edward Arnold, 1992). See in particular: William Spanos, 'The Detective and the Boundary: Some Notes on the Postmodern Literary Imagination', pp. 78–87; Leslie Fiedler, 'Cross the Border – Close the Gap', pp. 31–48; Susan Sontag, 'Against Interpretation', pp. 48–56; Ihab Hassan, from *Paracriticisms*, pp. 60–78.

mood or condition. Ihab Hassan described it as an 'antinomian movement that assumes a vast unmaking of the Western mind . . . an ontological rejection of the traditional full subject, the cogito of Western philosophy . . . an epistemological commitment to minorities in politics, sex or language . . . totalisation in human endeavour is potentially totalitarian'.[8] If foundationalism required confidence in the ability of the rational enquirer to arrive at foundations, then it would seem that the demise of one must entail the collapse of the other. Moreover, if the philosophical project of the Enlightenment was now under threat, if there could be no rational subject to be emancipated and if every collectivity represented a false and exclusive totality, then the political commitment to universal emancipation and justice must surely also be under threat. By the 1980s, it seemed that postmodernism had challenged every aspect of Enlightenment discourse and the entire foundation of modernity: the autonomy of art, the grounding of epistemological certainty in the rationalist subject, the political project of universal rights and emancipation and even the objectivity and truth of science.

Postmodernism and art: from autonomy to aestheticism

The shift from autonomy to aestheticism may be regarded as paradigmatic of the entire transition from modernism to postmodernism: in the relations of high art to mass culture; the relation of knowledge to historical and social contexts; of the concept of the self as a unified and rational whole; of the concept of history as a teleological structure underpinned by universal laws. Early literary postmodernism prefigures the later and broader cultural movement in addressing its relations with modernism primarily in terms of the concept of autonomy, a key term in the theorisation of modernism from the early 1920s. In 1913, Clive Bell's *Art* had argued for the absolute separation of life and art; T. S. Eliot's famous 1923 review of Joyce's *Ulysses* (in *The Dial*) would welcome his 'mythic method' as a deliverance from history;[9] in 1929, Eugene Jolas, the editor of the international modernist journal *transition* proclaimed that 'the epoch when the writer photographed the life about him . . . is happily drawing to a close. The new artist of the word has recognised the autonomy of language.'[10]

The crisis in this concept of autonomy is decisive for an understanding of the relationship between modernism and postmodernism in art, and also for

---

[8] Ihab Hassan, quoted in A. Wellmer, 'The Dialectic of Modernism and Postmodernism', *Praxis International* 4 (1985), p. 338.

[9] T. S. Eliot, '*Ulysses*, Order, and Myth', *Selected Prose of T. S. Eliot*, ed. Frank Kermode (London: Faber and Faber, 1975), pp. 175–178.

[10] Eugen Jolas, 'The Revolution of the Word and James Joyce', in *Our Exagmination round his Factification for Incamination of Work in Progress* (London: Faber, 1972), p. 80.

the entire postmodern critique of modernity. The modern idea of autonomy is derived from Kantian thought and is inextricably bound to the Kantian idea of freedom and truth. Autonomy involves the capacity to act in accordance with self-determined principles rationally formulated and not driven by irrational impulses from within or tyrannical pressures from without. To be autonomous is to transcend the phenomenality of material or historical determination and to give the law unto oneself in a space constituted by freedom. In Kantian ethics, it is associated with the idea of the categorical imperative: the unconditional rule that each individual is free if he or she acts in accordance with universalisable principles which respect other people as ends in themselves and not as means to one's own ends. Transferred to the aesthetic, Kantian universalism entails that art is its own end, that it creates its own universe, one structured according to internal rules not applicable or subordinate to or interchangeable with the imperatives of other orders outside the aesthetic: those of politics, morality, science or philosophy.

The postmodern critique of modernist literary autonomy has tended to pursue one of two paths. The first addresses the place of art in mass culture and, in particular, the process of 'dedifferentiation' whereby consumer culture appropriates the forms and surfaces of high art or where a highbrow literary culture gradually absorbs and reformulates the generic modes of popular and mass culture.[11] The second addresses the ethics of autonomy, the recognition that if the price of autonomy may be aesthetic withdrawal from historical engagement, then the price of aestheticisation might be a collapse of ethics and politics into art: the speculative projection of art onto history, and its dangerous degeneration into the kinds of unselfconscious mythmaking associated with recent fascist politics.

Advocates of postmodernism, however, regard the challenge to the concept of autonomy as an honest recognition of the complicity of all art with the cultural assumptions of its time and a welcome sign of the collapse of the cultural hegemony of a beleaguered leisure class anxious to defend its privileges against the tides of mass culture and political democratisation. For such commentatators, aesthetic autonomy was a way of refusing or containing radical energies or feelings and might therefore be seen as complicit with that 'iron cage of rationality' constitutive of bourgeois culture through its strategies and ethics of control.

Battle-lines have similarly been drawn over the issue of the ethical implications of the transition from autonomy to aestheticism. In a technologised mass society, human beings may begin to project their perfect aesthetic worlds onto history, to play God with the real. The religion of art within a secularised and urbanised culture might become a blueprint for pogroms, torture and genocide. It is all very well proclaiming the religion of art, but what are the

---

[11] See Scott Lash, *Sociology of Postmodernism* (London and New York: Routledge, 1990).

consequences if that religion begins to proselytise, to seek converts, to make claims for its powers to regenerate a consumer-driven world of history which is bereft of spiritual direction or formal coherence? Writers and artists in the 1960s seemed suddenly to recognise the fascistic potential of a liberated aestheticism, the force of Walter Benjamin's argument that it was the projection of a decadent aestheticist symbolism onto the sphere of history which had created the barbarous idealisms of Nazi Germany. In the early 1940s, Karl Popper had observed that art masquerading as science in the guise of metaphysics might produce a dangerous historicism, an aestheticist perfectionism. W. H. Auden's 'The Poet and the City' (1963), Borges' 'Tlön, Uqbar, Orbis Tertius' (1964), Frank Kermode's *The Sense of an Ending* (1967), Iris Murdoch's *The Flight From the Enchanter* (1956) were some of the earliest literary expressions of a recognition that heightened aesthetic self-reflexivity might be more than self-indulgent play with language games.[12] The metafictional strategies of postmodernism might serve an ethical function in a world which increasingly, and dangerously, neglects to discriminate between different orders of fictionality.

Postmodern writers have tended to adopt one of two responses to the difficulties thrown up by such insights: either to move further into aesthetic autonomy in a gesture of *reductio ad absurdum* which insulates art as absolute fictionality; or to self-consciously explore ways to retain art's magic without capitulation to a dangerous enchantment (the way of magic realism, historiographic metafiction, of novelists such as Calvino, Spark, Murdoch and Pynchon). Samuel Beckett, a writer whose work draws on both modes, and whose writing spans the period of high modernism *and* early postmodernism, was a crucial figure in the aesthetic transition from one to the other. In Beckett's parodic Cartesian universe, human consciousness, split off from that defective machine which is the body, longs to retreat into a purely rational or aesthetic space where internal coherence might subsume nature through language into the shape of a perfect Platonic circle. His works are full of *a priori* language games and much of the comedy is derived from the disjunction between the intensity of their pursuit and the futility of their import. The fascination with purely autonomous enclosed systems is both recognition of the seductions of syllogistic logic and a satire on its limitations. His characters, the Malones, Mahoods and Worms in *The Trilogy*, desperately but comically attempt to arrive at the certainty of selfhood as pure thinking, attempt to arrive, that is, at the condition of pure Cartesian reduction. Not only do they fail, of course, but the very effort is intended to bring the reader to a recognition that everything excluded as *waste* under the sign of pure autonomy also happens to be everything we normally value as *life*. Intelligibility does not arise out of the algorithmic self-reflexivity of the

---

[12] Iris Murdoch, *The Flight From the Enchanter* (London: Chatto and Windus, 1956).

autonomous system (whatever its seductions) and Beckett's avowed intention throughout his writing was to 'find a form in which to accommodate the mess'.[13] Postmodern self-reflexive play comes in many varieties; as with modernist aesthetics, blanket dismissals are as inappropriate as generalised paeans. Modernist autonomy might represent an aristocratic disdain for a vulgar and commercialised culture or a Nietzschean recommendation of aesthetic fictionality as a substitute for metaphysical presence; its repudiation or ironisation might represent a rejection of the former or an awareness of the potential dangers of the latter.

Politics, epistemology and postmodernism

How does the concern with autonomy enter the politics of the postmodern critique of modernity? Like its artists and writers, postmodern thinkers have recognised that one of the effects of modernity is that knowledge reflexively enters and shapes experience in the world and is then shaped by it in an unprecedentedly self-conscious fashion. Once knowledge is thus reconceived in constructivist or situational terms, however, then rationality may no longer be grounded in a self which is somehow transparent to itself; truth may no longer be discovered by a rationality capable of fathoming its own foundations. In this sphere of postmodernism, therefore, critique has focused on the modern idea of the autonomy of the self and of those metanarratives which have claimed to ground knowledge by standing outside of history. Postmodernism registers a pervasive crisis in the Romantic-modern understanding of selfhood as founded upon a unitary subjectivity striving towards a goal of perfect internal coherence and satisfying correspondence with the world outside the self (a crisis already implicit in the Marxist critique of Hegelian idealism, in the Freudian assault on rationality, in Nietzsche's deconstruction of metaphysics as an expression of the will-to-power and in the poststructuralist critique of representation). Postmodernism defines itself in contradistinction to earlier rationalist and empiricist modes of thinking: against a Platonic objective idealism in which truth resides in a transcendent sphere of ideal forms; against an empiricist reflectionism in which mind appears as a glassy essence; and against a Kantian transcendental idealism in which historical and contingent subjectivity is subsumed into categorical and *a priori* mental structures which provide the universal contours of space, time, identity and the conditions for knowledge.

Postmodern uncertainty thus replaces modern (pre-emptive) doubt. If it is impossible to move beyond and outside of our instruments of interrogation (primarily language) in order to make contact with truths in the world, then

[13] See Samuel Beckett, *Proust and Three Dialogues with Georges Duthuit* (London: Calder, 1965).

dialogue must replace dialectic (Socratic or Hegelian) and hermeneutic 'conversation' must be substituted for the rigours of Cartesian 'method'. In politics, there can be no universal subject of emancipation; no pure procedural justice derived from a 'view from nowhere' and grounding the discourse of equality and individual rights; no universally acknowledged concept of the 'good' derived from the telos of history. Liberalism and Marxism, the two main emancipatory discourses of modernity, can no longer legitimate themselves in universally acceptable terms. Politics therefore becomes 'micropolitics': the exercise at best of a situated rationality and a conversational practice grounded in the internal practices and claims of particular groups or communities. Claims to universality are to be regarded as strategies of exclusion and domination.

As with the issue of autonomy in the relations between aesthetic modernism and postmodernism, this epistemological critique of the autonomy of the subject and of subject-centred reason is at the heart of political debates between postmodernists and their critics. Feminists such as Hekman, Flax and Jardine have welcomed postmodernism as the most radical critique available of the 'masculinist epistemology of modernity'.[14] Communitarian post-Marxists such as Ernesto Laclau and Chantal Mouffe have viewed the postmodern critique of modernity as exposing the sterility of liberal proceduralism in its refusal to acknowledge the need for publicly debated and substantive vocabularies of the 'good'; and, secondly, the dangerous complicity of Marxism with an axiomatic rationality destructive of truly democratic community in its 'scientific' and non-negotiable outline of a metanarrative of history. For them, postmodernism has revealed that it is possible to explore ways to preserve the emancipatory ideals of modernity whilst dispensing with its epistemological foundations.[15]

Again, however, critics of postmodernism such as Christopher Norris, Terry Eagleton and John Gray have presented a very different picture of the political implications of postmodernism, regarding its strategies as a desperate and decadent pastiche of genuine political discourses of emancipation which require either a concept of subjectivity as a coherent and intentional agency and/or a structural understanding of cultural, economic and political realities which can provide a foundation for collective agreements about the nature of the good. In their view, postmodernism fails on both counts. On the one hand, it merely represents an absurd or facile *reductio ad absurdum* of the classic liberal principle of negative liberty into the restless and empty

[14] See S. Hekman, *Gender and Knowledge: Elements of a Postmodern Feminism* (Cambridge: Polity, 1990); Jane Flax, *Thinking Fragments: Psychoanalysis, Feminism and Postmodernism in the Contemporary West* (Berkeley: University of California Press, 1990); Alice Jardine, *Gynesis: Configurations of Woman and Modernity* (Ithaca and New York: Cornell University Press, 1985).

[15] Ernesto Laclau and Chantal Mouffe, 'Post-Marxism Without Apologies', *New Left Review* 166 (1987), pp. 79–106.

libertarianism of a subjectivity without a self caught in the ever-spiralling dialectic of need and desire of a self-perpetuating freemarket economy; and, on the other hand, it collapses into a paranoid neo-Hegelianism where the positive liberty of *Sittlichkeit* or the republican ideal of discovering the self within the practices of civil society is turned into a monolithic cultural determinism from which the only escape must be into a textualist void of freedom as *jouissance*, consumer hedonism or criticism as freeplay. Indeed, Eagleton views postmodernism as a kind of manic-depressive disorder, oscillating between the poles of textualist euphoria and constructivist dystopia, both underlyingly expressive of a desiring but decentred subjectivity, obsessed with freedom but with nothing to be free for, in a society which can only be regarded as an oppressive constraint and curb on such freefloating desire. In this analysis, if the only model of freedom is a kind of libertarian pastiche of negative liberty, where the self who might embody that freedom no longer exists, then the much vaunted 'difference' of postmodern politics simply becomes an end in itself with no other purposive goals.

Postmodernism as philosophical critique

Reading such polarised accounts of postmodernism, one wonders indeed if the various critics and commentators are actually talking about the same thing. Straw men are set up and knocked down at every turn of a postmodern discussion, so it comes as no surprise that one prominent social theorist has declared that postmodernism is 'the most sterile and boring intellectual movement ever to emerge'.[16] Perhaps one way to gain some purchase on these manouevres is to consider postmodernism as dividing into two modes derived from separate philosophical precursors: a strong and a weaker version, each with its own deconstructive and reconstructive orientation. Strong postmodernism emerges out of the poststructuralist reading of Nietzsche and weak postmodernism out of the hermeneutic reading of Heidegger.[17] Deconstructive versions usually concentrate on the critique of Enlightenment epistemology and reconstructive versions on the attempt to build an alternative system of values, a new ethics out of or in relation to this epistemological revision. Firstly let us consider the 'strong' version.

In a famous statement in *The Genealogy of Morals*, Nietzsche declared: 'Henceforth my dear philosophers, let us be on our guard against the

---

[16] See Christopher Norris, *What's Wrong with Postmodernism: Critical Theory and the Ends of Philosophy* (London and New York: Harvester Wheatsheaf, 1990); Terry Eagleton, *The Illusions of Postmodernism* (Oxford: Blackwell, 1996); John Gray, *Enlightenment's Wake: Politics and Culture at the Close of the Modern Age* (London and New York: Routledge, 1995).

[17] Bruno Latour, 'Postmodern? No, Simply Amodern! Steps Towards an Anthropology of Science', *Studies in the History and Philosophy of Science* 21 (1991), p. 147.

dangerous old conceptual fiction that posited a pure will-less, painless, time-less knowing subject . . . There is only a perspectival knowing.'[18] Nietzsche launched the first thoroughgoing critique of the idea of foundational truth and of the rational subject. For strong postmodernists, this position entails that philosophy must relinquish its claims to scientific status and embrace its true nature as poetry or art. Probably the most quoted sentence in the entire discourse of postmodernism is his assertion that truth is simply a 'mobile army of metaphors, metonyms and anthropomorphisms – in short a sum of human relations, which have been enhanced, transposed and embellished poetically and rhetorically'. Like 'coins which have lost their pictures', the his-torical origins of truth have simply been rubbed away and covered over with the rhetoric of objectivity and metaphysics. As far as human reason is con-cerned the only rational thing we know is what little reason we have. It is man's needs and not his reason which interpret the world and truth is simply 'the will to be master over the multiplicity of sensations – to classify phenom-ena into definite categories'.[19]

Accordingly, 'strong' deconstructive postmodernism tends to champion perspectivism in the mode of absolute 'difference'; to prefer nominalism over classification and to abhor 'totalities' as productive of a dangerous utopian-ism which would legislate for this world on the basis of an empty dream of the future. Its practitioners prefer performance and rhetoric over discovery and truth and, accepting the incommensurability of all language games, they also promote 'micropolitical action' over consensual or revolutionary politics. Axiomatic for this position is Lyotard's rejection of any claim to knowledge which makes an explicit appeal to some grand narrative. The Enlightenment pursuit of such 'grand narratives' is seen as a manifestation of the will to power. Seeking his telos in the mastery of nature, man has imposed on the living present the supreme fiction of an imaginary future of perfect justice, truth and emancipation. The postmodern repudiation of Enlightenment is synonymous with the refusal of Romantic-modern prometheanism, of 'the solace of good forms, the consensus of a taste which would make it possible to share collectively the nostalgia for the unattainable'.[20]

Richard Rorty may be considered, like Lyotard, to be a strong postmodern-ist. Though he shares Lyotard's anti-representationalism and his critique of metaphysical foundations, Rorty is less confident about the social effects of postmodern textualism. He sees the ironist theorist revelling in his experi-mental language games as a stimulus to his own private imagination, but one that is purchased at the expense of moral engagement and solidarity with his

[18] Friedrich Nietzsche, *The Genealogy of Morals*, trans. Walter Kaufmann (New York: Random House, 1969), §III, p. 3.
[19] Friedrich Nietzsche, *The Will to Power*, trans. Walter Kaufmann and R. J. Hollingdale (New York: Vintage Books, 1968), pp. 46–47 (p. 47); p. 280.
[20] Lyotard, *The Postmodern Condition*, p. xxiii; p. 81.

fellow human beings. For Rorty, the political agenda of the poststructuralist critique is largely wasted effort because its textualism is complicit with the idealism that it claims to overthrow and which was in any case also largely a distraction ('a sideshow') from that piecemeal, practical social reform which has been the real engine of progress.[21] Whereas, for Lyotard, consensus is an outmoded value and no longer a viable basis for a theory of justice, for Rorty, we must seek a 'detheoreticised sense of community' achieved through publicly shared vocabularies, 'beautiful ways of harmonising interests, rather than sublime ways of detaching oneself from others' interests'.[22] Both share the Nietzschean repudiation of metaphysical foundations and metanarratives of truth but whereas, for Lyotard, this entails an atomistic version of negative liberty, for Rorty, it requires the reconstruction of social consensus without recourse to final vocabularies and epistemological guarantees.

What makes Rorty 'strong' in his postmodernism, despite his defence of consensus as the basis for democracy, is the textualist insistence that society can only be transformed without violence through an aesthetic version of genetic engineering where it is vocabularies and not genes which determine the kind of life we shall lead. Rather than search for scientific proof or metaphysical certainty or even a structural analysis of social inequality, we should recognise that the way to improve the world is through the artificial mutation and manipulation of vocabularies: 'the method is to redescribe lots and lots of things in new ways, until you have created a pattern of linguistic behaviour which will tempt the rising generation to adopt it, thereby causing them to look for appropriate forms of non-linguistic behaviour'.[23] Though Rorty distances himself from strong postmodernism's deployment of rhetorics of the sublime, his own (admittedly slightly tongue-in-cheek) use of an aesthetic of the beautiful still places him in the textualist camp.

Just as Nietzsche may be regarded as the founding father of 'strong' postmodernism, so the legacy of Martin Heidegger, and the tradition of hermeneutics which arises from his philosophy of being-in-the-world, may be regarded as the significant starting point for what I have referred to as 'weak' postmodernism. Unlike strong postmodernism, the weak version may accept the human need to invest in grand-ish narratives, though its proponents reject the usefulness or validity of monocausal varieties and insist that all knowledge is embedded or situated in particular cultural practices or traditions. Weak deconstructive postmodernists vary in their evaluation of the 'Enlightenment project', but tend to be united in the view that the modern commitment to

[21] See Richard Rorty, 'Nineteenth-Century Idealism and Twentieth-Century Textualism', in *Consequences of Pragmatism* (New York and London: Harvester Wheatsheaf, 1982), pp. 139–160.

[22] Richard Rorty, 'Habermas and Lyotard on Postmodernity', in Richard J. Bernstein (ed.), *Habermas and Modernity* (Cambridge, Mass.: MIT Press, 1985), p. 174.

[23] Richard Rorty, *Contingency, Irony and Solidarity* (Cambridge: Cambridge University Press, 1989), p. 9.

justice and emancipation does not require metaphysical grounding. Their critique tends to focus on the sterile formalism of rationalist thought and on its mistaken ideal of homeless freedom. Although weak postmodernists oppose axiomatically the Cartesian attempt to split reason from custom, the body or tradition, they may sometimes wish to retain the ideal of a disembodied and transcendental subject as a regulative principle underpinning epistemological enquiry. The 'view from nowhere' is not entirely abandoned as a regulative principle, but is certainly shorn of its transcendental pretensions and presented simply as the capacity of the embodied subject to practice a negative capability which can imaginatively project itself into and inhabit the view of other embodied subjects in the world. So, for anti-Kantian and weak aestheticists such as Martha Nussbaum, the novel becomes a better way of doing moral philosophy than the attempt to arrive at ethical understanding through the abstract proceduralism of the categorical imperative. Weak postmodernists avoid the utopian seductiveness of the 'strong' perspectivism of a 'view from everywhere' and the protean, fluid and centreless subjectivity which underpins it, but they also insist that all understanding is situated and contextual.

For Heidegger, modernity is to be characterised by a denial or disavowal of being-in-the-world. A detached subjectivity has come to stand over against an inert nature, looking, speculating, fixing and judging for its own ends. Radically disembedded from the world, an instrumental rationalism distorts nature into the shape of its own fictionally projected telos. But, says Heidegger, 'in clarifying being-in-the-world we have shown that a bare subject without a world never . . . is . . . given'.[24] Heidegger's influence on weak deconstructive postmodernism is most obviously felt in the work of Hans-Georg Gadamer whose *Truth and Method* (1960) argues that there can be no Archimedean point outside of culture from which to achieve 'objective knowledge'. Understanding exists entirely in relation to the perspectives (or 'prejudices') provided for us through our cultural traditions. Critical knowledge is simply the partial recognition of particular prejudices through exposure to forms of relative otherness which allow one to repossess the self expanded through the incorporation of other (prejudicial) ways of seeing. Prejudice becomes the precondition for, rather than the negation of, Enlightenment, though neither world nor self can ever be possessed in any final sense.

Science, literature and literary criticism

The most recent and perhaps inevitable drift of the postmodern critique of epistemology, the move from autonomy to aestheticism, is into the realm of the cognitive in the shape of science. I say 'inevitable' since science must rep-

---

[24] Martin Heidegger, *Being and Time* (New York: Harper and Row, 1962), p. 152.

resent the last bastion of modernity and, indeed, some commentators have viewed postmodernism as an attempt to end the epistemic hegemony of science. On this terrain of what postmodernists regard as the 'culture wars' and scientists prefer to call the 'science wars', a triumphalist postmodern aestheticism encounters perhaps its most ferocious rival yet: a rejuvenated scientism, fortified most recently by molecular biology and the claim that genetics can explain everything from why we choose the partners we do to the way we use language and the reasons why nations go to war. As always, it would seem, postmodernism is curiously complicit with some aspects of this latest scientific thinking: both have deconstructed the humanist consciousness and both leave unresolved difficult ethical (and legal) questions about the nature of human responsibility in their respective deterministic landscapes. The two, however, are deeply at war. For the ire of scientists such as Lewis Wolpert, Richard Dawkins and Alan Sokal has been drawn not so much by the ongoing and *value-oriented* Romantic-hermeneutic critique of scientism (reaching back as far as Schiller's indictment of a Newtonian mechanics which had plunged the world into a value-shorn and 'monotonous round of ends', and now rejuvenated in the expressions of concern about the need for ethical constraints upon genetic engineering), but most emphatically by the far more radical postmodern critique of the very *epistemological* foundations of science.[25]

Sociologists of science have joined forces with postmodernists to claim not only the cultural situatedness and ideological constructedness of even scientific knowledge, but also the unverifiability of any reality affirmed by scientific claims or proofs. Scientific theory, it is argued, may be empirically adequate without necessarily describing the world at all. Scientific discourses use models and metaphors from everyday language already imbued with ideological slants and suggestive connotations. The idea of the autonomy of art as a unique kind of ostensive experience, one which could give back 'the world's body', was central in the Romantic-modern opposition to the calculative thinking of science. Again, in the move to postmodernism, the basic strategy is one of aestheticisation where science too will be exposed as fictionality, as yet another 'mobile army of metaphors'.

Lyotard would draw (often implicitly) on the radical interpretation of the epistemology of the New Sciences of the 1920s, to underpin his argument for the postmodern turn in knowledge as one involving a repudiation of modern pre-emptive Doubt for an all-pervasive and aestheticising postmodern Uncertainty. In effect, Lyotard's argument relies on the use of New Science to legitimate his argument for the end of the legitimacy of science. The move allows him to aestheticise science and then to exploit the fact that it is still, after all, science, to offer a legitimation of postmodern aestheticism, giving

[25] See in particular, Jean Bricmont and Alan Sokal, *Intellectual Impostures* (London: Profile Books, 1998).

postmodernism the borrowed authority of science on the grounds that aesthetic knowing was always the only kind of knowledge that we can have.[26] Not
only, however, is Lyotard still using science to legitimate his argument for the
end of science, he is still working implicitly with a correspondence model of
truth (even as he denies its very possibility), seeking a language authorised by
its mirroring of the external reality we call 'nature', but 'nature' reconstructed
as a radical indeterminacy.

Not surprisingly, literary criticism has been immensely receptive to these
ideas. There always was a problem for an increasingly professionalised discipline caught between the desire to be 'scientific', on the one hand, and to treat
the text as an object in the world, and the impulse to be creatively empathetic
on the other, and to recognise the text as the subjective expression of a unique
intentional consciousness. There still is a problem about reducing consciousness to an entity available to the procedures of 'objective' research. The pragmatist solution offered by postmodernism is useful because it circumvents
larger questions about mind and more specific problems about the nature of
critical knowledge or the possibility of a 'validity in interpretation' which
would not be the outcome of a reductive scientism. If we cannot establish the
grounds for believing one interpretation to be more 'true' than another, then
we can claim that the text is simply more useful for one set of purposes than
another and then pursue a 'strategic' reading (political, moral, social etc.). We
may then simply judge the text in terms of how well it does this job that we ask
of it, and thereby exclude the issue of whether it is appropriate in the first
place to demand of it this particular function. The position is summed up in
Stanley Fish's claim that 'interpretation is not the art of construing but the art
of constructing. Interpreters do not decode poems; they make them.'[27]
Knowledge is an art of invention and not a science of discovery.

Paradoxically, one might argue that the orientation towards relativism has
been further sustained because it appeals to the desire to give literary criticism
a clear political function in the world. Though relativism and politicisation
would seem to be naturally opposed (in that relativism must abandon the
Marxist distinction between 'truth' or 'science' and 'ideology' and because a
marginal position cannot therefore claim any greater truth status for itself
than a normative one), the assumption now seems to be that relativism at least
evens up the contest. Performance and rhetoric (Rorty's new vocabularies)
will then determine the outcome. To be authentic in this postmodern condition is simply to 'privilege' the reading that suits our purposes and to admit
the indistinguishable fictionality of all interpretative models. Within the logic
of incommensurability we cannot evaluate other language games within the
terms of our own (or even recognise them) and any attempt at old-fashioned

[26] Lyotard, *The Postmodern Condition*, p. 60.
[27] Stanley Fish, *Is There a Text in This Class?* (Cambridge: Cambridge University Press, 1980),
　　p. 327.

humanistic understanding will simply represent an imperialistic subsumption of the 'other' into the structures of our own desire. If we still desire to 'theorise', then we can practise postmodern theory as a game of (Popperian) pseudo-science, assuming that it is neither open to refutation nor verification. We can give up on the difficult business of Doubt as an open-ended struggle, actively seeking disconfirmation of premises and hypotheses in the evidence of the text before us or of history behind us, and simply enjoy the artistry of the patterns that we create.

This is something of a caricature of course. It is to play postmodernism at one of its own favourite games of *reductio ad absurdum*. It is also why the critical imperative now, for literary practitioners, philosophers and political theorists, must be that we learn from the lessons of postmodernism how to find a way out of the postmodern condition. Literary criticism can never be an exact 'science', but neither is it the same kind of fiction-making activity as 'art'. Postmodernism has taught us the importance of 'difference' and bequeathed an important legacy to postcolonialism, feminism and other kinds of political criticism. Its particular epistemological project, however, has reached a dead-end and there is little point any longer in shuffling amongst the remains. The exit from postmodernism for literary criticism lies somewhere in that excluded middle between the concepts of autonomy and aestheticisation, science and art, as delineated in this essay. It lies, in other words, in our capacity to continue struggling toward the discrimination of these orders without adopting either a naive aestheticism or an imperialistic scientism; it lies in our recognition of the need to preserve some distinction between intentional and natural objects; and in a continued resistance to the seductive temptation simply to subsume one into the other.

Philosophy, aesthetics and literary criticism

23

Words and things in phenomenology
and existentialism

CLIVE CAZEAUX

'To live or to recount . . . You have to choose.'[1] This is the dilemma facing
Roquentin in Sartre's *Nausea* (1938): one either involves oneself in the world
of action or exists in a state of distant, conceptual abstraction. Existentialism
is a philosophy of the gap, the gap between concepts and experience. It affects
both ethics and epistemology. On the one hand, how does one represent –
through art, literature or philosophy – lived experience? On the other, how
does one live in a world increasingly defined through representation, where
'representation' can extend from the self-image of the individual to the
human possibilities created by advances in technology? Sartre's disavowal of
the substantive Cartesian self might give the impression that he is advocating
an amoral nihilism. However, he in fact wants an immersed, committed existence, an adventure or a project, but is all too aware that the order granted by
concepts and grammar is only to be found in literature, and not available to
the individual. In this chapter, I examine the relationship between art, philosophy and experience in phenomenology and existentialism. I concentrate on
Sartre and suggest points of contact between his ideas and the work of
Nietzsche, Husserl, Levinas and Merleau-Ponty. The gap which Roquentin
opens for us between writing or living, I shall argue, is not another binarism
in the history of philosophy, demarcating two irreconcilable opposites, but a
state of affairs which, for Sartre, is an unavoidable aspect of our experiential
participation in the world.

Existentialism emerges from phenomenology, and this, in turn, derives
from transcendental idealism. The line can be traced back from de Beauvoir
and Sartre through Heidegger, Husserl, Nietzsche, Bergson, Brentano and,
ultimately, to Kant. Phenomenology asserts that we are immersed in the
world and implicated within it, as opposed to being observers whose
thoughts and actions are formulated at a distance from events. Kant is the
first to argue that our faculties are always already active in structuring the
world. His critical philosophy responds to the problems created by eighteenth-century rationalism and empiricism theorising experience in terms of
dualisms: the mental and the physical with the former, and impressions and
ideas with the latter. Kant suggests that we might have more success in the

---

[1] Jean-Paul Sartre, *Nausea*, trans. Robert Baldick (London: Penguin, 1988), p. 61.

task of metaphysics if we consider the hypothesis that our binary opposites are actually interrelated. His 'transcendental deduction' in the *Critique of Pure Reason* (1781, 1787) demonstrates that the conditions of possibility of subjectivity are, at one and the same time, the conditions of possibility of objectivity.[2]

Existentialism is a philosophy of action. The existentialist constructs him- and herself through action. Platonic and Cartesian epistemologies assert that human identities are determined either by substantive essences or by complexes of clear and distinct ideas. The problem of the relation between categoriality and action is considered by Kant in the *Critique of Practical Reason* (1788): how can a universal moral imperative supplied by reason in advance of experience show us how we ought to act in particular situations?[3] Although Kant shows that the *a priori* category anticipates and structures the empirical particular, Sartre nevertheless maintains that categorial values are too 'vague', 'too broad for the concrete and specific case'.[4] He rejects outright the thesis that we are defined and motivated by *a priori* concepts or essences: 'the act is everything. Behind the act there is neither potency nor "hexis" [a mysterious or magical impulse] nor virtue.'[5] He radically rethinks the relation between concept and identity to show that it is only through active transformation or engagement that people and things acquire meanings.

For both phenomenology and existentialism, art is the process of becoming *par excellence*. Phenomenology declares that past philosophy is misguided in seeking necessary truths about the world because these can never be answerable to the particularity and contingency of experience. In the absence of truth, there is only art. As Nietzsche argues in 'On Truth and Lie in an Extra-Moral Sense' (1873), there is no necessary correspondence between concept and object:

> For between two absolutely different spheres, as between subject and object, there is no causality, no correctness, and no expression; there is at most, an *aesthetic* relation: I mean, a suggestive transference, a stammering relation into a completely foreign tongue – for which there is required, in any case, a freely inventive intermediate sphere and mediating force . . . A painter without hands who wished to express in song the picture before his mind would, by means of this substitution of spheres, still reveal more about the essence of things than does the empirical world.[6]

[2] Immanuel Kant, *Critique of Pure Reason* (1781, 1787), trans. Norman Kemp Smith (London: Macmillan, 1990), A84–130, B116–169, pp. 120–175.

[3] Immanuel Kant, *Critique of Practical Reason* (1788), trans. Lewis White Beck (Indianapolis: Bobbs-Merrill, 1956).

[4] Jean-Paul Sartre, 'Existentialism and Humanism', trans. Bernard Frechtman, *Essays in Existentialism*, ed. Wade Baskin (New York: Citadel, 1995), p. 43.

[5] Jean-Paul Sartre, *Being and Nothingness* (1943), trans. Hazel Barnes (London: Routledge, 1990), p. xxii.

[6] Friedrich Nietzsche, 'On Truth and Lie in an Extra-Moral Sense', *Philosophy and Truth: Selections From Nietzsche's Notebooks of the Early 1870s*, ed. Daniel Breazeale (Hassocks: Harvester, 1982), pp. 86–87.

Removing the distinction between essence and appearance means the sensory material with which we come into immediate contact *is* reality. Art, no longer confined to surface impressions, becomes the process through which we shape the world.

How does art do this? How, for phenomenology, does art, literature or music impinge upon existence? In the phenomenological tradition from Kant to Merleau-Ponty, the ontological significance of art and representation is continually reasserted. Aesthetic experience is shown by Kant to be a state of conceptual freeplay in which we are motivated to find concepts that can begin to describe experience, and this process, he argues, is vital to the way in which we assign concepts in our theoretical and moral undertakings. Heidegger pursues the Kantian notion that there must be an *a priori*, preparatory structure which opens up the world to us in advance of experience. His fundamental ontology in *Being and Time* (1927) represents the conditions of possibility which must abide for ontic or empirical objects to come into being and, later, in 'The Origin of the Work of Art' (1935), this capacity for ontic 'disclosure' (*aletheia*) is ascribed to art.[7] Merleau-Ponty redefines the body as the refractory medium which creates experience and consciousness. The artist is someone who, more than most, lives and thinks through a medium, for instance, paint, stone, film, etc., and it is through the experience of art, Merleau-Ponty claims, that we overcome dualistic alienation and encounter the world-disclosing properties of our physical embodiment.[8]

Writing holds special significance for phenomenology because it entails the application of concepts to experience, of generalities to particularities. Phenomenology studies the conceptual distinctions we apply to experience and, in particular, reacts against the 'interior-exterior' dualism imposed on experience by empiricism and Cartesian rationalism. The fundamental premise of phenomenology is that consciousness is always consciousness of something: from the fact that we have experience, we can infer that this is experience of an object or realm which is independent of experience. Given this basic, intentional structure of experience, whereby one thing (experience) can open out to become two things (experience *of* something), phenomenology sets out to redescribe appearances. Questions regarding language and the nature of description become paramount.

Husserl's intention is to describe phenomena as they appear to consciousness, independent of an everyday, uncritical commitment to the existence of other people, places, physical objects, causality, etc. In his later philosophy – principally *Ideas Pertaining to a Pure Phenomenology and to a*

---

[7] Martin Heidegger, *Being and Time* (1927), trans. John Macquarrie and Edward Robinson (Oxford: Blackwell, 1995) and 'The Origin of the Work of Art', *Poetry, Language, Thought*, trans. Albert Hofstadter (New York: Harper and Row, 1975), pp. 15–87.

[8] See, for example, Maurice Merleau-Ponty, 'Eye and Mind', *Merleau-Ponty Aesthetics Reader*, ed. Galen Johnson (Evanston, Ill.: Northwestern University Press, 1993), pp. 121–160.

Phenomenological Philosophy (1913) and *Cartesian Meditations* (1931) – Husserl performs his phenomenological reduction in order to avoid the ontological naïvety which, he claims, characterises our natural attitude to the world:

This 'phenomenological epoché' or 'parenthesizing' of the objective world . . . does not leave us confronting nothing. On the contrary, we gain possession of something by it; and what we (or more accurately, what I, as the one who is meditating) acquire by it is my pure living, with all the pure subjective processes making this up, along with everything meant in them *purely as* meant in them; i.e., the world of *phenomena*.[9]

However, Husserl's *epoché* reduces the organisation of the world to the most general, undifferentiated level possible, that is, to a mere something. Consequently, how the philosopher proceeds from this bedrock of generality is going to be governed by the contingencies and vagaries of whatever he or she imports as their instruments of description. Derrida makes this point in *Speech and Phenomena* (1967) against Husserl's theory of meaning. Husserl claims it is possible to form 'objective expressions' which describe experience directly, free from any contingent bias or (in Derrida's words) 'indicative contamination'.[10] But, as Derrida shows, generating the objective expressions involves a series of phrase substitutions which means that the identity Husserl requires between word and phenomenon is not available to him.[11]

The question of writing is vital for Sartre. Writing introduces a gap between consciousness and experience. The way in which verbal description changes the experience to be described is transformed by Sartre into both a theory of the self and an account of the committed writer. In the first few pages of *Being and Nothingness* (1943), he draws our attention to the way in which language can isolate and give the appearance of free-standing objecthood to what is incapable of independent existence. With reference to Laporte, Sartre affirms that 'an abstraction is made when something not capable of existing in isolation is thought of as in an isolated state'.[12] For example, Husserl follows Berkeley in insisting that 'red is an abstraction because colour cannot exist without form'.[13]

---

[9] Edmund Husserl, *Cartesian Meditations* (1931), trans. Dorion Cairns (The Hague: Martinus Nijhoff, 1960), p. 20. See also Husserl, *Ideas Pertaining to a Pure Phenomenology and to a Phenomenological Philosophy* (1913), trans. F. Kersten (The Hague: Martinus Nijhoff, 1982). Husserl proposes three 'reductions': transcendental, eidetic and phenomenological. The phenomenological reduction combines the transcendental and the eidetic in that it concentrates upon our (transcendental) openness towards the essential (eidetic) givenness of objects.

[10] Jacques Derrida, *Speech and Phenomena and Other Essays on Husserl's Theory of Signs*, trans. David B. Allison (Evanston, Ill.: Northwestern University Press, 1973), p. 94. Derrida concentrates upon the the theory of meaning Husserl offers in *Logical Investigations* (1900), trans. J. N. Findlay (London: Routledge and Kegan Paul, 1970).   [11] *Ibid.*, pp. 99–100.

[12] Sartre, *Being and Nothingness*, p. 3.

[13] *Ibid.* Berkeley makes the same point against Locke's distinction between primary and secondary qualities and his abstract idea of substance.

Sartre's intention, in the opening sections of *Being and Nothingness*, is to examine the thought process which generates two things out of one. If the premise of your thesis is the mere fact that there is experience, how do you 'abstract' a world from this, how do you project yourself beyond subjectivity to make contact with reality? 'The first procedure of a philosophy', Sartre claims,

ought to be to expel things from consciousness and to re-establish its true connection with the world, to know that consciousness is a positional consciousness of the world. All consciousness is positional in that it transcends itself in order to reach an object, and it exhausts itself in this same positing.[14]

There is, he announces, an 'ontological proof' to show that consciousness can be consciousness of an object which is distinct from itself. The traditional epistemological contrast between essences and appearances (which are judged to conceal or mask their original essences in some way) is rejected in favour of the notion that an appearance is the disclosure or revealing of its essence: 'the essence of an existent is no longer a property sunk in the cavity of this existent; it is the manifest law which presides over the succession of its appearances, it is the principle of the series'.[15] However, an object does not disclose all its possible appearances in one moment. Experience is successive: a continuum in which aspects appear and disappear, in which appearances are revealed and then withdrawn. Impressions move on: this object is not present to me now in exactly the same way it was a moment ago. If all impressions were present in one instant, the objective 'would dissolve in the subjective'.[16] Concentrating on the object as 'the present impression', as Berkeley and Husserl do, does not create the ontological distance necessary to hold subject and object apart. It is the concept of temporal non-identity, the possibility of appearances other than the one I am currently having, which introduces the required sense of otherness. An object is distinguished from consciousness not by its presence but by its absence, 'not by its plenitude, but by its nothing-ness': 'to say that consciousness is consciousness of something is to say that it must produce itself as a revealed-revelation of a being which is not it and which gives itself as already existing when consciousness reveals it'.[17]

What is unique to consciousness is that it is the location of the perception of absence: it is only in consciousness that the impression of something not being the case can take place, for example, expecting to find thirty pounds in my wallet but finding only twenty, or waiting in a café for a friend who never turns up. As Sartre states:

Every question in essence posits the possibility of a negative reply. In a question we question a being about its being or its way of being. This way of being or this being is veiled; there always remains the possibility that it may unveil itself as a Nothingness.

[14] *Ibid.*, p. xxvii.   [15] *Ibid.*, p. xxii.   [16] *Ibid.*, p. xxxvii.   [17] *Ibid.*, pp. xxxvi, xxxviii.

But from the very fact that we presume that an Existent can always be revealed as *nothing*, every question supposes that we realize a nihilating withdrawal in relation to the given, which becomes a simple presentation, fluctuating between being and Nothingness.

It is essential therefore that the questioner have the permanent possibility of dissociating himself from the causal series which constitutes being and which can produce only being.[18]

It is the possibility of negation which disengages consciousness from the brute causal order of the world; 'this cleavage is precisely nothingness'.[19] A cleavage divides the present of consciousness from all its past, 'not as a phenomenon which it experiences, [but] rather as a structure of consciousness which it is'.[20] Because this rupture in the causal order of the world *is* the structure of consciousness for Sartre, there can never be a moment when consciousness is identical with a self which can influence or determine its actions. Consciousness is being-*for-itself* because it can never be identical with a content, cause or thing. There is nothing which can compel me to adopt a particular form of conduct.[21]

Nausea lets us see how the structures of consciousness and writing are linked for Sartre. The novel is a study of the non-identity between words and experience. The central character, Antoine Roquentin, is living in Bouville and trying to write a biography of the late eighteenth-century political activist Monsieur de Rollebon. However, he gives up the project when the minutiae of his own life encroach on him with ever increasing detail and sublimity, and convince him of the futility of trying to represent experience. The written word will always distance you from experience, will never allow you to be identical with the present. Writing alters the event. The novel's first page outlines the diarist's dilemma:

The best thing would be to write down everything that happens from day to day. To keep a diary in order to understand. To neglect no nuances or little details, even if they seem unimportant, and above all to classify them. I must say how I see this table, the street, people, my packet of tobacco, since *these* are the things which have changed. I must fix the exact extent and nature of this change.

---

[18] *Ibid.*, p. 23.   [19] *Ibid.*, p. 27.

[20] *Ibid.*, pp. 28–29. This is the condition Sartre (following Kierkegaard) refers to as 'anguish'. Anguish is not the same as fear: 'fear is fear *of* beings in the world whereas anguish is anguish *before* myself'. Anguish is created in situations when I distrust myself or, more especially, my reactions to the situation. Vertigo, Sartre suggests, is just as much fear of the precipice as it is anguish at the possibility of me throwing myself over.

[21] Human being cannot be defined or pinned-down conceptually in the same way that a thing can: 'the waiter in the café cannot be immediately a café waiter in the sense that this inkwell is an inkwell, or the glass is a glass' (*ibid.*, p. 59). A manufactured object is produced in accordance with a concept: it has a particular purpose or function and can be judged to be a superior or an inferior product depending upon how well it fulfils its task. Bad faith occurs when consciousness forgets 'the nothingness of its being' or, in other words, when the for-itself adopts the mode of the in-itself (*ibid.*, p. 47).

For example, there is a cardboard box which contains my bottle of ink. I ought to try to say how I saw it *before* and how I – – it now. Well, it's a parallelepiped rectangle standing out against – that's silly, there's nothing I can say about it. That's what I must avoid: I mustn't put strangeness where there's nothing. I think that is the danger of keeping a diary: you exaggerate everything, you are on the look-out, and you continually search the truth. On the other hand, it is certain that from one moment to the next – and precisely in connexion with this box or any other object – I may recapture this impression of the day before yesterday. I must always be prepared, or else it might slip through my fingers again. I must never – – anything but note down carefully and in the greatest detail everything that happens.[22]

The ellipses – 'how I – – it now' and 'I must never – – anything' – are acknowledged in the text with the respective footnotes: 'A word is missing here' and 'A word has been crossed out here (possibly "force" or "forge"), and another word has been written above it which is illegible.' By leaving these gaps, Sartre makes it apparent from the start that language introduces a specificity which is not present in experience. The crossings-out are important: 'force', an exertion of will or an impulse to change the state or position of an object; 'forge', on the one hand, to give shape to what was originally shapeless or, on the other, to copy, to fashion something which is inauthentic.

The task of verbal description, for Sartre, reflects the cognitive relationship between being-for-itself (*être-pour-soi*, human being) and being-in-itself (*être-en-soi*, the being of objects). Objects, he asserts, exist in themselves; they belong to the in-itself. The being of objects is 'full positivity': 'an immanence which cannot realize itself, an affirmation which cannot affirm itself, an activity which cannot act, because it is glued to itself'.[23] This makes objects opaque for us. Objects resist us in the world, assert a counter-pressure against perception, because they never disclose themselves all at once. It is precisely because things are to some degree closed to us that we have consciousness; consciousness is the partial, sequential disclosedness of things. Just as the appearance and disappearance of phenomena enable the perception of absence, so the application of general categories to particular experience puts experience at a distance, creates a phenomenological opening between writer and experience. As soon as Roquentin describes the bark of the tree-root as 'black', he feels 'the word subside, empty itself of its meaning with an extraordinary speed. Black? The root was not black, it was not the black there was on that piece of wood – it was . . . something else.'[24]

This opening occurs not just as a result of the difference between particular and universal, but also because judgement affects the situation. Writing gives order and significance to something which is 'not yet there':

When you are living, nothing happens. The settings change, people come in and go out, that's all. There are never any beginnings. Days are tacked on without rhyme or

---

[22] Sartre, *Nausea*, p. 9.   [23] Sartre, *Being and Nothingness*, p. xli.   [24] Sartre, *Nausea*, p. 186.

reason, it is an endless, monotonous addition . . . But when you tell about life, everything changes; only it's a change nobody notices: the proof of that is that people talk about true stories. As if there could possibly be such things as true stories; events take place one way and we recount them the opposite way. You appear to begin at the beginning: 'It was a fine autumn evening in 1922. I was a solicitor's clerk at Marommes.' And in fact you have begun at the end.[25]

Sartre is building on Heidegger here, in particular, the distinction he draws in *Being and Time* between 'readiness-to-hand' (*Zuhandenheit*) and 'presence-at-hand' (*Vorhandenheit*).[26] The former denotes the state of busy, immersed occupation in which we deal with everyday activities, where objects are simply zones of interaction diffused into the greater backdrop of our routine intentions. For example, you walk across the zebra-crossing on your way to work but are not aware of the exact number of stripes. 'Presence-at-hand' refers to occasions when, for whatever reason, we are stopped in our tracks and what was formerly the mere furniture of existence stands out as a thing, *against* a background, whose nature suddenly becomes of detached perceptual or conceptual interest. This, Sartre observes, is what writing does. Imposing a subject-predicate structure on otherwise diffuse interaction breaks (in Heidegger's idiom) the 'referential totality' of equipment and lights up the thing so that it 'announces itself afresh'.[27]

To write is to act. In the absence of any metaphysical given, order has to be made. *Nausea* can be regarded as the diary of someone coming to terms with the realisation that writing does not capture experience but, instead, disrupts experience, announces the existence of things, gives experience shape and form. Sartre has particular views on just how this takes place. In 'What is Writing?' (1947), he argues that, of all the arts, prose is the only form of representation which returns us to the world.[28] For the prose writer, he claims, words are 'transparent'.[29] This is an unfortunate metaphor, since it is associated historically with the philosophical ideal of passing through concepts to things in themselves. But this is not Sartre's meaning. The prose writer makes his or her words transparent so that their readers 'may assume full responsibility before the object which has been thus laid bare'.[30] Prose 'utilizes' words as signs: 'The ambiguity of the sign', he suggests, 'implies that one can penetrate it at will like a pane of glass and pursue the thing signified, or turn one's gaze towards its *reality* and consider it as an object'.[31] Sartre likens prose to an instrument:

Prose is first of all an attitude of mind. As Valéry would say, there is prose when the word passes across our gaze as the glass across the sun. When one is in danger or in

---

[25] *Ibid.*, pp. 61–63.   [26] Heidegger, *Being and Time*, §§15–16, pp. 95–107.
[27] *Ibid.*, §16, pp. 105–107. The interconnections between readiness-to-hand, presence-at-hand, and the further ontological categories of 'care' (*Sorge*) and 'worldhood' (*Weltlichkeit*) form part of Heidegger's 'preparatory fundamental analysis' of *Dasein* (human 'being'), §§39–44.
[28] Jean-Paul Sartre, 'What is Writing?', *What is Literature?*, trans. Bernard Frechtman (London: Routledge, 1998).   [29] *Ibid.*, p. 15.   [30] *Ibid.*, p. 14.   [31] *Ibid.*, p. 5.

difficulty one grabs any instrument. When the danger is past, one does not even remember whether it was a hammer or a stick; moreover, one never knew; all one needed was a prolongation of one's body, a means of extending one's hand to the highest branch. It was a sixth finger, a third leg, in short, a pure function which one assimilated. Thus, regarding language, it is our shell and our antennae; it protects us against others and informs us about them; it is a prolongation of our senses, a third eye which is going to look into our neighbour's heart.[32]

In contrast, the forms of painting, sculpture, music and poetry exist as things and, as such, have a density of their own which 'withdraws' the audience from the human condition:[33]

The writer can guide you and, if he describes a hovel, make it seem the symbol of social injustice and provoke your indignation. The painter is mute. He presents you with *a* hovel, that's all. You are free to see in it what you like. That attic window will never be the symbol of misery; for that, it would have to be a sign, whereas it is a thing. The bad painter looks for the type. He paints the Arab, the Child, the Woman; the good one knows that neither the Arab nor the proletarian exists either in reality or on his canvas. He offers a workman, a certain workman. And what are we to think about a workman? An infinity of contradictory things. All thoughts and feelings are there, adhering to the canvas in a state of profound undifferentiation. It is up to you to choose.[34]

Painting is phenomenal. Thus, Sartre reasons, the painter, in serving up another portion of material reality, is not taking a stance, is not contributing to moral discussion. After experiencing a painting, you are no better off than you were before. You are left with the same uninformed choice. Poetry is accused of amorality on similar grounds. As a result of the formalist and structuralist 'crises in language' at the turn of the century, Sartre suggests, poetry is now language made phenomenal. The poet no longer uses words as signs but as 'images' or 'things': traps 'to catch a fleeing reality rather than as indicators which throw him out of himself into the midst of things'.[35] Rimbaud's 'strangeness' 'is no longer a meaning but a substance'.[36]

We are dealing with an ontology of action. Shape has to be given to experience not in a way which isolates objects and distances us from them but in a way which makes them available to us. Sartre's main objection against the arts concerns their materiality. This is not meant in a literal sense, as poetry is included. Neither is it a condemnation of *mimesis*, as music and poetry are targeted. Instead, 'materiality' refers to the internal, substantive world created by a work: 'the significance of a melody – if one can still speak of significance – is nothing outside the melody itself'.[37] Modern poetry, he avows, manipulates words in a way which trips up the reader. The contrast is, once again, Heidegger's *Zuhandenheit-Vorhandenheit* distinction, but it is being put to a different use. Poetry, painting and music represent experiences as

[32] *Ibid.*, p. 11.   [33] *Ibid.*, p. 10.   [34] *Ibid.*, pp. 3–4.   [35] *Ibid.*, p. 6.
[36] *Ibid.*, p. 9.   [37] *Ibid.*, p. 3.

things present-at-hand, like broken implements, incapable of facilitating action in the world, whereas prose represents events in a way which carries a sense of 'ready-to-hand' engagement. Prose, for Sartre, organises experience in a manner which does not draw attention to itself as an external or extra-experiential form of organisation. This is an implicit form of Platonism: the thing-like phenomenality of the artwork deludes us into appreciating art for itself and distracts us from our true being in the world.

There is a difference of opinion among phenomenologists over verbal and visual signification. Whereas Sartre asserts that word and image signify in radically different respects, the two exist side-by-side in the dynamic Nietzsche creates between the Apollinian and the Dionysian. Words and images, Nietzsche argues in *The Birth of Tragedy* (1872), transform 'the inchoate, intangible reflection of the primordial pain in music' into 'a specific symbol or example'.[38] Under the lyric Apollinian dream inspiration, music reveals itself to the Dionysian artist as a *'symbolic dream image'*.[39] Furthermore, Nietzsche does not recognise the art versus reality divide to which Sartre seems to return. He constructs his dynamic in such a way that the distinction Sartre would like to make between art that points to the world and art that points to itself can never be firmly maintained. The 'beautiful illusion' of the Apollinian dream world always declares itself as 'mere appearance' and encourages us 'amid the dangers and terrors of dreams' to say 'It is a dream! I will dream on!'[40] But singing and dancing 'under the charm of the Dionysian', we become enchanted: we have 'forgotten how to walk and speak and [are] on the way toward flying into the air'.[41] Thus, Apollo veils reality under illusion, and Dionysius enchants us; neither gives us the world.

We only think the image distances us from the world, Merleau-Ponty declares, because we derive our understanding of it from the dualistic philosophies of rationalism and empiricism. Both epistemologies, he avers, configure knowledge as a binary relation between idea or impression and thing and so create for themselves the problem of a representation which stands before and conceals the world behind it. In response, he offers a theory which shows how knowledge and the traditional *dualities* of philosophy follow or emerge from our *monistic* condition as active, embodied entities located in the physical world. As he argues in 'Eye and Mind' (1961), an essay on contemporary drawing, the image does not stand before its object as a copy or a duplicate but, instead, is an expression of the gestural possibilities and restrictions which exist between artist, medium, and object.[42]

Levinas, however, would seem to share the Platonism underlying Sartre's distinction between word and image. In 'Reality and its Shadow', written in 1948, one year after Sartre's 'What is Writing?', Levinas argues that a 'fissure'

---

[38] Friedrich Nietzsche, *The Birth of Tragedy* (1872), trans. Walter Kaufman (New York: Vintage, 1967), §5, p. 49.   [39] *Ibid.*, §5, p. 49.   [40] *Ibid.*, §1, pp. 34–35.   [41] *Ibid.*, §1, p. 37.
[42] Merleau-Ponty, 'Eye and Mind', p. 144.

or an 'interval' (called the 'meanwhile') exists between art and reality. The gap comes about, he maintains, because art is a 'doubling of reality', like a shadow, and has a 'density of its own'.[43] Art is amoral, for Levinas, like Plato, in that it constitutes 'a dimension of evasion': we become preoccupied with it at the expense of our obligation to deal with the world.[44] It is only through conceptual, philosophical criticism that art can be re-integrated into human affairs. Critics work not with phenomenal particularities but with conceptual generalities. They lack 'the force to arouse realities' and so, instead, must 'speak in enigmas, by allusions, by suggestion, in equivocations'.[45] The inherent incompleteness of their medium, Levinas asserts (and here he departs from Plato), means they are more attentive to their rootedness in the world among others.

Sartre's distinction is between 'committed' art that points to the world and art that is pre-occupied with itself, 'art for art's sake'. The latter is being rebuked because it is a form of representation which does not offer any moral commentary. It is often assumed that the self-referentiality of an artwork precludes it from speaking about other things, but the assumption is false. The central question is whether or not an object's possessing one quality precludes it from possessing another. If an object is round, then it cannot be square, but an object can be *both* round and smooth or round and heavy, etc. The properties of self-referentiality and world-referentiality, I suggest, can similarly coexist. In the history of formalism and abstraction, claims are often made for the purity of a work which is devoid of all representational content, but these tend more to be rhetorical expressions of the work's novelty or to result from the speaker's inability to contextualise the piece within a history of more overtly representational forms. Some paintings will be less obviously representational than others, but if phenomenology is present in your working assumptions, from Kant, or Nietzsche, or Merleau-Ponty, then a strict demarcation between representation and reality is not an option. On this account, colours, sounds and language are forms of being in the world before they are objects of disinterested contemplation.

While it is possible to draw distinctions between the different *ways* in which prose, poetry, art and music point to the world, there is, I propose, no basis for a division on the grounds that some forms represent in a ready-to-hand fashion and others represent in a present-at-hand fashion. This point can be made against the later Sartre in two respects. Firstly, in *Nausea*, Sartre affirms that all conceptual judgement ruptures and, as a result, impedes the continuity of experience. Therefore, in this regard, prose is no different from poetry, painting or music.

The second point refers to an inconsistency in his concept of thinghood. The 'thing' as it is understood in 'What is Writing?' is not the same 'thing' which appears in *Nausea* and *Being and Nothingness*. In the former, the thing

[43] Emmanuel Levinas, 'Reality and its Shadow', *The Levinas Reader*, ed. Sean Hand (Oxford: Blackwell, 1996), p. 136.   [44] *Ibid.*, p. 141.   [45] *Ibid.*, p. 142.

exists isolated and at a distance from consciousness. It sits out of mind like a broken tool at the bottom of a drawer. The artistically produced thing, for Sartre, is alienated to the extent that he describes it as 'uncreated and eternal' and 'thickened and defaced'.[46] The painter, he affirms, always creates a thing in the sense that she is under no obligation to give their colours 'definable significance', that is, to have them 'refer particularly to another object'.[47] This is a concept of the thing which presents it as being external or opposite to any notion of interrelationship or engagement.

However, in *Nausea* and *Being and Nothingness*, what a thing is is inextricably bound up with consciousness: the opacity of objects is the texture or pressure in virtue of which we have consciousness. The object is 'an immanence which cannot realize itself' and it is in the gap left by the object never fully disclosing itself that awareness occurs.[48] Towards the end of *Nausea*, Roquentin realises that the complete description of experience – when the word captures the thing – is an impossibility and *it is the undecidability of description* which is 'the key to [his] Existence, the key to [his] Nausea'.[49] How should or could he describe the tree-root? 'Snake or claw or root or vulture's talon', 'a suction-pump', its 'hard, compact sea-lion skin', its 'oily, horny, stubborn look'; 'knotty, inert, *nameless*'.[50]

The object here is not something which opposes description or alienates the writer but something which establishes a moral contract between itself and consciousness. I say 'moral' because the metaphors that best describe the relationship come from the sphere of social interaction: objects 'invite', 'motivate', 'demand' or 'resist' representation. Whether one is confronting an inkwell, a tree-root or a painting, objects can only give themselves to the viewer incompletely and, therefore, in a way that requests or demands supplementation. The exchange is not necessarily a harmonious one, though. Finding the *right* word is often as difficult as deciding upon the *right* course of action. Similarly, Roquentin's moment of revelation is not beautiful but sublime. As Sartre has shown, there can be no moment of self-present, necessary correspondence between word and thing. One has to make a representation, choose a course of action. What the emphasis on the morality of description here achieves is to reassure Sartre that the thing, including the thing-like artwork, is not an entity which, by definition, leaves its perceiver unmoved or places itself outside any field of cognitive interaction.[51]

---

[46] Sartre, 'What is Writing?', p. 6.   [47] *Ibid.*, p. 2.   [48] Sartre, *Being and Nothingness*, p. xli.
[49] Sartre, *Nausea*, p. 185.   [50] *Ibid.*, pp. 185–186.
[51] The idea that the epistemological question of representation might have moral underpinnings is not new. Philosophy has shown on a number of occasions how understanding statements about what *is* the case requires an architectonic which can also account for statements about what *ought* to be the case, e.g., the Forms in Plato's *Republic*, Hume's concept of 'custom' in the *Treatise of Human Nature* (1739–40) and Kant's repositioning of the supersensible in relation to the sensible in his critical system. Even the idealised notion of concepts 'capturing' experience has its root in human situations.

As an illustration of art's affectability, one only has to recall that it is Roquentin's visit to the Bouville museum and, in particular, his viewing the portraits in the Bordurin-Renaudas Room, which prompts him to give up writing his biography of Rollebon.[52] The hundred and fifty portraits idealise their subjects and give them a presence which makes their actual lives seem all the more distant and intangible. The paintings draw attention to their own partiality: 'of this shrill-voiced little man, nothing would go down to posterity except a threatening face, a superb gesture, and the bloodshot eyes of a bull'.[53] Suddenly, the project of recovering Rollebon's past seems an impossibility. Rollebon had been Roquentin's prop: 'it was for him that I ate, for him that I breathed'.[54] Surrendering the project means that Roquentin no longer has past, retrievable experience to hide behind, and is forced to confront the nauseous, immediate play of phenomena and description which constitutes his own existence. His hand spread out on the table becomes a 'crab', showing its 'under-belly', then a 'fish'; his fingers become 'paws', then 'claws'.[55]

One of the main problems of epistemology is that we are always 'at a remove' from things, that there is always a gap between the world and our knowledge of it. What Sartre does, in keeping with the phenomenological tradition, is to show that this state of affairs is a condition of our rootedness in the world and not a deficiency which has to be overcome. When dealing with the situation in which we find ourselves, Sartre avers, we cannot expect the conceptual to determine or capture completely the particularity of the event. The structure of experience is such that a nothingness always insinuates itself between past and present, between concept and action, between description and experience, keeping the two apart. This structure, as I have shown, is particularly evident in writing: the descriptive sentence creates a specificity which cannot possibly be identical with experience.

A consequence of our accepting this gap as a necessary condition of experience is that it becomes something which we have to deal with, something which we have to act upon. An epistemological relation therefore rests upon questions of how we conduct ourselves in the world. The for-itself and the in-itself need each other, mutually define one another, on the Kantian or phenomenological grounds that experience is the necessary interaction between concept and intuition. Beyond this, however, objects do not simply exist waiting to be described. Rather, they are conceptually opaque to us, they resist us, they never disclose themselves to us all at once, and *it is in virtue of* this resistance that we are 'invited' or 'required' to offer conscious response. For the existentialist writer, the relationship between language and experience, I suggest, is a moral but uncertain one. Sartre maintains that prose, as

---

[52] Sartre, *Nausea*, pp. 120–138.   [53] *Ibid.*, p. 136.   [54] *Ibid.*, p. 143.
[55] *Ibid.*, pp. 143–144.

opposed to art, offers us ready-to-hand engagement with the world, but this fails to acknowledge that all writing, at some point, makes things present-at-hand. Art, including writing, changes and distorts experience, produces a 'thing' where there was nothing, but a thing, by Sartre's own definition, is that which motivates us to move on to *other* things.

24

Criticism, aesthetics and analytic philosophy

PETER LAMARQUE

The input to critical theory from so-called 'continental' (principally French and German) philosophy is well known and well documented. A somewhat less well known, less widely acknowledged, philosophical contribution to theoretical accounts of literature and criticism comes from 'analytic philosophy'. Nevertheless, there is a substantial body of work from the analytic tradition in what has come to be known as 'philosophy of literature' and it is by no means confined to the English-speaking world. This essay will map out this contribution and assess its significance.

Analytic philosophy and related movements

The very idea of 'analytic philosophy' is contested and resists uncontroversial definition. Philosophers as different as Gottlob Frege and G. E. Moore, Rudolf Carnap and J. L. Austin, W. V. O. Quine and P. F. Strawson, the Wittgenstein of the *Tractatus Logico-Philosophicus* and the Wittgenstein of the *Philosophical Investigations* have been called 'analytic' and it is hard to speak with confidence of common definitive elements. Nor is the epithet 'Anglo-American' (in contrast to 'continental') especially apt as leading figures, such as Frege, Wittgenstein, Friedrich Waismann, Moritz Schlick and other members of the Vienna Circle, came from Continental Europe. Other designations are sometimes used interchangeably with 'analytic philosophy', notably 'linguistic philosophy', 'ordinary language philosophy', even 'philosophy of language', but again only confusion results from running these together.

A good starting point in trying to pin down analytic philosophy is to notice two features on which there is wide agreement: the formative influence of Gottlob Frege and the idea of a 'linguistic turn' in philosophy (the anthology edited by Richard Rorty entitled *The Linguistic Turn* (1967) gave this expression currency). Significantly, Frege was a mathematician whose principal interest was the logical foundations of arithmetic.[1] He wrote little or nothing

[1] See, for instance, Gottlob Frege, *The Foundations of Arithmetic: A Logico-Mathematical Enquiry Into the Concept of Number* (*Grundgesetze der Arithmetik*, 1893, 1903), trans. J. L. Austin (Oxford: Blackwell, 1953) 2nd edn.

on the traditional problems of philosophy and even his central mathematical project, the attempt to reduce arithmetic to logic, proved unsuccessful. However, his contributions to logic became the starting point for an entirely new school of philosophy. His most influential ideas include: the representation of sentential structure in terms of function/argument and quantifiers, the context principle (only in the context of a sentence does a word have meaning), the distinction between sense and reference (*Sinn* and *Bedeutung*), anti-psychologism in logic (the idea that the laws of thought are not empirical), the distinction between objective, timeless, non-mentalistic thoughts (*Gedanken*) and subjective ideas (*Vorstellungen*), and the insight that meaning and truth are inextricably linked. Building on Frege's legacy, Bertrand Russell and Wittgenstein developed the idea of logical analysis as the search for the 'logical forms' of sentences, as distinct from their surface (often misleading) grammatical forms. From Russell's own analysis of definite descriptions (sometimes termed the 'paradigm of analysis') to Carnap's *Logische Syntax der Sprache* (1934), the uncovering of 'logical syntax' showed not only how to make patterns of inference perspicuous but more fundamentally how language itself 'latched onto' the world.

Thus was the linguistic turn born. An ambitious programme, as well as a methodology, in philosophy grew out of the revolution in logic. The new symbolism of Frege and Russell, which made logic a powerful tool of linguistic analysis, led to a focus on language unparalleled in the history of philosophy.

Richard Rorty defines 'linguistic philosophy' as 'the view that philosophical problems are problems which may be solved (or dissolved) either by reforming language, or by understanding more about the language we presently use'.[2] The disjunction points to two rather different developments in linguistic philosophy. In the first, the project was to 'reform language' or, in Quine's terms, 'regiment' it into a 'canonical notation', thereby eliminating vagaries and ambiguities in common usage and delivering a streamlined vehicle for science: Russell, Carnap and Quine led the way in this movement, stressing the efficacy of 'logical analysis'. The second approach, that of 'ordinary language philosophy', principally influenced by J. L. Austin in 1950s Oxford, rejected the need for 'regimentation' and maintained that attention to the nuances of common use could reveal important insights and distinctions missed by traditional philosophers; Gilbert Ryle, P. F. Strawson and A. R. White were influential here. A third development, logical positivism, based in Vienna in the 1930s, used the verification principle of meaning, which identified meaningfulness with empirical testability, to dismiss as meaningless (and thus 'dissolve', in Rorty's terms) the central tenets of metaphysics about substance, the soul, God, or Being. Finally, there was Wittgenstein himself, a crucial figure in linguistic philosophy, whose influence was felt in all three of

2 Richard Rorty (ed.), *The Linguistic Turn: Recent Essays in Philosophical Method* (Chicago: The University of Chicago Press, 1970), p. 3.

these groupings, even if he is not directly categorisable in any one. He described his method in *Philosophical Investigations* (1953) as 'grammatical' and insisted that problems could be solved by 'looking into the workings of our language', yet he held that philosophy 'may not advance any kind of theory' and 'neither explains nor deduces anything'.[3]

The optimism that linguistic analysis and ordinary language philosophy could afford genuine progress in the subject, sweeping away centuries of metaphysical muddle, began to dissipate in the 1960s. The interest in language and logic became focused into a relatively new inquiry, albeit inspired by Frege, namely, 'philosophy of language', which sought a clearer understanding of such concepts as meaning, truth, reference and indeed language itself, without harbouring any programmatic ambition towards solving all philosophical problems. By the 1970s few philosophers styled themselves as 'linguistic philosophers' or 'ordinary language philosophers' yet significantly the term 'analytic philosophy' grew in popularity. The Fregean tradition continued to inform philosophy of language but the original linguistic turn lost its revolutionary edge and settled down merely into a style of philosophising.

The recognisable traits of analytic philosophy are: the prominence of logic and conceptual analysis, the striving for clarity and rigour in argumentative strategy, the definition of terms, the explicit formulation of theses, the quasi-scientific dialectical method of hypothesis/counter-example/modification, the eschewing of rhetorical figures and the tendency to tackle narrowly defined problems. All areas of philosophy, including the moral and political, are amenable to the analytic approach and most conceivable stances have been adopted: realist and anti-realist, foundationalist and anti-foundationalist, relativist and absolutist, materialist and non-materialist. However, unlike its 'continental' counterpart, analytic philosophy shows a marked indifference to its own ideological or sociological presuppositions.

Analytic philosophy and the input to critical theory

There are two principal sources of input from analytic philosophy to the theory of literature: the first arising directly from topics in logic and philosophy of language, the second from analytic aesthetics, in particular its sub-branches of metacriticism and philosophy of literature. There is no clear line between these inputs as analytic aesthetics often draws on a background of logic and there are obvious overlaps between any logical enquiry into meaning, truth or reference and concerns related to literature or literary language. One fundamental question is whether there is any substantial division

---

[3] Ludwig Wittgenstein, *Philosophical Investigations*, trans. G. E. M. Anscombe (Oxford: Blackwell, 1953), §§ 109, 126.

of discourses between the literary and the non-literary and, if so, how it might be demarcated. Before turning to that issue, it is helpful to begin with the topic of fictionality and reference, which goes to the heart of the early analytic project.

The problem of non-existence arose in an acute form for the early analytic philosophers because of the close association of meaning and denotation. For those, like Russell, who held that the meaning of a name is the object it denotes, there was a deep problem accounting for sentences containing non-denoting expressions, such as 'the highest prime', 'the present King of France', 'phlogiston' or 'Pegasus'. Alexius Meinong stirred the debate in his theory of objects (*Gegenstandtheorie*) by admitting different levels of being (*Sosein, Sein, Aussersein*) thus allowing even contradictory expressions, e.g. 'the round square', to denote objects.[4] Although initially attracted, Russell came to reject the distinction between subsistence and existence, demanding a more 'robust sense of reality'. This led, on the one hand, to his analysis of definite descriptions, famously using the example 'the present King of France', in terms of quantifiers and propositional functions, and, on the other, to his view that proper names ('Pegasus' as well as 'Socrates') are not really names, i.e. denoting terms, but 'disguised descriptions', themselves amenable to the more general theory of descriptions. Russell thus showed that by logical paraphrase apparent reference to non-existent entities could be eliminated altogether.[5]

Russell's attempt to remove non-existent entities by analysis and Meinong's attempt to accommodate them set the parameters for later discussion. Terence Parsons has developed a sophisticated logical version of Meinong's theory and Charles Crittenden has defended Meinong's intuition that we can refer to what does not exist by appeal to ordinary language. Other accommodationists, bringing the debate nearer to literary concerns, have sought to attribute some kind of reality to the creatures of fiction. Peter van Inwagen describes fictional characters as 'theoretical entities of literary criticism', comparable in status to plots, metres and rhyme schemes. He distinguishes those properties 'ascribed' to characters ('being a butler', 'being called "Jeeves"'), which they do not literally possess, and those which characters 'exemplify' (like 'first appearing in Ch. 2', 'being created by P.G. Wodehouse', etc.).[6] Nicholas Wolterstorff holds that fictional characters are kinds, in the sense that the character Jeeves is a person-kind, though not a kind of person.

[4] Alexius Meinong, 'Theory of Objects', in R. M. Chisholm (ed.), *Realism and the Background of Phenomenology* (Glencoe, Ill.: Free Press, 1960), pp. 76–117.

[5] Bertrand Russell, *Logic and Knowledge*, ed. R. C. Marsh (London: George Allen and Unwin, 1956). This collection includes 'On Denoting' and 'The Philosophy of Logical Atomism', where Russell develops and applies his theory of descriptions and his conception of logical fictions.

[6] Peter van Inwagen, 'Creatures of Fiction', *American Philosophical Quarterly* 14 (1977), pp. 299–308.

One consequence is that characters not only exist (as kinds) but do so eternally. A writer 'selects' but does not strictly create characters, for the properties ('being a butler', etc.) which constitute the relevant kinds are not themselves created.

Other philosophers follow Russell in seeking to avoid such commitments to the existence of fictional entities. The trouble with Russell's analysis (and also Quine's)[7] is that it makes all sentences 'about fictional characters' turn out false. Yet arguably this fails to do justice to either fictional discourse or discourse about fiction. According to speech act theorists, fictional discourse as used by story-tellers should not be thought of as assertive, therefore not open to truth-assessment. Frege himself had implied that fictional stories lack truth-values. John Searle, a prominent speech act theorist, has argued that fiction is a kind of pretence, specifically a pretended illocutionary act.[8] In a similar vein, Gregory Currie claims that a story-teller's intention is that a reader make-believe rather than believe a proposition. In contrast, discourse about fiction can be genuinely assertive and does seem amenable to truth-assessment; 'Jeeves is a butler' is true while 'Jeeves is a woman' is false. Again it is hard to see how these intuitions can be captured without incurring undesirable ontological commitments. David Lewis, among others, sees them as truths about possible worlds. Kendall Walton, who rejects the possible world analysis, again invokes 'make-believe', defining fictions as 'props in games of make-believe'. In his idiom, *it is fictional* that Jeeves is a butler. This 'fictional truth' is not a special kind of truth but a fact about what is fictional: ultimately a fact about a game played with a text. Nelson Goodman is perhaps the most extreme eliminativist. In a paradigmatic use of logical analysis, in *The Languages of Art* (1968), he explains the status of pictures of (non-existent) unicorns by introducing the one-place predicate 'X is a unicorn-picture' which, unlike 'X is a picture of a unicorn', absolves commitment to referentiality. Curiously, in his later work, *Ways of Worldmaking* (1978), Goodman also wants to weaken the distinction between literary fiction and science, describing both as a species of 'worldmaking' or the 'fabrication of facts'.

The priority given by analytic philosophers to questions about reference and ontology, rather than, say, historical context or ideological content, when writing about fiction, seems to place their enquiry permanently at odds with that of literary critics.[9] Another important strand of debate on fictionality, which might have brought the different interests closer, concerns emotional

---

[7] W. V. O. Quine, 'On What There Is', *From a Logical Point of View* (Cambridge, Mass.: Harvard University Press, 1953).

[8] John Searle, 'The Logical Status of Fictional Discourse', *Expression and Meaning: Studies in the Theory of Speech Acts* (Cambridge: Cambridge University Press, 1979).

[9] See Peter Lamarque, *Fictional Points of View* (Ithaca, N. Y.: Cornell University Press, 1996), particularly chapter 4.

responses, although this too has largely failed to engage the critical community. Aristotle argued that the appropriate response to dramatic tragedy is fear and pity but logically-minded philosophers ask how pure fictions, known to be non-existent, can be the subject of such cognitive emotions (i.e. emotions presupposing beliefs). One line, offered by Colin Radford, is that humans are simply irrational, grieving over entities they know to be unreal. Others have followed Kendall Walton in supposing that spectators only 'make-believedly' fear and pity fictions, without really doing so.[10] A third suggestion, by Peter Lamarque and Noël Carroll, is that the emotions are caused by thoughts and as such sideline existential beliefs.

Truth and literature

It is not such a major step from analysing the truth-conditions of fictional sentences in purely logical terms to investigating the deeper more traditional problem of 'poetic truth'. The move is from logic to aesthetics. Analytic aestheticians have long engaged in the essentially humanistic debate about the 'cognitive value' of art, the ability of art – including literature *par excellence* – to convey knowledge and insight. Again there are distinctive features of the analytic approach. There is little concern for ideological truth, as discussed, say, by Theodor Adorno or in the debate between Gyorgy Lukács and Berthold Brecht about realism; nor is there an overt political dimension, as in Jean-Paul Sartre's 'la littérature engagée', or a metaphysical one as found in Martin Heidegger's conception of truth as 'unconcealment'. The analytic focus begins with definition and clarification. What could it mean to claim that fictional works of literature reveal truths? But it does not end there. Analytic philosophers have pressed the topic to the very heart of what counts as humanistic study.

Probably the best early ground-clearing operation comes in Monroe C. Beardsley's *Aesthetics: Problems in the Philosophy of Criticism* (1958) where he distinguishes reports and reflections, themes and theses, in an attempt to establish exactly what the truth bearers are (could be) in the literary case. Analytic philosophers are reluctant to assign truth to anything which is non-propositional in form. Thus while the theme, say, of unrequited love could not, they would claim, be a bearer of truth, the implied reflection or thesis that 'love is doomed' could be. Pure fictional reports, unasserted, have no truth-value. A truth bearer has now been found but logical questions remain:

[10] See Kendall L. Walton, *Mimesis as Make-Believe* (Cambridge, Mass.: Harvard University Press, 1990), chapters 5–7. Useful discussion of Walton and others is offered in Mette Hjort and Sue Laver (eds.), *Emotion and the Arts* (Oxford: Oxford University Press, 1997), and E. M. Dadlez, *What's Hecuba to Him? Fictional Events and Actual Emotions* (Philadelphia: Pennsylvania State University Press, 1997).

how are a work's theses discoverable? Must a work always have a thesis? Is the truth of a thesis a mark of a work's value? (It should also be noted that not all philosophers accept Beardsley's terminology.)

The truth debate, in the analytic tradition, is both about the presence of truth in works of literature and also about its relevance to literary value. Not all in the 'pro-truth' camp have felt constrained by the austere propositional conception of truth. A common suggestion is that works of art can exhibit truth in ways not amenable to science or philosophy and that therein lies their distinctive value. Literary works are described as being true to reality, or having 'authenticity', or ontological truth, or metaphorical truth, or offering knowledge how rather than knowledge that, or being a species of moral philosophy. Such accounts are often carefully worked out, but the suspicion remains, at least within the 'no-truth' camp, that in moving so far from the logical paradigm of truth it is only obfuscation to continue speaking of 'literary truth'. On the other hand, those analytic aestheticians who reject truth as a central value in literature are characteristically not committed to anti-humanism, nor to postmodernist scepticism about truth itself, nor to the essentially fictional status of literature. A more common attitude derives ultimately from Wittgenstein, namely that the 'language game' or 'practice' of literature is distinct from the truth-centred practices of science or philosophy and that literary value is a species of aesthetic value, not of cognition.

Defining literature

Underlying discussions of the 'truth' of literature are even more fundamental questions about the very nature of literature. Within analytic aesthetics the focus for these questions derives from parallel attempts to define art. Four principal approaches are discernible: formalist, functionalist, anti-essentialist and institutionalist.

Formalist theories are those that seek to define literature in terms of intrinsic textual properties of 'literariness'. One typical instance, from analytic philosophy, was the 'semantic definition' associated, again, with Monroe Beardsley,[11] developed at the very time that Beardsley was providing philosophical support for the principles underlying New Criticism. Echoing the prominence given by the New Critics to ambiguity, irony, paradox and 'tension' in literary works, the semantic definition proposed that literary discourse was distinctive for possessing a high degree of 'implicit meaning' or 'semantic density'. However, a forceful objection to the theory, applicable also to most other formalist accounts, is that the presence of such textual features

[11] Monroe C. Beardsley, *Aesthetics: Problems in the Philosophy of Criticism* (New York: Harcourt Brace, 1958), pp. 126–128.

could never be sufficient to identify a work as literary without some further explanation of how these features contribute to the *value* of the work. The assumption behind the objection is that 'literature' is not merely a descriptive category but also an honorific or merit-conferring concept.

Functionalist definitions can, although do not necessarily, address this point by identifying the functions fulfilled by literary discourse, including responses elicited from readers. Literary works are those that give aesthetic pleasure or offer an imaginative vision. John M. Ellis has compared the concept of literature with the concept of a weed, each definable not by intrinsic qualities but by attitudes taken to them.[12] Early appeals to the 'emotive' nature of literary language, inspired by positivism, gave way to more sophisticated attempts to employ speech act theory to define literary function. In one such, the ancient theory of *mimesis* is evoked, where what is mimetic is the 'illocutionary force' behind the sentences in a work.[13] Speech act theories, however, like theories of 'games of make-believe', seem unable to distinguish the literary from the merely fictional. Yet boldly to stipulate a higher value for the literacy is in danger either of arbitrariness or of begging the question as to what kinds of value are involved. Classical 'aesthetic attitude' theories, on which one such account might rest, have fared badly with analytic philosophers. Nevertheless, functionalist theories of a refined kind, which incorporate values and do not overly limit artistic functions, still find support among analytic aestheticians.[14]

An important overarching strand of analytic aesthetics is the debate between essentialists and anti-essentialists. The former believe, broadly, that art has an essence that can be captured in a definition with necessary and sufficient conditions, the latter deny this. One branch of anti-essentialism is associated with the Wittgensteinian school. Thus Morris Weitz argued, influentially, that 'art' is an open concept, inherently expansive, that any closed definition would make artistic creativity impossible, and that at most works of art share 'family resemblances'.[15] Although the 'family resemblance' view of art is now largely rejected, it did focus attention on the very enterprise of trying to define cultural objects. Intense and productive discussion has been addressed to this issue and emerging from it has come an increasing interest in 'institutional' theories.

Institutionalist definitions, which take many forms, afford a way of reviving

---

[12] John M. Ellis, *The Theory of Literary Criticism: A Logical Analysis* (Berkeley and Los Angeles: University of California Press, 1974).

[13] Richard Ohmann, 'Speech Acts and the Definition of Literature', *Philosophy and Rhetoric* 4 (1971), pp. 1–19; for a useful general survey, see Peter J. Rabinowitz, 'Speech Acts and Literary Studies', in Raman Selden (ed.), *The Cambridge History of Literary Criticism*, vol. 8 (Cambridge: Cambridge University Press, 1995), pp. 375–403.

[14] See, for example, Robert Stecker, *Artworks: Definition, Meaning, Value* (Philadelphia: Pennsylvania State University Press, 1997).

[15] Morris Weitz, 'The Role of Theory in Aesthetics', *Journal of Aesthetics and Art Criticism* 15 (1956), pp. 27–35.

essentialism without commitment to the existence of any set of *intrinsic* properties shared by all members of a class (art works, literary works). Some philosophers argue that what binds the class together are relational properties: for example, being related in an appropriate way to an 'artworld' (Arthur C. Danto), a 'practice' (Noël Carroll) or history (Jerrold Levinson). The idea has important repercussions for the literary case in removing the need to search for inherently 'literary' qualities and in re-introducing a role for authors and readers in a practice governed by *sui generis* conventions and concepts. Literary works, on this account, exist only relative to a practice of reading and appreciation, just as, say, 'castling' is possible only under the conventions of chess. Stein Haugom Olsen, who offers the most comprehensive institutionalist account of literature from the analytic perspective, has shown how literary works can be fully integrated into aesthetic theory through a revitalised conception of 'appreciation'. While appreciation, in this sense, follows familiar procedures of eliciting themes and assigning significance, it also transfigures textual features into aesthetic features, the latter 'emergent' from the former. A consequence is that there are no textual qualities *per se* – formal, semantic or rhetorical – which constitute literary discourse, and literary works are defined as those to which the 'literary stance' is most rewardingly applied.

Meaning, intention, interpretation

Given the central focus of analytic philosophy upon language and logic, it is not surprising that much attention has been given to meaning in the arts. In the literary case, the discussion nearly always begins, even if it goes beyond, the problem of intention. The argument for the irrelevance of authorial intention in constraining literary critical judgement was forcefully put in 'The Intentional Fallacy' (1946) by Monroe Beardsley and William K. Wimsatt, Jr.[16] The literary work, they claimed, is autonomous, 'detached from the author at birth', and the meanings it bears are those of a public language and culture. In *The Possibility of Criticism*, Beardsley went on to distinguish 'authorial' from 'textual' meaning, a distinction analogous to that drawn by philosophers of language between 'speaker's meaning' and 'sentence meaning', claiming that the latter alone is relevant to the critic. Precisely the opposite view was advanced by the literary critic E. D. Hirsch, who insisted in *Validity in Interpretation* that 'a text means what its author meant'.[17]

Underlying the debate are deeper issues about what kind of entity a literary work is and what kind of enterprise literary criticism should be. Hirsch's view

---

[16] Monroe C. Beardsley and William K. Wimsatt, 'The Intentional Fallacy', *On Literary Intention*, ed. David Newton-de Molina (Edinburgh: Edinburgh University Press, 1976).

[17] E. D. Hirsch, Jr., *Validity in Interpretation* (New Haven: Yale University Press, 1967).

presupposes not just that a work must 'represent one, particular, self-identical, unchanging complex of meaning' but also that a work itself has a determinate identity. The philosopher Joseph Margolis has challenged both assumptions in his view that works (of art) are 'culturally emergent entities', not determinate in the required sense, and open to plural interpretations which might be valid even where they contradict each other. Those who would not want to admit incompatible interpretations need not, however, restrict the constraints on interpretation to either authorial intention or semantic meaning.[18] Jerrold Levinson has offered a compromise between intentionalism and anti-intentionalism in what he styles 'hypothetical intentionalism'.[19] Not all philosophers, though, are persuaded that there is a useful distinction between these kinds of intentionalism.[20]

Analytic philosophers characteristically approach the topic of interpretation with theories of meaning drawn from outside literary criticism or aesthetics – speech act theory, semantics, Wittgensteinian language games, etc. – and the discussion proceeds by debating the appropriate model for the literary work: is it like an utterance, a conversation, a legal statute, a metaphor, an isolated sentence in a language?[21] Occasionally, though, resistance is shown to the importation of any such theories of meaning.[22] Philosophers have also been concerned with the kinds of reasoning involved in interpretation, enquiring into the status and possible resolution of critical disagreement, whether interpretative judgements are genuinely open to truth assessment, and what kinds of support are appropriate for them.[23]

Perhaps the most substantial interplay between philosophy of language and analytic aesthetics occurs in discussions of metaphor, on which there is now a vast and ever-expanding literature. Like the problem of fiction, the very existence of metaphor poses a challenge to orthodox logical conceptions of language. In fact parallels can be drawn with the treatment of fiction, for metaphor and fiction prompt similar questions: are they semantic or pragmatic phenomena? Are they open to truth-assessment? Do they possess a cognitive element? Or are they at root mere 'play'? How can they be accommodated into theories of meaning? Max Black's 'interaction' theory (1955) set the scene, according to which metaphors create new meanings

---

[18] For different strategies, see Michael Krautz, *Rightness and Reasons: Interpretations in Cultural Practices* (Ithaca, N.Y.: Cornell University Press, 1993).

[19] Jerrold Levinson, 'Intention and Interpretation: A Last Look', in Gary Iseminger (ed.), *Intention and Interpretation* (Philadelphia: Pennsylvania State University Press, 1992).

[20] See, for example, Stecker, *Artworks*, p. 201.

[21] For example, Noël Carroll, 'Art, Intention, and Conversation', in Iseminger (ed.), *Intention and Interpretation*; see also William E. Tolhurst, 'On What a Text is and How it Means', *British Journal of Aesthetics* 19 (1979), pp. 3–14.

[22] Stein Haugom Olsen, 'The "Meaning" of a Literary Work', in *The End of Literary Theory* (Cambridge: Cambridge University Press, 1987).

[23] See, for example, Annette Barnes, *On Interpretation: A Critical Analysis* (Oxford: Blackwell, 1988); also Krautz, *Rightness and Reasons*.

through the interaction, in tenor and vehicle, of systems of associated commonplaces.[24] There have been many attempts to establish a rigorous semantic theory along interactionist lines.[25] Other philosophers have followed Donald Davidson in rejecting a semantics of metaphor. For Davidson, there is no such thing as metaphorical meaning or metaphorical truth; metaphors possess only literal meaning and simply prompt us to think in novel ways.[26] Between these archetypical semantic and anti-semantic theories are various pragmatic approaches, appealing, for example, to speaker's meaning and speech acts,[27] or the 'cultivation of intimacy',[28] or varieties of comparisons.[29]

Other philosophical inputs

The aforementioned debates by no means exhaust the contribution of analytic aesthetics to the theory of criticism, even if they are characteristic of that contribution. Another topic, once again given impetus by Monroe Beardsley (in *Aesthetics*), is that of evaluation. For all their focus on logical analysis, aestheticians have not shied away from questions of value.[30] Beardsley proposed, controversially even at the time, objective criteria of value across the arts: notably unity, intensity and complexity. These are, he argued, formal aesthetic features without which a work of art could not have artistic value and which, on his instrumentalist view, help to fulfil the very purpose of art, producing aesthetic experiences. Although Beardsley's formalist criteria within an instrumentalist framework have come under fierce attack by other analytic philosophers, the search for criteria of value has by no means been abandoned.

Not unrelated to the question of value, there has been a recent revival of interest, influenced by the work of Iris Murdoch[31] (only tenuously an analytic philosopher) and Martha Nussbaum,[32] in literature and ethics. The debate

---

[24] Max Black, 'Metaphor', *Proceedings of the Aristotelian Society* 55 (1954–55), pp. 273–294.

[25] For instance, Eva Feder Kittay, *Metaphor: Its Cognitive Force and Structure* (Oxford: Clarendon Press, 1986).

[26] Donald Davidson, 'What Metaphors Mean', *Critical Inquiry* 5 (1978), pp. 31–47; also David E. Cooper, *Metaphor* (Oxford: Blackwell, 1986).

[27] John R. Searle, 'Metaphor', in Andrew Ortony (ed.), *Metaphor and Thought*, 2nd edn. (Cambridge: Cambridge University Press, 1993).

[28] Ted Cohen, 'Metaphor and the Cultivation of Intimacy', *Critical Inquiry* 5 (1978), pp. 3–12.

[29] Robert J. Fogelin, *Figuratively Speaking* (New Haven: Yale University Press, 1988).

[30] Direct treatment of value can be found in Mary Mothersill, *Beauty Restored* (Oxford: Clarendon Press, 1984); Anthony Savile, *The Test of Time* (Oxford: Clarendon Press, 1982); Malcolm Budd, *Values of Art: Pictures, Poetry and Music* (Harmondsworth: The Penguin Press, 1995).

[31] Iris Murdoch, *Metaphysics as a Guide to Morals* (London: Chatto & Windus, 1992).

[32] Martha Nussbaum, *Love's Knowledge: Essays on Philosophy and Literature* (Oxford: Oxford University Press, 1990); Martha Nussbaum, *Poetic Justice: The Literary Imagination and Public Life* (Cambridge, Mass.: Harvard University Press, 1995).

between 'moralists', who believe that the ethical implications of a work can affect its aesthetic value, and 'autonomists', who deny this, engages not only moral philosophy but also ontological and definitional questions about literature itself.[33]

Work by analytic philosophers on tragedy,[34] narrative identity,[35] mass art,[36] and feminist aesthetics,[37] only reinforces the view expressed at the beginning that analytic philosophy is a valuable contribution to literary criticism not only for the range of its topics but, perhaps more, for its distinctive logical methodology.

[33] See Jerrold Levinson (ed.), *Aesthetics and Ethics* (Cambridge: Cambridge University Press, 1997).
[34] See, for instance, Lamarque, *Fictional Points of View*, chapters 8, 9.
[35] David Novitz, *The Boundaries of Art* (Philadelphia: Temple University Press, 1992).
[36] Noël Carroll, *A Philosophy of Mass Art* (Oxford: Oxford University Press, 1998).
[37] Peggy Z. Brand and Carolyn Korsmeyer (eds.), *Feminism and Tradition in Aesthetics* (University Park: Pennsylvania State University Press, 1995).

25

Italian idealism

STEPHEN MOLLER

The roots of Italian idealism are to be found in the work of Giambattista Vico (1668–1744), professor of Latin Eloquence at the University of Naples. Years before Hegel's *Phenomenology of Spirit* (1807), Vico's *New Science* (1725) conceived of knowledge as acquired through a self-generative process. To Vico, thought in its development is first 'poetic wisdom' then becomes understanding and finally achieves unity of truth and certainty. Thought here does not merely represent, but actively creates reality. It is, moreover, conscious of its own generative process (*verum et factum convertuntur*).

Vico's epistemological idealism is bolstered by a religious metaphysics which postulates the unity of human thought with divine thought. The 'common sense' (*sensus communis*) of humanity, which orders the social and historical world is thus also identical with divine providence, and this identity acts to verify or ground the knowledge engendered by human thought.

Vico's ideas, however, won little recognition at the time. Thus the revival of idealism in Italy at the University of Naples, dating from 1840, was initially focused on Hegel, rather than Vico. The result was a Neapolitan school of Hegelianism. For A. Vera, leader of the 'orthodox Hegelians' at Naples, thought represented the 'absolute idea' in Hegelian terminology, which stood outside of human control. But two other central figures in Neapolitan Hegelianism, B. Spaventa (1813–83) and F. De Sanctis (1817–83), rejected this transcendence. Connecting Vico (whom they had rediscovered) to Hegelianism, Spaventa and De Sanctis defended a radical humanism that located all truth and reality solely in *this* world. Hence they reinterpreted Hegelian idealism so as to exclude any order of reality or truth which is not immanent to human consciousness, that is, they wished to exclude both the naturally and supernaturally transcendent. But whereas to Spaventa philosophy or knowledge of conscious reality was the sole 'category' containing all others, for De Sanctis art and literary criticism existed independently of philosophy. Spaventa's view was then reflected in the 'actualism' of Giovanni Gentile (1875–1944) and that of De Sanctis in the 'absolute historicism' of Benedetto Croce (1866–1952).

Croce and Gentile, each of them notable as a critic, philosopher and historian, came together in 1896 'to shake Italy out of the doze of naturalism and positivism and back to idealistic philosophy'.[1] The two formed an intellectual alliance in which each upheld ideas that matched the other's at many points. Their idealist teachings dominated Italian aesthetics and literary criticism for half a century, beginning with the founding of Croce's journal *La critica* in 1903. However, their association was marked by a gradually increasing rivalry. It was irreparably broken in 1925, when Gentile became the 'official' philosopher of fascism, Croce a leading antifascist. Yet, from 1925 to 1943, F. Flora, M. Fubini, L. Russo and other 'Crocean' critics were contributors to Gentile's *Enciclopedia italiana*, the testimony of the fascist regime in the field of culture. The reason for this apparently odd fact is that the fascist movement stemmed from a cultural situation of which Croce's idealism was already a vital part.

The ideal that Croce and Gentile as critics embodied was the union of literary theory and practical criticism: the philosopher-critic. Since artistic creation is a conscious activity necessarily related to the other activities of the mind, a theory of art must be viewed as an integral part of a philosophy that offers a systematic account of the mental processes through which humanity defines itself. To both Croce and Gentile the model critic was De Sanctis who had turned aesthetics into a highly developed instrument for the evaluation of literature.[2]

The idealism of Croce and Gentile derives from the concept that every reality, truth or value is realised only in and through the present activity of consciousness or 'spirit' (*spirito*), which is the only form of determinacy. Accordingly, spirit achieves its self-aware identity because it recognises its own universal characteristics and it is fully present to itself as self-consciousness, the absolute act by which mind makes itself its own object. Croce and Gentile hold that the process of spirit in all its formal dimensions is immanent and hence expresses itself similarly in every existent human individual.

The general ideas concerning the poem as a literary form that Croce and Gentile both accepted in the 1920s flow from this immanentism: the poem is understood as an original act in which aesthetic value is realised; 'form' and 'content' become one in the poetic act; the universal 'self' of the poet is realised in the poem, where the poem endeavours to remake the world out of an elemental sense of all human experience.

Yet Croce and Gentile diverged at a vital point. The essence of Croce's aesthetic is the autonomy of poetry, which it defines as pure 'intuition' (*intuizione*), and his criticism is the practical application of this idea. By contrast, Gentile identifies poetry with the primitive 'feeling' (*sentimento*) in which

---

[1] Introduction to D. Bigongiari's translation of Gentile's *La riforma dell'educazione* (New York: Harcourt Brace, 1922), p. vii.

[2] On De Sanctis and Croce, see E. E. Jacobitti, *Revolutionary Humanism and Historicism in Modern Italy* (New Haven: Yale, 1981), pp. 46–56; and G. Gentile, *The Philosophy of Art* (1931), trans. G. Gullace (Ithaca: Cornell University Press, 1972), pp. 285–290.

consciousness originates and whose realisation is its development into the act of self-consciousness (or *pensiero pensante*), which is the subject's philosophical awareness of itself as its own object. Gentile's criticism (unlike Croce's) thus insists on the idea that poetry is fused with philosophy and every other human activity.

Croce

Croce's artistic and literary theory evolved from a first phase as outlined in *Estetica come scienza dell'espressione e linguistica generale* (1902) ('Aesthetic as Science of Expression and General Linguistic'), to a final phase as set down in *La poesia: Introduzione alla critica e storia della poesia* (1936) ('Poetry: An Introduction to its Criticism and History'). Croce tested and exemplified his theories in a series of critical essays ranging over the whole of western literature from Homer to Ibsen. He identified four phases in his critical theory and practice, which he (but not all of his critics) viewed as forming a consistent development.[3]

Croce's *Estetica* presents a theory of art (where poetry is the true type of art) as a theory of the human spirit *in toto*. On Croce's scheme, reality lies in the connected activities of spirit. There are two main categories: theory and practice. Each of these manifests two distinct forms, related to one another as particular to general. Theory is first imagery or 'intuition'. The instant of pure intuition, before reflection and volition encroach upon it, is the work of the 'imagination' (*fantasia*) in presenting before the mind the particulars that form its world. This imaginative vision of particulars coincides with poetry, which Croce identifies with language and expression in their full, unanalysed concreteness. This equation of poetry and language thus depends on the idea of a phase of linguistic expression in which logical meaning has not yet appeared, parts of speech are not distinguished, and words are not discriminated as signs for objects, but language springs spontaneously from one's total 'state of being' (*stato d'animo*). Croce insists that intuition marks the essential character of poetry, however stylistically elaborated it may be.

The second form of theoretical activity, which presupposes intuition, is thought or 'logic' which relates the particulars of intuition to universals. The initial closeness of theory and poetry stresses the intuitive vision of the particular while the secondary link to logic brings out universal concepts and thus connects the particular to the universal.

The two practical forms, the 'economic', in which we intentionally envisage a particular end and the 'ethical' in which the particular is related to the

---

[3] B. Croce, *The Aesthetic as the Science of Expression and of the Linguistic in General* (1902), trans. C. Lyas (Cambridge: Cambridge University Press, 1992), pp. xxx–xxxiv.

universal end, depend upon and employ the theoretical. But while Croce holds that theory is the presupposition of practice, he also affirms that practice is no less the condition of knowledge. Poetry, logic, economic and moral willing thus constitute a complete cycle of activities, which are traversed by the mind in 'spirals'. Every cycle recommences at the point of experience to which the mind has been raised by what has previously been achieved. Thus poetry finds its 'kindling' in the products of the logical and of the practical. Poetry precedes all other experience in an ideal, not a temporal, sense.

For Croce, poetry (like logic, economic and moral willing) is self-determining and self-justifying: nothing counts but the perfection of the poetic act in itself and according to its own norm. True and false, real and unreal, good and bad are irrelevant to poetry. Here nothing counts but the adequacy of the poetic act in itself and by its own standard. Thus Croce means to rid poetry of *allotria*, of alien aims; of moral and intellectual 'instruction'; of the provocation of pleasure; of conformity to 'nature'; of 'appropriateness' in its subject matter. Nor does he allow that 'content' may dictate the mode of expression, that one theme must be treated in one form, and another theme in another form. The reason for this is that apart from the expression the content does not exist. Content and form are created *pari passu*; intuition-expression encompasses the two in one.

Specifically, to Croce all poetry consists in the production of an image. The image is the presentation of something concrete and definite either of outward sense (a person or object) or of inner sense (an emotion or mood), that has existence only in the mind that constructs and contemplates it and bears evidence only to itself. The image is a mental vision that exists only when produced in the act of imagination, and this act is only for the sake of producing the vision. Imagination, which thus encompasses both act and product, is not merely a private affair but universally human: what one person has imagined another is assumed to be able to imagine. Milton's Satan is such an image, a determinate mental picture. But also the whole poem in which this image appears (*Paradise Lost*) is an image, for it is a unified individual presentation, a single vision that integrates many images into a complex whole. The poem is thus understood as an image that is a tapestry of images.

For Croce imagination is a form of cognition that portrays but does not affirm. It is one with intuition and expression, two terms that he makes coincide. 'Intuition' stresses mainly the theoretical, but pre-conceptual, character of the image; 'expression' the distinctive quality of the constructive imagination by which expressive activity is differentiated from the passivity that marks mere 'impression'. Poetry is thus an intuition which is an expression of a sense impression that the poet feels driven to render present to consciousness by means of the image.

Croce stresses that a fully formed poetic image is a verbalised image, embodied in its appropriate words, in their appropriate order, and in the special patterns (metre, rhyme, cadence, etc.) that the words may assume. In a poem many details are fused together so as to form a concrete image; but the image is 'concrete' only if it is expressed in words.

This leads to Croce's theory of language. To Croce language does not exist *per se*, as a system of signs. Rather language is the utterance, the spoken sentence and the concrete pattern of phrases as they are spontaneously formed by the speaker. To support this point he assumes that dictionaries, grammars, treatises on metric, or poetic instructions, all presuppose the *continuum* of speech or the poem, from which they abstract their single words and rules. These *a posteriori* constructions have a practical value; they serve the speaker as reminders of tradition that one may accept, modify or reject, in accordance with one's mood.[4]

To Croce, then, language is the poetic act in ever-changing creativity, where the image is constituted in the act of expression. It follows that (1) synonyms and homonyms are impossible, for each word has the same unique individuality as the expression of intuition; (2) the only test of 'diction' is its appropriateness to the mood expressed by the poet; (3) metres are different in every poem or poet; (4) the parts of speech have no expressive value in isolation but become language only in actual speech. Accordingly, Croce's criticism abandons discussion of classes of words, grammatical categories and all such 'abstractions'; it attends instead to poetry as speech and holds that the meaning of its words cannot be detached from the poem and analysed 'materialistically'.

Similarly, Croce rejects 'genres' both as principles of composition and as critical categories. Each poem is *sui-generis*, a unique expression of its author. Hence no attempt should be made to compare one poem with another, still less to categorise it as 'lyric', 'epic' or 'dramatic'. Croce holds that the concepts of genres and all other such classifications (conventions, etc.) arise out of empirical generalisations and practical advice to poets; they are abstractions formed from single works and have no value for the judgement and for the history of poetry. Genre distinctions are merely useful, as aids to the recollection and identification of single works or as shorthand designations for groups of works.[5]

Accordingly, in place of the old history of genres (or of periods, national traditions, schools) Croce's criticism, as exemplified in *La letteratura della nuova Italia* (6 vols., 1904–1940), presents a series of monographs. The aim of these is to define the individuality of a poem, of the image and the mood which it expresses in their unique relationship; to determine whether the poem achieves a coherence among its images; and ultimately to place the poem in the total development of its author's 'poetic personality'.

Croce also denies the relevance to criticism of uncovering the author's

[4] *Ibid.*, pp. 156–164.   [5] *Ibid.*, pp. 36–43.

intentions. As the meaning of the poem is to be found in the poem, no judgement of intention (alleged aims quoted from some extra-poetic source) is relevant unless corroborated by the poem itself. Equally, Croce rejects the idea that criticism should refer to circumstances (political or otherwise extra-poetic) that transcend the poem. To view a poem in its cultural or historical context is to distort one's sense of that poem. The New Criticism of J. C. Ransom, C. Brooks and others, which was prominent in the 1940s, though not Crocean in inspiration, upheld a similar thesis.[6]

Croce's critical 'method' in the *Estetica* turns on the idea that to judge a poem is 'to reproduce it in oneself', where the only difference between the criteria informing the act of reproducing the poem ('taste') and those of producing it ('genius') is in the diversity of circumstances. To judge is to transfer oneself into the situation in which a poem was born in the mind of the poet, to reiterate the poet's vision.[7] There is then no real difference between critic and poet, only a distinction of degree, not of originality and authenticity.

In practice Croce soon extended the idea that criticism is reproduction of a previous expression. He began to view each poem in the light of the universal category of poetry and felt that it was necessary to describe this relationship in a unique way. Here criticism becomes the logical operation of applying a universal category (the concept of poetry) to a 'fact' (a poem or aesthetic intuition), an operation to which the process of reproduction is preparatory. As he put it in *Problemi di estetica* (1910): 'the aesthetic fact, as reproduced in the imagination, should be conceived as an aesthetic fact; ... from being contemplation it should become a logical act (subject, predicate and copula). Literary criticism consists in this simple act of adding a predicate to the subject of contemplation.'[8] This fresh approach enabled Croce to distinguish taste from criticism, and critic from poet. It also allowed him to assert the validity of the critical judgement for the decision of whether a given work is a work of poetry (an image expressive of a state of mind).[9]

By 1907, Croce had begun the second phase of his aesthetics, the theory of poetry as 'lyrical' (*liricità*) intuition. The 1902 *Estetica* had spoken vaguely of intuition as drawing its material from 'impressions'. But in his paper 'L'intuizione pura e il carattere lirico dell'arte' (1908) ('Pure Intuition and the Lyrical Character of Art') Croce makes it clear that the function of intuition is to express emotions arising from our practical life and that this determines poetry's lyrical character. It is the practical or ethical spirit alone that provides the material to which poetry gives form by means of integrating it into the content of intuition. In the *Brevario di estetica* (1913) (*The Essence of*

---

[6] See, for instance, J. C. Ransom, *The New Criticism* (Norfolk: New Directions, 1941).
[7] Croce, *Aesthetic*, pp. 132–152.
[8] B. Croce, *Problemi d'estetica* (Bari: Laterza, 1910), p. 52.   [9] *Ibid.*, p. 54.

Aesthetic), Croce redefines poetry as the '*a priori synthesis*' of image and emotion (form and content) in the intuition.[10]

The critic's task is now to define the emotion as crystallised in a poem's integral image and to declare judgement as to the unity, consistency and shapeliness of that image, as well as to the adequacy of the adjustment of the objective elements of the poem (metre, scenes, characters, plot) to its dominant emotion. The critic must decide how far the poem achieves expression of its lyrical 'motif' (*macchia*) and how far its expression is impeded by non-poetic intrusions (the promotion of political and other interests), pointing out where in the poem these occur, explaining why they are not poetic.

The third phase of Croce's thought, his theory that lyric intuition has a 'cosmic character' (*carattere cosmico*), is evident in the *Nuovi saggi di estetica* (1920).[11] On this theory, poetry is the intuition of the universally human in the individual: the poetic image is the universe in individual form. The material of poetry is composed of all the passions of human experience; in entering the poem these passions are transformed by the poet's sense of life into its content; and in becoming its content they become part of the image. The poem is then the poet's effort to articulate a universal emotion or sense of all human life, to make the world of the image adequate to that emotion. This ideal is for Croce the quality of being 'classic' (*classicità*). Here Croce distinguishes his view from both a Romantic notion of poetry as a mere effusion of emotion and a 'classicism' that stresses the formal element at the expense of the emotional in sober discursive prose.

Croce applied his 'cosmic' theory in essays on Ariosto (1918), Shakespeare (1919), Goethe (1919), Corneille (1920) and Dante (1921). These essays all aim at a synthesis of evaluation and 'characterisation' (*caratterizzazione*). Here the critic's job is to study the poem as the embodiment of an image expressing the poet's cosmic emotion. This gives the critic three aspects from which to grasp the poem: the image, the emotion and their reciprocal relation. The critic characterises the image, defines the emotion and evaluates their mutual adjustment. The conclusion that the image is an adequate expression of the dominant emotion is the critical judgement. It is the essay on Ariosto that best reflects Croce's cosmic view of poetry. By presenting Ariosto not as the poet of irony (as De Sanctis had done) but as the poet of harmony – the harmony which is the sum of all human passions felt with an intensity that makes it 'cosmic' – Croce gave new impetus to the study of this poet in Italy.

Croce came to believe the idea that poetry expresses not solely an individual reality but an entire universe. But, to his critics, Croce had not shown how this cosmic character could be reconciled with his earlier conception of

---

[10] B. Croce, *The Essence of Aesthetic* (1913), trans. D. Ainslie (London: Heinemann, 1921), pp. 39–40.

[11] Croce first announced his cosmic theory in 'Il carattere di totalità dell'espressione artistica', *La critica* 16 (1918), pp. 129–140.

poetry being the intuition of a definite, individual image.[12] The final 'phase' of Croce's thought is the theory of literature in *La poesia* (1936), a work intended to consolidate the preceding revisions of his aesthetic. *La poesia* offers, as a negative corollary of the theory of intuition, a definition of literature as everything that is not poetry. Croce identifies four kinds of expression: 'sentimental or immediate', 'poetic', 'prosaic' and 'rhetorical'. In true poetry intuition is not subservient to any extrinsic ends, such as intellectual instruction; it is pure lyrical expression. Thus Lucretius' *De rerum natura*, for instance, is held to be a work of literature, not of poetry, because its argument is more important than its form. In short, wherever verse lacks pure lyrical intuition one has literature, which Croce further subdivides into 'sentimental', 'moralistic', 'entertaining' and 'didactic' kinds.

La poesia is an apology for literature as ornament, decorum and restraint. Literature gives a poetic 'flavour' to 'expressions of civilisation'; its function is to satisfy the aesthetic exigencies of non-poetic expressions. This, however, renders it difficult to identify 'real' poetry, because the concept of aesthetic beauty now applies to both poetry and literature or the resemblance of poetry (since it falls short of authentic lyrical and cosmic intuition). Nevertheless, the basic task of the critic is still to distinguish between poetry and literature.

In sum, Croce denies that reflection is a necessary part of poetry. His criticism adopts a purely imagistic view of poetry. But this causes some obvious problems. An example is his verdict, in *La poesia di Dante* (1921), that Dante's *Commedia* is a theological novel and, as such, non-poetical, while the lyrical episodes that cover the theological structure alone are poetical. This reduces the poem to a selection of pieces that according to Croce are not spoilt by intellectualism, religious purposes, or allegorical constructions. Similar problems occur in Croce's negative judgements of Leopardi, Foscolo, Alfieri, Manzoni and others.

Moreover, Croce's treatment of imagination or poetry as essentially prior to conceptual thought is *philosophically* untenable. The image may be free from any explicit logical affirmation or judgement; but to call it an image means that it is discriminated by thought and referred to objective conditions. How can we have images of determinate, individual things (of 'this river', 'this lake', etc.) without concepts or categories, without the *de facto* working in our minds of the ideas of identity, distinction, substance, whole and part? That is, how can a definite image be other than an object of thought having identity, diversity and so on? Croce's idea of antedating language by comparison with conventional or logical meaning seems equally problematic. As R. G. Collingwood (who was generally sympathetic to Croce) pointed out, language is not language without its conceptual side; and to equate language

---

[12] See A. Tilgher, *Estetica: teoria generale dell'attività artistica* (Rome: Libreria di scienze e lettere, 1931) pp. 18–19.

with intuition, and detach intuition from thinking, is to undermine the conception of a unity of the human mind, upon which Croce also insists.

Gentile

Gentile's chief concern as a critic is with the relation between poetry and philosophy. His critical studies, which are fewer and narrower in scope than those of Croce, include *Gino Capponi e la cultura toscana nel secolo XIX* (1922); *Dante e Manzoni* (1923); *L'eredità di Vittorio Alfieri* (1926); *Manzoni e Leopardi: Saggi critici* (1928); *La profezia di Dante* (1933); and *Poesia e filosofia di G. Leopardi* (1939). The romantically exuberant *La filosofia dell'arte* (1931) (*The Philosophy of Art*), is Gentile's major work of aesthetic and literary theory, intended to rival that of Croce.

Before the emergence of his 'actualism' in 1912, Gentile adopted Croce's idea of the lyrical character of poetry that precedes reflective thought. Thus in 'La filosofia di Giacomo Leopardi' (1907),[13] Gentile regards the philosophy in Leopardi's *Zilbadone di pensieri* (*Notebook of Thoughts*) as just a record of different emotions or states of mind. True philosophy, however, transcends the personal feeling of its author; it is distinct from the pure lyric expression in images that characterises poetry.

But in a 1917 review of G. Bertacchi's book on Leopardi (*Un maestro di vita*), Gentile, in the light of his 'actualism', now sees Leopardi's poetry and his philosophy as inseparable.[14] Leopardi's poetry is produced by the feeling which is also the source of his philosophy. Conversely, his philosophy is transmuted into the rhythm of his poetic feeling. Thus his philosophy is not a system of ideas but is based on an elemental sense of what it means to be human.

In 'La poesia del Leopardi' (1927) and 'Poesia e filosofia del Leopardi' (1938), Gentile presses this view to its limit. He argues that Leopardi's poetry *is* his philosophy and vice versa. Leopardi's personality is realised in the unity of his feeling and thought. Here Gentile defends the essential unity of Leopardi's works: the philosophical feeling of pessimism (or *nòia*) with which Leopardi lives imbues all his writings. Thus Leopardi's *Operette morali* (satirical and ironical compositions) are as lyrical as his *Canti*, while the *Canti* express his philosophy in lyric notes.

The theory underlying Gentile's 'actualist' criticism recalls Croce's cosmic view: the poem is an original act in which the poet objectifies a fundamental feeling, into which is dissolved his whole past, all his passions both lived and fancied, and his sense of the hopes, pains, and joys of humankind. The poet

---

[13] This essay, and all of the other pieces by Gentile on Leopardi mentioned hereafter, are now in G. Gentile, *Manzoni e Leopardi, opere complete*, vol. XXIV, 2nd edn. (Florence: Sansoni, 1960).   [14] Gentile, *The Philosophy of Art*, pp. 216–219.

articulates this feeling objectively (in metre, scenes, plot, etc.), constructing a vision adequate to it, under the aegis of a pervasive self-awareness. The latter is the active 'moment' which unites feeling and expression, wherein the poet tries to make the vision of the poem adequate to the feeling, so that no objective element is devoid of feeling. For any such element is 'poetic' only insofar as it serves to illuminate feeling. Considered in itself, the objective element is non-poetic, a mere item of technique; but in a fully realised poem every such element will be synthesised by the poet with the poetry or pervasive feeling of the poem, so as to work as a vital part of the poetic act. Gentile defines this whole constructive process as an act of 'self-translation' (*autotradursi*).[15]

The critic studies a poem in the light of the concept of the universal poetic act, in which a feeling is objectified, and where the poem as expressive of the unique individuality of the poet is also a unique expression of universal humanity. The critic is to determine whether, and to what extent, a poem attains to an adequacy of the objective elements of the poet's vision to its original feeling, and to define the unique way in which it does so. This involves three stages. The critic analyses the 'poetics' (objective elements) of the poem; then moves from these to an appreciation of the feeling which gave them birth; then reconstructs the poem as a whole, viewing the objective elements as expressive of and integrated by the feeling of the poem or, conversely, the feeling as it develops into the world of the poem.[16]

Now to Croce the poem is never more than what the poet formed out of what he or she felt; it is sealed off both from the poet's past and that which follows it, including its criticism. Hence to Croce the critic is a 'philosopher added to artist'.[17] Gentile holds that the emotional experience of the poem also has its origin only in the poem. But for him the poet's effort to make a poem adequate to that feeling does not close the poem off from the critic. The poet cannot achieve an absolute adequacy because the feeling is inexhaustible.[18] Thus the attempt of the poet to articulate the feeling never achieves finality. Each new critic who tries to grasp how the individual movement of the poem embodies the feeling further defines the vision of the expression of its feeling. To Gentile, the critic is therefore an 'artist added to artist'.[19]

Also striking is Gentile's idea that the meaning of a work is produced by the reader, when it is being read, and not by the author who wrote it. This has some parallels with the theme of 'active interpretation' developed by post-structuralist criticism.[20] But Gentile links this idea to a complex theory of inter-personal understanding, to account for the transmission of meaning from author to reader or from one reader to another. The basis of this theory is that one can understand another person by transforming the facts of that

---

[15] *Ibid.*, pp. 219–222.   [16] *Ibid.*, pp. 219–225.
[17] B. Croce, *Nuovi saggi*, 4th edn. (Bari: Laterza, 1958), p. 79.
[18] Gentile, *The Philosophy of Art*, pp. 207–214.   [19] *Ibid.*, pp. 216–223.
[20] *Ibid.*, pp. 77–83.

person's life into actions, to be imagined and understood in the present act of thinking (*pensiero pensante*) of the one who would understand.

Gentile's critics (particularly Croce) allege that in poets such as Leopardi and Dante Gentile sees the philosopher rather than the poet, that he is blind to what makes poetry poetry.[21] True, he focuses on doctrinal poets who, to his view, expound a philosophical poetics of life; but he does not slight poetry. The aim of his 'actualist' criticism is to grasp the poet's philosophy in the images and the varied tone of the poem, and to show how poetry consists in the reflective-passionate content of the poem into which is concentrated the poet's whole personality. Gentile's insight is that there is no poet *per se*, no poet who is not also a thinker; for the poet cannot produce a poem in detachment from the act of thinking in which he or she articulates his or her feeling. Thus it is only by tracing the integral movement of this act that the critic can grasp all instances of poetic qualities, the specific formal skills in a poet, and objective elements of a poem, such as stanzaic form, plot and metre.

Italian idealistic criticism after Croce and Gentile

From 1903 to 1940 Italian criticism was marked by its strong sense of affiliation with the philosophical attitudes of idealism. Although there were several notable exceptions (including G. Toffanin, B. Nardi and C. Marchesi), most Italian critics born between 1890 and 1914 initially adopted the ideas of Croce or Gentile. However, by the early 1930s some of these critics were beginning to evolve positions that deviated from their masters' teachings at crucial points.

A main source of this divergence was the new historicism. This was a widespread critical movement in Italy after the 1930s (independent of the American new historicism) that stemmed from the work of L. Russo, and focused on the historical presuppositions of poetry. The best known of the new historicists (many of whom wrote for Russo's journal *Belfagor*) was Walter Binni who edited his own review *La Rassegna della letteratura italiana*. Other critics who took advantage of this movement included Umberto Bosco, N. Sapegno, G. Getto, and 'philological' critics, such as M. Marti, G. Contini and L. Caretti.

Now for Croce and Gentile the content of the poem, its emotion or feeling, is the content as formed only in the poem itself. It followed that all the poet's preparatory labours, private and social experience, intentions, beliefs and historical situation cannot be analysed as the 'cause' of the emotion of the poem. Any philological work that the critic undertakes is either preliminary to the criticism of the poem (Croce) or consists in an analysis of the objective

---

[21] B. Croce, *Conversazioni critiche*, vol. 4 (Bari: Laterza, 1951), p. 300.

moment of the poem itself (Gentile). Gentile, in particular, had stressed that the historical milieu in which the poem was created, as well as the emotional life and ideas of the poet, should be studied only as they are resolved in the 'timelessness' of the poem. But both Croce and Gentile ruled out any attempt to recognise the sense and value of the poem by more or less extensive researches on the circumstances out of which it emerged.

Binni, however, disputes the idea of the poem as an autogenetic act closed at its source from all antecedent conditions, and hence rejects the idea that the critic has no need to avert from the poem in order to understand or evaluate it. Instead, as in his *La nuova poetica leopardiana* (1947), he holds that criticism should attend not only to the expression of emotion but also to the *poetica*, to the ideas and literary orientation of the poet, to the historical links between the poem and the development of literary ideals.

But 'faithful' Croceans, such as M. Sansone, also began to study the ways in which the content of the poem had already been formed in the poet's everyday life, before it became poetry. The intention here (as with Russo and Binni) was not to replace the aesthetic criticism of Croce and Gentile but to supplement it with erudite research in the hope that a more complete 'method' would result. But any such extension conflicted with Croce's and Gentile's idea that the work of poetry and the mind of the poet are essentially unpredictable; they may hence turn out to be untraceable to any development unearthed by the critic.

In brief, the new historicism and the emergence of poetics as a major part of Italian literary theory undermined the idea of the unconditional originality of the poem that had been central to the absolute idealism of Croce and Gentile. But other factors, too, contributed to the gradual erosion of the authority of this idealism for Italian criticism.

Now to Croce and Gentile criticism was essentially one in its concept (as an evaluative criterion) and diverse only in its procedures. But after 1945 Italian critics – for instance, Russo in his *Problemi di metodo critico* (1950) and Mario Fubini, in his *Critica e poesia* (1973) – began to affirm only the need of a methodological diversity. By becoming a poetics, criticism could no longer be absolutely universal; rather each reading is a 'hypothesis' or a 'metacritical exercise'.

By the early 1950s, the main current of Italian criticism had moved away from the idealism of Croce and Gentile. Italian critics, older and younger, were forming new critical perspectives and becoming increasingly pluralistic in their approaches, drawing variously from Marxism, existentialism, pragmatism, hermeneutics, phenomenology, structuralism, semiotics or (in the case of at least one notable Crocean, Francesco Flora) Platonism.[22]

---

[22] For an account of this, see Vittorio Stella, 'Aspetti e tendenze dell' estetica italiana odierna (1945–1963)', *Giornale di metafisica*, a. XVIII, 6 (1963), pp. 576–621, and a. XIX, 1–2 (1964), pp. 41–74, 280–329.

At the same time these critics became more inclined to specialise and to leave the elemental questions to aestheticians. Or they saw no point in raising these old questions again: 'why illuminate the light'? To Croce and Gentile, it had been vital to know how we know: to accept a principle without grounding it in a theory of knowledge meant to surrender reason. But by the 1960s a growing number of Italian critics had abandoned the idea of tying literary criticism to a primary philosophy.

Today most Italian critics would regard themselves as *superatori* of Croce and Gentile. Having assimilated the teachings of idealism they are not about to revive the old ways of criticism, such as the theory of poetry as imitation; but they are not held in check by any sense of dependence upon those teachings.

Italian idealistic criticism outside Italy

Although he is still a well-known figure in Italy, elsewhere Gentile is hardly known as a critic, and his critical writings remain untranslated. The reasons for this neglect are not far to seek: Gentile wrote exclusively on Italian literature which, with the exception of Dante, has ceased to excite much general critical interest in the rest of the world. Moreover, to many, including his erstwhile English disciple R. G. Collingwood, Gentile's association with fascism was enough to discredit him permanently.[23] But it should be noted that Gentile never became a party hack and his scholarly work under fascism remained impressive.

Gentile deserves a wider consideration than he is currently getting. His contribution to contemporary criticism is significant, for it represents an original denunciation of those theories which view poetry as a 'quintessence' detached from the total rhythm of human life. More than anyone, Gentile has tried to show how poetry is the ground of our entire conscious life, of our moral values, ideals, science, philosophy and religious beliefs.

The situation is different with Croce, whose international reputation was enhanced by his opposition to fascism. Some of his critical writings have been translated into several languages; and (unlike Gentile) he appears in standard histories of aesthetics, though he is seldom mentioned in non-Italian works of literary criticism. It is difficult to trace precisely Croce's international influence, which is of a pervasive kind. He found several sympathetic expositors in the United States, including Joel E. Spingarn, and in England, notably Collingwood.[24] Though he wrote extensively on French literature, and was known to French critics such as Valéry, Croce was not greatly esteemed in

---

[23] R. G. Collingwood, *An Autobiography* (Oxford: Clarendon Press, 1939), p. 158.
[24] For Croce's impact in the U.S.A., see M. E. Moss, *Benedetto Croce: Essays on Literature and Literary Criticism* (Albany: SUNY, 1990), pp. 18–25.

France. His ideas (like those of Gentile) are essentially antithetical to the theoretical 'anti-humanism' of French structuralism and to other literary schools that no longer preserve humanistic perspectives.[25]

Croce's contribution to literary criticism should also be more widely appreciated outside Italy, for it represents a truly systematic and philosophically articulate attempt to defend the autonomy of poetry. In this, Croce exemplifies the ideal of the philosopher-critic to a remarkable degree; and much of his value as a critic stems from his acute sense of the theoretical implications of his practical criticism. Furthermore, he provides an able defence of criticism as an essentially rational undertaking. Finally, like Gentile, Croce preserves unwavering trust in the capacity of our thought to illuminate the structures of its own activity.

[25] On the contrast between Crocean idealism and structuralism, see P. Olivier, *Croce, ou l'affirmation de l'immanence absolue* (Paris: Seghers, 1975), e.g., pp. 43–44.

26

Spanish and Spanish American poetics and criticism

MANUEL BARBEITO VARELA

– 'The rest is silence', said Hamlet.
– 'Le rest est littérature', echoed Verlaine.
– 'Un no se qué que quedan balbuciendo'

(S. Juán de la Cruz)

The last decades of the nineteenth century and the early years of the twentieth century saw a major change in Spanish American arts and letters: Spanish intellectuals began to look north, reversing the European romantic artists' movement towards the south; at the same time the state of mutual ignorance that had existed before the 1890s between Spain and Spanish America was transformed by the springing up of new, fertile cultural relationships. This development was symbolically marked by the disintegration of the old Spanish empire in 1898, when the last of the old Spanish colonies finally gained independence. After 1898, intellectuals no longer saw Spain as the repressive power, they began to see it instead as a victim of emergent North American imperialism, already felt to be a threat to Spanish America.

Both Spanish and Spanish American writers were imbued with European philosophical, literary and artistic ideas. Spanish painters received grants to study in Europe, especially Italy; Zuloaga established himself in Paris; Sorolla won the Grand Prix of the Paris exhibition of 1900; Picasso and Gris made decisive contributions to the cubist revolution in Paris. In Spanish America, French symbolism and parnassianism in particular deeply influenced those forerunners of 'modernismo', such as the Mexican Gutiérrez Nájera (1859–95), the Colombian Asunción Silva (1865–96), and the Cuban independentist hero Martí (1853–95). In Spain, the members of the 98 Generation also delved into European literature and philosophy.

Several Spanish Americans such as Darío, Nervo and Borges wrote and published in Madrid during the last decade of the nineteenth and the first third of the twentieth centuries. It may have been evidence of such activities that tempted the Madrid review *La gaceta literaria* in 1927 to suggest the creation of a sort of cultural network by Spanish speaking intellectuals, an idea which was rejected by Spanish Americans such as Borges, Carpentier and others, who were jealous of their independence and of their recent ascendancy. Such intellectuals proposed instead a cultural community of Spanish American countries, but this was never really more than an ideal. Although neither of these proposals was carried out, shared elements such as language and cultural traditions, not to speak of the historical relationship, remained crucial for the development of Spanish and Spanish American literature.

The ideas belonging to 'modernismo' were disseminated in various American countries through the collaboration of the modernists in journals such as *La revista azul*, *La revista moderna* and *Helios*. The Nicaraguan Rubén Darío became the leader of the modernist movement in Buenos Aires, and he later took his ideas to Spain where he became associated with members of the 98 Generation. In his early phase of 'modernismo' Darío, like other modernists, was attracted by the concept of 'art for art's sake', showing little interest in everyday life and preferring artificial worlds, classic mythology, exotic images and themes. After 1898, however, Darío's art underwent a transformation and became preoccupied with existential and also political problems, such as the future of Spanish America.

'Modernismo' effected a major change from a complex to a more simple grammar. This suited the project of the 98 Generation who, in their desire to debunk the fantasy of Spanish imperial splendour, attacked the grand style with which they associated it. Thus Valle Inclán stated that: '[t]he way of the Indies is no longer ours, the popes are not Spanish, but the baroque style remains'. The 98 Generation shared the feeling, present in European culture since the eighteenth century, of a fall from 'true being' to a 'false modernity'. For them the ideal had indeed been a reality in the Middle Ages, typically expressed in the spontaneity and simplicity of poets like Berceo. Such a style had then been discarded to make way for a less truthful, more ornate mode of expression better fitted to celebrate the feats of the conquest.

The idea of Spain was central to the poetics of the 98 Generation. Moving against the ideas of positivism and naturalism, the dominant movements of the previous decades in Europe, they abandoned the attempt to explain human beings in terms of their environment. Moreover, rejecting the tradition of Pérez Galdós, they maintained that truth, whether personal or historical, could not be found in the sequence of events on which canonical history was based. As a foil to the idea of external history, Unamuno introduced the concept of 'intrahistory': while history, in the conventional sense of the term, deals with the great events of a nation's past, 'intrahistory' is concerned with habitual actions, popular tradition and one's own experience of the landscape of one's home (Azorín used the term 'sponge of memories' to express this idea). Neither great historical events nor objective description mattered for the 98 Generation. In line with the philosophy which privileged lived experience over intellect, their aim was to capture and express seemingly insignificant things made poetic by the intensity of the moment. Machado and Azorín held the belief that the aim of the poet was to eternalise the ephemeral living moment, and they considered the ability to express this moment to be the measure of this generation's achievement. In this they remained well within the Romantic tradition, but exhibited a distinctive flavour of their own in that it is the idea of the spirit of the race, a Spanish essence, that is the subject of the living moment. In literature this concept revolutionised the novel: in place of a rigid plot structure, artists explored new possibilities for capturing and representing these fragmentary moments.

These artists replaced traditional narrative with impressionistic description; moreover they established a close link between their impressionism and a particular view of the landscape. Laín Entralgo characterised the impressionism of the 98 Generation as one in which the idea of Spain mediated between the object and the image, in contrast to the immediacy that, according to Levenson, ruled the impressionism of the London Imagists.[1] Such an idea of Spain led to the differentiation between the historical persona considered as an intruder into the landscape, and the ideal persona who exists in harmony with nature.

In the interpretation of the aesthetic millenarianism of the 98 Generation, 'dream' is a key word in much the same way as it is for Yeats: what is only a ghostly presence for the materialists, constitutes the ultimate reality for the poet who, they thought, is able to divine a deeper truth in historical particularity ('reality does not matter; what matters is our dream', said Azorín); as a historical person, though, he must suffer from the phantasmagoric quality of his dream. They thought that the cause of the dream's ghostliness was a weakened will, which was also perceived as the cause of the decline of Spain. The solution to this decline was, therefore, not to be found in science and technology, dominant in materialist Europe, but in the empowering of the ideal. This ideal, according to Unamuno, was what the new-born quixotic Spain could impart to Europe; it was also essential if Spain was to avoid importing Europe's inhuman materialism along with its science and technology. The figures of the 98 Generation here differ significantly from the contemporary 'regenerationists' (Costa and Ramón y Cajal) who emphasised that Spain's future, like that of other European nations, lay in improving material living conditions by means of investment in science, education, transport and agriculture.

Such ideas dominated the literary and aesthetic criticism of the 98 Generation and were also reflected in the work of those artists that they brought to the forefront. Their favoured painters refused to paint historical themes and, like the impressionists, abandoned the study for the open air to paint the landscape and its inhabitants. They especially admired Zuloaga who, like Goya and El Greco, explored the aesthetic potential of black. The

---

[1] Cf. M. Levenson, *The Genealogy of Modernism* (Cambridge: Cambridge University Press, 1992); see also P. Laín Entralgo, *La generación del 98* (Madrid: Espasa Calpe, 1947).

classical Spanish writers and painters, on the other hand, were ignored except where they lent themselves to this modernist quest for the expression of the Spanish character. The figure of Menéndez Pidal illustrates the force of this idealism: in spite of the fact that it was he who introduced a positivist perspective into Spanish studies, his concept of tradition shows elements of transcendence, and his work was driven by an impulse to recover the old Spanish spirit, lost in modern times and wandering the fields of Castile.[2]

The younger writers of '98', also referred to as the 1914 generation (Ortega y Gasset, Castro, Marañón, Azaña, Madariaga), distanced themselves from their elders in several respects. First, they reacted against their pessimism. Secondly, instead of trying to locate the expression of a unique Spanish character in medieval literature, people like Castro studied the Golden Age of Spanish letters and tried to prove the existence of a Spanish Renaissance, to understand the Spanish spirit as the spirit of the age. Thirdly, in *Historia como sistema* (1935) ('History as System'), Ortega rejected any kind of transcendent spirit, and argued for the historicity of the human spirit. In *La rebelión de las masas* (1930) (*The Revolt of the Masses*), he made fun of those who believed in the existence of a Spanish or French spirit before the existence of either Spain or France. Fourthly, Ortega denied that pure realism was the essence of Spanish literature, arguing that *Don Quixote* drew on both irrealist and realist traditions.

Castro did not give up the search for a Spanish spirit, but refused to define it as a single essence and emphasised the diversity of its origins (attributing Spanish realism to Arab influence, for example). This idea had methodological consequences in that this spirit could no longer be thought of in abstract terms, but had to be studied in concrete sociological contexts. Castro himself underwent a methodological change: his *El pensamiento de Cervantes* (1925) had been influenced by Dilthey's abstract perspective on the history of thought, but by the time he wrote his *España en su historia* (revised edn. 1954), he had moved to this more contextualised approach.

In 1914, Ortega wrote two of his most important works on aesthetics and literary theory: *Ensayo de estética a manera de prólogo* ('Essay on Aesthetics by Way of Prologue'), and *Meditaciones del Quijote*. They establish the basis of his aesthetics and also reflect a critical attitude which resembles hermeneutics, but differs from immanent criticism.[3] In the 'Essay', Ortega pays tribute to a new kind of writing which he calls 'antihumanist', a style which is free from referentiality. Ortega is able to reject both immanentism and referentiality through a phenomenological aesthetics: this bypasses the referent by

---

[2] See Laín Entralgo, *La generación del 98*, and J. Portolés, *Medio siglo de filología española (1896–1952): positivismo e idealismo* (Madrid: Cátedra, 1986).

[3] A. Casas, 'Ejecutividad y crítica literaria en Ortega: algunas implicaciones del "Ensayo de estética a manera de prólogo"', in Pintos Peñaranda, Mª Luz and J. L. González López, *Fenomenología y ciencias humanas* (Santiago de Compostela: USC, 1998), pp. 315–327.

suspending (what Husserl called) 'the natural attitude' which confuses our representation of the world with reality. Thus, the text or image is no longer taken to be ruled by the identity of the referent, and the reader's identity also dissolves, or rather, is changed in the process of re-creating the work of art. These ideas came to be central to the work of the 1927 generation.

The 1920s is another celebrated period for Spanish twentieth-century arts and letters. It includes painters such as Dalí and Miró, film directors, such as Buñuel, musicians such as Roberto and Ernesto Halffter, and, most importantly, the 1927 generation of poets: García Lorca, Alberti, Guillén, Salinas, Cernuda, Aleixandre and others. This group of poets was much influenced by various literary innovations: the 'pure poetry' of Juán Ramón Jiménez, who advocated concision, the suppression of anecdote and free verse; also 'creationism', the Spanish version of 'ultraism' – a kind of experimental poetry from the early twenties that rejected tradition and advocated the creation of highly subjective imaginary worlds, daring juxtaposition of images, experiments with words and metrical innovations. 'Creationism' had been founded in Paris by Reverdy and the Chilean poet Huidobro; it had a substantial impact in Spanish America through the influence of Borges, and also in Spain where the poets Diego and Larrea were its main exponents.

Dámaso Alonso, the poet-critic of the generation, classified two phases in what was called the 27 Generation: the first was rather formalist and dehumanised; the second began when, after 1927, life and passion returned to their poetry. Surrealism developed during the twenties in Paris, and was adopted by Spanish artists such as Dalí, Miró and Buñuel; it also influenced some members of the 27 Generation such as Cernuda, and Spanish American writers such as Carpentier, who (together with the younger writers Paz and Cortázar) was to prolong the influence of surrealism well beyond the interwar period. To the poets' political involvement in the turbulent period of the thirties in Spain corresponded a poetry more concerned with social problems (for example Alberti; also Neruda who came to Spain in 1934). To add to the social upheaval, the Spanish Civil War destroyed the rich cultural atmosphere Spain had enjoyed in the first part of the century because the most important artists and intellectuals had backed the republican government and were now forced into exile.

In 1944 Dámaso Alonso published *Hijos de la ira* ('Children of Wrath'), which signified the return to a more humanistic understanding of art which was emerging throughout war-torn Europe. However, form continued to be essential for Alonso, and it was he who, together with Amado Alonso, broached stylistics as a critical discipline in Spain, and thus introduced a scientific element into the study of literary form and a change in the concept of literary history. Stylistics followed two main lines: Dámaso strove to find a method of analysing the distinctive language of poetry, whereas Amado tried to examine the way in which poetic feeling is objectivised in the work of art.

Though Dámaso Alonso's poetics was romantic in some aspects (he believed in the intuition of both poet and reader as the means of both creation and communication), his practice was influenced by the methodology of the natural sciences which led him to a detailed analysis of poetic form. His move to a humanised poetry did not stop him from practising immanent analysis, and in 1948 he wrote *Vida y obra de Medrano*, a formalist study. Dámaso Alonso did not go all the way towards formalism: in *Poesía española*, he returned to Crocean idealism, incorporating notions such as 'the signified' and 'the poet's feeling' rather than viewing the work of art as an autonomous object. Like the Russian formalists, Alonso was interested in the avant-garde and immanent critique; he also used structuralist terminology, but he did not follow through in his theory the implications either of this or of formalism itself.

Stylistics remained prominent throughout the fifties and dominated the Spanish critical scene until the arrival of structuralism in the sixties. The theoretical debate in the forties and fifties concentrated on the social function of art; moreover literature after the Spanish Civil War showed a marked drift away from pure poetry towards an art concerned with human affairs. The poet-critic Bousoño, who began his career in the forties, defined three modes through which a writer could tell the truth of his time at that moment in history: social literature, realism and existentialism (which last he himself favoured).[4] Social literature was taken up by poets who retained the hope that poetry could make something happen. Realism went through several stages in the novel: from the crude presentation of unpleasant aspects of reality ('Tremendismo': e.g. Cela's *La familia de Pascual Duarte*, 1942), to neo-realist objective presentation, influenced by the aesthetics of Italian cinema (e.g. Sanchez Ferlosio's *El Jarama*, 1956), to dialectical realism, in which the author is re-introduced and the reader involved in a play of identity and difference with the characters (e.g. Martín Santos' *Tiempo de silencio*, 1960).[5] The search for the writer's own voice led to an assault on language and to the displacement of the story in favour of discourse, which culminated in Goytisolo's *Reivindicación del conde don Julián* (1970) ('Vindication of Count don Julián'), a novel which Gimferrer considers a masterpiece of Spanish literature.[6] Realism in the novel continued up until the sixties, when myth and allegory made their appearance along with the fantastical (Cunqueiro, Sender) under the influence of Spanish American 'magic realism', still marginal in Spain at that time.

Rather like Amado Alonso, Bousoño tried to explain the poetic process

[4] C. Bousoño, *Antología poética 1945–1973* (Barcelona: Plaza y Janés, 1976), pp. 19–20.

[5] For a discussion of these three stages see R. Buckey's 'Etapas de la novela de la postguerra'; for a discussion of dialectical realism see F. Grande's 'Significado y estilo de *Tiempo de silencio*'; both essays are in D. Ynduráin (ed.), *Época contemporánea: 1939–1980*, vol. 8: *Historia y crítica de la literatura española* (Barcelona: Editorial Crítica, 1981).

[6] P. Gimferrer, 'El nuevo Juan Goytisolo', *Revista de occidente* 137 (1974), pp. 15–23.

itself, with special emphasis on the contribution of the artist. In his self-analysis, published as a long introduction to his *Antología poética 1945–1973* (1976), Bousoño explains the goal of his poetry as an 'aesthetics of surprise' achieved through the analysis of minute detail, a practice which also dominates his literary criticism. He uses a mechanism of metaphor characteristic of poetry at the time to illustrate his method: that in which the significatory dimension of the 'vehicle' far exceeds any observable similarity with the 'tenor'. An example here is Maiakovski's: 'I shall make me black trousers with the felt of my voice.' Juán Ramón Jiménez and the poets of the 27 Generation had already employed this technique, but Bousoño pushes it to the extreme. Here is the development of the metaphor of the passage of time in his poem 'El rio de las horas' ('The River of Hours'): 'It moves, silent, imperceptible/ ... astute, disguised as a wardrobe/ it moves through the room,/ still, like a coffin, it moves.' This style of language contrasts vividly with that of the pre-eminent poet-critic of the following generation, José Ángel Valente.

Octavio Paz once stated that, after the Spanish Civil War, between 1940 and 1960, the universalist impulse of Spanish culture, which had been so vitally present in the 98 and 27 Generations, disappeared.[7] The dialogue between Spain and the Spanish American writers broke down and contact with European culture faded. What Paz missed in Spanish literature was reflection on language, which had been replaced by a poetry more concerned with social and political problems. But Valente's career is evidence that this statement, though true to an extent, needs some qualification. Valente was deeply interested in Spanish American poetry (his first critical essay was significantly dedicated to Huidobro in 1950; later he wrote on César Vallejo, Borges, Lezama Lima and others) and devoted much attention to questions of language; in line with Cernuda, he also showed considerable interest in the English literary tradition. (It should be noted that Valente was not an isolated case: there were editorial projects such as the journal *Insula*, which attempted to keep Spanish thinkers in contact with the rest of the world during those difficult times.)

Like Bousoño, Valente reacted against the social poetry of the time, denouncing its abandonment of style in favour of a prosaic engagement with ideology. He contributed to the debate during the forties and fifties about the social function of art, which treated communication and knowledge as opposites. Those who defended the ideal of communication, the 'social poets', drew on Machado's idea of the primacy of content over form and also on that of the power of literature to heal (which Machado himself had applied to existential insecurity, but which they applied to social evils). In 1950, Aleixandre published two collections of aphorisms under the significant titles *Poesía, moral y público* and *Poesía: comunicación*,[8] which provoked Barral in

---

[7] In an interview with María Embeitia, 'Octavio Paz: poesía y metafísica', *Insula* 95 (1968), pp. 11–14.   [8] *Insula* 59 (1950), pp. 1–2, and *Espadaña* 48 (1950), pp. 1–2, respectively.

1953 to write 'Poesía no es comunicación', an essay whose importance has been compared to Paz's *El arco y la lira* (1956), and which accuses 'social poetry' of colloquialism and of reducing the reader to a passive recipient of the message.

Aleixandre, though, was insisting that poetic form serve an epistemological purpose (poetic 'iridescence . . . discovers the deep truth to be revealed'), and Valente follows this path in underlining the link between the process of poetic creation and knowledge. This kind of knowledge cannot be achieved through identity thinking (here Ortega's influence is felt, along with Heidegger's and Adorno's more specific usage of the term). Valente's criticism of convention and identity thinking works on two levels: true poetic creation as such is the indictment of stagnant ideology; on a different level, however, the attempt to uproot convention itself leads to the very edge of silence, hence Valente's interest in mysticism. The mystic exists at the limits of language insofar as he or she tries to express an inexpressible experience (whether understood as the experience of God, of an instant in the eternal Being, or as a privileged moment of transient being), where silence is, in absolute terms, the only adequate response. Valente conceives poetry as the 'explosion of a silence': this is to say that the words are taken to be scattered fragments of silence and are poetic in so far as they bear its traces. This is the reason why the investigation of rhythm, largely achieved through silence in poetry, is so important for Valente. It also explains his interest in Chillida's art, in which the plastic expression of silence, the void, is so prominent. Driven by the desire to master the blank page, Valente's poetry frees itself from the loquacious imagery of mystic poetry and concentrates on linguistic intensity.[9]

Gimferrer argues that after the Spanish Civil War, the project of the 27 Generation was continued in Spanish America as part of a larger endeavour which sought to bring about the transition from romanticism to symbolism.[10] It can be described as a move away from interest in the genius of the poet towards interest in the genius of language, which goes along with a shift from a poetry revolving round the vision of transcendent Being to one of a vision of nothingness. It requires that western metaphysics (which understood Being as substance) be replaced by one in which Being is no longer opposed to nothingness. From the *moment in* Being we move to the *moment of* being, or in Nietzsche's terms, eternity is replaced by a sense of transient vitality.

Octavio Paz searched for the expression of the unity of opposites (e.g. I and the other, spirit and body) beyond western philosophy, and found it in eastern tantric eroticism (*Ladera Este*, 1969 ['The Eastern Side']). However, in Paz's poetry critical awareness is never given up, and consequently a certain distance is maintained from any kind of mysticism. Gimferrer pointed out, refer-

[9] A. García Berrio, 'Valente: descensos antiguos a la memoria', *El silencio y la escucha: José Ángel Valente*, ed. T. Hernández (Madrid: Cátedra, 1995), pp. 15–28.
[10] P. Gimferrer, 'Convergencias', in P. Gimferrer (ed.), *Octavio Paz* (Madrid: Taurus, 1989).

ring to Paz's *El mono gramático* (1974) ('The Grammarian Ape'): the revelation of 'the unity of the world corresponds to its dissolution . . . totality and vacuity' are the same. Void and silence are central to Paz's poetics, as they are to Valente's.

1940 was a turning point in the Spanish American novel. The new novel was influenced by European literature, but it also gained independence from it. These writers shared with modernism the defence of the autonomy of the work of art, and even when they were politically engaged, often with the left, they claimed freedom both from referentiality and from ideology. They reacted against realism, questioned the world's intelligibility and probed the consequences of this for the novel. This necessarily led them to experiment. There is no longer any valid intepretation of the world ('poems have no contents', said Paz); the aesthetic fact, said Borges, is 'perhaps, the imminence of a revelation which does not take place'. Rather than receiving knowledge about reality, the reader is involved in the interrogation of language and, consequently, of his or her world.

Like the European modernists, these writers realised that the traditional opposition between reality and appearance was part of the ideological game, but they could see in the Spanish Civil War and in World War II how soon an ideology could become reality. In Borges' fiction, the interrogation of language goes hand in hand with the dissolution of the boundaries between the fantastic and the real. Reality is exposed as fantasy, and that which seemed to be fantastic is revealed to be in some ways a very accurate rendition of reality (e.g. Borges' *Deutsches Requiem*, 1946). Playing with the boundaries between literature and reality is an attempt to communicate this sense of things. In the last part of Cabrera Infante's *Tres tristes tigres* (1964) ('Three Sad Tigers'), the protagonist promises to recount the 'real' facts that the reader is reading in a future story.

Overturning normal notions of space and time is part of the experiment. Time can be reversible, either as a consequence of the literature-reality game that we have just described, or because a cyclical notion of time replaces a linear one. Individual identity falls a prey to the game in Borges' *La muerte y la brújula* (1944) ('Death and the Compass'), where the possibility that the pursuer can become pursued remains open; as in Yeats' great wheel, roles can be changed in a new phase of the cycle. The span of a lifetime can acquire cosmic proportions. In Carpentier's *Los pasos perdidos* (1953) ('The lost steps'), the action spans the time from the fourth day of the creation of the world to the apocalypse, described as a journey across periods and regions of a mythologised American reality.

The new Spanish American novel diverges both from its former tradition and from the conventions of modernism in its understanding of magic realism and of the character of the work of art, respectively. Modernism's defence of the autonomy of the work of art had produced a division between high and popular art. The new Spanish American writers struggled to overcome some of the basic binary distinctions of modernist art (escapist/engaged, high/popular) partly by restoring a basic sense of narrativity, a bond between the reader and the writer.[11] These novelists also aimed to overcome the opposition between the local and the universal which had hampered the Spanish American novel by finding similarities across cultures, and they tried to take account of the western literary tradition in their writings.

The great South American writers are among the most important contemporary critics in the Spanish language. This is partly because they did not limit themselves to literary criticism, but embarked on a critique which encompassed social problems and scientific issues. In their critical essays and in their works of fiction they merge artistic skill with questions of theory, blurring the boundaries between the genres. From the perspective of literary criticism, they are what T. S. Eliot called practitioners whose aim is to pave the way for their art. All this formed part of a style whose greatest merit is that of an unceasing self-interrogation. It allows the reader to participate in the process of creation and encourages him or her to engage in a complex critique of the workings of ideology.

---

[11] See 'Introduction', in D. Villanueva and J. Mª Viña, *Trayectoria de la novela hispanoamericana actual* (Madrid: Espasa Calpe, 1991).

27

American neopragmatism and its background

DAN LATIMER

The lure of euphoric certainty: C. S. Peirce and William James

Pragmatism may not be uniquely American in its origins. The German think-
ers F. A. Lange and Hans Vaihinger are pragmatist when they hold that believ-
ing something unproven by experiment could still be good for you. G. T.
Fechner and the French philosopher Charles Renouvier encouraged William
James to believe whatever James found to contribute in the long run to human
happiness.[1] Judith Ryan detects in James traces of Austrian thought, namely
Ernst Mach: 'What is valid for me is not what is true, but what I need.'[2]
Whatever its provenance, pragmatism comes to have an instinctive appeal to
Americans, with whom common sense comes robustly into play, the same
national feature that John Dewey in 'The Practical Character of Reality'
(1908) will call 'gumption' or 'horse sense', 'taking hold of things right end
up'.[3] Charles Sanders Peirce says that pragmatism is nothing more than the
application of the old saw that 'by their fruits ye shall know them', acknowledging James' view that the value of a concept lies in the future conduct that
issues from that concept.[4] The meaning of a belief is the action that the belief
makes possible. The Greek word *pragma*, as James points out, means action.[5]
It is a word from which 'practice' and 'practical' derive. Americans are
thought to be both restlessly active and future-oriented, hence the native
appeal to them of pragmatism.[6] They are said to be impatient with making
unnecessary, impractical distinctions. They are blessedly unreflective and
optimistic, hence their resentment at *Grübelsucht*, a word William James uses

---

[1] Frederick Copleston, *Modern Philosophy: Empiricism, Idealism, and Pragmatism in Britain
and America* (New York: Doubleday, 1994), pp. 344–345.
[2] Judith Ryan, 'American Pragmatism, Viennese Psychology', *Raritan* 8.3 (Winter 1989), p. 53.
[3] John J. McDermott (ed.), *The Philosophy of John Dewey*, 2 vols. in 1 (Chicago: University of
Chicago Press, 1973), p. 212.
[4] Justus Buchler (ed.), *Philosophical Writings of Peirce* (New York: Dover, 1955), p. 271.
[5] John J. McDermott (ed.), *The Writings of William James, A Comprehensive Edition* (Chicago
and London: University of Chicago Press, 1977), p. 377.
[6] Richard Shusterman, *Pragmatist Aesthetics: Living Beauty, Rethinking Art* (Oxford and
Cambridge, Mass.: Blackwell, 1992), pp. 196–197.

to refer to the morbid melancholy brooding supposedly characteristic of Germans.[7] Such 'theoretic grubbing and brooding', like 'sick shriekings of . . . dying rats' depress Americans and divert energies better suited, if not to primitive accumulation, then at least to hearty rushing about.[8]

On the other hand, Peirce points out in his 'Pragmatism in Retrospect: A Last Formulation' (1906) that pragmatism began as a Boston institution defiantly called 'The metaphysical club'.[9] Sometimes the club met in Peirce's study, sometimes in William James'. Oliver Wendell Holmes, the future chief justice, was a sometimes uneasy member. It was a club established by people who either wanted to be religious or wanted to be tolerant of those who were. The enemy was a kind of scientific empiricist type hard-minded enough to insist that religious belief attain the status of fact. Since religion seldom provides facts on such matters as the existence of God or the immortality of the soul, the empiricists, everywhere in the ascendency in 1874, were wont to treat our world as nothing but careening matter and its God as a 'gaseous vertebrate', to use Haeckel's cruel joke.[10] It is clear to anyone familiar with *The Varieties of Religious Experience* (1902) that the driving force behind James' book is the determination to save the religious view of the world from sneering *philosophes* exalting facts. There, with a tolerant irony which, however, can't conceal the most encyclopaedic patience and human sympathy, James enumerates all imaginable kinds of religiosity, each kind more delirious, morbid and 'psychopathic' than the next, and ranging from the 'mumbo-jumbo' of benighted 'savages', to the hallucinatory 'photisms' (visions) of Paul and Constantine, to the apoplectic convulsions of tent-revivalists, to the frosty Stoic chill of Marcus Aurelius, who has God doing a 'wholesale, not a retail, business', that is, concentrating on general laws and disdaining private visitations upon his writhing creatures here below.[11] From James' pragmatic point of view, we need spend no time proving that the God promoted by any given religious conception is empirically real or merely an emanation of someone's private insecurities. 'Does God exist?' is an irrelevant question. God is not known, nor is he understood. 'He is used.' The point of any religion is that it gets us a richer, more satisfying life than we would have if we believed the world was but a random convulsion of matter. Belief in God gets us more love of life. God is real because he produces real effects. He opens up new spheres of power for us, unlocking an interior world which otherwise would be an empty waste.

In 'The Fixation of Belief' (1877) Peirce agrees that doubt is unpleasant and

---

[7] H. S. Thayer (ed.), *Pragmatism: The Classic Writings* (Indianapolis, Indiana: Hackett, 1982), p. 159.
[8] William James, *The Varieties of Religious Experience* (1902) (New York and London: Collier, 1961), p. 47.   [9] Buchler (ed.), *Philosophical Writings*, p. 269.
[10] William James, *Pragmatism* (1907) (New York: Dover, 1995), p. 6.
[11] James, *Varieties*, pp. 383–384, 392.

belief must be stabilised, otherwise euphoric certainty remains out of reach.[12] Peirce has no patience with 'dilettanti' who revel in debauched uncertainty, in their fatiguing instability never caring whether the questions they ask get answered or not. He would disapprove in advance of much of recent French thought. We are reminded that American neopragmatism, including the anti-theory movement, begins to develop in response to the *Grübelei*, if not the sick shriekings, of post-Heideggerian theory and the admirers of Maurice Blanchot, for whom euphoric certainty is a suspicious human feature at best.[13] Even for Peirce some ways of inducing euphoric certainty are less respectable than others. Peirce's own golden 'bride', the Scientific Method, involves an ongoing struggle short on easy pleasure.[14] Richard Rorty will eventually deny Peirce's pragmatist credentials for the retrograde belief that human thought will one day harmonise with Being, rather than float unproblematically above Being in its own ungrounded realm.[15] For Rorty, James is the most authentic pragmatist of the two precursors. But in Peirce's terms, Jamesian certainty might seem tainted either by the tenacity method, by which we believe what we have to to make us happy, or by the *a priori* method, belief by harmonious parallels: waking after sleeping demonstrates life after death.[16] Indeed James seems at times to occupy the position of Sebastian Flyte of Evelyn Waugh's *Brideshead Revisited* who can believe in the manger, ox and ass, precisely because they are lovely ideas. The aesthetic justification of belief, the euphoric harmony flowing from shape, resolution and a sense of purpose, may be the principal seduction of American pragmatism. Both Peirce and James are accessible and pleasurable to read, a tradition continued by their recent disciples. If pleasure is *not* a conspicuous product of John Dewey's unwearied extrapolations, aesthetic harmony in principle certainly is.

The surprising case of John Dewey

Dewey is a thinker whose mind circles lovingly around images of harmony, whether physical, aesthetic or social. He is offended by imbalance – for example, by instances of elitism and privilege. The armature of injustice is the means/end distinction, which he seeks to undermine at all costs.[17] To consider the part as a mere means and not as an indispensable feature of the whole is to shatter organic unity. When we consider the labouring class as animated tools permitting leisure to the elite, we perpetuate the anti-banausic prejudices of

---

[12] Buchler (ed.), *Philosophical Writings*, p. 10.
[13] W. J. T. Mitchell (ed.), *Against Theory, Literary Studies and the New Pragmatism* (Chicago: University of Chicago Press, 1985), pp. 21ff.
[14] Buchler (ed.), *Philosophical Writings*, pp. 21–22.
[15] Richard Rorty, *Consequences of Pragmatism* (Minneapolis: University of Minnesota Press, 1982), p. 173.   [16] Buchler (ed.), *Philosophical Writings*, pp. 12–20.
[17] McDermott (ed.), *Philosophy of John Dewey*, pp. 302 ff.

the ancient Greeks, who regarded those who work with their hands as tainted by servility and instrumentality.[18] When one class exists as a means for the welfare of another, there is not only class oppression; there is a hierarchy debasing the body *vis-à-vis* the mind. There is a separation of the somatic from the psychic. Products of the intellective realm become separated and isolated from use, very much in the manner of Kantian aesthetic theory, according to which the beautiful is decorative design and of no practical use at all. Kant even rejects the use of figurative speech to move people to action, treating the blandishments of rhetoric as unworthy seduction. Kant separates the aesthetic from the appetitive, rejecting Burke's connection of a taste for canary wine with a taste for the beautiful.[19]

For Dewey, however, when the beautiful is separated from use, art becomes isolated and sterile. Museums take over. Beautiful things are torn from their living contexts, no longer enriching the lives of real human beings. High art reinforces class difference, arguing by its auratic presence the superiority of the collector possessing it. On a larger scale, national museums are places to store a nation's loot, gathered during eras of imperialism and militarism, arguing one nation's superiority over another. Beauty becomes a sublimation of ugly national impulses. Art becomes a civilisation's 'beauty parlor' and art works esoteric and alien. The artist is cut off from any healthy communal context. Dewey proposes to connect art to the 'activities of the live creature in its environment'. Siding with Kant's Iroquois sachem, who admired the Paris cook shops, Dewey says there is no reason why a meal in a Paris restaurant should not be the paradigm of an aesthetic experience, shapely and satisfying to every sense, from the candlelight and roses to the Sauce Robert. There is no reason why a neat room should not be aesthetically pleasing. If 'aesthetic' means that every bodily sense is on a heightened state of alert, we should also think of the live animal, its wary glances, its cocking of the ears, every one of its senses on the *qui vive*. The old man poking a fire on a cold winter night is warmed by his fire as an instrumentality but also excited aesthetically by the colourful drama of the fire and imaginatively participates in it. It is 'mere ignorance' that withholds aesthetic status to life experiences like these.[20]

Dewey's most formative intellectual experience as an undergraduate was a sudden sense of the 'interdependence and interrelated unity' of the parts of the human body to the whole. It was this experience that gave him his ultimate philosophical paradigm. Biological functions of the body are not external or servile to its intellective phantasmata. Biology and thought work together in a cooperative enterprise. The same paradigm informs the work of art. Paints are the means of a picture as an end, but the paints are also the picture itself. 'Tones . . . are the means of music, because they constitute, make, are,

---

[18] John Dewey, *Art as Experience* (1934) (New York: Perigee Books, 1980), p. 341.
[19] Immanuel Kant, *Critique of Judgement* (1790), trans. J. H. Bernard (New York: Hafner, 1951), pp. 38, 46.   [20] Dewey, *Art as Experience*, pp. 19, 27.

music.'[21] The materials of a house or the words of a poem cannot be seen apart from the form of the composition as a whole. In every part of a work, the end is present, nor would the end exist without the parts. Such notions of interrelated unity have drastic implications. To revise instrumentality at Dewey's level of intensity is not only to invalidate the privileging of soul over body, of the intellective over the banausic, of white over blue collar, fine art over useful artefacts, museums over ordinary life, theory over practice; at the political level it is to return to an egalitarianism so fundamental that it is inconceivable in the United States, whether in the eighteenth century or today. And yet Dewey insists on precisely this intimate relation between politics and beauty. The value of a given civilisation rests on its aesthetic life. All present vitiation of the aesthetic in American society is directly traceable to oligarchic control of labour for the purpose of private profit.[22]

Richard Rorty and the pragmatism of self-creation

It is the hypnotic Richard Rorty who has renewed pragmatism's hold over American philosophy and *belles lettres*. It is he who has renewed interest in John Dewey. Certainly he transmits the democratic, somatic naturalism of Dewey in an unexpected way, associating him as far as possible with Martin Heidegger.[23] Both Dewey and Heidegger reject analytic, scientistic philosophy. Both are anti-foundational in the sense that they do not believe that there are essences (of beauty, justice, truth) free from colouration by historical accident. In fact, there are no essences at all. Both Dewey and Heidegger are aggressive toward the philosophical tradition, casting out accumulated prejudice. Both want to emphasise the ties between poetry and philosophy. Both want philosophy to find honourable terms of surrender to poetry. Both abandon the correspondence theory of truth to promote 'truth' as strong self-expression, the creative invention of a new vocabulary which escapes the humiliation of belatedness, surely Rorty's own most representative idea, and precisely the one that attracts him to Heidegger.[24] Heidegger rejects the misguided rationalism that seeks to penetrate to ahistorical truth. He wants to see the philosophical tradition as a series of poetic achievements. He admires those who have spoken truths transcending mere reason. Poets are the true thinkers. They are irrational, unassimilable lightning bolts from the blue, blasting apart the inherited language of their tradition with startling new metaphors. Dewey too believes the imagination is the 'chief instrument of the

---

[21] McDermott (ed.), *Philosophy of John Dewey*, pp. 2, 309.
[22] Dewey, *Art as Experience*, pp. 326–343.   [23] Rorty, *Consequences of Pragmatism*, pp. 37 ff.
[24] Richard Rorty, *Essays on Heidegger and Others* (Cambridge: Cambridge University Press, 1991), pp. 15–17. See also Rorty, *Contingency, Irony, and Solidarity* (Cambridge: Cambridge University Press, 1989), p. 110.

good' and that 'art is more moral than moralities'.[25] But Dewey is a political, not a poetic pragmatist, persisting in a kind of 'social hope' which Heidegger abandoned in disgust, and which Rorty too finds naive.[26]

Rorty claims for himself an alignment closer to Dewey than to Heidegger, but his 'strong-poet' predilection is actually closer to Heidegger.[27] Rorty appreciates the democratic gregariousness of Dewey. Rorty hates cruelty and promotes human solidarity. But at bottom he is most impressed with the 'deconstructive' side of Heidegger, the side that celebrates the idiosyncratic *vates* (poet-seer) climbing the mountain path away from all clichés of empty chatter, mere *Gerede*, climbing away from modern technological frenzy to primal solitude, to gather Black Forest mushrooms and listen to the chime of stillness, eventually to reappear himself with flashing eyes and floating hair, to issue new lightning-bolt metaphors of his own. Even utopian political ideals are first the product of enthusiastic genius.[28] If we ever get what we want, or what Rorty wants, the strong poet will have provided it. 'What is lasting is the gift of the poets', as Hölderlin said.

Rorty makes a distinction between systematic philosophers and edifying philosophers. The first sort think they are providing truths about the world as it is. Their discourse is a 'mirror' of reality. They celebrate facts. The second sort insist that self-formation (*Bildung*) be substituted for knowledge as thinking's proper goal. The point of self-edification is not to get the facts right but to find a 'new and more interesting way to express ourselves'. Such activity is 'poetic' in the sense that it thrives on the 'abnormal'.[29] It takes us 'out of our old selves by the power of strangeness', aids us in 'becoming new beings'. The ultimate horror is to be passive, shoving around 'already coined pieces', accepting another's description of us.[30] The goal of the self is to create the self out of its own sheer strength. In constructing our own minds, we create the only part of ourselves that matters, that part that differentiates us from all the others.

We cannot really say these newly forged selves with their private salvational abnormality have any privileged ontological priority over the selves of plodding drudges.[31] The 'poem' that is the self of the pervert or the lunatic can be just as 'richly textured' as our own. No one vision of things can be raised on high as the one before which all others must prostrate themselves. Without foundations, the best we can do is tolerate each other's mighty poem, somehow keeping the conversation going between incommensurable selves as they all strive to escape the influence of every other self. What a liberal democ-

---

[25] Dewey, *Art as Experience*, p. 348.
[26] Richard Rorty, *Achieving Our Country* (Cambridge, Mass. and London: Harvard University Press, 1998), p. 104.   [27] Shusterman, *Pragmatist Aesthetics*, pp. 246 ff.
[28] Rorty, *Achieving Our Country*, p. 140.
[29] Richard Rorty, *Philosophy and the Mirror of Nature* (Princeton: Princeton University Press, 1979), pp. 360, 367.   [30] Rorty, *Contingency*, p. 29.
[31] Rorty, *Philosophy and the Mirror of Nature*, pp. 365–366.

racy means in fact is that everyone has the right to pursue self-realisation as long as that pursuit does not harm or humiliate someone else. We must hope that democratic society can get along without any other foundation and that, despite the competition of self-creation, people will nevertheless be willing to 'cling . . . together against the dark', as Rorty movingly puts it in a famous phrase.[32] After we have spent so much time, though, differentiating ourselves from others and disdaining conformity, it seems unlikely that our first impulse will be to fling ourselves into the arms of others, risk our lives for them, sacrifice ourselves for their sake, nor will they be delighted to receive us in the liberal democratic boat for the sake of our icon-shattering conversation. Moreover, the liberal democratic boat seems small when one takes a close look at it. Rorty thinks of U.S. society as a 'private club' where one retreats in relief after a long day at the 'bazaar', dealing with people who are 'irredeemably different'.[33] If we also seem alien to *them*, it is because we have wanted to be. Despite Rorty's assurances, it seems likely that, having pushed the envelope of the private psyche beyond the communal, we will find ourselves sitting alone in the dark when the dark comes.

Self-assertion and the community: the lesson of Stanley Fish

The foundational affinity between Richard Rorty and Stanley Fish is that there is no foundation, only a choice of language games. Pragmatists believe, with William James, what is profitable or expedient to believe. We have our being in surfaces, says Fish, and 'it is surfaces all the way down'.[34] Thomas Pavel reassuringly calls this pragmatist attitude '*la conscience aiguë de la contingence*',[35] an attitude which tempts Rorty toward avuncular sweetness, but Fish toward combativeness and intensified chutzpah. An acute sense of one's contingency does not exactly disarm one's enemies. There is a danger in milquetoast liberalism.[36] One must be ready for those full of passionate conviction. The threat from that quarter in fact is the reason why 'strong multiculturalism' is a contradiction in terms. 'Boutique multiculturalism' is the end of the liberal line. A taste for hummus will not lead to Hamas. No one will adopt a point of view that implies his own abolition. One just always is a 'uniculturalist', insists Fish.[37]

[32] Rorty, *Contingency*, pp. 38, 189 ff; *Consequences*, p. 166.
[33] Richard Rorty, *Objectivity, Relativism, and Truth* (Cambridge: Cambridge University Press, 1991), pp. 209–210.
[34] Stanley Fish, *Professional Correctness, Literary Studies and Political Change* (Oxford: Oxford University Press, 1995), p. 75.
[35] Thomas Pavel, 'Lettre d'Amérique: la liberté de parole en question', *Commentaire* 69 (Printemps 1995), p. 170.
[36] Stanley Fish, *There's No Such Thing As Free Speech and It's a Good Thing, Too* (New York and Oxford: Oxford University Press, 1994), p. 296.
[37] Stanley Fish, 'Boutique Multiculturalism, or Why Liberals are Incapable of Thinking about Hate Speech', *Critical Inquiry* 23 (Winter 1997), p. 384.

Rorty distinguishes between analytic and edifying philosophy, privileging the latter. Fish identifies the choice in literary research between the model of demonstration and the model of persuasion, privileging the latter.[38] If you adopt the former you consider yourself in humble service to a cause greater than yourself. The value of your work amounts to adequation to an iconic original, which will always be other than what is said about it. You add facts to a great heap of earlier research and so participate in mankind's standing ever taller, growing ever closer to ultimate truth. For Fish, as for Rorty, ultimate truth is as much a notion for the dustbin as modesty. The consumer of poetry takes priority over any objective item consumed. The activity of perception itself constitutes the object. What the perceiver understands *is* the realisation of the object's identity. What the perceiver sees is then retroactively, and incorrectly, attributed to the object. What the object *is* apart from its identity in the consumer Fish does not know, nor does anyone else. If the demonstration model is not bankrupt, why then, when a given Shakespeare sonnet is only fourteen lines long, has the ultimate truth about it not yet been demonstrated after four hundred years?[39]

Steven Knapp and Walter Benn Michaels admire the part of Fish's pragmatism that claims that there is just practice, that one does what one does, believes what one believes, without ever needing to reach a position outside practice where pure principles abide. Anyway, 'there are no such principles', says Fish.[40] Knapp and Michaels concur that truth is the same as what one happens to believe at the moment, *episteme* is *doxa*, in Plato's terms. Knowledge is true belief. They believe themselves more pragmatic than Fish, however, because Fish admits the possibility that his present belief may only *seem* better than his earlier belief, that progress from one to the other may be delusory, a thought that shows him to be in a realm of principle which he denies. Moreover Fish locates the act of interpretation in the reader. For Knapp and Michaels 'what a text means is just what its author intended it to mean'.[41] There are no intentionless meanings. 'My car ran out of gas' could consequently never mean 'my Pullman emerged from a cloud of argon' as long as the speaker lives on earth and owns a Ford. Richard Shusterman finds the Knapp/Michaels dislike of polysemy (uncontrolled signification) to be a position closer to old-fashioned empiricism than to true pragmatism, which is comfortable with pluralism.[42] Pragmatism moreover is future-oriented, rather than fixated on antecedent phenomena, as in this case on the intention of the author's speech act.

---

[38] Stanley Fish, *Is There a Text in This Class?: The Authority of Interpretive Communities* (Cambridge, Mass.: Harvard University Press, 1980), pp. 356–371.

[39] *Ibid.*, p. 367.

[40] Stanley Fish, *Doing What Comes Naturally, Change, Rhetoric, and the Practice of Theory in Literary and Legal Studies* (Durham: Duke University Press, 1989), pp. 13–14.

[41] Steven Knapp and Walter Benn Michaels, 'Against Theory', *Critical Inquiry* 8 (1982), pp. 723–742; rpt. in Mitchell (ed.), *Against Theory*, pp. 11–30 (pp. 13, 26).

[42] Shusterman, *Pragmatist Aesthetics*, pp. 96, 99.

Fish is more ego-driven than empirical.[43] He would claim that the private ego is constituted and wilfulness constrained by a community of interpreters, but this community is defined by its agreement with *him*.[44] There is no reason for doing what we do other than partisan and subjective concerns.[45] What counts, finally, is self-assertion, one's success in differentiating one's views in the literary culture from everyone else's, displacing earlier views, even one's own earlier views, and imposing new ones on everyone else.[46] One is driven to compete, persuade and dominate. The glory of the persuasion model is that it allows us total domination if we are good at it. The dinginess of the demonstrative model is that it is not adaptable to raw rhetorical coercion. The institutions we work for encourage the persuasion model, since the profession's greatest rewards go to those who play Fish's way. Given Fish's current ascendency in his profession, his point is hard to deny.[47] Not everyone has the skill, or the right, to perform as Fish does.[48] The level of anarchy is kept low because the 'interpretive community' doesn't listen to just anyone. They listen to their own, those whom they have admitted to their body. They know who they are. They have an institutional solidarity. They exert control over the proliferation of interpretive product. Some voices just are more important than others. For Northrop Frye to denounce the concept of the archetype is infinitely more important than for some community college nobody to do the same.[49]

Richard Shusterman and the return to Dewey

Richard Shusterman considers Fish's 'interpretive community' elitist and exclusionary.[50] He also takes issue with Rorty's definition of human nature as too exclusively linguistic, detecting in Rorty a puritanical revulsion for Dewey's 'raw feels', his solicitude for the body. Shusterman admits the centrality of language for high-grade reflection but wants to identify areas of human experience besides pain that escape linguistic formulation. There is a bodily understanding that precedes linguistic cogitation. Actual consciousness is only a small part of human experience, as Dewey said. There is also a whole universe of nonreflectional experience. Shusterman calls this world 'somatic understanding'. When we listen to music, the body listens. The body's organic responses to an allegro and to a largo are entirely different. The same holds for keys and chords. Peirce had also said that listening to music is not thinking.

[43] Fish, *Is There a Text*, p. 360; *Professional Correctness*, pp. 110–111.
[44] Fish, *Is There a Text*, pp. 173, 369; *Doing*, p. 244.
[45] Fish, *Doing*, pp. 343 ff.; *Professional Correctness*, pp. 112–113.
[46] Fish, *Is There a Text*, p. 367.
[47] Adam Begley, 'Souped-up Scholar', *The New York Times Magazine* (3 May 1992), p. 50.
[48] Fish, *Doing*, p. 175.   [49] Fish, *Doing*, p. 167.
[50] Shusterman, *Pragmatist Aesthetics*, p. 116.

Shusterman goes even farther. There are people who think without words, residing in 'unmanageably illiterate and darkly somatic neighborhoods of town that we philosophers . . . avoid and ignore'.[51] It is arrogant to say with Stanley Fish that high-level interpretation is the only game in town, that the unarticulated pleasure afforded by art to naive or non-professional consumers is less valuable than the misprisions of the mighty. An informal chat at the water cooler is also a work of literary criticism. We cannot dismiss the experiences of the dark somatic neighborhoods as inhuman because they have not been caught in the web of articulate language. For Wittgenstein, there are 'things that cannot be put into words'. Nietzsche insisted that the soma determines the psyche, and here Dewey would agree, who expends considerable effort in *Experience and Nature* promoting the theories of the 'Alexander technique' designed to enhance the continuity of mind and body.[52]

One advantage of Shusterman's pragmatism is that it provides a view of mass culture very much at variance with the snobbery both of high Marxism (Theodor Adorno) and that of right-wing Straussian reactionaries (Allan Bloom), who, though they agree on nothing else, can both condemn popular art as revolting trash. To follow Dewey implies a tolerant, inclusive sense of aesthetic experience. Broadening our conception of art to include rock and rap compositions opens us to communication not only with disadvantaged classes but to alternatives to the political status quo. Shusterman hopes that native American anti-intellectualism may mean more unimpeded access to the somatic aspects of life and to the arts associated with the body, arts like dancing, singing, yarn-spinning which were involved with work and physical activity and therefore disdained along with the undignified activities of the animated tool, the *doulos* or *thes*. Shusterman points out that rock music has its origins in an 'African aesthetic of vigorously active and communally impassioned engagement rather than dispassionate judgmental remoteness'.[53] Rock, as Allan Bloom recognised to his outrage, is *alogon*. It is 'regressive', as Adorno pointed out, an experience that bypasses the brain to become sensuous immediacy. Rock that is 'funky' implies 'sweatiness'. The very name of rock and roll, like jazz, implies making love. Pierre Bourdieu is wrong to say popular art is 'torpor-inducing' and involves a lack of active effort, a 'passive absent participation'.[54] To despise the sweating, copulating, energetically gyrating body is to be a Cartesian snob, an elitist and a Puritan. It is to deny the life-experiences of a particular part of society and all eternal verities that result in the 'blues', disappointed love, economic oppression, family conflict, drugs and violence. It is to privilege instead only those experiences that

---

[51] *Ibid.*, p. 128.
[52] Richard Shusterman, *Practising Philosophy, Pragmatism and the Philosophical Life* (New York: Routledge, 1997), p. 167.   [53] Shusterman, *Pragmatist Aesthetics*, p. 184.
[54] Pierre Bourdieu, *Distinction, a Social Critique of the Judgement of Taste*, trans. Richard Nice (Cambridge, Mass.: Harvard University Press, 1984), p. 386.

are 'novel and esoteric enough to escape the experience and comprehension of the general public'.[55]

Shusterman doesn't explain why he privileges Stetsasonic over Ola Bell Campbell Reed, whose working class credentials are impeccable. For him rap simply is the pragmatist art par excellence and the main focus of his experiment in 'somaesthetics'.[56] Rap revives Dewey's respect for the body without going as far as, say, the acephalicism of Georges Bataille. Rap conceives of art not as an end in itself, as a sacred icon of the museum, but as an instrumentality, as a means to improve life. The hated means/end distinction finally becomes tolerable in this democratic revalorisation of its terms. Art so conceived promotes a 'refreshed attitude toward the circumstances and exigencies of ordinary experience', as Dewey said. Such art is a deep and natural human need, our hunger for beauty 'hardly less' than for food itself. Art can be life-enhancing without yielding to anti-intellectual excesses. The best forms of rap unite the aesthetic (the sensuous) and the cognitive in a non-elitist medium that is both pragmatic and postmodern. Dewey insists that all ranking of art in terms of higher and lower is 'stupid'.[57] So the rap philosophers are really 'down with Dewey', their great white American guru, whether they know it or not.

If we ignore Dewey's occasional neo-Platonic remarks about popular art being 'cheap and vulgar' and music 'brutally organic', conducing to orgasms, we can grant Shusterman his point, especially if rap does what art for Dewey is supposed to do, make civilisation less uncivil, break through the barriers that divide human beings from each other, provide a religious, ritualistic focus of shared celebration, and remake the community itself in the direction of greater order and unity.[58] But even Shusterman admits that rap, with its confrontational opposition between 'you' and 'us', does not always have this unifying effect. He would invite those who feel confronted to join the higher 'we' of the rapper community. To refuse is to continue the racial *polemos* of our present society and deny the seamless unity of which Dewey dreamed in his aesthetic ideology.[59] But some might wonder why a pluralist pragmatic agenda would insist that everyone dance the same dance.[60] Aesthetic inducements to social unity, it seems, have not been invariably benign.

---

[55] Shusterman, *Pragmatist Aesthetics*, p. 187.   [56] *Ibid.*, p. 177.
[57] Dewey, *Art as Experience*, pp. 139, 227.   [58] *Ibid.*, pp. 6, 242, 238, 271, 81.
[59] Shusterman, *Pragmatist Aesthetics*, p. 201.
[60] Paul de Man, *Aesthetic Ideology*, ed. Andrzej Warminski (Minneapolis and London: University of Minnesota Press, 1996), pp. 154–155. See also Paul de Man, *The Rhetoric of Romanticism* (New York: Columbia University Press, 1984), pp. 263ff.

28

Ethics and literary criticism

GEOFFREY GALT HARPHAM

No single concept has had a more vital, complex and uncertain relation to literary criticism than ethics. While criticism has long been felt to represent in part an ethical enterprise, the origin and nature of the ethical obligation binding criticism has been a matter of great uncertainty. In part, this uncertainty reflects at a distance a parallel uncertainty concerning the relation of literature to ethics; in part, it is a feature of the practice of criticism or scholarship in any field; and in part it derives from the discourse of ethics itself.

While there are many different strands of ethical thinking, including those grounded in the thought of Aristotle, Augustine, Kant, Hegel, Marx, Nietzsche, Freud, John Rawls, Michel Foucault, Jacques Lacan, Jacques Derrida and others, a few very general statements can apply to all. Ethics is a way of putting things in which a given concept or term is set in relation to another concept or term in such a way that each exerts pressure on the other. In ethical discourse, 'inclination' might be set against 'duty', 'self-interest' against 'altruism', 'law' against 'custom', 'long-term interests' against 'short-term desires', 'facts' against 'values'; such oppositions become 'ethical' when they are seen to constitute a relation of 'otherness' in which the two terms are defined in mutual resistance.

The disputes arising from such a relation can only be settled by the imposition of an 'ought': one ought (for example) to behave out of respect for the law rather than simply pursuing the pleasures of the moment because, for whatever reason, adherence to the law possesses a higher value than the pursuit of pleasure. The central word of ethics, 'ought' represents neither a commandment of the sort that leaves no room for individual decision, nor a mere recommendation: it is an imperative, a form of urging that recognises that the issue is not pre-decided, for one is free not to follow it. The nature of one's response to an 'ethical' imperative says, therefore, a great deal about one's character, in a way that the nature of one's response to laws against sleeping under bridges, illegal parking or exceeding the speed of light does not.

Since the first extended reflections in English on the nature of literature, in the newly secularised climate of the Renaissance, the character of literature has been assessed in terms of just such oppositions, in debates about the joint roles in literary works of such terms as pleasure and instruction, invention and mimesis, fiction and reality, ideality and actuality, even form and content. Inasmuch as the relations between such general and imprecise terms always involve an element of contestation or resistance, with the claims of one term impinging on the domain of the other, the question of the ethics of literature has never been far from the surface, even of debates in which it does not appear to figure explicitly.

If, for example, a critic makes an argument for Shakespeare's 'realism', this argument might well have to contest another, perhaps implied, argument that insisted on the element of fantasy and sheer poetic invention in Shakespeare; and the discussion might take a quasi-ethical form, with the critic contending, ultimately, that Shakespeare, and perhaps literature generally, *ought* to be read in realist terms. In fact, the ethical question is often engaged in just this indirect form, through the structure rather than the explicitly stated terms of the argument.

Questions engaged in this way rarely achieve final resolution, and the question of the ethical status of literature remains unresolved. A long critical tradition promotes the ethical value of literature as a superior instrument of moral education, a fertile source of examples and precepts, an indispensable medium of self-knowledge. Literature, many have argued, refines the sensibilities, militates against egoistic self-enclosure, models choices, helps articulate goals, instructs people on how to understand situations, fosters individual and communal self-consciousness, and reveals consequences of acts, and so helps people improve themselves. But an equally long tradition asserts the transgressive amorality of literature, its indifference to law, regularity and virtues in general; its rich excessiveness, its indulgence in fantasy and fiction; its formal (i.e., ethically neutral) character; its preference for beauty over truth; the way in which it gives pleasure even while depicting wickedness; its endorsement of what William Blake called 'the devil's party'. As an institutional discourse, criticism is perhaps not so much undecided as doubly committed, or rather, committed to literature's ethical ambivalence.

This double commitment is plainly visible as early as Sir Philip Sidney's *An Apology for Poetry* (1595), where poetry is defended in neo-Horatian terms as a discourse that delights and teaches. A partial reading of selected passages would suggest that Sidney found the value of literature to reside in its potential for inculcating virtue by pitting the 'erected wit' against the 'infected will'.[1] But when Sidney describes the method by which poetry incites people to virtue, he lapses into a discourse of the infected will, even a rhetoric of seduction. 'For he doth not only show the way', Sidney says of the poet, 'but giveth so sweet a prospect into the way, as will entice any man to enter into it ... he cometh to you with words set in delightful proportion, either accompa-

---

[1] Philip Sidney, *An Apology for Poetry*, ed. Geoffrey Shepherd (Manchester: Manchester University Press, 1973), p. 101.

nied with, or prepared for, the well-enchanting skill of music'.[2] The poet, Sidney concludes with alarming candour, 'doth intend the winning of the mind with wickedness to virtue'. Tempting people to goodness, poetry engages in a decidedly risky enterprise.

The nature of this risk is dramatised in a famous passage where Sidney says that the poet 'nothing affirms'. Because he never insists to the reader that his utterances are true representations of fact, the poet never lies. Still, the poet's ethical credentials seem undeserved inasmuch as they depend on his finding a way around the entire problem of truthfulness rather than simply speaking the truth. In judging the poet's stratagem admirable even while noting its lack of forthrightness, Sidney anticipates the history of criticism with respect to the ethical ambivalence of literature.

Indeed, in a gesture that resonates throughout the history of criticism, Sidney nearly asserts that literature represents a force superior – richer, more powerful, more capacious – to ethics itself. Where philosophers might teach men the good, and preachers might exhort them to it, poetry, he suggests, represents a more complete engagement with the fullness and complexity of existence, including those aspects of life that cannot be brought under the rule of custom and the moral law – 'a very inspiring', as Sidney puts it, 'of a divine force, far above man's wit'. Representing this inspiration, serving as it were as its agent, mediating between the world and the daemonic, supra-ethical work of art, criticism stands in the middle, its own ethical status complicated by its double allegiance.

When, in the eighteenth century, English critics began to reflect not on literature but on the act of criticism itself, the emphasis fell on the frame of mind that was necessary to register the distinctive qualities of literature. The precondition for right judgement was considered to be a scrupulous neutrality, purified of distracting concerns, desires, or enthusiasms. 'Avoid extremes', Pope advised in *An Essay on Criticism*:

> ... and shun the fault of such
> Who still are pleased too little or too much.
> At every trifle scorn to take offense:
> That always shows great pride, or little sense...
> For fools admire, but men of sense approve.[3]

In almost ostentatiously artificial couplets, Pope urged the virtues of naturalness, modesty, justness of appreciation and moderation. Just criticism results, in other words, not from cognitive superiority or acquired learning, but first and foremost from a certain kind of virtue, as least as Pope defined that term.

This argument for a critical ethic based on the negation of merely

[2] *Ibid.*, p. 113.
[3] Alexander Pope, *Essay on Criticism*, in William K. Wimsatt (ed.), *Alexander Pope: Selected Poetry and Prose* (New York: Rinehart, 1955), II.384–391, p. 74.

subjective or personal impulses actually links criticism from the Age of Reason with subsequent criticism. Coleridge has little in common with Pope other than the belief that the critic should see with eyes purged of egoism. Whereas, for Pope, such a purging left an impersonal faculty of discrimination or appraisal, for Coleridge, what remained was an equally impersonal form of enthusiasm. Indifferent to the neo-classical project of discrimination, the Coleridgian critic manifested the 'steady fervour of a mind possessed and filled with the grandeur of its subject'. Such a mind is so dominated by the qualities of the work it beholds that it cannot judge, but only render its excellence. A third possibility for critical virtue is indicated by the example of Matthew Arnold, whose passionately ethical conception of criticism casts a very long shadow even today. For Arnold, literary pleasure was subordinated to instruction, and the task of criticism was to recognise this subordination, to confirm and augment it by explicit acts of evaluation and comparison, and to publicise its conclusions about 'the best that is known and thought in the world'. The crucial term in this critical virtue, far more recognisably modern than either moderation or fervour, is 'disinterestedness'.

In 'The Function of Criticism at the Present Time', Arnold holds up disinterestedness as the essence of criticism.[4] 'And how', he asked, 'is criticism to show disinterestedness? By keeping aloof from what is called "the practical view of things"; by resolutely following the law of its own nature, which is to be a free play of the mind on all subjects which it touches. By steadily refusing to lend itself to any of those ulterior, political, practical considerations about ideas.' Defined negatively, the 'nature' of criticism consists in its independence from all utilities, interests and ends, which Arnold represents in virtually ethical terms as temptations the critic must avoid. As, in another context, only the purest knight could seek the grail so, for Arnold, only the truly 'disinterested' critic could apprehend the literary artefact 'as in itself it really is' and bear its redemptive-transformative message to the world.

One of the most remarkable single facts about the history of literary criticism is that virtually all schools of thought, despite their profound differences, gather in consensus around the notion that criticism constitutes a kind of discipline for the critic, a refusal of temptations and an adherence to principle that takes nearly or virtually ethical form. Even in the case of those critics who promote apparently anti-ethical positions, for instance, Walter Pater or Oscar Wilde, the act of criticism is generally described in terms of obligation or fidelity to a certain set of principles, often with severe warnings about lapses or transgressions.

There is, indeed, a surprising consonance between the earnest Arnold and the scandalous Wilde. Like Arnold, Wilde believed that the aesthetic experience took place outside 'the practical view of things', although Arnold

---

[4] Matthew Arnold, 'The Function of Criticism at the Present Time', *Essays in Criticism: First Series* (London: Dent, 1964), pp. 9–34.

believed that art had profound culture-transforming powers and Wilde held that art was quite useless.[5] Moreover, both Arnold and Wilde subscribed to the notion of a distinct and separate art-object that stood in a luminous extra-social aesthetic space, a space that guaranteed the work's purity for Arnold and its triviality for Wilde. But Wilde explicitly stated one possible consequence of art's fundamental difference from worldliness, that art and ethics were 'absolutely distinct and separate', so that any 'ethical sympathy' in the artist was a kind of betrayal, 'an unpardonable mannerism of style'. Wilde's unwillingness to pardon the ethical artist signalled, however, yet another affinity with Arnold, the conviction that the task of the critic was to stand in the vacant space between the work and the world, policing the boundary, and judging both. The 'function of criticism' for each could be represented in ethical terms as a duty to preserve the proper relationship between art and culture. In other words, the differences even between such dissimilar figures can be represented not as a disagreement over whether criticism is or is not an ethically significant act, but rather as different ways of agreeing with the proposition that it is.

Since Wilde, the question of the ethics of criticism has taken two general forms. The first, whose roots we have been exploring and to which we shall return, concerns itself with the ethical dimension of criticism itself as an activity beset by temptation, subject to perversions and impurities, and bound by obligations. Criticism has, in this spirit, been variously characterised as a kind of rescue or emancipation of the text from misreadings, an interaction with the text in which 'misreading' is seen as inevitable, an appropriation for present purposes, a form of obeisance or deference towards the original creative act, a rewriting in which the creative text has no special authority, or even a prosecution of the text for the unenlightened values it supports. All of these frameworks can function as a set of guidelines and guardrails, steering criticism towards its proper function and marking deviations or derelictions. More will be said about the more recent forms of this consensus later.

The second general stream followed by the question of critical ethics concerns the critical representation of the ethics of literature itself. This issue arises in a climate of uncertainty about whether ethics and aesthetics are one, as writers from (at least) Shaftesbury through Wittgenstein and beyond assert; or whether they are two, as Pater, Wilde, Nabokov and others claim. If they are one, if the order of the aesthetic just is the order of the ethical, then ethical values self-evidently inhere in the artistic work, and criticism need not dwell on the fact. And if they are absolutely distinct, then the issue is resolved in the other direction, through a retreat from ethics altogether. If partisans of the first position tend to be preachers or revolutionary enthusiasts, partisans

---

[5] See Oscar Wilde, 'The Critic as Artist', in Richard Ellmann (ed.), *The Artist as Critic* (London: W. H. Allen, 1970), pp. 341–407.

of the second are decadents and aesthetes. Both extremes violate traditional understandings about the nature of literature itself, which is held to be distinct from sermons and from pure formal abstraction. It is only when the relation between aesthetics and ethics is uncertain that criticism discovers an ongoing and worthwhile project in articulating the precise nature of the relationship between them.

Typically, criticism concerned with the ethical force of the literary work proceeds on the assumption that the work is bound by and directed towards particular values, principles, obligations, imperatives, laws. The task of criticism becomes the description of the way these factors of closure bind what is, in superficial appearance, a free and fictive construct, so that the ethical relevance of the work may be made manifest. The governing presumption of such accounts is that literature has an ethical significance that operates in partial concealment, and so the work requires the clarifying agency of the critic to realise its full ethical potentiality.

Into this category fall such diverse figures as Arnold, the critic F. R. Leavis and the cultural theorist Raymond Williams. Arnold held that poetry was 'at bottom a criticism of life' that involved the 'application of ideas to life', to the question of 'how to live'.[6] But, as he argued in 'The Function of Criticism at the Present Time', the ethical genius of literature could only be disseminated in proper form by a vibrant criticism dedicated to seeing the object as in itself it really is. Criticism, rather than literature itself, created the freely flowing and revivifying 'current' of ideas on which cultural health and vitality depended. For Leavis, literary language constituted a cultural treasury and, more important, effected a 'training of sensibility'. Novels, at least those included in what Leavis called 'the great tradition', expressed and honed a national-cultural 'consciousness' and did so against the grain of 'mass culture', which threatened a general degradation in the 'quality of living'. The critic had to establish the kind of consciousness – cultural values, habits, traditions and the relationships between them – that determined the work, and, if that consciousness was sufficiently inspiriting, to urge its continuing relevance, even privilege, in contemporary culture. Williams used the term 'structure of feeling' rather than 'quality of living' but he conceived the ethical obligation of the critic in virtually identical terms: to identify, to discriminate and to promote desirable structures of feeling as instances of cultural 'creativity', an ongoing collective project of self-reformation and self-invention.

For Leavis, Williams and most twentieth-century critics, the issue of the ethics of literature emerges most often in the context of narrative, for narrative is the most 'world-like' and least artificial-seeming literary form, and therefore the one in which ethical concerns are most likely to be present in

---

[6] Matthew Arnold, 'Wordsworth', *Essays in Criticism: Second Series* (London: Macmillan, 1921), pp. 141–142.

some way within the aesthetic work. The ethics associated with narrative are likely to be, but are not necessarily, broadly 'humanistic'; indeed, the terms 'human' and 'humanist' often carry a heavy burden of implicit argumentation, especially when they are pitted against other terms suggesting ethical absolutism, technical impersonality, or inhuman rigour, terms that suggest a standard more divine or philosophical than worldly.

Narrative is thus seen by many as implicitly promoting a humanist ethic fitted to a flawed and imperfect world, at the expense of a strictly conceptual ethic fitted, perhaps, to a computer or a saint. Many who study ethics and narrative see the imperatives that emerge from a chronicle of life lived in time and contingency as guiding and advisory rather than obligatory or overpowering. A good model for these might be narrative 'form', that indwelling but elusive principle of structure that is seen by the reader to regulate in an all but invisible way, without ever being available to the consciousness of the characters or narrator, the apparently shapeless record of reflections, descriptions, and reports that constitute the narrative text. In the same way, it is sometimes argued, ethical principles, in the form of attitudes, values and presuppositions, guide people towards the right.

Form can actually be conceived in a way that brings it into more direct alignment with the concerns of ethics. Mikhail Bakhtin, whose work is not generally associated with a strong ethical impulse, argues, in *The Dialogic Imagination*, that the crucial structural principle in the novel is the ordeal or temptation. The fundamental organising idea in the novel, he argues, is that of the trial, which has survived from the Sophistic novel, through Christian legends and saints' lives, and on through the subsequent history of the modern novel, where it preserves its overwhelming organisational significance.[7] If form is conceived not as a principle of impersonal technique, but as a structure of trial or temptation, its ethical significance may lie closer to the thematic surface of the narrative than to the structural depths.

Another, more thematically neutral account of form was offered by the philosopher Alasdair MacIntyre in *After Virtue* (1981). Today's ethical vocabulary, MacIntyre argued, is degraded and confused in contrast to the vocabulary current in the classical world. Still, one resource for ethical thought remains vital, the telling of stories. Ethics, he points out, had always been taught by means of stories, and narrative is still capable of conferring coherence in the form of a narrative concept of selfhood in which an individual is oriented towards a future in which certain possibilities beckon us forward and others repel us.[8] Indeed, he argues, it is only by conceiving of life

---

[7] Mikhail Bakhtin, *The Dialogic Imagination: Four Essays*, ed. Michael Holquist, trans. Caryl Emerson and Michael Holquist (Austin: University of Texas Press, 1981).

[8] See particularly Alasdair MacIntyre's chapter, 'The Virtues, the Unity of a Human Life and the Concept of a Tradition', in *After Virtue: A Study in Moral Theory* (London: Duckworth, 1981), pp. 204–225.

in terms of narrative that people can be held accountable for their acts; for only narrative posits an integrated, self-consistent subject that remains in certain key respects constant over time. 'The unity of a human life', he concludes in a tone that resonates among many thinkers, 'is the unity of a narrative quest.'

MacIntyre is more sanguine than many about the ability of people to imagine and to live their lives as single unified narratives. But his interest in conceiving of ethics as communal custom rather than as abstract rule is shared by most critics who take up the issue of ethics through narrative. The figure of Aristotle, often explicitly contrasted with Kant or Nietzsche, tends to dominate such discussions, for Aristotle's ethics are markedly worldly and social, and are in this respect more consistent with the representational habits of narrative.

One such contemporary Aristotelian is the philosopher Richard Rorty. In a well known essay called 'Solidarity or Objectivity?' Rorty argues that human beings make sense of their lives by telling the story of their contribution to a community rather than by describing themselves in immediate relation to a nonhuman reality, for the simple reason, he says, that the first option is true and useful and the second is not.[9] Narrative, for Rorty, not only refutes philosophical accounts of ethics, but provides a superior *kind* of ethic, one more closely related to *ethos* than to obligation. In Rorty's ethics, self-understanding is more important than obedience, and self-understanding can only be reached by the construction of stories about the self. If, for MacIntyre, stories are valuable insofar as they foster accountability and a sense of unity, for Rorty, story-telling develops the indispensable ability to improvise an identity, to 'tailor a coherent self-image for ourselves'.[10]

Aristotle provides another kind of guidance to the philosopher Martha Nussbaum, who has made some of the most forceful and sweeping claims for the ethics of literature. Like Rorty, she favours narrative over philosophical discourse as an instrument of ethical education, but her ethic is centred not on self-fashioning, but on a highly developed sensitivity to nuances of character and circumstance. The abstractions of philosophy miss, she says, the concrete materiality and immediacy of actual life, and so work against what she describes as an ethic of perception and responsiveness. In the novels of Henry James, by contrast, such responsiveness is represented in such a vivid, extended and detailed way as to awaken, crystallise and fortify the reader's own responsiveness.[11]

---

[9] Richard Rorty, 'Solidarity or Objectivity?', in John Rajchman and Cornel West (eds.), *Post-Analytic Philosophy* (New York: Columbia University Press, 1985), pp. 3–19.

[10] Richard Rorty, 'Freud and Moral Reflection', in Joseph H. Smith and William Kerrigan (eds.), *Pragmatism's Freud: The Moral Disposition of Psychoanalysis* (Baltimore and London: The Johns Hopkins University Press, 1986), pp. 1–27.

[11] See e.g. Martha C. Nussbaum, *Love's Knowledge: Essays on Philosophy and Literature* (New York and Oxford: Oxford University Press, 1990), pp. 140–143.

More generally, Nussbaum argues, the reading of novels is moral in two senses. First, it exposes one to circumstances in which a character behaves sensitively or insensitively, and thus instructs readers how they ought to behave in similar circumstances. And second, the very reading of a narrative – especially a narrative constructed with Jamesian sensitivity – provides a 'school for moral sentiments', refashioning the reader's consciousness almost unconsciously. Nussbaum does not give extended consideration to narratives constructed boorishly, or sensitively to the wrong things such as money, advantage or desire. Nor does she explore cases where sensitivity itself can be put to unethical purposes, as in the novels of de Sade. And her claims for the ethical force of novels and novel-reading, it may be charged, achieve their unrestricted global scope only through this limitation of evidence. But she does argue a case that many have felt, that literature itself is not only concerned with the subject of ethics, but actually performs an ethical function.

Nussbaum is especially responsive to the neo-Aristotelian arguments of the eminent literary critic Wayne Booth in *The Company We Keep: An Ethics of Fiction* (1988), to the effect that the optimal relation between reader and book is like that of friendship – voluntary, free and mutually enriching.[12] Booth's understanding of ethics is exceptionally spacious, including every consideration that might be applied to the ancient question, 'how should one live?' Like Leavis, Booth is generally concerned with the 'sense of life' represented in and by a given literary work. This sense is suggested not only by characters and plot elements, but also by sentences, figures, all the various 'literary' or 'formal' aspects of the work: if style defines human identity, Booth argues, then ethical criticism must take account of style. Like Nussbaum, however, Booth is also sensitive to the reader, and to the reformation or reformatting of character in the reading process. Moreover, he understands – again like Nussbaum – that the reading experience is at least quasi-erotic, involving a kind of seduction, a readerly 'succumbing', an 'act of *assent*'. Such an assent, Booth implies, defines the appeal of the literary text, which engages affections and sympathies in a way that texts on engineering, water management policy or even philosophical issues often do not.

Through this breadth of appeal, Booth contends, literature engages the whole person and serves to activate elements of responsiveness that can become inactive or dormant in the course of daily life. Booth is less precise than MacIntyre or Nussbaum in stipulating the optimal human condition, and in fact seems far more comfortable with a genuine diversity of human types than either. In fact, Booth argues for virtually the precise opposite of MacIntyre's case, insisting in effect that narrative is not a unifying factor but a kind of discursive shrine to 'pluralism', and that, consequently, the ethics of

---

[12] Wayne Booth, *The Company We Keep: An Ethics of Fiction* (Chicago: University of Chicago Press, 1988).

narrative consist not in a gathering together of disparate elements, but rather in an expansion of human possibilities.

Booth's sunny liberalism is not shared by those who are sensitive to the dangers presented by literature to the stability of the polis. Iris Murdoch, for one, defends a more restrictive account of literature's relation to ethics than Booth, one that begins with a warm appreciation of Plato's 'banishment of the artists'. One of the most distinguished novelists in the world, Murdoch fully grasps Plato's case that art invites distraction and fantasising, representing, as she puts it, a pseudo-spirituality, and even a defeat of the discursive intelligence. The pleasures of art, she contends, are seductive in a bad sense in that they are ethically and spiritually dangerous, being impure and indefinite and secretly in league with egoism.[13]

Still, Murdoch concludes that, read rightly, Plato also provides a defence and reasonable critique of art as essentially more free than philosophy, more able to enjoy the ambiguity of the whole person. But it is not ambiguity or even the wholly human that really interests Murdoch. For her own defence of literature is based on its 'symbolic force', which is capable of providing 'a stirring image of a pure transcendent value, a steady visible enduring higher good . . . [a clear] *experience* of something grasped as separate and precious and beneficial and held quietly and unpossessively in the attention'.[14] In this way, great art 'points in the direction of the good', and art that does not cannot be placed at the pinnacle of artistic achievement. The message of great literature is in this sense always the same: overcome personal fantasy and egoistic anxiety and self-indulgent daydream.[15]

A more recent non-classical account of the impact of literature on the reader has been elaborated by Adam Zachary Newton in *Narrative Ethics* (1995). Newton speaks not of the 'ethics of narrative' but of 'narrative as ethics', in order to draw attention to the readerly act of engaging the concrete, immediate problems represented by the narrative text. For Newton, as for several others discussed above, ethics is a matter of 'intersubjectivity' rather than abstraction, universal law or even Murdoch's 'higher good'. Unlike those in the neo-Aristotelian line, however, he promotes a sharp-edged version of ethical obligation. The kind of ethical forces that influence the individual are, in Rorty, beveled and merely advisory; but for Newton, ethics is focused in the experience of obligation, and obligation issues not from a community of like citizens but from the traumatic intervention of a starkly anonymous 'other'.

For the experience of encounter, Newton draws on the work of Bakhtin, whose theory of 'dialogism' emphasised social interaction between different kinds of people; and for the sense of trauma, he appropriates the Jewish Lithuanian philosopher, or anti-philosopher, Emmanuel Levinas, whose

---

[13] Cf. Iris Murdoch, *The Fire and the Sun: Why Plato Banished the Artists* (Oxford: Clarendon Press, 1977), p. 41.   [14] *Ibid.*, pp. 76–77.   [15] *Ibid.*, p. 77, cf. also p. 59.

fierce account of absolute obligation arising from 'the other' had been widely influential in philosophy, but not in literary criticism. If Rorty's account of narrative stresses community-building and the construction of personal identity, Newton emphasises dis-integration at all levels: face-to-face encounters between strangers introduce a principle of incommensurability, even incoherence, into the flow of narrative, the homogeneity of the community and the production of a coherent self-image. This principle of incommensurability, which Newton advocates as an ethical desideratum, emerges not as a set of consciously maintained principles or values, but rather in 'relations of provocation, call and response that bind narrator and listener, author and character, or reader and text'.

For the Marxist critic Fredric Jameson, by contrast, 'narrative as ethics' is not an end in itself, but merely an ideologically generated screen for a deeper political content – class inequities and the resulting conflicts – that cannot be represented directly. According to Jameson's *The Political Unconscious* (1981), these macro-struggles are subject to ideological working that produces a representation not of classes, or of history, but of individuals. Worked in this way, a class conflict that is, because of its magnitude, inconceivable and (short of revolution) unresolvable shrinks, when cast into narrative form, into a simple choice between alternative values; politics takes on the diminished form of what Jameson calls ethics – the predominant code, he says, in which the question 'What does it mean?' tends to be answered. The ethical dimension of narrative is, for Jameson, the problem rather than the solution, the starting point for a critical project whose goal is the decoding of those narrative moments of individual decision in an effort to recuperate the deeper but distorted political content.

The other form of critical ethics, which centres not on literature but on the act of criticism itself, has evolved dramatically in recent years, when criticism has assumed, in the eyes of some, greater cultural prominence. Since Poe denounced the 'didactic heresy', criticism has been aware of the threat of corruption in artistic practice; but with the New Criticism of the 1940s and 1950s, criticism came to see itself as vulnerable. The 'affective' and 'intentional' fallacies (Wimsatt and Beardsley), the 'personal heresy' (C. S. Lewis), the 'heresy of paraphrase' (Cleanth Brooks), the 'heresy of omnipossibilism' (E. D. Hirsch), the 'fallacy of unmediated expression' and the 'fallacy of finite interpretation' (Paul de Man) – all these reflect the anxious sense that criticism, an ethically significant activity in its own right, has a tendency to stray from the straight and narrow path of rightness. Particularly in the climate of professionalism that has dominated literary criticism since the end of the Second World War, criticism has become transformed from an amateur practice of appreciation to a 'discipline', with all the ethical overtones that term implies.

Any particular conception of the act of criticism includes some specification of a proper procedure or methodology – a critical duty – and some account of transgression. Every school of critical practice defines its own understanding of an imperative. Critics of diverse persuasions find a ground of accord in the proposition that the primary imperative is provided by the text. As a material document, a record of authorial intentions at a given moment, the text – the luminous object that critics strive to see clearly and whole – stands decisively outside the subjective impulses of the critic, and thus functions as a test of critical humility. The first requirement for the critic, T. S. Eliot said, was 'a sense of fact', and the material text is the main fact that a critic must recognise. This recognition will only come to those sufficiently humble, modest, patient and deferential to be able to clear out those obstacles to clear perception, prejudices and presuppositions.

Overshadowed by the artist and humbled by the text, criticism becomes a secondary, belated activity that must constantly keep its own creative or initiatory impulses under control, for these represent forms of self-indulgence or narcissism. Under this austere dispensation, criticism can assume a wide range of forms, including philological enquiry, textual study, reception history or formalist study. It cannot, however, indulge in subjective speculation or merely private assertions.

Of course, people read for private and subjective reasons, including entertainment, distraction, amusement, consolation, instruction, information, advice and more. But it is the belief in the invalidity of the average reader's response that unifies numerous 'schools' of critical practice. The German philosopher Hans-Georg Gadamer speaks for a consensus position in this respect when he argues that 'all correct interpretation must be on guard against the arbitrary fancies and the limitations imposed by imperceptible habits of thought and direct its gaze "on the things themselves" . . . For it is necessary to keep one's gaze fixed on the thing throughout all the distractions that the interpreter will constantly experience and which originate in himself.'[16]

From this disciplinary point of view, any kind of pleasure or gratification that the reader may experience becomes ethically suspect, a temptation to be resisted. Indeed, one may well argue that the professional study of literature comes into being precisely as just such an ethical resistance to the immediate responses of the average reader. Even those critics who advocate, in Roland Barthes' phrase, the 'pleasures of the text', outline some principle of duty set against a principle of indulgence. In Barthes' idiosyncratic argument, the concept of structure is represented as a temptation to believe in a stable epistemological ground. This temptation can be resisted, Barthes says, by submitting it to the experience of reading, an honest experience of which constitutes a permanent haemmorhage that renders structure hysterical.[17]

Barthes appears to revolutionise everything by removing the element of

---

[16] Hans-Georg Gadamer, *Truth and Method* (New York: Seabury Press, 1975), p. 236.
[17] Roland Barthes, *The Rustle of Language*, trans. Richard Howard (New York: Hill and Wang, 1986).

dubiety or embarrassment from the individual, temporal reading experience. But two considerations moderate this promise of readerly liberation. First, such a liberation would render the reading experience exciting, perhaps, but so unsystematic that it could not be the object of a professional discourse, which must be based on a methodology oriented towards consensus. But an even more telling point is that while Barthes has reversed some conventional formulae, the basic concept of an ethical reading practice threatened by temptation remains, with the reading experience and the form of the text simply changing places. For Barthes, the reader *ought* to permit his or her subjective experience to flourish, and *ought not* indulge in any arbitrary fantasies of a stable form.

Such an ethics of criticism appears in other surprising places as well. Deconstruction, as practised primarily during the 1970s and 1980s, seemed at first to define itself in stark opposition to all the key terms of ethics, including responsibility, obligation, imperative, virtue, right and even the subject itself. But an ethical imperative appeared in unexpected ways throughout the main texts of the movement. Paul de Man, for example, dismissed conventional notions of ethics (e. g., the subject's 'free' obedience to a fixed law) as so many sentimental illusions. He promoted not an ethics of criticism but rather a 'rigorous' analysis that would focus on the rhetorical aspects of a text. But 'rigour' could only be achieved, as he put it in 'Semiology and Rhetoric', by negating the reader's will or wishes; a given reading could be certified to be cleanly technical only if it could be shown to be not 'our' reading because it employed only the linguistic elements provided by the text itself.[18] In de Man, the ethics of criticism reassert themselves in the form of the chastened reading subject, his or her desires humbled by a methodology.

The ethical potentiality of de Man's critical position is made much more explicit in his colleague J. Hillis Miller's *The Ethics of Reading* (1987). According to Miller, the text compels from the reader a 'properly and independently ethical' act of self-evacuation, ending in an 'I must'.[19] The reader – if he or she is reading properly – derives from the text a powerful impression of its own stark indifference to edification, consolation, information, guidance, pleasure, or anything but its own silent textuality. Bound by the text to respect its inhuman otherness, the reader 'must' register the illegitimacy of interpretive closure. So, Miller concludes an account striking for its radically truncated sense of ethical responsibility, reading is an ethically assessable act, one that is performed well when the reader becomes, while reading, not a human subject so much as a relay station in a strictly linguistic transaction.

Derrida's practice is more exuberant, spontaneous and excessive than de

[18] Paul de Man, 'Semiology and Rhetoric', *Allegories of Reading: Figural Language in Rousseau, Nietzsche, Rilke, and Proust* (New Haven and London: Yale University Press, 1979), pp. 3–19.

[19] J. Hillis Miller, *The Ethics of Reading: Kant, de Man, Eliot, Trollope, James, and Benjamin* (New York: Columbia University Press, 1987).

Man's and Miller's, and less given to such bleak or severe pronouncements. Indeed, Derrida has been associated, at least in the popular imagination, not with a negation or redefinition of ethical terms, but with a total abandonment of the entire ethical problematic. He has been seen by many to represent the total collapse of all the hardwon standards and procedures not just of criticism but of reason itself. He has, however, been seen by others as the defender of reason (and ethics) in the contemporary world, a thinker in the great Enlightenment tradition who, unlike most others in this tradition, does not close his eyes to the forces of unreason in the world and in the text. His thinking has, in other words, been seen by some as a form of anti-ethical licence and irrationality, and by others as tempered by the full, unillusioned exposure to such irrationality.

Derrida himself attempted to settle the issue in two texts written during the 1980s, 'Afterword: Toward an Ethic of Discussion', and 'Racism's Last Word'. In the latter, he called for an 'unconditional' opposition to apartheid, explicitly invoking Kant's categorical imperative.[20] And in the former, he generalised his position on ethics and criticism which, he said, was enacted in two distinct but interrelated layers or moments.[21] In the first, the critic, acting according to an 'ethical-political duty', produced a 'doubling commentary', a lucid, exact, and minute description of the object – a 'minimal consensus' on the 'relatively stable' meaning of a text. Without such a commentary, one could, Derrida pointed out, 'just say anything at all'. This layer or moment of scrupulosity was then to be complemented by a second, 'productive' layer or moment of 'interpretation', which could claim to be principled only insofar as it was based on the ground of doubling commentary. Here, Derrida established not just his own claim to ethical responsibility, but the conditions of such responsibility generally.

Derrida's understanding of ethics is deeply informed by that of Levinas, the author of such texts as *Totality and Infinity* (French original 1961) and *Otherwise than Being* (French original 1974), whose influence on Newton was noted earlier.[22] In fact, while Levinas is one of the most remarkably idiosyncratic thinkers in any field, his work on ethics touches on, and in a sense underlies, many of the aspects of ethics just delineated. For Levinas, whose abstract, obscure and often contradictory thinking is commonly smoothed out and banalised by his admirers in the course of 'applying' it, the core of ethics is the absolute, unquestionable and infinite obligation owed to the

---

[20] Jacques Derrida, 'Racism's Last Word', in Henry Louis Gates (ed.), *'Race', Writing, and Difference* (Chicago and London: University of Chicago Press, 1986), pp. 329–338.

[21] Jacques Derrida, 'Afterword: Toward an Ethic of Discussion', *Limited Inc*, trans. Samuel Weber and Jeffrey Mehlman (Evanston: Northwestern University Press, 1988), pp. 111–160.

[22] Emmanuel Levinas, *Otherwise Than Being or Beyond Essence*, trans. Alphonso Lingis (The Hague: Nijhoff, 1981); *Totality and Infinity: An Essay on Exteriority*, trans. Alphonso Lingis (Pittsburgh, Duquesne University Press, 1969).

shadowy figure Levinas calls only 'the other'. This other might be conceived as the literary text, in which case Levinas has articulated an ethics of criticism of a particularly austere kind, one that requires the virtual self-annihilation of the critic in the luminous presence of a text whose truth the critic humbly aspires to articulate. The other might, however, be understood to be a human being, in which case Levinas is speaking of the concrete social world, the world represented in literature. Under this dispensation, Levinas could be seen as promoting literature, with its multiple voices and characters, its divided or conflicted subjects, as a way of understanding oneself and the world that is superior to philosophy, which is hostage to mere concepts and to the exaltation of mastery in the form of critical understanding. Literature could be said to represent the Levinasian ethical circumstance – the encounter between self and other – in all its irreducible particularity and concreteness, in a spirit of 'infinity' as opposed to 'totality'. By insisting so relentlessly on the single principle of the priority of the other to the self, Levinas has raised a host of issues applicable to an ethics of criticism and of literature.

Critical and literary ethics are bound up with a host of issues concerning the status of the reader, the nature of textuality, the status of 'literature', the character of ethical imperatives and the relation between literature and ethics. Anchored in such volatile and uncertain issues, it is likely that ethics will remain a fertile source of questions, rather than answers, in the context of literary study.

Interdisciplinary approaches

29

Literature and theology

KEVIN MILLS

Introduction

The specific and identifiable movement in literary criticism which might be referred to as 'literature and theology', or 'literature and religion', developed in western Christian cultures during the second half of the twentieth century. This is not to claim that there are no other, equally important approaches to the relationship between religious discourses and works of literature, or that such relationships cannot fruitfully be explored in non-Christian contexts. Neither is it to obscure the extent to which Christian interpretive practice has been questioned and complicated in encounters with other traditions. It is merely to observe that a set of theological discourses are historically and culturally interwoven with literary criticism in the Christian west, and that this coalescence has shaped a discernible critical movement in the last fifty or sixty years.

I would argue that the peculiar relationship between the study of literature and Christian theology in the west is a context coterminous with what Jacques Derrida refers to as the theological age of the linguistic sign:[1] in Christian cultures, language has been thought to encode the divine sanction implied in the creation of the world by the Word or logos: 'God said "Let there be . . ." And there was . . .' In this epoch, the combining of *theos* and *logos* in its very name predisposes theology toward the study of language, and literary criticism towards theology. The deconstruction of 'logocentric' modes of thought (i.e., those discourses which seek to provide texts with fixed, determinate meanings) raises questions of particular difficulty for critical practices which incorporate a relegous lineage and commitment. It is with these questions in mind that I explore the relationship between literature and theology in the following pages.

From book to text

In 1990, a volume of essays appeared under the title *The Book and the Text*. It comprises a series of analyses of biblical texts by a number of accomplished scholars, each practising some specialised mode of textual interpretation.

[1] Jacques Derrida, *Of Grammatology*, trans. Gayatri Chakravorty Spivak (Baltimore: Johns Hopkins University Press, 1976), p. 14.

The Bible is here brought into dialogue with various currents in contemporary theory such as structuralism, deconstruction, semiotics, hermeneutics, feminism, psychoanalytic interpretation and political thought. The book's title already tells the story of that dialogue, by juxtaposing two overdetermined literary terms; the subtitle, *The Bible and Literary Theory*, repeats the gesture. The word 'bible', after all, is no more than the anglicised form of the Greek word *biblion*, meaning simply 'book'. But in western Christian cultures, the Bible has never been just *a* book; it has always been *the* book: the definitive, self-contained expression of its author's being. Furthermore, Christ's portrayal as the incarnate Word and as Immanuel – God with(in) us – produced a belief that the recoverability of the author's presence in the process of reading was a religious truth. As Valentine Cunningham puts it:

The sense of the plenitudes of books was rooted in a sense of the plenitudes of God's Book. The felt capacity of words to make things, people, ideas present was founded in the notion of the Word becoming flesh. Once it was accepted that Christ could be made present through the Word, it was a short step to thinking that any person or thing could be manifested in language.[2]

Believed to be the word of God in written form, the Bible attracted to itself the adjective 'holy', and was long treated as sacrosanct, as being beyond question or criticism. But the privileged status of the Bible as the definitively closed book and as sacred text *par excellence* has always depended upon something other than what the reader actually finds in its pages: its status derives, in part, from a certain interpretative context. In other words, the reception of the Bible has a traceable history during the course of which it has gathered many layers of protective commentary and interpretation which have influenced, if not dictated, the way in which it has been read. The difficulty of penetrating such a thick outer skin of cultural insulation might be thought to account for its long-preserved immunity to critical analysis. While this immunity broke down in the eighteenth century, with the consequence that the Bible gradually lost its culturally dominant position, western thought, until comparatively recently, continued to view books as though each one were a kind of second-class bible – a type or shadow of the real book. Which is to say that books have enjoyed a privileged status in the creation and transmission of knowledge, seeming to offer a localised, scaled-down version of the plenitude, fullness and incontrovertibility of the archetypal book.

Like the Bible as a whole, its constituent texts have their own, pre-canonical reception-history, so that what is actually meant by 'The Bible' is not an ahistorical given. For Jews, the Bible does not include the Christian books of the so-called 'New Testament'; the Protestant Church does not include the 'apocryphal' or 'deutero-canonical' books in its Bible, while the Catholic

---

[2] Valentine Cunningham, *In the Reading Gaol: Postmodernity, Texts and History* (Oxford and Cambridge, Mass.: Blackwell, 1994), p. 203.

Church does include them; the Bible of the eastern orthodox Churches does not include the book of Revelation. Such differences in content point to the fact that there is something external to the texts themselves at work in the way in which they have been read and collated. In his discussion of the historical processes of canon-formation David Lawton writes:

Certainly, the criteria are partly scholarly: the spurious is expunged, the fake and the forged are exposed. But they are also critical: readers exclude what they do not wish to read, and they also exclude what appears to conflict with the rest. Such readers begin not with the Book, but with the Faith, and admit into that book only what strengthens faith. That is what the early Christians did, quite self-consciously.[3]

This tells us something important about the relationship between the book and the text in Christian cultures: that there are distinct and divergent ways of thinking about written matter. The book as a self-enclosed, unitary entity is constituted by considerations which are not internal to it. The text, on the other hand, is incomplete, open to scrutiny, to question and to challenge. To characterise a book as a text, therefore, is to draw attention to the fact that interpretative contexts are external to, and discontinuous with, the documents interpreted.

The struggle between these two versions of reading (book *versus* text) has been characteristic of literary criticism in the second half of the twentieth century, and especially so of the branch of literary study with which this article is concerned: the interdisciplinary approach to literature and theology. The book as a closed unit, sealed in the name of an author (for whom God – as Author of the world and of the Word – is the ultimate role model) who remains the possessor of its true meaning, is the product of theological interpretative discourses. In sharp contrast to, and in rebellion against, such approaches, recent literary criticism, characteristically, has rejected authorial control and has, with increasing fervour, celebrated the autonomy of the text and the role of the reader in the creation of meaning. Thus, in attempting to bring together two disciplines with a shared prehistory, but with divergent aims, the pioneers of interdisciplinary approaches to literary criticism and theology in the early post-war years helped to create a modern conflict of interpretations which is still current. Amos Wilder and Nathan A. Scott are often credited with opening the way for literature and theology as a distinct field of study. Both men were influenced by the prevailing critical modes of their day – the New Criticism in literary studies, and the New Hermeneutic in theology.

The latter emerged from Martin Heidegger's philosophical appropriation of attempts by the nineteenth-century thinkers Friedrich Schleiermacher and Wilhelm Dilthey to systematise interpretative practice. In Heidegger's

---

[3] David Lawton, *Faith, Text and History: The Bible in English* (New York: Harvester Wheatsheaf, 1990), p. 17.

thought hermeneutics became an approach to the question of Being, capable of divesting it of the metaphysical trappings which it had acquired through the philosophical tradition coming down from Plato and Aristotle. A hermeneutics of Being, he contended, would let Dasein – the mode of Being peculiar to humans – appear on its own terms. While the German Bible critic Rudolf Bultmann followed Heidegger in attempting to rediscover the meaning of human existence by 'demythologising' the Bible's message, attending chiefly to the existential import of the Christian proclamation, Gerhard Ebeling and Ernst Fuchs, the two thinkers most closely associated with the New Hermeneutic, assimilated from Heidegger an interest in the language of the gospel. Their chief concern was to translate New Testament vocabulary, images and representations into a language comprehensible to modern society. It is this focus which finds its way into the work of Wilder and Scott, and which they attempted to blend with aspects of the New Critical approach to literature. Wilder especially appealed to New Critical canons of poetry in dealing with the biblical text: 'We should reckon with what we can learn about metaphorical and symbolic language from students of poetry: that it cannot really be translated, least of all into prose; that its meaning is to be thought in terms of its own distinctive mode of communication.'[4]

T. S. Eliot was a key figure in the development of both the New Criticism and the interdisciplinary work of Wilder and Scott. His 1935 essay entitled 'Religion and Literature' set the terms of the engagement for many years to come when it characterised the relationship in terms of completion: 'Literary criticism should be completed by criticism from a definite ethical and theological standpoint.'[5] It is hard not to hear in this formulation echoes of the process of canon-formation by which the disparate texts which make up the Christian Bible came to be bound together and consecrated into the sacred book. It advocates a completeness which can only be imposed upon texts from the outside by some value-system or moral code such as that which Eliot's Anglo-Catholicism provided.

Just such commitments underlay both the founding of literature and theology as a discernible movement in the history of literary criticism, and the New Critical project. If the latter tended to isolate literary works from their authorial meanings, it remained within the book-based model of reading by virtue of an interpretative canon which characterised works of literature as 'verbal icons' (to borrow W. K. Wimsatt's resounding phrase). An icon, in this sense, is a self-contained, ahistorical artifact, which can be interrogated using a set of prescribed critical tools (such as 'tension', 'irony', 'paradox', etc.). The religious resonance of the term recalls the Protestant reverence of Scripture as

[4] Amos N. Wilder, *Early Christian Rhetoric: The Language of the Gospel* (London: SCM Press, 1964), p. 133.
[5] T. S. Eliot, 'Religion and Literature', *T.S. Eliot: Selected Prose*, ed. John Hayward (Harmondsworth: Penguin, 1953), pp. 31–42 (p. 31).

a unitary, self-authenticating whole, capable of transcending the conditions in which it was written by means of the revelation of timeless truths, or, for the less theologically minded, by means of sublime language and imagery. So,while the role of the author took second place to that of the competent New Critical reader, the work of literature remained a self-identical, complete, masterable presence.

The emergence of structuralism from the model of language proposed in Ferdinand de Saussure's *Course in General Linguistics* (original, French version, 1916), gave rise to a mode of criticism which promised to bring literary criticism and biblical studies into a new kind of proximity. In Britain, the anthropologist Edmund Leach published a structuralist reading of Genesis in 1969, while, in America, structuralism-inspired readings of biblical texts were produced by Daniel Patte and John Dominic Crossan in the mid 1970s. It is noteworthy that these works, and the majority of those that followed their lead, concentrate on narrative forms. To a greater extent than any other literary-critical endeavour, the study of narrative was transformed by structuralism, and it is in this field that its most enduring impact has been felt. This has been due, in large part, to the emergence of a number of extremely able exponents of what has become known as 'narratology', whose work has focused on biblical narratives. While its origins are in Russian Formalism and French structuralism, narrative poetics has evolved beyond the assignation of participant roles and the identification of lexical codes with which it began. Mieke Bal, in particular, has developed the work of earlier narrative semioticians such as Vladimir Propp, Viktor Shklovsky and A-J. Greimas, synthesising elements of their theories with poststructuralist and feminist methods to produce a distinctive and powerful analytical model. Her studies of the narratives recorded in the book of Judges, as cognisant of the history of biblical criticism as of semiotic theory, reveal how generations of male critics have failed to assign full significance to the female participants, and, as a direct result, have produced skewed interpretations of the text.[6]

An essay by Roland Barthes: 'Wrestling with the Angel: Textual Analysis of Genesis 32:23–33', despite its poststructuralist emphasis on detailed scrutiny of the text, is often cited as exemplary of applied structuralism.[7] But Barthes' work led beyond the elaboration of narrative patterns and verbal taxonomies typical of structural analysis. His prolix and detailed treatment of a short story by Balzac, in *S/Z* (French original, 1970), demonstrated the incapacity of

---

[6] Mieke Bal, *Murder and Difference: Gender, Genre and Scholarship on Sisera's Death* (Bloomington: Indiana University Press, 1988) and *Death and Dissymmetry: The Politics of Coherence in the Book of Judges* (Chicago: University of Chicago Press, 1988).

[7] Roland Barthes, 'Wrestling with the Angel: Textual Analysis of Genesis 32:23–33', *Image, Music, Text*, trans. Stephen Heath (Glasgow: Fontana, 1977), pp. 125–141. This point is made by Kevin Hart, 'The Poetics of the Negative', *Reading the Text: Biblical Criticism and Literary Theory*, ed. Stephen Prickett (Oxford and Cambridge, Mass.: Basil Blackwell, 1991), pp. 281–340 (p. 300).

this kind of approach to exhaust the possible meanings of a literary text: rather than trapping meaning in a well-constructed cage of semiotic possibilities, the process tended to cause an inexhaustible proliferation of meaning which could never be controlled by the intention of the absent author. Since a written text is, of necessity, detached from its authorial origins, and since language is, for the structuralist, a closed system of signs unanchored in external reality, texts are open to the multiple meanings constructed for them by their readers. Barthes concluded that the author is dead – a declaration fraught with theological implications: 'Once the Author is removed, the claim to decipher a text becomes quite futile. To give a text an Author is to impose a limit on that text, to furnish it with a final signified, to close the writing ... to refuse to fix meaning is, in the end, to refuse God.'[8] What Friedrich Nietzsche had declared a century earlier in the context of philosophical inquiry was now announced in literary criticism: God is dead.

The effect of Jacques Derrida's deconstruction of Saussurean linguistics, and of the whole structuralist enterprise, in his germinal work *Of Grammatology* (French original, 1967), was even more devastating to theological criticism. Not only did Derrida argue that the external discourses used to ratify certain interpretations of texts, to delimit their meanings, were ideological impositions, he also struck at the heart of Christian reading practice by undermining the concept of the 'transcendental signified', or ultimate guarantee of linguistic meaning. This concept derives, in western metaphysics, from the Greek *logos*, a term familiar to readers of the Christian Bible from John's gospel, where it is identified with Christ. Derrida's deconstructive strategy involves replacing the positive, active *logos* with the 'trace'. Unlike the *logos*, the trace is characterised as a movement rather than as a static, self-identical being or thing. A never-present non-origin which is disguised by the very meaning-effects of language to which it gives rise, '*the trace is in fact the absolute origin of sense in general. Which amounts to saying ... that there is no absolute origin of sense in general*' (original emphasis).[9] On this account, the history of metaphysics, including that of Christianity's theologically determined modes of interpretation, can be read as the systematic covering over of the shifting, unrepresentable 'trace' with the static presence of the *logos*. Contemporary critical theory after the death of the author, and in the wake of deconstruction, has presented Christian thinkers engaged in literary study with a profound problem for precisely this reason: it proclaims, in Derrida's words, 'the end of the book and the beginning of writing'.[10]

Christian approaches to the problems of interpretation thrown up by contemporary theory have often been informed by the work of the French philos-

[8] Roland Barthes, 'The Death of the Author', *Image, Music, Text*, pp. 142–148 (p. 147).
[9] Derrida, *Of Grammatology*, p. 65.   [10] *Ibid.*, heading I, p. 1.

opher Paul Ricoeur. He has been of the highest significance for the study of literature and theology through the years during which the emergence of hermeneutics, structuralism, deconstruction and postmodernism, have revolutionised critical thought. Offering allegiance to no one school of thought, Ricoeur has contributed to a wide range of crucial debates over five decades, attempting always to reconcile the most fruitful ideas from a variety of disciplines and positions. His interdisciplinary approach to the problems of interpretation, his interest in biblical criticism and his elaboration of a post-Heideggerian hermeneutical theory that preserves the possibility of faith have made his work of special interest to scholars in literature and theology. His work is too voluminous and wide-ranging to summarise here, but the indication of three specific aspects of it may serve to suggest its importance in this field of study.

Firstly, while Ricoeur shares a number of philosophico-interpretative attitudes with Derrida, he seeks to elucidate hermeneutical processes in order to promote the understanding of human existence, while Derrida's work insistently uncovers the inherent strains and contradictions which disrupt the apparently unitary meanings to which texts (especially philosophical texts) lay claim. Ricoeur's commitment to ontologically directed interpretation makes his work particularly appealing to critics with theological or religious sympathies. Secondly, his espousal of hope as a directing impulse in the reading process gives Ricoeur's hermeneutic an orientation towards which Christian criticism is predisposed. This hope (which owes much to Jürgen Moltmann's theological appropriation of the work of Ernst Bloch) appears as a feature of his attempt to complete the work of Heidegger and Kant. The limitation placed on the scope of knowledge by Kant (as against Hegel's positing of 'absolute knowledge'), leaves room for hope within philosophical speculation, and Ricoeur exploits this in order to criticise Heidegger's notion of authentic existence as 'being-towards-death'. Thirdly, acknowledging the significance for interpretation of the work of Nietzsche, Marx and Freud (whom he calls the 'masters of suspicion'), Ricoeur's complex and broad-based hermeneutical theory attempts to state the case for a mode of interpretation which moves beyond suspicion (of conceptuality, ideology and psychological naïvety), on the basis of 'a trust in the power to say, in the power to do, in the power to recognize oneself as a character in a narrative'.[11] This emphasis on trust might be thought of as the converse of Barthes' refusal of God through the denial of authorial meaning: if to deny meaning is to reject God, then to interpret is to approach a theology. This is not to return to a pre-critical faith; rather, it is to allow the emergence of a hermeneutical dialectic of faith and suspicion.

[11] Paul Ricoeur, *Oneself as Another*, trans. Kathleen Blamey (Chicago: Chicago University Press, 1992), p. 22.

Religious readings

In attending to the current state of the interrelationships between literature, criticism, theory and religion, a few additional factors should be borne in mind. The cultural context of English literature makes it impossible to mark a true starting point for the interdisciplinary study of literature and theology. One has only to think of the theological import of Milton's *Paradise Lost*, of the renegotiation of biblical themes in the poetry of William Blake, and of the intellectual interests and achievements of nineteenth-century British thinkers such as Thomas Carlyle, George Eliot and Matthew Arnold, or of the American transcendentalists, Ralph Waldo Emerson, Nathaniel Hawthorne and David Henry Thoreau, to appreciate the difficulty. A theological and biblical tone has persisted in both literature and criticism, and continues even today.

It should also be remembered that certain critics, whose work has not been swayed by winds of theoretical change, have pursued interests in the Bible as literature, and in the influence of the Bible upon English literature. Prominent examples might be C. S. Lewis's essays on the literary impact of the authorised version of the Bible, and on John Bunyan's allegorical vision, as well as the influence of literary study on his apologetical works. More recently Northrop Frye's *The Great Code* (1981) has examined the Bible as a means of decoding all manner of western literary forms. But such approaches, while they have proved stimulating to generations of readers (both those with and those without specific theological interests), have failed to engage with the major theoretical challenges of their day. When, for example, C. S. Lewis wrote of the contrast between New Testament imitative practice and the language of 'creative', 'original' and 'spontaneous' art, his target seems to have been Romantic aesthetics rather than contemporaneous ideas about tradition and the 'escape from personality' propounded by T. S. Eliot.[12] Similarly, Frye's work lacks the critical force to engage with more recent theoretical challenges (such as the deconstruction of theological conceptuality) because, as Robert Detweiler and Vernon K. Robbins have observed, 'he does not consider language itself to be an essential part of the hermeneutical problematic'.[13]

Contemporary criticism of a religious or theological cast can ill afford to ignore the profound upheavals, linguistic, philosophical and cultural, which have defined the contemporary scene, and there is evidence to suggest that thinkers in this interdisciplinary region are no longer content to do so. A recent article by Lloyd Davies in the American journal *Christianity and*

[12] C. S. Lewis, 'Christianity and Literature', *Rehabilitations and Other Essays* (Oxford: Oxford University Press, 1939), pp. 181–197 (p. 191).
[13] Robert Detweiler and Vernon K. Robbins, 'From New Criticism to Poststructuralism: Twentieth-Century Hermeneutics', *Reading the Text*, ed. Stephen Prickett, pp. 225–280 (p. 265).

Literature indicates the extent to which theologically minded critics have begun to engage with contemporary theoretical issues from a religious stand-point.[14] At the same time the fact that these critical modes, directly or indi-rectly, depend upon insights derived from the speculative 'death of God' make such engagements both necessary and extremely difficult. This is true not only of approaches to deconstruction and generic poststructuralism, but also of interpretative negotiations with those other significant movements which have shaped contemporary thought.

Michel Foucault's work on the history of cultural formations and on the epistemological significance of a Nietzschean genealogy of concepts has served to unsettle the foundations of belief upon which an earlier generation of literature and theology scholars were able to rest secure. Jean-François Lyotard's critique of metanarratives – the grand explanatory systems such as political ideologies, philosophical schemata and religious doctrines, used to legitimate knowledge as a graspable whole – has called into question the legit-imacy of interpretations based upon the undifferentiated application of pre-formed beliefs, dogmas and world-views. Jean Baudrillard's diagnosis of postmodern 'hyperreality', in which the 'real' world is replaced by a multi-layered palimpsest of epistemologically unstable simulacra, has disturbed religious belief in the 'world' as the object (or totalisable field) of God's love and of Christ's redemptive work. Of course, such 'postmodern' interpreta-tions of contemporary cultural proclivities are susceptible to counter-argu-ments and critiques from a variety of philosophical positions; even on their own terms they are not necessarily accurate or intelligible accounts of the phenomena they purport to explain. Christopher Norris, in particular, has mounted a sustained critique of postmodern ideas over the last decade, sub-jecting them to stringent examination in the light of rational, materialist thought. Nevertheless, they have had a profound effect on a wide range of lit-erary critical theories and practices.

The deepest theologico-literary appreciation of what these modes of 'post-modern' discourse entail is to be found in the works of those like René Girard, Burton Mack, Robert Detweiler, David Jasper and Stephen D. Moore whose approach to the Bible, culture, art and literature has been materially altered by their encounter with the work of Derrida, de Man, Foucault and others. In writers who have been thus influenced, it is not difficult to detect the proble-matical character which their faith, whether in God, the text, or the reliability of inherited modes of thought, has assumed in the encounter. Thus Moore testifies to a need to question interpretative categories once taken for granted; he is '[c]onvinced now of the necessity of an iconoclastic moment in biblical studies . . . a revision, though not a rejection, of foundational concepts such

---

[14] Lloyd Davies, 'Covenantal Hermeneutics and the Redemption of Theory', *Christianity and Literature* 46.3–4 (Spring–Summer 1997), pp. 1–41.

as Bible and exegesis'.[15] For Jasper too, the Bible needs to be re-read with the clear objective of releasing it from 'the strait-jacket of its sacrality'.[16] Such revisions and re-readings, enabled by the new theoretical models, have been driven by such forces for change as the rise of feminist criticism and the re-emergence of Jewish scholarship and interpretive practice.

While it is not difficult to identify ways in which patriarchal and misogynist values operate in some biblical texts, feminist critics have tended to show more interest in fostering positive, creative engagements with the canon of scripture. This has often meant seeking out the places and spaces in which women can be understood to play a significant role in proceedings, or have a major impact on situations. The work of theologians and critics such as Elizabeth Schussler Fiorenza, Daphne Hampson, Alicia Ostriker, Rosemary Radford Reuther and Phylis Trible, has had the effect of raising consciousness of the extent to which the reading of the Bible within the Christian tradition has tended to play down, sometimes to elide altogether, the role of women as agents as well as sufferers in its pages. Trible has argued that the Bible needs to be re-read today with this 'depatriarchalising principle' in mind.[17]

If male bias has been exposed by feminist readings of the Bible, Christian bias has appeared in sharp relief against the background of re-emergent Jewish scholarship. Susan Handelman's book, *The Slayers of Moses* (1982), drew attention to the fact that Jewish scholars such as Harold Bloom, Jacques Derrida and Geoffrey Hartman had been working with derivatives of Rabbinic exegetical practices and techniques (frowned upon by western practitioners of the so-called 'higher criticism' and its later cognates) for more than a decade. Other scholars, such as Robert Alter, Daniel Boyarin, Harold Fisch and Meir Sternberg have concentrated critical attention on the Hebrew (rather than the Christian) Bible. Boyarin's work, in particular, has made clear the relationship between contemporary notions of intertextuality and midrashic modes of reading. Handelman's book, along with *Midrash and Literature* (1986) – a volume of essays by Jewish scholars – has had a profound impact on the relationship between literary criticism and biblical studies, not only by virtue of its challenge to the hegemony of western, historical modes of interpretation, but also because the work of critics who are both conversant with hebraic reading practices and competent in the biblical languages has exposed the ideological character of interpretations constructed within the Christian tradition.

[15] Stephen D. Moore, *Literary Criticism and the Gospels: The Theoretical Challenge* (New Haven and London: Yale University Press, 1989), p. 176.

[16] David Jasper, *Readings in the Canon of Scripture: Written for our Learning* (London: Macmillan, 1995), p. xv.

[17] Phylis Trible, 'Depatriarchalizing in Biblical Interpretation', *Journal of the American Academy of Religion* 41 (1973), p. 48.

Another factor in this process of change is the burgeoning awareness, in the multi-cultural societies of the west, of non-Judeo-Christian religions and their reading practices. While inter-faith hermeneutical exchanges have yet to produce new theoretical models, some critics within the Christian tradition have begun to acknowledge the need to question the interpretative presuppositions imposed by a specific theology or religious formation. At this point it becomes important to note that so far in this discussion, in the interests of clarity and of brevity, I have elided the difference between 'theology' and 'religion'. This is partly justified by the fact that despite the liberalism suggested by the north American use of the description 'literature and religion' rather than 'literature and theology', both British and American scholars have tended to remain within a (broadly) conservative interpretive framework. But, as I have already intimated, there are exceptions to this rule. The work of Robert Detweiler in north America, and of David Jasper in the United Kingdom has begun the task of rethinking this relationship in a way which promises to break the constraints of Christian, ontotheological criticism in favour of what they jointly refer to as 'religious reading'.

Detweiler's notion of 'religious reading', taken up and developed by Jasper,[18] is characterised by five specific concerns: (1) a stress on friendship over conflict in interpretation, based on the belief that texts do not require a *right* analysis which has to be defended; (2) the communal 'construction of myths and rituals against chaos', which can counteract the failure of the 'rational objectivising mind' to resolve the chaotic potential of reality; (3) communal readings and discussions of texts in an atmosphere of celebration, serving as a counterweight to private thought and writing *about* them; (4) an interest in metaphor (in literary texts) as a mechanism for dealing with a surplus of meaning (relating it to Freud's theory that religion developed out of the need to domesticate behavioural excess by means of ritual and festival); (5) attention to the irreducibility of literary form as a means of rescuing it from the traditional (Aristotelian) mode of analysis by which it has been defined in western criticism. In what might be thought of as an inversion of Eliot's anti-secularist 'principled criticism', religious reading, as theorised and practised by Detweiler and Jasper, stresses the corporeality of texts (rather than seeking out the supernatural in their language and themes) as a way of reading which expresses and celebrates immanence rather than transcendence.

Jasper also emphasises the need for reading practice to resist the exclusivity of older modes of explication for which canonicity and interpretive orthodoxy were so important, and to usher in 'a different kind of politics which is reactive to situations of power and establishment, truly concerned with issues

---

[18] Robert Detweiler, *Breaking the Fall: Religious Readings of Contemporary Fiction* (San Francsico: Harper and Row, 1989); Jasper, *Readings in the Canon of Scripture*.

of freedom, the liberation of values'.[19] Towards the end of 'Religion and Literature' (the essay already quoted), T. S. Eliot expressly derogates those who 'demand more or less drastic changes' in the social order, because they are concerned only 'with changes of a temporal, material, and external nature'. On Eliot's terms, then, the political aspect of religious reading insisted upon by Jasper would be a (deplorable) species of 'secularism'. The reasons for the opening up of this great gulf between Eliot's stress on Christian critical practice as an embattled moral discourse 'shored against [the] ruins' of godless literature, and the contemporary stress on the body and political inclusivity, are explicable, at least in part, as the outcome of the processes which this article has attempted to trace.

These processes have combined to precipitate something of a crisis in the interdisciplinary study of literature and theology. Both terms have become subject to increasingly unanswerable questions of demarcation and definition which complicate any attempt to bring them into fruitful dialogue. Scholars are no longer able to take for granted that 'literature' is a stable, meaningful category, nor that the term 'theology' has an ultimately valid referent. The philosophical and critical death of God and of the author, and the problematising of linguistic reference, along with the increased awareness of global damage and appalling human suffering relayed by ever faster and more efficient telecommunication systems, have combined to return theological speculation to the age-old theme of theodicy. For these reasons it is, perhaps, now more appropriate, following David Jasper's lead, to speak of 'the textuality of theodicy' than of 'literature and theology'.[20]

---

[19] *Ibid.*, p. 137.
[20] David Jasper, *The Study of Literature and Religion* (London: Macmillan, 1989), p. 135.

30

Literary theory, science and philosophy of science

CHRISTOPHER NORRIS

Literary criticism and philosophy of science might appear to have few interests in common. After all, the main concern of philosophy of science – at least on one fairly standard conception – is to offer a justificatory account of how scientific theories achieve progress by providing an ever more detailed descriptive and depth-explanatory knowledge of physical objects, processes and events. Ideas may differ as to just how this should be done, whether (for example) through a 'top-down' method which seeks to derive empirical predictions from high-level covering-law statements or – conversely – through a 'bottom-up' inductive approach which starts out from the empirical data and treats them as the basis for constructing theories of the widest generality and scope.[1] There are many other fundamental issues on which philosophers of science divide, among them the question (first raised by Hume) as regards the validity of inductive arguments in whatever form and the problem of justifying causal explanations (or appeals to putative 'laws of nature') which necessarily transcend the limits of observed regularity or Humean 'constant conjunction'.[2] So philosophy of science is far from presenting a united front in these matters. All the same it may be thought that such issues are worlds apart from the kinds of concern that typically preoccupy literary critics and theorists. For them, what counts is not so much a theory's truth or explanatory power but rather its capacity to capture certain salient aspects of our subjective reponse to literary works, or perhaps – in formalist terms – its ability to locate certain salient attributes of poetic or narrative structure. Such approaches may be thought to give criticism a more 'scientific' status, that is, a claim to utilise methods which emulate those of the physical sciences rather than appealing to the vagaries of mere individual reader-response. But there is still a fairly obvious sense in which literary theory – unlike philosophy of science – has to do with matters of cultural-linguistic or interpretative understanding where such scientific models would seem to have limited applicability.[3]

[1] See for instance Karl Popper, *The Logic of Scientific Discovery*, 2nd edn. (New York: Harper & Row, 1959); Bertrand Russell, *On the Philosophy of Science* (Indianapolis: Bobbs-Merrill, 1965).
[2] David Hume, *A Treatise of Human Nature* (1740), ed. L. A. Selby-Bigge (Oxford: Clarendon Press, 1888). See also David M. Armstrong, *What is a Law of Nature?* (Cambridge: Cambridge University Press, 1983); Nancy Cartwright, *How the Laws of Physics Lie* (Oxford: Oxford University Press, 1983).
[3] See Paisley M. Livingston, *Literary Knowledge: Humanistic Inquiry and the Philosophy of Science* (Ithaca, N.Y.: Cornell University Press, 1988).

At any rate the two disciplines would appear to involve very different criteria of validity and truth. One could perhaps state the difference most clearly by saying that literary criticism always involves a hermeneutic dimension, a point at which – *pace* the formalists and structuralists – issues of applied methodology give way to issues of meaning and interpretation. However this is just where the picture begins to get more complicated with regard to recent developments in philosophy of science from the mid-twentieth century. What has occurred – in brief – is a questioning (some would say a radical transformation) of received disciplinary standards and values whose effect has been to challenge any straightforward acceptance of conventional boundary-lines. On the one hand some philosophers of science have become more receptive to a range of ideas – about paradigm-shifts, the role of metaphor in scientific theories, the 'linguistic construction of reality' and so forth – which are highly congenial to literary theorists with an interest in staking their own special claim to a measure of acquired expertise in such matters.[4] On the other those theorists have detected evidence of a breakdown (or a deep-laid Kuhnian 'crisis') in the discourse of the physical sciences, one that admits of no progress or solution through classically accepted modes of scientific reason. Its symptoms include the above-mentioned openness to new ways of thinking along with the challenge to received ideas of objectivity and truth that is inescapably posed – so they argue – by recent developments in the physical sciences. One may suspect that literary and cultural theorists – especially those of a postmodernist persuasion – have pursued their own agenda by exploiting certain vaguely suggestive analogies with quantum uncertainty, wave/particle dualism, mathematical undecidability, the limits of precise measurement, chaos-theory and so forth.[5] Nor is it by any means clear that Kuhnian or other such paradigm-relativist approaches to the history and philosophy of science have gained the upper hand over rival (realist or causal-explanatory) accounts. But it is certainly the case that debates in this area are a great deal more complex than they must have appeared to anyone writing on the topic a century ago.

Science as threat: Richards to the New Criticism

In the early twentieth century the issue would most likely have been posed in terms deriving from Matthew Arnold and his ideas about the function of poetry (or imaginative literature) in a science-dominated culture. For Arnold,

---

[4] See for instance Bruce Gregory, *Inventing Reality: Physics as Language* (New York: Wiley, 1988); Mary Hesse, *Models and Analogies in Science* (London: Sheed & Ward, 1963).
[5] For a prime exhibit see Jean-François Lyotard, *The Postmodern Condition: A Report on Knowledge*, trans. Geoff Bennington and Brian Massumi (Manchester: Manchester University Press, 1984).

science posed a threat to such values through its relentless disenchantment of the world, its stripping-away of all the comforts and assurances – as well as the tragic intimations – that had once played a role in the human relationship to nature and the physical cosmos.[6] More than that, it raised the distinctly uncomfortable question as to whether poetry had anything significant to say in an age given over to science-based conceptions of knowledge and cultural advancement. Arnold's response – like that of later critics such as T. S. Eliot and I. A. Richards – was to deny that there existed any such relation (and hence any such potential conflict) between imaginative truth and the standards of veridical utterance that applied in the physical sciences. Such truth had to do with the fuller cultivation of human creative and spiritual values and was therefore simply not a candidate for assessment according to those other standards. Eliot continued the Arnoldian line of defence by calling for a 'complete severance' between poetry and belief, such that poetry could minister to needs which were wholly unmet by the material benefits of a modern technocratic culture.[7]

For Richards the issue was in some ways more pressing since his approach to literary criticism was much influenced by the methods of empirical science, especially in the fields of psychology and anthropology.[8] He was also impressed by the logical-positivist case that the only classes of properly meaningful statement were those that expressed either analytic truths (self-evident to reason in virtue of their logical structure) or empirical claims whose content could be verified by means of observation or experiment.[9] Otherwise it was a matter of using language in a non-truth-functional way to convey various attitudes, feelings, sentiments or subjective mind-states. This category would include most of our everyday utterances along with expressions of ethical or aesthetic judgement whose content is merely 'emotive' and in no sense capable of reasoned justification. Richards was therefore driven to conclude that any ostensible statements encountered in a poem must be treated as 'pseudo-statements', since their function was not to assert some verifiable truth-claim but rather to call out a range of complex affective responses in the reader. Only thus – he believed – could poetry be saved from the encroachments of a scientific world-view that could otherwise find no room for such forms of imaginary self-indulgence.

Of course there were other, more assertive or uncompromising modes of response even at the time when Richards was developing his emotivist theory of

---

[6] See especially Matthew Arnold, 'The Study of Poetry', in D. J. Enright and E. de Chickera (eds.), *English Critical Texts* (Oxford: Oxford University Press, 1972), pp. 260–285.

[7] T. S. Eliot, *Selected Essays* (London: Faber, 1951) and *The Use of Poetry and the Use of Criticism*, 2nd edn. (London: Faber, 1964).

[8] I. A. Richards, *Principles of Literary Criticism* (London: Kegan Paul, Trench & Trubner, 1924).

[9] I. A. Richards, *Science and Poetry* (London: Kegan Paul, Trench & Trubner, 1926); rev. and expanded edn., *Sciences and Poetries* (London: Routledge and Kegan Paul, 1970).

poetic meaning. Among them was F. R. Leavis' argument – again much indebted to Arnold – for the absolute centrality of literary studies as the sole means of preserving essential human values and a sense of cultural continuity despite and against the looming threat of 'technologico-Benthamite' civilisation.[10] The American New Critics took over some elements of Richards' thinking – especially his stress on the richness and metaphorical complexity of poetic language – while rejecting what they saw as his overly subjective or psychologistic approach.[11] Rather, those qualities should be located in 'the words on the page', that is to say, in the various closely wrought rhetorical structures – of ambiguity, irony or paradox – which enabled the poem to endure as a 'verbal icon' throughout and despite all the changing vicissitudes of cultural reception or individual reader-response. Only thus (they believed) could poetry fulfil its role as a locus of resistance to the forces of a technocratic reason whose effect was to negate or devalue any mode of experience that could not be reduced to its own narrowly instrumental concepts and categories.

This emphasis on poetry's redemptive power – its capacity to give back 'the world's body' through a jointly intuitive and suprarational appeal beyond the limits of plain-prose sense – went along with the New Critics' agrarian values and their collective identity as a deep-south U.S. literary movement strongly opposed to the 'northern' ethos of modernising secular progress.[12] Those values were premised on a conservative and nostalgic myth of origin where the antebellum South played much the same role as pre-civil war England in Eliot's theory of poetic tradition and his idea of a drastic cultural change – the 'dissociation of sensibility' – which supposedly occurred during the mid seventeenth century.[13] In each case science was equated with the rise of a technocratic ethos whose effect was to impose a rigid divorce between intellect and emotion, thought and sensibility, conceptual and intuitive modes of understanding. In each case, moreover, the response was to elaborate a conception of poetic meaning that removed it from the realm of rational prose statement and located its value in a separate domain where altogether different criteria applied. But there was still a broad acceptance – in Eliot as in Richards – that the scientific way of knowing had the kind of self-evident truth or validity on its own terms that required literary critics to make peace with it as best they could.

[10] F. R. Leavis, *For Continuity* (Cambridge: Minority Press, 1933) and *Revaluation: Tradition and Development in English Poetry* (London: Chatto & Windus, 1936).

[11] See for instance Cleanth Brooks, *Modern Poetry and the Tradition* (Chapel Hill: University of North Carolina Press, 1939) and *The Well Wrought Urn: Studies in the Structure of Poetry* (New York: Harcourt Brace, 1947); John Crowe Ranson, *The World's Body* (New York: Scribner, 1938) and *The New Criticism* (New York: New Directions, 1941); W. K. Wimsatt, *The Verbal Icon: Studies in the Meaning of Poetry* (Lexington: University of Kentucky Press, 1954).

[12] See especially John Fekete, *The Critical Twilight: Explorations in the Ideology of Anglo-American Literary Theory from Eliot to McLuhan* (London: Routledge & Kegan Paul, 1977).

[13] T. S. Eliot, 'Tradition and the Individual Talent' and 'The Metaphysical Poets', in *Selected Essays*, pp. 3–11 and 241–250.

Post-empiricist directions: the 'hermeneutic turn'

This will all seem very remote to anyone who has kept up with developments in literary theory and philosophy of science over the past two decades. One measure of the changed situation is the sheer unlikelihood that any present-day literary theorist would feel such a need to accommodate their thinking to the presumed self-evidence of progress and achievement in the physical sciences. This change has come about for two main reasons, having to do with recent (post-1950) developments in philosophy of science and with the transformation of literary theory into a discipline far less prone to cast itself in a defensive or supplicant role *vis-à-vis* the claims of scientific method. Firstly, logical positivism ran into various problems, among them the fact that its central doctrine – the verification principle – could not be specified in terms that met its own criteria for genuine (truth-evaluable) statements, namely that these should be either logically self-evident or empirically verifiable. This case was pressed further by W. V. Quine in his landmark essay 'Two Dogmas of Empiricism' which denied the very possibility of distinguishing analytic statements (or 'truths of reason') from synthetic statements that asserted some claim with regard to contingent matters of fact or empirical truths-of-observation.[14] Thus, according to Quine, it is an error to think that observations, predictions, inductive hypotheses, etc., can be checked off one by one against the evidence and then brought under some covering-law theory whose statements can likewise be confirmed or disconfirmed by appeal to the relevant items of empirical data.[15] Rather such statements must be treated holistically, that is, as deriving their truth-evaluable content from the entire 'web' or 'fabric' of interconnected beliefs which forms the currency of scientific knowledge at any given time.

In this case there is no statement that might not conceivably be subject to revision under pressure from 'recalcitrant' evidence, whether at the outermost edges of the fabric where beliefs take shape under the barrage of incoming sensory stimuli, or even at the core where reasoning is constrained by what presently count as logical 'laws of thought'. For we can always conceive of circumstances in which we might be forced to revise those laws, as for instance – Quine's example – with regard to quantum physics and the proposal for suspending certain axioms of logic in order to accommodate classically unthinkable phenomena such as wave/particle dualism. And conversely, there is no observation-statement – no statement of empirical fact – that can stand proof against revision should it come into conflict with firmly entrenched beliefs or

---

[14] W. V. Quine, 'Two Dogmas of Empiricism', in *From a Logical Point of View*, 2nd edn. (Cambridge, Mass.: Harvard University Press, 1961), pp. 20–46.

[15] Quine's argument is directed most explicitly against the version of this logical-empiricist theory proposed in a number of influential works by the philosopher Rudolf Carnap. See especially Carnap, *The Logical Structure of the World and Pseudo-Problems in Philosophy*, trans. R. George (Berkeley and Los Angeles: University of California Press, 1967).

theoretical commitments. That is to say, we still have the option of devising some different (theory-preservative) construal of the evidence currently to hand, perhaps by adducing perceptual distortion or the limits of our best (even if technologically assisted) observational powers. From which it follows that theories will always be 'underdetermined' by the best available evidence, while that evidence will always be 'theory-laden' insofar as it entails a certain (potentially challengeable) range of beliefs, hypotheses, working assumptions, ontological commitments and so forth. Thus, according to Quine, the 'unit of empirical significance' for scientific theory-assessment is the entire existing body of beliefs held true at any given time, rather than a well-defined subset which can be tested (so to speak) in safe isolation from other beliefs that strike us as belonging to different parts of the fabric. For however well-attested the truth-claim in question – whether by the ground-rules of logical reason or by strength of empirical warrant – there remains the possibility of adducing auxiliary hypotheses that can be shown to play a role in its acceptance and hence to leave room for some alternative construal that would challenge its seeming self-evidence. Thus (to repeat) there is no statement that can be held immune from revision should one decide – on pragmatic grounds or in the interests of conserving some cherished theory – to meet the challenge of recalcitrant evidence by redistributing predicates or truth-values over the fabric as a whole.

I have discussed Quine's essay at length because it signalled a change in the dominant way of thinking not only about epistemology and philosophy of science but also with regard to the relationship between those disciplines and other fields of enquiry, among them literary criticism and the human or social sciences. After all, some version of the holistic or contextualist principle had long been standard among literary theorists – from the Romantics to the New Critics – who argued that poetry could not be analysed in reductive (atomistic) terms but should rather be treated as the product of a complex interplay between various organically related elements of meaning, structure and form. This idea becomes prominent in Richards' middle-period writings where he abandons the theory of poetic 'pseudo-statements' and adopts a more hermeneutic approach where words acquire meaning very largely through a process of reciprocal adjustment or inter-definition within various contexts of usage.[16] There was also an emergent sense, among literary critics, that science no longer presented a threat through its claim to monopolise the discourse of reason and truth, or its sheer self-evidence as a mode of knowledge with unrivalled descriptive, predictive and causal-explanatory power. As philosophers of science (or some of them) began to question such claims, so literary theorists became more confident in asserting that *their* kinds of knowledge – interpretative, hermeneutic, narrative, metaphorical, semantically overdetermined

---

[16] See for instance I. A. Richards, *Interpretation in Teaching* (New York: Harcourt Brace, 1938).

– should in no way be viewed as generically inferior or as requiring some kind of special defence when compared with those of the natural sciences.

This change had various other contributory sources, among them Thomas Kuhn's widely influential theory of scientific paradigm-change.[17] Kuhn followed Quine in adopting a thoroughly holistic approach, in stressing the underdetermination of theory by evidence and the theory-laden character of observation-statements, and in relativising 'truth' to the entire going range of beliefs-held-true at any given time. His approach also found support from developments in philosophy of language, especially the idea (much influenced by Wittgenstein's later writing) that there existed as many legitimate ways of making sense as there existed language-games or cultural 'forms of life', all of them perfectly intelligible by their own immanent criteria and none of them possessing a privileged claim to lay down terms or validity-conditions by which others should be understood.[18] Thus literary critics – along with sociologists, historians, ethical theorists, aestheticians, theologians and others – were simply mistaken if they felt any need to defend or justify their claims vis-à-vis those of logic or the natural sciences. Rather they should see that this compulsion came about through a false and reductive understanding of language, one that Wittgenstein had himself subscribed to (albeit with certain significant reservations) in his own early thinking but had then shown up as the merest of old-style positivist illusions.[19]

For some – including disciples of Leavis – the chief lessons to be learned from Wittgenstein were the autonomy of literary-critical judgement as an evaluative discourse strictly unbeholden to any such extraneous standards and (following from this) the irrelevance of literary theory as a pseudo-discipline that aped the natural sciences in a different field of study. At about the same time – from the early 1960s on – there was a growing awareness among Anglophone critics of the various hermeneutically inspired theories of language and interpretation whose sources lay in the mainly German tradition of thought descending from Schleiermacher and Dilthey to thinkers such as Heidegger and Gadamer.[20] Here again the chief result was to encourage a less defensive, indeed a more self-assertive attitude which rejected any notion of physical science as a paradigm of method or a privileged truth-telling discourse, and which stressed the various background contexts – of language, culture, tradition, life-form, communal 'horizons' of belief – that were

---

[17] Thomas S. Kuhn, *The Structure of Scientific Revolutions*, 2nd edn. (Chicago: University of Chicago Press, 1970).

[18] Ludwig Wittgenstein, *Philosophical Investigations*, trans. G. E. M. Anscombe (Oxford: Blackwell, 1958).

[19] See especially Peter Winch, *The Idea of a Social Science and its Relation to Philosophy* (London: Routledge & Kegan Paul, 1958).

[20] See Kurt Müller-Vollmer, *The Hermeneutics Reader* (Oxford: Blackwell, 1986); Richard E. Palmer, *Hermeneutics: Interpretation Theory in Schleiermacher, Dilthey, Heidegger, and Gadamer* (Evanston: Northwestern University Press, 1969).

presupposed by every kind of knowledge, scientific knowledge included. Heidegger's influence has no doubt been strongest in promoting the view of technology as a form of instrumental or means-end reasoning that is deeply complicit with the history of 'western metaphysics', that is, the legacy of philosophic thought (from ancient Greece to the present) which ignores the primordial question of Being through a relentless will to extend its conceptual grasp over nature and humankind alike.[21] Thus Heidegger's critique of techno-scientific modes of knowledge goes along with the appeal to poetry – especially in his later writings – as a language that can still vouchsafe such truth through the power of 'unconcealment' (or authentic revelation) to which it alone has moments of privileged access.[22]

Hence the distinctly hermeneutic 'turn' that has characterised a good deal of recent work in those quarters of Anglo-American philosophy of science where the continental influence has been most marked. Hence also the idea that this signals a decisive shift away from the predominance not only of the physical sciences with regard to the humanities and social-science disciplines but also of science-based epistemologies or theories of meaning and truth in relation to other, more interpretative or hermeneutically oriented kinds of approach. The extreme position here is that adopted by a 'strong'-descriptivist like Richard Rorty who would urge that science can best make progress by having the courage of its most inventive or adventurous metaphors and rejecting the idea of truth as a matter of literal 'correspondence' with the way things notionally stand 'in reality'.[23] Thus there is no rule of method (inductive, hypothetico-deductive, causal-explanatory or whatever) which constitutes a canon of valid scientific reasoning and which thereby draws a demarcation-line between genuine science and 'knowledge' that cannot aspire to such status. On the contrary: what occurs when science undergoes some radical Kuhnian paradigm-shift is very like what transpires when a strong-willed revisionist interpreter – say Blake on Milton or Harold Bloom on the entire western canon – comes along to transform our preexisting sense of literary history and the place of various poets within it. In both cases the result is a radical Nietzschean transvaluation of values that leaves nothing untouched since it changes all the organising concepts (or the dominant metaphors and narratives, as Rorty would have it) by which we had hitherto sought to impose some order on the otherwise inchoate flux of experience and memory.

Thus science does best when it gives up the attachment to old methods and

---

[21] See Martin Heidegger, *The Question Concerning Technology and Other Essays*, trans. William Lovitt (New York: Harper & Row, 1977); also Michael E. Zimmerman, *Heidegger's Confrontation with Modernity: Technology, Politics, Art* (Bloomington, Ind.: Indiana University Press, 1991).

[22] See especially Heidegger, *On the Way to Language*, trans. Peter D. Hertz (New York: Harper & Row, 1971).

[23] See Richard Rorty, *Consequences of Pragmatism* (Brighton: Harvester, 1982).

paradigms – like those which prevail in periods of Kuhnian 'normal' enquiry – and ventures into new 'revolutionary' seas of thought. We should likewise jettison the old idea (a throwback to the heyday of logical positivism) that the various disciplines can be firmly ranked on a 'hard-to-soft' scale with physics at the top, followed by chemistry and biology, and then descending *via* anthropology, sociology and psychology to such ill-defined subject-areas as ethics, aesthetics and literary criticism. The middle-range disciplines on this scale can in turn be subdivided – so the argument goes – to the extent that they incline toward either an empirical (scientific) methodology or a purely interpretative (hence subjectivist and scientifically vacuous) mode of understanding.[24] Such was the view propounded by advocates of the 'unity of science' movement, a programme that achieved wide acceptance during the 1940s and 50s, though thereafter increasingly subject to attack not only from disgruntled workers at the 'lower' (humanities) end of the scale but also from those – including biologists and chemists – who challenged the assumed priority of physics as the most fundamental branch of the natural sciences.[25] What comes across strikingly in Rorty's case is the reaction against such thinking that has taken hold in at least some quarters of literary academe. 'Literary', that is, in the sense that Rorty, although trained as an academic philosopher – indeed, one whose early work stood squarely within the mainstream analytic tradition – now prefers to be thought of as a literary critic or as a cultural conversationalist with no allegiance to those old (science-led) ideas of analytic rigour, conceptual precision or constructive problem-solving power. Thus he seizes every chance to make the case for privileging metaphor over concept, rhetoric over logic, narrative understanding over modes of rational reconstruction and hermeneutical (or strong-descriptivist) approaches over anything that resembles the deluded quest for an objective knowledge transcending the horizon of our present-day cultural needs and interests. This in turn works out – at its most provocative – as the claim that (say) nuclear physicists or molecular biologists might have more to learn in the way of new and productive metaphors not from their own intradisciplinary colleagues but rather from poets, novelists, or literary critics.[26]

I have cited Rorty as one (albeit extreme) example of the way that thinking can go under the influence of various contemporary schools of thought such as hermeneutics, Nietzschean genealogy, poststructuralism, postmodernism

[24] See Otto Neurath, Rudolf Carnap and Charles Morris (eds.), *Foundations of the Unity of Science: Towards an International Encyclopedia of Unified Science* (Chicago: University of Chicago Press, 1955–70); also Carnap, *The Unity of Science*, ed. Max Black (Bristol: Thoemmes Press, 1995) and Robert L. Causley, *Unity of Science* (Dordrecht: D. Reidel, 1977).

[25] For a sceptical discussion of the 'unity of science' programme, see John Dupré, *The Disorder of Things: Metaphysical Foundations of the Disunity of Science* (Cambridge, Mass.: Harvard University Press, 1993).

[26] See especially Rorty, 'Texts and Lumps', in *Objectivity, Relativism, and Truth* (Cambridge: Cambridge University Press, 1991), pp. 78–92.

and the 'strong' programme in sociology of knowledge or science studies. What these all have in common is their tendency toward a low valuation of scientific method and a high valuation of the power of language, discourse or narrative to shape our very sense of what counts as reality or truth.[27] Hence the sharp contrast between present-day sceptical-relativist approaches to the sociology of science and Robert Merton's pioneering studies in the field which took for granted such traditional scientific values as the quest for truth and the striving for rational consensus among a suitably qualified community of thinkers with shared interests and commitments.[28] Postmodernist thinkers often claim that science has itself now moved on to a stage far beyond those classical certitudes, a stage where – as Jean-François Lyotard argues – scientific research, 'by concerning itself with such things as undecidables, the limits of precise control, conflicts characterised by incomplete information, "*fracta*", catastrophes, and pragmatic paradoxes . . . is theorizing its own evolution as discontinuous, catastrophic, non-rectifiable and paradoxical'.[29] Such – we are told – is the current postmodern condition as it pertains to the natural sciences, physics in particular, as likewise to every other form of knowledge in a period when 'constative' (truth-apt) standards of assertoric warrant have given way to 'performative' criteria, that is, to the sheerly pragmatic measure of how far theories or research programmes can win support in virtue of their proven suasive-rhetorical power. In which case *dissensus* – rather than rational consensus – is the mark of a vibrant scientific culture which prizes the multiplicity of viewpoints or theories on offer and which strives so far as possible not to impose some crampingly orthodox normative conception of objectivity, method and truth.

No doubt the above-cited passage from Lyotard is an extreme instance of the kind. Nevertheless it has the merit – as with Rorty – of showing just how far such arguments can be pushed in order to challenge the kinds of epistemic privilege standardly accorded to the physical sciences. Also it suggests that postmodernism is still fighting old battles, not least with a bugbear image of scientific method whose source – so far as one can tell from Lyotard's pronouncements – is the positivist idea of truth and knowledge as consisting in a straightforward one-to-one correspondence between veridical statements and discrete items of empirical fact. In other words things have not moved on quite so far as might be supposed from a text-book survey of literary theory from Richards to Lyotard.

[27] On the 'strong programme', see for instance Barry Barnes, *About Science* (Oxford: Blackwell, 1985); David Bloor, *Knowledge and Social Imagery* (London: Routledge & Kegan Paul, 1976); Steve Fuller, *Social Epistemology* (Bloomington, Ind.: Indiana University Press, 1988); Steve Woolgar (ed.), *Knowledge and Reflexivity: New Frontiers in the Sociology of Knowledge* (London: Sage, 1988).
[28] See for instance Robert K. Merton, *Science, Technology and Society in Seventeenth Century England* (New York: Howard Fertig, 1970).
[29] Lyotard, *The Postmodern Condition*, p. 112.

Literary criticism and the new physics

Of course there is a sense in which certain developments during this century lend credence to the notion of physical science as having entered a new and problematical phase where a good many hitherto well-established values, methods and beliefs are henceforth open to question. Relativity-theory is most often invoked in this context although it is not so often acknowledged that Einstein's was in most respects a 'classical' theory, one that denied any ultimate rest-frame for observed values of position or momentum but which none the less took the speed of light as an absolute constant by which to assign such values in objective (non-observer-relative) terms.[30] Thus there is room for doubt when literary critics draw comparisons between Einstein's conceptual revolution and the kinds of development that were taking place in the period of high literary modernism that produced such multiplex spatio-temporal constructs as Eliot's *The Waste Land*, Joyce's *Ulysses* or Pound's *Cantos*.

Analogies with quantum mechanics are perhaps more to the point since it is here, in the microphysical domain, that science has posed its greatest challenge to classical (post-Newtonian) conceptions of reality, objectivity and truth.[31] Indeed it was Einstein's steadfast refusal to accept the dictates of orthodox quantum thinking that drove his persistent – some would say stubborn – quest for an alternative account compatible with the framework of relativity-theory and with a realist construal of the evidence.[32] Thus, in Einstein's view, the standard interpretation was self-evidently 'incomplete' since it claimed no more than empirical (predictive-observational) adequacy, and expressly renounced any aim to describe the reality behind quantum appearances. Moreover, it entailed certain highly paradoxical consequences – among them several placidly endorsed by Lyotard in the passage quoted above – which Einstein considered an affront to scientific reason and as further evidence that the authorised version was merely a stopgap theory adopted for want of anything better. Among them was the idea of superposed quantum-states that were somehow 'collapsed', that is, reduced to one or another determinate (wave or particle) form only through the act of observation; Heisenberg's famous uncertainty-principle concerning the limits of precise measurement at a subatomic level; and, above all, the postulate of superluminal (faster-than-light) 'entanglement' between particles that had once

[30] Albert Einstein, *Relativity: The Special and the General Theories* (London: Methuen, 1954).

[31] For some good introductory accounts see Paul Davies, *Other Worlds* (London: Dent, 1980); John Gribbin, *In Search of Schrödinger's Cat: Quantum Physics and Reality* (New York: Bantam Books, 1984).

[32] See Niels Bohr, 'Discussion with Einstein on Epistemological Problems in Atomic Physics', in P. A. Schilpp (ed.), *Albert Einstein: Philosopher-Scientist* (La Salle, Ill.: Open Court, 1969), pp. 199–241; A. Einstein, B. Podolsky and N. Rosen, 'Can Quantum-Mechanical Description of Reality be Considered Complete?', in *Physical Review*, ser. 2, vol. XLVII (1935), pp. 777–80; also, for a detailed and balanced assessment of Einstein's case, Arthur Fine, *The Shaky Game: Einstein, Realism and Quantum Theory* (Chicago: University of Chicago Press, 1986).

interacted and thereafter moved apart to a large (maybe astronomical) distance of spacetime separation.[33] This is clearly not the place for a detailed discussion of the complex scientific and philosophical issues raised by quantum mechanics.[34] What is worth remarking is the readiness of many literary and cultural theorists to seize upon its more paradoxical or even bizarre implications in order to enlist 'scientific' support for their own vaguely kindred claims with regard to the demise of realist world-views and the supersession of those old 'grand narratives' (of reason, progress, truth at the end of enquiry) that supposedly went along with them. Such verdicts may be thought at very least premature given that there exist alternative construals of quantum mechanics which entail nothing like so radical a break with just about every preexisting notion of scientific truth and method.[35]

Other critics – William Empson among them, as early as 1930 in his classic *Seven Types of Ambiguity* – have shown a greater knowledge of the relevant scientific theories and responded to them in a far more intelligent, less sweeping and doctrinaire fashion. Thus Empson has some speculative passages discussing Heisenberg's Uncertainty-Principle in relation to the issue of just how far poetic meaning can be thought of as objectively 'there' in the words on the page, or whether it should rather be viewed as a product of the complex reciprocal exchange between text and reader.[36] I. A. Richards – Empson's tutor at Cambridge – started out (as we have seen) by espousing an emotivist theory of poetic language under pressure from logical positivism and its hardline verificationist doctrine. Later on, however, he found a way forward from that unsatisfactory position in Niels Bohr's philosophy of 'complementarity', that is, the idea that certain quantum phenomena – such as wave/particle dualism – require that one adopt two different (complementary) descriptive frameworks or conceptual schemes which are mutually exclusive yet noncontradictory and each borne out by the empirical evidence.[37] Like Bohr himself, Richards thought that this theory held the answer to problems far beyond the

---

[33] See Tim Maudlin, *Quantum Non-Locality and Relativity: Metaphysical Intimations of Modern Science* (Oxford: Blackwell, 1993); and Michael Redhead, *Incompleteness, Nonlocality and Realism: A Prolegomenon to the Philosophy of Quantum Mechanics* (Oxford: Clarendon Press, 1987).

[34] See for instance Christopher Norris, *Quantum Theory and the Flight From Realism: Philosophical Responses to Quantum Mechanics* (London: Routledge, 2000).

[35] See especially David Bohm, *Causality and Chance in Modern Physics* (London: Routledge & Kegan Paul, 1957); David Bohm and B. J. Hiley, *The Undivided Universe: An Ontological Interpretation of Quantum Theory* (London: Routledge, 1993); Peter Holland, *The Quantum Theory of Motion: An Account of the de Broglie-Bohm Causal Interpretation of Quantum Mechanics* (Cambridge: Cambridge University Press, 1993).

[36] William Empson, *Seven Types of Ambiguity* (1930), 3rd edn., revised (Harmondsworth: Penguin, 1961), pp. 248ff.

[37] See Niels Bohr, *Atomic Physics and Human Knowledge* (New York: Wiley, 1958) and *The Philosophical Writings of Niels Bohr*, 3 vols. (Woodbridge, Conn.: Ox Bow Press, 1987); also Henry J. Folse, *The Philosophy of Niels Bohr: The Framework of Complementarity* (Amsterdam: North-Holland, 1985).

field of theoretical physics, including those that were often encountered in the social, ethical, political and (not least) aesthetic domains. Thus it promised to resolve such longstanding quandaries as the freewill-determinism issue, the fact/value dichotomy, and – most crucially in this context – the place of literary meaning and imaginative experience in a culture so largely given over to science-led conceptions of knowledge and truth.[38] Bohr's arguments are often rather fuzzily expressed and Richards' writing has nothing like the sheer analytical acuity of Empson on quantum-related themes. All the same it fares well by comparison with the current postmodernist fashion for talk about quantum physics as marking the demise of such old-fashioned 'enlightenment' values as truth, reason and reality.

Gaston Bachelard: metaphor, criticism and theory-change

It is worth noting here that there exists a strong tradition in French philosophy of science which goes clean against any stereotyped idea of Anglo-French intellectual and cultural differences. It can best be brought out by reference to Gaston Bachelard's conception of scientific paradigm-change and of the role in that process which has often been played by metaphors, analogies and modes of 'naive' (anthropomorphic or image-based) thinking.[39] For Bachelard, science can no more dispense with such heuristic aids and devices than it can dispense with the labour of conceptual analysis – of ongoing 'rectification and critique' – whereby they are progressively developed and refined to the stage of more adequate scientific grasp. This is what Bachelard means by his phrase 'applied rationalism' (*le rationalisme appliqué*): a process of rigorously critical reflection on the sources of scientific knowledge which allows for the role of concepts, intuitions, thought-processes, etc., but which treats them as always susceptible to change – sometimes to radical transformation – under newly emergent conditions of scientific practice. In part this is a matter of philosophy's need to catch up with developments (such as non-Euclidean geometry, relativity theory and quantum mechanics) that present large obstacles to any theory based on Cartesian – or indeed Kantian – notions of a self-assured access to truth through the mind's innate powers of intuitive-conceptual grasp. But it can also be seen as rejecting the idea – the typically 'analytic' idea – that philosophy of science should always be conducted in the mode of 'rational reconstruction', that is, by applying covering-law theories or hypothetico-deductive principles that are answerable only to our present

---

[38] See I. A. Richards, *Speculative Instruments* (London: Routledge & Kegan Paul, 1955) and *Complementarities: Uncollected Essays and Reviews*, ed. J. P. Russo (Cambridge, Mass.: Harvard University Press, 1976).

[39] Gaston Bachelard, *La formation de l'ésprit scientifique* (Paris: Corti, 1938); *Le rationalisme appliqué* (Paris: Presses Universitaires de France, 1949).

best standards of rational enquiry, and which need not at any point go by way of whatever is supposed to have occurred in the mind of this or that enquirer.

Thus knowledge could never have advanced beyond the stage of naive sense-certainty were it not for this capacity of critical thought to revise and modify its own preconceptions in response to new challenges or obstacles. These latter may arise in the form of anomalous experimental findings or theories that are based on the best current evidence but which then turn out to entail problematical or strongly counter-intuitive consequences. Or again, they may result from the kind of 'internal' blockage that occurs when thought is too rigidly bound by certain fixed habits of belief. Such would be, for instance, the concepts supposedly self-evident to reason that Descartes took as his epistemological anchor-point, or primordial intuitions (such as those of the classical Newtonian space-time framework) which Kant considered to be given *a priori* as the very condition of possibility for human knowledge and experience. This is not to deny that metaphors and images can play a role – sometimes a decisive role – in the progress toward more adequate scientific concepts. Bachelard's work itself provides many striking examples of the way that such advances in knowledge come about through the process of ongoing rectification and critique. However, that process cannot be understood unless in the context of a jointly historical and epistemological enquiry into the various episodes which constitute its development to date. This in turn requires that it take due account of the various 'obstacles' that thought confronted as well as the various means through which it overcame them, whether by replacing intuitive metaphors with more adequate concepts, refining certain useful or productive metaphors to a higher degree of conceptual precision, or – in some cases – adopting heuristic metaphors that go beyond the limits of existing (inadequate) descriptive or explanatory concepts. Which is also to say that philosophy of science must always at some point concern itself with issues of epistemology or with the genesis of scientific theories through acts of consciousness that mark a definite stage of advance in the production of scientific knowledge. And this despite Bachelard's insistence that ultimately the truth of theories is in no way dependent on their intuitive appeal, their (supposed) *a priori* warrant or other such epistemological criteria. For it is precisely his point that some of the most signal advances in fields such as geometry, mathematics and subatomic physics have been achieved *despite and against* what appeared self-evident to previous enquirers. Indeed, those beliefs may remain self-evident at a commonsense-intuitive level and yet have been rendered scientifically obsolete through just this kind of critical-evaluative process.

Thus Bachelard firmly rejects the 'ornamentalist' notion of metaphor and stresses its role as a vital resource in the acquisition of scientific knowledge. However he also insists (unlike Rorty and the current 'strong' textualists) that scientific metaphors are always open to criticism since they can work just as

often to retard that process as to bring about new discoveries. So it is wrong –
explanatorily vacuous – to treat them as so many optional 'language-games'
or Rortian 'final vocabularies', invented mainly out of boredom with old ways
of talking and therefore best dropped as soon as they become literalised in the
discourse of 'normal', workaday science. For this is to abandon every last distinction between concept and metaphor, knowledge and belief, progressive
and degenerating research-programmes, or scientific truth – as defined by our
current best theories and methods of enquiry – and what once passed for scientific truth according to some then-prevalent way of thinking. It is an
outlook that falls in readily with the so-called 'strong' programme in sociology of knowledge and with other movements of thought – such as its offshoot
discipline of 'science studies' – which likewise operate on a strict principle of
parity as between various belief-systems past and present, scientific and non-
scientific, or 'true' and 'false' according to our own (culture-specific) lights.[40]

Bachelard's thought has been subject to various revisionist readings – or
sometimes downright misconstruals – in its course of migration from philosophy and history of science to critical, cultural and literary theory. For Louis
Althusser, seeking to justify the claims of Marxist 'theoretical practice', it
offered the idea of a decisive epistemological break (*coupure epistemolo-
gique*) between the realm of ideological (imaginary) misrecognition and the
standpoint of a genuine Marxist 'science' that would enable the theorist to
achieve at least a momentary view from outside that realm.[41] Thus
Althussser's project of (so-called) 'structural Marxism' preserved this main
feature of Bachelard's critical epistemology even though it involved some considerable stretching of terms – 'science' among them – and also gave rise to
many other problems for his Marxist disciples and exegetes. In Foucault's
early work, conversely, the notion of 'epistemological breaks' took on such a
wide and loose application that it became pretty much synymous with Kuhn's
idea of 'paradigm-change'.[42] That is to say, it is envisaged as a large-scale shift
of interpretative framework occurring at certain vaguely defined historical
junctures for no specifiable reason and amounting to a kind of random drift
which somehow affects all the discourses of knowledge from one *episteme* (or
order of knowledge and representation) to the next. Foucault's main interest
in *The Order of Things* is directed toward those middle-range disciplines on
the standard 'hard-to-soft' scale – biology (or the life-sciences), economics (or

---

[40] See for instance Barry Barnes, *About Science* (Oxford: Blackwell, 1985); David Bloor,
Knowledge and Social Imagery (London: Routledge & Kegan Paul, 1976); Steven Shapin and
Simon Shaffer, *Leviathan and the Air-Pump: Hobbes, Boyle, and the Experimental Life*
(Princeton: Princeton University Press, 1985).

[41] Louis Althusser, *For Marx*, trans. Ben Brewster (London: Allen Lane, 1969); *Philosophy and
the Spontaneous Philosophy of the Scientists, and Other Essays*, trans. Gregory Elliott
(London: Verso, 1991).

[42] Michel Foucault, *The Order of Things: An Archaeology of the Human Sciences*, trans Alan
Sheridan (London: Tavistock, 1970).

the earlier 'analysis of wealth'), sociology, psychology, philology, historiography – which have undergone various marked transformations in their scope of 'legitimate' enquiry, and whose scientific status has often been a matter of methodological dispute. Still it is strongly implied that this approach would have equal validity if extended to disciplines, such as physics or chemistry, that are thought to occupy the 'hard' (objective) end of the scale. Thus Foucault comes out largely in agreement with Kuhn – and deeply at odds with Bachelard – on the 'radical' (world-transformative) nature of paradigm-shifts and the lack of any rational standards or criteria for judgements of trans-paradigm scientific progress.

Crossing the disciplines

In this chapter I have focused mainly on prominent trends and movements which have marked various stages in the shifting relationship between science, philosophy of science and literary theory. That is to say, I have singled out certain major issues and representative viewpoints which I hope will serve as a route-map for readers largely unfamiliar with the territory. Of course this has meant leaving out a great range of more specialised thematic or period-specific studies which otherwise – given more space – would have merited inclusion here. Thus, for instance, there has been some innovative work on the rise of early modern science in relation to changing modes of literary and cultural production;[43] on the rhetoric of empiricism and the problems it encountered in attempting to naturalise its own select range of favoured representational devices;[44] on the advent of field-theoretical concepts (from Faraday to Maxwell and beyond) with reference to ideas of literary genre and spatio-temporal form;[45] on the impact of Darwinian-evolutionary thinking as displayed by various nineteenth-century poets and novelists, not only at a straightforward thematic level but also through organicist metaphors of growth and development;[46] on the history of optics (whether theories of vision or technological adjuncts like the microscope and telescope) in com-

---

[43] For extensive documentation see Walter Schatzberg, Ronald A. Waite and Jonathan K. Jackson (eds.), *The Relations of Literature and Science: An Annotated Bibliography of Scholarship, 1880–1980* (New York: Modern Language Association of America, 1987).

[44] See especially Andrew Benjamin, Geoffrey N. Cantor and John R. Christie (eds.), *The Figural and the Literal: Problems in the History of Science and Philosophy, 1630–1800* (Manchester: Manchester University Press, 1987).

[45] See for instance Gillian Beer, *Open Fields: Science in Cultural Encounter* (Oxford: Clarendon Press, 1996); N. Katherine Hayles, *The Cosmic Web: Scientific Field Models and Narrative strategies in the Twentieth Century* (Ithaca, N.Y.: Cornell University Press, 1984).

[46] Gillian Beer, *Darwin's Plots: Evolutionary Narrative in Darwin, George Eliot and Nineteenth-Century Fiction* (London: Routledge & Kegan Paul, 1983); George Levine, *Darwin and the Novelists: Patterns of Science in Victorian Fiction* (Cambridge, Mass.: Harvard University Press, 1988).

parison to shifts in narrative viewpoint or authorial perspective;[47] on chaos-theory as a source of suggestive metaphors for the tension between orderly and disorderly elements in the dynamics of literary response;[48] and on the role of metaphor and figural language more generally as a point of intersection or productive exchange between literary and scientific modes of knowledge.[49] Needless to say this amounts to no more than a brief and selective survey of work that covers so vast a range of historical and disciplinary subject-areas.

In some cases that work has involved a traditional kind of comparative scholarship which adopts a fairly standard source-documentary or history-of-ideas approach and which thus – for better or worse – remains little affected by recent theoretical debates. More often, however, those debates have left their mark through the greater confidence of literary critics in challenging established disciplinary bounds while also (paradoxically enough) evincing a far greater degree of caution with regard to the status or authority of their own claims. Yet perhaps this is not so surprising after all. For a similar point could just as well be made about the most advanced fields of current scientific research, prone as they are – most strikingly in the case of quantum mechanics – to generate problems of conceptual-interpretative grasp in direct proportion to the progress achieved in terms of empirical warrant or predictive power. That literary and cultural theorists are so much at home with these problems is perhaps one reason why they have taken so readily to the kinds of debate thrown up by the demise of logical positivism and the advent of post-Kuhnian philosophy of science. Whether this will turn out, with benefit of hindsight, to have been an unusually protracted period of Kuhnian pre-revolutionary 'crisis' is among the questions that will no doubt preoccupy contributors to some future edition of the Cambridge *History*.

---

[47] For a classic early study, see Marjorie Hope Nicolson, *Science and Imagination* (Ithaca, N.Y.: Great Seal Books, 1956).

[48] See James Gleick, *Chaos: Making a New Science* (New York: Viking, 1987); also Harriett Hawkins, *Strange Attractors: Literature, Culture and Chaos Theory* (Hemel Hempstead: Harvester Wheatsheaf, 1995); N. Katherine Hayles, *Chaos Bound: Orderly Disorder in Contemporary Literature and Science* (Ithaca, N.Y.: Cornell University Press, 1990); N. Katherine Hayles (ed.), *Chaos and Order: Complex Dynamics in Literature and Science* (Chicago: University of Chicago Press, 1991).

[49] Andrew Ortony (ed.), *Metaphor and Thought* (Cambridge: Cambridge University Press, 1979).

Bibliography

Historicism and historical criticism

Primary sources

Adorno, Theodor W., *The Culture Industry*, ed. J. Bernstein, London: Routledge, 1991.

Aristotle, *The Poetics*, trans. and introd. Malcolm Heath, London: Penguin, 1996.

Benjamin, Walter, *Illuminations*, trans. Harry Zorn, foreword by Hannah Arendt, London: Fontana, 1973.

Bossuet, J.-B., *Discourse on Universal History* (1681), trans. E. Forster, introd. Leonard Krieger, Chicago and London: University of Chicago Press, 1976.

Condorcet, Marie-Jean-Antoine-Nicolas-Caritat, Marquis de, *Sketch for a Historical Picture of the Human Mind* (1795), trans. J. Barraclough, introd. Stuart Hampshire, London: Weidenfeld and Nicolson, 1955.

De Man, Paul, *Aesthetic Ideology*, ed. and introd. Andrzej Warminski, Minneapolis and London: University of Minnesota Press, 1996.

Deleuze, Gilles, *Difference and Repetition*, trans. P. Patton, London: Athlone Press, 1994.

Foucault, Paris: Les Editions de minuit, 1986.

Derrida, Jacques, *Specters of Marx: The State of the Debt, the Work of Mourning, and the New International*, trans. Peggy Kamuf, introd. Bernd Magnus and Stephen Cullenberg, New York and London: Routledge, 1994.

Fanon, Franz, *The Wretched of the Earth*, trans. Constance Farrington, Harmondsworth: Penguin, 1967.

Foucault, Michel, *Language, Counter-Memory, Practice: Selected Essays and Interviews*, ed. and introd. D. Bouchard, Oxford: Basil Blackwell, 1977.

Gadamer, Hans-Georg, *Philosophical Hermeneutics*, trans. and ed. D. E. Linge, Los Angeles: University of California Press, 1976.

Truth and Method, trans. J. Weinsheimer and D. G. Marshall, London: Sheed and Ward, 1989.

Hegel, G. W. F., *The Phenomenology of Spirit* (1807), trans. A. V. Miller, foreword by J. N. Findlay, New York and Oxford: Oxford University Press, 1977.

Jameson, Fredric, *The Political Unconscious: Narrative as a Socially Symbolic Act*, London: Methuen, 1981.

Jauss, Hans Robert, *Towards an Aesthetic of Reception*, trans. Timothy Bahti, Minneapolis: University of Minnesota Press, 1982.

Kierkegaard, Soren, *Fear and Trembling, Repetition*, trans. and introd. H. V. Hong and E. H. Hong, Princeton: Princeton University Press, 1983.

Kuhn, Thomas, *The Structure of Scientific Revolutions*, 2nd edn., enlarged, Chicago: University of Chicago Press, 1970.

Nietzsche, Friedrich, 'On the Uses and Disadvantages of History for Life', in *Untimely Meditations*, trans. R. J. Holingdale, introd. J. P. Stern, Cambridge: Cambridge University Press, 1983.

Plato, *Phaedo* and *Meno*, in *The Collected Dialogues of Plato Including the Letters*, eds. E. Hamilton and H. Cairns, Bollingen Series LXXI, Princeton: Princeton University Press, 1963.

Popper, Karl, *The Poverty of Historicism*, London: Routledge and Kegan Paul, 1986.

Schleiermacher, F. D. E., *Hermeneutics: The Handwritten Manuscripts*, ed. Heinz Kimmerle, trans. James Duke and Jack Forstman, Atlanta: Scolars Press, 1977.

Simmel, G., *The Problem of the Philosophy of History* (2nd edn., 1905), trans. and ed. Guy Oakes, London and New York: Macmillan, 1977.

Spivak, Gayatri Chakravorty, *In Other Worlds: Essays in Cultural Politics*, London: Methuen, 1987.

Secondary sources

Clark, Lorraine, *Blake, Kierkegaard, and the Spectre of Dialectic*, Cambridge: Cambridge University Press, 1991.

Greer, Germaine, *The Whole Woman*, London: Doubleday, 1999.

Hamilton, Paul, *Historicism*, London: Routledge, 1996.

McGann, Jerome J., 'The Third World of Criticism', in Marjorie Levinson, Marilyn Butler, Jerome McGann, Paul Hamilton (eds.), *Rethinking Historicism: Critical Readings in Romantic History*, Oxford: Basil Blackwell, 1989, pp. 85–108.

Pocock, J. G. E., *The Machiavellian Moment: Florentine Political Thought and the Atlantic Republican Tradition*, Princeton: Princeton University Press, 1975.

Politics, Language and Time: Essays on Political Thought and History, Chicago: Chicago University Press, 1971.

Said, Edward, *Culture and Imperialism*, London: Vintage, 1994.

Orientalism, London: Routledge and Kegan Paul, 1978.

White, Hayden, *Metahistory*, Baltimore: Johns Hopkins University Press, 1973.

Literary criticism and the history of ideas

Primary sources

Auerbach, Erich, *Mimesis: The Representation of Reality in Western Literature*, trans. Willard Trask, Princeton: Princeton University Press, 1953.

Scenes from the Drama of European Literature, trans. Ralph Mannheim, New York: Meridian, 1959.

Curtius, Ernst Robert, *European Literature and the Latin Middle Ages*, trans. Willard Trask, New York: Pantheon, 1953.

De Man, Paul, 'The Rhetoric of Temporality', in Charles Singleton (ed.), *Interpretation: Theory and Practice*, Baltimore: Johns Hopkins University Press, 1968, pp. 173–209.

Hegel, Georg Wilhelm Friedrich, *Aesthetics: Lectures on Fine Art*, 2 vols., trans. T. M. Knox, Oxford: Clarendon, 1975.

Lovejoy, Arthur O., *Essays in the History of Ideas*, Baltimore: Johns Hopkins University Press, 1948.
  The Great Chain of Being: A Study of the History of an Idea, Cambridge, Mass.: Harvard University Press, 1936.
Spitzer, Leo, *Representative Essays*, eds. Alban Forcione, Herbert Lindenberger and Madeleine Sutherland, Stanford: Stanford University Press, 1988.
Wellek, René and Austin Warren, *Theory of Literature*, 3rd edn., New York: Harcourt, Brace & World, 1962.

Secondary sources

Bahti, Timothy, *Allegories of History: Literary Historiography after Hegel*, Baltimore: Johns Hopkins University Press, 1992.
Macksey, Richard, 'History of Ideas', in Michael Groden and Martin Kreiswirth (eds.), *The Johns Hopkins Guide to Literary Theory and Criticism*, Baltimore: Johns Hopkins University Press, 1994, pp. 388–392.
Wellek, René, *Concepts of Criticism*, ed. Stephen G. Nichols, Jr., New Haven: Yale University Press, 1963.
  A History of Modern Criticism, 1750–1950, 5 vols., New Haven: Yale University Press, 1955–93.

Cultural materialism

Barker, Francis, *The Tremulous Private Body: Essays on Subjection*, London: Methuen, 1984.
Barthes, Roland, *Mythologies*, trans. Annette Lavers, London: Cape, 1972.
Belsey, Catherine, *Critical Practice*, London: Methuen, 1980.
  The Subject of Tragedy, London: Methuen, 1985.
Bennett, Tony, *Formalism and Marxism*, London: Methuen, 1979.
Brannigan, John, *New Historicism and Cultural Materialism*, Basingstoke: Macmillan Press Ltd., 1998.
Cohen, Walter, *Drama of a Nation: Public Theater in Renaissance England and Spain*, Ithaca and London: Cornell University Press, 1985.
Coward, Rosalind and John Ellis, *Language and Materialism: Developments in Semiology and the Theory of the Subject*, London: Routledge & Kegan Paul, 1977.
Derrida, Jacques, *Of Grammatology*, trans. Gayatri Chakravorty Spivak, Baltimore: Johns Hopkins University Press, 1976.
  Writing and Difference, trans., with introduction and notes, Alan Bass, London: Routledge & Kegan Paul, 1978.
Dollimore, Jonathan, *Death, Desire and Loss in Western Culture*, London: Allen Lane The Penguin Press, 1998.
  Radical Tragedy: Religion, Ideology and Power in the Drama of Shakespeare and his Contemporaries, Brighton: Harvester, 1984; 2nd edn., New York and London: Harvester Wheatsheaf, 1989.
  Sexual Dissidence: Augustine to Wilde, Freud to Foucault, Oxford: Clarendon, 1991.
Dollimore, Jonathan and Alan Sinfield, *Political Shakespeare: New Essays in Cultural Materialism*, Manchester: Manchester University Press, 1985.

Drakakis, John (ed.), *Alternative Shakespeares*, London: Methuen, 1985; 2nd edn., Manchester: Manchester University Press, 1994.

(ed.), *Shakespearean Tragedy*, Harlow: Longman, 1992.

Eagleton, Terry, *Criticism and Ideology*, London: New Left Books, 1976.

Easthope, Antony, *British Post-Structuralism Since 1968*, London: Routledge, 1988.

Foucault, Michel, *Madness and Civilization: A History of Insanity in the Age of Reason*, trans. Richard Howard (abridged), London: Tavistock Publications, 1967.

Greenblatt, Stephen, *Renaissance Self-Fashioning from More to Shakespeare*, Chicago and London: University of Chicago Press, 1980.

Shakespearean Negotiations: The Circulation of Social Energy in Renaissance England, Oxford: Clarendon Press, 1988.

Hall, Stuart and Tony Jefferson (eds.), *Resistance Through Rituals: Youth Subcultures in Post-War Britain*, London: Hutchinson, 1976.

Harris, Marvin, *Cultural Materialism: The Struggle for a Science of Culture*, New York: Random House, 1979.

Hawkes, Terence, *Meaning by Shakespeare*, London: Routledge, 1992.

Shakespeare's Talking Animals: Language and Drama in Society, London: Edward Arnold, 1975.

Structuralism and Semiotics, London: Methuen, 1977.

That Shakespeherian Rag, London: Methuen, 1986.

(ed.), *Alternative Shakespeares 2*, London: Routledge, 1996.

Hebdige, Dick, *Subculture: The Meaning of Style*, London: Methuen, 1979.

Hoggart, Richard, *The Uses of Literacy: Aspects of Working-Class Life, with Special Reference to Publications and Entertainments*, London: Chatto and Windus, 1957.

Holderness, Graham (ed.), *The Shakespeare Myth*, Manchester: Manchester University Press, 1988.

Lacan, Jacques, *The Four Fundamental Concepts of Psycho-Analysis*, ed. Jacques-Alain Miller, trans. Alan Sheridan, London: Hogarth Press, 1977.

Lever, J. W., *The Tragedy of State: A Study of Jacobean Drama*, London: Methuen, 1987.

Macherey, Pierre, *A Theory of Literary Production*, trans. Geoffrey Wall, London: Routledge and Kegan Paul, 1978.

Norris, Christopher, *Deconstruction: Theory and Practice*, London: Methuen, 1982.

Norris, Christopher and Richard Machin (eds.), *Post-Structuralist Readings in English Poetry*, Cambridge: Cambridge University Press, 1987.

Sinfield, Alan, *Cultural Politics – Queer Reading*, London: Routledge, 1994.

Faultlines: Cultural Materialism and the Politics of Dissident Reading, Oxford: Clarendon Press,1992.

Literature in Protestant England 1560–1660, London: Croom Helm, 1983.

Literature, Politics and Culture in Postwar Britain, Oxford: Blackwell, 1989; 2nd edn., London: Athlone Press, 1997.

The Wilde Century: Effeminacy, Oscar Wilde and the Queer Moment, London: Cassell, 1994.

Stallybrass, Peter and Allon White, *The Politics and Poetics of Transgression*, London: Methuen, 1986.

Steiner, George, *The Death of Tragedy*, London: Faber and Faber, 1961.
Thompson, E. P., *The Making of the English Working Class*, London: Gollancz, 1980.
Widdowson, Peter (ed.), *Re-Reading English*, London: Methuen, 1982.
Williams, Raymond, *The Long Revolution*, London: Chatto & Windus, 1961.
  Marxism and Literature, Oxford: Oxford University Press, 1977.
  Problems in Materialism and Culture, London: Verso, 1980.
Wilson, Scott, *Cultural Materialism: Theory and Practice*, Oxford: Blackwell, 1995.

New historicism

Primary sources

Bloom, Harold, *Shakespeare: The Invention of the Human*, London: Fourth Estate, 1999.
Brannigan, John, *New Historicism and Cultural Materialism*, Basingstoke: Macmillan, 1998.
Cole, Steven E., 'Evading Politics:The Poverty of Historicizing Romanticism', *Studies in Romanticism* 34.1 (1995), pp. 29–50.
Colebrook, Claire, *New Literary Histories: New Historicism and Contemporary Criticism*, Manchester and New York: Manchester University Press, 1997.
Dollimore, Jonathan and Alan Sinfield (eds.), *Political Shakespeare: New Essays in Cultural Materialism*, 2nd edn., Manchester: Manchester University Press, 1994.
Foucault, Michel, *Madness and Civilization: A History of Insanity in the Age of Reason*, trans. Richard Howard, London: Tavistock Publications, 1967.
Geertz, Clifford, 'History and Anthropology', *New Literary History* 21.2 (1990), pp. 321–336; and Renato Rosaldo's reply, pp. 337–342.
  The Interpretation of Cultures: Selected Essays, London: Hutchinson, 1975.
  Works and Lives: The Anthropologist as Author, Cambridge: Polity Press, 1988.
Greenblatt, Stephen J., 'Interviewed by Noel King', *Textual Practice* 6.2 (1994), pp. 114–127.
  Learning to Curse: Essays in Early Modern Culture, New York and London: Routledge, 1990.
  Marvellous Possessions: The Wonder of the New World, Chicago: University of Chicago Press, 1991.
  Renaissance Self-Fashioning: From More to Shakespeare, Chicago: University of Chicago Press, 1980.
Greenblatt, Stephen and Giles Gunn (eds.), *Redrawing the Boundaries: The Transformation of English and American Literary Studies*, New York: Modern Language Association, 1992.
Howard, Jean E., 'The New Historicism in Renaissance Studies', *English Literary Renaissance* 16.1 (1986), pp. 13–43.
Jardine, Lisa, *Reading Shakespeare Historically*, New York and London: Routledge, 1996.
Levinson, Marjorie, 'The New Historicism: Back to the Future', in Marjorie Levinson, Marilyn Butler, Jerome McGann and Paul Hamilton (eds.), *Rethinking Historicism: Critical Readings in Romantic History*, Oxford: Basil Blackwell, 1989.

Liu, Alan, 'The Power of Formalism: The New Historicism', *English Literary History* 56.4 (1989), pp. 721–772.

Montrose, Louis, 'New Historicisms', in Greenblatt and Gunn (eds.), *Redrawing the Boundaries*, pp. 392–418.

'Renaissance Literary Studies and the Subject of History', *English Literary Renaissance* 16.1 (1986), pp. 5–12.

Mullaney, Steven, 'After the New Historicism', in T. Hawkes (ed.), *Alternative Shakespeares*, vol. 2, New York and London: Routledge, 1996.

Pechter, Edward, 'The New Historicism and its Discontents: Politicizing Renaissance Drama', *PMLA* 102.3 (May 1987), pp. 293–303.

Ross, Marlon B., 'Contingent Predilections: The Newest Historicisms and the Question of Method', *The Centennial Review* 34 (1990), pp. 485–538.

Simpson, David, 'Literary Criticism and the Return to "History"', *Critical Inquiry* 14.4 (1988), pp. 721–747.

Thomas, Brook, *The New Historicism and other Old-Fashioned Topics*, Princeton: Princeton University Press, 1991.

Veeser, H. A., *The New Historicism*, New York and London: Routledge, 1989.

The New Historicism: A Reader, New York and London, 1994.

Wilson, Richard and Richard Dutton (eds.), *New Historicism and Renaissance Drama*, London and New York: Longman, 1992.

Secondary sources

Barton, Ann, 'The Perils of Historicism', *The New York Review of Books*, 24 January (1991), pp. 8–10.

Belsey, Catherine, 'The Subject in Danger: A Reply to Richard Levin', *Textual Practice* 3 (1989), pp. 187–90.

'Richard Levin and In-Different Reading', *New Literary History* 21.3 (1990), pp. 449–456.

Clare, Janet, 'Historicism and the Question of Censorship in the Renaissance', *English Literary Renaissance* 27. 2 (Spring 1997), pp. 155–176.

Cressy, David, 'Foucault, Stone and Social History', in *English Literary Renaissance* 21.2 (1991), pp. 121–133.

Dusinberre, Juliet, *Shakespeare and the Nature of Women,* 2nd ed. London: Macmillan, 1998.

Grady, Hugh, *The Modernist Shakespeare*, Oxford: Clarendon Press, 1991.

Holstun, James, 'Ranting at the New Historicism', *English Literary Renaissance* 19 (1989), pp. 89–225.

Honigmann, E. A. J., 'The New Shakespeare?', *The New York Review of Books* 31 March, 35.5 (1988), pp. 32–35.

Kamps, Ivo, *Shakespeare Left and Right*, New York and London: Routledge, 1991.

Lentricchia, Frank, 'Foucault's Legacy: A New Historicism?', in Veeser, *The New Historicism*, 1989, pp. 231–242.

Levin, Richard, 'Bashing the Bourgeois Subject', *Textual Practice* 3.1 (1989), pp. 76–86.

'Feminist Thematics and Shakespearean Tragedy', *PMLA* 103.1 (1988), pp. 125–138; letter in reply, 'Feminist Criticism', *PMLA* 104.1 (1989), pp. 77–78.

'Reply to Catherine Belsey and Jonathan Goldberg', *New Literary History* 21.3 (1990), pp. 463–470.

'Unthinkable Thoughts in the New Historicizing of English Renaissance Drama', *New Literary History* 21.3 (1990), pp. 433–448.

Liu, Alan, *Wordsworth: The Sense of History*, Stanford: Stanford University Press, 1989.

McGann, Jerome, *The Beauty of Inflections: Literary Investigations in Historical Method and Theory*, Oxford: Oxford University Press, 1985.

Social Values and Poetic Acts: The Historical Judgment of Literary Work, Cambridge, Mass. and London: Harvard University Press, 1988.

Miller, J. Hillis, 'Presidential Address 1986: The Triumph of Theory, the Resistance to Reading, and the Question of the Material Base', *PMLA* 102 (1987), pp. 281–291.

Porter, Carolyn, 'Are We Being Historical Yet?', *South Atlantic Quarterly* 87 (1988), pp. 743–786.

'History and Literature: "After the New Historicism"', *New Literary History* 21.2 (Winter 1990), pp. 253–272; Porter's reply to Rena Fraden, pp. 279–282.

Ross, Marlon B., 'Contingent Predilections: The Newest Historicisms and the Question of Method', *The Centennial Review* 34 (Fall 1990), pp. 485–538.

Veyne, Paul, 'The Final Foucault and His Ethics', *Critical Inquiry* 20.1 (Autumn 1993), pp. 1–9.

Vickers, Brian, *Appropriating Shakespeare: Contemporary Critical Quarrels*, New Haven and London: Yale University Press, 1993.

Wilson, Scott, *Cultural Materialism: Theory and Practice*, Oxford: Basil Blackwell, 1995.

Fascist politics and literary criticism

Almgren, Birgitta, *Germanistik und Nationalsozialismus: Affirmation, Konflikt und Protest: Traditionsfelder und zeitgebundene Wertung der Sprach- und Literaturwissenschaft am Beispiel der Germanisch-Romanischen Monatsschrift 1929–1943*, Acta Universitatis Upsaliensis, Studia Germanistica Upsaliensia, 36 (1997).

Aron, Paul, Dirk De Geest, Pierre Halen and Antoon Vanden Braembussche (eds.), *Leurs occupations: l'impact de la seconde guerre mondiale sur la littérature en Belgique*, Bruxelles: Textyles-CREHSGM, 1997.

Benjamin, Walter, 'Das Kunstwerk im Zeitalter seiner technischen Reproduzierbarkeit', in *Illuminationen: ausgewählte Schriften*, Frankfurt: Suhrkamp, 1977, pp. 136–169.

Berghaus, Günter, *Futurism and Politics: Between Anarchist Rebellion and Fascist Reaction, 1909–1944*, Providence: Berghahn, 1996.

(ed.), *Fascism and Theatre: Comparative Studies on the Aesthetics and Politics of Performance in Europe, 1925–1945*, Providence: Berghahn, 1996.

Berman, Russell A., 'Aestheticization of Politics: Walter Benjamin on Fascism and the Avant-garde', *Modern Culture and Critical Theory*, Madison: University of Wisconsin Press, 1989.

Carroll, David, *French Literary Fascism: Nationalism, Anti-Semitism, and the Ideology of Culture*, Princeton: Princeton University Press, 1995.

Conway, Martin, *Collaboration in Belgium: Léon Degrelle and the Rexist Movement, 1940–1945*, New Haven: Yale University Press, 1993.

De Geest, Dirk, Eveline Vanfraussen, Marnix Beyen and Ilse Mestdagh, *Collaboratie of cultuur?: een Vlaams tijdschrift in bezettingstijd (1941–1944)*, Antwerp/Amsterdam: Meulenhoff/Kritak/Soma, 1997.

De Graef, Ortwin, *Serenity in Crisis: A Preface to Paul de Man, 1939–1960*, Lincoln: University of Nebraska Press, 1993.

Titanic Light: Paul de Man's Post-Romanticism, 1960–1969, Lincoln: University of Nebraska Press, 1995.

De Man, Paul, *Aesthetic Ideology*, ed. and introd. Andrzej Warminski, Minneapolis: University of Minnesota Press, 1996.

Wartime Journalism, 1939–1943, eds. Werner Hamacher, Neil Hertz and Thomas Keenan, Lincoln: University of Nebraska Press, 1988.

De Wever, Bruno, *Greep naar de Macht: Vlaams-nationalisme en Nieuwe Orde: Het VNV 1933–1945*, Tielt: Lannoo, 1994.

Friedländer, Saul, *Reflets du nazisme*, Paris: Seuil, 1982.

Golsan, Richard J. (ed.), *Fascism, Aesthetics, and Culture*, Hanover: University Press of New England, 1992.

Griffin, Roger, *The Nature of Fascism*, London: Pinter, 1991.

(ed.), *Fascism*, Oxford Readers Series, Oxford: Oxford University Press, 1995.

Hamacher, Werner, Neil Hertz and Thomas Keenan (eds.), *Responses: On Paul de Man's Wartime Journalism*, Lincoln: University of Nebraska Press, 1989.

Hewitt, Andrew, *Fascist Modernism: Aesthetics, Politics, and the Avant-Garde*, Stanford: Stanford University Press, 1993.

Kaplan, Alice Yaeger, *Reproductions of Banality: Fascism, Literature, and French Intellectual Life*, foreword by Russel Berman, Minneapolis: University of Minnesota Press, 1986.

Ketelsen, Uwe-Karsten, *Literatur und Drittes Reich*, Vierow bei Greifswald: SH-Verlag, 1994.

Lacoue-Labarthe, Philippe, *La fiction du politique*, Paris: Bourgois, 1987.

Lacoue-Labarthe, Philippe and Jean-Luc Nancy, *Le mythe nazi*, Paris: l'Aube, 1996.

Retreating the Political, ed. Simon Sparks, London: Routledge, 1997.

Lacqueur, Walter (ed.), *Fascism: A Reader's Guide*, London: Wildwood House, 1976.

Loiseaux, Gérard, *La littérature de la défaite et de la collaboration, d'après Phönix oder Asche? (Phénix ou cendres?) de Bernhard Payr*, Paris: Fayard, 1995.

Martin, Bernd (ed.), *Martin Heidegger und das 'Dritte Reich': ein Kompendium*, Darmstadt: Wissenschaftliche Buchgesellschaft, 1989.

Milza, Pierre and Serge Berstein, *Dictionnaire historique des fascismes et du nazisme*, Bruxelles: Complexe, 1992.

Mosse, George L., *Der national-sozialistische Alltag*, Frankfurt a.M.: Hain, 1993.

Norris, Christopher, *Paul de Man: Deconstruction and the Critique of Aesthetic Ideology*, London: Routledge, 1988.

O'Sullivan, Noël, *Fascism*, London: J. M. Dent, 1983.

Reichel, Peter, *Der schöne Schein des dritten Reiches: Faszination und Gewalt des Faschismus*, Frankfurt: Fischer, 1993.

Rioux, Jean-Pierre (ed.), *La vie culturelle sous Vichy*, Bruxelles: Complexe, 1990.

Sirinelli, Jean-François (gen. ed.), *Histoire des droites en France*, 3 vols. Paris: Gallimard, 1992.

Spackman, Barbara, *Fascist Virilities: Rhetoric, Ideology, and Social Fantasy in Italy*, Minneapolis: University of Minnesota Press, 1996.

Sternhell, Zeev, *La Droite révolutionnaire, 1885–1914: les origines françaises du fascisme*, Paris: Seuil, 1978.

Maurice Barrès et le nationalisme français, Paris: Colin, 1972.

Ni droite, ni gauche: l'idéologie fasciste en France, rev. edn., Bruxelles: Complexe, 1987, 1st edn. 1983.

Sternhell, Zeev, Mario Sznajder, and Maia Ashéri, *Naissance de l'idéologie fasciste*, Paris: Gallimard, 1989.

Tabor, Jan (ed.), *Kunst und Diktatur: Architektur, Bildhauerei und Malerei in Österreich, Deutschland, Italien und der Sowjetunion, 1922–1956*, 2 vols. Baden: Grasl, 1994.

Theweleit, Klaus, *Männerphantasien*, vol. 2: *Männerkörper – zur Psychoanalyse des weissen Terrors*, Reinbek bei Hamburg: Rowohlt, 1980.

Verhoeyen, Etienne, *België Bezet, 1940–1944: een synthese*, Brussel: BRTN, 1993.

Welch, David, *The Third Reich: Politics and Propaganda*, London: Routledge, 1995.

Woolf, S. J. (ed.), *Fascism in Europe* (previously published as *European Fascism*, 1968), London: Methuen, 1981.

Marxism and literary criticism

Adorno, Theodor W., *Minima Moralia*, trans. E. Jephcott, London: Verso, 1974.

Althusser, Louis, *For Marx*, trans. Ben Brewster, London: Verso, 1969.

Lenin and Philosophy and Other Essays, trans. Ben Brewster, London: Verso, 1971.

Althusser, Louis and Etienne Balibar, *Reading Capital*, trans. Ben Brewster, London: Verso, 1970.

Anderson, Perry, *Considerations on Western Marxism*, London: New Left Books, 1976.

The Origins of Postmodernity, London: Verso, 1998.

Benjamin, Walter, *Charles Baudelaire*, trans. Harry Zohn, London: New Left Books, 1973.

Illuminations, trans. Harry Zohn, introd. Hannah Arendt, London: Jonathan Cape, 1970.

One-Way Street and Other Writings, trans. E. Jephcott and Kingsley Shorter, London: New Left Books, 1979.

Understanding Brecht, trans. Anna Bostock, London: New Left Books, 1973.

Bloch, Ernst, *et al.*, *Aesthetics and Politics*, London: New Left Books, 1977.

Callinicos, Alex, *Against Postmodernism*, Cambridge: Polity, 1989.

Cohen, G.A., *Karl Marx's Theory of History*, Oxford: Clarendon, 1978.

Eagleton, Terry, *Criticism and Ideology*, London: New Left Books, 1976.

Literary Theory, Oxford: Blackwell, 1986.

Marxism and Literary Criticism, London: Methuen, 1976.

Walter Benjamin, or, Towards a Revolutionary Criticism, London: Verso, 1981.

Jameson, Fredric, *Marxism and Form*, Princeton: Princeton University Press, 1971.

The Political Unconscious, London: Methuen, 1981.

Postmodernism, or the Cultural Logic of Late Capitalism, London: Verso, 1991.

Kermode, Frank, *History and Value*, Oxford: Clarendon, 1988.

Labriola, Antonio, *Essays on the Materialistic Conception of History*, Chicago: Kerr, 1908.

Laclau, Ernesto and Chantal Mouffe, *Hegemony and Socialist Strategy*, London: Verso, 1985.

Lukács, Gyorgy, *The Historical Novel*, trans. Hannah and Stanley Mitchell, London: Merlin, 1962.

History and Class Consciousness, trans. R. Livingstone, London: Merlin, 1971.

The Meaning of Contemporary Realism, trans. John and Necke Mander, London: Merlin, 1963.

Macherey, Pierre, *A Theory of Literary Production*, trans. G. Wall, London: Routledge and Kegan Paul, 1978.

Nelson, Cary and Lawrence Grossberg (eds.), *Marxism and the Interpretation of Culture*, Houndmills: Macmillan, 1988.

Prawer, S. S., *Karl Marx and World Literature*, Oxford: Oxford University Press, 1978.

Trotsky, Leon, *Literature and Revolution* (1923), Ann Arbor: University of Michigan Press, 1971.

On Literature and Art, New York: Pathfinder, 1970.

Willett, John (ed.), *Brecht on Theatre*, London: Methuen, 1978.

Williams, Raymond, *Marxism and Literature*, Oxford: Clarendon, 1977.

Marxism and poststructuralism

Baudrillard, Jean, *A Critique of the Political Economy of the Sign*, trans. Charles Levin, St. Louis: Telos Press, 1981.

Fatal Strategies, trans. Philip Beitchman and W. G. J. Niesluchowski, New York: Semiotext(e)/Pluto, 1990.

The Gulf War Did Not Happen, trans. Paul Patton, Bloomington: Indiana University Press, 1995.

The Mirror of Production, trans. Mark Poster, St. Louis: Telos Press, 1975.

Seduction, trans. Brian Singer, New York: St. Martin's Press, 1990.

Simulations and Simulacra, trans. Sheila Faria, Ann Arbor: The University of Michigan Press, 1994.

Symbolic Exchange and Death, trans. Iain Hamilton Grant, London: Sage, 1993.

The System of Objects, trans. James Benedict, New York: Verso, 1996.

Caudwell, Christopher, *Illusion and Reality*, New York: International Publishers, 1947.

Studies in a Dying Culture, London: John Lane, 1938.

Deleuze, Gilles, *Difference and Repetition*, trans. Paul Patton, New York: Columbia University Press, 1994.

The Logic of Sense, trans. Mark Lester and Charles Stivale, New York: Columbia University Press, 1990.

Nietzsche and Philosophy, trans. Hugh Tomlinson, New York: Columbia University Press, 1983.

Deleuze, Gilles and Félix Guattari, *The Anti-Oedipus: Capitalism and Schizophrenia*, trans. Robert Hurley, Mark Seem, Helen R. Lane, Minneapolis: University of Minnesota Press, 1983.

A Thousand Plateaus: Capitalism and Schizophrenia, Vol. 2, trans. Brian Massumi, Minneapolis: University of Minnesota Press, 1987.

Derrida, Jacques, *Of Grammatology*, trans. Gayatri Chakravorty Spivak, Baltimore: Johns Hopkins University Press, 1976.

Specters of Marx: The State of Debt, the Work of Mourning, and the New International, trans. Peggy Kamuf, New York: Routledge, 1994.

Speech and Phenomena, trans. David B. Allison, Evanston: Northwestern University Press, 1973.

Writing and Difference, trans. Alan Bass, Chicago: University of Chicago Press, 1978.

Foucault, Michel, *Discipline and Punish*, trans. Alan Sheridan, New York: Vintage, 1979.

The History of Sexuality, trans. Robert Hurley, New York: Vintage, 1988–90.

Madness and Civilization: A History of Insanity in the Age of Reason, trans. Richard Howard, New York: Vintage, 1965.

The Order of Things: An Archaeology of the Human Sciences, trans. Alan Sherian, London: Tavistock, 1974.

Kristeva, Julia, *Desire in Language: A Semiotic Approach to Literature and Art*, trans. Thomas Gora, Alice Jardine, Leon S. Roudiez, New York: Columbia University Press, 1980.

Revolution in Poetic Language, trans. Margaret Waller, New York: Columbia University Press, 1984.

Lukács, Gyorgy, *The Historical Novel*, trans. Hannah and Stanley Mitchell, Lincoln: University of Nebraska Press, 1983.

Lyotard, Jean François, *Dérive a partir de Marx et Freud* (1975), Paris: Galilée, 1994.

Discours/figure, Paris: Klincksieck, 1971.

The Post-Modern Condition, trans. Geoff Bennington and Brian Massumi, Minneapolis: University of Minnesota Press, 1984.

Macherey, Pierre, *A Theory of Literary Production*, trans. G. Wall, London: Routledge & Kegan Paul, 1978.

Adorno and the early Frankfurt School

Primary sources

Adorno, Theodor W., *Aesthetic Theory*, trans. C. Lenhardt, eds. Gretel Adorno and Rolf Tiedemann, London: Routledge and Kegan Paul, 1984.

The Culture Industry: Selected Essays on Mass Culture, ed. and introd. J. M. Bernstein, London: Routledge, 1991.

Notes to Literature, trans. Shierry Weber Nicholsen, ed. Rolf Tiedemann, New York: Columbia University Press, 1991, 1992.

Prisms, trans. Samuel and Shierry Weber, Cambridge, Mass.: MIT Press, 1981.

Adorno, Theodor W. and Max Horkheimer, *Dialectic of Enlightenment*, trans. John Cumming, London: Allen Lane, 1973.

Arato, A. and E. Gebhardt (eds.), *The Essential Frankfurt School Reader*, Oxford: Blackwell, 1978.

Bronner, S. E. and D. M. Kellner (eds.), *Critical Theory and Society: A Reader*, London: Routledge, 1989.

Horkheimer, Max, *Critical Theory: Selected Essays*, trans. Matthew J. O'Connell, New York: Continuum, 1982.

Lowenthal, Leo, *Literature and the Image of Man: Sociological Studies of the European Drama and Novel, 1600–1900*, New York: Beacon Press, 1957.

Marcuse, Herbert, *Negations: Essays in Critical Theory*, Harmondsworth: Penguin, 1968.

Secondary sources

Held, David, *Introduction to Critical Theory: Horkheimer to Habermas*, London: Hutchinson, 1980.

Jarvis, Simon, *Adorno: A Critical Introduction*, Cambridge: Polity Press, 1998.

Rose, Gillian, *The Melancholy Science: An Introduction to the Thought of Theodor W. Adorno*, London: Macmillan, 1978.

Wiggerhaus, Rolf, *The Frankfurt School: Its History, Theories and Political Significance*, Cambridge: Polity Press, 1994.

The 'German-French' debate: critical theory, hermeneutics and deconstruction

Primary sources

Bohrer, Karl Heinz, *Das absolute Präsens: die Semantik ästhetischer Zeit*, Frankfurt a. M.: Suhrkamp, 1994.

Plötzlichkeit: zum Augenblick des ästhetischen Scheins, Frankfurt a. M.: Suhrkamp, 1981.

Bürger, Peter, *Theorie der Avantgarde*, Frankfurt a. M.: Suhrkamp, 1982.

Zur Kritik der idealistischen Ästhetik, Frankfurt a. M.: Suhrkamp, 1983.

Derrida, Jacques, *L'écriture et la différence*, Paris: Points, 1967.

Marges de la philosophie, Paris: Minuit, 1972.

Frank, Manfred, *Grenzen der Verständigung: ein Geistergespräch zwischen Lyotard und Habermas*, Frankfurt: Suhrkamp, 1988.

Das Individuelle-Allgemeine: Textstrukturierung und -interpretation nach Schleiermacher, Frankfurt: Suhrkamp, 1977.

Das Sagbare und das Unsagbare, Frankfurt a. M.: Suhrkamp, 1989 (part translation, *The Subject and the Text: Essays in Literary Theory and Philosophy*, introd. Andrew Bowie, Cambridge: Cambridge University Press, 1997).

Was ist Neostrukturalismus?, Frankfurt a. M.: Suhrkamp, 1984.

Gadamer, Hans-Georg, *Hermeneutik: Wahrheit und Methode, 2 Ergänzungen, Register*, Tübingen: J. C. B. Mohr, 1986.

Wahrheit und Methode, Tübingen: J. C. B. Mohr, 1975.

Habermas, Jürgen, *Der philosophische Diskurs der Moderne*, Frankfurt: Suhrkamp, 1985.

Henrich, Dieter, *Selbstverhältnisse*, Stuttgart: Reclam, 1982.

Lyotard, Jean-François, *Le différend*, Paris: Minuit, 1983.

Menke, Christoph, *Die Souveränität der Kunst: Ästhetische Erfahrung nach Adorno und Derrida*, Frankfurt: Suhrkamp, 1991.

Michelfelder, Diane P. and Richard E. Palmer (eds.), *Dialogue and Deconstruction: The Gadamer-Derrida Encounter*, Albany: SUNY Press, 1989.

Wellmer, Albrecht, *Zur Dialektik von Moderne und Postmoderne*, Frankfurt: Suhrkamp, 1985.

Welsch, Wolfgang, *Vernunft: die zeitgenössische Vernunftkritik und das Konzept der transversalen Vernunft*, Frankfurt a. M.: Suhrkamp, 1996.

Secondary sources

Bowie, Andrew, *Aesthetics and Subjectivity: From Kant to Nietzsche*, Manchester: Manchester University Press, 1993 (rev. edn., forthcoming).

From Romanticism to Critical Theory: The Philosophy of German Literary Theory, London, New York: Routledge, 1997.

Dews, Peter, *The Limits of Disenchantment*, London and New York: Verso, 1995.

Logics of Disintegration, London, New York: Verso, 1987.

Gasché, Rodolphe, *The Tain of the Mirror: Derrida and the Philosophy of Reflection*, Cambridge, Mass.: Harvard University Press, 1986.

Holub, Robert, *Crossing Borders: Reception Theory, Poststructuralism, Deconstruction*, Madison: University of Wisconsin Press, 1992.

Post-war Italian intellectual culture: from Marxism to cultural studies

Agamben, Giorgio, *The Coming Community*, trans. Michael Hardt, Minneapolis: Minnesota University Press, 1993.

Asor Rosa, Alberto, *Sintesi di storia della letteratura italiana*, Florence: La Nuova Italia, 1975

Birnbaum, Lucia Chiavola, *Liberazione della donna: feminism in Italy*, Middletown, Conn: Wesleyan University Press, 1986.

Bodei, Remo, *Repenser l'Europe*, Brussels: Editions de l'Université de Bruxelles, 1996.

Bono, Paola and Sandra Kemp (eds.), *Italian Feminist Thought: A Reader*, Oxford: Basil Blackwell, 1991.

Cacciari, Massimo, *Geo-filosofia dell'Europa*, Milan: Adelphi, 1994.

Krisis: saggio sulla crisi del pensiero negativo da Nietzsche a Wittgenstein, Milan: Feltrinelli, 1976.

Carravetta, Peter, 'Repositioning Interpretive Discourse: From "A Crisis of Reason" to "Weak Thought"', *Differentia, Review of Italian Thought* 2 (1988), pp. 83–126.

Calefato, Patrizia, *Europa fenicia, identità linguistica, comunità, linguaggio come pratica sociale*, Milan: Franco Angeli, 1994.

Colletti, Lucio, *Marxism and Hegel*, trans. Lawrence Garner, London: Verso, 1973.

D'Alema, Massimo, Claudio Verlardi, and Gianni Cuperlo, *Un paese normale*, Milan: Mondadori, 1995.

Dalla Costa, Mariarosa, *Donne, sviluppo e lavoro di riproduzione: questioni delle lotte e dei movimenti*, Milan: Franco Angeli, 1996.

Paying the Price: Women and the Politics of International Economic Strategy (1993), London: Zed Books, 1995.

della Volpe, Galvano, *Critique of Taste*, trans. Michael Casar, London: MLB, 1978.

Logica come scienza storica, Rome: Riuniti, 1969.

Rousseau e Marx, Rome: Riuniti, 1974; first edn. 1956.

Diotima (group), *Il cielo stellato dentro di noi: l'ordine simbolico della madre*, Milan: Tartaruga, 1992.

Mettere al mondo il mondo: oggetto e oggettività alla luce della differenza sessual, Milan: Tartaruga, 1990.

Eco, Umberto, *Semiotics and the Philosophy of Language*, Bloomington: Indiana University Press, 1984.

A Theory of Semiotics, Bloomington: Indiana University Press, 1976.

Ferraris, Maurizio, *History of Hermeneutics*, trans. Luca Somigli, Atlantic Heights, N.J.: Humanities Press, 1996.

Foa, Vittorio and Paul Ginsborg, *Le virtù della repubblica: dalla crisi del sistema e dal ricambio della class politica lo spazio per una nuova cultura di governo*, Milan: Il Saggiatore, 1994.

Forgacs, David and Robert Lumley (eds.), *Italian Cultural Studies: An Introduction*, Oxford: Oxford University Press, 1996.

Fraser, John, *An Introduction to the Thought of Galvano della Volpe*, London: Lawrence and Wishart, 1977.

Gargani, Aldo (ed.), *Crisi della ragione: nuovi modelli nel rapporto tra sapere e attività umane*, Turin: Einaudi, 1979.

Gramsci, Antonio, *Selections from the Prison Notebooks of Antonio Gramsci*, eds. and trans. Quintin Hoare and Geoffrey Nowell Smith, London: Lawrence & Wishart, 1971.

Holub, Renate, *Antonio Gramsci: Beyond Marxism and Postmodernism*, London: Routledge, 1992.

'The Cultural Politics of the CPI 1944–1956', *Yale Italian Studies* 2 (1978), pp. 261–283.

'Strong Ethics and Weak Thought: Feminism and Postmodernism in Italy', *Annali d'Italianistica* 9 (1991), pp. 124–143.

'Towards a New Rationality? Notes on Feminism and Current Discursive Practices in Italy', *Discourse: Berkeley Journal for Theoretical Studies in Media and Culture* 4 (1981–82), pp. 89–108.

Macciocchi, Maria Antonietta, *Letters from Inside the Italian Communist Party to Louis Althusser*, trans. Stephen M. Hellman, London: MLB, 1975.

Manacorda, Giuliano, *Storia della letteratura italiana contemporanea (1940–1965)*, Rome: Editori Riuniti, 1974; 1st edn. 1967.

Negri, Antonio, *Marx beyond Marx* (1979), ed. Jim Fleming, trans. Harry Cleaver, Michael Ryan and Maurizio Viano, South Hadley, Mass.: Bergin and Garvey, 1984.

Passerini, Luisa, *Identità culturale europea*, Florence: La Nuova Italia, 1999.

Petrilli, Susan (ed.), *Between Signs and Non-Signs*, Amsterdam and Philadelphia: Benjamins, 1992.

Petronio, Giuseppe, *Letteratura e società: storia e antologia della letteratura italiana*, Palermo: Palumba, 1972.

Ponzio, Augusto, *Produzione linguistica e ideologia sociale*, Bari: Di Donato, 1973.

Signs, Dialogue and Ideology, Amsterdam: Benjamins, 1992.

Rossanda, Rossana, *Anche per me: donna, persona, memoria dal 1973–1986*, Milan: Feltrinelli, 1986.

Rossi-Landi, Ferruccio, *Language as Word and Trade: Semiotic Homology for Linguistics and Economics*, South Hadley, Mass.: Bergin and Garvey, 1983.

Linguistics and Economics, The Hague: Mouton, 1977.

Marxism and Ideology, trans. Roger Griffin, Oxford: Clarendon Press, 1990.

Rusconi, Gian Enrico, *Nazione, etnia, cittadinanza in Italia e in Europa*, Brescia: La Scuola, 1993.

La teoria critica della società, Bologna: Il Mulino, 1968.

Salinari, Carlo, *Profilo storico della letteratura Italiana*, Rome: Editori Riuniti, 1972.

Storia d'Italia, dall'unità a oggi, Turin: Einaudi, 1975.

Touraine, Alain, *Pourrons nous vivre ensemble? Egaux et différents*, Paris: Fayard, 1997.

Vattimo, Gianni, *La società trasparente*, Milan: Garazanti, 1989.

Il soggetto e la maschere: Nietzsche e il problema della liberazione, Milan: Bompiani, 1974.

Vattimo, Gianni and Pier Aldo Rovatti (eds.), *Il pensiero debole*, Milan: Feltrinelli, 1983.

Veltroni, Walter, *La bella politica: un intervista di Stefano del Re*, Milan: Rizzoli, 1995.

Mikhail Bakhtin: historical becoming in language, literature and culture

Primary sources

Bakhtin, Mikhail, *Art and Answerability: Early Philosophical Essays by M. M. Bakhtin*, eds. Michael Holquist and Vadim Liapunov, trans. Vadim Liapunov and Kenneth Brostrom, Austin, Tex.: University of Tex. Press, 1990 (contains the early philosophical fragment 'Author and Hero in Aesthetic Activity', fragments of Bakhtin's *Bildungsroman* project, pieces on linguistics from the 1950s and late philosophical notes).

The Dialogic Imagination: Four Essays by M. M. Bakhtin, ed. Michael Holquist, trans. Caryl Emerson and Michael Holquist, Austin, Tex.: University of Texas Press, 1981.

'Lektsii i vystupleniia M. M. Bakhtina 1924–1925 gg. v zapisiakh L. V. Pumpianskogo' ('Lectures and Interventions by M. M. Bakhtin in 1924–1925, from Notes by L. V. Pumpiansky'; Bakhtin's contributions to the Leningrad philosophical seminar), in L. A. Gogotishvili and P. S. Gurevich (eds.), *M. M. Bakhtin kak filosof*, Moscow: Nauka, 1992, pp. 221–252.

Literaturno-kriticheskie stat'i ('Literary-Critical Articles'), eds. S. G. Bocharov and V. V. Kozhinov, Moscow: Khudozhestvennaia literatura, 1986.

Problems of Dostoevsky's Poetics (1963), ed. and trans. Caryl Emerson, Manchester: Manchester University Press, 1984.

Problemy tvorchestva Dostoevskogo ('Problems of Dostoevsky's Art'), Leningrad: Priboi, 1929.

Rabelais and His World, trans. Hélène Iswolsky, Cambridge, Mass.: MIT Press, 1968.

Sobranie sochinenii v semi tomakh, tom 5, Raboty 1940-kh – nachala 1960-kh godov ('Collected Works in Seven Volumes', Vol. 5: 'Works from the 1940s to the Beginning of the 1960s'), eds. S. G. Bocharov and L. A. Gogotishvili, Moscow: Russkie slovari, 1996.

Speech Genres and Other Late Essays, eds. Caryl Emerson and Michael Holquist, trans. Vern W. McGee, Austin, Tex.: University of Texas Press, 1986.

Towards a Philosophy of the Act, trans. Vadim Liapunov, eds. Vadim Liapunov and Michael Holquist, Austin, Tex.: University of Tex. Press, 1993.

Tvorchestvo Fransua Rable i narodnaia kul'tura srednevekov'ia i renessansa (1940) ('The Art of François Rabelais and the Popular Culture of the Middle Ages and Renaissance'), Moscow: Khudozhestvennaia literatura, 1965; reprinted with new pagination in 1990.

Voloshinov, Valentin, *Marxism and the Philosophy of Language* (1929), trans. Ladislav Matejka and I. R. Titunik, New York: Seminar Press, 1973.

Secondary sources

Barsky, Robert and Michael Holquist (eds.), *Bakhtin and Otherness; Discours Social / Social Discourse* 3.1–2 (1990).

Bibler, V. S., *M. M. Bakhtin, ili poetika kul'tury*, Moscow: Progress-Gnozis, 1991.

Myshlenie kak tvorchestvo: vvedenie k logiku myshlennogo dialoga, Moscow: Izd. politicheskoi literatury, 1975.

Bocharov, Sergei, 'Sobytie bytiia: o Mikhaile Mikhailoviche Bakhtine', *Novyi mir* 11 (1995), pp. 211–221.

Bocharov, S. G., 'Ob odnom razgovore i vokrug nego', *Novoe literaturnoe obozrenie* 2 (1993), pp. 70–89; abridged translation by Vadim Liapunov and Stephen Blackwell, 'Conversations with Bakhtin', *PMLA* 109.5 (1994), pp. 1009–1024.

Bonetskaia, N. K., 'Bakhtin's Aesthetics as a Logic of Form', in David Shepherd (ed.), *The Contexts of Bakhtin: Philosophy, Authorship, Aesthetics*, New York: Harwood Academic Press, 1998.

Clark, Katerina and Michael Holquist, *Mikhail Bakhtin*, Cambridge, Mass. and London: Harvard University Press, 1985.

Coates, Ruth, *Christianity in Bakhtin*, Cambridge: Cambridge University Press, 1999.

Emerson, Caryl, *The First Hundred Years of Mikhail Bakhtin*, Princeton: Princeton University Press, 1997.

Hale, Dorothy, *Social Formalism: The Novel in Theory from Henry James to the Present*, Stanford, Calif.: Stanford University Press, 1998.

Hitchcock, Peter (ed.), *Bakhtin/'Bakhtin': Studies in the Archive and Beyond*, South Atlantic Quarterly 97.3–4 (1998).

Holquist, Michael, *Dialogism: Bakhtin and his World*, London and New York: Routledge, 1990.

Howes, Craig, 'Rhetorics of Attack: Bakhtin and the Aesthetics of Satire', *Genre* 19.3 (1986), pp. 231–243.

Kagan, M. I., 'Evreistvo i krizis kul'tury' ('Judaism and the Crisis of Culture', 1923), *Minuvshee* 6 (1981), pp. 229–236.

Konkin, S. S. and L. S. Konkina, *Mikhail Bakhtin: stranitsy zhizni i tvorchestva*, Saransk: Mordovskoe knizhnoe izdatel'stvo, 1993.

Medvedev, Iu. P., '"Nas bylo mnogo na chelne . . ."', *Dialog Karnaval Khronotop* 1 (1992), pp. 89–108.

Mihailovic, Alexander, *Corporeal Words: Mikhail Bakhtin's Theology of Discourse*, Evanston, Ill.: Northwestern University Press, 1997.

Morson, Gary Saul and Caryl Emerson, *Mikhail Bakhtin: Creation of a Prosaics*, Stanford, Calif.: Stanford University Press, 1990.

Pechey, Graham, 'Boundaries versus Binaries: Bakhtin in/against the History of Ideas', *Radical Philosophy* 54 (1990), pp. 23–31.

'Modernity and Chronotopicity in Bakhtin', in David Shepherd (ed.), *The Contexts of Bakhtin: Philosophy, Authorship, Aesthetics*, New York: Harwood Academic Press, 1998.

'Philosophy and Theology in "Aesthetic Activity"', *Dialogism* 1 (1998), pp. 57–73.

Poole, Brian, 'Bakhtin and Cassirer: The Philosophical Origins of Bakhtin's Carnival Messianism', *South Atlantic Quarterly* 97.3–4 (1998), pp. 537–578.

'From Phenomenology to Dialogue: Max Scheler's Phenomenological Tradition and Mikhail Bakhtin's Development from *Towards a Philosophy of the Act* to his Study of Dostoevsky', in Ken Hirschkop and David Shepherd (eds.), *Bakhtin and Cultural Theory*, 2nd rev. edn., Manchester: Manchester University Press, forthcoming.

'"Nazad k Kaganu"', *Dialog Karnaval Khronotop* 1 (1995), pp. 38–48.

Segre, Cesare, 'What Bakhtin Left Unsaid: The Case of the Medieval Romance', in Kevin Brownlee and Marina Scordiles Brownlee (eds.), *Romance: Generic Transformations From Chrétien de Troyes to Cervantes*, Hanover, N.H.: University Press of New England, 1985.

Shepherd, David (ed.), *The Contexts of Bakhtin: Philosophy, Authorship, Aesthetics*, New York: Harwood Academic Publishers, 1998.

Stallybrass, Peter and Allon White, *The Politics and Poetics of Transgression*, London: Methuen, 1986.

Stam, Robert, *Subversive Pleasures: Bakhtin, Cultural Criticism, and Film*, Baltimore and London: The Johns Hopkins University Press, 1989.

Thomson, Clive and Hans Raj Dua (eds.), *Dialogism and Cultural Criticism*, London, Canada: Mestengo Press, 1995.

Tihanov, Galen, 'Bakhtin's Essays on the Novel (1935–41): A Study of their Intellectual Background and Innovativeness', *Dialogism* 1 (1998), pp. 30–56.

'Bakhtin, Lukács and German Romanticism: The Case of Epic and Irony', in Carol Adlam *et al.* (eds.), *Face to Face: Bakhtin in Russia and the West*, Sheffield: Sheffield Academic Press, 1997.

Todorov, Tzvetan, *Mikhail Bakhtin: The Dialogical Principle*, trans. Wlad Godzich, Manchester: Manchester University Press, 1984.

Williams, Raymond, 'The Uses of Cultural Theory', *New Left Review* 158 (1986), pp. 19–31.

Cultural studies

Arnold, Matthew, *Culture and Anarchy and Other Writings*, ed. Stefan Collini, Cambridge: Cambridge University Press, 1993.

Batsleer, Janet, Tony Davies, Rebecca O'Rourke and Chris Weedon, *Rewriting English: Cultural Politics of Gender and Class*, London: Methuen, 1985.

Belsey, Catherine, *Critical Practice*, London: Methuen, 1980.

Bourdieu, Pierre and Jean-Claude Passeron, *Reproduction in Education, Society, and Culture*, trans. R. Nice, London and Newbury Park, Calif.: Sage (in association with the Theory, Culture and Society Department, Teesside Polytechnic), 1990.

Eagleton, Terry, *Criticism and Ideology*, London: New Left Books, 1976.

Easthope, Antony, *Literary into Cultural Studies*, London: Routledge, 1991.

Hall, Stuart and Paddy Whannel, *The Popular Arts*, London: Hutchinson Educational, 1964.

Hoggart, Richard, *Speaking to Each Other*, vol. 1: *About Society*, London: Chatto and Windus, 1970.

The Uses of Literacy, London: Chatto and Windus, 1957.

Leavis, F. R, *The Common Pursuit*, Harmondsworth: Penguin, 1962.

Mass Civilization and Minority Culture, Cambridge: Gordon Fraser, 1930.

Leavis, F. R. and Denys Thompson, *Culture and Environment*, London: Chatto and Windus, 1933.

Macherey, Pierre, *A Theory of Literary Production*, trans. G. Wall, London: Routledge and Kegan Paul, 1978.

Mathieson, Margaret (ed.), *The Preachers of Culture*, London: Allen and Unwin, 1975.

Milner, Andrew, *Literature, Culture and Society*, London: UCL Press, 1996.

Mulhern, Francis, *The Moment of 'Scrutiny'*, London: New Left Books, 1979.

Newbolt Report, *The Teaching of English in England*, London: Board of Education, HMSO, 1921.

Sampson, George, *English for the English*, Cambridge: Cambridge University Press, 1921.

Steele, Tom, *The Emergence of Cultural Studies 1945–65: Cultural Politics, Adult Education and the English Question*, London: Lawrence and Wishart, 1997.

Turner, Graeme, *British Cultural Studies: An Introduction*, 2nd edn., London: Routledge, 1996.

Williams, Raymond, *Communications*, Harmondsworth: Penguin, 1962.

Culture and Society, London: Chatto and Windus, 1958.

Keywords: A Vocabulary of Culture and Society, London: Fontana, 1976.

The Long Revolution, Harmondsworth: Pelican, 1965.

Marxism and Literature, Oxford: Oxford University Press, 1977.

Television: Technology and Cultural Form, London: Fontana, 1974.

Literature and the institutional context in Britain

Primary sources

Chambers, R.W., 'The Teaching of English in the Universities of England', *English Association Pamphlet* 53 (1922).

Daiches, David (ed.), *The Idea of a New University: An Experiment in Sussex*, London: Andre Deutsch, 1964.

Leavis, F. R., *Education and the University*, London: Chatto and Windus, 1943.

Newman, John Henry, *The Idea of the University*, London: Image Books, 1959.

Potter, Stephen, *The Muse in Chains: A Study in Education*, London: Jonathan Cape, 1937.

Tillyard, E. M. W., *The Muse Unchained*, London: Bowes and Bowes, 1958.

The National Committee of Inquiry into Higher Education: Higher Education in the Learning Society (The Dearing Report), London: HMSO, 1997.

The Teaching of English in England: Being the Report of the Departmental Committee Appointed by the President of the Board of Education to Inquire into the Position of English in the Education System (The Newbolt Report), London: HMSO, 1921.

Thompson, E. P., *Warwick University Ltd*, London: Merlin, 1970.

Secondary sources

Baldick, Chris, *Criticism and Literary Theory 1890 to the Present*, London: Longman, 1996.

Doyle, Brian, *English and Englishness*, London: Routledge 1988.

Halsey, A. H., *Decline of Donnish Dominion: The British Academic Professions in the Twentieth Century*, Clarendon: Oxford, 1992.

Moodie, Graeme and Rowland Eustace, *Power and Authority in British Universities*, London: George Allen and Unwin, 1974.

Palmer, D. J., *The Rise of English Studies: An Account of the Study of English Language and Literature From Its origins to the Making of the Oxford English School*, London: University of Hull and Oxford University Press, 1965.

Sanderson, Michael, *The Universities and British Industry: 1850–1970*, London: Routledge, 1972.

Scott, Peter, *The Meanings of Mass Higher Education*, Buckingham: Open University Press, 1995.

Taper, Ted and Brian Salter, *Oxford, Cambridge and the Changing Idea of the University: The Challenge to Donnish Dominion*, Buckingham: Open University Press, 1992.

Literary criticism and psychoanalytic positions

Primary sources

Freud, Sigmund, *The Pelican Freud Library*, 15 vols., trans. James Strachey, eds. Angela Richards and Albert Dickson, London: Penguin, 1973–85.

Separate volumes:

Art and Literature, trans. James Strachey, ed. Albert Dickson, *Pelican Freud Library*, vol XIV.

On Metapsychology: The Theory of Psychoanalysis, trans. James Strachey, ed. Angela Richards, *Pelican Freud Library*, vol. XI.

The Origins of Religion, trans. James Strachey, ed. Albert Dickson, *Pelican Freud Library*, vol. XIII.

Studies on Hysteria, trans. James Strachey, ed. Angela Richards, *Pelican Freud Library*, vol. III.

Jung, Carl Gustav, *Collected Works*, trans. R. F. C. Hull, eds. Herbert Read, Michael Fordham, and Gerhard Adler, 20 vols. (and 4 unnumbered vols.), London: Routledge and Kegan Paul, 1959.

Klein, Melanie, *Contributions to Psycho-Analysis 1921–1945*, International Psycho-Analytical Library, 34, London: Hogarth Press, 1968.

Envy and Gratitude and Other Works 1946–63, London: Virago, 1988.

Love, Guilt and Reparation and Other Works 1921–45, London: Virago, 1988.

Kristeva, Julia, *Desire in Language: A Semiotic Approach to Literature and Art*, trans. and ed. Leon S. Roudiez, Oxford: Blackwell, 1980.

Powers of Horror: An Essay on Abjection, trans. and ed. Leon S. Roudiez, European Perspectives Series, New York: Columbia University Press, 1982.

Lacan, Jacques, *Écrits*, trans. Alan Sheridan, London: Tavistock, 1977.

The Four Fundamental Concepts of Psycho-Analysis, trans. Alan Sheridan, ed. Jacques-Alain Miller, New York and London: Norton, 1978 .

Winnicott, D.W., *Playing and Reality*, Harmondsworth: Penguin, 1974.

Secondary sources

Berman, Jeffrey, *The Talking Cure: Literary Representations of Psychoanalysis*, New York: New York University Press, 1985.

Brooks, Peter, *Psychoanalysis and Storytelling*, Oxford: Blackwell, 1993.

Ellmann, Maud (ed.), *Psychoanalytic Literary Criticism*, Longman Critical Readers Series, London and New York: Longman, 1994.

Felman, Shoshana, *Writing and Madness: Literature/Philosophy/Psychoanalysis*, Ithaca: Cornell University Press, 1985.

(ed.), *Literature and Psychoanalysis: The Question of Reading: Otherwise*, Baltimore: Johns Hopkins University Press, 1982.

Gunn, Daniel, *Psychoanalysis and Fiction: An Exploration of Literary and Psychoanalytical Borders*, Cambridge: Cambridge University Press, 1988.

Hartman, Geoffrey (ed.), *Psychoanalysis and the Question of the Text: Selected Papers From the English Institute, 1976–77*, Baltimore and London: Johns Hopkins University Press, 1978.

Kofman, Sarah, *Freud and Fiction*, Cambridge: Polity, 1991.

Kurzweil, Edith and William Phillips (eds.), *Literature and Psychoanalysis*, Ithaca: Cornell University Press, 1983.

Lechte, John (ed.), *Writing and Psychoanalysis: A Reader*, London and New York: Arnold, 1996.

Rimmon-Kenan, Shlomith (ed.), *Discourse in Psychoanalysis and Literature*, London: Methuen, 1987.

Royle, Nicholas and Ann Wordsworth (eds.), *Psychoanalysis and Literature: New Work*, special edition of *The Oxford Literary Review*, 12.1–2 (1990).

Williams, Linda Ruth, *Critical Desire: Psychoanalysis and the Literary Subject*, Interrogating Texts Series, London and New York: Arnold, 1995.

Vice, Sue (ed.), *Psychoanalytic Criticism: A Reader*, Cambridge: Polity, 1996.

Wright, Elizabeth, *Psychoanalytic Criticism: Theory in Practice*, New Accents Series, London and New York: Methuen, 1984.

The history of feminist criticism

Primary sources

Barrett, Michèle, *Women's Oppression Today: Problems in Marxist Feminist Analysis*, London: Verso, 1980.

Cixous, Hélène, 'The Laugh of the Medusa', trans. Keith Cohen and Paula Cohen, *Signs* 1.4, 1976, pp. 875–894.

Daly, Mary, *Gyn/ecology*, London: The Women's Press, 1979.

De Beauvoir, Simone, *The Second Sex* (1949), trans. H. M. Parshley, Harmondsworth: Penguin, 1972.

Ellmann, Mary, *Thinking About Women*, New York: Harcourt, 1968.

Firestone, Shulamith, *The Dialectic of Sex: The Case for Feminist Revolution*, London: The Women's Press, 1970.

Friedan, Betty, *The Feminine Mystique*, Harmondsworth: Penguin, 1982.

Gilbert, Sandra M. and Susan Gubar, *The Madwoman in the Attic*, New Haven: Yale University Press, 1979.

Greer, Germaine, *The Female Eunuch*, London: Paladin, 1971.

Irigaray, Luce, *Speculum of the Other Woman*, trans. Gillian G. Gill, Ithaca: Cornell University Press, 1985 (*Spéculum de l'autre femme*, 1974).

Kristeva, Julia, *Revolution in Poetic Language*, trans. Margaret Waller, New York: Columbia University Press, 1980 (*Révolution du langage poétique*, 1974).

Millett, Kate, *Sexual Politics*, New York: Avon Books, 1970.

Mitchell, Juliet, *Psychonanalysis and feminism*, Harmondsworth: Penguin, 1974.

'Women: The Longest Revolution', *New Left Review* 40 (1966), pp. 1–39.

Moers, Ellen, *Literary Women: The Great Writers*, New York: Doubleday, 1976.

Moi, Toril, *Sexual/Textual Politics: Feminist Literary Theory*, London: Methuen, 1985.

Moraga, Cherríe and Gloria Anzaldúa (eds.), *This Bridge Called my Back: Writings by Radical Women of Color*, New York: Kitchen Table Press, 1983.

Morgan, Robin (ed.), *Sisterhood is Powerful: An Anthology of Writings from the Women's Liberation Movement*, New York: Random House, 1970.

Olsen, Tillie, *Silences*, London: Virago, 1972.

Rich, Adrienne, 'Compulsory Heterosexuality and Lesbian Existence', in E. Abel and E. K. Abel (eds.), *The Signs Reader: Woman, Gender and Scholarship*, Chicago: Chicago University Press, 1983, pp. 139–168.

Of Woman Born: Motherhood as Experience and Institution, London: Virago, 1977.

Rowbotham, Sheila, *Woman's Consciousness, Man's World*, Harmondsworth: Penguin, 1973.

Rubin, Gayle, 'The Traffic in Women', in Linda Nicholson (ed.), *The Second Wave: A Reader in Feminist Theory*, ed. Linda Nicholson, New York: Routledge, 1997, pp. 27–62.

Showalter, Elaine, *A Literature of Their Own: British Women Novelist from Brontë to Lessing*, Princeton: Princeton University Press, 1977.

Spender, Dale, *Man Made Language*, London: Routledge and Kegan Paul, 1980.

Mothers of the Novel: 100 Good Women Writers Before Jane Austen, London: Pandora, 1986.

Woolf, Virginia, *A Room of One's Own* (1928), Harmondsworth: Penguin, 1973.

Three Guineas (1938), Harmondsworth: Penguin, 1977.

Zimmerman, Bonnie, 'What Has Never Been: An Overview of Lesbian Feminist Criticism', in Gayle Greene and Coppélia Kahn (eds.), *Making a Difference: Feminist Literary Criticism*, London: Methuen, 1985, pp. 177–210.

Secondary sources

Butler, Judith, *Gender Trouble: Feminism and the Subversion of Identity: Essays on Theory, Film, and Fiction*, New York: Routledge, 1990.

Carby, Hazel V., *Reconstructing Womanhood: The Emergence of the Afro-American Woman Novelist*, Oxford: Oxford University Press, 1987.

Christian, Barbara, *Black Feminist Criticism*, Oxford: Pergamon, 1985.

Gallop, Jane, *Feminism and Psychoanalysis: The Daughter's Seduction*, London: Macmillan, 1982.

Hartsock, Nancy, *Money, Sex and Power*, New York: Longman, 1983.

Humm, Maggie (ed.), *Feminisms: A Reader*, New York: Harvester Wheatsheaf, 1992.

Todd, Janet, *Feminist Literary History*, Cambridge: Polity Press, 1988.

Weedon, Chris, *Feminism, Theory and the Politics of Difference*, Oxford: Blackwell, 1999.

Feminist Practice and Poststructuralist Theory, Oxford: Blackwell, 1987.

Feminism and deconstruction

Brown, Wendy, *States of Injury: Power and Freedom in Late Modernity*, Princeton: Princeton University Press, 1995.

Butler, Judith, *Bodies That Matter: On the Discursive Limits of 'Sex'*, New York: Routledge, 1993.

Gender Trouble: Feminism and the Subversion of Identity: Essays on Theory, Film, and Fiction, New York: Routledge, 1990.

'Imitation and Gender Insubordination', in Diana Fuss (ed.), *Inside/Out: Lesbian Theories, Gay Theories*, New York: Routledge, 1991.

Cixous, Hélène and Catherine Clement, *The Newly Born Woman*, trans. Betsy Wing, Minneapolis: University of Minnesota Press, 1986.

Cornell, Drucilla, *Beyond Accommodation: Ethical Feminism, Deconstruction, and the Law*, New York: Routledge, 1991.

'Gender, Sex, and Equivalent Rights', in Judith Butler and Joan Wallach Scott (eds.), *Feminists Theorize the Political*, New York: Routledge, 1992, pp. 280–296.

The Philosophy of the Limit, New York: Routledge, 1992.

De Lauretis, Teresa, *Technologies of Gender: Essays on Theory, Film, and Fiction*, Bloomington: Indiana University Press, 1987.

Derrida, Jacques, 'Afterword: Toward an Ethic of Discussion', *Limited Inc*, Evanston, Ill.: Northwestern University Press, 1988, pp. 111–160.

'Deconstruction in America', *Critical Exchange* 17 (Winter 1985), pp. 1–33.

'The Double Session', in *Dissemination*, trans. Barbara Johnson, Chicago: The University of Chicago Press, 1981, pp. 173–286.

'Sending: On Representation', *Social Research* 49.2 (Summer 1982), pp. 294–326.

Spurs: Nietzsche's Styles, trans. Barbara Harlow, Chicago: University of Chicago Press, 1978.

'Women in the Beehive: A Seminar with Jacques Derrida', in Alice Jardine and Paul Smith (eds.), *Men in Feminism*, New York: Methuen, 1987.

Derrida, Jacques and Christie McDonald, 'Choreographies', *Diacritics* 12.2 (Summer 1982), pp. 66–76.

Elam, Diane, *Feminism and Deconstruction: ms. en abyme*, London: Routledge, 1994.

Feder, Ellen K. and Mary C. Rawlinson (eds.), *Derrida and Feminism: Recasting the Question of Woman*, New York: Routledge, 1997.

Holland, Nancy (ed.), *Feminist Interpretations of Jacques Derrida*, University Park: Penn State University Press, 1997.

Irigaray, Luce, *This Sex Which is Not One*, trans. Catherine Porter, Ithaca: Cornell University Press, 1985.

Johnson, Barbara, 'Apostrophe, Animation, and Abortion', *A World of Difference*, Baltimore and London: The Johns Hopkins University Press, 1987.

Riley, Denise, '*Am I That Name?': Feminism and the Category of 'Women' in History*, Minnesota: University of Minnesota Press, 1988.

Scott, Joan Wallach, *Gender and the Politics of History*, New York: Columbia University Press, 1988.

Spivak, Gayatri Chakravorty, 'Displacement and the Discourse of Woman', in Mark Krupnick (ed.), *Displacement: Derrida and After*, Bloomington, Ind.: Indiana University Press, 1987, pp. 169–195.

Tomkins, Jane, 'Me and My Shadow', in Linda Kauffman (ed.), *Gender and Theory: Dialogues on Feminist Criticism*, Oxford: Blackwell, 1989, pp. 121–139.

Trinh Minh-ha, *Woman, Native, Other: Writing Postcoloniality and Feminism*, Bloomington: Indiana University Press, 1989.

Whitford, Margaret, *Luce Irigaray: Philosophy in the Feminine*, London: Routledge, 1991.

Gay, lesbian, bisexual, queer and transgender criticism

Primary sources

Abbott, Sidney and Barbara Love, *Sappho was a Right-On Woman: A Liberated View of Lesbianism*, New York: Stein and Day, 1972.

Altman, Dennis, *Homosexual: Oppression and Liberation*, rev. edn., London: Allen Lane, 1974.

Anzaldúa, Gloria, 'La consciencia de la mestiza: towards a new consciousness', in Alma M. García, (ed.), *Chicana Feminist Thought: The Basic Historical Writings*, New York: Routledge, 1997.

BI ACADEMIC INTERVENTION (Phoebe Davidson, Jo Eadie, Clare Hemmings, Ann Kaloski and Merl Storr) (eds.), *The Bisexual Imaginary: Representation, Identity and Desire*, London: Cassell, 1997.

Butler, Judith, *Gender Trouble: Feminism and the Subversion of Identity*, New York: Routledge, 1990.

  'Imitation and Gender Insubordination', in Diana Fuss (ed.), *Inside/Out: Lesbian Theories, Gay Theories*, New York: Routledge, 1991.

D'Emilio, John, *Sexual Politics, Sexual Communities: The Making of a Homosexual Minority in the United States, 1940–1970*, Chicago: University of Chicago Press, 1983.

Donoghue, Emma, *Passions Between Women: British Lesbian Culture, 1668–1801*, London: Scarlet Press, 1993.

Faderman, Lillian, *Surpassing the Love of Men: Romantic Friendship and Love Between Women from the Renaissance to the Present Day*, New York: William Morrow, 1981.

Foster, Jeannette H., *Sex-Variant Women in Literature*, 3rd edn., Tallahassee, Fla.: Naiad Press, 1985.

Foucault, Michel, *The History of Sexuality: Vol. 1: An Introduction*, trans. Robert Hurley, London: Allen Lane, 1979.

Johnston, Jill, *Lesbian Nation: The Feminist Solution*, New York: Simon and Schuster, 1973.

Lorde, Audre, *Sister Outsider: Essays and Speeches*, Freedom, Calif.: The Crossing Press, 1984.

Nestle, Joan, *A Restricted Country: Essays and Short Stories*, London: Sheba, 1988.

Prosser, Jay, *Second Skins: The Body Narratives of Transsexuality*, New York: Columbia University Press, 1998.

Raymond, Janice G., *The Transsexual Empire*, London: Women's Press, 1980.

Rubin, Gayle, 'The Leather Menace: Comments on Politics and S/M', in SAMOIS (ed.), *Coming to Power: Writings and Graphics in Lesbian S/M*, Berkeley: SAMOIS, 1981.

Sedgwick, Eve Kosofsky, *Between Men: English Literature and Male Homosocial Desire*, New York: Columbia University Press, 1985.

Epistemology of the Closet, Hemel Hempstead: Harvester Wheatsheaf, 1991.

Warner, Michael (ed.), *Fear of a Queer Planet: Queer Politics and Social Theory*, Minneapolis: University of Minnesota Press, 1993.

Weeks, Jeffrey, *Coming Out: Homosexual Politics in Britain from the Nineteenth Century to the Present*, rev. edn., London: Quartet, 1990.

Wittig, Monique, *The Straight Mind and Other Essays*, Hemel Hempstead: Harvester Wheatsheaf, 1992.

Secondary sources

Abelove, Henry, Michèle Aina Barale, and David M. Halperin (eds.), *The Lesbian and Gay Studies Reader*, New York: Routledge, 1993.

Bland, Lucy, and Laura Doan (eds.), *Sexology Uncensored: The Documents of Sexual Science*, Cambridge: Polity Press, 1998.

Dollimore, Jonathan, *Sexual Dissidence: Augustine to Wilde, Freud to Foucault*, Oxford: Clarendon Press, 1991.

Gay Left Collective (eds.), *Homosexuality*, London: Allison and Busby, 1980.

Hamer, Emily, *Britannia's Glory: A History of Twentieth-Century Lesbians*, London: Cassell, 1996.

McIntosh, Mary, 'The Homosexual Role', *Social Problems*, 16 (1968), pp. 182–192.

White, Chris (ed.), *Nineteenth-Century Writings on Homosexuality: A Sourcebook*, London: Routledge, 1999.

Post-colonial theory

Ahmad, Aijaz, *In Theory: Classes, Nations, Literatures*, London: Verso, 1992.

Ashcroft, Bill, Gareth Griffins, and Helen Tiffin, *The Empire Writes Back: Theory and Practice in Post-Colonial Literatures*, London: Routledge, 1989.

Azim, Firdous, *The Colonial Rise of the Novel*, London: Routledge, 1993.

Bhabha, Homi, *The Location of Culture*, London: Routledge, 1994.

Chaudhuri, N. C., *Bangali jibane ramani*, Calcutta: Mitra and Ghose Publishers Ltd., 1968.

Dabydeen, David, *The Black Presence in English Literature*, Manchester: Manchester University Press, 1985.

Fanon, Frantz, *Black Skin, White Masks*, London: Pluto Press, 1986.

The Wretched of the Earth, Harmondsworth: Penguin, 1967.

Guha, Ranajit, 'On Some Aspects of the Historiography of Colonial India', in R. Guha (ed.), *Subaltern Studies 1: Writings on South Asian History and Society*, New Delhi: Oxford University Press, 1982, pp. 1–8.

Gupta, Akhil, *Postcolonial Developments: Agriculture in the Making of Modern India*, London and Durham: Duke University Press, 1988.

Mani, Lata, 'Contentious Traditions: The Debate of Sati in Colonial India', in K. Sangari and S. Vaid (eds.), *Recasting Women: Essays in Colonial History*, New Delhi: Kali for Women, 1989, pp. 88–126.

Ngugi Wa Thiongo, *Decolonising the Mind: The Politics of Language in African Literature*, Nairobi: Heinemann, 1988.

Parry, Benita, 'Problems in Current Theories of Colonial Discourse', *Oxford Literary Review* 9 (1987), pp. 27–58.

Rajan, Rajeswari, *Real and Imagined Women*, London: Routledge, 1993.

Said, Edward, *Culture and Imperialism*, London: Chatto and Windus, 1993.

Orientalism, London: Routledge and Kegan Paul, 1978.

Senghor, Leopold, 'Negritude: A Humanism of the Twentieth Century', in L. Chrisman and P. Williams (eds.), *Colonial Discourse and Post-Colonial Theory: A Reader*, London: Harvester Wheatsheaf, 1993, pp. 27–35.

Spivak, Gayatri, 'Can the Subaltern Speak', in L. Chrisman and P. Williams (eds.), *Colonial Discourse and Post-Colonial Theory: A Reader*, London: Harvester Wheatsheaf, 1993, pp. 66–111.

A Critique of Postcolonial Reason: Toward a History of the Vanishing Present, Cambridge, Mass.: Harvard University Press, 1999.

In Other Worlds: Essays in Cultural Politics, London: Methuen, 1987.

Outside in the Teaching Machine, London: Routledge, 1994.

'Three Women's Texts and a Critique of Imperialism', *Critical Inquiry* 12.1 (1985), pp. 243–261.

Viswanathan, Gauri, *Masks of Conquest: Literary Study and British Rule in India*, London: Faber and Faber, 1990.

African American literary history and criticism

Primary sources

Du Bois, W. E. B. *The Souls of Black Folk: Essays and Sketches*, ed. and introd. David W. Blight and Robert Gooding-Williams, Boston: Bedford Books, 1997.

Gates, Jr., Henry Louis and Nellie Y. Mckay (eds.), *The Norton Anthology of African American Literature*, New York: W. W. Norton and Company, 1997.

Gayle, Jr., Addison (ed.), *The Black Aesthetic*, New York: Doubleday and Company, 1971.

Locke, Alain (ed.), *The New Negro*, ed. and introd. Arnold Rampersad, New York: Atheneum, 1992.

Mitchell, Angelyn (ed.), *Within the Circle: An Anthology of African American Literary Criticism from the Harlem Renaissance to the Present*, Durham: Duke University Press, 1994.

Secondary sources

Andrews, William L., Frances Smith Foster, and Trudier Harris (eds.), *The Oxford Companion to African American Literature*, New York: Oxford University Press, 1997.

Baker, Jr., Houston, A., *Blues, Ideology, and Afro-American Literature*, Chicago: University of Chicago Press, 1984.

Modernism and the Harlem Renaissance, Chicago: University of Chicago Press, 1987.

Davis, Charles T. and Henry Louis Gates, Jr. (eds.), *The Slave's Narrative*, Oxford: Oxford University Press, 1985.

Eze, Emmanuel Chukwudi (ed.), *Race and the Enlightenment: A Reader*, Cambridge, Mass.: Blackwell, 1997.

Gates, Jr., Henry Louis, 'Canon-Formation, Literary History, and the Afro-American Tradition: From the Seen to the Told', in Houston A. Baker, Jr. and Patricia Redmond (eds.), *Afro-American Literary Study in the 1990s*, Chicago: University of Chicago Press, 1989.

Figures in Black: Words, Signs and the 'Racial' Self, New York: Oxford University Press, 1989.

'Introduction: "Tell Me, Sir, . . . What *is* 'Black' Literature?"', *PMLA* 105 (1990), pp. 11–22.

Gilroy, Paul, *The Black Atlantic: Modernity and Double Consciousness*, London: Verso, 1993.

Huggins, Nathan Irvin, *The Harlem Renaissance*, New York: Oxford University Press, 1971.

Lewis, David Levering, *When Harlem Was in Vogue*, New York: Oxford University Press, 1989.

Stepto, Robert, 'Afro-American Literature', in Emory Elliot (ed.), *Columbia Literary History of the United States*, New York: Columbia University Press, 1988.

Sundquist, Eric J., *To Wake the Nations: Race in the Making of American Literature*, Cambridge, Mass.: Belknap/Harvard University Press, 1993.

Wonham, Henry B. (ed.), *Criticism and the Color Line: Desegregating American Literary Studies*, New Brunswick: Rutgers University Press, 1996.

Anthropological criticism

Achebe, Chinua, *Hopes and Impediments*, Oxford: Heinemann International, 1988.

Arnold, Matthew, *Culture and Anarchy* (1869), ed. J. Dover Wilson, Cambridge: Cambridge University Press, 1960.

Bhabha, Homi K., 'Postcolonial Authority and Postmodern Guilt', in Lawrence Grossberg, Cary Nelson, and Paula A. Treichler (eds.), *Cultural Studies*, London: Routledge, 1992, pp. 56–66.

Clifford, James, 'Travelling Cultures', in Lawrence Grossberg, Cary Nelson, and Paula A. Treichler (eds.), *Cultural Studies*, London: Routledge, 1992, pp. 96–112.

Clifford, James, and G. E. Marcus (eds.), *Writing Culture: The Poetics and Politics of Ethnography*, Berkeley and London: University of California Press, 1986.

Derrida, Jacques, *Of Grammatology*, trans. Gayatri Chakavorty Spivak, Baltimore: Johns Hopkins University Press, 1982.

Writing and Difference, trans. Alan Bass, London: Routledge and Kegan Paul, 1981.

Douglas, Mary, *Implicit Meanings: Essays in Anthropology*, London: Routledge and Kegan Paul, 1975.

Eagleton, Terry, *The Function of Criticism: From 'The Spectator' to Poststructuralism*, London: Verso, 1985.

Literary Theory: An Introduction, 2nd edn., Oxford: Blackwell, 1996.

Eliot, T. S., 'Ulysses, Order and Myth', *The Dial* 75 (1923), pp. 480–483.

Frye, Northrop, *Anatomy of Criticism: Four Essays*, New York: Atheneum/Princeton University Press, 1957.

The Critical Path, Bloomington: Indiana University Press, 1971.

The Stubborn Structure, Ithaca: Cornell University Press, 1970.

Geertz, Clifford, *The Interpretation of Cultures*, New York: HarperCollins, 1973.

Grossberg, Lawrence, Cary Nelson, and Paula A. Treichler (eds.), *Cultural Studies*, London: Routledge, 1992.

Harvey, Paul, and J. E. Heseltine, *The Oxford Companion to French Literature*, Oxford: Oxford University Press, 1969.

Hawkes, Terence, *Structuralism and Semiotics*, London: Routledge, 1992.

Jameson, Fredric, *The Political Unconscious: Narrative as a Socially Symbolic Act*, Ithaca: Cornell University Press, 1981.

Leitch, Vincent, *American Literary Criticism from the Thirties to the Eighties*, New York: Columbia University Press, 1988.

Lévi-Strauss, Claude, *The Elementary Structures of Kinship* (1969), trans. James Harle, Boston: Beacon Press, 1977.

Mulhern, Francis, *The Moment of 'Scrutiny'*, London: Verso, 1981.

(ed.), *Contemporary Marxist Literary Criticism*, Harlow: Longman, 1992.

Nicholls, Peter, *Modernisms: A Literary Guide*, Basingstoke: Macmillan, 1995.

Norris, Christopher, *The Truth About Postmodernism*, Oxford: Blackwell, 1993.

Ortner, Sherry B., 'Is Female to Male as Nature is to Culture?', in M. Z. Rosaldo and L. Lamphere (eds.), *Woman, Culture and Society*, Stanford: Stanford University Press, 1974, pp. 67–87.

Rabinow, Paul, 'Representations are Social Facts: Modernity and Post-Modernity in Anthropology', in James Clifford and G. E. Marcus (eds.), *Writing Culture: The Poetics and Politics of Ethnography*, Berkeley and London: University of California Press, 1986, pp. 234–261.

Rubin, Gayle, 'The Traffic in Women: Notes on the "Political Economy" of Sex', in R. Reiter (ed.), *Toward an Anthropology of Women*, New York and London: Monthly Review Press, 1975, pp. 157–210.

Spivak, Gayatri Chakravorty, *In Other Worlds*, London: Methuen, 1987.

Wellek, René, *The Rise of English Literary History*, New York: McGraw-Hill, 1966.

Young, Robert, *Torn Halves: Political Conflict in Literary and Cultural Theory*, Manchester: Manchester University Press, 1996.

Modernism, modernity, modernisation

Adorno, Theodor, *Aesthetic Theory*, London: Routledge, 1984.
  Prisms, Cambridge: MIT Press, 1981.
Benjamin, Walter, *Illuminations*, New York: Schocken, 1969.
Berman, Marshall, *All That is Solid Melts Into Air*, New York: Simon and Schuster, 1982.
Blumenberg, Hans, *The Legitimation of the Modern Age*, Cambridge, Mass.: MIT Press, 1983.
Bradbury, Malcolm, and James McFarlane (eds.), *Modernism: A Guide to European Literature 1890–1930*, London: Penguin, 1991.
Bürger, Peter, *Theory of the Avant-Garde*, Minneapolis: University of Minnesota Press, 1984.
Eysteinsson, Astradur, *The Concept of Modernism*, Ithaca: Cornell University Press, 1990.
Habermas, Jürgen, 'Modernity versus Postmodernity', *New German Critique* 22 (1981), pp. 3–14.
  The Philosophical Discourse of Modernity, Cambridge, Mass.: MIT Press, 1987.
  The Theory of Communicative Action, 2 vols., Boston: Beacon Press, 1984, 1987.
Hall, Stuart, *et al.*, *Modernity: An Introduction to Modern Societies*, Cambridge: Polity Press, 1995.
Harvey, David, *The Condition of Postmodernity*, London: Blackwell, 1990.
Horkheimer, Max, and Theodor Adorno, *Dialectic of Enlightenment*, New York: Herder and Herder, 1972.
Huyssen, Andreas, *After the Great Divide: Modernism, Mass Culture, Postmodernism*, Bloomington: Indiana University Press, 1986.
Jauss, Hans Robert, *Literaturgeschichte als Provokation*, Frankfurt: Suhrkamp, 1970.
Luhmann, Niklas, *Social Systems*, Stanford: Stanford University Press, 1995.
Nicholls, Peter, *Modernisms: A Literary Guide*, Berkeley: University of California Press, 1995.
Passerin d'Entrèves, Maurizio, and Seyla Benhabib (eds.), *Habermas and the Unfinished Project of Modernity: Critical Essays on 'The Philosophical Discourse of Modernity'*, Cambridge, Mass.: MIT Press, 1997.
Poggioli, Renato, *The Theory of the Avant-Garde*, Cambridge, Mass.: Harvard University Press, 1968.
Reis, Timothy, *The Discourse of Modernism*, Ithaca: Cornell University Press, 1982.
Weber, Max, *Economy and Society*, Berkeley: University of California Press, 1978.
  From Max Weber: Essays in Sociology, New York: Oxford University Press, 1946.
  The Protestant Ethic and the Spirit of Capitalism, New York: Charles Scribner's Sons, 1958.

Postmodernism

Primary sources

Barth, John, 'Postmodernism Revisited', *Review of Contemporary Fiction* 8.3 (1988), pp. 16–24.
Baudrillard, Jean, *Simulations*, New York: Semiotext(e), 1983.

During, Simon, 'Postmodernism or Post-Colonialism Today', *Textual Practice* 1.1 (1987), pp. 32–47.

Eagleton, Terry, *The Illusions of Postmodernism*, Oxford: Blackwell, 1996.

Graff, Gerald, 'The Myth of the Postmodernist Breakthrough', *Triquarterly* 26 (1973), pp. 383–417.

Habermas, Jürgen, 'Modernity versus Postmodernity', *New German Critique* 22 (1981), pp. 3–14.

Hassan, Ihab, *Paracriticisms: Seven Speculations of the Times*, Urbana: University of Illinois Press, 1975.

Jameson, Fredric, 'Postmodernism, or the Cultural Logic of Late Capitalism', *New Left Review* 146 (1984), pp. 53–92.

   Postmodernism, or the Cultural Logic of Late Capitalism, Durham, N.C.: Duke University Press, 1991.

Jencks, Charles, *The Language of Post-Modern Architecture*, London: Academy, 1977.

Lyotard, Jean-François, *The Postmodern Condition: A Report on Knowledge*, Minneapolis: University of Minnesota Press, 1984.

Norris, Christopher, *What's Wrong with Postmodernism: Critical Theory and the Ends of Philosophy*, London and New York: Harvester Wheatsheaf, 1990.

Rorty, Richard, *Consequences of Pragmatism*, Minneapolis: University of Minnesota Press, 1982.

   'Postmodernist Bourgeois Liberalism', *Journal of Philosophy* 80 (1983), pp. 583–589.

Secondary sources

Arac, Jonathan, *Postmodernism and Politics*, Minneapolis: University of Minnesota Press, 1986.

Connor, Stephen, *Postmodern Culture*, Oxford and New York: Blackwell, 1989.

Foster, Hal, *The Anti-Aesthetic: Essays in Postmodern Culture*, Port Townsend, Wash.: Bay Press, 1983.

Harvey, David, *The Condition of Postmodernity: An Enquiry into the Origins of Cultural Change*, Oxford and Cambridge: Blackwell, 1989.

Heller, Agnes and Ferenc Feher, *The Postmodern Political Condition*, Oxford: Blackwell, 1988.

Hutcheon, Linda, *A Poetics of Postmodernism: History, Theory, Fiction*, New York and London: Routledge, 1988.

Huyssen, Andreas, 'Mapping the Postmodern', *New German Critique* 33 (1984), pp. 5–52.

Lash, Scott, *Sociology of Postmodernism*, London and New York: Routledge, 1990.

McGowan, John, *Postmodernism and its Critics*, Ithaca, N.Y.: Cornell University Press, 1991.

McHale, Brian, *Postmodernist Fiction*, London and New York: Methuen, 1987.

Nicholson, Linda, *Feminism/Postmodernism*, New York and London: Routledge, 1990.

Spanos, William V., *Repetitions: The Postmodern Occasion in Literature and Culture*, Baton Rouge: Louisiana State University Press, 1987.

Ward, Stephen, *Reconfiguring Truth: Postmodernism, Science Studies, and the Search for a New Model of Knowledge*, Maryland and London: Rowman and Littlefield, 1996.

Waugh, Patricia, *Practising Postmodernism/Reading Modernism*, London and New York: Edward Arnold, 1992.

Words and things in phenomenology and existentialism

Primary sources

Brentano, Franz, *Psychology from an Empirical Standpoint*, trans. A. C. Rancurello, D. B. Terrell, and L. L. McAlister, London: Routledge and Kegan Paul, 1973.

De Beauvoir, Simone, *The Ethics of Ambiguity*, trans. Bernard Frechtman, Secaucus, N.J.: Citadel, 1980.

The Second Sex, trans. H. M. Parshley, Harmondsworth: Penguin, 1972.

Derrida, Jacques, *Speech and Phenomena and Other Essays on Husserl's Theory of Signs*, trans. David B. Allison, Evanston, Ill.: Northwestern University Press, 1973.

Heidegger, Martin, *Basic Writings*, ed. David Farrell Krell, London: Routledge, 1993.

Being and Time (1927), trans. John Macquarrie and Edward Robinson, Oxford: Blackwell, 1995.

Poetry, Language, Thought, trans. Albert Hofstadter, New York: Harper and Row, 1975.

Husserl, Edmund, *Cartesian Meditations* (1931), trans. Dorion Cairns, The Hague: Martinus Nijhoff, 1960.

Logical Investigations (1906), trans. J. N. Findlay, London: Routledge and Kegan Paul, 1970.

Kant, Immanuel, *Critique of Judgement* (1790), trans. Werner S. Pluhar, Indianapolis: Hackett, 1987.

Critique of Practical Reason (1788), trans. Lewis White Beck, Indianapolis: Bobbs-Merrill, 1956.

Critique of Pure Reason (1781, 1787), trans. Norman Kemp Smith, London: Macmillan, 1990.

Levinas, Emmanuel, *Collected Philosophical Papers*, trans. Alphonso Lingis, Dordrecht: Martinus Nijhoff, 1987.

The Levinas Reader, ed. Sean Hand, Oxford: Blackwell, 1989.

Merleau-Ponty, Maurice, *Merleau-Ponty Aesthetics Reader*, ed. Galen Johnson, Evanston, Ill.: Northwestern University Press, 1993.

Phenomenology of Perception, trans. Colin Smith, London: Routledge, 1996.

Nietzsche, Friedrich, *The Birth of Tragedy* (1872), trans. Walter Kaufman, New York: Vintage, 1967.

'On Truth and Lie in an Extra-Moral Sense', *Philosophy and Truth: Selections from Nietzsche's Notebooks of the Early 1870s*, ed. Daniel Breazeale, Hassocks: Harvester, 1982, pp. 79–97.

Sartre, Jean-Paul, *Being and Nothingness* (1943), trans. Hazel Barnes, London: Routledge, 1990.

Essays in Existentialism, ed. Wade Baskin, New York: Citadel, 1995.

Nausea (1938), trans. Robert Baldick, London: Penguin, 1988.
What is Literature?, trans. Bernard Frechtman, London: Routledge, 1998.

Secondary sources

Caws, Peter, *Sartre*, London: Routledge and Kegan Paul, 1979.
Danto, Arthur, *Sartre*, London: Fontana Modern Masters, 1975.
Golomb, Jacob, *In Search of Authenticity*, London: Routledge, 1995.
Guignon, Charles (ed.), *Cambridge Companion to Heidegger*, Cambridge: Cambridge University Press, 1993.
Howells, Christina (ed.), *Cambridge Companion to Sartre,* Cambridge: Cambridge University Press, 1995.
Kaelin, Eugene F., *An Existentialist Aesthetic: The Theories of Sartre and Merleau-Ponty*, Madison: University of Wisconsin Press, 1962.
Macann, Christopher, *Four Phenomenological Philosophers*, London: Routledge, 1993.
Magnus, Bernd and Kathleen Higgins (eds.), *Cambridge Companion to Nietzsche*, Cambridge: Cambridge University Press, 1996.
Matthews, Eric, *Twentieth Century French Philosophy*, Oxford: Opus, 1996.
Priest, Stephen, *Merleau-Ponty: Arguments of the Philosophers*, London: Routledge, 1998.
Sprigge, T. L. S., *Theories of Existence*, London: Penguin, 1990.
Warnock, Mary, *The Philosophy of Sartre*, London: Hutchinson, 1965.
West, David, *An Introduction to Continental Philosophy*, London: Polity, 1996.
Wood, David, *Philosophy at the Limit*, London: Unwin Hyman, 1990.

Criticism, aesthetics and analytic philosophy

Barnes, Annette, *On Interpretation: A Critical Analysis*, Oxford: Blackwell, 1988.
Beardsley, Monroe C., *Aesthetics: Problems in the Philosophy of Criticism*, New York: Harcourt Brace, 1958.
  The Possibility of Criticism, Detroit: Wayne State University Press, 1970.
Black, Max, 'Metaphor', *Proceedings of the Aristotelian Society* 55 (1954–55), pp. 273–294.
Brand, Peggy Z. and Carolyn Korsmeyer (eds.), *Feminism and Tradition in Aesthetics*, University Park, Pa.: Pennsylvania State University Press, 1995.
Budd, Malcolm, *Values of Art: Pictures, Poetry and Music*, Harmondsworth: The Penguin Press, 1995.
Carroll, Noël, *A Philosophy of Mass Art*, Oxford: Oxford University Press, 1998.
Cooper, David E., *Metaphor*, Oxford: Blackwell, 1986.
Crittenden, Charles, *Unreality: The Metaphysics of Fictional Objects*, Ithaca, N.Y.: Cornell University Press, 1991.
Currie, Gregory, *The Nature of Fiction*, Cambridge: Cambridge University Press, 1990.
Dadlez, E. M., *What's Hecuba to Him? Fictional Events and Actual Emotions*, Philadelphia: Pennsylvania State University Press, 1997.
Danto, Arthur C., *The Transfiguration of the Commonplace*, Cambridge, Mass.: Harvard University Press, 1981.

Davidson, Donald, 'What Metaphors Mean', *Critical Inquiry* 5 (1978), pp. 31–47.

Davies, Stephen, *Definitions of Art*, Ithaca, N.Y.: Cornell University Press, 1991.

Dickie, George, *The Art Circle: A Theory of Art*, New York: Haven, 1984.

Dummett, Michael, *Origins of Analytical Philosophy*, Cambridge, Mass.: Harvard University Press, 1994.

Eldridge, Richard, *On Moral Personhood: Philosophy, Literature, Criticism, and Self-Understanding*, Chicago: Chicago University Press, 1989.

Ellis, John M., *The Theory of Literary Criticism: A Logical Analysis*, Berkeley and Los Angeles: University of California Press, 1974.

Falck, Colin, *Myth, Truth and Literature*, Cambridge: Cambridge University Press, 1989.

Feagin, Susan L., *Reading with Feeling: The Aesthetics of Appreciation*, Ithaca, N.Y.: Cornell University Press, 1996.

Fogelin, Robert E., *Figuratively Speaking*, New Haven: Yale University Press, 1988.

Frege, Gottlob, *The Foundations of Arithmetic: A Logico-Mathematical Enquiry into the Concept of Number* (Grundgesetze der Arithmetik, 1893, 1903), trans. J. L. Austin, Oxford: Blackwell, 1953, 2nd edn.

Goodman, Nelson, *The Languages of Art*, New York: Bobbs-Merrill, 1968.

Ways of Worldmaking, Brighton: Harvester Press, 1978.

Hirsch, E. D. Jr., *Validity in Interpretation*, New Haven: Yale University Press, 1967.

Hjort, Mette and Sue Laver (eds.), *Emotion and the Arts*, Oxford: Oxford University Press, 1997.

Hospers, John, *Meaning and Truth in the Arts*, Chapel Hill: University of North Carolina Press, 1946.

Iseminger, Gary (ed.), *Intention and Interpretation*, Philadelphia: Pennsylvania State University Press, 1992.

Kittay, Eva Feder, *Metaphor: Its Cognitive Force and Structure*, Oxford: Clarendon Press, 1986.

Krautz, Michael, *Rightness and Reasons: Interpretation in Cultural Practices*, Ithaca, N.Y.: Cornell University Press, 1993.

Lamarque, Peter, *Fictional Points of View*, Ithaca, N.Y.: Cornell University Press, 1996.

Lamarque, Peter and Stein Haugom Olsen, *Truth, Fiction, and Literature: A Philosophical Perspective*, Oxford: Clarendon Press, 1994.

Levinson, Jerrold (ed.), *Aesthetics and Ethics*, Cambridge: Cambridge University Press, 1997.

Music, Art, and Metaphysics: Essays in Philosophical Aesthetics, Ithaca, N.Y.: Cornell University Press, 1990.

Lewis, David, 'Truth in Fiction', *American Philosophical Quarterly* 15 (1978), pp. 37–46.

Livingston, Paisley, *Literary Knowledge: Humanistic Enquiry and the Philosophy of Science*, Ithaca, N.Y.: Cornell University Press, 1990.

Margolis, Joseph, *Art and Philosophy: Conceptual Issues in Aesthetics*, Atlantic Highlands, N.J.: Humanities Press, 1980.

Interpretation; Radical but not Unruly: The New Puzzle of the Arts and History, Berkeley: University of California Press, 1995.

Meinong, A., *On Assumptions*, ed. and trans. James Keanue, Berkeley: University of California Press, 1983.

Miller, Richard W., 'Truth in Beauty', *American Philosophical Quarterly* 16 (1979), pp. 317–325.

Newton-de Molina, David (ed.), *On Literary Intention*, Edinburgh: Edinburgh University Press, 1976.

Novitz, David, *Knowledge, Fiction and Imagination*, Philadelphia: Temple University Press, 1987.

Nussbaum, Martha, *Love's Knowledge: Essays on Philosophy and Literature*, Oxford: Oxford University Press, 1990.

Poetic Justice: The Literary Imagination and Public Life, Boston: Beacon Press, 1995.

Murdoch, Iris, *Metaphysics as a Guide to Morals*, London: Chatto & Windus, 1992.

Olsen, Stein Haugom, *The End of Literary Theory*, Cambridge: Cambridge University Press, 1987.

The Structure of Literary Understanding, Cambridge: Cambridge University Press, 1978.

Ortony, Andrew (ed.), *Metaphor and Thought*, 2nd edn., Cambridge: Cambridge University Press, 1993.

Parsons, Terence, *Nonexistent Objects*, New Haven: Yale University Press, 1980.

Quine, W. V. O., *From a Logical Point of View*, Cambridge, Mass.: Harvard University Press, 1953.

Radford, Colin, 'How Can We be Moved by the Fate of Anna Karenina?', *Proceedings of the Aristotelian Society*, suppl. vol. 49 (1975), pp. 67–80.

Richards, I. A., *Principles of Literary Criticism*, London: Paul Trench Trubner, 1924.

Rorty, Richard (ed.), *The Linguistic Turn: Recent Essays in Philosophical Method*, Chicago: The University of Chicago Press, 1970.

Russell, Bertrand, *Logic and Knowledge*, ed. R. C. Marsh, London: George Allen and Unwin, 1956.

Searle, John R., *Expression and Meaning: Studies in the Theory of Speech Acts*, Cambridge: Cambridge University Press, 1979.

Shusterman, Richard, *Pragmatist Aesthetics: Living Beauty, Rethinking Art*, Oxford: Blackwell, 1992.

Stecker, Robert, *Artworks: Definition, Meaning, Value*, Philadelphia: Pennsylvania State University Press, 1997.

Walsh, Dorothy, *Literature and Knowledge*, Middletown, Conn.: Wesleyan University Press, 1969.

Walton, Kendall L., *Mimesis as Make-Believe*, Cambridge, Mass.: Harvard University Press, 1990.

Weitz, Morris, *'Hamlet' and the Philosophy of Literary Criticism*, London: Faber & Faber, 1965.

Wittgenstein, Ludwig, *Philosophical Investigations*, trans. G. E. M. Anscombe, Oxford, Blackwell, 1953.

Italian idealism

Primary sources

Binni, Walter, *Poetica, critica e storia letteraria*, Bari: Laterza, 1964.

Croce, Benedetto, *The Aesthetic as the Science of Expression and of the Linguistic in General* (1902), trans. C. Lyas, Cambridge: Cambridge University Press, 1992.

Ariosto, Shakespeare and Corneille (1918–20), trans. D. Ainslie, London: Allen and Unwin, 1920.

Benedetto Croce's Poetry and Literature: An Introduction to its Criticism and History, trans. G. Gullace, Carbondale: Southern Illinois University Press, 1981.

'Il carattere di totalità dell'espressione artistica', *La critica* 16 (1918), pp. 129–140.

Conversazioni critiche, 5 vols., Bari: Laterza, 1918–40.

The Essence of Aesthetic (1913), trans. D. Ainslie, London: Heinemann, 1921.

La letteratura della nuova Italia, 6 vols., Bari: Laterza, 1914–40.

Nuovi saggi di estetica, Bari: Laterza, 1920.

Philosophy, Poetry, History, trans. C. Sprigge, London: Oxford University Press, 1966.

Poesia e non poesia, Bari: Laterza, 1923.

Problemi di estetica, 4th edn., Bari: Laterza, 1949.

Ultimi saggi, Bari: Laterza, 1935.

Gentile, Giovanni, *Dante e Manzoni*, Florence: Vallecchi, 1923.

Frammenti di estetica e letteratura, Lanciano: Carabba, 1920.

Lettere a Benedetto Croce, 5 vols., Florence: Casa Editrice Le Lettere, 1992.

Manzoni e Leopardi, opere complete, vol. XXIV, 2nd edn., Florence: Sansoni, 1960.

Manzoni e Leopardi: saggi critici, Milan: Treves, 1928.

Il pensiero di Leopardi, Florence: Sansoni, 1941.

The Philosophy of Art (1931), trans. G. Gullace, Ithaca: Cornell University Press, 1972.

Poesia e filosofia di G. Leopardi, Florence: Sansoni, 1939.

Getto, Giovanni, *Letteratura e critica nel tempo*, Milan: Marzorati, 1954.

Storia delle storie letterarie, 2nd edn., Milan: Bompiani, 1946.

Russo, Luigi, *La critica letteraria contemporanea*, new edn., Florence: Sansoni, 1967.

Sapegno, Natalino, *Compendio di storia della letteratura italiana*, 17th edn., 3 vols. Florence: La Nuova Italia, 1960.

Secondary sources

Borsari, Silvano, *L' opera di Benedetto Croce*, Naples: Nella Sede dell'Istituto, 1964.

Brown, Merle E., 'Italian Criticism after Croce', *Philological Quarterly* 47 (1968), pp. 92–116, 253–279.

Neo-Idealistic Aesthetics: Croce-Gentile-Collingwood, Ithaca: Cornell University Press, 1960.

Collingwood, R. G., *An Autobiography*, Oxford: Clarendon Press, 1939.

De Feo, Italo, *Croce: l'uomo e l'opera*, Milan: Mondadori, 1975.

Flora, Francesco (ed.), *Benedetto Croce*, Milan: Malfasi, 1953.

Jacobitti, E. E., *Revolutionary Humanism and Historicism in Modern Italy*, New Haven: Yale, 1981.

Moss, M. E., *Benedetto Croce: Essays on Literature and Literary Criticism*, Albany: SUNY, 1990.

Olivier, P., *Croce, ou l'affirmation de l'immanance absolue*, Paris: Seghers, 1975.

Orsini, Gian N. G., *Benedetto Croce: Philosopher of Art and Literary Critic*, Carbondale: Southern Illinois University Press, 1961.

Piccoli, Raffaello, *Benedetto Croce*, London: Cape, 1922.

Puppo, Mario, *Benedetto Croce e la critica letteraria*, Florence: Sansoni, 1974.
Ransom, J. C., *The New Criticism*, Norfolk: New Directions, 1941.
Sansone, Mario, *Interpretazioni crociane*, Bari: Laterza, 1965.
Stella, Vittorio, 'Aspetti e tendenze dell'estetica italiana odierna (1945–1963)', *Giornale di metafisica*, a. XVIII, 6 (1963), pp. 576–621, and a. XIX, 1–2 (1964), pp. 41–74, 280–329.
Tilgher, A., *Estetica: teoria generale dell'attività artistica*, Rome: Libreria di scienze e lettere, 1931.

Spanish and Spanish American poetics and criticism

Primary sources

Aleixandre, V., 'Poesía, moral, público', *Insula* 59 (1950), pp. 1–2.
Alonso, Amado, *Poesía y estilo de Pablo Neruda*, Madrid: Gredos, 1997.
Alonso, Dámaso, *Poesía española*, Madrid: Gredos, 1976.
Azorín, José, *La voluntad*, Madrid: Cátedra, 1977.
Barral, C., 'Poesía no es comunicación', *Laye* 23 (1953), pp. 23–26.
Borges, J. L., *Discusión*, Buenos Aires: Emecé, 1975.
Bousoño, C., *Teoría de la expresión poética*, Madrid: Gredos, 1985.
Carpentier, A., *Tientos y diferencias*, La Habana: UNEAC, 1966.
Castro, Américo, *España en su historia: cristianos, moros y judíos*, Barcelona: Grijalbo, 1996.
Cernuda, L., *Poesía y literatura*, 2 vols., Barcelona: Seix Barral, 1960–65.
Cortázar, J., *Obra crítica*, 3 vols., Madrid: Alfaguara, 1994.
Fuentes, C., *La nueva novela hispanoamericana*, México: Joaquín Mortiz, 1972.
García Márquez, Gabriel and E. Vargas Llosa, *La novela en América Latina: diálogo*, Lima: Carlos Milla Batres-Edics. UNI, 1968.
Goytisolo, J., *El furgón de cola*, Barcelona: Seix Barral, 1976.
Menéndez Pidal, R., *Poema del mio cid*, Madrid: DGAB, 1961.
Ortega y Gasset, J., *Meditaciones del Quijote*, ed. J. Marías, Madrid: Cátedra, 1984.
Paz, Octavio, *El arco y la lira: el poema, la revelación poética, poesía e historia*, México: Fondo de Cultura Económica, 1992.
Ribes, F. (ed.), *Poesía última*, Madrid: Taurus, 1963.
Sánchez Ferlosio, R., *Las semanas del jardín*, Madrid: Alianza, 1981.
Unamuno, M., *Vida de don Quijote y Sancho*, Madrid: Cátedra, 1988.
Valente, J.A., *Las palabras de la tribu*, Madrid: Siglo XXI, 1971.

Secondary sources

Ancet, J. *et al.*, *En torno a la obra de José Ángel Valente*, Madrid: Alianza, 1996.
Chicharro Chamorro, A., *Teoría, crítica e historia literarias españolas,* Sevilla: Alfar, 1993.
Díaz-Plaja, G., *Estructura y sentido del novecentismo español*, Madrid: Alianza, 1975.
Goic, C., *Historia crítica de la novela hispanoamericana*, vol. III, Barcelona: Editorial Crítica, 1988.
Gimferrer, P. (ed.), *Octavio Paz*, Madrid: Taurus, 1989.

454   Bibliography

Laín Entralgo, P., *La generación del 98*, Madrid: Espasa Calpe, 1998.
López, S. L. and D. Villanueva (eds.), *Critical Practices in Post-Franco Spain*,
     Minneapolis: University of Minnesota Press, 1994.
Portolés, J., *Medio siglo de filología española (1896–1952): positivismo e idealismo*,
     Madrid: Cátedra, 1986.
Rico, F. (ed.), *Historia y crítica de la literatura española*, vols. VI, VII, VIII, IX,
     Barcelona: Crítica, 1992–1995.
Rodríguez Monegal, E., 'La narrativa hispanoamericana: hacia una nueva "poética"',
     in Sanz Villanueva (ed.), *Teoría de la novela*, Madrid: SGEL, 1976.
Volek, E., *Cuatro claves para la modernidad: Aleixandre, Borges, Carpentier, Cabrera
     Infante*, Madrid: Gredos, 1984.
Wahnon, S, *Estética y crítica literaria en España (1910–1930)*, Granada: University of
     Granada, 1988.

                  American neopragmatism and its background

Appleby, Joyce, Lynn Hunt, and Margaret Jacob, *Telling the Truth About History*,
     New York: Norton, 1994.
Begley, Adam, 'Souped-Up Scholar', *The New York Times Magazine*, 3 May, 1992, pp.
     38–52.
Bloom, Allan, *The Closing of the American Mind*, New York: Simon and Schuster, 1987.
Bourdieu, Pierre, *Distinction, A Social Critique of the Judgement of Taste*, trans.
     Richard Nice, Cambridge, Mass.: Harvard University Press, 1984.
Buchler, Justus (ed.), *Philosophical Writings of Peirce*, New York: Dover, 1955.
Copleston, Frederick, *Modern Philosophy: Empiricism, Idealism, and Pragmatism in
     Britain and America*, New York: Doubleday, 1994.
De Man, Paul, *Aesthetic Ideology*, ed. Andrzej Warminski, Minneapolis and London:
     University of Minnesota Press, 1996.
     The Rhetoric of Romanticism, New York: Columbia University Press, 1984.
Dewey, John, *Art as Experience* (1934), New York: Berkley Perigree Books, 1980.
Fish, Stanley, 'Boutique Multiculturalism, or Why Liberals are Incapable of Thinking
     about Hate Speech', *Critical Inquiry* 23 (Winter 1997), pp. 378–395.
     *Doing What Comes Naturally: Change, Rhetoric, and the Practice of Theory in
     Literary and Legal Studies*, Durham: Duke University Press, 1989.
     Is There a Text in This Class?: The Authority of interpretive communities,
     Cambridge, Mass.: Harvard University Press, 1980.
     Professional Correctness, Literary Studies and Political Change, Oxford: Oxford
     University Press, 1995.
     There's No Such Thing as Free Speech and It's a Good Thing, Too, New York and
     Oxford: Oxford University Press, 1994.
Heidegger, Martin, *Being and Time*, trans. John Macquarrie and Edward Robinson,
     New York and Evanston: Harper and Row, 1962.
James, William, *Pragmatism* (1907), New York: Dover, 1995.
     Varieties of Religious Experience (1902), New York and London: Collier Books,
     1961.
Kant, Immanuel, *Critique of Judgement* (1790), trans. J. H. Bernard, New York:
     Hafner, 1951.

McDermott, John J. (ed.), *The Philosophy of John Dewey*, vol. 1, Chicago and London: University of Chicago Press, 1973.

The Writings of William James, A Comprehensive Edition, Chicago and London: University of Chicago Press, 1977.

Menand, Louis (ed.), *Pragmatism, A Reader*, New York: Random House, 1997.

Mitchell, W. J. T. (ed.), *Against Theory, Literary Studies and the New Pragmatism*, Chicago: University of Chicago Press, 1985.

Norris, Christopher, *What's Wrong with Postmodernism, Critical Theory and the Ends of Philosophy*, New York: Harvester Wheatsheaf, 1990.

Pavel, Thomas, 'Lettre d'Amérique: la liberté de parole en question', *Commentaire 69* (Printemps 1995), pp. 163–173.

Rorty, Richard, *Achieving our Country*, Cambridge, Mass. and London: Harvard University Press, 1998.

Consequences of Pragmatism, Minneapolis: University of Minnesota Press, 1982.

Contingency, Irony, and Solidarity, Cambridge: Cambridge University Press, 1989.

Essays on Heidegger and Others, Cambridge: Cambridge University Press, 1991.

Objectivity, Relativism, and Truth, Cambridge: Cambridge University Press, 1991.

Philosophy and the Mirror of Nature, Princeton: Princeton University Press, 1979.

Ryan, Judith, 'American Pragmatism, Viennese Psychology', *Raritan* 8.3 (Winter 1989), pp. 45–54.

Shusterman, Richard, *Practising Philosophy, Pragmatism and the Philosophical Life*, New York and London: Routledge, 1997.

Pragmatist Aesthetics: Living Beauty, Rethinking Art, Oxford and Cambridge, Mass.: Blackwell Publishers, 1992.

Thayer, H. S. (ed.), *Pragmatism, The Classic Writings*, Indianapolis and Cambridge: Hackett, 1982.

Ethics and literary criticism

Arnold, Matthew, 'The Function of Criticism at the Present Time', in *Essays in Criticism: First Series*, London: Dent, 1964, pp. 9–34.

Bakhtin, Mikhail, *The Dialogic Imagination: Four Essays*, ed. Michael Holquist, trans. Caryl Emerson and Michael Holquist, Austin: University of Texas Press, 1981.

Barthes, Roland, *The Rustle of Language*, trans. Richard Howard, New York: Hill and Wang, 1986.

Booth, Wayne, *The Company We Keep: An Ethics of Fiction*, Chicago: University of Chicago Press, 1988.

De Man, Paul, *Allegories of Reading: Figural Language in Rousseau, Nietzsche, Rilke, and Proust*, New Haven and London: Yale University Press, 1979.

Derrida, Jacques, 'Afterword: Toward an Ethic of Discussion', *Limited Inc*, trans. Samuel Weber and Jeffrey Mehlman, Evanston: Northwestern University Press, 1988, pp. 111–160.

'Racism's Last Word', in Henry Louis Gates (ed.), *'Race', Writing, and Difference*, Chicago and London: University of Chicago Press, 1986, pp. 329–338.

Gadamer, Hans-Georg, *Truth and Method*, New York: Seabury Press, 1975.

Harpham, Geoffrey Galt, *Getting it Right: Language, Literature, and Ethics*, Chicago and London: University of Chicago Press, 1992.

Jameson, Fredric, *The Political Unconscious: Narrative as a Socially Symbolic Act*, Ithaca: Cornell University Press, 1981.

Kant, Immanuel, 'Metaphysical Foundations of Morals', in Carl J. Friedrich (trans. and ed.), *The Philosophy of Kant: Immanuel Kant's Moral and Political Writings*, New York: Random House, 1977, pp. 140–208.

Levinas, Emmanuel, *Otherwise Than Being or Beyond Essence*, trans. Alphonso Lingis, The Hague: Nijhoff, 1981.

   Totality and Infinity: An Essay on Exteriority, trans. Alphonso Lingis, Pittsburgh: Duquesne University Press, 1969.

MacIntyre, Alasdair, *After Virtue: A Study in Moral Theory*, London: Duckworth, 1981.

Miller, J. Hillis, *The Ethics of Reading: Kant, de Man, Eliot, Trollope, James, and Benjamin,* New York: Columbia University Press, 1987.

Murdoch, Iris, *The Fire and the Sun: Why Plato Banished the Artists*, Oxford: Oxford University Press, 1977.

Newton, Adam Zachary, *Narrative Ethics*, Cambridge, Mass. and London: Harvard University Press, 1995.

Nietzsche, Friedrich, *On the Genealogy of Morals*, in Walter Kaufmann (trans.), *On the Genealogy of Morals and Ecce Homo*, New York: Random House, 1969.

Nussbaum, Martha C., *Love's Knowledge: Essays on Philosophy and Literature,* New York and Oxford: Oxford University Press, 1990.

Rainsford, Dominic, *Authorship, Ethics and the Reader: Blake, Dickens, Joyce,* New York: St. Martin's Press, 1997.

Rorty, Richard, 'Freud and Moral Reflection', in Joseph H. Smith and William Kerrigan (eds.), *Pragmatism's Freud: The Moral Disposition of Psychoanalysis,* Baltimore: The Johns Hopkins University Press, 1986, pp. 1–27.

   'Solidarity or Objectivity?', in John Rajchman and Cornel West (eds.), *Post-Analytic Philosophy,* New York: Columbia University Press, 1985, pp. 3–19.

Siebers, Tobin, *The Ethics of Criticism*, Ithaca: Cornell University Press, 1988.

Williams, Raymond, *Marxism and Literature*, Oxford and New York: Oxford University Press, 1977.

Literature and theology

Primary sources

Alter, Robert, *The Art of Biblical Narrative*, New York: Basic Books, 1981.

Bal, Mieke, *Death and Dissymmetry: The Politics of Coherence in the Book of Judges*, Chicago: University of Chicago Press, 1988.

   Murder and Difference: Gender, Genre and Scholarship on Sisera's Death, Bloomington: Indiana University Press, 1988.

Bloom, Harold, *Ruin the Sacred Truths: Poetry and Belief from the Bible to the Present*, Cambridge, Mass.: Harvard University Press, 1989.

Boyarin, Daniel, *Intertextuality and the Reading of Midrash*, Bloomington: Indiana University Press, 1990.

Cunningham, Valentine, *In the Reading Gaol: Postmodernity, Texts and History*, Oxford and Cambridge, Mass.: Blackwell, 1994.

Derrida, Jacques, *Of Grammatology*, trans. Gayatri Chakravorty Spivak, Baltimore: Johns Hopkins University Press, 1976.

Detweiler, Robert, *Breaking the Fall: Religious Readings of Contemporary Fiction*, San Francisco: Harper and Row, 1989.

Eliot, T. S., 'Religion and Literature', *T. S. Eliot: Selected Prose*, ed. John Hayward, Harmondsworth: Penguin, 1953, pp.31–42.

Fisch, Harold, *Poetry With a Purpose: Biblical Poetics and Interpretation*, Bloomington: Indiana University Press, 1988.

Frei, Hans W., *The Eclipse of Biblical Narrative: A Study in Eighteenth and Nineteenth-Century Hermeneutics*, New Haven: Yale University Press, 1974.

Frye, Northrop, *The Great Code: The Bible and Literature*, London: Routledge and Kegan Paul, 1981.

Handelman, Susan, *The Slayers of Moses: The Emergence of Rabbinic Interpretation in Modern Literary Theory*, Albany: State University of New York Press, 1982.

Hart, Kevin, *The Trespass of the Sign: Deconstruction, Theology and Philosophy*, Cambridge: Cambridge University Press, 1989.

Hartman, Geoffrey H. and Sanford Budick (eds.), *Midrash and Literature*, New Haven: Yale University Press, 1986.

Jasper, David, *The Study of Literature and Religion*, London: Macmillan, 1989.

  Readings in the Canon of Scripture: Written for Our Learning, London: Macmillan, 1995.

Jay, Elisabeth, *The Religion of the Heart: Anglican Evangelicalism and the Nineteenth-Century Novel*, Oxford: Clarendon Press, 1979.

Kermode, Frank, *The Genesis of Secrecy*, Cambridge, Mass.: Harvard University Press, 1979.

Moore, Stephen D., *Literary Criticism and the Gospels: The Theoretical Challenge*, New Haven and London: Yale University Press, 1989.

Moore, Stephen D., *Mark and Luke in Poststructuralist Perspectives: Jesus Begins to Write*, New Haven and London: Yale University Press, 1992.

Prickett, Stephen, *Words and the Word: Language, Poetics and Biblical Interpretation*, Cambridge: Cambridge University Press, 1986.

Ricoeur, Paul, *Essays on Biblical Interpretation*, ed. Lewis S. Mudge, London: SPCK, 1981.

  Interpretation Theory: Discourse and the Surplus of Meaning, Fort Worth: Texas Christian University Press, 1976.

Ryken, Leland, *The New Testament in Literary Criticism*, New York: Frederick Ungar, 1984.

Scott, Nathan A., Jr, *The Broken Center: Studies in the Theological Horizon of Modern Literature*, New Haven and London: Yale University Press, 1966.

Sternberg, Meir, *The Poetics of Biblical Narrative: Ideological Literature and the Drama of Reading*, Bloomington: Indiana University Press, 1985.

Trible, Phylis, *Texts of Terror: Literary-Feminist Readings of Biblical Narratives*, London: SCM Press, 1984.

Wilder, Amos N., *Early Christian Rhetoric: The Language of the Gospel*, London: SCM Press, 1964.

  Theology and Modern Literature, Cambridge Mass.: Harvard University Press, 1958.

Wright, T. R., *Theology and Literature*, Oxford: Basil Blackwell, 1988.

Secondary sources

Barratt, David, Roger Pooley, and Leland Ryken (eds.), *The Discerning Reader: Christian Perspectives on Literature and Theory*, Leicester: Apollos/Grand Rapids: Baker, 1995.

Gearon, Liam (ed.), *Theology in Dialogue: English Literature and Theology*, London: Cassell, 1999.

Prickett, Stephen (ed.), *Reading the Text: Biblical Criticism and Literary Theory*, Oxford and Cambridge, Mass.: Basil Blackwell, 1991.

Schad, John, (ed.), *The Bodies of Christ: Writing the Church, From Carlyle to Derrida*, London: Macmillan, 2000.

Schwartz, Regina M., (ed.), *The Book and the Text: The Bible and Literary theory*, Oxford and Cambridge, Mass.: Basil Blackwell, 1990.

Walhout, Clarence, and Leland Ryken (eds.), *Contemporary Literary Theory: A Christian Appraisal*, Grand Rapids: Eerdmans, 1991.

Literary theory, science and philosophy of science

Achinstein, Peter, *Law and Explanation: An Essay in the Philosophy of Science*, Oxford: Clarendon Press, 1971.

Althusser, Louis, *For Marx*, London: Allen Lane, 1969.

Philosophy and the Spontaneous Philosophy of the Scientists, and Other Essays, trans. Gregory Elliott, London: Verso, 1991.

Angel, R. B., *Relativity: The Theory and its Philosophy*, Oxford: Pergamon Press, 1980.

Ayer, A. J. (ed.), *Logical Positivism*, New York: Free Press, 1959.

Bachelard, Gaston, *La formation de l'ésprit scientifique*, Paris: Corti, 1938.

Le rationalisme appliqué, Paris: Presses Universitaires de France, 1949.

Barnes, Barry, *About Science*, Oxford: Blackwell, 1985.

Beer, Gillian, *Darwin's Plots: Evolutionary Narrative in Darwin, George Eliot and Nineteenth-Century Fiction*, London: Routledge & Kegan Paul, 1983.

Open Fields: Science in Cultural Encounter, Oxford: Clarendon Press, 1996.

Benjamin, Andrew, Geoffrey N. Cantor, and John R. Christie (eds.), *The Figural and the Literal: Problems in the History of Science and Philosophy, 1630–1800*, Manchester: Manchester University Press, 1987.

Bloor, David, *Knowledge and Social Imagery*, London: Routledge & Kegan Paul, 1976.

Bohr, Niels, *Atomic Physics and Human Knowledge*, New York: Wiley, 1958.

The Philosophical Writings of Niels Bohr, 3 vols., Woodbridge, Conn.: Ox Bow Press, 1987.

Carnap, Rudolf, *An Introduction to the Philosophy of Science*, New York: Basic Books, 1974.

Cohen, Murray, *Sensible Words: Linguistic Practice in England, 1640–1785*, Baltimore: Johns Hopkins University Press, 1977.

Davies, Paul, *Other Worlds*, London: Dent, 1980.

Einstein, Albert, *Relativity: The Special and the General Theories*, London: Methuen, 1954.

Empson, William, *Seven Types of Ambiguity*, 3rd edn., revised, Harmondsworth: Penguin, 1961.

Folse, Henry J., *The Philosophy of Niels Bohr: The Framework of Complementarity*, Amsterdam: North-Holland, 1985.

Foucault, Michel, *The Order of Things: An Archaeology of the Human Sciences*, London: Tavistock, 1970.

van Fraassen, Bas, *The Scientific Image*, Oxford: Oxford University Press, 1980.

Gardner, Martin, 'Is Quantum Logic Really Logic?', *Philosophy of Science* 38 (1971), pp. 508–529.

Gibbins, Peter, *Particles and Paradoxes: The Limits of Quantum Logic*, Cambridge: Cambridge University Press, 1987.

Gleick, James, *Chaos: Making a New Science*, New York: Viking, 1987.

Grandy, Richard E. (ed.), *Theories and Observation in Science*, Englewood Cliffs, N.J.: Prentice-Hall, 1973.

Gribbin, John, *In Search of Schrödinger's Cat: Quantum Physics and Reality*, New York: Bantam Books, 1984.

Haack, Susan, *Deviant Logic: Some Philosophical Issues*, Cambridge: Cambridge University Press, 1974.

Hacking, Ian (ed.), *Scientific Revolutions*, Oxford: Oxford University Press, 1981.

Harding, Sandra G. (ed.), *Can Theories Be Refuted? Essays on the Duhem-Quine Thesis*, Dordrecht and Boston: D. Reidel, 1976.

Hawkins, Harriett, *Strange Attractors: Literature, Culture and Chaos Theory*, Hemel Hempstead: Harvester Wheatsheaf, 1995.

Harré, Rom, *Laws of Nature*, London: Duckworth, 1993.

   The Philosophies of Science, Oxford: Oxford University Press, 1972.

Harré, Rom and E. H. Madden, *Causal Powers*, Oxford: Blackwell, 1975.

Hayles, N. Katherine, *Chaos Bound: Orderly Disorder in Contemporary Literature and Science*, Ithaca, N.Y.: Cornell University Press, 1990.

   The Cosmic Web: Scientific Field Models and Narrative Strategies in the Twentieth Century, Ithaca, N.Y.: Cornell University Press, 1984.

Heidegger, Martin, *The Question Concerning Technology and Other Essays*, trans. William Lovitt, New York: Harper & Row, 1977.

Hesse, Mary, *Revolutions and Reconstructions in the Philosophy of Science*, Brighton: Harvester, 1980.

Horwich, Paul (ed.), *The World Changes: Thomas Kuhn and the Nature of Science*, Cambridge, Mass.: MIT Press, 1993.

Kuhn, Thomas S., *The Structure of Scientific Revolutions*, 2nd edn., Chicago: University of Chicago Press, 1970.

Law, Jules David, *The Rhetoric of Empiricism: Language and Perception from Locke to I. A. Richards*, Ithaca, N.Y.: Cornell University Press, 1993.

Leatherdale, W. H., *The Role of Analogy, Model and Metaphor in Science*, Amsterdam: North-Holland, 1974.

Levine, George, *Darwin and the Novelists: Patterns of Science in Victorian Fiction*, Cambridge, Mass.: Harvard University Press, 1988.

Lindberg, David C. and Robert S. Westman (eds.), *Reappraisals of the Scientific Revolution*, Cambridge: Cambridge University Press, 1990.

Lindley, David, *Where Does the Weirdness Go? Why Quantum Physics is Strange, but Not So Strange as You Think*, London: Vintage, 1997.

Merton, Robert K., *Science, Technology and Society in Seventeenth Century England*, New York: Howard Fertig, 1970.

Misak, C. J., *Verificationism: Its History and Prospects*, London: Routledge, 1995.

Newton-Smith, W. H., *The Rationality of Science*, London: Routledge & Kegan Paul, 1981.

Nicolson, Marjorie Hope, *Science and Imagination*, Ithaca, N.Y.: Great Seal Books, 1956.

Ortony, Andrew (ed.), *Metaphor and Thought*, Cambridge: Cambridge University Press, 1979.

Papineau, David (ed.), *The Philosophy of Science*, Oxford: Oxford University Press, 1996.

Parkinson, G. H. R. (ed.), *The Theory of Meaning*, Oxford: Oxford University Press, 1976.

Polkinghorne, John, *The Quantum World*, Harmondsworth: Penguin, 1986.

Putnam, Hilary, 'How to Think Quantum-Logically', *Synthèse* (1974), pp. 55–61.

Quine, W. V., 'Two Dogmas of Empiricism', in *From a Logical Point of View*, 2nd edn., Cambridge, Mass.: Harvard University Press, 1961, pp. 20–46.

Reiss, Timothy J., *The Discourse of Modernism*, Ithaca, N.Y.: Cornell University Press, 1982.

Richards, I. A., *Science and Poetry*, London: Kegan Paul, Trench and Trubner, 1926; revised and expanded edn, *Sciences and Poetries*, London: Routledge and Kegan Paul, 1970.

Ricoeur, Paul, *Hermeneutics and the Human Sciences*, Cambridge: Cambridge University Press, 1981.

Rorty, Richard, *Contingency, Irony, and Solidarity*, Cambridge: Cambridge University Press, 1989.

   Objectivity, Relativism, and Truth, Cambridge: Cambridge University Press, 1991.

Ross, Andrew, *Strange Weather: Science and Technology in the Age of Limits*, London: Verso, 1991.

Salmon, Wesley C., *Four Decades of Scientific Explanation*, Minneapolis: University of Minnesota Press, 1989.

   Scientific Explanation and the Causal Structure of the World, Princeton: Princeton University Press, 1984.

Schatzberg, Walter, Ronald A. Waite, and Jonathan K. Jackson (eds.), *The Relations of Literature and Science: An Annotated Bibliography of Scholarship, 1880–1980*, New York: Modern Language Association of America, 1987.

Shapin, Steven, *The Scientific Revolution*, Chicago: University of Chicago Press, 1996.

Shapin, Steven and Simon Schaffer, *Leviathan and the Air-Pump: Hobbes, Boyle, and the Experimental Life*, Princeton: Princeton University Press, 1985.

Thomas, David Wayne, 'Gödel's Theorem and Postmodern Theory', *PMLA* 110.2 (March 1995), pp. 248–261.

Tooley, M., *Causation: A Realist Approach*, Oxford: Blackwell, 1988.

Index

Rossanda, Rossana, 140
Rossetti, Christina, 226
Rossi-Landi, Ferrucci, 134,138
Rousseau, Jean-Jacques, 42, 122, 268
Rowbotham, Sheila, 204
Rubin, Gayle, 201, 229, 230, 271
Rushdie, Salman, 244, 289
Russell, Bertrand, 2, 7, 291–2, 324,
    326–7
Russo, L., 336, 345, 346
Ryan, Judith, 359
Ryle, Gilbert, 271, 324

Sade, Marquis de, 379
Said, Edward, 242, 265
    on binary oppositions, 271
    Orientalism, 237, 238, 239, 243
    relation to Foucault, 22
Salinari, Carlo, 136
Salinas, Pedro 353
Sanchez Ferlosio, Rafael, 354
Sand, George (see Bradley, Katherine),
    226
Sansone, M., 346
Sapegno, N., 345
Sappho, 225, 226
Sartre, Jean-Paul, 309–322, 102, 226,
    265, 328
Saussure, Ferdinand de, 185, 232, 270,
    393, 394
    (see linguistics, structuralist)
Scheler, Max, 148
Schelling, F. W. J., 124, 125
Schiller, Friedrich, 303
Schlegel, Friedrich, 10, 125
Schleiermacher, Friedrich, 21, 125, 130,
    391, 407
Schlick, Moritz, 323
Schoenberg, Arnold, 11, 95
Schreiner, Olive, 194, 204
Schubert, Franz, 11
science, 25, 26, 147, 165, 167, 279, 281,
    291, 292, 295, 296, 329, 350,
    401–17
    death of, 289
    Frankfurt School on, 114–15
    Marx on, 304

and postmodernism, 291, 293–4, 302–5
    western, 284
scientism, 303, 304, 305
Scott, Edmund, 64
Scott, Joan 210
Scott, Nathan A., 391, 392
Scott, Peter, 170, 172
Screen, 45, 47, 163
Scrutiny (1932–53), 45, 157, 158, 266
Searle, John, 7, 327
secularism, 285, 400
Sedgwick, Eve Kosofsky, 224–5, 231
self, the, 231, 291, 292, 294, 364
    Caudwell on, 100
    Jung on, 180
    Klein on, 183
    Sartrean theory of, 312–14
semantics 36, 201, 332, 333
semanalysis (Kristeva), 184
semiotics (and semiology), 10, 44, 59, 61,
    133, 137, 138, 161, 163, 271, 346,
    390, 393, 394
    Baudrillard on, 105
    in Klein, 183
    Kristeva on, 103, 184
Sender, Ramón José, 354
Senghor, Leopold, 242
sexology, 218–19, 223, 231
sexuality, 209, 223
    in bisexual criticism, 231
    construction of sexual identities,
        232–3, 234
    critiques of, 220
    in feminism, 229
    Foucault on, 107, 231–2
    Millett on, 198
    and representation, 202–4
    repression of, 221
Shaftesbury, Earl of, 375
Shakespeare, William, 22, 48, 49, 50, 57,
    60–1, 62, 65, 66, 67, 100, 113, 118,
    177, 243, 341, 372
Shelley, Mary, 241
Shklovsky, Viktor, 91, 393
Showalter, Elaine, 199, 200, 202
Shusterman, Richard, 366, 367–9
Sidney, Sir Philip, 372–3

DATE DUE

DEC 04 2004			

#47-0108 Peel Off Pressure Sensitive